Conversion Tables

Conversion Tables
Volume 2

Dewey–LC

Third Edition

Mona L. Scott

LIBRARIES
UNLIMITED
A Member of the Greenwood Publishing Group

Westport, Connecticut • London

Library of Congress Cataloging-in-Publication Data

Scott, Mona L.
    Conversion tables / by Mona L. Scott.
      p. cm.
      ISBN 1-59158-348-9 (set : alk. paper) — ISBN 1-59158-315-2 (v. 1 :
    alk. paper) — ISBN 1-59158-346-2 (v. 2 : alk. paper)
      —ISBN 1-59158-347-0 (v. 3 : alk. paper)
    1. Classification, Library of Congress. 2. Classification,
    Dewey decimal. 3. Reclassification (Libraries) I. Title.
    Z696.U4S36 2006
    025.4'33—dc22   2005030846

British Library Cataloguing in Publication Data is available.

Library of Congress Catalog Card Number:
ISBN: 1-59158-315-2 (Volume 1)
        1-59158-346-2 (Volume 2)
        1-59158-347-0 (Volume 3)
        1-59158-348-9 (Set)

First published in 2006

Libraries Unlimited, 88 Post Road West, Westport, CT 06881
A Member of Greenwood Publishing, Inc.
www.lu.com

Printed in the United States of America

The paper used in this book complies with the
Permanent Paper Standard issued by the National
Information Standards Organization (Z39.48–1984).

10 9 8 7 6 5 4 3 2 1

Contents

Introduction

The third edition of *Conversion Tables: LC–Dewey; Dewey–LC* contains extensive updates of Dewey numbers that reflect the 22nd edition of the Dewey Decimal Classification. Also included are almost one thousand additional sets of class numbers and corresponding Library of Congress (LC) subject headings. These include new subjects that reflect today's world, such as the September 11, 2001, Terrorist Attacks; the War on Terrorism; the Afghan War of 2001; and the Iraq War of 2003. There are also classification and subject sets that broaden areas that were found in the earlier editions, such as Druids and Druidism; World War, 1939–1945—Campaigns—Burma; 401(k) plans; Cosmic noise; Butterfly gardens; Anorexia; CPR (First aid); Computer art; and many ethnic groups found in Africa.

Materials referenced in the *Conversion Tables* are the 22nd edition of the Dewey Decimal Classification (DDC) and the most current editions of the various volumes of the Library of Congress classification schedules and LC Subject Headings available. Library of Congress authority files were consulted regularly to maintain the currency of country or nation names.

Conversion Tables was conceived as a cataloging tool or standard reference in any cataloging department for daily copy cataloging activities, the converting of classifications of individual MARC (machine readable cataloging) records from bibliographic utilities that include only one of the classifications. The LC subject heading table also can be used as call a number assigning tool for both LC and DDC classifications.

The LC and DDC classification schemes approach the organization of knowledge from different perspectives. This can be seen in how LC and Dewey view language and the literatures of each language. LC classes them together in the Ps, whereas Dewey separates them, placing language in the 400s and literature in the 800s. Similarly, LC places military and naval sciences in stand-alone classes, U for military science and V for naval sciences; Dewey places both in the so-called megaclass 300s, which includes virtually all of social and political sciences.

Becasue the two schemes differ so greatly in basic concepts, it was necessary to analyze the concepts of each order to select the corresponding numbers or alphanumeric notations to construct the tables. Ultimately, it involved assigning tens of thousands of class notations.

Structure of the Tables

This cataloging tool is arranged in three sections, each in its own volume: LC to Dewey, Volume 1; Dewey to LC, Volume 2; and Subject Headings with corresponding classifications, Volume 3. Thus each volume contains the same list of classifications in the two systems and corresponding subject headings but is arranged differently.

Example:

LC to Dewey tables

LC	Dewey	Subject Heading
DS79.76	956.70443	Iraq War, 2003

Dewey to LC tables

Dewey	LC	Subject Heading
956.70443	DS79.76	Iraq War, 2003

Subject Heading tables

Subject Heading	LC	Dewey
Iraq War, 2003	DS79.76	956.70443

The notation for a general concept such as Philosophy, which is 100 in Dewey and B in the Library of Congress Classification, will have divisions and subdivisions broken down into smaller concepts and thus more detailed notations ("Philosophy—Congresses" is 105 in Dewey and B20 in LC).

The differences just discussed also result in more than one notation corresponding to the other, or even a whole range of numbers and alphanumeric notations corresponding to the other. For example, 951.041 in the Dewey schedule under the history of China corresponds to seven LC notations in these tables, in the range DS773.83 to DS777.45.

Dates in the LC and Dewey schemes are a problem. The two schedules often do not agree on the date that an event occurred. For example, the LC classification indicates that the Time of Troubles in Russian history was from 1598–1613, but the Dewey scheme uses the date 1605–1613. In other places, however, the dates match perfectly, as in the history of Tunisia. To aid in the conversion, I have often used a range of dates from Table 1 in the Dewey Classification to indicate a century, rather than the single date.

The following conventions have been used:

- Diacritics have not been included in the subject headings.

- Within the class numbers and subject headings, "/" indicates a choice and is usually contained within parentheses or brackets.

- As in conventional cataloging rules, brackets [ ] contain words added by the author.

Instructions for Use of the Tables

To convert a classification from LC to Dewey or Dewey to LC, find the volume containing the table from which you wish to convert. Locate the classification from which you wish to convert in the left column. As indicated earlier, it may be included in a range of "numbers" or alphanumeric notations that correspond to the other classification, or it may fall between two classifications. In these cases, locate the class nearest in concept by using the Subject Headings. The classification to which you wish to convert is in the middle column, with the subject heading on the right.

The Subject Heading section provides a shortcut to the call-number assigning process. Using that section, you can search for the subject heading that reflects or approximates the subject matter of the item that is being cataloged and note the appropriate classifications next to it. This notation may be the classification that is needed, or it will lead you to the appropriate one in the schedules.

Subject Headings—Dewey and LC

Dewey	LC	Subject Heading
001.2	AZ	Learning and scholarship
001.201	AZ101-111	Learning and scholarship—Philosophy
001.2090	AZ200-361	Learning and scholarship—History
001.20902	AZ321	Learning and scholarship—History—Medieval, 500-1500
001.2094	AZ600-765	Learning and scholarship—Europe
001.2095	AZ770-795	Learning and scholarship—Asia
001.2096	AZ800-821	Learning and scholarship—Africa
001.2097	AZ501-516	Learning and scholarship—North America
001.20973	AZ503-513	Learning and scholarship—United States
001.2098	AZ517-588	Learning and scholarship—Latin America
001.2099	AZ850-881	Learning and scholarship—Australia
001.40681	Q180.55.G7	Endowment of research
001.4226	HA31	Statistics—Graphic methods
001.94	CB156	Civilization—Extraterrestrial influences
001.94	GN750-751	Lost continents
001.942	TL789-.6	Unidentified flying objects
001.944	QL89.2.C53	Champ (Monster)
001.944	QL89.2.S2	Sasquatch
001.96	AZ999	Errors, Popular
001.96	AZ999	Superstition
001.96	BF1001-1999	Superstition
003	QA402-.37	System analysis
003.01	Q295	System theory
003.2	CB158-161	Forecasting
003.20904	CB160-161	Twentieth century—Forecasts
003.3	QA76.9.C65	Computer simulation
003.5	Q300-390	Cybernetics
003.5	Q317-321	Bionics
003.503	Q304	Cybernetics—Dictionaries
003.5071	Q316	Cybernetics—Study and teaching
003.509	Q305	Cybernetics—History
003.54	Q350-390	Information theory
003.7	Q325-390	Self-organizing systems
003.83	QA402	Discrete-time systems
003.857	Q172.5.C45	Chaotic behavior in systems
004	QA75.5-.95	Computers
004	QA76.9.C64	Computer literacy
004	QA76.9.D6	Electronic data processing documentation
004.019	QA76.9.H85	Human-computer interaction
004.03	QA76.15	Computers—Dictionaries
004.09	QA76.17	Computers—History
004.1	QA76.6-.66	Electronic digital computers—Programming
004.1	QA76.85	Fifth generation computers
004.11	QA76.88	Supercomputers
004.16	QA76.89	Pen-based computers
004.22	QA76.9.A73	Computer architecture
004.33	QA76.54-.545	Real-time data processing
004.35	QA76.5	Multiprocessors
004.35	QA76.5	Parallel computers
004.36	QA76.9.C55	Client/server computing
004.36	QA76.9.D5	Electronic data processing—Distributed processing
004.6	TK5105.5-.9	Computer networks
004.67	TK5105.87-.888	Wide area networks (Computer networks)
004.678	TK5105.875.I57	Internet (Computer network)
004.68	TK5105.7-.85	Local area networks (Computer networks)
004.692	TK5105.73	Electronic mail systems
005	QA76.76.C64	Software compatibility
005	QA76.9.T48	Text processing (Computer science)
005.1	QA76.6-.66	Programming (Electronic computers)
005.1	QA76.758	Software engineering
005.1	QA76.9.A43	Computer algorithms
005.112	QA76.6	Modular programming
005.115	QA76.63	Logic programming
005.117	QA76.64	Object-oriented programming (Computer science)
005.13	QA76.5	EGPS (Computer program language)
005.13	QA76.7-.73	Programming languages (Electronic computers)
005.16	QA76.76.S64	Software maintenance
005.3	QA76.75-.9	Computer software
005.3	QA76.76.D63	Software documentation
005.3	QA76.76.S46	Shareware (Computer software)
005.3	TK5105.9	Communications software
005.43	QA76.6.U84	Utilities (Computer programs)
005.43	QA76.76.S95	Systems software
005.43	QA76.76.O63	Operating systems (Computers)

1

Dewey	LC	Subject Heading	Dewey	LC	Subject Heading
005.437	QA76.9.U83	User interfaces (Computer systems)	006.4	Q327	Pattern perception
			006.6	T385	Computer graphics
005.4476	QA76.76.063	Distributed operating systems (Computers)	006.7	QA76.575	Multimedia systems
			006.7	QA76.76.I59	Interactive multimedia
005.45	QA76.6	Macro processors	006.7	TK6687	Interactive video
005.452	QA76.6	Interpreters (Computer programs)	010	Z1001-9000	Bibliography
			011.7	AY2001	Directories
005.453	QA76.76.C65	Compilers (Computer programs)	015	Z1201-4980	Bibliography, National
			015.4	Z2000-2959	Bibliography, National—Europe
005.5	QA76.76.A65	Application software			
005.52	HF5548.115	Word processing	015.47	Z3401-3409	Bibliography, National—Asiatic Russia
005.7	QA76.55-.57	Online data processing—Downloading	015.4756	Z3461-3465	Bibliography, National—Armenia
005.713	QA76.76.D49	Device drivers (Computer programs)	015.5	Z3126-3415	Bibliography, National—Asia
005.72	QA76.9.D337	Electronic data processing—Data entry	015.55	Z3366-3370	Bibliography, National—Iran
005.72	QA76.9.D345	Electronic data processing—Data preparation	015.56	Z3013-3028	Bibliography, National—Middle East
005.74	QA76.9.D26	Database design	015.5691	Z3481-3485	Bibliography, National—Syria
005.74	QA76.9.D3	Database management			
005.74	QA76.9.D32	Databases	015.5692	Z3466-3470	Bibliography, National—Lebanon
005.74	QA76.9.F53	File processing (Computer science)	015.5694	Z3476-3480	Bibliography, National—Israel
005.741	QA76.9.F5	File organization (Computer science)	015.59	Z3221-3415	Bibliography, National—Asia, Southeastern
005.746	QA76.9.D33	Data compression (Computer science)	015.6	Z3501-3975	Bibliography, National—Africa
005.758	QA76.9.D3	Distributed databases	015.71	Z1365-1401	Bibliography, National—Canada
005.8	QA76.76.P76	Software protection			
005.8	QA76.9.A25	Computer security	015.72	Z1411-1431	Bibliography, National—Mexico
005.8	QA76.9.D314	Database security	015.729	Z1501-1595	Bibliography, National—West Indies
005.84	QA76.76.C68	Computer viruses			
005.86	QA76.9.B32	Electronic data processing—Backup processing alternatives	015.73	Z1215-1363	Bibliography, National—United States
005.86	QA76.9.D348	Data recovery (Computer science)	015.8	Z1601-1939	Bibliography, National—South America
006.3	Q334-342	Artificial intelligence	015.94	Z4001-4439	Bibliography, National—Australia
006.3	Q337	Distributed artificial intelligence			
006.3	BC137-138	Logic machines	016	AI	Indexes
006.31	Q325.5-.78	Machine learning	016.07	AI21	Newspapers—Indexes
006.31	Q325.6	Reinforcement learning (Machine learning)	016.78	ML111-158	Music—Bibliography
			017.4	Z998-1000.5	Catalogs, Booksellers'
006.32	QA76.87	Neural computers	020	Z	Library Science
006.32	QA76.87	Neural networks (Computer science)	020	Z665-720	Library science
			020.92	Z720	Librarians
006.33	QA76.76.E95	Expert systems (Computer science)	021.65	Z674.7-.83	Library information networks
			023.2	Z682-.4	Librarians
006.33	QA76.9.D32	Deductive databases	023.2	Z682.4.C65	Library consultants
006.332	Q387-.5	Knowledge representation (Information theory)	023.4	Z682.4.A45	Library administrators
			025.1	Z678-.88	Library administration
006.35	QA76.9.N38	Natural language processing (Computer science)	025.11	Z683-.2	Library finance

Dewey	LC	Subject Heading	Dewey	LC	Subject Heading
025.173409(4-9)	CD101-392	Government publications—[By region or country]	026.6	T11.9	Archives, Technical
			026.61	R119.8	Archives, Medical
			026.6176	Z675.D3	Dental libraries
025.1734094	CD101-215	Government publications—Europe	026.62913	Z675.A5	Aeronautical libraries
			027	CD	Archives
025.1734094	CD271-272	Government publications—Australia	027	CD921-4280	Archives
			027	Z662-664	Libraries
025.1734095	CD221-254	Government publications—Asia	027.001	CD947	Archives—Philosophy
			027.0021	Z683	Library statistics
025.1734096	CD255-269	Government publications—Africa	027.0021	Z711.3	Library statistics
			027.0025	CD941	Archives—Directories
025.17340971	CD331-332	Government publications—Canada	027.0028	CD973	Archives—Methodology
			027.003	CD945	Archives—Dictionaries
025.17340972	CD333-334	Government publications—Mexico	027.005	CD921	Archives—Periodicals
			027.0071	CD987-988	Archives—Study and teaching
025.173409728	CD335-350	Government publications—Central America	027.009	CD995-4280	Archives—History
			027.009	Z721-871	Libraries—History
025.173409729	CD351-362	Government publications—Caribbean Area	027.0(4-9)	CD1000-4280	Archives—[By region or country]
025.17340973	CD309-311	Government publications—United States	027.04	CD1000-2000	Archives—Europe
			027.041	CD1040-1199.5	Archives—Great Britain
025.1734098	CD365-392	Government publications—South America	027.043	CD1220-1234.5	Archives—Germany
			027.0436	CD1120-1149.5	Archives—Austria
			027.0437	CD1150-1169.5	Archives—Czechoslovakia
025.1734099	CD291	Government publications—Oceania	027.0438	CD1740-1759.5	Archives—Poland
025.2	Z689-.8	Acquisitions (Libraries)	027.0439	CD1170-1189.5	Archives—Hungary
025.21	Z689-.5	Book selection	027.044	CD1190-1219.5	Archives—France
025.26	Z675.D4	Depository libraries	027.045	CD1400-1658	Archives—Italy
025.2761	Z688.M4	Acquisition of medical literature	027.046	CD1850-1879.5	Archives—Spain
			027.0469	CD1880-1899.5	Archives—Portugal
025.277	Z688.A7	Acquisition of art catalogs	027.047	CD1710-1739.5	Archives—Russia
025.28305	Z692.S5	Acquisition of serial publications	027.0481	CD1810-1829.5	Archives—Norway
			027.0485	CD1830-1849.5	Archives—Sweden
025.284	Z692.D38	Acquisition of databases	027.0489	CD1770-1789.5	Archives—Denmark
025.286	Z692.M3	Acquisition of maps	027.04912	CD1790-1809.5	Archives—Iceland
025.31	Z695.83	Catalogs, Union	027.0492	CD1690-1733.3	Archives—Netherlands
025.31	Z710	Library catalogs	027.0493	CD1670-1689.5	Archives—Belgium
025.3132	Z678.9-.93	Libraries—Automation	027.0494	CD1900-1929.5	Archives—Switzerland
025.3132	Z678.93.D85	Dynix (Computer system)	027.0496	CD1930-1989.5	Archives—Balkan Peninsula
025.3132	Z699-.5	Machine-readable bibliographic data	027.05	CD2001-2291	Archives—Asia
			027.051	CD2030-2059.5	Archives—China
025.32	Z693-695.83	Descriptive cataloging	027.052	CD2160-2189.5	Archives—Japan
025.52	Z674.2-.5	Information services	027.054	CD2080-2099.5	Archives—India
025.56	Z704	Library rules and regulations	027.05694	CD2010-2919.5	Archives—Israel
025.56	Z711.2	Library orientation	027.06	CD2300-2491	Archives—Africa
025.58	Z711.3	Library use studies	027.071	CD3620-3649.6	Archives—Canada
025.7	Z700.9-701.5	Books—Conservation and restoration	027.072	CD3650-3679.5	Archives—Mexico
			027.0728	CD3690-3859.5	Archives—Central America
025.82	Z702	Book thefts	027.0729	CD3860-3985	Archives—Caribbean area
025.84	Z701.3.D4	Books—Deacidification	027.073	CD3020-3615	Archives—United States
026	Z675.A2	Special libraries	027.07(4-9)	CD3070-3609	Archives—[United States, By state]
026.1	Z987-997.2	Book collecting			
026.3046	Z675.D28	Demographic libraries	027.08	CD4000-4279.5	Archives—South America

Dewey	LC	Subject Heading	Dewey	LC	Subject Heading
027.091734	Z675.V7	Rural libraries	060	AS	Academies and learned societies
027.093	CD2570-2789.5	Archives—New Zealand	060	AS	Learned institutions and societies
027.094	CD2500-2529.5	Archives—Australia			
027.09(5-6)	CD2795	Archives—Oceania	060	AS6	Congresses and conventions
027.1	CD977	Personal archives			
027.2	Z675.P85	Proprietary libraries	060.9	AS5	Learned institutions and societies— History
027.3	Z675.R4	Rental libraries			
027.5	Z675.C8	Public libraries			
027.5	Z675.G7	Government libraries	069	AM	Museums
027.662	Z675.H7	Hospital libraries	069	AM	Collectors and collecting
027.665	Z675.P8	Prison libraries	069.01	AM111-157	Museums—Methodology
027.67	Z675.C5	Church libraries	069.0681	AM122	Museum finance
027.69	Z675.B8	Business libraries	069.083	AM8	Children's museums
027.7	LB3044.7-.74	Instructional materials centers	069.09	AM10-101	Museums—[By region or country]
027.7	Z675.U5	Academic libraries	069.094	AM40-70	Museums—Europe
027.8	Z675.S3	School libraries	069.0941	AM41-43	Museums—Great Britain
028	Z1003-.5	Books and reading	069.0943	AM49-51	Museums—Germany
028.7	Z711	Reference books	069.0944	AM46-48	Museums—France
030	AY	Directories	069.0945	AM54-55	Museums—Italy
030.9	AY30-39	Almanacs—History	069.0946	AM65	Museums—Spain
031	AY51-381	Almanacs—America	069.09469	AM66	Museums—Portugal
031	AY67.N5	Almanacs, American	069.0947	AM60-61	Museums—Russia
031.0971	AY410-425	Almanacs—Canada	069.0948	AM61.5-64	Museums—Scandinavia
032	AY830-839	Almanacs—Great Britain	069.09495	AM52-53	Museums—Greece
032.0994	AY1600-1636	Almanacs—Australia	069.09496	AM69	Museums—Balkan Peninsula
033.1	AY850-860	Almanacs—Germany			
035.1	AY890-899	Almanacs—Italy	069.095	AM71-79	Museums—Asia
036.1	AY1000-1009	Almanacs—Spain	069.0951	AM72	Museums—China
036.9	AY1010-1019	Almanacs—Portugal	069.0952	AM77-78	Museums—Japan
050	AI11	Periodicals—Indexes	069.096	AM80-91	Museums—Africa
050	AP	Periodicals	069.0971	AM21-22	Museums—Canada
050	PN4700-5650	Periodicals	069.0972	AM23-24	Museums—Mexico
050	AY	Yearbooks	069.09728	AM25-27	Museums—Central America
050.835	AP200-230	Youths' periodicals	069.0973	AM11-13	Museums—United States
051	PN4840-4899	American newspapers	069.098	AM33-35	Museums—South America
051	PN4901-4920	Canadian periodicals	069.0993	AM96-98	Museums—New Zealand
052	PN5111-5130	English periodicals	069.0994	AM93-95	Museums—Australia
052	AP2-9	English periodicals	069.099(5-6)	AM99-100	Museums—Oceania
053.1	PN5201-5220	German periodicals	069.5	AM200-401	Collectors and collecting
053.1	AP30-36.7	German periodicals	069.509	AM221	Collectors and collecting—History
053.931	AP14-17	Dutch periodicals			
053.931	AP14-17	Flemish periodicals	069.509(4-9)	AM301-396	Collectors and collecting—[By region or country]
054.1	AP20-28.7	French periodicals			
054.1	PN5171-5790	French periodicals			
055.1	PN5241-5250	Italian periodicals	069.5094	AM342-371	Collectors and collecting—Europe
055.1	AP37-39	Italian periodicals			
056.1	PN5317.P4	Spanish periodicals	069.50941	AM343-347	Collectors and collecting—Great Britain
056.9	PN5321-5330	Portuguese periodicals			
058	PN5280.5-5310	Scandinavian periodicals	069.50943	AM350	Collectors and collecting—Germany
058.81	PN5281-5290	Danish periodicals			
059.89	AP85	Greek periodicals	069.50944	AM349	Collectors and collecting—France
059.9171	PN5271-5280	Russian periodicals			
059.924	AP91-93	Jewish periodicals	069.50946	AM362	Collectors and collecting—Spain

Dewey	LC	Subject Heading	Dewey	LC	Subject Heading
069.509469	AM363	Collectors and collecting—Portugal	070.520973	KF3084	Authors and publishers—United States
069.50947	AM356	Collectors and collecting—Russia	070.592	Z231.5.L5	Small presses
069.5095	AM372-385	Collectors and collecting—Asia	070.594	Z286.S37	Scholarly publishing
			071	PN4840-4900	American periodicals
069.5096	AM387-389	Collectors and collecting—Africa	072.(1-8)	PN5111-5129	English newspapers
			073-078	PN5110-5355	European periodicals
069.50971	AM313	Collectors and collecting—Canada	078.489	PN5281-5289	Danish newspapers
			079.5	PN5360-5449	Asian periodicals
069.509728	AM314	Collectors and collecting—Mexico	079.6	PN5450-5499	African periodicals
			079.8	PN5000-5106	South American periodicals
069.509728	AM315-322	Collectors and collecting—Central America	079.94	PN5510-5590	Australian periodicals
			080	AC	Collections
069.509729	AM323-329	Collectors and collecting—West Indies	080	LC6501-6560.4	Lectures and lecturing
			081	AC1-8	American essays
069.50973	AM303-311	Collectors and collecting—United States	083	AC16-19	Dutch essays
			083.1	AC30-35	German essays
069.5098	AM330-341	Collectors and collecting—South America	083.91	AC103-104	Yiddish essays
			084.1	AC20-25	French essays
069.50993	AM393	Collectors and collecting—New Zealand	085.1	AC40-45	Italian essays
			086.(1 or 9)	AC70-75	Spanish and Portuguese essays
069.50994	AM390-391	Collectors and collecting—Australia	089.91992	AC132-133	Armenian essays
069.5099(5-6)	AM395-396	Collectors and collecting—Oceania	089.924	AC101-102	Hebrew essays
			089.927	AC105-106	Arabic essays
069.53	AM141-145	Museum conservation methods	089.945	AC80-85	Finno-Ugric essays
			089.951	AC149-150	Chinese essays
070.172	AN	Newspapers	089.956	AC145-146	Japanese essays
070.172	PN4700-5650	Press	089.96	AC177-189	African essays
070.175	PN4784.N5	Newsletters	089.97	AC195	Indian essays
070.4	PN4700-5650	Journalism	089.99221	AC168-169	Indonesian essays
070.4	PN4749	Journalism—Social aspects	091.09495	PA3301-3371	Manuscripts, Greek (Papyri)
070.4071	PN4785-4823	Journalism—Study and teaching	092	Z240-241.5	Block books
			096.2	Z1030	Vellum printed books
070.4074	PN4720	Journalism—Exhibitions	098.3	PN171.F6-.F7	Literary forgeries and mystifications
070.41	PN4778	Journalism—Editing			
070.43	PN4781	Reporters and reporting			
070.4333092	PN4823	War correspondents	100	B	Philosophy
070.435	PN4784.E53	Electronic news gathering	100	BD	Philosophy
070.444	PN6700-6790	Comic books, strips, etc.	103	B40-48	Philosophy—Dictionaries
070.44932	PN4751	Journalism—Political aspects	103	B49-50	Philosophy—Terminology
			105	B1-8	Philosophy—Periodicals
070.449796	PN4784.S6	Sports journalism	106	B11-18	Philosophy—Societies, etc.
070.484	PN4882.5	Afro-American press	106	B20	Philosophy—Congresses
070.484	PN4882.5	Afro-American newspapers	107.1	B52-.65	Philosophy—Study and teaching
070.49	TR820	Photojournalism			
070.49	TR820.5	Documentary photography	109	B69-4695	Philosophy—History
070.49796	TR821	Photography of sports	109.22	B104	Philosophers
070.5	Z278-550	Publishers and publishing	110	BD95-131	Metaphysics
070.5	Z549	Book clubs	110	BD331	Spiritualism (Philosophy)
070.5	Z1008	Book clubs	111	B836	Relationism
070.509(4-9)	Z289-550	Publishers and publishing—[By region or country]	111	BD300-450	Ontology
			111	BD331	Reality
070.52	PN163	Literary agents	111.1	BD331	Substance (Philosophy)

Dewey	LC	Subject Heading	Dewey	LC	Subject Heading
111.5	BD398	Nothing (Philosophy)	121.6	BD183	Inquiry (Theory of knowledge)
111.6	BD411	Finite, The			
111.6	BD411	Infinite	121.6	BD215	Belief and doubt
111.6	BD416	Absolute, The	121.63	BC141	Probabilities
111.8	BD352	Attribute (Philosophy)	121.63	BD171	Certainty
111.82	BD236	Identity	121.65	BC171-173	Evidence
111.82	BD396	Whole and parts (Philosophy)	121.68	B105.M4	Meaning (Philosophy)
			121.68	B820	General semantics
111.8503	BH56	Aesthetics—Dictionaries	121.68	BD240-241	Hermeneutics
111.8505	BH1-8	Aesthetics—Periodicals	121.8	BD232	Values
111.8506	BH19	Aesthetics—Congresses	121.8	BD430-435	Values
111.85071	BH61-62	Aesthetics—Study and teaching	122	BD530-595	Causation
			123	B105.D47	Determinism (Philosophy)
111.8509	BH81-208	Aesthetics—History	123.3	BC141	Chance
111.850901	BH91-116	Aesthetics, Ancient	123.3	BD595	Chance
111.850902	BH131-137	Aesthetics, Medieval	123.7	BD417	Necessity (Philosophy)
111.850903	BH151-208	Aesthetics, Modern	124	BD530-595	Teleology
111.8509031	BH161-168	Aesthetics, Modern—16th century	126	BD331	Personality
			127	BF1001-1389	Subconsciousness
111.8509032	BH171-178	Aesthetics, Modern—17th century	128	B105.B64	Body, Human (Philosophy)
			128	B105.I56	Intentionality (Philosophy)
111.8509033	BH181-188	Aesthetics, Modern—18th century	128	BD450	Philosophical anthropology
			128.1	BD419-428	Soul
111.8509034	BH191-198	Aesthetics, Modern—19th century	128.2	BD418-.5	Philosophy of mind
			128.3	BD181.7	Memory (Philosophy)
111.850904	BH201-208	Aesthetics, Modern—20th century	128.37	B105.E3	Emotions (Philosophy)
			128.37	B815	Emotions
111.8509495	BH221.B	Aesthetics, Byzantine	128.46	BD436	Love
11.85095	BH101-102	Aesthetics, Oriental	133	BF1001-1999	Supernatural
111.850971	BH221.C	Aesthetics, Canadian	133	BF1001-1389	Parapsychology
113	BD493-708	Cosmology	133	BF1404-2050	Occultism
113	BD581	Philosophy of nature	133.025	BF1409	Occultism—Directories
113	BD645	Harmony of the spheres	133.03	BF1025	Parapsychology—Dictionaries
113.09	BD494-497	Cosmology—History			
113.0901	BD495	Cosmology, Ancient	133.03	BF1407	Occultism—Dictionaries
113.0902	BD495.5	Cosmology, Medieval	133.05	BF1001-1008	Parapsychology—Periodicals
113.8	BD430-435	Life			
114-115	BD620-655	Space and time	133.06	BF1021	Parapsychology—Congresses
115	BD638	Time			
116	BD373	Change	133.06	BF1404	Occultism—Congresses
117	B105.O7	Order (Philosophy)	133.071	BF1040.5	Parapsychology—Study and teaching
117	BD331	Matter			
117	BD493-708	Matter	133.09	BF1028-.5	Parapsychology—History
119	B105.Q34	Quantity (Philosophy)	133.09	BF1421-1429	Occultism—History
121	B820.3	Epistemics	133.09(4-9)	BF1434	Occultism—[By region or country]
121	BC171	Truth			
121	BC181	Judgment (Logic)	133.092	BF1026-1027	Parapsychology— Biography
121	BD143-237	Knowledge, Theory of	133.092	BF1408-.2	Occultists
121	BD171	Error	133.1	BF1444-1486	Apparitions
121.2	BD201	Skepticism	133.1	BF1444-1486	Ghosts
121.35	BD214	Senses and sensation	133.122	BF1475	Haunted houses
121.4	B105.I54	Innate ideas (Philosophy)	133.142	BF1483	Poltergeists
121.4	BD220	Objectivity	133.3	BF1045.D42	Decision-making—Psychic aspects
121.4	BD222	Subjectivity			
121.5	BD215	Belief and doubt	133.3	BF1745-1779	Divination

Dewey	LC	Subject Heading	Dewey	LC	Subject Heading
133.3	BF1845-1891	Fortune-telling	133.892	BF1389.A8	Aura
133.322	BF1335	Crystal gazing	133.9	B841	Spiritualism (Philosophy)
133.323	BF1628	Dowsing	133.9	BF1228-1389	Spiritualism
133.323	BF1628	Dowsers	133.9	BF1275.G85	Guides (Spiritualism)
133.32424	BF1879.T2	Tarot	133.9	BF1389.T7	Transfiguration (Spiritualism)
133.3248	BF1745-1779	Sibyls			
133.3248	BF1745-1779	Oracles	133.9013	BF1045.N4	Near-death experiences
133.32480938	DF125	Oracles, Greek	133.9013	BF1063.D4	Deathbed hallucinations
133.32480938	DF261.D35	Delphian oracle	133.91	BF1281-1315	Channeling (Spiritualism)
133.33	BF1623.S9	Symbolism	133.92	BF1375	Table-moving (Spiritualism)
133.3337	BF1779.F4	Feng-shui	133.92	BF1378	Materialization
133.334	BF1777	Omens	133.92	BF1385	Levitation
133.335	BF1623.P9	Numerology	133.95	BF1389.A7	Astral projection
133.3359	BF1623.P9	Symbolism of numbers	135.3	BF1074-1099	Dreams
133.42	BF1501-1562	Demonology	135.47	BF1585-1623	Cabala
133.422	BF1546-1561	Devil	137	BF889-905	Graphology
133.422	BF1546-1550	Satanism	138	BF839.8-861	Physiognomy
133.423	BF1556	Vampires	139	BF866-885	Phrenology
133.425	BF1553	Evil eye	141	B823	Idealism
133.425	GN475.6	Evil eye	141.3	B823	Transcendentalism
133.426	BF1555	Demoniac possession	141.3	B905	Transcendentalism (New England)
133.427	BF1559	Exorcism			
133.43	BF1562.5-1584	Witchcraft	141.4	B824	Individualism
133.43	BF1585-1623	Magic	141.5	B828.5	Personalism
133.43	GN475.3	Magic	142.7	B829.5	Phenomenology
133.44	BF1558	Incantations	142.7	BD352	Phenomenalism
133.44	BF1561	Talismans	142.78	B818.5	Existential phenomenology
133.5	BF1651-1729	Astrology	142.78	B819	Existentialism
133.52	BF1716-.28	Houses (Astrology)	144	B778	Humanism
133.52	BF1716.28	Eighth house (Astrology)	144	B821	Humanism
133.5262	BF1727	Aries (Astrology)	144.3	B831.5	Pragmatics
133.5263	BF1727.2	Taurus (Astrology)	144.3	B832	Pragmatism
133.5264	BF1727.25	Gemini (Astrology)	144.6	B843	Utilitarianism
133.5265	BF1727.3	Cancer (Astrology)	145	B823.3	Ideology
133.5266	BF1727.35	Leo (Astrology)	146	B828.2	Naturalism
133.5267	BF1727.4	Virgo (Astrology)	146.32	B809.8	Dialectical materialism
133.5272	BF1727.45	Libra (Astrology)	146.4	B831	Positivism
133.5273	BF1727.5	Scorpio (Astrology)	146.42	B824.6	Logical positivism
133.5274	BF1727.6	Sagittarius (Astrology)	146.44	B816	Empiricism
133.5275	BF1727.65	Capricorn (Astrology)	146.5	BD646	Atomism
133.5276	BF1727.7	Aquarius (Astrology)	146.7	B818	Evolution
133.5277	BF1727.75	Pisces (Astrology)	147.4	B812	Dualism
133.5832	BF1729.P6	Astrology and politics	147.4	BD394	Pluralism
133.585	BF1729.S34	Science and astrology	148	B814	Eclecticism
133.5861	BF1718	Medical astrology	149.2	B835	Realism
133.593927	BF1714.A6	Astrology, Arab	149.3	B828	Mysticism
133.59443	BF1714.B7	Buddhist astrology	149.5	B829	Optimism
133.59444	BF1714.J28	Jaina astrology	149.6	B829	Pessimism
133.59445	BF1714.H5	Hindu astrology	149.7	B833	Rationalism
133.6	BF908-940	Hand	149.73	B779	Skepticism
133.6	BF910-940	Palmistry	149.73	B837	Skepticism
133.82	BF1161-1171	Telepathy	149.8	HX914-917	Nihilism
133.88	BF1371-1389	Psychokinesis	149.91	B839	Neo-Scholasticism
133.89	BF1111-1156	Hypnotism	149.91	B839	Scholasticism

Dewey	LC	Subject Heading	Dewey	LC	Subject Heading
149.91	BD125	Scholasticism	152.4	BF575.D57	Disappointment
149.94	B828.36	Ordinary-language philosophy	152.4	BF575.E53	Embarrassment
			152.4	BF575.G8	Guilt
149.96	B841.4	Structuralism	152.4	BF575.H3	Hate
150	BF	Psychology	152.41	BF575.E55	Empathy
150	BF150-172	Mind and body	152.41	BF575.L8	Love
150.1	BF38.5-39.8	Psychology—Methodology	152.42	BF515	Pleasure
150.14	BF32	Psychology—Terminology	152.42	BF575.H27	Happiness
150.192	BF204.5	Existential psychology	152.46	BF575.A6	Anxiety
150.192	BF204.5	Phenomenological psychology	152.46	BF575.F2	Fear
			152.46	BF575.W8	Worry
150.1943	BF199	Behaviorism (Psychology)	152.47	BF575.A5	Temper
150.195	BF173-175.5	Psychoanalysis	152.47	BF575.A5	Anger
150.195	BF175.4.C68	Psychoanalytic counseling	152.47	BF575.F7	Frustration
150.195	BF175.5.C37	Castration complex	152.47	RC569.5.A53	Anger
150.1953	BF175.5.A33	Adlerian psychology	152.47	BF575.H6	Hostility (Psychology)
150.198	BF204	Humanistic psychology	152.48	BF575.J4	Jealousy
150.198	BF204.7	Transpersonal psychology	153	BF201	Cognitive psychology
150.1982	BF203	Gestalt psychology	153	BF309-499	Cognition
150.287	BF176-.5	Psychological tests	153	BF309-499	Consciousness
150.3	BF31	Psychology—Dictionaries	153	BF311	Cognitive styles
150.5	BF1-8	Psychology—Periodicals	153	BF337.C62	Cognitive balance
150.6	BF20	Psychology—Congresses	153	BF444	Human information processing
150.71	BF77-80.7	Psychology—Study and teaching	153.12	BF370-387	Memory
150.72	BF76.5-.6	Psychology—Research	153.12	BF376	Memory disorders
150.724	BF76.6.E94	Experiential research	153.12	BF378.S54	Short-term memory
150.8996073	BF109	Afro-American psychologists	153.123	BF365-395	Reproduction (Psychology)
150.9	BF81-105	Psychology—History	153.123	BF378.R44	Reminiscing
150.92	BF109	Psychologists	153.124	BF378.R4	Recognition (Psychology)
152.1	BF231-299	Senses and sensation	153.14	BF380-387	Mnemonics
152.14	BF241	Visual perception	153.15	BF318-319.5	Learning, Psychology of
152.1423	BF311	Pattern perception	153.15	LB1060-1091	Learning, Psychology of
152.1423	QP360	Pattern perception	153.15	LB1060	Learning
152.15	BF205.N6	Noise	153.152	LB1067.5	Visual learning
152.15	BF251-.5	Hearing	153.1523	BF357	Imitation
152.15	BF353.5.N65	Noise—Psychological aspects	153.1526	BF319.5.O6	Operant conditioning
			153.1526	BF319.5.P34	Paired-association learning
152.166	BF271	Odors	153.1532	LB1065	Attention
152.166	BF271	Smell	153.1533	LB1065	Interest (Psychology)
152.167	BF261	Taste	153.1533	BF321.I5	Interest (Psychology)
152.182	BF275	Touch	153.1533	BF575.E6	Enthusiasm
152.182	BF285	Muscular sense	153.154	LB1059	Transfer of training
152.1882	BF299.O7	Orientation (Psychology)	153.2	BF365-395	Association of ideas
152.1886	BF482	Fatigue	153.3	BF408-426	Creative thinking
152.1886	LB1075	Mental fatigue	153.3	BF408	Creative ability
152.3	BF295-.5	Movement, Psychology of	153.3	BF410	Inspiration
152.33	BF335-337	Habit	153.32	BF367	Eidetic imagery
152.33	BF337.B74	Habit breaking	153.32	BF367	Imagery (Psychology)
152.334	BF295-.5	Perceptual-motor learning	153.32	BF408-426	Imagination
152.335	LB1123	Left- and right-handedness	153.35	BF408-426	Creation (Literary, artistic, etc.)
152.4	BF327	Attitude (Psychology)			
152.4	BF511-593	Emotions	153.35	BH301.C84	Creation (Literary, artistic, etc.)
152.4	BF575.A45	Ambivalence			

Dewey	LC	Subject Heading	Dewey	LC	Subject Heading
153.42	BF441-449.5	Thought and thinking	154.4	BF209.M4	Mescaline
153.42	LB1590.3-.5	Thought and thinking	154.4	BF491-493	Hallucinations and illusions
153.43	BF442	Reasoning (Psychology)	154.4	BF1045.A48	Altered states of consciousness
153.44	BF315.5	Intuition (Psychology)	154.4	BF1045.D76	Drugs—Psychic aspects
153.45	BF778	Values	154.6	BF1068-1073	Sleep
153.6	BF455-463	Speech	154.6	BF1073.S56	Sleep positions
153.6	LB1139.L3	Speech	154.63	BF1099.F34	Family in dreams
153.68	B105.L54	Listening (Philosophy)	154.63	BF1099.L82	Lucid dreams
153.68	BF323.L5	Listening	154.63	BF1099.N53	Nightmares
153.69	BF637.N66	Nonverbal communication (Psychology)	154.63	RC499.D7	Dreams
153.69	BF637.N66	Body language	154.64	BF1073.S58	Sleeptalking
153.73	BF321-323	Apperception	154.7	BF1111-1156	Mesmerism
153.73	LB1067	Apperception	154.7	BF1156.S8	Mental suggestion
153.733	BF321-323	Attention	154.7	RC490-499	Hypnotism
153.733	BF323.L5	Listening	154.72	QH504	Biomagnetism
153.736	BF323.S8	Subliminal perception	155	BF697.5.S44	Self-presentation
153.736	RC499.S92	Subliminal perception	155	BF712-724.85	Developmental psychology
153.752	BF467-475	Space and time	155	BF720.P56	Symbolic play
153.752	BF469	Spatial behavior	155.2	BF175.5.E35	Ego (Psychology)
153.752	BF469	Space perception	155.2	BF697-.5	Self
153.753	BF468	Time perception	155.2	BF697-.5	Individuality
153.753	BF475	Rhythm	155.2	BF697-.5	Self psychology
153.8	BF199	Motivation (Psychology)	155.2	BF698.35.I55	Inner child
153.8	BF501-505	Achievement motivation	155.2	BF818-839	Character
153.8	BF608-635	Will	155.2	RC473.D43	Defense Mechanisms Inventory
153.8	BF611	Self-efficacy			
153.8	LB1071	Will	155.2076	BF818-839	Character tests
153.8	BF632	Self-control	155.232	BF575.A3	Aggressiveness (Psychology)
153.83	BF448	Decision-making			
153.85	BF210	Electronic behavior control	155.232	BF575.B3	Bashfulness
153.85	BF319.5.R4	Reinforcement (Psychology)	155.232	BF575.D34	Dependency (Psychology)
153.85	BF505.R48	Reward (Psychology)	155.232	BF575.H4	Helplessness (Psychology)
153.85	BF637.B4	Behavior modification	155.232	BF575.S39	Self-confidence
153.852	BF774	Influence (Psychology)	155.232	BF698.35.A87	Authoritarianism (Personality trait)
153.853	BF633	Brainwashing			
153.9	BF431-433	Intellect	155.232	BF698.35.C45	Charisma (Personality trait)
153.9	LB1134	Learning ability	155.232	BF698.35.D64	Dogmatism
153.93	BF431-433	Ability—Testing	155.232	BF698.35.N44	Negativism
153.93	BF431-432.5	Intelligence tests	155.232	BF698.35.O57	Optimism
153.93	BF432.5.N64	Non-Verbal Ability Tests	155.232	BF698.35.P36	Passivity (Psychology)
153.93	BF432.5.N65	Nonverbal intelligence tests	155.232	BF698.35.P43	Pedantry
153.94	BF432.5.D53	Differential Aptitude Tests	155.232	BF698.35.P47	Perfectionism (Personality trait)
153.94	BF432.5.M85	Multidimensional Aptitude Battery	155.232	BF698.35.P49	Pessimism
			155.232	BJ1477	Optimism
153.98	BF412-426	Genius	155.232	RC569.5.D47	Dependency (Psychology)
154.2	BF175.5.S92	Sublimation	155.234	BF698.35.D48	Determination (Personality trait)
154.2	BF175.5.S93	Superego			
154.2	BF315	Subconsciousness	155.24	BF335-337	Adjustment (Psychology)
154.2	RC473.E36	Ego Function Assessment	155.25	BF723.M54	Moral development
154.2	RC489.T73	Transference (Psychology)	155.26	BF795-811	Temperament
154.2	RC569.5.C68	Complexes (Psychology)	155.28	BF698.4-.8	Personality assessment
154.3	P96.F36	Fantasy in mass media	155.282	RC473.G7	Graphology
154.4	BF209.L9	LSD (Drug)			

Dewey	LC	Subject Heading	Dewey	LC	Subject Heading
155.283	BF698.8.D9	Dynamic personality inventory	155.66	BF724.6-.65	Middle age—Psychological aspects
155.283	BF698.8.M5	Minnesota Multiphasic Personality Inventory	155.67	BF724.8-.85	Aged—Psychology
			155.7	BF699-711	Genetic psychology
155.283	BF698.8.P48	Personality questionnaires	155.82	GN270-279	Ethnopsychology
155.284	BF698.7	Projective techniques	155.82	GN502-517	Ethnopsychology
155.2842	BF698.8.R5	Rorschach Test	155.8496073	E185.625	Afro-Americans—Psychology
155.3	BF692-.5	Sex (Psychology)	155.8497	E98.P95	Indians of North America—Psychology
155.3	BF692.15	Sexual animosity			
155.3	BF723.S4	Psychosexual development	155.9	BF353-.5	Environmental psychology
155.3	BF723.S42	Sex role in children	155.9	BF353-.5	Man—Influence of environment
155.332	BF692.5	Masculinity (Psychology)			
155.334	BF692.2	Androgyny (Psychology)	155.9042	BF575.S75	Stress (Psychology)
155.4	BF721-723	Child psychology	155.915	BF353.5.W4	Weather—Psychological aspects
155.4	BF721-723	Child mental health			
155.4	BF723.E598	Emotional problems of children	155.92	BF575.L7	Loneliness
			155.93	BF575.D35	Loss (Psychology)
155.4	LB1101-1139	Child development	155.93	RC455.4.L67	Loss (Psychology)
155.412	BF720.E45	Emotions in children	155.93083	BF723.L68	Loss (Psychology) in children
155.412	BF723.E6	Emotions in children			
155.412	BF723.F4	Fear in children	155.935	BF789.D5	Disasters—Psychological aspects
155.41246	BF723.A5	Anxiety in children			
155.41247	BF723.A4	Temper tantrums in children	155.937	BF175.5.D4	Death instinct
155.41247	BF723.F7	Frustration in children	155.937	BF789.D4	Death—Psychological aspects
155.413	BF723.C5	Cognition in children			
155.4133	BF723.C7	Creative ability in children	155.962	HV6089	Prison psychology
155.4133	BF723.D7	Drawing ability in children	156	BF660-685	Psychology, Comparative
155.41332	BF723.F28	Fantasy in children	158	BF636-637	Psychology, Applied
155.4138	BF723.S25	Self-control in children	158	BF637.S8	Success
155.4139	BF723.A25	Ability in children	158.1	BF637.S4	Self-actualization (Psychology)
155.418	BF723.S75	Stress in children			
155.4182	BF723.S24	Self in children	158.1	BF697.5.S46	Self-esteem
155.418232	BF723.A35	Aggressiveness in children	158.1	BF698-.9	Personality
155.41825	BF723.P4	Personality development	158.125	BF637.T68	Transcendental Meditation
155.422	BF719-720	Infant psychology	158.2	BF637.C45	Interpersonal communication
155.42221	BF720.S45	Sensory stimulation in newborn infants	158.2	RC489.A77	Assertiveness training
			158.25	BF575.F66	Friendship
155.42221532	BF720.A85	Attention in newborn infants	158.3	BF637.C56	Psychological consultation
155.42224	BF720.E45	Emotions in infants	158.3	BF637.C6	Counseling
155.42239	BF720.A24	Ability in infants	158.3	RC466-.3	Mental health counseling
155.443	BF723.S43	Sibling rivalry	158.35	BF637.C6	Group counseling
155.444	BF723.T9	Twins—Psychology	158.39	BF761-768	Interviewing
155.455	BF723.G5	Gifted children	158.4	BF637.L4	Leadership
155.4567	GN372	Feral children	158.5	BF637.N4	Negotiation
155.4567	RJ507.F47	Feral children	158.7	BF481	Work—Psychological aspects
155.5	BF724-.3	Adolescent psychology			
155.5	BF724-.3	Youthfulness	158.7	BF481	Work
155.5	LB1135	Adolescence	158.7	HF5548.7-.85	Psychology, Industrial
155.51	BF710	Maturation (Psychology)	158.7	RC967.5	Industrial psychiatry
155.512	BF724.3.E5	Emotions in adolescence	158.72	HF5548.85	Job stress
155.51247	BF724.3.A34	Aggressiveness (Psychology) in youth	158.723	BF481	Burn out (Psychology)
			160	BC	Logic
155.51247	BF724.3.A34	Aggressiveness (Psychology) in adolescence	160	BC25-32	Logic, Ancient
			160	BC34-35	Logic, Medieval
155.633	HQ1206-1216	Women—Psychology			

Dewey	LC	Subject Heading	Dewey	LC	Subject Heading
160	BC38-39	Logic, Modern	171	BJ10.E8	Ethical culture movement
160	BC177	Reasoning	171.2	BJ1340	Existential ethics
160	BC181	Proposition (Logic)	171.2	BJ1360	Humanistic ethics
160	BC199.D8	Duality (Logic)	171.2	BJ1365-1385	Ethics, Positivist
160.1	BC50-57	Logic—Methodology	171.2	BJ1475.3	Humanitarianism
160.5	BC1	Logic—Periodicals	171.4	BJ1491	Hedonism
160.6	BC5	Logic—Congresses	171.7	BJ1298-1335	Ethics, Evolutionary
160.71	BC59	Logic—Study and teaching	171.7	BJ1388	Socialist ethics
160.9	BC11-39	Logic—History	171.7	BJ1390-.5	Communist ethics
161	BC80-99	Induction (Logic)	171.8	BJ1474	Altruism
165	BC175	Fallacies (Logic)	171.9	BJ1474	Egoism
165	BC199.C6	Contradiction	171.9	BJ1474	Self-interest
165	BC199.F5	Fictions, Theory of	174	BJ1498	Work
165	BC199.P2	Paradox	174	BJ1725	Professional ethics
167	BC183	Hypothesis	174.2	R724-726	Medical ethics
169	BD190	Analogy	174.2	RC455.2.E8	Psychotherapists—Professional ethics
170	BJ	Ethics			
170	BJ991-1185	Ethics—Textbooks	174.2	RC455.2.E8	Psychiatric ethics
170	BJ1400-1408.5	Good and evil	174.2	RK52.7	Dental ethics
170	BJ1410-1418	Right and wrong	174.2	RS100.5	Pharmaceutical ethics
170	BJ1450-1458	Duty	174.2	RT85	Nursing ethics
170	BJ1471	Conscience	174.2	SF756.39	Veterinarians—Professional ethics
170	BJ1480-1486	Happiness			
170.1	BJ37-60	Ethics—Philosophy	174.4	HF5387	Business ethics
170.202	BJ1075-1077	Ethics—Outlines, syllabi, etc.	174.915	BF76.4	Psychologists—Professional ethics
170.3	BJ63	Ethics—Dictionaries	174.9375	LB3609	Student ethics
170.44	BJ1545-1697	Conduct of life	174.957	QH332	Bioethics
170.5	BJ1-8	Ethics—Periodicals	174.962	TA157	Engineering ethics
170.6	BJ10-11	Ethics—Societies, etc.	174.972	NA1995	Architects—Professional ethics
170.6	BJ19	Ethics—Congresses	174.97914	PN2056	Actors—Professional ethics
170.71	BJ66-68	Ethics—Study and teaching	174.98	PN154	Literary ethics
170.9	BJ71-982	Ethics—History	175	PN1995.5	Motion pictures—Moral and ethical aspects
170.902	BJ231-255	Ethics, Medieval			
170.90(23-31)	BJ271-285	Ethics, Renaissance	175	BJ1498	Leisure
170.903	BJ301-982	Ethics, Modern	176	BJ1533.C4	Chastity
170.9033	BJ311	Ethics, Modern—18th century	176	HQ31-64	Sexual ethics
170.9034	BJ315	Ethics, Modern—19th century	176.082	HQ46	Sexual ethics for women
			176.0835	HQ35	Sexual ethics for teenagers
170.904	BJ319	Ethics, Modern—20th century	177.1	BJ1520-1688	Courtesy
			177.1	BJ1533.C9	Courtesy
170.935	BJ136-138	Ethics, Assyro-Babylonian	177.2	BJ1535.G6	Gossip
170.938	BJ160-224	Ethics, Greek	177.3	BJ1420-1428.3	Truthfulness and falsehood
170.943	BJ751-759	Ethics, Germanic	177.3	BJ1500.P7	Promises
170.9438	BJ847-850	Ethics, Polish	177.3	BJ1535.S6	Slander
170.944	BJ701-704	Ethics, French	177.62	BJ1533.F8	Friendship
170.9495	BJ801-804	Ethics, Greek	177.7	BJ1476	Forgiveness
170.95	BJ116-118	Ethics, Chinese	177.7	BJ1533.K5	Kindness
170.95	BJ961-977	Ethics, Oriental	178	BJ1535.A8	Avarice
170.951	BJ965-968	Ethics, Chinese	179	BJ1535.C7	Cruelty
170.9519	BJ973-976	Ethics, Korean	179.3	HV4701-4890.7	Animal rights
170.952	BJ969-971	Ethics, Japanese	179.5	BJ1535.S9	Swearing
170.954	BJ121-123	Ethics, Indic	179.6	BJ1533.C8	Courage

Dewey	LC	Subject Heading	Dewey	LC	Subject Heading
179.7	R726	Assisted suicide	184	B398.L9	Platonic love
179.7	R726	Euthanasia	184	B491.R44	Refutation (Logic)
179.8	BJ1534-1535	Vices	186	B525	Skeptics (Greek philosophy)
179.8	BJ1534-1535	Vice	186.3	B271	Eclecticism
179.8	BJ1535.A6	Anger	186.4	B517	Neoplatonism
179.8	BJ1535.P9	Pride and vanity	186.4	B645	Neoplatonism
179.9	BJ1430-1438	Compromise (Ethics)	188	B528	Stoics
179.9	BJ1477-1486	Cheerfulness	189	B630-708	Philosophy, Ancient
179.9	BJ1518-1691	Virtue	189	B720-785	Philosophy, Medieval
179.9	BJ1533.C5	Cheerfulness	189.4	B734	Scholasticism
179.9	BJ1533.D49	Self-control	189.5	B728	Mysticism
179.9	BJ1533.G8	Gratitude	190	B770-785	Philosophy, Renaissance
179.9	BJ1533.H7	Honesty	190	B790-5739	Philosophy, Modern
179.9	BJ1533.M73	Modesty	190	B802	Enlightenment
179.9	BJ1533.P3	Patience	191	B850-945	Philosophy, American
179.9	BJ1533.P9	Prudence	191	B981-995	Philosophy, Canadian
179.9	BJ1533.S27	Self-reliance	192	B1111-1674	Philosophy, English
180	B108-708	Philosophy, Ancient	193	B2521-3396	Philosophy, German
181	B121-162.7	Philosophy, Oriental	194	B1801-2430	Philosophy, French
181	B5000-5295	Philosophy, Oriental	195	B3551-3656	Philosophy, Italian
181.043	B162	Philosophy, Buddhist	196.1	B4561-4568	Philosophy, Spanish
181.044	B162.5	Jaina philosophy	196.9	B4591-4598	Philosophy, Portuguese
181.06	B154-157	Philosophy, Jewish	197	B4201-4279	Philosophy, Russian
181.06	B157.C65	Jewish cosmology	198.1	B4411-4445	Philosophy, Norwegian
181.07	B740-753	Philosophy, Islamic	198.5	B4455-4495	Philosophy, Swedish
181.09561	B162.6	Philosophy, Shinto	198.8	B4711-4800	Philosophy, Finnish
181.11	B125-128	Philosophy, Chinese	198.9	B4325-4395	Philosophy, Danish
181.11	B5230-5234	Philosophy, Chinese	199.437	B4801-4805	Philosophy, Czech
181.112	B127.C65	Philosophy, Confucian	199.438	B4687-4691	Philosophy, Polish
181.112	B127.N4	Neo-Confucianism	199.439	B4811-4815	Philosophy, Hungarian
181.114	B163	Philosophy, Taoist	199.492	B4041-4095	Philosophy, Dutch
181.119	B139.1-.4	Philosophy, Korean	199.493	B4151-4175	Philosophy, Belgian
181.12	B135-138	Philosophy, Japanese	199.494	B4628-4651	Philosophy, Swiss
181.12	B5243-5244	Philosophy, Japanese	199.495	B3500-3515	Philosophy, Greek (Modern)
181.2	B140-143	Philosophy, Egyptian	199.498	B4821-4825	Philosophy, Romanian
181.3	B755-759	Philosophy, Jewish	199.561	B4871-4875	Philosophy, Turkish
181.3	B5025-5099	Philosophy, Middle Eastern	199.6	B5300-5320	Philosophy, African
181.3	B5055-5059	Philosophy, Israeli	199.72	B1015-1019	Philosophy, Mexican
181.4	B130-133	Hinduism	199.728	B1025-1026	Philosophy, Central American
181.45	B132.Y6	Yoga			
181.482	B132.A3	Advaita	199.729	B1028-1029	Philosophy, West Indian
181.5	B150-153	Philosophy, Iranian	199.8	B1030-1084	Philosophy, South American
181.(6-8)	B5025-5099	Philosophy, Middle Eastern			
181.6	B145-148	Philosophy, Babylonian	200	BL	Religion
181.92	B740-753	Philosophy, Arab	200	BL48-50	Religion
181.92	B5295	Philosophy, Arab	200.25	BL35	Religion—Directories
182	B193	Atomism	200.5	BL1-10	Religion—Periodicals
183	B279	Hedonism	200.71	BL41	Religion—Study and teaching
183.1	B288	Sophists (Greek philosophy)			
183.6	B285	Megarians (Greek philosophy)	200.8	BL65.R3	Race—Religious aspects
			200.8	BL458	Sexism in religion
184	B398.C34	Plato's cave (Allegory)	200.8	BL65.E68	Equality—Religious aspects
184	B398.G6	God (Greek religion)	200.94	BL690-980	Europe—Religion
184	B398.I3	Idea (Philosophy)	200.956	BL660-687	Middle East—Religion

Dewey	LC	Subject Heading	Dewey	LC	Subject Heading
201.3	BL300-325	Mythology	203.37	BL406.C7	Crosses
201.3094	BL689-980	Mythology, European	203.4	BL570	Sacrifice
201.42	GN799.R4	Religion, Prehistoric	203.5	BL580-586	Shrines
201.44	BF1585-1623	Shamanism	203.6	BL619.S3	Sacred meals
201.44	BL2370.S5	Shamanism	203.7	BL600-620	Symbolism
201.615	BL53	Psychology, Religious	203.7	BL603	Emblems
201.65	BL239-265	Religion and science	203.7	BL604.C5	Circle—Religious aspects
201.7	BL55	Religion and civilization	203.7	BL604.S8	Swastika
201.7	BL60	Religion and sociology	203.7	BL604.V2	V symbol
201.7	BL65.C8	Religion and culture	203.8	BL600-619	Rites and ceremonies
201.72	BL65.P7	Religion and politics	203.8	BL590	Fasts and feasts
201.72	BL65.S8	Religion and state	203.8	BL600-619	Ritual
201.72	BL65.C58	Civil rights—Religious aspects	203.8	GN473	Rites and ceremonies
			204	BL624-627	Religious life
201.72	BL65.L33	Religion and law	204.2	BL626	Ecstasy
201.7621	BL65.M4	Medicine—Religious aspects	204.2	BL53	Experience (Religion)
			204.22	BL625	Mysticism
202.1	BL473	Gods	204.3	BL560	Prayer
202.1	BL525	Transmigration	204.3	BL560	Prayers
202.1	GN471	Animism	204.35	BL627	Meditation
202.1	GN472	Fetishism	204.47	BJ1491	Asceticism
202.11	GN489	Totemism	204.47	BL625	Asceticism
202.11	GN491	Totems	205	BJ47	Religion and ethics
202.114	BL325.M6	Mother goddesses	205	BJ1188-1295	Religious ethics
202.12	BL438	Moon worship	205.22	BL65.J87	Religion and justice
202.12	BL444	Tree worship	205.695	BV4627.B6	Blasphemy
202.12	BL325.M63	Mountain gods	206	BL11-21	Religion—Societies or Congresses
202.12	BL435-457	Nature worship			
202.12	BL438	Sun worship	206.1	BL635	Priests
202.12	BL439-443	Animal worship	206.1	BL475	Messiah
202.12	BL441	Serpent worship	206.5	BL632	Religious communities
202.12	BL447	Mountain worship	208.2	BL70-71	Sacred books
202.12	BL453	Fire-worshipers	210	BL51	Religion—Philosophy
202.13	BL465	Emperor worship	210	BL51	Knowledge, Theory of (Religion)
202.13	BL467	Ancestor worship			
202.15	BL477	Angels	210	BL51	Fictions, Theory of
202.16	BL480	Satanism	210	BL175-190	Natural theology
202.16	BL480	Demonology	210	BL210	Analogy (Religion)
202.16	BL480	Devil	211	BL215	Anthropomorphism
202.16	BL480	Satanism	211.2	BL220	Pantheism
202.18	BL485	Idols and images—Worship	211.3	BD555	Theism
202.22	BL256	Man (Theology)	211.3	BL200	Theism
202.22	BL290	Soul	211.32	BL217	Polytheism
202.3	BL500-547	Eschatology	211.33	BL218	Dualism (Religion)
202.3	BL503	Resurrection	211.34	BL221	Monotheism
202.3	BL535-547	Future life	211.4	BL2700-2790	Skepticism
202.3	BL545	Hell	211.4	BL2700-2790	Rationalism
202.37	BL515	Reincarnation	211.6	BL2700-2790	Secularism
203	BL550-620	Worship	211.7	BL2700-2790	Agnosticism
203	GN470-474	Worship	211.8	BL2700-2790	Atheism
203	GN475.3	Magic	213	BL263	Evolution—Religious aspects
203.1	BL325.H4	Healing gods			
203.2	BL613	Oracles	213	BL224-226	Creation
203.2	BL613	Divination	220	BS	Bible

Dewey	LC	Subject Heading	Dewey	LC	Subject Heading
220.(4-5)	BS420-429	Bible—Concordances	221.68	BS1183	Myth in the Old Testament
220.(4-5)	BS537	Bible—Language, style	221.7	BS1143-1158	Bible. O.T.—Commentaries
220.046	BS646	Apocalyptic literature	221.837	BS1199.E38	Education in the Bible
220.071	BS585-613	Bible—Study and teaching	221.92	BS1199.P7	Priests, Jewish
220.076	BS612	Bible—Examinations, questions, etc.	222.1	BS1221-1285.5	Bible. O.T. Pentateuch
			222.106	BS1225	Documentary hypothesis (Pentateuchal criticism)
220.0846	BS680.A34	Aged in the Bible			
220.09	BS445-460	Bible—History	222.11	BS658	Deluge
220.092	BS570-580	Bible—Biography	222.11	BS1237	Eden
220.1	BS480	Bible—Evidences, authority, etc.	222.11	BS1237	Forbidden fruit
			222.11	BL325.D4	Noah's ark
220.13	BS480	Bible—Inspiration	222.110922	BS573	Patriarchs (Bible)
220.15	BS647-649	Bible—Prophecies	222.1109505	BS658	Noah's ark
220.4	BS450-460	Bible—Versions	222.12	BS1245	Manna
220.49	BS560	Hieroglyphic Bibles	222.16	BS1281-1285.5	Ten commandments
220.5	BS405-408	Bible—Abridgments	223	BS1401-1405.5	Hebrew poetry, Biblical
220.5	BS450-460	Bible—Versions	223.2	BS1419-1450	Bible. O.T. Psalms
220.51	BS1-3	Bible. Polyglot	223.2	BS1445.M4	Royal Psalms
220.52	BS135-198	Bible. English	223.9	BS1481-1490	Bible. O.T. Song of Solomon
220.6	BS500-534.8	Bible—Criticism, interpretation, etc.	224	BS1501-1675.5	Prophets
220.6	BS1181.17	D document (Biblical criticism)	225.(4-5)	BS1901	Bible. N.T.—Versions
			225.(4-5)	BS2301-2308	Bible. N.T.—Concordances
220.6	BS1181.2	E document (Biblical criticism)	225.071	BS2525-2544	Bible. N.T.—Study and teaching
220.64	BS477	Symbolism in the Bible	225.09	BS2315-2318	Bible. N.T.—History
220.64	BS478	Typology (Theology)	in0225.6	BS2350-2393	Bible. N.T.—Criticism, interpretation, etc.
220.68	BS520.5	Myth in the Bible			
220.7	BS482-498	Bible—Commentaries	225.68	BS2378	Demythologizcation
220.817	BS680.E84	Ethics in the Bible	225.7	BS2333-2348	Bible. N.T.—Commentaries
220.8301	BS670	Sociology, Biblical	225.92	BS580.A3	Abraham (Biblical patriarch) in the New Testament
220.83058	BS661	Ethnology in the Bible			
220.83067	BS680.S5	Sex in the Bible	225.92	BS2440	Apostles
220.830685	BS680.F3	Family—Biblical teaching	225-228	BS1901-2970	Bible. N.T.
220.8330	BS670	Economics in the Bible	226	BS2549	Bible. N.T. Gospels
220.83638	BS680.F32	Famines in the Bible	226.6	BS26S20-2628	Bible. N.T. Acts
220.837	BS680.E3	Education in the Bible	226.8	BS680.P3	Bible—Parables
220.85	BS660-667	Nature in the Bible	226.8	BT373-378	Jesus Christ—Parables
220.852	BS655	Astronomy in the Bible	226.8	BT378.D5	Rich man and Lazarus (Parable)
220.9	BS569	Genealogy in the Bible			
220.9	BS635-636	Bible—History of Biblical events	226.8	BT378.G6	Good Samaritan (Parable)
			226.8	BT378.G7	Great supper (Parable)
220.9	BS637	Bible—Chronology	226.8	BT378.M8	Mustard seed (Parable)
220.9505	BS546-559	Bible stories	226.8	BT378.P	Pearl of great price (Parable)
221.(4-5)	BS701-1013	Bible. O.T.—Versions			
221.(4-5)	BS1121-1128	Bible. O.T.—Concordances	226.9	BT380-.2	Sermon on the mount
221.071	BS1193-1195	Bible. O.T.—Study and teaching	226.93	BT382	Beatitudes
			227	BS2630-2815.5	Bible. N.T. Epistles
221.09	BS1130-1134	Bible. O.T.—History	227	BS2640-2815.5	Bible. N.T. Pauline Epistles
221.092	BS580	Bible. O.T.—Biography	228	BS646	Revelation
221.47	BS767-815	Bible. O.T. Latin	228	BS2820-2827	Four Horsemen of the Apocalypse
221.48	BS737-765	Bible. O.T. Greek			
221.6	BS1160-1191.5	Bible. O.T.—Criticism, interpretation, etc.	229	BS1691-1830	Bible. O.T. Apocrypha
			229	BS2831-2970	Apocryphal books (New Testament)
221.65	BS1104	Bible. O.T.—Harmonies			

Dewey	LC	Subject Heading	Dewey	LC	Subject Heading
230	BR	Christianity	231.73	BS2545.M5	Miracles
230	BR1-129	Christianity	231.73	BT97-.2	Miracles
230	BR115.C5	Civilization, Christian	231.74	BT126-127.5	Revelation
230	BR115.H5	History (Theology)	231.74	BX8643.R4	Revelation (Mormon theology)
230	BS2397	Bible. N.T.—Theology	231.745	BX8643.P7	Prophets (Mormon theology)
230	BT	Doctrinal theology			
230	BT19-33	Dogma	231.76	BT155	Covenant theology
230	BV	Practical theology	231.765	BS651-652	Creation
230.01	BT40-55	Philosophical theology	231.765	BS651-652	Biblical cosmology
230.041	BS543	Bible—Theology	231.765	BT98-102	God—Proof, Cosmological
230.0411	BS1192.5	Bible. O.T.—Theology	231.765	BX8643.C68	Mormon cosmology
230.046	BR1615-1617	Liberalism (Religion)	231.7652	BS651-652	Creationism
230.046	BT82.25	Dominion theology	231.8	BT137	God—Goodness
230.0464	BT83.57	Liberation theology	231.8	BT160-162	Theodicy
230.071	BV4019-4180	Theology—Study and teaching	231-239	BT65-84	Theology, Doctrinal
			232	BT198-590	Jesus Christ
230.071	BV4163	Pretheological education	232	BT306	Jesus Christ—Words
230.0711	BV4019-4160	Theological seminaries	232.1	BT220	Incarnation
230.0711	BV4164	Seminary extension	232.1	BT225	Typology (Theology)
230.082	BT83.55	Feminist theology	232.1	BT230-245	Jesus Christ—Messiahship
230.08996	BT82.7	Black theology	232.2	BT210	Logos
230.09	BT20-30	Theology, Doctrinal—History	232.8	BT198-590	Jesus Christ—Person and offices
230.1	BT1115	Apologetics—Early church, ca. 30-600	232.9	BT232	Son of Man
			232.901	BT300-302	Jesus Christ—Biography
230.2	BX1746-1755	Catholic Church—Doctrines	232.903	BT304-.97	Jesus Christ—Character
230.2	BX1752	Catholic Church—Apologetic works	232.91	BT595-680	Mary, Blessed Virgin, Saint
			232.91	BT610-660	Mary, Blessed Virgin, Saint—Theology
230.342	BX5137-5140	Church of England—Doctrines	232.911	BT620	Immaculate Conception
230.373	BX5929-5930.2	Episcopal Church—Doctrines	232.917	BT650-660	Visions
			232.917	BT650-654	Mary, Blessed Virgin, Saint—Apparitions and miracles
230.42	BX9420-9422.2	Reformed Church—Doctrines			
230.6(1-5)	BX6330-6331.2	Baptists—Doctrines	232.921	BT317	Virgin birth
230.7	BX8330-8331.2	Methodist Church—Doctrines	232.923	BT315	Magi
			232.95	BT340-500	Jesus Christ—Biography—Public life
230-299	BL74-98	Religions			
231	BT98-180	God			
231	BT99	God—Biblical teaching	232.954	BS2415-2417	Jesus Christ—Teachings
231	BT124	Immanence of God	232.955	BTB363-367	Jesus Christ—Miracles
231	BT153.S8	Suffering of God	232.956	BT410	Jesus Christ—Transfiguration
231	BT180.G6	Glory of God			
231.042	BT98-101	God—Proof, Ontological	232.957	BT420	Last Supper
231.044	BT109-115	Trinity	232.96	BT414	Holy Week
231.09	BT98	God—History of doctrines	232.96	BT430-470	Jesus Christ—Passion
231.3	BT117-123	Holy Spirit	232.963	BT465	Holy Cross
231.4	BT130-157	God—Attributes	232.966	BT587	Jesus Christ—Relics
231.4	BT131	God—Omniscience	232.966	BT587.S4	Holy Shroud
231.4	BT133	God—Omnipotence	233	BS661	Man (Theology)
231.5	BT95-96.2	Providence and government of God	233	BT700-745	Man (Christian theology)
			233	BT700-745	Man (Theology)
231.5	BT135	Providence and government of God	233	BT704	Woman (Christian theology)
231.72	BT94	Kingdom of God	233.14	BT710	Fall of man
231.73	BS1199.M5	Miracles			

Dewey	LC	Subject Heading	Dewey	LC	Subject Heading
233.14	BT715-722	Sin	236.9	BT885-886	Second Advent
233.14	BT720	Sin, Original	236.9	BT890-891	Millennium
233.5	BT708	Sex—Religious aspects—Christianity	238	BT990-1010	Creeds
			238	BT990	Creeds, Ecumenical
233.5	BT740-743	Soul	238	BT1029-1040	Catechisms
234	BT750-810.2	Salvation	238	BX8068-8070	Catechetics
234	BT755	Salvation outside the Catholic Church	238.2	BX1958-1968	Catholic Church—Catechisms
234	BT759	Salvation outside the church	238.373	BX5939	Episcopal Church—Creeds
			238.373	BX6074	Episcopal Church—Creeds
234	BT760-769	Grace (Theology)	238.58	BX7235-7236.2	Congregational churches—Creeds
234	BT773	Merit (Christianity)			
234	BT809-810.2	Election (Theology)	238.6	BX6335	Baptists—Creeds
234.13	BT123	Baptism in the Holy Spirit	238.6(1-5)	BX6336	Baptists—Catechisms
234.13	BT767.3	Gifts, Spiritual	238.7	BX8335	Methodist Church—[Catechisms/Creeds]
234.131	BT732.5-.56	Spiritual healing			
234.166	BX5949.C6	Confession	239	BT1095-1255	Apologetics
234.23	BT770-772	Faith	239.09	BT1109-1115	Apologetics—History
234.3	BT775	Redemption	239.7	BT1209-1211	Rationalism
234.4	BT790	Regeneration (Theology)	240-248	BV1-4	Theology, Practical
234.5	BT263-268	Atonement	241	BJ1188.5-1278	Christian ethics
234.5	BT795	Forgiveness of sin	241	BV4618	Human acts
234.5	BT800	Repentance	241	BV4625-4780	Christian ethics
234.7	BT763-764.2	Justification	241	BJ1188.5-1278	Christian ethics
234.8	BT767	Holiness	241.1	BV4615	Conscience
234.9	BT809-810.2	Predestination	241.1	BX2377	Conscience, Examination of
235	BT960-962	Spirits	241.2	BT95-97	Law (Theology)
235.2	BT683-694	Saints	241.3	BR115.W2	Evil, Non-resistance to
235.2	BV890	Relics	241.3	BT721	Sin, Unpardonable
235.2	BX380	Christian saints	241.3	BT725	Temptation
235.2	BX575-577.5	Christian saints	241.3	BV4625-4627	Sins
235.2	BX577	Relics	241.3	BV4625-4627	Vices
235.2	BX2315	Relics	241.3	BV4625	Sin
235.24	BX576	Canonization	241.3	BV4626	Deadly sins
235.24	BX2330	Canonization	241.3	BV4627.H8	Hypocrisy
235.3	BT960-968	Angels	241.3	BV4627.Q	Quarreling
235.3	BT968.M5	Michael (Archangel)	241.3	BV4627.R4	Revenge
235.4	BT850-860	Limbo	241.3	BV4627.S6	Slander
235.4	BT980-981	Devil	241.3	BV4627.S9	Swearing
236	BT819-891	Eschatology	241.3	BV4630-4647	Vice
236	BT985	Antichrist	241.3	BV4726.S2	Sacrilege
236.2	BT899-940	Future life	241.31	BV4625.6-.7	Sin, Venial
236.21	BT910-912	Eternity	241.4	BR1610	Religious tolerance
236.22	BT919-925	Immortality	241.4	BV1518-1533	Virtues
236.23	BT919-925	Conditional immortality	241.4	BV4625-4627	Virtues
236.23	BT930	Annihilationism	241.4	BV4630-4647	Virtue
236.24	BT844-849	Heaven	241.4	BV4635-4639	Theological virtues
236.24	BT844-849	Paradise	241.4	BV4637	Faith
236.25	BT834-838	Hell	241.4	BV4639	Charity
236.4	BT830	Intermediate state	241.4	BV4645	Cardinal virtues
236.5	BT840-842	Purgatory	241.4	BV4647.D6	Discretion
236.8	BT870-872	Resurrection	241.4	BV4647.M2	Magnanimity
236.9	BT875-891	End of the world	241.4	BV4647.M3	Meekness
236.9	BT880-882	Judgment Day	241.4	BV4647.M4	Corporal works of mercy

Dewey	LC	Subject Heading	Dewey	LC	Subject Heading
241.4	BV4647.M4	Spiritual works of mercy	248.29	BV5090-5091	Trance
241.4	BV4647.M4	Mercy	248.29	BV5091.E3	Ecstasy
241.4	BV4647.P5	Piety	248.29	BV5091.R4	Private revelations
241.4	BV4647.S4	Self-denial	248.29	BV5091.R4	Revelation
241.4	BV4647.T4	Temperance (Virtue)	248.29	BV5091.V6	Visions
241.5	BV4720-4730	Commandments of the church	248.3	BV5-530	Worship
			248.309	BV5-8	Worship—History
241.52	BV4655-4710	Ten commandments	248.30901	BV6	Worship—History—Early church, ca. 30-600
241.54	BV4715	Golden rule			
241.62	BV4647.J	Justice (Virtue)	248.34	BV4800-4870	Meditations
241.66	BV4647.C5	Virginity	248.34	BV5091.C7	Contemplation
241.66	BV4647.C5	Chastity	248.34	BX2177-2198	Meditations
242	BS617.8	Bible—Devotional use	248.4	BV4500-4595	Christian life
242	BV4800-4895	Devotional literature	248.47	BV5015-5068	Asceticism
242	BV4815	Devotion	248.47	BV5055	Fasting
242	BX2177-2198	Devotional literature	248.47	BV5099	Quietism
242.2	BV283.G7	Grace at meals	248.470901	BV5023	Asceticism—History—Early church, ca. 30-600
242.2	BV283.S3	Schools—Prayers			
242.2	BV287	Prayer groups	248.470902	BV5025	Asceticism—History—Middle Ages, 600-1500
242.3	BV4810-4812	Devotional calendars			
242.4	BV4900-4911	Consolation	248.5	BV4520	Witness bearing (Christianity)
242.5	BS680.P64	Bible—Prayers			
242.72	BV194.D	Doxology	248.6	BV772	Stewardship, Christian
242.74	BT303	Mysteries of the Rosary	248.6	BX5165	Tithes
242.74	BX2310.R7	Rosary	248.6	BX8643.T5	Tithes—Mormon Church
242.8	BV245-283	Prayer-books	248.83	BV4530-4579	Youth—Religious life
242.802	BX2050-2155	Catholic Church—Prayer-books and devotions	248.85	BV4580	Aged—Religious life
			248.88	BV4593	Working class—Religious life
242.802	BX2080	Books of hours	249	BV200	Family—Religious life
242.82	BV283.B7	Boys—Prayer-books and devotions	249	BV1590	Religious education—Home training
246.55	BV150-168	Symbolism	250	BV637.8	Small churches
246.55	BV150-168	Signs and symbols	250	BV652.9	Church controversies
246.55	BV150-155	Emblems	250.91732	BV637	City churches
246.558	BV160	Crosses	250.91733	BV637.7	Suburban churches
246.558	CC300-350	Crosses	250.91734	BV638-.8	Rural churches
246.6	BV165	Colors, Liturgical	251	BV4200-4317	Preaching
246.6	BX8643.T4	Mormon temples	251	BV4235.B56	Biographical preaching
246.75	BV301-530	Hymns	251	BV4235.E8	Extemporaneous preaching
246.75	BV520	Sunday schools—Hymns	251	BV4235.L3	Lay preaching
247.1	BV195-196	Altars	251	BV4235.L43	Lectionary preaching
247.1	BV863.P4	Pews and pew rights	251	BV4235.T65	Topical preaching
248	BV4800-4897	Devotional exercises	251.009	BV4207-4208	Preaching—History
248.2	BR110	Experience (Religion)	252	BV4239-4316	Sermons
248.2	BR112	Enthusiasm	252	BV4254.2	Occasional sermons
248.2	BR114	Fanaticism	252	BV4257.5	Communion sermons
248.2	BV4912-4915	Experience (Religion)	252	BV4307.D5	Dialogue sermons
248.22	BV5070-5095	Mysticism	252.02	BX1756	Catholic Church— Sermons
248.22	BV5095	Mystics	252.03	BX5008	Anglican Communion—Sermons
248.24	BR110	Conversion			
248.24	BT780	Conversion	252.041	BX8066	Lutheran Church—Sermons
248.24	BV4912-4950	Conversion			
248.24	BV4930-4935	Converts	252.042	BX9426	Reformed Church—Sermons
248.29	BV5083	Discernment of spirits			

17

Dewey	LC	Subject Heading	Dewey	LC	Subject Heading
252.046	BX8577	Moravians—Sermons	254.5	BV4523	Church attendance
252.05	BX9178	Presbyterian Church—Sermons	254.7	BV636	Church buildings—Interdenominational use
252.058	BX7233	Congregational churches—Sermons	254.8	BV770-777	Church finance
252.06(1-5)	BX6333	Baptists—Sermons	254.8	BV771	Tithes
252.067	BX6123	Adventists—Sermons	254.8	BV772	Christian giving
252.091	BX9843	Unitarian Universalist churches—Sermons	254.8	BV772.5	Church fund raising
			254.8	BX1950	Catholic Church—Finance
252.09134	BX9943	Universalism—Sermons	255.00901	BV761.A1-.A5	Church orders, Ancient
252.093	BX8639	Mormon Church— Sermons	255.(1-7)	BX2400-4560	Monasticism and religious orders
252.094	BX8724	New Jerusalem Church—Sermons	255.(1-7)	BX2435	Monastic and religious life
252.096	BX7733	Society of Friends—Sermons	255.(1-7)	BX2460-2749	Monasteries
			255.(1-7)	BX4668.2-.3	Ex-monks
252.097	BX8127	Mennonites—Sermons	255.(1-7)009	BX2460-2749	Monastic and religious life—History
252.097	BX8129.A1	Mennonites—Parties and movements	255.(1-7)0094	BX2631-2676	Monasticism and religious orders—Europe
252.098	BX9777	Shakers—Sermons	255.(1-7)0095	BX2677-2731	Monasticism and religious orders—Asia
252.1	BV4275	Funeral sermons			
252.3	BV3797	Evangelistic sermons	255.(1-7)0096	BX2732-2740	Monasticism and religious orders—Africa
252.53	BV4315	Children's sermons			
252.55	BV4310	Youth sermons	255.(1-7)00971	BX2527-2529	Monasticism and religious orders—Canada
252.6	BV4254.3	Festival-day sermons			
252.6	BV4270	Fast-day sermons	255.(1-7)00972	BX2530-2532	Monasticism and religious orders—Mexico
252.61	BV40	Advent sermons			
252.615	BV4257	Christmas sermons	255.(1-7)00973	BX2505-2525	Monasticism and religious orders—United States
252.63	BV4259	Easter—Sermons			
252.68	BV4255	Baccalaureate addresses	255.(1-7)06	BX2436-2437	Monasticism and religious orders—Rules
252.68	BV4260-4261	Election sermons			
252.68	BV4262	Execution sermons	255.2	BX3501-3556	Dominicans
252.68	BV4282	New Year sermons	255.(2-3)	BX2820	Friars
252.7	BV4290	Installation (Clergy)	255.3	BX3601-3656	Franciscans
252.7	BX8333	Methodist Church—Sermons	255.3	BX3651-3653	Secular Franciscans
			255.4	BX2901-2956	Augustinians
253	BV4000-4470	Pastoral theology	255.7	CR5547-5575	Orders of knighthood and chivalry, Papal
253	BV4335	Pastoral medicine			
253.2	BV4327	Clergy—Political activity	255.791	CR4701-4731	Orders of knighthood and chivalry, Papal
253.2	BV4395.5	Clergy—Divorce			
253.22	BV4396	Clergy—Family relationships	255.791	CR5547-5577	Papal decorations
253.25	BV4390	Celibacy	255.7914	CR4759-4775	Teutonic Knights
253.252	BX1912.9	Catholic Church—Clergy—Sexual behavior	255.7914	DK4600.P77	Teutonic Knights
			255.8	BV4405-4408	Monasticism and religious orders, Protestant
253.5	BV4012.2	Pastoral counseling	255.819	BX385	Monasticism and religious orders
253.5	BV4012.25	Pastoral counseling centers			
253.52	BV4012-.3	Pastoral psychology	255.819	BX580-583	Monasticism and religious orders
253.53	BV5053	Spiritual direction			
253.53	BX382.5	Spiritual direction	255.83	BX5178	Anglican orders
253.53	BX2350.7	Spiritual direction	255.83	BX5970-5974	Monasticism and religious orders, Anglican
254	BV168.S7	Staff, Pastoral			
254	BV652-.9	Church management	255.9(1-7)	BX4200-4556	Sisterhoods
254.4	BV652.95-657	Church publicity	255.9(1-7)	BX4200-4563	Monasticism and religious orders for women
254.4	BV653	Advertising—Churches			
254.5	BV652.25	Church growth	255.972	BX4337-.5	Dominican sisters
254.5	BV820	Church membership	255.973	BX4361-4364	Franciscans

Dewey	LC	Subject Heading	Dewey	LC	Subject Heading
255.983	BX5185	Sisterhoods	262.096	BX7740-7746	Society of Friends—Government
258.0835	BV4427-4430	Youth in church work			
259.082	BV4445.5	Abused women—Pastoral counseling of	262.098	BX9776	Shakers—Government
			262.1	BV652.1	Christian leadership
261	BV601.3	Church—Catholicity	262.1	BV705	Church officers
261	BV601.8	Mission of the church	262.1	BX8659.5	Aaronic Priesthood (Mormon Church)
261.2	BR127-128	Christianity and other religions			
			262.12	BV669-670.2	Episcopacy
261.5	BT738-.5	Sociology, Christian	262.12	BX5176-5178	Episcopacy
261.7	BV629-631	Church and state	262.12	BX5179	Archdeacons
261.7	BX1790-1795	Church and state—Catholic Church	262.122	BX1905	Catholic Church—Bishops
			262.13	BX400-440	Patriarchs and patriarchate
261.8	HT910-921	Slavery and the church	262.13	BX950-961	Papacy
261.83	HN30-39	Church and social problems	262.13	BX958.A23	Popes—Abdication
262	BT1010	Covenants (Church polity)	262.13	BX958.V7	Papal visits
262	BV590-640	Church	262.13	BX1001-1378	Popes
262.0011092	BX6.7-.8	Ecumenists	262.13	BX1805-1810	Popes
262.0017	BV600	Church renewal	262.13	CR5547-5577	Nobility, Papal
262.009	BR97-99	Ecclesiastical geography	262.131	BX1806	Popes—Infallibility
262.01947	BX520-558	Orthodox Eastern Church—Government	262.14	BV659-683	Priests
			262.14	BV659-683	Clergy
262.02	BX1800-1920	Catholic Church—Government	262.14	BV674	Associate clergy
			262.14	BV675	Group ministry
262.02	BX1911	Archdeacons	262.14	BV675.7	Clergy couples
262.02	BX1912	Deacons	262.14	BV676	Women clergy
262.02	BX1939.A3	Administrators apostolic	262.14	BV676	Ordination of women
264.02(1-9)	BX1999.8-2047	Catholic Church—Liturgy—Texts	262.14	BV680	Deacons
			262.14	BV685	Ordination
262.03	BX5175-5182.5	Priests	262.14	BV830	Ordination
262.03	BX5175-5182.5	Church of England—Clergy	262.14	BV4423-4425	Deaconesses
262.03	BX5179	Archdeacons	262.14091732	BV637.5	City clergy
262.0342	BX5150-5182.5	Church of England—Government	262.142	BX1910	Vicars apostolic
			262.142	BX1910	Vicars-general
262.0373	BX5950-5968	Episcopal Church—Government	262.142	BX1912-1914.5	Priests
262.0373	BX6076	Episcopal Church—Government	262.142	BX1912-1914.5	Catholic Church—Clergy
			262.15	BV677	Lay readers
262.041	BX8071-.2	Lutheran Church—Clergy	262.15	BV687	Laity
262.042	BX9425	Reformed Church—Government	262.152	BX1920	Laity—Catholic Church
			262.17092	BX4663-4665	Cardinals
262.05	BX9190-9195	Presbyterian Church—Government	262.26	BV4405-4406	Christian communities
			262.3	BX837.5	Episcopal conferences (Catholic)
262.058	BX7240-7246	Congregational churches—Government			
			262.3	BX838	Diocesan pastoral councils
262.06(1-5)	BX6340-6346.3	Baptists—Government	262.5	BV626	Local church councils
262.13090 (1 to 23)	BX965-1263	Papacy—History—To 1309	262.52	BX820-838	Councils and synods, Episcopal (Catholic)
			262.73	BT972	Communion of saints
262.(4-5)	BV710	Councils and synods	262.8	BT20-30	Heresies, Christian
262.07	BX8340-8345.5	Methodist Church—Government	262.8	BT88-92	Authority—Religious aspects
262.091	BX9850	Unitarian Universalist churches—Government	262.8	BT91	Church—Authority
			262.9	BV759-763	Ecclesiastical law
262.094	BX8737	New Jerusalem Church—Government	262.90901	BV761	Canon law—Early church, ca. 30-600
262.095	BX6958	Christian Science—Government	262.91	BX860	Encyclicals, Papal

Dewey	LC	Subject Heading	Dewey	LC	Subject Heading
262.91	BX863	Letters, Papal	264.02	BX2015.5.H	Dog Mass
262.932	BX1939.A	Abbots (Canon law)	264.02	BX2045.E96	Exultets (Liturgy)
262.932	BX1939.C665	Clergy (Canon law)	264.02	BX2230-2234	Mass
262.932	BX1939.P47	Persons (Canon law)	264.02	BX2347-2348	Catholic Church—
262.933	BX1939.A	Absolution (Canon law)			Liturgy—Theology
262.933	BX1939.B3	Baptism (Canon law)	264.02036	BX2215-2239	Lord's Supper
262.933	BX1939.C3	Catechetics (Canon law)	264.02036	BX2215.A1	Eucharistic congresses
262.933	BX1939.C72	Confirmation (Canon law)	264.02036	BX2220	Transubstantiation
262.934	BX1939.T65	Trial practice (Canon law)	264.02036	BX2231.7	Private masses
263.04	BX2323	Christian pilgrims and	264.02036	BX2237	First communion
		pilgrimages	264.02036	BX2307.3	Baptismal water
263.042	BX2320-2321	Christian shrines	264.0207	BX2290	Extreme unction
263.3	BV107-133	Sunday	264.0208	BX2200-2292	Sacraments (Liturgy)
263.9	BV30-135	Fasts and feasts	264.02084	BX2240	Ordination—Catholic
263.9	BV30-135	Church year			Church
263.9	BV50.A4	All Souls' Day	264.02085	BX2045.W34	Wake services
263.9	CE81	Fasts and feasts	264.02085	BX2250-2254	Marriage service
263.915	BV50.E7	Epiphany	264.02086	BX2260-2283	Penance
263.92	BV53	Palm Sunday	264.020862	BX2262-2267	Confession
263.92	BV85-95	Lent	264.020866	BX2279-2283	Indulgences
263.925	BT414	Holy Week	264.0209	BX2295-2310	Sacramentals
263.925	BV90-95	Holy Week	264.0209	BX2310.A	Agnus Dei (Sacramental)
263.925	BV95	Good Friday	264.02092	BX2305	Consecration of virgins
263.93	BV55	Paschal mystery	264.02094	BX2340	Exorcism
263.93	BV55	Easter	264.023	BX2015-2016	Missals
263.93	BV57	Ascension Day	264.023	BX2037	Sacramentaries
263.94	BT122.5	Pentecost	264.024	BX2000-.68	Breviaries
263.94	BV60	Pentecost Festival	264.0274	BX2040	Stations of the Cross
263.94	BV61-63	Pentecost season	264.03	BX5123	Ritualism
263.97	BV50.A7	Feast of the Assumption of	264.03	BX5145	Church of England—
		the Blessed Virgin			Prayer-Books and devotions
263.97	BV50.H6	Feast of the Holy Innocents	264.03	BX5149.C5	Lord's Supper
263.97	BV50.I6	Feast of the Immaculate	264.03	BX5940-5948	Episcopal Church—Liturgy
		Conception	264.03	BX5943-5945	Episcopal Church—
263.97	BV64.J4	Feast of Jesus Christ the			Prayer-books and devotions
		King	264.03	BX6075	Episcopal Church—Liturgy
263.97	BV64.S3	Feast of the Sacred Heart	264.0342	BX5140.5-5147	Church of England— Liturgy
263.97	BV75	Thanksgiving Day	264.035	BX5148-5149	Sacraments—Church of
263.98	BV67	All Saints' Day			England
264	BV5-25	Public worship	264.035	BX5949	Episcopal Church
264	BV169-199	Liturgics	264.03562	BX5149.C6	Confession
264	BV169-199	Rites and ceremonies	264.041	BX8067	Lutheran Church—Liturgy
264	BV180-181	Ritualism	264.04108	BX8072-8073.5	Sacraments—Lutheran
264	BV186.7	Ecumenical liturgies			Church
264	BV196.C	Censers	264.042	BX9427-.5	Reformed Church—Liturgy
264	BV198-199	Liturgies	264.05	BX9185-9187	Presbyterian Church—
264.01	BV185	Liturgies, Early Christian			Liturgy
264.019	BX350-376	Orthodox Eastern	264.05	BX9188-9189	Sacraments—Presbyterian
		Church—Liturgy			Church
264.019	BX377-378	Sacraments—Orthodox	264.058	BX7237	Congregational
		Eastern Church			churches—Liturgy
264.01947	BX560-563	Orthodox Eastern	264.05808	BX7238-7239	Sacraments—
		Church—Russia			Congregational churches
264.02	BX1970	Liturgical language	264.06(1-5)	BX6337	Baptists—Liturgy
264.02	BX1970.A7-.Z	Catholic Church—Liturgy	264.06708	BX6124.3-.6	Sacraments—Adventists

Dewey	LC	Subject Heading	Dewey	LC	Subject Heading
264.07	BX8337	Methodist Church—Liturgy	266.00946	BV3120-3127	Missions—Spain
264.0708	BX8338	Sacraments—Methodist Church	266.0095	BV3149-3487	Missions—Asia
			266.00952	BV3440-3457	Missions—Japan
264.0913308	BX9854	Sacraments—Unitarianism	266.0096	BV3500-3630	Missions—Africa
264.0913408	BX9954	Sacraments—Universalism	266.00971	BV2810-2820	Missions—Canada
264.09308	BX8655-.3	Sacraments—Mormon Church	266.00994	BV3650-3660	Missions—Australia
			266.0099(3-6)	BV3640-3680	Missions—Oceania
264.09408	BX8736	Sacraments—New Jerusalem Church	266.022	BV2650	Home missions
			266.2	BV2130-2300	Catholic Church— Missions
264.095	BX6960	Christian Science—Liturgy	266.373	BX5969	Episcopal Church— Missions
264.13	BV197.B5	Benediction			
264.13	BV205-287	Prayer—Christianity	266.93	BX8661	Mormon Church— Missions
264.13	BV228-284	Prayers	267	BV900-1450	Church societies
264.13	BV250-254	Pastoral prayers	267	BV950-1220	Brotherhoods
264.13	BX2048.B5	Benediction	267.16	BJ10.M6	Moral re-armament
264.36	BV820	Close and open communion	267.3	BV1000-1220	Young Men's Christian associations
264.36	BV823-828	Lord's Supper			
264.9	BV197.S5	Cross, Sign of the	267.5	BV1300-1393	Young Women's Christian associations
264.9	BV875-885	Sacramentals			
265	BV199.R5	Responsive worship	268	BV1500-1578	Sunday schools
265	BV800-873	Sacraments	268	BV1585	Vacation schools, Religious
265.1	BV803-814	Baptism	268.3	BV1531	Directors of religious education
265.1	BV814	Baptism for the dead			
265.12	BV813-.2	Infant baptism	268.432	BV1474-1475.2	Christian education of children
265.2	BV815	Confirmation			
265.5	BV835-838	Marriage	268.6	BV1534-1536	Religious education— Teaching methods
265.6	BV840-850	Penance			
265.62	BV845-847	Confessors	268.6	BV4560-4579	Sunday school literature
265.62	BV845-847	Confession	268.635	BV1535	Religious education— Audio-visual aids
265.62	BX5949.C6	Confession			
265.85	BV199.F8	Funeral service	268.67	BV1534.4	Drama in Christian education
265.9	BV199	Occasional services			
265.9	BV873.F7	Foot washing (Rite)	268.82	BX895-939	Catholic Church— Education
265.9	BV873.L3	Imposition of hands			
265.92	BV199.D4	Dedication services	268.82	BX1968	Catechetics
265.92	BV4501	Consecration	268.8373	BX5850-5876	Episcopal Church— Education
265.94	BV873.E8	Exorcism			
266	BV2000-3705	Missions	268.8373	BX6061-6064.5	Episcopal Church— Education
266	BV2082.A9	Aeronautics in missionary work			
			268.846	BX8561-8564.5	Moravians—Education
266	BV2082.I6	Missions—Interdenominational cooperation	268.85	BX8917-8925	Presbyterian Church—Education
266	BV2350-2595	Protestant churches—Missions	268.858	BX7119-7127	Congregational churches—Education
266	BV2619-2623	Missions to Jews	268.86(1-5)	BX6219-6227	Baptists—Education
266	BV2625-2626.4	Missions to Muslims	268.87	BX8219-8227	Methodist Church—Education
266	BV2637	Missions to lepers			
266.0083	BV2617	Youth in missionary work	268.891	BX9817-9823	Unitarian Universalist churches—Education
266.009	BV2400-2595	Protestant churches— Missions—History	268.89134	BX9917-9923	Universalism—Education
			268.893	BX8610	Mormon Church— Education
266.0092	BV3700-3705	Missionaries			
266.0094	BV2855-3145	Missions—Europe	268.894	BX8714	New Jerusalem Church—Education
266.00941	BV2860-2895	Missions—Great Britain			
266.00943	BV2950-2957	Missions—Germany	268.895	BX6917	Christian Science— Education
266.00944	BV2940-2945	Missions—France			

Dewey	LC	Subject Heading	Dewey	LC	Subject Heading
268.896	BX7619-7627	Society of Friends—Education	273.4	BT1350	Arianism
			273.4	BT1370	Donatists
268.898	BX9761-9764	Shakers—Education	273.7	BR1650-1653	Pietism
269.2	BV3750-3799	Evangelistic work	273.9	BT82	Modernism
269.2	BV3793	Evangelistic invitations			
269.2	BV4487.E9	Evangelical academies	274-279	BR500-1500	[By region or country]—Church history
269.2	BX5925	Evangelicalism—Episcopal Church	274.1	BR740-799	Great Britain—Church history
269.2092	BV3780-3785	Evangelists	274.10902	BR745-754	England—Church history—1066-1485
269.24	BV3750-3799	Revivals			
269.24	BV3798-3799	Camp-meetings	274.109021	BR749	England—Church history—449-1066
269.24	BX6475-6476	Church camps—Baptists	274.10903	BR750	England—Church history—1485-
269.24	BX8475-8476	Camp-meetings			
269.6	BV5068.R4	Retreats	274.109031	BR755-757	England—Church history—16th century
269.6	BX2375-2376	Retreats—Catholic Church			
269.6	BX2375	Parish missions	274.109032	BR756	England—Church history—17th century
270	BT1313-1480	Theology—History			
270	BX940-1745	Catholic Church—History	274.109033	BR758	Evangelical Revival
270.01	BR138	Church history— Philosophy	274.10904	BR759	England—Church history—20th century
270.03	BR95	Church history—Dictionaries			
270.05	BR1-9	Church history— Periodicals	274.3	BR850-856.35	Germany—Church history
270.06	BR21-29	Church history—Societies, etc.	274.4	BR748	Celtic Church
			274.4	BR794	Celtic Church
270.06	BR41-43	Church history—Congresses	274.4	BR840-849	France—Church history
			274.6	BR1020-1029	Spain—Church history
270.089	BT734-.3	Race—Religious aspects—Christianity	274.7	BR930-939	Russia—Church history
			274.8	BR970-1019	Scandinavia—Church history
270.089	BT734-.3	Race			
270.092	BR60-67	Fathers of the church	275	BR1060-1357	Asia—Church history
270.092	BR1690-1725	Church history—Biography	275.1	BR1280-1297	China—Church history
270.092	BR1690-1725	Christian biography	275.19	BR1320-1337	Korea—Church history
270.092	BR1705	Fathers of the church	275.2	BR1300-1317	Japan—Church history
270.092	BX2325-2333	Christian saints	275.4	BR1150-1156	India—Church history
270.(1-8)	BR160-481	Church history—[By date]	275.9	BR1178-1261	Asia, Southeastern—Church history
270.(1-2)	BR160-240	Church history—Primitive and early church, ca. 30-600			
			276	BR1359-1470	Africa—Church history
270.(1-2)	BS2410	Christianity—Early church, ca. 30-600	276.1	BR1369-1415	Africa, North—Church history
			276.6	BR1460-1463	Africa, West—Church history
270.1092	BR60-67	Apostolic Fathers	276.7	BR1430	Africa, Central—Church history
270.3	BR160-270	Church history—Middle Ages, 600-1500			
			276.76	BR1440-1445	Africa, East—Church history
270.(5-8)	BR290-481	Church history—Modern period, 1500-	276.8	BR1446-1458	Africa, Southern—Church history
270.6	BR295	Reformation—Early movements			
			277.2	BR610-615	Mexico—Church history
270.6	BR300-420	Reformation	277.28	BR620-625	Central America—Church history
270.6	BR307	Reformation—Causes			
270.6	BR430	Counter-Reformation	277.29	BR655	Caribbean Area—Church history
270.82	BR1644-.5	Pentecostalism			
270.82	BT82.2	Fundamentalism	277.3	BR513-569	United States—Religion
272	BR1600-1609	Persecution	277.3081	BR520	Great Awakening
272.2	BX1700-1745	Inquisition	278	BR660-730	South America—Church history
273.1	BT1390	Gnosticism			

Dewey	LC	Subject Heading	Dewey	LC	Subject Heading
279.4	BR1480-1483	Australia—Church history	281.9	BX200-754	Orthodox Eastern Church
279.9(5-6)	BR1490-1495	Oceania—Church history	281.9436	BX630-639	Orthodox Eastern Church—Austria
280	BR157	Christian sects			
280	BX	Christian denominations	281.9439	BX630-639	Orthodox Eastern Church—Hungary
280.042	BV625	Interdenominational cooperation	281.947	BX460-605	Orthodox Eastern Church
280.042	BX1-9.5	Christian union	281.94709	BX485-492	Orthodox Eastern Church—History
280.042	BX9.5.A37	Ecumenical movement—African influences	281.9495	BX610-619	Orthodox Eastern Church—Greece
280.042	BX9.5.E94	Evangelicalism and Christian union	282	BX800-4795	Catholic Church
280.042	BX9.5.L55	Liturgics and Christian union	282.03	BX841	Catholic Church—Dictionaries
280.042	BX9.5.P29	Papacy and Christian union	282.05	BX800-806	Catholic Church—Periodicals
280.042	BX9.5.V45	Veneration of saints and Christian union	282.06	BX808-816	Catholic Church—Societies, etc.
280.0420835	BX9.5.Y68	Youth in the ecumenical movement	282.08996073	BX1407.N4	Afro-American Catholics
280.4	BX4800-9999	Protestant churches	282.09	BX940-1745	Catholic Church—History
280.4	BX4800-4946	Protestantism	282.092	BX4650-4705	Catholic Church—Biography
280.4	BX4818-.3	Protestant churches—Relations	282.0922	BX4654-4662	Martyrs—Legends
280.405	BX4800	Protestantism— Periodicals	282.4	BX1490-1612	Catholic Church—Europe
280.409	BX4804-4807	Protestantism—History	282.41	BX1491-1514	Catholic Church—Great Britain
280.4092	BX4800-9890	Protestants	282.43	BX1534-1539	Catholic Church—Germany
280.4094	BX4837-4854	Protestant churches—Europe	282.44	BX1528-1533	Catholic Church—France
280.40941	BX4838-4840	Protestant churches—Great Britain	282.45	BX1543-1548	Catholic Church—Italy
			282.46	BX1583-1588	Catholic Church—Spain
280.40941	BX5200-5207	Dissenters, Religious—England	282.47	BX1558-1560	Catholic Church—Russia
			282.5	BX1615-1673	Catholic Church—Asia
280.40943	BX4844-.5	Protestant churches—Germany	282.5	BX1662-1670.7	Catholic Church—East Asia
280.40944	BX4843	Protestant churches—France	282.56	BX1617-1636	Catholic Church—Middle East
280.40945	BX4847	Protestant churches—Italy	282.6	BX1675-1682	Catholic Church—Africa
280.40946	BX4851	Protestant churches—Spain	282.71	BX1419-1424	Catholic Church—Canada
			282.72	BX1427-1431	Catholic Church—Mexico
280.4095	BX4857	Protestant churches—Asia	282.728	BX1432-1447	Catholic Church—Central America
280.40972	BX4833	Protestant churches—Mexico	282.729	BX1448-1459	Catholic Church—West Indies
280.409728	BX4833.5-4834	Protestant churches—Central America	282.73	BX1407.A5	Americanism (Catholic controversy)
280.409729	BX4835	Protestant churches—West Indies	282.73	BX1404-1418	Catholic Church—United States
280.4098	BX4836	Protestant churches—South America	282.73	BX4600-4644	Catholic Church—[By region or country]
281.5	BX100-189	Eastern churches	282.8	BX1460-1489	Catholic Church—South America
281.5	BX4711.11-.995	Catholic Church— Byzantine rite	282.9(3 or 4)	BX1685-1692	Catholic Church—[New Zealand or Australia]
281.509495	BX4711.231-.2395	Catholic Church— Byzantine rite, Greek	283	BX5001-5009	Anglican Communion
			283	BX5721-5740	Church of England—Oceania
281.62	BX120-129	Armenian Church	283.09	BX5005	Anglican Communion—History
281.8	BT1440	Nestorians			
281.8	BX150-159	Nestorian Church			

23

Dewey	LC	Subject Heading	Dewey	LC	Subject Heading
283.0972092	BX5619-5620	Church of England—Biography	284.2492	BX9470-9479	Reformed Church—Netherlands
283.415	BX5410-5595	Church of Ireland	284.2494	BX9430-9439	Reformed Church—Switzerland
283.41509	BX5500-5510	Church of Ireland—History	284.25	BX9615	Reformed Church—Asia
283.415092	BX5590-5595	Church of Ireland—Biography	284.26	BX9618-9640	Reformed Church—Africa
283.42	BX5011-5740	Church of England	284.271	BX9596-9598	Reformed Church—Canada
283.42	BX5115-5126	Church of England— Parties and movements	284.273	BX9495-9593	Reformed Church—United States
283.42	BX5127-5129.8	Church of England—Relations	284.3	BX4900-4906	Lollards
			284.3	BX4913-4918	Hussites
283.42025	BX5031	Church of England—Directories	284.3	BX4929-4946	Anabaptists
283.4205	BX5011	Church of England—Periodicals	284.4	BX4872-4883	Waldenses
			284.5	BX9450-9459	Huguenots
283.4209	BX5051-5101	Church of England— History	284.6	BX8551-8593	Moravians
283.42092	BX5197-5199	Church of England—Biography	284.606	BX8553	Moravians—Societies, etc.
			284.609	BX8565-8569	Moravians—History
283.429	BX5596-5598	Church of England—Wales	284.6092	BX8591-8593	Moravians—Biography
283.5	BX5661-5680.7	Church of England—Asia	284.8	BX1301	Schism, The Great Western, 1378-1417
283.6	BX5681-5700.9	Church of England—Africa			
283.72	BX5601-5620	Church of England—Canada	284.84	BX4718.5-4735	Jansenists
			284.9	BX6195-6197	Arminianism
283.72	BX5610-5613	Church of England—Canada—History	285	BX8901-9225	Presbyterian Church
			285.092	BX9220-9225	Presbyterians—Biography
283.73	BX5926-5928.5	Episcopal Church—Relations	285.1	BX8960-8968	Presbyterian Church in the U.S.
283.7305	BX6051	Episcopal Church—Periodicals	285.1	BX8950-8958	Presbyterian Church in the U.S.A.
283.7308996 + 073	BX5979	Afro-American Episcopalians	285.(1-2)	BX8901-9225	Presbyterianism
			285.(1-2)06	BX8905	Presbyterian Church—Societies, etc.
283.7309	BX5879-5919	Episcopal Church—History			
283.7309	BX6065-6069	Episcopal Church—History	285.(1-2)09	BX8930-9169	Presbyterian Church—History
283.73092	BX5800-6093	Episcopalians			
283.73092	BX5990-5995	Episcopalians—Biography	285.(1-2)4	BX9050-9140	Presbyterian Church—Europe
283.73092	BX6091-6093	Episcopalians—Biography	285.(1-2)41	BX9052-9105	Presbyterian Church—Great Britain
283.9(3 or 4)	BX5701-5720.8	Church of England—[New Zealand/Australia]	285.(1-2)5	BX9150-9151	Presbyterian Church—Asia
284.1	BX8001-8080	Lutheran Church	285.(1-2)6	BX9160-9162	Presbyterian Church—Africa
284.104	BX8001	Lutheran Church—Periodicals	285.(1-2)71	BX9001-9003	Presbyterian Church—Canada
284.109	BX8018-8063	Lutheran Church—History	285.(1-2)8	BX9011-9043	Presbyterian Church— Latin America
284.1092	BX8079-8080	Lutherans—Biography			
284.14	BX8020-8040.5	Lutheran Church—Europe	285.136	BX8990-8998.38	Reformed Presbyterian Church
284.143	BX8020-8023	Lutheran Church—Germany	285.233	BX9075-9095	Church of Scotland
284.173	BX8041-8061	Lutheran Church—United States	285.733	BX9551-9593	Reformed Church in the United States
284.2	BX9401-9640	Calvinism	285.8	BX7101-7260	Congregationalism
284.2	BX9401-9640	Reformed Church	285.8	BX7101-7260	Congregational churches
284.205	BX9401	Calvinism—Periodicals	285.806	BX7105	Congregational churches—Societies, etc.
284.206	BX9403	Reformed Church—Societies, etc.			
284.209	BX9415	Reformed Church—History	285.806	BX7106-7109	Congregational churches—Congresses
284.24	BX9430-9480	Reformed Church—Europe			
284.244	BX9450-9459	Reformed Church—France			

134000

Dewey	LC	Subject Heading	Dewey	LC	Subject Heading
289.605	BX7601-7795	Society of Friends	292.13	BL820.L25	Ladon (Greek mythology)
289.605	BX7601	Society of Friends—Periodicals	292.13	BL820.M37	Medea (Greek mythology)
			292.13	BL820.M63	Minotaur (Greek mythology)
289.606	BX7606.5-7608	Society of Friends—Congresses	292.13	BL820.P	Pandora (Greek mythology)
			292.13	BL820.P4	Pegasus (Greek mythology)
289.609	BX7630-7728	Society of Friends— History	292.13	BL820.P5	Perseus (Greek mythology)
289.6092	BX7790-7795	Quakers—Biography	292.13	BL820.T6	Titans (Mythology)
289.64	BX7675-7710	Society of Friends— Europe	292.2113	BL820.A25	Adonis (Greek deity)
289.641	BX7676-7693	Society of Friends—Great Britain	292.2113	BL820.A4	Aesculapius (Greek deity)
			292.2113	BL820.A25	Adonis (Greek deity)
289.65	BX7715-7716	Society of Friends—Asia	292.2113	BL820.A4	Aesculapius (Greek deity)
289.66	BX7720-7723	Society of Friends—Africa	292.2113	BL820.B2	Dionysia
289.671	BX7650-7653	Society of Friends—Canada	292.2113	BL820.J8	Jupiter (Roman deity)
			292.2113	BL820.M26	Marsyas (Greek deity)
289.673	BX7635-7649	Society of Friends—United States	292.2113	BL820.06	Ops (Roman deity)
			292.2113	BL820.P2	Pan (Greek deity)
289.68	BX7671-7673	Society of Friends—South America	292.2113	BL870.S29	Saturn (Roman deity)
			292.2114	BL820.C5	Demeter (Greek deity)
289.694	BX7725-7726	Society of Friends—Australia	292.2114	BL820.C5	Ceres (Roman deity)
289.709	BX8115-8119	Mennonites—History	292.2114	BL820.D54	Diktynna (Greek deity)
289.7092	BX8101-8143	Mennonites	292.2114	BL820.E5	Eileithyia (Greek deity)
289.7092	BX8129.043	Old Order Mennonites	292.2114	BL820.F7	Fortuna (Roman deity)
289.7092	BX8141-8143	Mennonites—Biography	292.2114	BL820.M6	Athena (Greek deity)
289.73092	BX8129.A5-.A6	Amish	292.2114	BL820.M65	Mother goddesses, Greek
289.771	BX8118.5-.7	Mennonites—Canada	292.2114	BL820.P7	Persephone (Greek deity)
289.773	BX8116-8118	Mennonites—United States	292.28	BL735	Hell
289.8	BX9751-9793	Shakers	292.61	BL815.V4	Vestals
289.806	BX9755	Shakers—Congresses	293	BL830-875	Germanic peoples—Religion
289.809	BX9765-9769	Shakers—History			
289.8092	BX9791-9793	Shakers—Biography	293.13	BL870.F28	Fafnir (Germanic mythology)
289.809(4-9)	BX9766-9769	Shakers—[By region or country]	293.2113	BL870.B3	Balder (Norse deity)
			294	BL2000-2016	Mythology, Indic
289.80973	BX9766-9768	Shakers—United States	294.3	BQ	Buddhism
289.9	BX7433	Dukhobors	294.3	BQ1-9999	Buddhism
289.9	BX7990.H6	Snake cults (Holiness churches)	294.305	BQ1-10	Buddhism—Periodicals
			294.309	BQ251-799	Buddhism—History
289.92	BX8525-8528	Jehovah's Witnesses	294.30901	BQ287-296	Buddhism—History—To ca. 100 A.D.
289.94	BX8762-8780	Pentecostal churches			
291.2130937	DG124	Emperor worship, Rome	294.3092	BQ840-845	Buddhists—Biography
292.07	BL800-820	Rome—Religion	294.3094	BQ700-709	Buddhism—Europe
292.07	BL800-820	Rome—Religion	294.3095	BQ610-699	Buddhism—East Asia
292.08	BL780-795	Greece—Religion	294.30951	BQ620-649	Buddhism—China
292.13	BL700-820	Mythology, Classical	294.309519	BQ650-669	Buddhism—Korea
292.13	BL820.A6	Amazons	294.30952	BQ670-699	Buddhism—Japan
292.13	BL820.A63	Amycus (Greek mythology)	294.30954	BQ330-349	Buddhism—India
292.13	BL820.A8	Jason (Greek mythology)	294.3095493	BQ350-379	Buddhism—Sri Lanka
292.13	BL820.C	Centaurs	294.3095496	BQ380-396	Buddhism—Nepal
292.13	BL820.D	Dryads	294.30958	BQ570-609	Buddhism—Asia, Central
292.13	BL820.D25	Daedalus (Greek mythology)	294.30959	BQ440-509	Indochina—Religion
292.13	BL820.F8	Furies (Roman mythology)	294.309591	BQ416-439	Buddhism—Burma
292.13	BL820.F8	Erinyes (Greek mythology)	294.309593	BQ550-568	Buddhism—Thailand
292.13	BL820.G7	Gorgons (Greek mythology)	294.309595	BQ540-549	Buddhism—Malaysia
292.13	BL820.G8	Graces, The	294.309598	BQ510-539	Buddhism—Indonesia
292.13	BL820.H5	Heracles (Greek mythology)	294.3096	BQ710-719	Buddhism—Africa

Dewey	LC	Subject Heading	Dewey	LC	Subject Heading
294.309(7-8)	BQ720-760	Buddhism—America	294.3438	BQ7982.3	Gcod (Bonpo rite)
294.30971	BQ740-749	Buddhism—Canada	294.344	BQ4330	Bodhisattva stages (Mahayana Buddhism)
294.30973	BQ730-739	Buddhism—United States			
294.3099(3-6)	BQ770-799	Buddhism—[New Zealand/Australia/Oceania]	294.344	BQ4965-5030	Buddhism—Customs and practices
294.32	BQ4170	Buddhism—Catechisms	294.344	BQ5595-5630	Devotion (Buddhism)
294.32	BQ4170	Buddhism—Creeds	294.3443	BQ5595-5630	Prayer—Buddhism
294.333	BQ5741-5755	Mythology, Buddhist	294.34433	BQ5535-5594	Buddhism—Prayer-books and devotions
294.3372	BQ4600-4610	Buddhism—Relations			
294.3375	BL1493	Zen Buddhism—Psychology	294.3444	BQ9288	Spiritual life—Zen Buddhism
294.3375	BQ4570.P76	Buddhism—Psychology	294.3444	BQ5360-5680	Religious life—Buddhism
294.3378	BQ5851-5899	Buddhism—Charities	294.34447	BQ6200-6240	Asceticism—Buddhism
294.33783	BQ5851-5899	Buddhism and social problems	294.35	BJ1289	Buddhist ethics
			294.35	BJ1289.5.Y6	Youth, Buddhist—Conduct of life
294.3378344	BQ4570.W6	Woman (Buddhism)			
294.34	BQ4195-4250	Dharma (Buddhism)	294.35	BQ4401-4430	Virtues (Buddhism)
294.34	BQ4240	Causation (Buddhism)	294.35	BQ4425-4430	Vice (Buddhism)
294.342	BQ4050	Buddhism—Apologetic works	294.361	BQ5140-5355	Priests, Buddhist
			294.361	BQ7930	Dalai lamas
294.342	BQ4061-4570	Buddhism—Doctrines	294.363	BQ922	Gautama Buddha—Footprints
294.342	BQ4360	Compassion (Buddhism)			
294.342	BQ5485-5525	Five Precepts (Buddhism)	294.363	BQ935	Gautama Buddha—Enlightenment
294.342	BQ5485-5530	Buddhist precepts			
294.342	BQ5485-5530	Buddhism—Doctrines	294.363	BQ938	Gautama Buddha—Date of death
294.34209	BQ4080-4125	Buddhism—Doctrines—History			
			294.363	BQ4180	Buddha (The concept)
294.34211	BQ4690.M3	Maitreya (Buddhist deity)	294.363	BQ4670-4690	Buddhas
294.34211	BQ4750.D33	Dakini (Buddhist deity)	294.365	BQ12-93	Buddhism—Societies, etc.
294.34211	BQ4750.Y35	Yama (Buddhist deity)	294.3657	BL1478	Profession (Buddhist monastic orders)
294.34211	BQ4860.A4	Acala (Buddhist deity)			
294.34211	BQ4890.D33-.D334	Dam-tshig-rdo-rje (Buddhist deity)	294.3657	BQ6001-6160	Monasticism and religious orders, Buddhist
294.3423	BQ4475-4525	Eschatology, Buddhist	294.372	BQ5901-5975	Buddhism—Missions
294.343	BQ7982.4	Bonpo incantations	294.375	BQ171-199	Buddhist education of children
294.3435	BL1477.8.D4	Temples, Buddhist—Dedication			
			294.375	BQ141-209	Buddhist education
294.3435	BQ5130-5137	Temples, Buddhist	294.382	BQ1100-3340	Tripitaka
294.3435	BQ6300-6388	Buddhist shrines	294.382	BQ1100-3340	Buddhism—Sacred books
294.3435	BQ6460	Gautama Buddha—Shrines	r294.39	BQ7530-7950	Dge-lugs-pa (Sect)
294.34351	BQ6400-6495	Buddhist pilgrims and pilgrimages	294.39	BQ7669	Bka'-rgyud-pa (Sect)
			294.39	BQ7960-7989	Bonpo (Sect)
294.3437	BQ4570.A4	Amulets (Buddhism)	294.39	BQ8000-9800	Buddhist sects
294.3437	BQ4570.A4	Charms (Buddhism)	294.39	BQ8000-8049	Abhayagiri (Sect)
294.3437	BQ5070-5075	Buddhism—Liturgical objects	294.391	BQ7100-7285	Theravada Buddhism
			294.392	BQ7300-7522	Mahayana Buddhism
294.3437	BQ5070-5075	Altars, Buddhist	294.3923	BQ7530-7950	Buddhism
294.3438	BL1477.8.F8	Funeral rites and ceremonies, Buddhist	294.3926	BQ8500-8769	Pure Land Buddhism
			294.3927	BQ9250-9519	Zen Buddhism
294.3438	BQ4965-5030	Buddhism—Rituals	294.4	BL1300-1365	Jainism
294.3438	BQ5005	Confirmation (Buddhist rite)	294.4	BL1300-1365	Jains
294.3438	BQ5035-5065	Chants (Buddhist)	294.42	BL1356-1375	Jainism—Doctrines
294.3438	BQ5700-5720	Fasts and feasts—Buddhism	294.43	BL1376-1380	Worship (Jainism)
			294.434	BL1375.P	Penance (Jainism)
294.3438	BQ7699.G36	Gcod (Buddhist rite)	294.437	BL1377.3	Jaina mantras

Dewey	LC	Subject Heading	Dewey	LC	Subject Heading
294.438	BL1355.5	Fasts and feasts—Jainism	295.82	BL1510-1525	Zoroastrianism—Sacred books
294.4422	BL1378.8	Mysticism—Jainism	296	BM	Judaism
294.4436	BL1375.Y63	Yoga (Jainism)	296.025	BM55-65	Judaism—Directories
294.482	BL1310-1314.2	Jainism—Sacred books	296.03	BM50	Judaism—Dictionaries
294.493	BL1380.D	Digambara (Jaina sect)	296.05	BM11	Judaism—Periodicals
294.5	BL1100-1270	Hinduism	296.09	BM150-449	Judaism—History
294.5	BL1100-1245	Brahmanism	296.09014	BM165-178	Judaism—History—To 70 A.D.
294.5	BL1241.46	Brahmans	296.0902	BM180-185	Judaism—History—Medieval and early modern, 425-1789
294.5	BL2000-2030	Hinduism			
294.513	BL1225.M	Manus (Hindu mythology)	296.09033	BM190-199	Judaism—History—Modern period, 1750-
294.517	BL1215.S64	Sociology, Hindu			
294.5175	BL2015.K3	Karma	296.092	BM652	Rabbis
294.52	BL1213.32-1215	Hinduism—Doctrines	296.094	BM290-376	Judaism—Europe
294.5211	BL1200-1225	God (Hinduism)	296.0941	BM292-305	Judaism—Great Britain
294.5211	BL1214.32.B53	Bhakti	296.0943	BM316-318	Judaism—Germany
294.52113	BL1225.A	Aatimna (Hindu deity)	296.09436	BM307-309	Judaism—Austria
294.52113	BL1225.A42	Adityas (Hindu deities)	296.09438	BM337-339	Judaism—Poland
294.52113	BL1225.D3	Dattatreya (Hindu deity)	296.0944	BM313-315	Judaism—France
294.52113	BL1225.D48	Devanarayana (Hindu deity)	296.0945	BM322-324	Judaism—Italy
294.52114	BL1216	Goddesses, Hindu	296.0946	BM354-356	Judaism—Spain
294.52114	BL1225.A4	Aditi (Hindu deity)	296.09469	BM328-330	Judaism—Portugal
294.52114	BL1225.D8	Durga (Hindu deity)	296.0947	BM331-333	Judaism—Russia
294.5213	BL1171	Alvars	296.0948	BM340-353	Judaism—Scandinavia
294.5213	BL1171	Hindu saints	296.09481	BM348-350	Judaism—Norway
294.522	BL1215.M3	Man (Hinduism)	296.09485	BM351-353	Judaism—Sweden
294.522	BL1215.S8	Soul (Hinduism)	296.09489	BM342-344	Judaism—Denmark
294.53	BL1226	Worship (Hinduism)	296.094897	BM334-336	Judaism—Finland
294.534	BL1236.76.S23	Sacrifice	296.09492	BM325-327	Judaism—Netherlands
294.535	BL1243.72-.78	Temples, Hindu	296.09493	BM310-312	Judaism—Belgium
294.5351	BL1239.32	Hindu pilgrims and pilgrimages	296.09494	BM357-359	Judaism—Switzerland
			296.09495	BM319-321	Judaism—Greece
294.536	BL1213.D87	Durga-puja (Hindu festival)	296.094971	BM373-375	Judaism—Yugoslavia
294.538	BL1226.2	Chants (Hindu)	296.09498	BM370-372	Judaism—Romania
294.538	BL1239.72-.82	Fasts and feasts—Hinduism	296.09499	BM364-366	Judaism—Bulgaria
294.5422	BL1215.M9	Mysticism—Hinduism	296.095	BM377-431	Judaism—Asia
294.544	BL1228	Religious life—Hinduism	296.0951	BM423-425	Judaism—China
294.5441	BL1226.82.M3	Marriage customs and rites, Hindu	296.0952	BM426-428	Judaism—Japan
			296.0953	BM393-395	Judaism—Arabia
294.5447	BL1215.F3	Fasting (Hinduism)	296.0954	BM406-410	Judaism—India
294.55	BL1245.A1	Hindu sects	296.0955	BM396-398	Judaism—Iran
294.5514	BL1282.2-.292	Shaktism	296.09567	BM386.4-.6	Judaism—Iraq
294.5514	BL1141.2-1142.6	Tantrism	296.095691	BM387-389	Judaism—Syria
294.5657	BL1238	Monasticism and religious orders, Hindu	296.095694	BM390-392	Judaism—Israel
			296.095694	BM387-389	Judaism—Palestine
294.5921	BL1112.2	Vedas	296.09581	BM400	Judaism—Afghanistan
294.5924	BL1245.B5	Bhagavatas	296.096	BM432-440	Judaism—Africa
294.6	BL2017-2018.7	Sikhism	296.0962	BM434-436	Judaism—Egypt
294.6	BL2020.S5	Sikhs	296.0968	BM437	Judaism—South Africa
294.682	BL2017.2-.4	Sikhism—Sacred books	296.0971	BM227-229	Judaism—Canada
294.69	BL2018.7	Sikh sects	296.0972	BM230-232	Judaism—Mexico
294.69	BL2018.7.K44	Khalsa (Sect)	296.09728	BM233-247	Judaism—Central America
295	BL1500-1590	Zorastrianism	296.09729	BM248-260	Judaism—West Indies
295	BL1500-1590	Parsees			

Dewey	LC	Subject Heading	Dewey	LC	Subject Heading
296.0973	BM205-225	Judaism—United States	296.481	BM693.P5	Pilgrim Festivals (Judaism)
296.098	BM261-289	Judaism—South America	296.61	BM652.5	Pastoral counseling (Judaism)
296.099(3 or 4)	BM443-445	Judaism—[New Zealand/Australia]	296.65	BM653-655	Synagogues
296.099(5-6)	BM447-449	Judaism—Oceania	296.67	BM1	Judaism—Societies, etc.
296.1	BM495-532	Rabbinical literature	296.67	BM21-30	Judaism—Congresses
296.12	BM500-509	Talmud	296.68	BM70-135	Jews—Education
296.120092	BM177	Tannaim	296.7	BM650-747	Judaism—Customs and practices
296.14	BM511-518	Midrash			
296.16	BM525	Cabala	296.7	BM723	Jewish way of life
296.18	BM729.S85	Summer (Jewish law)	296.72	BM729.C6	Consolation (Judaism)
296.19	BM516-.5	Aggada	296.73	BM710	Jews—Dietary laws
296.3	BM600-603	Judaism—Doctrines	296.8	BM175	Jewish sects
296.3	BM945	Samaritan theology	296.81	BM185-.4	Karaites
296.311	BM610	God (Judaism)	296.812	BM175.P4	Pharisees
296.31172	BM612.5	Covenants—Judaism	296.813	BM175.S2	Sadducees
296.32	BM630	Sin (Judaism)	296.814	BM175.E8	Essenes
296.32	BM729.F3	Faith (Judaism)	296.82	BM199.S3	Sabbathaians
296.336	BM615	Messiah—Judaism	296.82092	BX9680.S3	Sabbatarians
296.336	BM615	Jewish messianic movements	296.8332	BM198	Hasidism
			296.834	BM197.8	Humanistic Judaism
296.36	BJ1279-1287	Ethics, Jewish	296.8342	BM197.5	Conservative Judaism
296.36	BJ1286.G64	Golden rule	297	BP	Islam
296.4	BM656-685	Worship (Judaism)	297	BP1-223	Islam
296.41	BM685	Sabbath	297.03	BP40	Islam—Dictionaries
296.43	BM690-720	Fasts and feasts— Judaism	297.05	BP1-9	Islam—Periodicals
296.43	BM690	Religious calendars— Judaism	297.122	BP100-134	Koran
			297.12209	BP134.E5	Egypt in the Koran
296.43	BM970	Fasts and feasts— Samaritan religion	297.122092	BP133.7.A3	Adam (Biblical figure) in the Koran
296.431	BM693.H5	High Holidays	297.122092	BP133.7.D38	David, King of Israel, in the Koran
296.4315	BM695.N5	Rosh ha-Shanah			
296.432	BM675.A8	Yom Kippur	297.122092	BP133.7.M67	Moses (Biblical leader) in the Koran
296.432	BM695.A8	Yom Kippur			
296.435	BM657.H3	Hanukkah lamp	297.12286413	BP134.F58	Food in the Koran
296.435	BM657.M35	Menorah	297.124	BP135	Hadith
296.435	BM695.H3	Hanukkah	297.124	BP193.25-.28	Hadith (Shiites)
296.437	BM675.P3	Passover	297.18	BP137-.5	Legends, Islamic
296.437	BM695.P3	Passover	297.2	BP165.5-166.94	Islam—Doctrines
296.437	BM695.P35	Seder	297.21	BP166.89	Spirits (Islam)
296.4391	BM720.S2	Sabbatical year (Judaism)	297.21	BP166.89	Discernment of spirits (Islam)
296.4424	BM707-.4	Confirmation (Jewish rite)			
296.4424	BM707.4	Bar Mitzvah	297.211	BP166.2	Word of God (Islam)
296.4434	BM707-.4	Bat Mitzvah	297.211	BP166.2	God (Islam)
296.444	BM713	Marriage customs and rites, Jewish	297.2115	BP166.6	Revelation (Islam)
			297.215	BP166.89	Angels (Islam)
296.445	BM712	Mourning customs, Jewish	297.216	BP166.89	Demonology, Islamic
296.45	BM669	Prayer—Judaism	297.216	BP166.89	Devil (Islam)
296.45	BM675.D3	Siddurim	297.22	BP166.75	Sin (Islam)
296.4615	BM657.T6	Torah scrolls	297.22	BP166.78	Faith (Islam)
296.4615	BM659.S3	Scribes, Jewish	297.22	BP166.7	Man (Islam)
296.462	BM658.2	Cantors (Judaism)	297.225	BP166.73	Soul (Islam)
296.47	BM730	Jewish preaching	297.227	BP166.3	Predestination—Islam
296.4731	BM746	High Holiday sermons	297.227	BP166.3	Free will and determinism (Islam)
296.4737	BM747.P3	Passover sermons			

Dewey	LC	Subject Heading	Dewey	LC	Subject Heading
297.23	BP166.8	Eschatology, Islamic	297.87	BP62.N4	Muslims, Black
297.23	BP166.83	Resurrection (Islam)	297.87	BP221-223	Black Muslims
297.23	BP166.85	Judgment Day (Islam)	297.92	BP340	Babism
297.23	BP166.87	Paradise (Islam)	297.93	BP300-395	Bahai faith
297.246	BP166.4	Prophets, Pre-Islamic	297.93435	BP380	Bahai meditations
297.27	BP173.25-.45	Sociology, Islamic	299.14122	BL2035	Pakistan—Religion
297.3	BP184.2	Worship (Islam)	299.15	BL1590.R5	Rider-gods
297.31	BP176	Pillars of Islam	299.155	BL2270-2280	Iran—Religion
297.35	BP187	Muslim pilgrims and pilgrimages	299.16	BL910	Druids and Druidism
297.35	BP194.6	Shiite shrines	299.2	BL1600-1710	Semites—Religion
297.352	BP187.3	Muslim pilgrims and pilgrimages—Saudi Arabia—Mecca	299.21	BL1620-1625	Assyro-Babylonian religion
			299.21	BL1625.A5	Anu (Assyro-Babylonian deity)
297.362	BP183.6	Ramadan sermons	299.21	BL1625.M37	Marduk (Babylonian deity)
297.37	BP183.6	Islamic sermons	299.21	BL1625.P3	Panbabylonism
297.37	BP184.25	Islamic preaching	299.26	BL1671	Baal (Deity)
297.38	BM184	Judaism—Liturgy	299.3	BL2462	Africa, North—Religion
297.38	BP184.4	Purity, Ritual—Islam	299.31	BL2420-2460	Egypt—Religion
297.382	BP178	Prayer—Islam	299.31	BL2450.A45	Amon (Egyptian deity)
297.385	BP184.9.F8	Funeral rites and ceremonies, Islamic	299.31	BL2450.A89	Atum (Egyptian deity)
			299.31	BL2450.G6	Gods, Egyptian
297.39	BP190.5.A5	Amulets (Islam)	299.31	BL2450.N45	Neith (Egyptian deity)
297.4	BP189	Mysticism—Islam	299.31	BL2450.O7	Osiris (Egyptian deity)
297.4	BP189	Sufism	299.31	BL2450.S27	Satis (Egyptian deity)
297.4092	BP189.33	Muslim saints	299.5	BL1000-2370	Mythology, Oriental
297.4382	BP189.62	Sufi meditations	299.5	BL2050-2150	Asia, Southeastern—Religion
297.48	BP189.7.B4-.B42	Bektashi			
297.5	BJ1291-1292	Islamic ethics	299.51	BL1800-1975	China—Religion
297.53	BP179	Fasting (Islam)	299.512	BL1830-1875	Confucianism
297.53	BP186	Fasts and feasts—Islam	299.514	BL1900-1940	Taoism
297.57	BP188	Religious life—Islam	299.5145	BL1290.8	Taoist ethics
297.57	BP188.3.Y6	Youth, Muslim—Religious life	299.56	BL2200-2228	Japan—Religion
			299.56	BL2211.D33	Daikokuten (Japanese deity)
297.574	BP170.5	Muslim converts	299.56	BL2211.E24	Ebisu (Japanese deity)
297.574	BP170.5	Muslim converts from Christianity	299.56	BL2211.E46	Emperor worship—Japanese
297.574092	BP170.5	Muslim converts from Christianity—Biography	299.561	BL2216-2227.8	Shinto
			299.56135	BL2224.9-2225.3	Shinto shrines
297.576	BP190.5.A75	Asceticism—Islam	299.56136	BL2224.3	Shinto devotional calendars
297.577	BP190.5.S4	Sex—Religious aspects—Islam	299.56138	BL2224.2	Shinto—Rituals
			299.56182	BL2217-.5	Shinto—Sacred books
297.61	BP184	Pastoral theology (Islam)	299.5619	BL2222.H5	Hinomoto (Sect)
297.63	BP75-77.5	Muhammad, Prophet, d. 632	299.6	BL2400-2490	Africa—Religion
			299.675	BL2490	Voodooism
297.63	BP75.8	Muhammad, Prophet, d. 632—Miracles	299.6869	BL2480.Y6	Sopono (Cult)
			299.6869	BL2480.Y6	Egungun (Cult)
297.65	BP10-15	Islam—Congresses	299.7	E98.R3	Indians of North America—Religion
297.72	BP182	Jihad			
297.74	BP170.85	Dawah (Islam)	299.7138	E98.D2	Eagle dance
297.77	BP42-48	Islamic religious education	299.7138	E98.D2	Sun dance
297.81	BP175.S8	Sunnites	299.7138	E98.R2	Wolf ritual
297.82	BP193	Shiites	299.74	E98.D2	Indian dance—North America
297.822	BP195.A8	Assassins (Ismailites)			
297.85	BL1695	Druzes	299.78452013	F1219.76.R45	Aztec mythology

Dewey	LC	Subject Heading	Dewey	LC	Subject Heading
299.8	BL2580-2592	South America—Religion	302.208996073	P94.5.A37	Afro-Americans—Communication
299.891	BL2590.B7	Afro-Brazilian cults			
299.92	BL2600-2630	Oceania—Religion	302.222	GR780-790	Flower language
299.924	BL2620.P6	Mythology, Polynesian	302.23	TR835	Microfilm readers
299.9294	BL740-760	Etruscans—Religion	302.23	P95.8	Mass media policy
299.9295	BL1616.E54	Enki (Sumarian deity)	302.23	P96.A83	Audiences
299.93	BF638-648	New Thought	302.23089	P94.5.M55	Ethnic mass media
299.93	BP605.G68	Great White Brotherhood	302.3	HM291	Social interaction
299.93	BP605.N48	New Age movement	302.32082	HQ1201-1216	Women—Socialization
299.934	BP500-585	Theosophy	302.33	HM281-283	Crowds
299.934	BP573.R5	Reincarnation	302.33	HM281-283	Mobs
299.935	BP595-597	Anthroposophy	302.34	GN486.3	Friendship
299.957	BL2230-2240	Korea—Religion	302.34	HM132.5	Friendship—Sociological aspects
300	H	Social sciences	302.34083	HQ784.F7	Friendship in children
300.1	H61-.4	Social sciences—Methodology	302.4	HM291	Social interaction
			302.54	BJ1533.A4	Ambition
300.5	H1-8	Social sciences—Periodicals	302.54	HM136-146	Individualism
			303.32	GN510	Socialization
300.6	H21-29	Social sciences—Congresses	303.32	HQ783	Socialization
			303.34	HM141	Leadership
300.71	H62-.5	Social sciences—Study and teaching	303.34	HM259	Social influence
			303.36	HM271-276	Authority
300.72	H62-.5	Social sciences— Research	303.372	HM216	Social ethics
300.724	H62	Social sciences—Experiments	303.375	HM263	Propaganda
			303.38	HM261	Public opinion
300.9	H51-53	Social sciences—History	303.380723	HM261	Public opinion polls
300.92	H57-59	Social sciences—Biography	303.4	HM101-121	Social change
			303.44	CB155	Progress
301	GN	Anthropology	303.44	HM101-121	Progress
301	HM	Sociology	303.482	GN345.6	Intercultural communication
301.01	GN33-34.3	Anthropology—Methodology	303.482	GN345.65	Cross-cultural orientation
			303.482	HM258	Intercultural communication
301.01	HM24-37	Sociology—Methodology	303.482	JV6342	Assimilation (Sociology)
301.028	GN34.3.A35	Aerial photography in anthropology	303.483	T14.5	Technology—Social aspects
			303.483	T174.5	Technology assessment
301.03	HM17	Sociology—Dictionaries	303.483	Q175.5	Science—Social aspects
301.05	HM1-7	Sociology—Periodicals	303.4833	HC79.I55	Information technology
301.06	HM13	Sociology—Congresses	303.6	HM281-283	Violence
301.071	HM45-47	Sociology—Study and teaching	303.6	P96.V5	Violence in mass media
			303.623	HM281-283	Riots
301.072	GN42-46	Anthropology—Research	303.625073	HV6432	Nuclear terrorism—United States
301.09	HM19-22	Sociology—History			
301.09	HM104	Historical sociology	303.62509538	HV6430.B55	Terrorists—Saudi Arabia—Biography
301.092	GN20-21	Anthropologists			
301.7	GN406-498	Society, Primitive	303.6250973	HV6432	Terrorism—United States—Prevention
302	HM132	Interpersonal relations			
302	HM251-291	Social psychology	303.64	HM281-283	Revolutions
302.015195	HM253	Sociometry	304.2	GE51-71	Man—Influence of environment
302.12	BF323.S63	Social perception			
302.14	HN49.V64	Voluntarism	304.2	GF	Human ecology
302.14	RC455.4.S67	Social adjustment	304.2	GF1-900	Human ecology
302.2	P87-96	Communication	304.2	GF24	Applied human geography
302.2	P95.8	Communication policy	304.2	HM206-208	Social ecology
302.2	GN799.T73	Communication, Prehistoric	304.20913	GF895	Human ecology—Tropics

Dewey	LC	Subject Heading	Dewey	LC	Subject Heading
304.209(4-9)	GF500-895	Human ecology—[By region or country]	304.60944	HB3593-3594	Demography—France
			304.60944949	HB3594.5	Demography—Monaco
304.20973	GF503-504	Human ecology—United States	304.60945	HB2059-2060	Population geography—Italy
			304.60945	HB3599-3600	Demography—Italy
304.25	GF71	Man—Influence of climate	304.60946	HB2079-2080	Population geography—Spain
304.5	GN365.9	Sociobiology			
304.5	HM121	Heredity	304.60946	HB3619-3620	Demography—Spain
304.6	GN33.5	Demographic anthropology	304.609469	HB2081-2082	Population geography—Portugal
304.6	HB	Demography			
304.6	HB848-3697	Demography	304.609469	HB3621-3622	Demography—Portugal
304.6	HB848-3697	Population	304.6094698	HB2128.5	Population geography—Madeira Islands
304.6	HB887	Demographic transition			
304.605	HB848	Demography—Periodicals	304.6094698	HB3668.5	Demography—Madeira Islands
304.6072	HB850-.5	Population Research			
304.60723	HB849.49	Demographic surveys	304.6094699	HB2127.5	Population geography—Azores
304.609	HB851-853	Population—History			
304.60942(9)	HB2045-2046	Population geography—England and Wales	304.6094699	HB3667.5	Demography—Azores
			304.60947	HB2067-2068.2	Population geography—Russia
304.60942(9)	HB3585-3586	Demography—England and Wales	304.60947	HB3607-3608.2	Demography—Russia
304.6091724	HB884	Developing countries—Population	304.609481	HB2075-2076	Population geography—Norway
304.6091734	HB2371-2578	Rural population	304.609481	HB3615-3616	Demography—Norway
304.6092	HB855-865	Demography—Biography	304.609485	HB2077-2078	Population geography—Sweden
304.609411	HB2047-2048	Population geography—Scotland			
			304.609485	HB3617-3618	Demography—Sweden
304.609411	HB3587-3588	Demography—Scotland	304.609489	HB2071-2072	Population geography—Denmark
304.609415	HB2049-2050	Population geography—Ireland			
			304.609489	HB3611-3612	Demography—Denmark
304.609415	HB3589-3590	Demography—Ireland	304.6094897	HB2068.3	Population geography—Finland
304.609416	HB2048.5	Population geography—Northern Ireland			
			304.6094897	HB3608.3	Demography—Finland
304.609416	HB3588.5	Demography—Northern Ireland	304.6094912	HB2073-2074	Population geography—Iceland
304.60943	HB2055-2056	Population geography—Germany	304.6094912	HB3613-3614	Demography—Iceland
			304.609492	HB2065-2066	Population geography—Netherlands
304.60943	HB3595-3596.5	Demography—Germany			
304.609436	HB2051-2052	Population geography—Austria	304.609492	HB3605-3606	Demography— Netherlands
			304.609493	HB2063-2064	Population geography—Belgium
304.609436	HB3591-3592	Demography—Austria			
304.60943648	HB2052.9	Population geography—Liechtenstein	304.609493	HB3603-3604	Demography—Belgium
			304.6094935	HB2066.5	Population geography—Luxembourg
304.60943648	HB3592.9	Demography—Liechtenstein			
			304.6094935	HB3606.5	Demography— Luxembourg
304.609437	HB2052.3	Population geography—Czechoslovakia	304.609494	HB2083-2084	Population geography—Switzerland
304.609437	HB3592.3	Demography—Czechoslovakia	304.609494	HB3623-3624	Demography—Switzerland
			304.609495	HB2092.5	Population geography—Greece
304.609438	HB2068.7	Population geography—Poland			
			304.609495	HB3632.5	Demography—Greece
304.609438	HB3608.7	Demography—Poland	304.6094965	HB2086.5	Population geography—Albania
304.609439	HB2052.5	Population geography—Hungary			
			304.6094965	HB3626.5	Demography—Albania
304.609439	HB3592.5	Demography—Hungary	304.609497	HB2088.5	Population geography—Yugoslavia
304.60944	HB2053-2054	Population geography—France			
			304.609497	HB3628.5	Demography—Yugoslavia

Dewey	LC	Subject Heading	Dewey	LC	Subject Heading
304.609498	HB2091-2092	Population geography—Romania	304.6095493	HB2096.8	Population geography— Sri Lanka
304.609498	HB3631-3632	Demography—Romania	304.6095493	HB3636.8	Demography—Sri Lanka
304.609499	HB2087-2088	Population geography—Bulgaria	304.6095495	HB2131.5	Population geography—Maldives
304.609499	HB3627-3628	Demography—Bulgaria	304.6095495	HB3671.5	Demography—Maldives
304.60951	HB2114	Population geography—China	304.6095496	HB2096.9	Population geography—Nepal
304.60951	HB3654	Demography—China	304.6095496	HB3636.9	Demography—Nepal
304.60951249	HB2116	Population geography—Taiwan	304.6095498	HB2100.3	Population geography—Bhutan
304.60951249	HB3656	Demography—Taiwan	304.6095498	HB3640.3	Demography—Bhutan
304.6095125	HB2117	Population geography—Hong Kong	304.60955	HB2096.4	Population geography—Iran
304.6095125	HB3657	Demography—Hong Kong	304.60955	HB3636.4	Demography—Iran
304.6095126	HB2115	Population geography—Macao	304.609561	HB2093.4	Population geography—Turkey
304.6095126	HB3655	Demography—Macao	304.609561	HB3633.4	Demography—Turkey
304.609517	HB2112.8	Population geography—Mongolia	304.609567	HB2096.3	Population geography—Iraq
304.609517	HB3652.8	Demography—Mongolia	304.609567	HB3636.3	Demography—Iraq
304.609519	HB2112.5-.6	Population geography—Korea	304.6095691	HB2093.7	Population geography—Syria
304.609519	HB3652.5-.6	Demography—Korea	304.6095691	HB3633.7	Demography—Syria
304.60952	HB2111-2112	Population geography—Japan	304.6095692	HB2093.9	Population geography—Lebanon
304.60952	HB3651-3652	Demography—Japan	304.6095692	HB3633.9	Demography—Lebanon
304.609533	HB2094.9-2095	Population geography—Yemen	304.6095693	HB2093.5	Population geography—Cyprus
304.609533	HB3634.9-3635	Demography—Yemen	304.6095693	HB3633.5	Demography—Cyprus
304.6095353	HB2095.3	Population geography—Oman	304.6095694	HB2094	Population geography—Israel
304.6095353	HB3635.3	Demography—Oman	304.6095694	HB3634	Demography—Israel
304.6095357	HB3635.5	Demography—United Arab Emirates	304.6095695	HB2094.3	Population geography—Jordan
304.6095363	HB2095.7	Population geography—Qatar	304.6095695	HB3634.3	Demography—Jordan
304.6095363	HB3635.7	Demography—Qatar	304.609581	HB2096.6	Population geography—Afghanistan
304.6095365	HB2095.9	Population geography—Bahrain	304.609581	HB3636.6	Demography—Afghanistan
304.6095365	HB3635.9	Demography—Bahrain	304.609591	HB2096.7	Population geography—Burma
304.6095367	HB2096	Population geography—Kuwait	304.609591	HB3636.7	Demography—Burma
304.6095367	HB3636	Demography—Kuwait	304.609593	HB2104.55	Population geography—Thailand
304.609538	HB2094.7	Population geography—Saudi Arabia	304.609593	HB3644.55	Demography—Thailand
304.609538	HB3634.7	Demography—Saudi Arabia	304.609594	HB2104.4	Population geography—Laos
304.60954	HB2099-2100	Population geography—India	304.609594	HB3644.4	Demography—Laos
304.60954	HB3639-3640	Demography—India	304.609595	HB2104.6	Population geography—Malaysia
304.6095491	HB2100.5	Population geography—Pakistan	304.609595	HB3644.6	Demography—Malaysia
304.6095491	HB3640.5	Demography—Pakistan	304.609596	HB2104.3	Population geography—Cambodia
304.6095492	HB2100.6	Population geography—Bangladesh	304.609596	HB3644.3	Demography—Cambodia
304.6095492	HB3640.6	Demography—Bangladesh	304.609597	HB2104.5	Population geography—Vietnam

Dewey	LC	Subject Heading	Dewey	LC	Subject Heading
304.609597	HB3644.5	Demography—Vietnam	304.6096652	HB2126.2	Population geography—Guinea
304.609598	HB2107-2108	Population geography—Indonesia	304.6096652	HB3666.2	Demography—Guinea
304.609598	HB3647-3648	Demography—Indonesia	304.6096657	HB2127.3	Population geography—Guinea-Bissau
304.609599	HB2109-2110	Population geography—Philippines	304.6096657	HB3667.3	Demography—Guinea-Bissau
304.609599	HB3649-3650	Demography—Philippines	304.6096658	HB2129.5	Population geography—Cape Verde
304.609611	HB2121.5	Population geography—Tunisia	304.6096658	HB3669.5	Demography—Cape Verde
304.609611	HB3661.5	Demography—Tunisia	304.6096662	HB2127.2	Population geography—Liberia
304.609612	HB2121.6	Population geography—Libya	304.6096662	HB3667.2	Demography—Liberia
304.609612	HB3661.6	Demography—Libya	304.6096668	HB2126	Population geography—Cote d'Ivoire
304.60962	HB2121.7	Population geography—Egypt	304.6096668	HB3666	Demography—Cote d'Ivoire
304.60962	HB3661.7	Demography—Egypt	304.609667	HB2126.8	Population geography—Ghana
304.609624	HB2121.8	Population geography—Sudan	304.609667	HB3666.8	Demography—Ghana
304.609624	HB3661.8	Demography—Sudan	304.6096681	HB2125.8	Population geography—Togo
304.60963	HB2122	Population geography—Ethiopia	304.6096681	HB3665.8	Demography—Togo
304.60963	HB3662	Demography—Ethiopia	304.6096683	HB2125.7	Population geography—Benin
304.60964	HB2121.3	Population geography—Morocco	304.6096683	HB3665.7	Demography—Benin
304.60964	HB3661.3	Demography—Morocco	304.609669	HB2126.7	Population geography—Nigeria
304.609648	HB2127.4	Population geography—Western Sahara	304.609669	HB3666.7	Demography—Nigeria
304.609648	HB3667.4	Demography—Western Sahara	304.6096711	HB2125.4	Population geography—Cameroon
304.609649	HB2129	Population geography—Canary Islands	304.6096711	HB3665.4	Demography—Cameroon
304.609649	HB3669	Demography—Canary Islands	304.6096715	HB3664.7	Demography—Sao Tome and Principe
304.60965	HB2121.4	Population geography—Algeria	304.6096718	HB2124.6	Population geography—Equatorial Guinea
304.60965	HB3661.4	Demography—Algeria	304.6096718	HB3664.6	Demography—Equatorial Guinea
304.609661	HB2126.6	Population geography—Mauritania	304.6096721	HB2124.9	Population geography—Gabon
304.609661	HB3666.6	Demography—Mauritania	304.6096721	HB3664.9	Demography—Gabon
304.6096623	HB2126.3	Population geography—Mali	304.6096724	HB2125	Population geography—Congo (Brazzaville)
304.6096623	HB3666.3	Demography—Mali	304.6096724	HB3665	Demography—Congo (Brazzaville)
304.6096625	HB2126.4	Population geography—Burkina Faso	304.609673	HB2124.4	Population geography—Angola
304.6096625	HB3666.4	Demography—Burkina Faso	304.609673	HB3664.4	Demography—Angola
304.6096626	HB2125.9	Population geography—Niger	304.6096741	HB2125.2	Population geography—Central African Republic
304.6096626	HB3665.9	Demography—Niger	304.6096741	HB3665.2	Demography—Central African Republic
304.609663	HB2126.5	Population geography—Senegal	304.6096743	HB2125.3	Population geography—Chad
304.609663	HB3666.5	Demography—Senegal	304.6096743	HB3665.3	Demography—Chad
304.609664	HB2126.9	Population geography—Sierra Leone	304.6096751	HB2124.5	Population geography—Zaire
304.609664	HB3666.9	Demography—Sierra Leone	304.6096751	HB3664.5	Demography—Zaire
304.6096651	HB2127	Population geography—Gambia			
304.6096651	HB3667	Demography—Gambia			

Dewey	LC	Subject Heading	Dewey	LC	Subject Heading
304.60967571	HB2122.7	Population geography—Rwanda	304.6096981	HB2133.5	Population geography—Reunion
304.60967571	HB3662.7	Demography—Rwanda	304.6096981	HB3673.5	Demography—Reunion
304.60967572	HB2122.8	Population geography—Burundi	304.6096982	HB2133	Population geography—Mauritius
304.60967572	HB3662.8	Demography—Burundi	304.6096982	HB3673	Demography—Mauritius
304.6096761	HB2122.6	Population geography—Uganda	304.609699	HB2134	Population geography—Kerguelen Islands
304.6096761	HB3662.6	Demography—Uganda	304.609699	HB3674	Demography—Kerguelen Islands
304.6096762	HB2122.5	Population geography—Kenya	304.60971	HB1989-1990	Population geography—Canada
304.6096762	HB3662.5	Demography—Kenya	304.60971	HB3529-3530	Demography—Canada
304.6096771	HB2122.3	Population geography—Djibouti	304.60972	HB1991-1992	Population geography—Mexico
304.6096771	HB3662.3	Demography—Djibouti	304.60972	HB3531-3532	Demography—Mexico
304.6096773	HB2122.2	Population geography—Somalia	304.6097281	HB1999	Population geography—Guatemala
304.6096773	HB3662.2	Demography—Somalia	304.6097281	HB3539	Demography—Guatemala
304.609678	HB2122.9	Population geography—Tanzania	304.6097282	HB1995-1996	Population geography—Belize
304.609678	HB3662.9	Demography—Tanzania	304.6097282	HB3535-3536	Demography—Belize
304.609679	HB2123	Population geography—Mozambique	304.6097283	HB2000	Population geography—Honduras
304.609679	HB3663	Demography—Mozambique	304.6097283	HB3540	Demography—Honduras
304.60968	HB2123.4	Population geography—South Africa	304.6097284	HB2004	Population geography—El Salvador
304.60968	HB3663.4	Demography—South Africa	304.6097284	HB3544	Demography—El Salvador
304.6096881	HB2124.2	Population geography—Namibia	304.6097285	HB2001	Population geography—Nicaragua
304.6096881	HB3664.2	Demography—Namibia	304.6097285	HB3541	Demography—Nicaragua
304.6096883	HB2123.9	Population geography—Botswana	304.6097286	HB1997-1998	Population geography—Costa Rica
304.6096883	HB3663.9	Demography—Botswana	304.6097286	HB3537-3538	Demography—Costa Rica
304.6096885	HB2123.7	Population geography—Lesotho	304.6097287	HB2002-2003	Population geography—Panama
304.6096885	HB3663.7	Demography—Lesotho	304.6097287	HB3542-3543	Demography—Panama
304.6096887	HB2123.8	Population geography—Swaziland	304.6097291	HB2009-2010	Population geography—Cuba
304.6096887	HB3663.8	Demography—Swaziland	304.6097291	HB3549-3550	Demography—Cuba
304.6096894	HB2123.6	Population geography—Zambia	304.6097292	HB2013-2014	Population geography—Jamaica
304.6096894	HB3663.6	Demography—Zambia	304.6097292	HB3553-3554	Demography—Jamaica
304.6096897	HB2124	Population geography—Malawi	304.6097293	HB2012	Population geography—Dominican Republic
304.6096897	HB3664	Demography—Malawi	304.6097293	HB3552	Demography—Dominican Republic
304.609691	HB2123.2	Population geography—Madagascar	304.6097294	HB2011	Population geography—Haiti
304.609691	HB3663.2	Demography— Madagascar	304.6097294	HB3551	Demography—Haiti
304.609694	HB2132.5	Population geography—Comoro Islands	304.6097296	HB2007-2008	Population geography—Bahamas
304.609694	HB3672.5	Demography—Comoro Islands	304.6097296	HB3547-3548	Demography—Bahamas
304.609696	HB2132	Population geography—Seychelles	304.609729722	HB3556.3	Demography—Virgin Islands of the United States
304.609696	HB3672	Demography—Seychelles			

Dewey	LC	Subject Heading	Dewey	LC	Subject Heading
304.60972973	HB2016.72	Population geography—Anguilla	304.60972986	HB3557.36	Demography—Bonaire
			304.60972986	HB3557.37	Demography—Curacao
304.60972973	HB2016.78	Population geography—St. Kitts and Nevis	304.6097299	HB2128	Population geography—Bermuda Islands
304.60972973	HB3556.72	Demography—Anguilla	304.6097299	HB3668	Demography—Bermuda Islands
304.60972973	HB3556.78	Demography—Saint Kitts and Nevis			
304.60972974	HB2016.74	Population geography—Antigua	304.60973	HB1965-1987	Population geography—United States
304.60972974	HB3556.74	Demography—Antigua	304.60973	HB3505-3527	Demography—United States
304.60972975	HB2016.76	Population geography—Montserrat	304.6097(4-9)	HB1985	Population geography—[United States, By state]
304.60972975	HB3556.76	Demography—Montserrat	304.6097(4-9)	HB1987	Population geography—[United States, By city]
304.60972976	HB2017.7	Population geography—Guadeloupe	304.6097(4-9)	HB3525	Demography—[United States, By State]
304.60972976	HB3557.7	Demography—Guadeloupe	304.6097(4-9)	HB3527	Demography—[United States, By City]
304.60972977	HB2017.385	Population geography—Saint Eustatius (Netherlands Antilles)	304.60981	HB2023-2024	Population geography—Brazil
304.60972977	HB2017.39	Population geography—Saint Martin	304.60981	HB3563-3564	Demography—Brazil
304.60972977	HB3557.38	Demography—Saba (Netherlands Antilles)	304.60982	HB2019-2020	Population geography—Argentina
304.60972977	HB3557.385	Demography—Saint Eustatius (Netherlands Antilles)	304.60982	HB3559-3560	Demography—Argentina
			304.60983	HB2025-2026	Population geography—Chile
304.60972977	HB3557.39	Demography—Saint Martin	304.60983	HB3565-3566	Demography—Chile
304.60972981	HB2016.57	Population geography—Barbados	304.60984	HB2021-2022	Population geography—Bolivia
304.60972981	HB3556.57	Demography—Barbados	304.60984	HB3561-3562	Demography—Bolivia
304.60972982	HB2017.9	Population geography—Martinique	304.60985	HB2035-2036	Population geography—Peru
304.60972982	HB3557.9	Demography—Martinique	304.60985	HB3575-3576	Demography—Peru
304.60972983	HB2017	Population geography—Trinidad and Tobago	304.609861	HB2027-2028	Population geography—Colombia
304.60972983	HB3557	Demography—Trinidad and Tobago	304.609861	HB3567-3568	Demography—Colombia
304.609729841	HB2016.93	Population geography—Dominica	304.609866	HB2029-2030	Population geography—Ecuador
304.609729841	HB3556.93	Demography—Dominica	304.609866	HB3569-3570	Demography—Ecuador
304.609729843	HB2016.97	Population geography—Saint Lucia	304.60987	HB2039-2040	Population geography—Venezuela
304.609729843	HB3556.97	Demography—Saint Lucia	304.60987	HB3579-3580	Demography—Venezuela
304.609729844	HB2016.99	Population geography—Saint Vincent	304.609881	HB2032.3	Population geography—Guyana
304.609729844	HB3556.99	Demography—Saint Vincent	304.609881	HB3572.3	Demography—Guyana
304.609729845	HB2016.95	Population geography—Grenada	304.609882	HB2032.7	Population geography—French Guiana
304.609729845	HB3556.95	Demography—Grenada	304.609882	HB3572.7	Demography—French Guiana
304.60972986	HB2017.35	Population geography—Aruba	304.609883	HB2032.5	Population geography—Surinam
304.60972986	HB2017.36	Population geography—Bonaire	304.609883	HB3572.5	Demography—Surinam
304.60972986	HB2017.37	Population geography—Curacao	304.609892	HB2033-2034	Population geography—Paraguay
304.60972986	HB3557.35	Demography—Aruba	304.609892	HB3573-3574	Demography—Paraguay
			304.609895	HB2037-2038	Population geography—Uruguay

Dewey	LC	Subject Heading	Dewey	LC	Subject Heading
304.609895	HB3577-3578	Demography—Uruguay	304.609973	HB3670.5	Demography—Tristan da Cunha
304.60993	HB2152.5	Population geography—New Zealand	304.60998	HB3695	Demography—Arctic Regions
304.60993	HB3692.5	Demography—New Zealand	304.60998	HB2155	Population geography—Arctic regions
304.60994	HB2135-2136	Population geography—Australia	304.609982	HB2156	Population geography—Greenland
304.60994	HB3675-3676	Demography—Australia	304.609982	HB3696	Demography—Greenland
304.609953	HB2152.8	Population geography—Papua New Guinea	304.61	HB1953	Population density
304.609953	HB3692.8	Demography—Papua New Guinea	304.63	HQ759.98	Family demography
304.6099593	HB2153	Population geography—Solomon Islands	304.63	HQ760-767.7	Family size
			304.6309(1-9)	HQ762	Family size—[By region or country]
304.6099593	HB3693	Demography—Solomon Islands	304.632	HB901-1108	Fertility, Human
304.6099595	HB2153.4	Population geography—Vanuatu	304.632091724	HB1108	Fertility, Human—Developing countries
304.6099595	HB3693.4	Demography—Vanuatu	304.63209(4-9)	HB901-1108	Fertility, Human—[By region or country]
304.6099597	HB2153.3	Population geography—New Caledonia	304.64	HB1321-1528	Mortality
304.6099597	HB3693.3	Demography—New Caledonia	304.64021	HB1322	Mortality—Tables
			304.64083	HB1323.C5	Children—Mortality
304.6099611	HB2153.5	Population geography—Fiji	304.6408996 +073	HB1323.B5	Afro-Americans—Mortality
304.6099611	HB3693.5	Demography—Fiji			
304.6099612	HB2153.6	Population geography—Tonga	304.6451724	HB1528	Mortality—Developing countries
304.6099612	HB3693.6	Demography—Tonga	304.645(4-9)	HB1335-1526	Mortality—[By region or country]
304.6099613	HB2153.7	Population geography—American Samoa	304.666	HQ763-767.52	Birth control
304.6099613	HB3693.7	Demography—American Samoa	304.8	D135-149	Migrations of nations
			304.8	D145	Lombards
304.6099614	HB2153.8	Population geography—Western Samoa	304.8	GN370	Man—Migrations
			304.808939	D139	Vandals
304.6099614	HB3693.8	Demography—Western Samoa	305	GN478-491.7	Social structure
304.609962	HB2153.9	Population geography—French Polynesia	305	HM131-134	Social groups
			305	HM146	Equality
304.609962	HB3693.9	Demography—French Polynesia	305.2	HB1531-1738	Age distribution (Demography)
304.6099623	HB2153.65	Population geography—Cook Islands	305.209(4-9)	HB1541-1737	Age distribution—[By region or country]
304.6099623	HB3693.65	Demography—Cook Islands	305.20973	HB1545-1567	Age distribution (Demography)—United States
304.609967	HB2152.7	Population geography—Guam	305.2097(4-9)	HB1565	Age distribution (Demography)—[United States, By state]
304.609967	HB3692.7	Demography—Guam			
304.6099681	HB2152.9	Population geography—Kiribati	305.23	HQ767.8-792.2	Children
304.6099681	HB3692.9	Demography—Kiribati	305.2308996 + 073	E185.86	Afro-American children
304.6099711	HB2131	Population geography—Falkland Islands	305.2309	HQ767.87	Children—History
			305.23091732	HT206	City children
304.6099711	HB3671	Demography—Falkland Islands	305.232	HQ774	Infants
304.609973	HB2130	Population geography—Saint Helena	305.232	HQ774	Infants—Development
			305.232	HQ774.5	Toddlers
304.609973	HB2130.5	Population geography—Tristan da Cunha	305.232	HQ779-.5	Baby books
304.609973	HB3670	Demography—Saint Helena	305.233	HQ774.5	Preschool children

Dewey	LC	Subject Heading	Dewey	LC	Subject Heading
305.234	HQ778.6	School-age child care	305.8	GN301-673	Ethnology
305.235	GN483-484	Adolescence	305.8	GN325	Ethnology
305.235	HQ793-799.9	Youth	305.8	GN380	Indigenous peoples
305.235	HQ798	Teenage girls	305.8	GN492.5	Tribes
305.235	HQ799.5-.9	Young adults	305.8	GN495.4	Ethnic groups
305.23509(4-9)	HQ799	Youth—[By region or country]	305.8	GN495.6	Ethnicity
			305.8	GN496-498	Ethnic relations
305.24	HQ799.95-.97	Adulthood	305.8	GN496-498	Race relations
305.244	HQ1059.4-.5	Middle age	305.8	HT	Race
305.26	HQ1060-1064	Aged	305.8	HT1501-1595	Race
305.26	P96.A38	Aged in mass media	305.8	HT1501-1595	Race relations
305.26091734	HQ1060-1064	Rural aged	305.8001	GN468	Ethnophilosophy
305.3	HB1741-1948	Sex distribution (Demography)	305.8001	HM24	Ethnomethodology
			305.80074	GN35-41	Ethnological museums and collections
305.3	HQ77.7-.95	Transsexualism			
305.3	HQ1075-.5	Sex role	305.8009	GN345.2	Ethnohistory
305.3	P96.S48	Sexism in communication	305.8009	HT1507	Race relations—History
305.3	P96.S5	Sex role in mass media	305.80094	GN575-585	Ethnic groups—Europe
305.30973	HB1755-1777	Sex distribution (Demography)—United States	305.80095	GN625-635	Ethnic groups—Asia
			305.80096	GN643-661	Ethnic groups—Africa
			305.80097	GN550-560	Ethnic groups—North America
305.3097(4-9)	HB1775	Sex distribution (Demography—[United State, By state]	305.80098	GN562-564	Ethnic groups—South America
305.3097(4-9)	HB1777	Sex distribution (Demography)—[United States, By city]	305.80099(5-6)	GN662-671	Ethnic groups—Oceania
			305.8034	GN537	Caucasian race
			305.8034	HT1575-1577	Caucasian race
305.31	HQ1088-1090.7	Men's studies	305.8044	GN645	Mulattoes
305.3899	GN372	Wild men	305.8073	E184-185.98	United States—Race relations
305.4	HQ1101-2030.7	Women			
305.407	HQ1180-1186	Women's studies	305.8073	E184.A1	United States—Ethnic relations
305.409	HQ1121-1172	Women—History			
305.409	HQ1139	Amazons	305.8096	GN664.N3	Negritos
305.409(4-9)	HQ1400-1870.5	Women—[By region or country]	305.8152	HQ800.3	Bachelors
			305.83	GN549.G4	Germanic peoples
305.40973	HQ1402-1439	Women—United States	305.83	GN549.T4	Teutonic race
305.42	HQ1121-1870.5	Women—Social conditions	305.892	GN547	Semites
305.42	HQ1190	Feminist theory	305.8924	DS145-146	Antisemitism
305.48696	HQ1172	Jewish women	305.8924	GN547	Jews
305.486971	HQ1170	Muslim women	305.8942	GN548	Mongols
305.48969	GN372	Wild women	305.896073	E185.61	Afro-Americans—Segregation
305.5	HT	Social classes			
305.5	HT601-1444	Social classes	305.89912	GN664.P2	Papuans
305.5072	HT608	Social classes—Research	305.89915	GN666	Australian aborigines—Ethnic identity
305.509	HT607	Social classes—History			
305.5122	GN491.4	Caste	305.8995	GN671.B5	Gunantuna (Melanesian people)
305.5122	HT713-725	Caste			
305.51220954	DS422.C3	Caste	305.89952	GN669	Micronesians
305.52	HT647-653	Aristocracy (Social class)	305.906918	GN387	Nomads
305.522	HT647-653	Nobility	305.963	HT421	Farm life
305.5232	HT657	Gentry	306	GN400-406	Culture
305.55	HT680-690	Middle class	306	GN493.3	Social norms
305.5509(4-9)	HT690	Middle class—[By region or country]	306	HM101-121	Culture
			306	HN25	Quality of life
305.8	CB195-197	National characteristics	306.2	GN492-495	Political anthropology

Dewey	LC	Subject Heading	Dewey	LC	Subject Heading
306.27	UH750-769	Military social work	306.7	HQ801-.83	Man-woman relationships
306.3	GN448-450.7	Economic anthropology	306.70816	HQ30.5	Handicapped—Sexual behavior
306.3	HM35	Economics—Sociological aspects	306.7082	HQ29	Women—Sexual behavior
306.36	HD6951-6957	Industrial sociology	306.7083	HQ784.S45	Children—Sexual behavior
306.361	HD6951-6957	Quality of work life	306.70835	HQ27-.5	Young adults—Sexual behavior
306.3613	HD4905-.3	Work ethic	306.70846	HQ30	Aged—Sexual behavior
306.362	HT851-1444	Slavery	306.7088375	HQ27	Students—Sexual behavior
306.362090 + (1-5)	HT863-867	Slavery—History	306.73	HQ12-18	Sex customs
306.362094	HT1155-1240	Slavery—Europe	306.73	HQ801.8	Interracial dating
306.3620941	HT1161-1165	Slavery—Great Britain	306.73	HQ801.83	Dating violence
306.3620943	HT1181	Slavery—Germany	306.73	HQ961-967	Free love
306.3620944	HT1176-1180	Slavery—France	306.73	HX546	Free love
306.3620945	HT1191-1194	Slavery—Italy	306.732	HQ800.15	Celibacy
306.3620946	HT1216-1220	Slavery—Spain	306.736	HQ806	Adultery
306.3620947	HT1206-1209	Slavery—Russia	306.74	HQ101-440.7	Prostitution
306.36209492	HT1196-1203	Slavery—Benelux countries	306.7409	HQ111-117	Prostitution—History
306.36209494	HT1227-1228	Slavery—Switzerland	306.7409(4-9)	HQ141-270.7	Prostitution—[By region or country]
306.36209495	HT1234	Slavery—Greece			
306.362095	HT1240.5-1315	Slavery—Asia	306.765	HQ74-.2	Bisexuality
306.3620951	HT1241-1244	Slavery—China	306.766	HQ75-76.95	Homosexuality
306.3620952	HT1276	Slavery—Japan	306.766	HQ76.5-.8	Gay liberation movement
306.36209599	HT1271	Slavery—Philippines	306.7662	HQ75.8	Gay men
306.362096	HT1321-1427	Slavery—Africa	306.7663	HQ75.3-.6	Abused lesbians
306.3620971	HT1051-1052	Slavery—Canada	306.7663	HQ75.3-.6	Lesbianism
306.3620972	HT1053-1054	Slavery—Mexico	306.77	HQ79	Fetishism (Sexual behavior)
306.36209728	HT1055-1056	Slavery—Central America	306.772	HQ447	Masturbation
306.36209729	HT1071-1119	Slavery—West Indies	306.775	HQ79	Sadism
306.362098	HT1121-1152	Slavery—South America	306.775	HQ79	Sadomasochism
306.3620994	HT1431	Slavery—Australia	306.778	HQ76.97-77.2	Transvestites
306.363	HD4871-4875	Indentured servants	306.8	HQ503-1064	Family
306.365	HT751-815	Serfdom	306.8	HQ503-1064	Home
306.36509(4-9)	HT781-815	Serfdom—[By region or country]	306.81	GN480	Marriage
			306.81	GN480.4	Cross-cousin marriage
306.3650941	HT781	Serfdom—Great Britain	306.81	HQ	Marriage
306.3650943	HT791-801	Serfdom—Germany	306.81	HQ503-1064	Marriage
306.36509436	HT803	Serfdom—Austria	306.81021	HB1111-1317	Marital status—Statistics
306.3650944	HT785	Serfdom—France	306.81087	HQ1036-1043	Handicapped—Marriage
306.3650947	HT807-809	Serfdom—Russia	306.810872	HQ1040	Deaf—Marriage
306.38	HD7105.2-.25	Disability retirement	306.8109	HB1121-1317	Marital status—[By region or country]
306.38	HD7110-.5	Early retirement			
306.42	GN451-477.7	Intellectual life	306.8109	HQ503-518	Marriage—History
306.42	HM213	Intellectuals	306.8109(4-9)	HQ531-727.9	Marriage—[By region or country]
306.43	LB45	Educational anthropology			
306.43	LC189-214.53	Educational sociology	306.81094	HQ611-662.7	Marriage—Europe
306.44	P40	Sociolinguistics	306.810941	HQ613-618.5	Marriage—Great Britain
306.46	HM221	Technology—Sociological aspects	306.810943	HQ625-626.5	Marriage—Germany
			306.810944	HQ623-624	Marriage—France
306.482	GN454.6	Gambling	306.810945	HQ629-630	Marriage—Italy
306.483	GN454-455	Sports	306.810946	HQ649-650	Marriage—Spain
306.7	HQ	Sex	306.810947	HQ637-638	Marriage—Russia
306.7	HQ12-449	Sex	306.8109492	HQ631-636.5	Marriage—Benelux Countries
306.7	HQ19-30.7	Sexual instinct	306.8109494	HQ653-654	Marriage—Switzerland

Dewey	LC	Subject Heading	Dewey	LC	Subject Heading
306.8109495	HQ662.5	Marriage—Greece	306.8740835	HQ759.64	Teenage parents
306.81095	HQ663-690.5	Marriage—Asia	306.874084	HQ755.86	Parent and adult child
306.810951	HQ684	Marriage—China	306.874087	HQ759.912	Handicapped parents
306.810952	HQ681-682	Marriage—Japan	306.874087	HQ759.913	Parents of handicapped children
306.810954	HQ669-670	Marriage—India	306.8740879	HQ759.913	Parents of exceptional children
306.810955	HQ666.4	Marriage—Iran			
306.8109567	HQ666.3	Marriage—Iraq	306.8742	HQ756-.7	Fatherhood
306.81095694	HQ664	Marriage—Israel	306.8742	HQ756-.7	Fathers
306.8109599	HQ679-680	Marriage—Philippines	306.8742	HQ756	Stepfathers
306.81096	HQ691-697.4	Marriage—Africa	306.874208653	HQ756	Divorced fathers
306.810971	HQ559-560	Marriage—Canada	306.8743	HQ759-.6	Motherhood
306.810972	HQ561-562	Marriage—Mexico	306.8743	HQ759-.6	Mothers
306.8109728	HQ563-574	Marriage—Central America	306.8743	HQ759.3	Absentee mothers
306.8109729	HQ575-587.9	Marriage—West Indies	306.8743	HQ759.48	Working mothers
306.810973	HB1125-1126	Marital status—United States	306.8743	HQ759.5	Surrogate mothers
306.810973	HQ535-557	Marriage—United States	306.87430835	HQ759.4	Teenage mothers
306.81097(4-9)	HB1145	Marital status—[United States, By state]	306.8745	HQ759.9	Grandparenting
			306.875	GN63.6	Quintuplets
306.81097(4-9)	HB1147	Marital status—[United States, By city]	306.875	GN63.6	Quadruplets
			306.875	GN63.6	Twins
306.81098	HQ588-610	Marriage—South America	306.875	GN63.6	Triplets
306.810994	HQ705-706	Marriage—Australia	306.877	GN480.3	Incest
306.815	HQ800-.4	Single people	306.877	HQ71	Incest
306.8153	HQ800.2	Single women	306.88	HQ805	Desertion and non-support
306.82	GN480.3	Endogamy and exogamy	306.880973	HQ833-836	Desertion—United States
306.83	GN480-.65	Kinship	306.8809(4-9)	HQ837-960.9	Desertion—[Other countries]
306.83	GN480	Double descent (Kinship)			
306.84	HQ803	Temporary marriage	306.8809(4-9)	HQ831-960.7	Divorce—[By region or country]
306.84	HQ803	Marriage, Companionate			
306.84	HQ1018-1019	Remarriage	306.882	HQ1058-.5	Widowers
306.84	HQ1028	Marriage with deceased wife's sister	306.883	HQ1058-.5	Widows
			306.89	HQ811-960.7	Divorce
306.842	HQ981-996	Group marriage	306.9	HQ1073-.5	Thanatology
306.8423	GN480.33-.36	Polygamy	306.9	HQ1073-.5	Death
306.8423	GN480.6	Polyandry	307	HM131-134	Community life
306.8423	HQ981-996	Polygamy	307	HT	Communities
306.843	HQ1031	Interfaith marriage	307	HT51-65	Human settlements
306.843083	HQ777.9	Children of interracial marriage	307	HT101-395	Cities and towns
			307.1209(4-9)	HT392-395	Regional planning—[By region or country]
306.846	E185.62	Miscegenation			
306.846	GN254	Miscegenation	307.120973	HT392-394	Regional planning—United States
306.846	HQ1031	Interracial marriage			
306.85	GN480-.65	Family	307.1216	HT165.5-169.5	City planning
306.85	HQ	Family	307.121609 (4-9)	HT167-169.54	City planning—[By region or country]
306.85	HQ734	Family			
306.850896073	E185.86	Afro-American families	307.12160973	HT167-168	City planning—United States
306.859	GN497.5	Matriarchy			
306.87	HQ777.2	First-born children	307.14	GF101-127	Human settlements
306.87	HQ777.22	Second-born children	307.14	HN49.C6	Community development
306.874	HQ755.7-759.92	Parenting	307.24	HB1955	Rural-urban migration
306.874	HQ755.7-759.92	Parenthood	307.26	HB1956-2157	Urban-rural migration
306.874	HQ755.85	Abused parents	307.26	HT381	Urban-rural migration
306.874	HQ799.15	Parent and teenager	307.3364	HV4023-4170.7	Slums
306.874	HQ998-999	Illegitimacy	307.3416	HT170-178	Urban renewal

Dewey	LC	Subject Heading	Dewey	LC	Subject Heading
307.341609 (4-9)	HT178	Urban renewal—[Other countries]	314.15	HA1170.1-.5	Ireland—Census
307.34160973	HT175-177	Urban renewal—United States	314.16	HA1141-1150	Northern Ireland—Census
			314.29	HA1161-1170	Wales—Census
307.72	HT401-485	Sociology, Rural	314.3	HA1231-1349	Germany—Census
307.72090(1-5)	HT415	Sociology, Rural—History	314.36	HA1171-1190	Austria—Census
307.74	HT351-352	Suburban life	314.3648	HA1210.5	Liechtenstein—Census
307.76	GN395	Urban anthropology	314.37	HA1191-1200	Czechoslovakia—Census
307.76	HT101-395	Sociology, Urban	314.38	HA1451-1460	Poland—Census
307.76	HT156	Inner cities	314.39	HA1201-1210	Hungary—Census
307.76	HT161-165	Garden cities	314.4	HA1211-1230	France—Census
307.76072	HT110	Sociology, Urban—Research	314.5	HA1361-1379	Italy—Census
			314.6	HA1541-1560	Spain—Census
307.7609	HT111-150	Sociology, Urban—History	314.69	HA1571-1580	Portugal—Census
307.760902	D134	Cities and towns, Medieval	314.698	HA2285	Madeira Islands—Census
307.760902	HT115	Cities and towns, Medieval	314.699	HA2280	Azores—Census
307.76091724	HT149.5	Sociology, Urban—Developing countries	314.7	HA1431 -1450.12	Russia—Census
307.76093	HT114	Cities and towns, Ancient	314.81	HA1501-1520	Norway—Census
307.76094	HT131-145	Sociology, Urban—Europe	314.85	HA1521-1540	Sweden—Census
307.760941	HT133	Sociology, Urban—Great Britain	314.89	HA1471-1490	Denmark—Census
			314.897	HA1450.5	Finland—Census
307.760943	HT137	Sociology, Urban—Germany	314.912	HA1491-1500	Iceland—Census
			314.92	HA1381-1390	Netherlands—Census
307.760944	HT135	Sociology, Urban—France	314.93	HA1391-1410	Belgium—Census
307.76095	HT147	Sociology, Urban—Asia	314.935	HA1411-1420	Luxembourg—Census
307.76096	HT148	Sociology, Urban—Africa	314.94	HA1591-1610	Switzerland—Census
307.760971	HT127	Sociology, Urban—Canada	314.95	HA1351-1359	Greece—Census
307.760972	HT127.7	Sociology, Urban—Mexico	314.965	HA1620.5	Albania—Census
307.7609728	HT128	Sociology, Urban—Central America	314.97	HA1631-1635	Yugoslavia—Census
			314.98	HA1641-1650	Romania—Census
307.760973	HT123-.5	Sociology, Urban—United States	314.99	HA1621-1630	Bulgaria—Census
			315.1	HA4631-4640	China—Census
307.76098	HT129	Sociology, Urban—South America	315.1249	HA4646-4650	Taiwan—Census
			315.125	HA4651-4655	Hong Kong—Census
307.760994	HT149	Sociology, Urban—Australia	315.126	HA4641-4645	Macao—Census
			315.17	HA4630.8	Mongolia—Census
307.768	HT169.55-.57	Planned communities	315.19	HA4630.5-.6	Korea—Census
307.768	HT169.55-.57	New towns	315.2	HA4621-4630	Japan—Census
307.774	HQ970-975.7	Communal living	315.33	HA4564	Yemen—Census
310	HA	Statistics	315.353	HA4565	Oman—Census
310	HA154-4737	Vital statistics	315.357	HA4566	United Arab Emirates—Census
310	HA175-4737	Census			
310.0223	GA109.8	Maps, Statistical	315.363	HA4567	Qatar—Census
310.0723	HA31.2	Sampling (Statistics)	315.365	HA4568	Bahrain—Census
310.1	HA29-32	Statistics—Methodology	315.38	HA4563	Saudi Arabia—Census
310.1	HA30.6	Spatial analysis (Statistics)	315.4	HA4581-4590	India—Census
310.5	HA1	Statistics—Periodicals	315.491	HA4590.5	Pakistan—Census
310.72	HA31.3	Correlation (Statistics)	315.492	HA4590.6	Bangladesh—Census
310.72	HA35	Statistics—Research	315.493	HA4570.8	Sri Lanka—Census
310.9	HA19	Statistics—History	315.495	HA2300	Maldives—Census
310.92	QA276.17	Statistical consultants	315.496	HA4570.9	Nepal—Census
314	HA1107-1650	Europe—Census	315.498	HA4590.3	Bhutan—Census
314.1	HA1121-1170	Great Britain—Census	315.5	HA4570.2	Iran—Census
314.11	HA1151-1160	Scotland—Census	315.61	HA4556.5	Turkey—Census

41

Dewey	LC	Subject Heading	Dewey	LC	Subject Heading
315.67	HA4569	Iraq—Census	316.761	HA4694	Uganda—Census
315.691	HA4558	Syria—Census	316.762	HA4693	Kenya—Census
315.692	HA4559	Lebanon—Census	316.771	HA4691	Djibouti—Census
315.693	HA4557	Cyprus—Census	316.773	HA4690	Somalia—Census
315.694	HA4560	Israel—Census	316.78	HA4697	Tanzania—Census
315.695	HA4561	Jordan—Census	316.79	HA4698	Mozambique—Census
315.81	HA4570.6	Afghanistan—Census	316.8	HA4701	South Africa—Census
315.91	HA4570.7	Burma—Census	316.881	HA4708	Namibia—Census
315.93	HA4600.55	Thailand—Census	316.883	HA4706	Botswana—Census
315.94	HA4600.4	Laos—Census	316.885	HA4704	Lesotho—Census
315.95	HA4600.6	Malaysia—Census	316.887	HA4705	Swaziland—Census
315.96	HA4600.3	Cambodia—Census	316.89	HA4702	Zimbabwe—Census
315.97	HA4600.5	Vietnam—Census	316.894	HA4703	Zambia—Census
315.98	HA4601-4610	Indonesia—Census	316.897	HA4707	Malawi—Census
315.99	HA4611-4620	Philippines—Census	316.91	HA4699	Madagascar—Census
316.11	HA4684	Tunisia—Census	316.94	HA2303	Comoro Islands—Census
316.12	HA4685	Libya—Census	316.96	HA2301	Seychelles—Census
316.2	HA4686	Egypt—Census	316.981	HA2307	Reunion—Census
316.24	HA4687	Sudan—Census	316.982	HA2305	Mauritius—Census
316.3	HA4689	Ethiopia—Census	316.99	HA2309	Kerguelen Islands— Census
316.4	HA4682	Morocco—Census	317.1	HA741-750	Canada—Census
316.48	HA4737	Western Sahara—Census	317.2	HA761-770	Mexico—Census
316.49	HA2287	Canary Islands—Census	317.281	HA811-820	Guatemala—Census
316.5	HA4683	Algeria—Census	317.282	HA791-800	Belize—Census
316.61	HA4730	Mauritania—Census	317.283	HA821-830	Honduras—Census
316.623	HA4727	Mali—Census	317.284	HA841-850	El Salvador—Census
316.625	HA4728	Burkina Faso—Census	317.285	HA831-840	Nicaragua—Census
316.626	HA4724	Niger—Census	317.286	HA801-810	Costa Rica—Census
316.63	HA4729	Senegal—Census	317.287	HA851-854	Panama—Census
316.64	HA4733	Sierra Leone—Census	317.295	HA901-910	Puerto Rico—Census
316.651	HA4734	Gambia—Census	317.297	HA866-.9	Leeward Islands (West Indies)—Census
316.652	HA4726	Guinea—Census			
316.657	HA4736	Guinea-Bissau—Census	317.29722	HA911-915	Virgin Islands of the United States—Census
316.658	HA2289	Cape Verde—Census			
316.662	HA4735	Liberia—Census	317.2976	HA918.7	Guadeloupe—Census
316.668	HA4725	Cote d'Ivoire—Census	317.2981	HA865	Barbados—Census
316.67	HA4732	Ghana—Census	317.2982	HA918.9	Martinique—Census
316.681	HA4723	Togo—Census	317.2983	HA867	Trinidad and Tobago—Census
316.683	HA4722	Benin—Census			
316.69	HA4731	Nigeria—Census	317.2986	HA917-.78	Netherlands Antilles—Census
316.711	HA4719	Cameroon—Census			
316.715	HA4713	Sao Tome and Principe—Census	317.299	HA921-930	Bermuda Islands—Census
			317.3	HA201-730	United States—Census
316.718	HA4712	Equatorial Guinea— Census	317.3	HA201-214	United States—Statistics, Vital
316.721	HA4715	Gabon—Census			
316.724	HA4716	Congo (Brazzaville)—Census	317.3	HA201-214	United States—Statistics
			317.7(4-9)	HA221-730	[United States, By state]—Census
316.73	HA4710	Angola—Census			
316.741	HA4717	Central African Republic—Census	318.1	HA971-990	Brazil—Census
			318.2	HA941-960	Argentina—Census
316.743	HA4718	Chad—Census	318.3	HA991-1010	Chile—Census
316.751	HA4711	Zaire—Census	318.4	HA961-970	Bolivia—Census
316.7571	HA4695	Rwanda—Census	318.5	HA1051-1070	Peru—Census
316.7572	HA4696	Burundi—Census	318.61	HA1011-1020	Colombia—Census
			318.66	HA1021-1030	Ecuador—Census

Dewey	LC	Subject Heading	Dewey	LC	Subject Heading
318.7	HA1091-1100	Venezuela—Census	320.54	JC311-314	Nationalism
318.81	HA1033	Guyana—Census	320.5409	DS38	Panarabism
318.82	HA1037	French Guiana—Census	+ 174927		
318.83	HA1035	Surinam—Census	320.54095694	DS149-151	Zionism
318.92	HA1041-1050	Paraguay—Census	320.85	JS	Local government
318.95	HA1071-1090	Uruguay—Census	320.85	JS113	Municipal home rule
319.3	HA3171-3190	New Zealand—Census	320.9174927	JQ1850	Arab countries—Politics and government
319.4	HA3001-3010	Australia—Census			
319.53	HA4013	Papua New Guinea—Census	320.932	JC66	Egypt—Politics and government
319.593	HA4014	Solomon Islands—Census	320.933	JC67	Jews—Politics and government
319.595	HA4015.5	Vanuatu—Census	320.9376	JC81-89	Rome—Politics and government
319.597	HA4015	New Caledonia—Census			
319.611	HA4016	Fiji—Census	320.938	JC71-75	Greece—Politics and government—To 146 B.C.
319.612	HA4017	Tonga—Census			
319.613	HA4018.5	American Samoa—Census	320.938	JC75.D	Deme
319.623	HA4017.5	Cook Islands—Census	320.94	JN12	Europe—Politics and government—20th century
319.67	HA4012	Guam—Census			
319.681	HA4016.7	Kiribati—Census	320.940948	D2009	Europe—Politics and government—1989-
319.71	HA2295	Falkland Islands—Census			
319.73	HA2291	Saint Helena—Census	320.941	JN101-1371	Great Britain—Politics and government
319.82	HA740	Greenland—Census			
319.89	HA4020-.5	Antarctica	320.9410902	JN137-158	Great Britain—Politics and government—1066-1485
320	B65	Political science	+ (1-4)		
320	HM33	Political science	320.941090	JN175-231	Great Britain—Politics and government—1485-
320	J	Political science	+ (3-511)		
320	JA	Political science	320.9411	JN1187-1371	Scotland—Politics and government
320.011	JC	State, The			
320.011	JC578	Justice	320.9415	JN1405-1571.5	Ireland—Politics and government
320.05	JA1-26	Political science—Periodicals	320.9416	JN1572	Northern Ireland—Politics and government
320.05	JA51	Political science—Periodicals	320.9429	JN1150-1159	Wales—Politics and government
320.06	JA27-34	Political science—Societies, etc.	320.943	JN3201-4944	Germany—Politics and government
320.06	JA35.5	Political science—Congresses	320.9436	JN1601-2041	Austria—Politics and government
320.071	JA86-88	Political science—Study and teaching	320.9437	JN2210-2229	Czechoslovakia—Politics and government
320.09	JA81-84	Political science—History	320.9438	JN6750-6769	Poland—Politics and government
320.0975	JK9661-9993	Confederate States of America—Politics and government	320.944	JN2301-3007	France—Politics and government
320.11	GN492.6	State, The—Origin	320.946	JN8101-8399	Spain—Politics and government
320.11	JA81-84	Social contract			
320.11	JC336	Social contract	320.9469	JN8423-8661	Portugal—Politics and government
320.12	CC600-605	Boundary stones	320.947	JN6500-6598	Russia—Politics and government
320.12	JC319-323	Political geography			
320.12	JC319-323	Geopolitics	320.948	JN7011-7066	Scandinavia—Politics and government
320.12	JC323	Boundaries			
320.120973	JK2556	United States—Territories and possessions	320.9481	JN7401-7695	Norway—Politics and government
320.15	JC327	Sovereignty	320.9485	JN7721-7995	Sweden—Politics and government
320.404	JF229	Separation of powers			
320.533	JC481	Fascism			

43

Dewey	LC	Subject Heading	Dewey	LC	Subject Heading
320.9489	JN7101-7367	Denmark—Politics and government	320.955	JQ1780-1789	Iran—Politics and government
320.94897	JN7390-7399	Finland—Politics and government	320.956	JQ	Middle East—Politics and government
320.94912	JN7370-7379	Iceland—Politics and government	320.9561	JQ1800-1809	Turkey—Politics and government
320.9492	JN5701-5999	Netherlands—Politics and government	320.9567	JQ1849	Iraq—Politics and government
320.9493	JN6101-6371	Belgium—Politics and government	320.95691	JQ1826	Syria—Politics and government
320.9494	JN8701-9599	Switzerland—Politics and government	320.95692	JQ1828	Lebanon—Politics and government
320.9495	JC91-93	Byzantine Empire—Politics and government	320.95693	JQ1811	Cyprus—Politics and government
320.9495	JN5001-5191	Greece—Politics and government	320.95694	JQ1830	Israel—Politics and government
320.9496	JN9600-9689	Balkan Peninsula—Politics and government	320.95695	JQ1833	Jordon—Politics and government
320.95	JQ	Asia—Politics and government	320.9581	JQ1760-1769	Afghanistan—Politics and government
320.95	JQ21-1825	Asia—Politics and government	320.9593	JQ1740-1749	Thailand—Politics and government
			320.9594	JQ950-959	Laos—Politics and government
320.951	JQ1500-1519	China—Politics and government	320.9595	JQ751	Burma—Politics and government
320.951249	JQ1520-1539	Taiwan—Politics and government	320.9596	JQ930-939	Cambodia—Politics and government
320.9519	JQ1720-1729.5	Korea—Politics and government	320.9597	JQ800-899	Vietnam—Politics and government
320.952	JQ1600-1699	Japan—Politics and government	320.9598	JQ760-779	Indonesia—Politics and government
320.9533	JQ1842	Yemen—Politics and government	320.9599	JQ1250-1419	Philippines—Politics and government
320.95353	JQ1843	Oman—Politics and government	320.96	JQ	Africa—Politics and government
320.95357	JQ1844	United Arab Emirates—Politics and government	320.96	JQ1870-3981	Africa—Politics and government
320.95363	JQ1845	Qatar—Politics sand government	320.971	JL	Canada—Politics and government
320.95365	JQ1846	Bahrain—Politics and government	320.971	JL1-500	Canada—Politics and government
320.95367	JQ1848	Kuwait—Politics and government	320.971090 + (1-33)	JL41-45	Canada—Politics and government—To 1763
320.9538	JQ1841	Saudi Arabia—Politics and government	320.97109033	JL48	Canada—Politics and government—1763-1791
320.954	JN5201-5690	Italy—Politics and government	320.9710903 + (3-4)	JL53	Canada—Politics and government—1791-1841
320.954	JQ200-620	India—Politics and government	320.97109034	JL55	Canada—Politics and government—1841-1867
320.95491	JQ629	Pakistan—Politics and government	320.971090 + (34-511)	JL65	Canada—Politics and government—1867-
320.95492	JQ630-639	Bangladesh—Politics and government	320.972	JL1200-1299	Mexico—Politics and government
320.95493	JQ650-659	Sri Lanka—Politics and government	320.9728	JL	Central America—Politics and government

Dewey	LC	Subject Heading	Dewey	LC	Subject Heading
320.97281	JL1480-1499	Guatemala—Politics and government	320.982	JL2000-2099	Argentina—Politics and government
320.97282	JL670-679	Belize—Politics and government	320.983	JL2600-2699	Chile—Politics and government
320.97283	JL1520-1539	Honduras—Politics and government	320.984	JL2200-2299	Bolivia—Politics and government
320.97284	JL1560-1579	El Salvador—Politics and government	320.985	JL3400-3499	Peru—Politics and government
320.97285	JL1600-1619	Nicaragua—Politics and government	320.9861	JL2800-2899	Colombia—Politics and government
320.97286	JL1440-1459	Costa Rica—Politics and government	320.9866	JL3000-3099	Ecuador—Politics and government
320.9729	JL	Caribbean Area—Politics and government	320.987	JL3800-3899	Venezuela—Politics and government
320.97291	JL1000-1019	Cuba—Politics and government	320.9881	JL680-689	Guyana—Politics and government
320.97292	JL630-639	Jamaica—Politics and government	320.9882	JL810-819	French Guiana—Politics and government
320.972921	JL629.5	Cayman Islands—Politics and government	320.9883	JL780-789	Surinam—Politics and government
320.97293	JL1120-1139	Dominican Republic—Politics and government	320.9892	JL3200-3299	Paraguay—Politics and government
320.97294	JL1080-1099	Haiti—Politics and government	320.9895	JL3600-3699	Uruguay—Politics and government
320.97295	JL1040-1059	Puerto Rico—Politics and government	320.99(5-6)	JQ5995-6651	Oceania—Politics and government
320.97296	JL610-619	Bahamas—Politics and government	320.99711	JL690-699	Falkland Islands—Politics and government
320.97297	JL640-649.7	Leeward Islands (West Indies)—Politics and government	320.9982	JN7380-7389	Greenland—Politics and government
320.972976	JL820-829	Guadeloupe—Politics and government	321	JC374-408	Kings and rulers
320.972982	JL830-839	Martinique—Politics and government	321.02	JC355	Federal government
			321.02	K3285	Federal government
320.972983	JL650-659	Trinidad and Tobago—Politics and government	321.03094	D352.1	Royal houses
			321.03094	D412.7	Royal houses
			321.030944	JC359	Bonapartism
320.9729845	JL629.6	Grenada—Politics and government	321.04094	D1060	European federation
			321.04094	JN15	European federation
320.972986	JL770-779	Curacao—Politics and government	321.06	JC352	City-states
			321.06	JC365	States, Small
320.97299	JL590-599	Bermuda Islands—Politics and government	321.07	HX	Utopias
			321.07	HX806-811	Utopias
320.973	JK	United States—Politics and government	321.08	JV	Colonies
			321.09	JC492	Counterrevolutions
320.9730903	JK54-103	United States—Politics and government—To 1775	321.09	JC494	Coups d'etat
			321.094	JC491	Revolutions
320.97309034	JK320	United States—Politics and government—1861-1865	321.1	GN479.6	Patriarchy
			321.3	D131	Feudalism
320.97309034	JK321	United States—Politics and government— 1865-1877	321.3	JC109-121	Feudalism
			321.5	JC20-89	Theocracy
320.98	JL	South America—Politics and government	321.5	JC419	Oligarchy
			321.6	D226.7	Royal houses
320.981	JL2400-2499	Brazil—Politics and government	321.6	JC375-393	Monarchy
			321.6	JC375-392	Despotism
			321.6	JC389	Divine right of kings
			321.6	JC391	Coronations

Dewey	LC	Subject Heading
321.60901	GN495.5	Kings and rulers, Ancient
321.8	JC421-423	Democracy
321.8042	JF285	Heads of state—Succession
321.80420973	E176.4	Presidents—United States—Mistresses
321.86	JC421-458	Republics
321.9	JC480-481	Totalitarianism
321.9092	JC495	Dictators
321.92	JC474	Communist state
321.94	HD3611-4730.9	Corporate state
321.94	JC478	Corporate state
322.1	BL65.S8	Religion and state
322.1	K3280-3282	Church and state
322.4	JC328.3	Civil disobedience
322.42	JC328.5	Insurgency
322.4.099747	F128.44	Draft Riot, New York, N.Y., 1863
322.5	JF195	Civil-military relations
323	JC571-628	Human rights
323	JC571-628	Civil rights
323	JC571-605	Individualism
323.044	JC328.3	Government, Resistance to
323.044	JC585-599	Political persecution
323.0440951	HV6335.C	Red Brigades
323.0941	JN900-1088	Political rights—Great Britain
323.0973	JK1717-2217	Political rights—United States
323.1	JC312	Minorities
323.1196073	E185.61	Afro-Americans—Civil rights
323.34	HQ1236-.5	Women's rights
323.42	JC575-578	Equality
323.44	JC585-599	Liberty
323.442	BL640	Freedom of religion
323.442	BV741	Freedom of religion
323.442	BV741	Liberty of conscience
323.445	Z657-659	Book burning
323.48	JC609	Petition, Right of
323.480973	JK1731	Petition, Right of
323.6	JC328	Allegiance
323.6	JC328	Treason
323.6	JF801	Citizenship
323.60973	JK1758-1759	Patriotism—United States
323.60973	JK1758	Americanization
323.631	HV8652-8654	Asylum, Right of
324	JF1001-1048	Elections
324.0973	JK524-529	Presidents—United States—Election
324.2	JF2011-2112	Political parties
324.241	JN1111-1129	Political parties—Great Britain
324.24102	JN1129.T7	Tories, English
324.273015	JK2063-2075	Nominations for office
324.2730154	JK2071-2077	Primaries

Dewey	LC	Subject Heading
331.8892	HD4903-.5	Right to labor
331.8892	HD6488-.2	Open and closed shop
331.8896	HD6972.5	Grievance procedures
331.89	HD6971.5-.65	Collective bargaining
331.8912	HD6490.07	Trade-unions—Organizing
331.8912	HD6490.R4	Trade-unions—Recognition
331.89143	HD5481-5630.7	Arbitration, Industrial
331.892	HD5306-5474	Strikes and lockouts
331.892	HD5309	Strikes and lockouts, Sympathetic
331.892	HD5311	Wildcat strikes
331.8925	HD5307	General strikes
331.89250941	HD5366	General strike, Great Britain, 1926
331.892509416	HD5368	General strike, Northern Ireland, 1974
331.8927	HD5468	Picketing
331.89280943	HD5379.C6	Eles (Firm) Strike, Bleidenstadt, Ger., 1975
331.89280952	HD5427	Daiichi Tokyo Kabushiki Kaisha Strike, 1970-1975
331.893	HD5461	Boycotts
331.893	HD5473	Sabotage
331.894	HD5306-5474	Strikes and lockouts
332	HG	Finance
332	HG1-9999	Financial institutions
332	HG1655	Acceptances
332.021	HG176-.5	Finance—Statistics
332.024	HG179	Finance, Personal
332.0240145	HD7105.4-.45	401(k) plans
332.024092	HG179.5	Financial planners
332.025	HG64-96	Finance—Directories
332.03	HG151	Finance—Encyclopedias
332.041	HB501	Capital
332.041	HC79.C3	Capital
332.0414	HG4028.C4	Capital investments
332.0415	HG7920-7933	Saving and thrift
332.042	HG3879-4000	International finance
332.042	HG3891	Capital movements
332.05	HG1-61	Finance—Periodicals
332.06	HG63	Finance—Congresses
332.071	HG152-.5	Finance—Study and teaching
332.09	HG171	Finance—History
332.1	HG1501-3550	Banks and banking
332.1	HG1616.C34	Bank capital
332.1	HG1656	Bank reserves
332.10285	HG1709	Banks and banking—Computer programs
332.10285	HG1710-.5	Electronic funds transfer
332.109(4-9)	HG2401-3542.7	Banks and banking—[By region or country]

Dewey	LC	Subject Heading	Dewey	LC	Subject Heading
332.10973	HG2401-2626	Banks and banking—United States	332.4042	HG289	Gold
			332.4042	HG321	Gold—Minting
332.110973	HG2559-2565	Federal Reserve banks	332.40420973	HG551-566	Coinage
332.12	HG2301-2351	Clearinghouses (Banking)	332.40420973	HG551	Gold
332.123	HG1978-2031	Private banks	332.4044	HG348-353.5	Paper money
332.152	HG3882-3890	Balance of payments	332.4044	HG348-353.5	Bank notes
332.16	HG1722	Bank mergers	332.40440973	HG604	Greenbacks
332.17	HG1616.C87	Banks and banking—Customer services	332.40440973	HG607-610	Bank notes
			332.4089973	E98.M7	Wampum
332.17	HG1711-1712	Home banking services	332.41	HG223	Value
332.1752	HG1660	Bank deposits	332.41	HG229-.5	Purchasing power
332.1752	HG1660	Bank accounts	332.41	HG229-.5	Prices
332.1752	HG1660	Savings accounts	332.41	HG229-.5	Deflation (Finance)
332.1752	HG1691-1704	Checking accounts	332.414	HG226.5	Demand for money
332.1753	HG1641-1643	Commercial loans	332.42	HG361-363	Legal tender
332.1753	HG1641-1643	Bank loans	332.4222	HG297	Gold standard
332.1753	HG1641-1643	Term loans	332.4223	HG301-309	Silver
332.1754	HG1616.I5	Bank investments	332.45	HG381-421	Coinage, International
332.178	HG1643	Bank credit cards	332.45	HG3810-4000	Foreign exchange
332.178	HG1643	Affinity credit cards	332.4503	HG3810.5	Foreign exchange—Encyclopedias
332.178	HG1643	Check credit plans	332.4509	HG3811-3815	Foreign exchange—History
332.178	HG2251-2256	Safe-deposit boxes	332.4509(4-9)	HG3901-4000	Foreign exchange—[By region or country]
332.21	HG1881-1966	Savings banks			
332.22	HG1951-1956	Postal savings banks	332.490973	HG641-645	Counterfeits and counterfeiting
332.26	HG4301-4480.9	Trust companies			
332.26025	HG4307	Trust companies—Directories	332.49(4-9)	HG451-1496	Money—[By region or country]
332.2609	HG4311	Trust companies—History	332.4973	HG451-645	Money—United States
332.2609(4-9)	HG4341-4480.9	Trust companies—[By region or country]	332.55	HG1685-1704	Drafts
			332.6	HG4501-6051	Investments
332.260973	HG4341-4356	Trust companies—United States	332.6	HG4529.5	Portfolio management
			332.6	HG4530	Investment clubs
332.2609(4-9)	HG4357-4480.9	Trust companies—[Other countries]	332.609(4-9)	HG4901-5993	Investments—[By region or country]
332.28	HG1975-1976	Development banks	332.60973	HG4905-5131	Investments—United States
332.31	HG2041-2051	Agricultural cooperative credit associations	332.609(4-9)	HG5151-5993	Investments—[Other countries]
332.31	HG2041-2051	Land banks	332.62	HG4621	Discount brokers
332.32	HG2039.5-2040.5	Mortgage banks	332.62	HG4621	Stockbrokers
332.32	HG2121-2156	Savings and loan associations	332.63	AM237	Collectibles as an investment
332.34	HG2070-2106	Pawnbroking	332.63	HD9677	Diamonds as an investment
332.37	HG1970-1971	Merchant banks	332.63	N8600	Art as an investment
332.4	GN435.7-450.5	Shell money	332.632	HG4650-4930.5	Securities
332.4	GN436.2	Stone money	332.6322	HG4028.T4	Tender offers (Securities)
332.4	HG201-1496	Money	332.6322	HG4661	Stocks
332.4	HG235	Shell money	332.63221	HG4028.D5	Dividend reinvestment
332.4	HG321-329	Mints	332.63221	HG4028.V3	Valuation
332.4	HG353.5	Military currency	332.63228	HG6042	Stock options
332.401	HG226.6	Quantity theory of money	332.63228	HG6043	Stock index futures
332.4021	HG3854-3858	Money—Tables	332.6323	HB531-549	Interest rates
332.404	HG393	Decimal system	332.6323	HG4028.B6	Bond transfer
332.4042	HG258-312	Precious metals	332.6323	HG4651	Bonds
332.4042	HG261-315	Coinage	332.63232	HG4701-4726	Government securities

Dewey	LC	Subject Heading	Dewey	LC	Subject Heading
332.632320973	HG4931-4955	Government securities—United States	333.33	HD1334-1335	Consolidation of land holdings
332.63233	HG4726	Municipal bonds	333.33	HD1361-1395.5	Real estate business
332.63244	HG4655	Mortgages	333.335	HD1471	Haciendas
332.6327	HG4530	Mutual funds	333.335563	HD1478	Sharecropping
332.6328	HG6046-6051	Commodity futures	333.5	HB401	Rent
332.642	HG4551-4598	Stock-exchanges	333.7	GE300-350	Environmental management
332.642	HG4621	Floor traders (Finance)	333.7	GE	Environmental sciences
332.64273	HG4571-4575.3	Wall Street	333.7	SH327.5	Fishery resources
332.644	HG6046-6051	Commodity exchanges	333.7071	GF70-90	Environmental education
332.645	HG6001-6051	Speculation	333.72	GE195-199	Green movement
332.6452	HG3853	Foreign exchange futures	333.72	GE195-199	Environmentalism
332.6452	HG6024-6051	Futures	333.72	JA75.8	Green movement
332.6452	HG6024.3-.9	Financial futures	333.72	S900-954	Conservation of natural resources
332.6722	HG1723	Bank stocks			
332.673	HG4538	Investments, Foreign	333.72071	S946	Environmental education
332.7	HG3691-3769	Credit	333.73	HD101-1131	Land use
332.7	HG3746	Documentary credit	333.7309	HD113-156	Land use—History
332.7	HG3751.5-.9	Credit ratings	333.7309411	HD611-620	Land use—Scotland
332.7	HG3752.3	Accounts receivable loans	333.7309415	HD621-630	Land use—Ireland
332.71	HD1439-1440	Agricultural credit	333.7309416	HD620.5	Land use—Northern Ireland
332.72	HD1443	Mortgages	333.730942	HD601-610	Land use—England
332.72	HG2039.5-2040.5	Mortgage loans, Reverse	333.730943	HD651-660.5	Land use—Germany
332.72	HG2040.2	Discrimination in mortgage loans	333.7309436	HD631-640	Land use—Austria
			333.730943648	HD640.9	Land use—Liechtenstein
332.722	HG2040.4	Home improvement loans	333.7309437	HD640.3	Land use—Czechoslovakia
332.722	HG2040.45	Home equity loans	333.7309438	HD726-729.5	Land use—Poland
332.742	HG3751-3754.5	Commercial credit	333.7309439	HD640.5	Land use—Hungary
332.742	HG3753-3754	Export credit	333.730944	HD641-650	Land use—France
332.743	HG3755-3756	Consumer credit	333.730944949	HD650.5	Land use—Monaco
332.743	HG3755-3756	Loans, Personal	333.730945	HD671-680	Land use—Italy
332.743	HG3755.5	Installment plan	333.730946	HD771-780	Land use—Spain
332.75	HG3705-3711	Credit control	333.7309469	HD781-790	Land use—Portugal
332.75	HG3760-3769	Bankruptcy	333.73094698	HD1028.5	Land use—Madeira Islands
332.75	HG3760-3769	Business failures	333.73094699	HD1028	Land use—Azores
332.75	HG3773	Receivers	333.730947	HD711-720	Land use—Russia
332.76	HG1692	Check collection systems	333.7309481	HD751-760	Land use—Norway
332.76	HG1692	Check float	333.7309485	HD761-770	Land use—Sweden
332.76	HG1710.5	Debit cards	333.7309489	HD731-740	Land use—Denmark
332.77	HG1689	Bills of exchange	333.73094897	HD721-725	Land use—Finland
332.77	HG3745	Letters of credit	333.73094912	HD741-750	Land use—Iceland
332.8	HG1621-1623	Interest rates	333.7309492	HD701-710	Land use—Netherlands
332.83	HB551	Usury	333.7309493	HD691-700	Land use—Belgium
332.84	HG1651-1654	Discount houses (Finance)	333.73094935	HD710.5	Land use—Luxembourg
332.84	HG1651-1654	Discount	333.7309494	HD791-800	Land use—Switzerland
332.9	HG1696-1698	Forgery	333.7309495	HD840.5	Land use—Greece
332.90973	HG335-341	Counterfeits and counterfeiting	333.73094965	HD810.5	Land use—Albania
			333.7309497	HD821-825	Land use—Yugoslavia
333.14	HD1301-1339	Land, Nationalization of	333.7309498	HD831-840	Land use—Romania
333.2	HD1286-1289	Commons	333.7309499	HD811-820	Land use—Bulgaria
333.3	HD1241-1339	Land tenure	333.730951	HD921-930	Land use—China
333.30973	HD251-279	Real property	333.730951249	HD936-940	Land use—Taiwan
333.31	HD1332-1333.5	Land reform	333.73095125	HD941-945	Land use—Hong Kong
333.32	HD1336-1339	Peasantry	333.73095126	HD931-935	Land use—Macao

Dewey	LC	Subject Heading	Dewey	LC	Subject Heading
333.7309517	HD920.8	Land use—Mongolia	333.73096662	HD1025	Land use—Liberia
333.7309519	HD920.5-.6	Land use—Korea	333.73096668	HD1015	Land use—Cote d'Ivoire
333.730952	HD911-920	Land use—Japan	333.7309667	HD1022	Land use—Ghana
333.7309533	HD854-.5	Land use—Yemen	333.73096681	HD1013	Land use—Togo
333.73095353	HD855	Land use—Oman	333.73096683	HD1012	Land use—Benin
333.73095357	HD856	Land use—United Arab Emirates	333.7309669	HD1021	Land use—Nigeria
333.73095363	HD857	Land use—Qatar	333.73096711	HD1009	Land use—Cameroon
333.73095365	HD858	Land use—Bahrain	333.73096715	HD1003	Land use—Sao Tome and Principe
333.73095367	HD859	Land use—Kuwait	333.73096718	HD1002	Land use—Equatorial Guinea
333.7309538	HD853	Land use—Saudi Arabia	333.73096721	HD1005	Land use—Gabon
333.730954	HD871-880	Land use—India	333.73096724	HD1006	Land use—Zaire
333.73095491	HD880.5	Land use—Pakistan	333.7309673	HD1000	Land use—Angola
333.73095492	HD880.6	Land use—Bangladesh	333.73096741	HD1007	Land use—Central African Republic
333.73095493	HD860.8	Land use—Sri Lanka	333.73096743	HD1008	Land use—Chad
333.73095495	HD1029.7	Land use—Maldives	333.73096751	HD1001	Land use—Congo (Democratic Republic)
333.73095496	HD860.9	Land use—Nepal	333.730967571	HD985	Land use—Rwanda
333.73095498	HD880.3	Land use—Bhutan	333.730967572	HD986	Land use—Burundi
333.730955	HD860.2	Land use—Iran	333.73096761	HD984	Land use—Uganda
333.7309561	HD846.5	Land use—Turkey	333.73096762	HD983	Land use—Kenya
333.7309567	HD860	Land use—Iraq	333.73096771	HD981	Land use—Djibouti
333.73095691	HD848	Land use—Syria	333.73096773	HD980	Land use—Somalia
333.73095692	HD849	Land use—Lebanon	333.7309678	HD987	Land use—Tanzania
333.73095693	HD847	Land use—Cyprus	333.7309679	HD988	Land use—Mozambique
333.73095694	HD850	Land use—Israel	333.730968	HD991	Land use—South Africa
333.73095695	HD851	Land use—Jordan	333.73096881	HD998	Land use—Namibia
333.7309581	HD860.6	Land use—Afghanistan	333.73096883	HD996	Land use—Botswana
333.7309591	HD860.7	Land use—Burma	333.73096885	HD994	Land use—Lesotho
333.7309593	HD890.55	Land use—Thailand	333.73096887	HD995	Land use—Swaziland
333.7309594	HD890.4	Land use—Laos	333.7309689	HD992	Land use—Zimbabwe
333.7309595	HD890.6	Land use—Malaysia	333.73096894	HD993	Land use—Zambia
333.7309596	HD890.3	Land use—Cambodia	333.73096897	HD997	Land use—Malawi
333.7309597	HD890.5	Land use—Vietnam	333.7309691	HD989	Land use—Madagascar
333.7309598	HD891-900	Land use—Indonesia	333.7309694	HD1030	Land use—Comoro Islands
333.7309599	HD901-910	Land use—Philippines	333.7309696	HD1029.9	Land use—Seychelles
333.7309611	HD974	Land use—Tunisia	333.73096981	HD1030.5	Land use—Reunion
333.7309612	HD975	Land use—Libya	333.73096982	HD1030.3	Land use—Mauritius
333.730962	HD976	Land use—Egypt	333.7309699	HD1030.7	Land use—Kerguelen Islands
333.7309624	HD977	Land use—Sudan	333.730971	HD311-320	Land use—Canada
333.730963	HD979	Land use—Ethiopia	333.730972	HD321-330	Land use—Mexico
333.730964	HD972	Land use—Morocco	333.73097281	HD351-360	Land use—Guatemala
333.7309648	HD1027	Land use—Western Sahara	333.73097282	HD336-340	Land use—Belize
333.7309649	HD1028.7	Land use—Canary Islands	333.73097283	HD361-370	Land use—Honduras
333.730965	HD973	Land use—Algeria	333.73097284	HD391-400	Land use—El Salvador
333.7309661	HD1020	Land use—Mauritania	333.73097285	HD371-380	Land use—Nicaragua
333.73096623	HD1017	Land use—Mali	333.73097286	HD341-350	Land use—Costa Rica
333.73096625	HD1018	Land use—Burkina Faso	333.73097287	HD381-385	Land use—Panama
333.73096626	HD1014	Land use—Niger	333.730972875	HD386-390	Land use—Panama Canal Zone
333.7309663	HD1019	Land use—Senegal	333.73097291	HD411-420	Land use—Cuba
333.7309664	HD1023	Land use—Sierra Leone	333.73097292	HD431-440	Land use—Jamaica
333.73096651	HD1024	Land use—Gambia			
333.73096652	HD1016	Land use—Guinea			
333.73096657	HD1026	Land use—Guinea Bissau			
333.73096658	HD1028.9	Land use—Cape Verde			

Dewey	LC	Subject Heading	Dewey	LC	Subject Heading
333.73097293	HD426-430	Land use—Dominican Republic	333.73099611	HD1126	Land use—Fiji
			333.73099612	HD1127	Land use—Tonga
333.73097294	HD421-425	Land use—Haiti	333.73099613	HD1128	Land use—American Samoa
333.73097295	HD441-450	Land use—Puerto Rico			
333.73097296	HD406-410	Land use—Bahamas	333.7309962	HD1129.5	Land use—French Polynesia
333.7309 + 729722	HD450.3	Land use—Virgin Islands of the United States	333.73099623	HD1127.5	Land use—Cook Islands
333.730972973	HD453.2	Land use—Anguilla	333.7309967	HD1121.5	Land use—Guam
333.730972973	HD453.8	Land use—Saint Kitts and Nevis	333.73099681	HD1122.3	Land use—Kiribati
			333.7309971	HD1029.5	Land use—Falkland Islands
333.730972974	HD453.4	Land use—Antigua	333.7309973	HD1029	Land use—Saint Helena
333.730972975	HD453.6	Land use—Montserrat	333.7309973	HD1029.3	Land use—Tristan da Cunha
333.730972976	HD458	Land use—Guadeloupe			
333.730972977	HD456.8	Land use—Saba (Netherlands Antilles)	333.730998 + (1-8)	HD1130	Land use—Arctic regions
333.730972977	HD456.85	Land use—Saint Eustatius (Netherlands Antilles)	333.7309982	HD1130.5	Land use—Greenland
			333.73137	HD1665-1671	Waste lands
333.730972977	HD456.9	Land use—Saint Martin	333.7316	S439-481	Green Revolution
333.730972981	HD451.5	Land use—Barbados	333.736153	HD1711-1741	Desert reclamation
333.730972982	HD459	Land use—Martinique	333.736153	TC801-957	Desert reclamation
333.730972983	HD455	Land use—Trinidad and Tobago	333.740973	HD241	Grazing
			333.75	SD387.043	Old growth forests
333.7309 + 729841	HD454.3	Land use—Dominica	333.7511	SD426-428	Forest reserves
333.7309 + 729843	HD454.7	Land use—Saint Lucia	333.76	HD101-1131	Land capability for agriculture
333.7309 + 729844	HD454.9	Land use—Saint Vincent	333.76	HD1393	Farms—Valuation
			333.77	HD1393.5	Industrial districts
333.7309 + 729845	HD454.5	Land use—Grenada	333.7717	HT169.6-.9	Zoning
			333.780973	E160	National parks and reserves—United States
333.730972986	HD456.5	Land use—Aruba	333.7816	QH75-77	Nature conservation
333.730972986	HD456.6	Land use—Bonaire	333.784	GV191.67.F6	Forest reserves—Recreational use
333.730972986	HD456.7	Land use—Curacao			
333.73097299	HD1028.3	Land use—Bermuda Islands	333.79	HD9502-.5	Energy policy
333.730973	HD170-279	Land use—United States	333.79	TN263.5	Energy minerals
333.730981	HD491-500	Land use—Brazil	333.7923	HD9681	Solar energy industries
333.730982	HD471-480	Land use—Argentina	333.7924	HD9698-.5	Nuclear industry
333.730983	HD501-510	Land use—Chile	333.7932	HD9685-9695	Electric utilities
333.730984	HD481-490	Land use—Bolivia	333.8509162	TN264	Marine mineral resources
333.730985	HD551-560	Land use—Peru	333.850973	HD242.5	Mineral lands
333.7309861	HD511-520	Land use—Colombia	333.91	HD1690-1702	Water resources development
333.7309866	HD521-530	Land use—Ecuador			
333.730987	HD571-580	Land use—Venezuela	333.9164	GC1000-1023	Marine resources
333.7309881	HD540.3	Land use—Guyana	333.916416	GC1018	Marine resources conservation
333.7309882	HD540.7	Land use—French Guiana			
333.7309883	HD540.5	Land use—Surinam	333.91816	QH75-77	Wetland conservation
333.7309892	HD541-550	Land use—Paraguay	333.95	QH75-77	Biological diversity conservation
333.7309895	HD561-570	Land use—Uruguay			
333.730993	HD1120.5	Land use—New Zealand	333.95	QH75-77	Biosphere reserves
333.730994	HD1031-1040	Land use—Australia	333.95	QH541.15.B56	Biological diversity
333.7309953	HD1122	Land use—Papua New Guinea	333.953	QK86-.4	Plant conservation
333.73099593	HD1123	Land use—Solomon Islands	333.95416	QL81.5-84.7	Wildlife conservation
333.73099595	HD1125	Land use—Vanuatu	333.95416	QL83.4	Wildlife reintroduction
			333.95416	SF996.45	Wildlife rehabilitation
333.73099597	HD1124	Land use—New Caledonia	333.958	QL676.5-.57	Bird refuges

Dewey	LC	Subject Heading	Dewey	LC	Subject Heading
333.95816	SK351-579	Birds, Protection of	336.01473	HJ9141-9343	Local finance—United States
334	HD2951-3575	Cooperation	336.014(4-9)	HJ9350-9695	Local finance—[Other countries]
334.06	HD2952	Cooperation—Societies, etc.	336.02	HJ2240-7395	Revenue
334.09	HD2956	Cooperation—History	336.090(1-5)	HJ210-240	Finance, Public—History
334.1	HD7287.7-.72	Housing, Cooperative	336.16	HJ5301-5508	Licenses
334.2	HG2032-2039	Banks and banking, Cooperative	336.1609(4-9)	HJ5321-5510	Licenses—[By region or country]
334.22	HG2032-2039	Credit unions	336.160973	HJ5321-5374	Licenses—United States
334.5	HD3271-3575	Consumers' leagues	336.17	HG6105-6270.9	Lotteries
334.5	HD3271-3575	Consumer cooperatives	336.170973	HG6126-6134	Lotteries—United States
334.509	HD3281-3410.9	Consumer cooperatives—[By region or country]	336.2	HJ3241	Tax assessment
334.6	HD3120-3260.9	Producer cooperatives	336.20015195	HJ2351.4	Tax revenue estimating
334.609(4-9)	HD3131-3260.9	Producer cooperatives—[By region or country]	336.2009	HJ2250-2279	Taxation—History
334.683	HD1483-1491.5	Agriculture, Cooperative	336.2009(4-9)	HJ2361-3192.7	Taxation—[By region or country]
334.683	HD1492-.5	Collective farms	336.200973	HJ2361-2442	Taxation—United States
334.683	HD1492-.5	Collectivization of agriculture	336.2009(4-9)	HJ2449-3192.7	Taxation—[Other regions or countries]
334.683	HD1493-.5	State farms	336.200973	HJ2361	Internal revenue—United States
334.683	HX550.A37	Communism and agriculture	336.20097(4-9)	HJ2391-2442	Taxation—[United States, By state]
334.7	HG9201-9245	Friendly societies	336.2014	HJ9115-9123	Municipal revenue
334.7	HS1501-1510	Friendly societies	336.206	HJ2336-2337	Tax exemption
335	HX	Collectivism	336.207	HD2753	Corporations—Taxation
335	HX	Socialism	336.22	HJ4101-4936	Property tax
335	HX1-550	Socialism	336.23	HJ4581-4601	Taxation of personal property
335.0071	HX19-.2	Socialism—Study and teaching	336.2309(4-9)	HJ4120-4460	Property tax—[By region or country]
335.009	HX21-54	Socialism—History	336.24	HJ4621-4830	Income tax
335.009(4-9)	HX80-517.5	Socialism—[By region or country]	336.2424	HJ4639	Capital gains tax
335.1209	HX626-632	Utopian socialism—History	336.24240973	HJ4653.C3	Capital gains tax
335.1209(4-9)	HX651-780.7	Utopian socialism—[By region or country]	336.24320973	HJ4653.E8	Excess profits tax
335.1209694	HX742.2	Kibbutzim	336.27	HJ5711-5715	Turnover tax
335.15	HD6479	Guild socialism	336.271	HJ5730-5731	Excise tax
335.4	HB97.5	Marxian economics	336.271	HJ5771-5797	Luxuries—Taxation
335.412	HB206	Labor theory of value	336.2713	HJ5711-5721	Sales tax
335.43	HX1-780.9	Communism	336.2714	HJ5711-5715	Value-added tax
335.43	HX77	Democratic centralism	336.272	HJ5315	Revenue-stamps
335.43092	HX518.L4	Communist leadership	336.276	HJ5801-5823	Inheritance and transfer tax
335.7	HX51-54	Socialism, Christian	336.27863371	HD9130-9149	Tobacco industry
335.82	HD6477	Syndicalism	336.293	HJ2326-2327	Progressive taxation
335.83	HX821-970.7	Anarchism	336.294	HJ2321-2323	Tax incidence
335.8309(4-9)	HX841-970.7	Anarchism—[By region or country]	336.294	HJ5250-5255	Indirect taxation
336	HJ	Finance, Public	336.294	HJ3863-3925	Direct taxation
336	HJ2240-7395	Taxation	336.29409(4-9)	HJ3925.A-.Z	Direct taxation—[By region or country]
336.005	HJ9-99.8	Finance, Public—Periodicals	336.34	HJ8003-8899	Debts, External
336.014	HJ9103-9695	Local finance	336.34	HJ8001-8899	Debts, Public
336.014(4-9)	HJ9141-9695	Local finance—[By region or country]	336.3409(4-9)	HJ8101-8899	Debts, Public—[By region or country]
336.01405	HJ9103	Local finance—Periodicals	336.363	HJ8052	Sinking-funds

Dewey	LC	Subject Heading	Dewey	LC	Subject Heading
336.368	HJ8061	State bankruptcy	338.2741	HD9536	Gold mines and mining
336.39	HJ7461-7977	Expenditures, Public	338.27633	HD9585.B67 .B674	Borax
336.39	HJ7543	Entitlement spending			
336.3909(4-9)	HJ7537-7977	Expenditures, Public—[By region or country]	338.2768	HD9999.C36	Chalk
			338.372072	SH343.4	Fishery research vessels
336.390973	HJ7537-7654	Expenditures, Public—United States	338.3727	SH334	Fisheries subsidies
			338.4	HD9980-9990	Service industries
336.3909(4-9)	HJ7663-7977	Expenditures, Public—[Other countries]	338.47004	HD9696.D54- .D544	Digital computer industry
336.73	HJ241-785	Finance, Public—United States	338.4702504	HD9696.D36- .D364	Database industry
336.7(4-9)	HJ285-785	Finance, Public—[United States, By state]	338.47355	HD9743-9744	Defense industries
			338.47355092	HD8039.M9	Defense industries—Employees
337	HF1351-1532.935	International economic relations			
			338.473621	RA410-415	Medical economics
337.14	HG3896	Euro-bond market	338.4738773	HD9711-.2	Aircraft industry
337.(4-9)	HF1451-1647	International economic relations—[By region or country]	338.4739142	HD9948.3	Lingerie industry
			338.4754786	HD9660.D84- .D844	Dye industry
338	HD	Production (Economic theory)	338.476151	HD9665-9675	Nonprescription drug industry
338	HD2321-4730.9	Industries	338.476153137	HD9675.A7-.A74	Aspirin
338	HD2329	Industrialization	338.4762161	HD9705.5.F35- .F354	Fans (Machinery) industry
338	T58.7-.8	Industrial capacity			
338.04	HB615	Entrepreneurship	338.476218	HD9705-9705.5	Machinery industry
338.06	HD56-57.5	Industrial productivity	338.4762382	VM298.5-301	Shipbuilding industry
338.068	HD30.22	Managerial economics	338.47624	HD9715-9717.5	Construction industry
338.0999	TL797	Space industrialization	338.4762912	HD9711.5	Aerospace industries
338.1	SB107-109	Botany, Economic	338.47637143	HD9275-9283.7	Dairy products industry
338.13	HD1447	Agricultural prices	338.47641815	HD9057-9058	Bakers and bakeries
338.16	HD1401-2210	Farms	338.476453	HD9939	Drapery industry
338.16	HD1470-1476	Farms, Size of	338.4764795	TX901-946.5	Food service
338.16	S494.5.P75	Agricultural productivity	338.4764793 + 0068	TX911.3.M27	Food service management
338.163	HD1549	Gleaning			
338.17	HD9000-9019	Farm produce	338.4765173	HD9999 .T34- .T344	Telephone answering services
338.17311	HD9049.W3-.W5	Durum wheat industry			
338.17351	HD9070-9093	Cotton growing	338.4766	HD9650-9660	Chemical industry
338.173577	HD9019.A43- .A434	Agave products industry	338.4766316	HD9390-9395	Distilling industries
			338.4766468	HD9330.B2-.B23	Baking powder
338.17498	HD9750-9769	Forest products	338.476655	HD9490-.5	Oil industries
338.17498	SD430-557	Timber	338.476655384	HD9579.D5-.D54	Diesel fuels industry
338.176	HD9778-.5	Hides and skins	338.476682	HD9660.G58-.G6	Glycerin
338.181	HD1428-1431	Agriculture—International cooperation	338.476683	HD9999.A4 - .A44	Adhesives industry
338.2025	TN12	Mineral industries—Directories	338.4767	HD7406-7510	Factories
			338.4767	HD9720-9739	Manufactures
338.203	TN9-10	Mineral industries—Dictionaries	338.4767482	HD9750-9769	Coopers and cooperage
			338.4767634	HD9971.5.T32- .T324	Disposal tableware industry
338.205	TN1-4	Mineral industries—Periodicals			
			338.476774742	HD9929.5.A2 79274	Acrylic fiber industry
338.206	TN5	Mineral industries—Congresses	338.47678	HD9662.E42- .E423	Elastomer industry
338.2074	TN6	Mineral industries—Exhibitions			
			338.4768111	HD9999.C6	Clocks and watches
338.209	TN15-124	Mineral industries— History	338.476816	HD9801	Electronic office machine industry
338.2724	HD9540-9559	Coal			

Dewey	LC	Subject Heading	Dewey	LC	Subject Heading
338.47681761	HD9995 .D54-.D544	Diagnostic equipment industry	338.74094	HD2844-2891.84	Corporations—Europe
338.476834	HD9744.F55- .F554	Firearms industry and trade	338.740941	HD2845-2847.5	Corporations—Great Britain
			338.740943	HD2857-2860.5	Corporations—Germany
338.476887221	HD9993 .D65-.D654	Doll industry	338.740944	HD2853-2856	Corporations—France
			338.740945	HD2862-2865	Corporations—Italy
338.47694	HD9716 .C3-.C33	Carpentry	338.740946	HD2885-2888	Corporations—Spain
			338.7409469	HD2889	Corporations—Portugal
338.4791	G154.9	Tourist trade	338.740947	HD2874-2877	Corporations—Russia
338.5	HB615	Risk	338.7409492	HD2865.5-2873.5	Corporations—Benelux countries
338.516	HB601	Profit			
338.516	HC79.P7	Profit	338.7409495	HD2891.83	Corporations—Greece
338.52	HB143	Shadow prices	338.740951	HD2910	Corporations—China
338.52	HB221-236	Prices	338.740952	HD2907	Corporations—Japan
338.52	HD6977-7080	Prices	338.740954	HD2897-2900	Corporations—India
338.52	HF5417	Price cutting	338.740955	HD2892.56	Corporations—Iran
338.521	HB201-206	Value	338.7409561	HD2891.93	Corporations—Turkey
338.521	HB201-206	Supply and demand	338.7409567	HD2892.55	Corporations—Iraq
338.526	HB236	Prices—Government policy	338.74095694	HD2892.2	Corporations—Israel
338.528	HB225	Consumer price indexes	338.7409598	HD2904	Corporations—Indonesia
338.542	HB3711-3840	Business cycles	338.7409599	HD2905	Corporations—Philippines
338.542	HB3711-3840	Depressions	338.74096	HD2917-2929.3	Corporations—Africa
338.542	HB3722-3725	Financial crises	338.740971	HD2807-2810	Corporations—Canada
338.542	HB3729	Long waves (Economics)	338.740972	HD2811	Corporations—Mexico
338.54209(4-9)	HB3741-3840	Business cycles—[By region or country]	338.7409728	HD2813.5-2819	Corporations—Central America
			338.7409729	HD2820.5-2825.9	Corporations—West Indies
338.544	HD30.27	Business forecasting	338.740973	HD2771-2798.5	Corporations—United States
338.6	HD51	Division of labor			
338.6	HD2756-.2	Diversification in industry	338.74098	HD2827-2843	Corporations—South America
338.6041	HG4001-4285	Business enterprises—Finance	338.740994	HD2930	Corporations—Australia
338.6042	HD5708.5-.55	Plant shutdowns	338.749	HD3840-4420.8	Government ownership
338.6048	HB238	Competition, Imperfect	338.749	HD3850	Corporations, Government
338.6048	HD41	Competition	338.76313	HD9486-.6	Agricultural machinery industry
338.6048	HF1414	Competition			
338.634	HD2331-2336.35	Home labor	338.7637143	HD9282	Dried milk industry
338.634	HD2331-2336.35	Home-based businesses	338.790896073	E185.8	Afro-Americans in business
338.634	HD2336.2-.25	Cottage industries	338.8042	HD2756-.2	Conglomerate corporations
338.6420681	HG4027.7	Small business—Finance	338.82	HD2709-2932	Monopolies
338.644	HD2350.8-2356	Big business	338.82	HD2757-2768	Oligopolies
338.65	HD2350.8-2356	Factory system	338.83	HD2746.5-.55	Consolidation and merger of corporations
338.69	HD5650-5660	Employee ownership			
338.7	HC79.D5	Business relocation	338.83	HG4028.M4	Consolidation and merger of corporations
338.7	HD62.25	Family-owned business enterprises			
			338.86	HD2709-2932	Stock companies
338.7	HD62.27	Couple-owned business enterprises	338.87	HD2757.5	Cartels
			338.9	HD72-88	Economic development
338.7	HF5001-6182.2	Business	338.9	HD82-85	Autarchy
338.74	HD59	Corporations—Investor relations	338.9	HD87-88	Economic policy
			338.901	HD108-.8	Economic development—Methodology
338.74	HD59.2	Corporate image			
338.74	HD2709-2932	Corporations	338.926	T174.3	Technology transfer
338.74	HG4001-4285	Corporations—Finance	339.21	HB401	Rent
338.7409	HD2770-2930.7	Corporations—[By region or country]	339.23	HB142	Input-output analysis
			339.27421	HD9536	Silver mines and mining

Dewey	LC	Subject Heading	Dewey	LC	Subject Heading
339.42	HD6977-7080	Cost and standard of living	340.972	K7350	Conflict of laws—Sales
339.46	HC79.P6	Poverty	340.982	K7380-7384	Conflict of laws—Banking
339.47	HB801-843	Consumption (Economics)	340.986	K7470	Conflict of laws— Insurance
339.47	HC79.C6	Consumption (Economics)	340.996	K7360-7370	Conflict of laws—
339.47092	HC79.C6	Consumers			Negotiable instruments
339.5	HB145	Equilibrium (Economics)	341	K540-5570	International law
339.5	HB3732	Economic stabilization	341.0711	KF285	Law School Admission Test
340-349	K	Law	341.2422	HC241.2-.25	European Economic
340.0207	K183-184.7	Law—Humor			Community literature
342.0297(4-9)	JK2413-2428	Constitutions, State	341.28	K3375	Colonies—Law and
340.03	K50-54	Law—Dictionaries			legislation
340.071	K100-103	Law—Study and teaching	341.47	K4135	Space law
340.0711	LC1101-1261	Law schools	341.7	K7051-7054	Law—International
340.09	K140-165	Law—History			unification
340.092	K170	Law—Biography	342	K3150	Public law
340.0973	KF338	Lawyer referral	342	K3154-3367	Constitutional law
		service—United States	342.029	K3161	Constitutional history
340.11	K280-286	Law—Sources	342.0292	JF71-99	Constitutional conventions
340.11	KF382	Rule of law—United States	342.03288	K970	Reparation
340.115	K368-380	Sociological jurisprudence	342.041	K3220-3225	Public policy (Law)
340.18	BM523.5.S53	Shaving (Jewish law)	342.0418	JK371.P7-.P8	Police power
340.2	K583-591	Comparative law	342.042	K7000-7720	Conflict of laws
340.52	K190-195	Law, Primitive	342.062	K3332-3351	Executive power
340.550942	KD834-839	Feudal law—England	342.066	K3400-3431	Administrative law
340.59	BP140-165	Islamic law	342.068	K3440-3460	Civil service
340.59	BP140-165	Islamic law	342.08	K3224-3229	People (Constitutional law)
340.9	K7680	Judgments, Foreign	342.08	K3290-3304	People (Constitutional law)
340.912	K7120-7197	Conflict of laws—Persons	342.084	RA1067	Abortion
340.913	K7145-7148	Conflict of laws—Juristic	342.085	K3236-3268	Civil rights
		persons	342.085	K3236-3268	Human rights
340.915	K7155-7197	Conflict of laws— Domestic	342.085	K3252	Right to life
		relations	342.4105	KD4190-4381	Great Britain. Parliament.
340.917	K7181-7197	Conflict of laws—Parent	342.4106	KD4430-4531	Monarchy—Great Britain
		and child	342.4106	KD4462	Prime ministers—Great
340.918	K7197	Conflict of laws—Guardian			Britain
		and ward	342.411	KDC750-785	Scotland—Constitutional
340.92	K7260-7335	Conflict of laws—			law
		Obligations	342.415	KDK1200-1350	Ireland—Constitutional law
340.92	K7265-7305	Conflict of laws— Contracts	342.416	KDE410-462	Northern
340.929	K7310	Conflict of laws—Quasi			Ireland—Constitutional law
		contracts	342.42	KD3931-4645	England—Constitutional law
340.93	K7315-7335	Conflict of laws—Torts	342.42029	KD3931-3966	England—Constitutional
340.94	K7200-7218	Conflict of laws—Property			history
340.948	K7550-7582	Conflict of laws—	342.420412	KD4030	England—Foreign
		Intellectual property			relations—Law and
340.948	K7570-7582	Conflict of laws—Industrial			legislation
		property	342.42042	KD680-685	Conflict of laws—England
340.9482	K7555-7557	Conflict of laws—Copyright	342.42044	KD4000-4010	Separation of
		licenses			powers—England
340.952	K7230-7245	Conflict of laws—	342.42083	KD4050-4058	Citizenship—England
		Inheritance and succession	342.42083	KD4130-4139	Aliens—England
340.966	K7490-7495	Conflict of laws—	342.42085	KD4080-4119	Civil rights—England
		Corporations	342.4209	KD4746-4840	Local government—Law
340.97	K7340-7512	Conflict of laws—			and legislation—England
		Commercial law	342.421	KD8996-9142	Statutes—London
340.97	K7350-7444	Conflict of laws— Contracts			

Dewey	LC	Subject Heading	Dewey	LC	Subject Heading
342.71	KE4125-4775	Canada—Constitutional law	343.01	K4720-4760	Military readiness—Law and legislation
342.710412	KE4310	Canada—Foreign relations—Law and legislation	343.014	UB790-795	Military discipline
			343.014	VB840-845	Naval discipline
342.710418	KE5006-5010	Police power—Canada	343.0143	UB850-857	Courts-martial and courts of inquiry
342.71042	KE470-474	Conflict of laws—Canada			
342.7105	KE4533-4665	Canada. Parliament	343.0143	VB800-807	Courts-martial and courts of inquiry
342.7106	KE4730	Prime ministers—Canada			
342.71085	KE4381-4430	Civil rights—Canada	343.019	VB350-785	Naval law
342.7109	KE4900-4995	Local government—Law and legislation—Canada	343.02	K3476-3558	Public domain
			343.02	K3558-3560	Government property
342.73	KF4501-5130	Constitutional law—United States	343.0252	K3511-3512	Eminent domain
			343.03	K4430-4675	Finance, Public—Law and legislation
342.73024	JK301	Constitutional conventions			
342.73032	KF4555-4558	Constitutional amendments—United States	343.03	K4650-4675	Local finance—Law and legislation
			343.04	K4456-4590	Taxation—Law and legislation
342.730413	KF4635	Law—United States—Territories and possessions	343.052	K4501-4550	Income tax—Law and legislation
342.730418	KF4695	Police power—United States	343.053	K4568	Inheritance and succession
342.730418	KF5399-.5	Police power—United States	343.054	K4560-4564	Property tax—Law and legislation
342.73042	JK311-325	States rights	343.0553	K4572-4580	Excise tax—Law and legislation
342.73042	JK310-331	Secession			
342.73042	KF410-418	Conflict of laws—United States	343.056	K4600-4640	Tariff—Law and legislation
			343.07	K3840-4375	Commercial law
342.73042	KF4600-4629	Federal government—United States	343.08	K3842-3862	Trade regulation
			343.082	HF5833	Advertising laws
342.73044	JK305	Separation of powers	343.09	K3978-3990	Public utilities—Law and legislation
342.73044	KF4565-4579	Separation of powers—United States	343.0924	K3496-3501	Water-supply—Law and legislation
342.7305	KF4930-5005	Legislative bodies—United States	343.093	K4021-4025	Transportation—Law and legislation
342.730509	JK1033-1059	United States. Congress—History	343.0942	K3492	Highway law
342.7306	KF5050-5125	Executive departments—United States	343.0942	K4028-4042	Highway law
			343.095	K4061-4070	Railroad law
342.73066	KF5401-5425	Administrative law—United States	343.096	K7449-7460	Conflict of laws—Maritime law
342.73068	KF5336-5398	Civil service—United States	343.0967	K4182-4194	Inland navigation—Law and legislation
342.7308	KF4881-4921	People (Constitutional law)—United States	343.0967	K4198-4200	Harbors—Law and legislation
342.73082	KF4794-.5	Passports—United States			
342.73083	KF4700-4720	Citizenship—United States	343.097	K4091-4124	Aeronautics—Law and legislation
342.73083	KF4800-4848	Aliens—United States	343.098	K4080	Local transit—Law and legislation
342.730852	KF4865-4869	Church and state—United States			
342.73087	KF4788	Political parties—United States	343.0992	K4245-4254	Postal service—Law and legislation
342.730872	KF8201-8228	Indians of North America—Legal status, laws, etc.	343.0994	K4301-4339	Telecommunication—Law and legislation
			343.37604	KJA3210	Taxation (Roman law)
342.7309	KF5300-5332	Local government—Law and legislation—United States	343.(4-9)01	UB461-736	Military law—[By region or country]
			343.401	UB590-684	Military law—Europe

Dewey	LC	Subject Heading	Dewey	LC	Subject Heading
343.41103	KDC807-825	Finance, Public—Law and legislation—Scotland	343.42(1-9)03	KD5710-5752	Local finance—Law and legislation—England
343.41503	KDK1430-1526	Finance, Public—Law and legislation—Ireland	343.4301	UB620-624	Military law—Germany
343.41507	KDK550-769	Commercial law—Ireland	343.4401	UB615-619	Military law—France
343.41607	KDE235-282	Commercial law—Northern Ireland	343.4501	UB640-644	Military law—Italy
			343.4601	UB660-664	Military law—Spain
343.4201	KD6000-6355	Military readiness—Law and legislation—England	343.46901	UB650-654	Military law—Portugal
343.4202	KD1034-1107	Government property—England	343.4701	UB655-659	Military law—Russia
			343.49501	UB630-634	Military law—Greece
343.420252	KD1185-1189	Eminent domain—England	343.501	UB685-710	Military law—Asia
343.420256	KD1195	Public works—Law and legislation—England	343.5101	UB690-694	Military law—China
			343.5201	UB700-704	Military law—Japan
343.4203	KD5280-5752	Finance, Public—Law and legislation—England	343.5401	UB695-699	Military law—India
			343.601	UB715-729	Military law—Africa
343.42032	KD5284-5286	Money—Law and legislation—England	343.7101	KE6800-7240	Military readiness—Law and legislation—Canada
343.42032	KD5288	Foreign exchange—Law and legislation—England	343.7101	UB505-509	Military law—Canada
			343.7102	KE5105-5420	Government property—Canada
343.42034	KD5292	Budget—Law and legislation—England	343.7103	KE5600-6328	Finance, Public—Law and legislation—Canada
343.42037	KD5300	Debts, Public—Law and legislation—England	343.7107	KE1935-1999	Commercial law—Canada
			343.71076	KE1671-1745	Agricultural laws and legislation—Canada
343.4204	KD5351-5605	Taxation—Law and legislation—England	343.7107692	KE1760-1765	Fishery law and legislation—Canada
343.42205242	KD3241-3250	Social security—Law and legislation—England	343.71077	KE1790-1802	Mining law—Canada
343.42056	KD5641-5694	Tariff—Law and legislation—England	343.71078624	KE1915	Construction industry— Law and legislation
343.4207	KD2455-2530	Commercial law—England	343.7108	KE1591-1660	Trade regulation—Canada
343.42072	KD2225-2226	Competition, Unfair—England	343.71082	KE1610-1614	Advertising laws—Canada
343.420721	KD2218-2220	Antitrust law—England	343.71082	KE1616-1618	Labels—Law and legislation—Canada
343.42075	KD2230-2231	Containers—Law and legislation—England	343.7109	KE2020-2061	Public utilities—Law and legislation—Canada
343.42076	KD2241-2295	Agricultural laws and legislation—England	343.71093	KE1099-1135	Carriers—Law and legislation—Canada
343.4207692	KD2310-2315	Fishery law and legislation—England	343.71093	KE2071-2649	Transportation—Law and legislation—Canada
343.42077	KD2331-2370	Mining law—England	343.7201	UB510-514	Military law—Mexico
343.4207833 + 847664	KD2405-2430	Food law and legislation—England	343.72801	UB515-519	Military law—Central America
343.42078624	KD2435	Construction industry—Law and legislation	343.72901	UB520-524	Military law—West Indies
343.4208	KD2204-2231	Trade regulation—England	343.7301	KF5900-6075.5	War and emergency legislation—United States
343.42082	KD2206	Advertising laws—England	343.730143	KF7625-7659	Courts-martial and courts of inquiry—United States
343.42082	KD2208-2209	Labels—Law and legislation—England	343.7302	KF5500-5865	Government property—United States
343.42083	KD2215	Price regulation—England	343.730252	KF5599	Eminent domain—United States
343.4209	KD2535-2560	Public utilities—Law and legislation—England	343.730253	KF5670-5673	Homestead law—United States
343.42093	KD1800-1847	Carriers—Law and legislation—England	343.730253	KF5675-5677	Land grants—Law and legislation—United States
343.42093	KD2571-2838	Transportation—Law and legislation—England			
343.420942	KD1040-1048	Highway law—England			

Dewey	LC	Subject Heading	Dewey	LC	Subject Heading
343.7303	KF6200-6795	Finance, Public—Law and legislation—United States	343.73082	KF1619-1620	Labels—Law and legislation
343.73032	KF6201-6219	Money—Law and legislation—United States	343.73093	KF1091-1137	Carriers—Law and legislation—United States
343.73034	KF6221-6227	Budget—Law and legislation—United States	343.73093	KF2161-2654	Transportation—Law and legislation—United States
343.73034	KF6231-6239	Finance, Public—Auditing—Law and legislation—United States	343.730942	KF5521-5536	Highway law—United States
			343.801	UB530-589	Military law—South America
343.73036	KF6251-6708	Internal revenue law—United States	343.8201	UB530-534	Military law—Argentina
			343.8301	UB545-549	Military law—Chile
343.73037	KF6241-6245	Debts, Public—Law and legislation—United States	343.86101	UB550-554	Military law—Colombia
			343.8701	UB585-589	Military law—Venezuela
343.7304	KF6271-6636	Taxation—Law and legislation—United States	343.9(5-6)01	UB735-736	Military law—Oceania
			343.9401	UB730-734	Military law—Australia
343.7304	KF6329-6330	Tax exemption—Law and legislation—United States	344	K1701-2000	Social legislation
			344.01	K1701-1841	Labor laws and legislation
			344.01712	K4360-4375	Professions—Law and legislation
343.73043	KF6770-6795	Local finance—Law and legislation—United States	344.01893	K2320	Injunctions
343.73052	KF6351-6499	Income tax—Law and legislation—United States	344.0316	K1960-2000	Public welfare—Law and legislation
			344.04	K3566-3597	Public health laws
343.7305242	KF3641-3664	Social security—United States	344.0411	RA1056.5	Medical personnel—Malpractice
343.730526	KF6598-6609	Indirect taxation—Law and legislation—United States	344.042	K3651-3654	Alcohol—Law and legislation
343.73054	KF6525-6558	Property tax—Law and legislation—United States	344.04232	K3626-3633	Food law and legislation
			344.04633	SB970-.4	Pesticides—Government policy
343.73056	KF6651-6708	Tariff—Law and legislation—United States	344.049	K3615-3617	Veterinary hygiene—Law and legislation
343.7307	KF1600-2940	Commercial law—United States	344.05242	K1861-1929	Social security—Law and legislation
343.7307	KF1659-.1	Small business—Law and legislation—United States	344.0533	K3661	Weapons—Law and legislation
343.73072	KF1601-1611	Competition, Unfair—United States	344.063635	K3550-3553	Public housing—Law and legislation
343.73072	KF1631-1657	Monopolies—United States	344.07	K3740-3762	Educational law and legislation
343.73072	K3195-3198	Competition, Unfair—United States	344.09	K3770	Research—Law and legislation
343.73075	KF1665-1666	Weights and measures—Law and legislation—United States	344.411	KDC635-674	Social legislation—Scotland
343.73076	KF1681-1755	Agricultural laws and legislation—United States	344.411041	KDC690-695	Medical laws and legislation—Scotland
343.7307692	KF1770-1773	Fishery law and legislation—United States	344.415	KDK800-895	Social legislation—Ireland
343.73077	KF1801-1873	Mining law—United States	344.415041	KDK926-932	Medical laws and legislation—Ireland
343.73078	KF1875-1893	United States—Manufactures—Law and legislation	344.416	KDE320-348	Social legislation—Northern Ireland
343.73078624	KF1950	Construction industry— Law and legislation—United States	344.42	KD3000-3315	Social legislation—England
			344.4201	KD3001-3177	Labor laws and legislation—England
343.7308	KF1085-1087	Commodity exchanges—Law and legislation—United States	344.4201542	KD1638-1642	Labor contract—England
			344.420316	KD3291-3315	Public welfare—Law and legislation
343.73082	KF1614-1617	Advertising laws—United States			

Dewey	LC	Subject Heading	Dewey	LC	Subject Heading
344.4204	KD3351-3375	Public health laws—England	344.7303288	KF9763	Victims of crimes—United States
344.4204	KD3395-3413	Medical laws and legislation—England	344.7304	KF3775-3816	Public health laws—United States
344.42042	KD3466-3480	Alcohol—Law and legislation—England	344.73041	KF3821-3829	Medical laws and legislation—United States
344.4204233	KD3460-3462	Drugs—Law and legislation—England	344.73042	KF3945-3965	Product safety—Law and legislation—United States
344.42047	KD3510	Accident law—England	344.7304232	KF1900-1944	Food law and legislation—United States
344.42049	KD3420-3422	Veterinary hygiene—Law and legislation—England	344.73047	KF3970	Accident law—United States
344.420533	KD3492	Weapons—Law and legislation—England	344.73048	KF3832	Sterilization, Eugenic— Law and legislation— United States
344.420535	KD6340	Civil defense—Law and legislation—England	344.73049	KF3835-3838	Veterinary hygiene—Law and legislation—United States
344.4207	KD3600-3689	Educational law and legislation			
344.4209	KD4650	Emblems, National—England	344.7305	KF3901-3925	Alcohol—Law and legislation—United States
344.42092	KD3746	Library legislation—England	344.7305	KF4850-4856	Internal security—United States
344.42092	KD3753-3755	Archives—Law and legislation—England	344.730533	KF3941-3942	Weapons—Law and legislation—United States
344.42093	KD3736	Museums—Law and legislation—England	344.7305348	KF3750	Disaster relief—Law and legislation—United States
344.42097	KD3720-3731	Performing arts—Law and legislation—England	344.730535	KF7685	Civil defense—Law and legislation–United States
344.42099	KD3523	Amusements—Law and legislation—England	344.7305377	KF3975-3977	Fire prevention—Law and legislation—United States
344.42099	KD3525	Sports—Law and legislation—England	344.730542	KF1241	Contracts, Aleatory—United States
344.42099	KD3527	Gambling—Law and legislation—England	344.730542	KF3992	Lotteries—Law and legislation—United States
344.429071	KD9460	Law—Wales—Study and teaching	344.7306	KF5865	Public works—Law and legislation—United States
344.71	KE3098-3542	Social legislation—Canada			
344.710189	KE928-936	Labor contract—Canada	344.73063635	KF5721-5740	Housing—Law and legislation—United States
344.71041	KE3575-3635	Public health laws—Canada	344.730655168	KF5594	Weather control—Law and legislation—United States
344.71041	KE3646-3660	Medical laws and legislation—Canada	344.7307	KF4101-4257	Educational law and legislation—United States
344.7104232	KE1867-1906	Food law and legislation—Canada	344.7307	KF4192-.5	School employees—Legal status, laws, etc.—United States
344.7104233	KE3714-3725	Drugs—Law and legislation—Canada			
344.7107	KE3805-3917	Educational law and legislation—Canada	344.7307	KF4195-4223	Educational law and legislation—United States
344.71097	KE3968	Law and art—Canada	344.73074	KF4225-4257	Education, Higher—Law and legislation—United States
344.73	KF3300-3771	Social legislation—United States			
344.7301	KF3301-3580	Labor laws and legislation—United States	344.73076	KF4125-4143	Education—Finance—Law and legislation—United States
344.7301542	KF898-905	Contracts for work and labor—United States			
344.7301712	KF2900-2940	Professions—Law and legislation—United States	344.73078	KF4175-4190	Teachers—Legal status, laws, etc.—United States
344.730316	KF3720-3745	Public welfare—Law and legislation–United States	344.73079	KF4150-4166	Students—Legal status, laws, etc.—United States

Dewey	LC	Subject Heading	Dewey	LC	Subject Heading
344.7309	KF5150	Emblems, National—United States	345.73026	KF9350-9379	Offenses against property—United States
344.73092	KF4315-4319	Library legislation—United States	345.73052	KF9635	Extradition—United States
344.73092	KF4325	Archives—Law and legislation—United States	345.730522	KF9630	Searches and seizures—United States
344.73093	KF4305	Museums—Law and legislation—United States	345.730527	KF9625	Arrest—United States
			345.73056	KF9632	Bail—United States
344.73094	KF4310-4312	Historic buildings—Law and legislation—United States	345.7306	KF9660-9678	Evidence, Criminal—United States
344.73099	KF3987	Amusements—Law and legislation—United States	345.7307	KF219-224	Trials—United States
			345.73072	KF9640-9642	Indictments—United States
344.73099	KF3989	Sports—Law and legislation—United States	345.73072	KF9645-9650	Arraignment—United States
			345.73075	KF9680	Jury—United States
345	K5011-5316	Criminal law	345.73077	KF9695	Pardon—United States
345.01	K5036-5048	Criminal jurisdiction	345.730773	KF9725	Capital punishment—United States
345.01	K5423	Criminal jurisdiction			
345.04	K5064-5083	Criminal liability	346	K623-968	Civil law
345.05	HV7231-9960	Criminal justice, Administration of	346.015	K670-709	Domestic relations
			346.02	K830-968	Obligations (Law)
345.05	K5401-5570	Criminal procedure	346.02	K840-917	Contracts
345 0509(4-9)	HV9950-9960	Criminal justice, Administration of—[By region or country]	346.02	K1024-1132	Contracts
			346.023	HD3860-3861	Public contracts
			346.029	K920	Quasi contracts
345.050973	HV9950	Criminal justice, Administration of	346.03	K923-968	Torts
			346.043	JK318	Squatter sovereignty
345.052	JF781	Extradition	346.044	K3478-3486	Natural resources—Law and legislation
345.06	K5465-5490	Evidence, Criminal			
345.072	K5425	Indictments	346.045	K3531-3544	Regional planning—Law and legislation
345.075	K5460-5492	Trials			
345.075	K5492	Jury	346.047	K783-793	Personal property
345.0772	K5510-5560	Sentences (Criminal procedure)	346.048	K1401-1578	Intellectual property
			346.048	K1500-1578	Industrial property
345.08	K5575-5582	Juvenile courts	346.0482	K1411-1485	Copyright
345.411	KDC910-920	Criminal law—Scotland	346.0482	Z649.T7	Copyright—Transfer
345.415	KDK1750-1782	Criminal law—Ireland	346.052	K805-821	Inheritance and succession
345.41675	KDE550-557	Criminal procedure—Northern Ireland	346.07	K1001-1388	Commercial law
			346.07	K1010-1014	Business law
345.42	KD7850-8090	Criminal law—England	346.082	HG1725-1778	Banking law
345.4205	KD8220-8464	Criminal procedure—England	346.082	K1066-1088	Banking law
			346.086	HG9733-9735	Insurance, Fire—Law and legislation
345.429	KD9490	Criminal law—Wales			
345.42907	KD9423	Trials—Wales	346.086	K1241-1287	Insurance law
345.71	KE8801-9112	Criminal law—Canada	346.08632	HG8901-8914	Insurance, Life—Law and legislation
345.73	KF9201-9479	Criminal law—United States			
345.7301	JK1548.P8	Public defenders	346.092	K1100-1108	Security (Law)
345.7302	KF221.B74	Trials (Bribery)—United States	346.092	K1112-1116	Investments—Law and legislation
			346.096	K1054-1065	Negotiable instruments
345.730207	KF221.C6	Trials (Conspiracy)— United States	346.411012	KDC350-378	Persons (Law)—Scotland
345.730231	KF224.W	Watergate Trial, Washington, D.C., 1973	346.411052	KDC462-470	Inheritance and succession—Scotland
			346.415012	KDK185-205	Persons (Law)—Ireland
345.730233	KF6334	Tax evasion—United States	346.41502	KDK370-437	Contracts—Ireland
345.73025	KF9304-9329	Offenses against the person—United States	346.41503	KDK450-469	Torts—Ireland

Dewey	LC	Subject Heading	Dewey	LC	Subject Heading
346.415052	KDK360-365	Inheritance and succession—Ireland	346.420862	KD1845-1847	Insurance, Marine—England
346.416012	KDE90-98	Persons (Law)—Northern Ireland	346.42092	KD1774-1787	Investments—Law and legislation—England
346.416052	KDE145-151	Inheritance and succession—Northern Ireland	346.42096	KD1695-1699	Negotiable instruments—England
			346.71004	KE457	Equity—Canada
346.42004	KD674	Equity—England	346.71012	KE498-606	Persons (Law)—Canada
346.42012	KD723-785	Persons (Law)—England	346.71015	KE531-606	Domestic relations—Canada
346.42015	KD750-785	Domestic relations—England	346.7102	KE850-1225	Contracts—Canada
346.4202	KD1554-1920	Contracts—England	346.7102	KE1328-1332	Agency (Law)—Canada
346.42025	KD1679-1685	Bailments—England	346.71025	KE970-972	Bailments—Canada
346.42029	KD1924	Quasi contracts—England	346.7103	KE1232-1309	Torts—Canada
346.42029	KD2022	Power of attorney—England	346.71043	KE625-754	Real property—Canada
346.4203	KD1941-1980	Torts—England	346.71045	KE5258-5284	Regional planning—Law and legislation—Canada
346.42043	KD821-1195	Real property—England	346.71047	KE765-781	Personal property— Canada
346.420432	KD833-960	Land tenure—Law and legislation—England	346.71048	KE2771-2998	Intellectual property—Canada
346.420432	KD841-960	Estates (Law)—England	346.71052	KE806-833	Inheritance and succession—Canada
346.4204364	KD1010-1016	Mortgages—England			
346.420437	KD810-815	Possession (Law)— England	346.71064	KE1351-1361	Unincorporated societies—Canada
346.42045	KD1125-1162	Zoning law—England	346.71066	KE1369-1465	Corporation law—Canada
346.42046	KD1035	Natural resources—Law and legislation—England	346.71073	KE1030-1034	Loans—Law and legislation—Canada
346.4204691	KD1070	Water—Law and legislation—England	346.71078	KE1491-1506	Bankruptcy—Canada
346.42047	KD1205-1465	Personal property—England	346.71082	KE991-1026	Banking law—Canada
346.42048	KD1238-1450	Intangible property—England	346.71086	KE1141-1220	Insurance law—Canada
			346.71092	KE1042-1056	Securities—Canada
346.42048	KD1261-1450	Intellectual property—England	346.71092	KE1060-1089	Investments—Law and legislation—Canada
346.42048	KD1450	Business names—England	346.71096	KE980-986	Negotiable instruments—Canada
346.420482	KD1281-1325	Copyright—England			
346.420484	KD1345	Design protection—England	346.73004	KF398-400	Equity—United States
346.420486	KD1361-1413.3	Patent laws and legislation—England	346.73012	KF465-553	Persons (Law)—United States
346.4205	KD1497	Estate planning—England	346.73015	KF501-553	Domestic relations— United States
346.42052	KD1500-1534	Inheritance and succession—England	346.7302	KF801-1241	Contracts—United States
346.4206	KD2228	Trade associations—Law and legislation—England	346.73025	KF939-951	Bailments—United States
			346.73029	KF1244-.5	Quasi contracts—United States
346.42064	KD2046-2054	Unincorporated societies—England	346.73029	KF1341-1348	Agency (Law)—United States
346.42064	KD2061-2062	Nonprofit organizations—Law and legislation	346.7303	KF1246-1329	Torts—United States
346.42066	KD2057-2127	Corporation law—England	346.73043	KF566-698	Real property—United States
346.420682	KD2049-2054	Partnership—England			
346.42073	KD1740-1742	Loans—Law and legislation—England	346.73044	KF5505-5510	Conservation of natural resources—United States
346.42074	KD1752	Suretyship and guaranty—England	346.73045	KF5691-5710	City planning and redevelopment law—United States
346.42078	KD2141-2164	Bankruptcy—England			
346.42082	KD1715-1737	Banking law—England			
346.42086	KD1851-1913	Insurance law—England			

Dewey	LC	Subject Heading	Dewey	LC	Subject Heading
346.7304691	KF5551-5590	Water resources development—Law and legislation—United States	347.41105	KDC840-915	Procedure (Law)— Scotland
			347.41107	KDC184-188	Trials—Scotland
			347.41505	KDK1580-1713	Procedure (Law)—Ireland
346.73047	KF701-720	Personal property—United States	347.41507	KDK102-106	Trials—Ireland
346.73048	KF2971-3193	Intellectual property—United States	347.41605	KDE510-530	Procedure (Law)— Northern Ireland
346.730482	KF2986-3080	Copyright—United States	347.42	KD720-721	Civil law—England
346.730484	KF3086	Design protection—United States	347.4201	KD4645	Courts—England
			347.42013	KD327-332	Judicial statistics— England
346.730486	KF3091-3193	Patent laws and legislation—United States	347.4203	KD7132-7216	Appellate courts—England
			347.4205	KD6850-7640	Procedure (Law)—England
346.73052	KF753-780	Inheritance and succession—United States	347.42055	KD318	Forms (Law)—England
			347.4207	KD370-379.5	Trials—England
346.7306	KF1355-1480	Associations, institutions, etc.—Law and legislation—United States	347.4209	KD7645-7647	Arbitration and award— England
			347.42901	KD9480-9484	Courts—Wales
346.73064	KF1361-1381	Unincorporated societies—United States	347.71	JL87-111	Executive departments— Canada
346.73064	KF1388-1390	Nonprofit organizations—Law and legislation	347.71	KE495	Civil law—Canada
			347.7101	KE4775	Courts—Canada
			347.7101	KE8200-8605	Courts—Canada
346.73064	KF1661	Trade associations—Law and legislation—United States	347.71013	KE198-206	Judicial statistics—Canada
			347.7105	KE8341-8605	Procedure (Law)—Canada
			347.7107	KE225-237	Trials—Canada
346.73066	KF1384-1480	Corporation law—United States	347.7109	KE8618	Arbitration and award—Canada
346.73066	KF1396-1477	Corporations—Law and legislation—United States	347.7301	JK1606	Courts—United States
			347.7301	KF101-153	Courts—United States
346.73067	KF1480	Corporations, Government—Law and legislation—United States	347.73012	KF5130	Judicial power—United States
			347.73013	KF180-185	Judicial statistics—United States
346.7307	KF1970-2105	Business law—United States	347.7305	KF8700-9075	Procedure (Law)—United States
346.73073	KF1035-1040	Loans—Law and legislation—United States	347.7305	KF8741-8752	Appellate procedure—United States
346.73074	KF1045	Suretyship and guaranty—United States	347.7305	KF8810-9075	Civil procedure—United States
346.73078	KF1501-1548	Bankruptcy—United States	347.73051	KF8816-8821	Court rules—United States
346.73082	KF966-1032	Banking law—United States	347.73051	KF8858-8861	Jurisdiction—United States
346.73086	KF1146-1238	Insurance law—United States	347.73052	KF8890-8896.5	Parties to actions—United States
346.73092	KF1046-1062	Security (Law)—United States	347.73053	KF8863-8865	Actions and defenses—United States
346.73092	KF1066-1084	Investments—Law and legislation—United States	347.7306	KF8931-8969	Evidence (Law)—United States
346.73096	KF956-962	Negotiable instruments—United States	347.7307	KF8910-8986	Trials—United States
347.012	JF711	Judicial review	347.73072	KF8866-8885	Pleading—United States
347.012	K3367	Judicial power	347.73072	KF8900-8902	Pre-trial procedure—United States
347.035	K5495	Appellate procedure			
347.05	K2100-2385	Procedure (Law)	347.73075	KF8911-8925	Trial practice—United States
347.05	K2201-2385	Civil procedure			
347.07	K540-546	Trials	347.730752	KF8971-8984	Jury—United States
347.09	K7690	Conflict of laws—Arbitration and award	347.73077	KF8990-9002	Judgments—United States
347.41103	KDC110-113	Appellate courts— Scotland	347.7309	KF9085-9086	Arbitration and award—United States

Dewey	LC	Subject Heading	Dewey	LC	Subject Heading
347.731(4-6)	KF8771-8807	Courts—United States—Officials and employees	349.45	KKH	Law—Italy
			349.4585	KKK1000-1499	Law—Malta
348.022	K7010-7011	Statutes	349.46	KKT	Law—Spain
348.41504	KDK61-80	Law reports, digests, etc.—Ireland	349.469	KKQ	Law—Portugal
			349.481	KKN	Law—Norway
348.416041	KDE55-60	Law reports, digests, etc.—Northern Ireland	349.485	KKV	Law—Sweden
			349.489	KJR	Law—Denmark
348.42022	KD125-150	Statutes—England	349.4897	KJT	Law—Finland
348.42041	KD187-291	Law reports, digests, etc.—England	349.4912	KKG	Law—Iceland
			349.492	KKM	Law—Netherlands
348.429022	KD9407	Statutes—Wales	349.493	KJK	Law—Belgium
348.429041	KD9410-9417	Law reports, digests, etc.—Wales	349.4935	KKK0-499	Law—Luxembourg
			349.494	KKW	Law—Switzerland
348.71041	KE132-156	Law reports, digests, etc.—Canada	349.495	KKE	Law—Greece
			349.4965	KJG	Law—Albania
348.7301	KF16-22	Bills, Legislative—United States	349.497	KKZ	Law—Yugoslavia
			349.498	KKR	Law—Romania
348.73022	KF50-70	Statutes—United States	349.499	KJM	Law—Bulgaria
348.73041	KF255	Law reporting—United States	349.561	KKX	Law—Turkey
			349.5645	KJN	Law—Cyprus
348.7(4-9)	KF165	Uniform state laws	349.71	KE	Law—Canada
349.411	KDC	Law—Scotland	349.71	KE335-355	Lawyers—Canada
349.411	KDC225-247	Lawyers—Scotland	349.71071	KE273-322	Law—Study and teaching—Canada
349.411003	KDC152	Law—Scotland—Dictionaries	349.71072	KE250-259	Legal research—Canada
349.415	KDK	Law—Ireland	349.71(1-9)	KEZ	Law—[Canada, By city]
349.415	KDK120-134	Lawyers—Ireland	349.711	KEB	Law—British Columbia
349.41503	KDK84	Law—Ireland— Dictionaries	349.7123	KEA	Law—Alberta
349.416	KDE	Law—Northern Ireland	349.7124	KES	Law—Saskatchewan
349.42	KD	Law—England	349.7127	KEM	Law—Manitoba
349.42	KD460-472	Lawyers—England	349.713	KEO	Law—Ontario
349.42	KD5020-5025	Commonwealth countries	349.714	KEQ	Law—Quebec
349.42	KD8850-9355	Statutes—England	349.7151	KEN0-599	Law—New Brunswick
349.4203	KD313	Law—England—Dictionaries	349.716	KEN7400-7999	Law—Nova Scotia
			349.717	KEP	Law—Prince Edward Island
349.42071	KD419-452	Law—Study and teaching—England	349.718	KEN1200-1799	Law—Newfoundland
			349.7191	KEY	Law—Yukon Territory
349.42072	KD392-400	Legal research—England	349.72	KGF	Law—Mexico
349.4209	KD530-632	Law—England—History	349.7281	KGD	Law—Guatemala
349.4234	KDG	Law—Channel Islands	349.7282	KGA	Law—Belize
349.42341	KDG220-380	Law—Jersey (Channel Islands)	349.7283	KGE	Law—Honduras
			349.7284	KGC	Law—El Salvador
349.42342	KDG421-440	Law—Guernsey (Channel Islands)	349.7285	KGG	Law—Nicaragua
			349.7286	KGB	Law—Costa Rica
349.4279	KDG26-170	Law—Isle of Man	349.7287	KGH	Law—Panama
349.429	KD9400-9500	Law—Wales	349.729	KGJ	Law—West Indies
349.42903	KD9420	Law—Wales—Dictionaries	349.7291	KGN	Law—Cuba
349.43	KK	Law—Germany	349.7292	KGT0-499	Law—Jamaica
349.436	KJJ	Law—Austria	349.7293	KGQ	Law—Dominican Republic
349.43648	KKJ	Law—Liechtenstein	349.7294	KGS	Law—Haiti
349.437	KJP	Law—Czechoslovakia	349.7295	KGV	Law—Puerto Rico
349.438	KKP	Law—Poland	349.7296	KGL0-499	Law—Bahamas
349.439	KKF	Law—Hungary	349.729722	KGZ0-499	Law—Virgin Islands of the United States
349.44	KJV	Law—France			
349.44949	KKL	Law—Monaco			

Dewey	LC	Subject Heading	Dewey	LC	Subject Heading
349.729725	KGL4000-4499	Law—British Virgin Islands	349.758	KFG0-599	Law—Georgia
349.72973	KGJ7000-7499	Law—Anguilla	349.759	KFF0-599	Law—Florida
349.72973	KGW2000-2499	Law—Saint Kitts and Nevis	349.761	KFA0-599	Law—Alabama
349.72974	KGK0-499	Law—Antigua	349.762	KFM6600-7199	Law—Mississippi
349.72975	KGT2000-2499	Law—Montserrat	349.763	KFL0-599	Law—Louisiana
349.72976	KGR3000-3499	Law—West Indies, French	349.764	KFT1200-1799	Law—Texas
349.72976	KGR5000-5499	Law—Guadeloupe	349.766	KFO1200-1799	Law—Oklahoma
349.72977	KGW0-499	Law—Saba (Netherlands Antilles)	349.767	KFA3600-4199	Law—Arkansas
			349.768	KFT0-599	Law—Tennessee
349.72977	KGW7000-7499	Law—Saint Eustatius (Netherlands Antilles)	349.769	KFK1200-1799	Law—Kentucky
			349.771	KFO0-599	Law—Ohio
349.72977	KGW8000-8499	Law—Saint Martin	349.773	KFI1200-1799	Law—Illinois
349.72981	KGL1000-1499	Law—Barbados	349.774	KFM4200-4799	Law—Michigan
349.72982	KGT1000-1499	Law—Martinique	349.775	KFW2400-2999	Law—Wisconsin
349.72983	KGX0-499	Law—Trinidad and Tobago	349.776	KFM5400-5999	Law—Minnesota
349.729841	KGP2000-2499	Law—Dominica	349.777	KFI4200-4799	Law—Iowa
349.729843	KGW3000-3499	Law—Saint Lucia	349.778	KFM7800-8399	Law—Missouri
349.729844	KGW5000-5499	Law—Saint Vincent	349.781	KFK0-599	Law—Kansas
349.729845	KGR4000-4499	Law—Grenada	349.782	KFN0-599	Law—Nebraska
349.72986	KGK1000-1499	Law—Aruba	349.783	KFS3000-3599	Law—South Dakota
349.72986	KGL2000-2499	Law—Bonaire	349.784	KFN8600-9199	Law—North Dakota
349.72986	KGP0-499	Law—Curacao	349.786	KFM9000-9599	Law—Montana
349.72986	KGR1000-1499	Law—Netherlands Antilles	349.787	KFW4200-4799	Law—Wyoming
349.73	KF	Law—United States	349.788	KFC1800-2399	Law—Colorado
349.73	KF297-338	Lawyers—United States	349.789	KFN3600-4199	Law—New Mexico
349.7303	KF156	Law—United States—Dictionaries	349.791	KFA2400-2999	Law—Arizona
			349.792	KFU0-599	Law—Utah
349.73071	KF261-292	Law—United States—Study and teaching	349.793	KFN 600-1199	Law—Nevada
			349.794	KFC0-1199	Law—California
349.73072	KF240-247	Legal research—United States	349.795	KFO2400-2999	Law—Oregon
			349.796	KFI0-599	Law—Idaho
349.730899 + 6073	KF299.A35	Afro-American lawyers	349.797	KFW0-599	Law—Washington
			349.798	KFA1200-1799	Law—Alaska
349.7309	KF350-374	Law—United States—History	349.8	KH	Law—South America
349.7(4-9)	KFX	Law—[United States, By city]	349.81	KHD	Law—Brazil
			349.82	KHA	Law—Argentina
349.741	KFM0-599	Law—Maine	349.83	KHF	Law—Chile
349.742	KFN1200-1799	Law—New Hampshire	349.84	KHC	Law—Bolivia
349.743	KFV0-599	Law—Vermont	349.85	KHQ	Law—Peru
349.744	KFM2400-2999	Law—Massachusetts	349.861	KHH	Law—Columbia
349.745	KFR0-599	Law—Rhode Island	349.866	KHK	Law—Ecuador
349.746	KFC3600-4199	Law—Connecticut	349.87	KHW	Law—Venezuela
349.747	KFN5000-6199	Law—New York (State)	349.882	KHM	Law—French Guiana
349.748	KFP0-599	Law—Pennsylvania	349.883	KHS	Law—Surinam
349.749	KFN1800-2399	Law—New Jersey	349.892	KHP	Law—Paraguay
349.75	KFZ8600-9199	Law—Confederate States of America	349.895	KHU	Law—Uruguay
			349.969	KFH0-599	Law—Hawaii
349.751	KFD0-599	Law—Delaware	349.9711	KHL	Law—Falkland Islands
349.752	KFM1200-1799	Law—Maryland	350	JF	Public administration
349.753	KFD1200-1799	Law—Washington, D.C.	351	JF1501-1521	Civil service
349.754	KFW1200-1799	Law—West Virginia	351.056	JS7435-7520	Local government—Middle East
349.755	KFV2400-2999	Law—Virginia			
349.756	KFN7400-7999	Law—North Carolina	351.4	JS3000-6949.8	Local government— Europe
349.757	KFS1800-2399	Law—South Carolina			

Dewey	LC	Subject Heading	Dewey	LC	Subject Heading
351.41	JN309-678	Public administration—Great Britain	352.130973	JK2403-9593	State governments—United States
351.41	JS3001-4295	Local government—Great Britain	352.1309(4-9)	JK2701-9593	State governments—[United States, By state]
351.43	JS5301-5598	Local government—Germany	352.1309(4-9)	JK2443-2525	Public administration—[United States, By state]
351.436	JS4501-4655	Local government— Austria			
351.439	JS4661-4696	Local government—Hungary	352.133	JK2441	Interstate agreements
			352.1406	JS42	Local government—Societies, etc.
351.44	JS4801-5250	Local government—France			
351.45	JS5701-5925	Local government—Italy	352.14071	JS49	Local government—Study and teaching
351.46	JS6301-6335	Local government—Spain	352.1409	JS55-67	Local government—History
351.469	JS6341-6375	Local government—Portugal	352.150973	JS411	County government—United States
351.47	JS6051-6109	Local government—Russia			
351.485	JS6251-6285	Local government—Sweden	352.16	JS261	Boroughs
351.489	JS6151-6185	Local government—Denmark	352.16092	JS148-155	Municipal officials and employees
351.492	JS5931-5998	Local government—Netherlands	352.16097(4-9)	JS422	Metropolitan government—[United States, By state]
351.493	JS6001-6048	Local government—Belgium	352.16097(4-9)	JS504-1583	Municipal government—[United States, By city]
351.494	JS6401-6889	Local government—Switzerland			
351.496	JS6899.5-6949.8	Local government—Balkan Peninsula	352.23	GN492.7	Kings and rulers
351.5	JS6950-7520	Local government—Asia	352.23	JF251-289	Heads of state
351.51	JS7351-7365	Local government—China	352.23	JF255	Presidents
351.52	JS7371-7385	Local government—Japan	352.23	JF286	Heads of state—Term of office
351.54	JS7001-7090	Local government—India			
351.599	JS7301-7335	Local government—Philippines	352.230973	JK511-609	Presidents—United States
			352.232130973	JK2447-2454	Governors—United States
351.6	JS7525-7819	Local government—Africa	352.23216	JS143-163	Mayors
351.71	JL1-500	Public administration—Canada	352.2330941	JN331-389	Great Britain—Kings and rulers
351.71	JS1701-1800	Local government—Canada	352.235	JF251-289	Executive power
351.72	JS2101-2143	Local government—Mexico	352.238	J80-82	Presidents—Messages
351.728	JS2145-2219	Local government—Central America	352.2380973	J82	Presidents—United States—Messages
351.729	JS1840-2058	Local government—West Indies	352.2390973	JK609.5	Vice-Presidents—United States
351.73063	JK631-868	Civil service			
351.7(4-9)	JS300-1583	Local government—United States	352.2390973	JK2459	Lieutenant governors—United States
351.75	JK9720-9770	Executive departments—Confederate States of America	352.24	JF331-341	Cabinet system
			352.240973	JK610-616	Cabinet officers
			352.250973	JS342-343	Municipal government by commission
351.8	JS2300-2778	Local government—South America	352.266	HD3840-4420.8	Government ownership
351.824	Z551-656	Copyright	352.266	HD3850	Corporations, Government
351.93	JS8331-8399	Local government—New Zealand	352.266	HD4421-4730.9	Municipal ownership
351.94	JS8001-8310	Local government—Australia	352.44809(4-9)	HJ6622-7390	Customs administration—[By region or country]
351.9(5-6)	JS8450-8490	Local government—Oceania	352.2660973	HD3881-4420.8	Corporations, Government—United States

Dewey	LC	Subject Heading	Dewey	LC	Subject Heading
352.26609(4-9)	HD4001-4420.7	Corporations, Government—[Other countries]	353.60607(4-9)	RA15-182	Health boards—[United States, By city]
352.283	JF225	Delegation of powers	353.60608	RA198-235	Health boards—South America
352.283	JS113	Decentralization in government	353.606094	RA371-372	Health boards—Australia
352.293	JF341	Ministerial responsibility	353.88284	LB2331.6-.615	Universities and colleges—Accreditation
352.33	JF1525.D4	Public administration—Decision making	354.094	JN	Europe—Politics and government
352.35	JF1621	Administrative responsibility	354.37	QC875	Meteorological services
352.448	HJ6603-7390	Customs administration	354.7299	JL131-179	Canada. Parliament
			355	U	Military art and science
352.4480973	HJ6622-6731	Customs administration—United States	355	U130-135	Military art and science—Officers' handbooks
352.44809(4-9)	HJ6750-7390	Customs administration—[Other countries]	355.0019	U22.3	Psychology, Military
			355.0021	UA19	Military statistics
			355.003	U24-26	Military art and science—Dictionaries
352.48	HJ2005-2216	Budget	355.006	U7	Military art and science—Congresses
352.5	JF1525.P7	Government property			
352.530973	HJ2050-2053	United States—Appropriations & expenditures	355.0071	U400-714	Military education
			355.00710(4-9)	U407-714	Military education—[By region or country]
352.63	HD5713.5-.6	Public service employment	355.007104	U505-630	Military education—Europe
352.63	HD8001-8013	Civil service	355.0071041	U510-549.3	Military education—Great Britain
352.63	JK765-770	Civil service—Personnel management	355.0071043	U570-574.54	Military education—Germany
352.63	JS148-153	Civil service	355.00710436	U550-554	Military education—Austria
352.630971	JL106-111	Civil service—Canada	355.007105	U635-660	Military education—Asia
352.630973	JK681	Civil service reform	355.0071051	U640-644	Military education—China
352.630973	JK771-794	United States—Officials and employees—Salaries, etc.	355.0071052	U650-654	Military education—Japan
			355.0071054	U645-649	Military education—India
352.885	JF1621	Government liability	355.0071055	U655-659	Military education—Iran
353	JK404-1685	Public administration—United States	355.007106	U670-695	Military education—Africa
			355.007107(4-9)	U409	Military education—[United States, By state]
353.00074	JK4	Freedom Train			
353.15	JV412-461	Colonies—Administration	355.0071071	U440-444	Military education—Canada
353.15	JV443	Civil service, Colonial	355.0071072	U445-449	Military education—Mexico
353.15092	JV431	Viceroyalty	355.00710728	U450-454	Military education—Central America
353.36	HV7935-8025	Police administration			
353.549	JF1671	Civil service—Pensions	355.00710729	U455-459	Military education—West Indies
353.596	RA405	Death—Proof and certification	355.0071073	U408-439	Military education—United States
353.606	RA10-388	Health boards			
353.60604	RA239-299	Health boards—Europe	355.0071073	U410.E9	Hazing
353.60605	RA303-340	Health boards—Asia	355.007108	U465-499	Military education—South America
353.60606	RA345-352	Health boards—Africa			
353.606071	RA184-186	Health boards—Canada	355.0071094	U700-704	Military education—Australia
353.606072	RA187-188	Health boards—Mexico			
353.6060728	RA191	Health boards—Central America	355.0074	U13	Military art and science—Exhibitions
353.606073	RA11-182	Health boards—United States	355.0074	U13	Military museums
			355.008996073	E185.63	United States—Armed Forces—Afro-Americans

Dewey	LC	Subject Heading	Dewey	LC	Subject Heading
355.009	U27-43	Military art and science—History	355.0218	D25.5	Guerrillas
			355.0218	U240	Guerrilla warfare
355.009	D25-.4	Military history	355.0218	U241	Counterinsurgency
355.00901	U29-35	Military art and science—History—To 500	355.031	UA12	Mutual security program, 1951-
355.00903	D214	Military history—Modern	355.032	UA16	Military missions
355.0092	U1-145	Soldiers	355.03305	UA830	East Asia—Strategic aspects
355.0092	U51-55	Military art and science—Biography	355.0335	UA11	Military policy
355.0092	U51-55	Generals	355.07	U390-395	Military research
355.0092	U750-773	Soldiers	355.113	UB280-285	Military passes
355.009402	D128	Military history—Medieval	355.12	UB400-405	Military dependents
355.00941	DA49-69.3	Great Britain—History, Military	355.123	U22	Morale
			355.13323	UB820-825	Military police
355.00943	DD99-104	Germany—History, Military	355.13325	UB810-815	Corporal punishment
355.00943	DD354	Prussia (Germany)—History, Military	355.1334	UB780-789	Military offenses
			355.1334	UB787	Mutiny
355.009436	DB42-44	Austria—History, Military	355.1334	UB788	Desertion, Military
355.00944	DC44-47	France—History, Military	355.1334	UB789	Insubordination
355.00945	DG480-484	Italy—History, Military	355.134	UB430-435	Military decorations
355.00946	DP76-78	Spain—History, Military	355.1342	UB430-435	Decorations of honor
355.009469	DP547	Portugal—History, Military	355.13420941	UB435.G	Distinguished Conduct Medal (Great Britain)
355.00947	DK50-54	Soviet Union—History, Military	355.13420973	UB433	Distinguished Service Cross (U.S.)
355.009492	DH113	Netherlands—History, Military	355.13420973	UB433	Medal of Honor
355.009492	DJ124	Netherlands—History, Military	355.13420973	UC533	United States. Army—Medals, badges, decorations
355.009493	DH540-545	Belgium—History, Military			
355.009494	DQ59	Switzerland—History, Military	355.13420973	VB333	Navy Cross (Medal)
			355.14	UC480-485	Military uniforms
355.009495	DF543	Byzantine Empire—History, Military	355.14	UC530-535	Insignia
			355.15	UC590-595	Standards, Military
355.009495	DF765	Greece—History, Military	355.15	UC590-595	Guidons
355.009497	DR1250-1251	Yugoslavia—History, Military	355.15	UC590-595	Flags
355.009498	DR219	Romania—History, Military	355.17	U350-365	Military ceremonies, honors, and salutes
355.009499	DR70	Bulgaria—History, Military	355.17	U350-355	Weddings, Military
355.00951	DS775.4	China—History, Military—1912-1949	355.22	UA17.5	Manpower
			355.223	UB320-345	Recruiting and enlistment
355.00951	UA835	China—Armed Forces	355.2230973	UB323	United States. Army—Recruiting, enlistment, etc.
355.00951	DS777.65	China—History, Military			
355.009561	DR448	Turkey—History, Military	355.2236	UB320-338	Advertising—Recruiting and enlistment
355.00971	F1028	Canada—History, Military			
355.00973	E181	United States—History, Military	355.22362	UB320-325	Military service, Voluntary
			355.22363	UB340-355	Draft
355.00973	E181	United States. Army—History	355.224	UB341-342	Conscientious objectors
			355.225	UB350-355	Draft
355.02	U	War	355.26	UA18	Industrial mobilization
355.0213	U21	Militarism	355.28	UA910-915	Armed forces—Mobilization
355.0213	UA10	Militarism	355.28	UC15	Requisitions, Military
355.0215	UA11.5	Limited war	355.306073	UB233	United States—Armed Forces—Headquarters
355.0217	U162.6	Deterrence (Strategy)			
355.0217	U263	Nuclear warfare	355.30973	UA24-39	United States. Army
355.0217	U263	Nuclear crisis stability			
355.0217	U264	No first use (Nuclear strategy)			

Dewey	LC	Subject Heading
355.30973	UA23-25	United States. Army—History
355.30973	UA24.A7	United States. Army—Appropriations and expenditures
355.309730216	U11	United States. Army—Registers
355.30975	UA580-585	Confederate States of America. Army
355.31	UA	Armies
355.33041	UB210	Command of troops
355.33041	UB210	Leadership
355.3308351	UB418.B69	Boys as soldiers
355.332	UB410-415	Armies—Officers
355.3320973	UB408-.5	United States—Armed Forces—Warrant officers
355.3320973	UB412-414	United States. Army—Officers
355.341	UC750-755	Canteens (Establishments)
355.3410973	UC723	United States—Armed Forces—Messes
355.3432	UB250-271	Military intelligence
355.3432	UB265	Military interrogation
355.3432092	UB270-271	Spies
355.3434	UB275-277	Psychological warfare
355.345	UH	War—Relief of sick and wounded
355.345	UH201-551	War—Relief of sick and wounded
355.345	UH201-515	Medicine, Military
355.345	UH420-425	Pharmacy, Military
355.345	UH490-495	Military nursing
355.345	UH600-629.5	Military hygiene
355.345	UH650-655	Veterinary service, Military
355.345021	UH215-325	War—Casualties (Statistics, etc.)
355.34506	UH205	Medicine, Military—Congresses
355.345071	UH398-399	Medicine, Military—Study and teaching
355.34509	UH215-324	Medicine, Military—History
355.345092	UH341-347	Medicine, Military—Biography
355.345092	UH400	Physicians
355.345094	UH255-295	Medicine, Military—Europe
355.345094	UH321-322	Medicine, Military—Australia
355.3450941	UH257-264	Medicine, Military—Great Britain
355.3450943	UH273-274	Medicine, Military—Germany
355.3450944	UH271-272	Medicine, Military—France
355.3450945	UH279-280	Medicine, Military—Italy
355.3450946	UH287-288	Medicine, Military—Spain
355.34509469	UH283-284	Medicine, Military—Portugal
355.3450947	UH285-286	Medicine, Military—Russia
355.3450948	UH286.5	Medicine, Military—Scandinavia
355.34509495	UH275-276	Medicine, Military—Greece
355.345095	UH299-313	Medicine, Military—Asia
355.3450951	UH301-302	Medicine, Military—China
355.3450952	UH305-306	Medicine, Military—Japan
355.3450954	UH303-304	Medicine, Military—India
355.345096	UH315-319	Medicine, Military—Africa
355.3450971	UH226-227	Medicine, Military—Canada
355.3450972	UH228-229	Medicine, Military—Mexico
355.34509728	UH230-231	Medicine, Military—Central America
355.34509729	UH232-233	Medicine, Military—West Indies
355.3450973	UH223-224	Medicine, Military—United States
355.345098	UH234-254	Medicine, Military—South America
355.3450982	UH236-237	Medicine, Military—Argentina
355.3450983	UH243-244	Medicine, Military—Chile
355.34509861	UH245-246	Medicine, Military—Colombia
355.3450987	UH254	Medicine, Military—Venezuela
355.345099(5-6)	UH323-324	Medicine, Military—Oceania
355.3460973	U56-59	United States—Armed Forces—Officers' clubs
355.347	UH20-25	Chaplains
355.3480973	UA45	United States—Armed Forces—Women's reserves
355.35	U370-375	Garrisons
355.35	UA12.8	Guard troops
355.350973	U173	United States. Army—Field service
355.350975	U173.5	Confederate States of America. Army—Field service
355.351	U230	Riots
355.352	UA14	Armies, Colonial
355.354	G539	Soldiers of fortune
355.37	UA13	Militia
355.37097(4-9)	UA50-549	United States—Armed Forces—Reserves, [United States, By state]
355.370973	UA42-560	United States—National Guard
355.370973	UA42-560	United States—Militia
355.370973	UA42-560	United States—Armed Forces—Reserves
355.3709741	UA230-239	Maine—National Guard
355.3709742	UA330-339	New Hampshire—National Guard
355.3709743	UA490-499	Vermont—National Guard
355.3709744	UA250-259	Massachusetts—National Guard

Dewey	LC	Subject Heading	Dewey	LC	Subject Heading
355.3709745	UA430-439	Rhode Island—National Guard	355.3709797	UA510-519	Washington (State)—National Guard
355.3709746	UA100-109	Connecticut—National Guard	355.3709798	UA60-69	Alaska—National Guard
			355.3709969	UA159.1-.9	Hawaii—National Guard
355.3709747	UA360-369	New York (State)—National Guard	355.4	D25	Battles
355.3709748	UA420-429	Pennsylvania—National Guard	355.4	U161-163	Operational art (Military science)
355.3709749	UA340-349	New Jersey—National Guard	355.4	U167.5.A35	Advanced guard (Military science)
355.3709751	UA110-119	Delaware—National Guard	355.4	U225	Combat survival
355.3709752	UA240-249	Maryland—National Guard	355.4	U250-255	Military maneuvers
355.3709753	UA120-129	Washington (D.C.)—National Guard	355.4	U865	Swordplay
			355.4(8)	U280-285	Staff rides
355.3709754	UA520-529	West Virginia—National Guard	355.40285	UG478	Military art and science—Automation
355.3709755	UA500-509	Virginia—National Guard	355.40973	U253	United States. Army—Maneuvers
355.3709756	UA370-379	North Carolina—National Guard	355.41	UG447.7	Smoke screens
355.3709757	UA440-449	South Carolina—National Guard	355.41	UG449	Camouflage (Military science)
355.3709758	UA150-159	Georgia—National Guard	355.411	U168	Logistics
355.3709759	UA140-149	Florida—National Guard	355.411	U168	Integrated logistic support
355.3709761	UA50-59	Alabama—National Guard	355.413	U190	Scouts and scouting
355.3709762	UA280-289	Mississippi—National Guard	355.413	U220	Military reconnaissance
355.3709763	UA220-229	Louisiana—National Guard	355.42	U161-163	Strategy
355.3709764	UA470-479	Texas—National Guard	355.42	U164-167.5	Tactics
355.3709766	UA400-409	Oklahoma—National Guard	355.422	U167	Friendly fire (Military science)
355.3709767	UA80-89	Arkansas—National Guard	355.422	U167	Ambushes and surprises
355.3709768	UA460-469	Tennessee—National Guard	355.422	U167.5.E57	Envelopment (Military science)
355.3709769	UA210-219	Kentucky—National Guard	355.422	U167.5.L5	Lightning war
355.3709771	UA390-399	Ohio—National Guard	355.422	U167.5.R34	Raids (Military science)
355.3709772	UA180-189	Indiana—National Guard	355.422	U190-195	Guard duty
355.3709773	UA170-179	Illinois—National Guard	355.422	U200	Landing operations
355.3709774	UA260-269	Michigan—National Guard	355.422	U210	Skirmishing
355.3709775	UA530-539	Wisconsin—National Guard	355.422	U215	Rearguard action (Military science)
355.3709776	UA270-279	Minnesota—National Guard	355.422	U262	Commando troops
355.3709777	UA190-199	Iowa—National Guard	355.423	U167.5.J8	Jungle warfare
355.3709778	UA290-299	Missouri—National Guard	355.423	U167.5.W5	Winter warfare
355.3709781	UA200-209	Kansas—National Guard	355.423	U205	Stream crossing, Military
355.3709782	UA310-319	Nebraska—National Guard	355.44	UG443-449	Siege warfare
355.3709783	UA450-459	South Dakota—National Guard	355.44	UG446	Intrenchments
355.3709784	UA380-389	North Dakota—National Guard	355.45	UA10.7	Civilian-based defense
			355.45	UG410-442	Coast defenses
355.3709786	UA300-309	Montana—National Guard	355.45	UG448	Coast defenses
355.3709787	UA540-549	Wyoming—National Guard	355.450973	UA23	United States—Defenses
355.3709789	UA350-359	New Mexico—National Guard	355.450975	UA580-585	Confederate States of America—Defenses
355.3709791	UA70-79	Arizona—National Guard	355.46	U260	Combined operations (Military science)
355.3709792	UA480-489	Utah—National Guard	355.46	U261	Amphibious warfare
355.3709793	UA320-329	Nevada—National Guard			
355.3709794	UA90-99	California—National Guard	355.47	UA985-997	Military geography
355.3709795	UA410-419	Oregon—National Guard	355.47	UA985-997	Maps, Military
355.3709796	UA160-169	Idaho—National Guard			

Dewey	LC	Subject Heading	Dewey	LC	Subject Heading
358.400942	DA89.5	England. Royal Air force	355.640973	UC70-75	United States. Army—Pay, allowances, etc.
355.48	U310	War games	355.685	UB240-245	Military inspectors general
355.48	U313	Imaginary wars and battles	355.6850973	UB243	United States. Army—Inspection
355.480285	U310	Computer war games			
355.480285	U310	AGATE (Computer war game)	355.693	UH80-85	Postal service
			355.7	UB390-395	Military reservations
355.5	U110-115	Military art and science—Soldiers' handbooks	355.7	UF540-545	Arsenals
			355.71	UC400-440	Barracks
355.5	U290-295	Military training camps	355.71	UC410	Soldiers—Billeting
355.5	U300-305	Bombing and gunnery ranges	355.72	UH460-485	Military hospitals
			355.75	UA	Armories
355.5	U320-325	Physical education and training, Military	355.8	U800-897	Weapons
			355.8	UC260-267	Military supplies
355.5071	U715-717	Soldiers—Education, Non-military	355.8	UH87-100	Animals—War use
			355.8094	UC158-233	Europe—Armed Forces—Supplies and stores
355.50973	U323	United States. Army—Physical training	355.80941	UC184-187	Great Britain—Armed Forces—Supplies and stores
355.50973	U408.3	Experimental Volunteer Army Training Program			
355.5470973	U113	United States. Army—Handbooks, manuals, etc.	355.80943	UC180-183	Germany—Armed Forces—Supplies and stores
			355.8095	UC234-245	Asia—Armed Forces—Supplies and stores
355.6	UB	Military administration			
355.605	UB1	Military administration—Periodicals	355.80952	UC241	Japan—Armed Forces—Supplies and stores
355.609	UB15	Military administration—History	355.8096	UC247-253	Africa—Armed Forces—Supplies and stores
			355.80971	UC90-93	Canada—Armed forces—Supplies and stores
355.60943	UB73-74	Germany—Armed Forces—Management			
355.60947	UB85-86	Russia—Armed Forces—Management	355.80972	UC94-97	Mexico—Armed forces—Supplies and stores
355.60951	UB101-102	China—Armed Forces—Management	355.809728	UC98-99	Central America—Armed Forces—Supplies and stores
355.60952	UB105-106	Japan—Armed Forces—Management			
355.60973	UA23.2-.6	United States. Dept. of Defense	355.80973	UC523	United States. Army—Equipment
355.60973	UB23-25	United States—Armed Forces—Management	355.80973	UF523-563	United States. Army—Ordnance and ordnance stores
355.60973	UB163	United States. Army—Records and correspondence	355.8098	UC106-154	South America—Armed Forces—Supplies and stores
355.62	UC700-780	Armies—Commissariat			
355.620973	UC40-44	United States. Army—Commissariat	355.80994	UC255-256	Australia—Armed Forces—Supplies and stores
355.620975	UC85-86	Confederate States of America. Army—Commissariat	355.81	U825	Helmets
			355.81	UC460-465	Armies—Equipment
			355.81	UC570-575	Tents
355.6212	UC260	Armed forces—Procurement	355.824	U167.5.H3	Flexible weapons (Hand-to-hand fighting)
355.62120973	UC260-267	United States—Armed Forces—Procurement			
355.62120973	UC263	United States. Army—Procurement	355.8241	U850-872	Swords
			355.8241	U850-863	Sabers
355.62137	UC260-267	Surplus military property	355.8241	U875	Ballista
355.622	UA17	Armies, Cost of	355.8241	U875	Catapult
355.622	UA17	War, Cost of	355.8241	U877-878	Bow and arrow

Dewey	LC	Subject Heading	Dewey	LC	Subject Heading
355.82420975	UD383.5	Confederate States of America. Army—Firearms	357.0482	UE420-425	Sabers
			357.048241	UE420-425	Swords
355.825119	U264	Nuclear weapons	357.06	UE1	Cavalry—Societies, etc.
355.83	UC320-325	Transports	357.09	UE15	Cavalry—History
355.83	UC330-335	Airlift, Military	357.09(4-9)	UE21-124	Cavalry—[By region or country]
355.83	UC330-335	Airdrop			
355.83	UC340-345	Motorization, Military	357.094	UE55-95	Cavalry—Europe
355.83	UH500-505	Transportation, Military	357.0941	UE57-64	Cavalry—Great Britain
355.85	UA940-945	Communications, Military	357.0943	UE73-74	Cavalry—Germany
355.88	UH440-445	Medical supplies	357.0944	UE71-72	Cavalry—France
356.1	UD	Infantry	357.0945	UE79-80	Cavalry—Italy
356.106	UD1	Infantry—Societies, etc.	357.0946	UE87-88	Cavalry—Spain
356.109	UD15	Infantry—History	357.09469	UE83-84	Cavalry—Portugal
356.10973	UA28-29	United States. Army—Infantry	357.0947	UE85-86	Cavalry—Russia
			357.0948	UE86.5	Cavalry—Scandinavia
356.10973	UD23	United States. Army—Infantry	357.09495	UE75-76	Cavalry—Greece
			357.095	UE99-113	Cavalry—Asia
356.114	UD310-315	Marching	357.0951	UE101-102	Cavalry—China
356.114	UD330-335	Sharpshooting (Military science)	357.0952	UE105-106	Cavalry—Japan
			357.0954	UE103-104	Cavalry—India
356.114	UD330-335	Sniping (Military science)	357.096	UE115-119	Cavalry—Africa
356.1154	UD157-302	Infantry drill and tactics	357.0971	UE26-27	Cavalry—Canada
356.11547	UD330-335	Shooting, Military	357.0972	UE28-29	Cavalry—Mexico
356.118	UD370-375	Infantry—Equipment	357.09728	UE30-31	Cavalry—Central America
356.1182	UD380-415	Firearms	357.09729	UE32-33	Cavalry—West Indies
356.1182	UD390	Firearms—Sights	357.0973	UE23-25	Cavalry—United States
356.118241	UD340-345	Bayonets	357.098	UE34-54	Cavalry—South America
356.118241	UD400	Bayonets	357.0982	UE36-37	Cavalry—Argentina
356.118241	UD420-425	Swords	357.0983	UE43-44	Cavalry—Chile
356.1182425	UD390-395	Assault rifles	357.09861	UE45-46	Cavalry—Colombia
356.1182425	UD390-395	Rifles	357.0987	UE54	Cavalry—Venezuela
356.1182425 + 0973	UD395.M17	M1 carbine	357.099(5-6)	UE123-124	Cavalry—Oceania
			357.0994	UE121-122	Cavalry—Australia
356.1182425 + 973	UD395.E	Enfield rifle	357.10973	UA30-31	United States. Army—Cavalry
356.1182432	UD410-415	Pistols	357.184	UE157-302	Cavalry drill and tactics
356.1182436	UD410-415	Revolvers	357.2	UC600-695	Horses
356.16	U262	Special operations (Military science)	357.2	UC600-695	Remount service
			357.2	UE460-475	War horses
356.16	UG633	Special forces (Military science)	357.2	UE460-475	Horses
			357.2	UE460-475	Horsemanship
356.160973	U262	Special forces (Military science)—United States—History	358.12	UF	Artillery
			358.12	UF400-445	Artillery, Field and mountain
			358.12	UF628	Antitank weapons
356.160973	UA34.S64	United States. Army—Special Forces—History	358.12006	UF1	Artillery—Societies, etc.
			358.1203	UF9	Artillery—Dictionaries
356.164	UD460-465	Mountain warfare	358.12074	UF6	Military museums
356.164	UD470-475	Ski troops	358.1209	UF15	Artillery—History
356.166	UD480-485	Parachute troops	358.1209(4-9)	UF21-124	Artillery—[By region or country]
356.1660973	UD483	United States—Armed Forces—Airborne troops			
			358.12094	UF55-95	Artillery—Europe
356.1660973	UD483	United States—Armed Forces—Parachute troops	358.120941	UF57-64	Artillery—Great Britain
			358.120943	UF73-74	Artillery—Germany
356.4	UD460-465	Military maneuvers	358.120944	UF71-72	Artillery—France
357	UE	Cavalry			
357.04144	UE440-445	Cavalry—Uniforms			

Dewey	LC	Subject Heading
358.120945	UF79-80	Artillery—Italy
358.120946	UF87-88	Artillery—Spain
358.1209469	UF83-84	Artillery—Portugal
358.120947	UF85-86	Artillery—Russia
358.120948	UF86.5	Artillery—Scandinavia
358.1209495	UF75-76	Artillery—Greece
358.12095	UF99-113	Artillery—Asia
358.120951	UF101-102	Artillery—China
358.120952	UF105-106	Artillery—Japan
358.120954	UF103-104	Artillery—India
358.12096	UF115-119	Artillery—Africa
358.120971	UF26-27	Artillery—Canada
358.120972	UF28-29	Artillery—Mexico
358.1209728	UF30-31	Artillery—Central America
358.1209729	UF32-33	Artillery—West Indies
358.120973	UA32-33	United States. Army—Artillery
358.120973	UF23-25	Artillery—United States
358.120973	UF23	United States. Army—Artillery
358.12098	UF34-54	Artillery—South America
358.120982	UF36-37	Artillery—Argentina
358.120983	UF43-44	Artillery—Chile
358.1209861	UF45-46	Artillery—Colombia
358.120987	UF54	Artillery—Venezuela
358.12099(5-6)	UF123-124	Artillery—Oceania
358.120993	UF122.5	Artillery—New Zealand
358.120994	UF121-122	Artillery—Australia
358.124	UF157-302	Artillery drill and tactics
358.1240973	UF160-162	United States. Army—Artillery—Drill and tactics
358.125	UF340-345	Target practice
358.128	UF560-565	Ordnance, Rapid-fire
358.128	UF845	Telescopes
358.1280287	UF890	Ordnance testing
358.1282	UF520-780	Ordnance
358.1282	UF560-565	Howitzers
358.1282	UF563.A77	Trench mortars
358.1282	UF620	Machine-guns
358.1282	UF656	Recoilless rifles
358.1282	UF700-770	Ammunition
358.1282	UF765	Grenades
358.1282	UF780	Electric detonators
358.12822	UF470-475	Howitzers
358.1282356	UF767	Rockets (Ordnance)
358.128251	UF767	Projectiles, Aerial
358.1282513	UF750-770	Projectiles
358.128255	UF740-745	Cartridges
358.1382	UF625	Antiaircraft guns
358.16	UF450-455	Artillery, Coast
358.171	UG740-745	Ballistic missile defenses
358.174	UF625	Surface-to-air missiles
358.1754	UG1312.B34	Ballistic missiles
358.1754	UG1312.I2	Intercontinental ballistic missiles
358.1883	UG446.5	Centurion (Tank)
358.1883	UG446.5	M1 (Tank)
358.1883	UG446.5	Armored personnel carriers
358.1883	UG446.5	Half-track vehicles, Military
358.1883	UG446.5	Tanks (Military science)
358.22	UG	Military engineering
358.22	UG360-390	Military field engineering
358.22	UG375	Obstacles (Military science)
358.2206	UG1	Military engineering—Societies, etc.
358.2206	UG5	Military engineering—Congresses
358.22071	UG157	Military engineering—Study and teaching
358.2209	UG15	Military engineering—History
358.2209(4-9)	UG21-124	Military engineering—[By region or country]
358.22092	UG127-128	Tank engineers
358.23	UG370	Demolition, Military
358.24	UG570-613.5	Signals and signaling
358.25	UC	Transportation, Military
358.25	UC270-360	Transportation, Military
358.25	UC300-305	Pack transportation
358.250973	UC273	United States. Army—Transportation
358.32	V795	Ships of the line
358.34	UG447-.5	Gases, Asphyxiating and poisonous—War use
358.34	UG447.5.M8	Mustard gas
358.34	UG447-.65	Chemical warfare
358.3482	UG447.5-.65	Chemical weapons
358.38	UG447.8	Biological warfare
358.38820947	UG447.8	Biological weapons—Soviet Union
358.4	UG622-1425	Air forces
358.4	UG630-670	Aeronautics, Military
358.4	UG630	Air warfare
358.4006	UG622	Air forces—Societies, etc.
358.4006	UG623	Air forces—Congresses
358.4009	UG625	Air forces—History
358.40092	UG626-.2	Air pilots, Military
358.40092	UG626.2.D66	Generals—United States – Biography
358.400973	UG633-634.5	United States. Air Force
358.400973	UG633	United States. Air Force—History
358.413380973	UG823	United States. Air Force—Non-commissioned officers—History
358.414	UG730-735	Airborne warning and control systems
358.414	UG730-735	Air defenses
358.414	UG1180-1185	Air forces—Insignia

Dewey	LC	Subject Heading	Dewey	LC	Subject Heading
358.41422	UG700	Air interdiction	359.007106	V660-680	Naval education—Africa
358.4183	UG1240-1242	Airplanes, Military	359.0071071	V440-444	Naval education—Canada
358.42	UG1242.A28	Dauntless (Dive bomber)	359.0071072	V445-449	Naval education—Mexico
358.42	UG1312.C7	Cruise missiles	359.00710728	V450-453	Naval education—Central America
358.428251	UG1282.N48	Neutron bomb			
358.4283	UG1242.A25	Antisubmarine aircraft	359.00710729	V455-458	Naval education—West Indies
358.4283	UG1242.A28	Dive bombers			
358.42830973	UG1242.B6	B-52 bomber	359.0071073	V411-437	Naval education—United States
358.43	UG1242.A28	Attack planes			
358.4303	UG1242.F5	Night fighter planes	359.0071073	V415	Midshipmen
358.43092	UG626-.2	Fighter pilots	359.0071075	V438	Naval education—Confederate States of America
358.430973	UG703	Fighter plane combat—United States			
358.434	UG700-705	Fighter plane combat	359.007108	V465-496	Naval education—South America
358.4383	UG1230-1235	Attack helicopters			
358.4383	UG1233	Apache (Attack helicopter)	359.0071094	V690-694	Naval education—Australia
358.4383	UG1242.F5	Fighter planes	359.0074	V13	Naval museums
358.4483	UG1232.T72	Chinook (Military transport helicopter)	359.009	V25-55	Naval art and science—History
358.4483	UG1232.T72	Choctaw (Military transport helicopter)	359.009	VD23-25	Sailors—United States
			359.009	D27	Naval history
358.45	UG760-765	Aerial reconnaissance	359.00901	D95	Naval history, Ancient
358.45	UG1242.R4	Reconnaissance aircraft	359.0092	V61-65	Naval biography
358.450941	UG765.G	Aerial reconnaissance, British	359.0092	VD	Sailors
			359.0092	VD15	Sailors—History
358.450973	UG763	Aerial reconnaissance, American	359.0092	VD21-124	Sailors—[By region or country]
358.8	UG1500-1530	Space surveillance	359.0094	D436	Naval history, Modern—20th century
358.8	UG1530	Space warfare			
359	V	Naval art and science	359.00943	DA70-89.1	Great Britain—History, Naval
359	V	War			
359	VA	Naval districts	359.00943	DD106	Germany—History, Naval
359	VA37-42	Navies	359.00941	DD358	Prussia (Germany)—History, Naval
359.00289	V383	United States. Navy—Safety measures			
359.003	V23-24	Naval art and science—Dictionary	359.00943	DB45	Austria—History, Naval
			359.00944	DC49-53	France—History, Naval
359.003	V23-24	Naval art and science—Terminology	359.00946	DP80-81	Spain—History, Naval
			359.009469	DP550-551	Portugal—History, Naval
359.005	V1-5	Naval art and science—Periodicals	359.009492	DH121	Netherlands—History, Naval
			359.009492	DJ130-138	Netherlands—History, Naval
359.006	V7	Naval art and science—Congresses	359.009493	DH551	Belgium—History, Naval
			359.009495	DF544	Byzantine Empire—History, Naval
359.0071	V400-695	Naval education			
359.00710(4-9)	V411-695	Naval education—[By region or country]	359.009497	DR1252-1253	Yugoslavia—History, Naval
			359.009498	DR225	Romania—History, Naval
359.007104	V500-623	Naval education—Europe	359.009561	DR451	Turkey—History, Naval
359.0071041	V510-530	Naval education—Great Britain	359.00971	F1028.5	Canada—History, Naval
			359.00973	E182	United States. Navy—History
359.0071043	V570-574.54	Naval education—Germany	359.00973	E182	United States—History, Naval
359.007105	V625-650	Naval education—Asia			
359.0071051	V630-634	Naval education—China	359.00973	VA49-395	United States. Navy—Organization
359.0071052	V640-644	Naval education—Japan			
359.0071054	V635-639	Naval education—India	359.00975	E591-600	Confederate States of America—History, Naval
359.0071055	V645-649	Naval education—Iran			

Dewey	LC	Subject Heading
359.00975	E591-600	Confederate States of America. Navy—History
359.310973	VD403	United States. Navy—Small-boat service
359.00947	DK55-59	Russia—History, Naval
359.07	V390-395	Naval research
359.13323	VB920-925	Military police
359.13325	VB910	Corporal punishment
359.1334	VB850-880	Naval offenses
359.1334	VB860-867	Mutiny
359.1334	VB870-875	Desertion, Naval
359.1334	VB880	Insubordination
359.1342	VB330-335	Military decorations
359.1342	VC345	Insignia
359.15	V300-305	Flags
359.1509(4-9)	V305	Flags—[Other countries]
359.150973	V303-304	Flags—United States
359.17	V310	Naval ceremonies, honors, and salutes
359.2236	VB260-275	Recruiting and enlistment
359.22360973	VB263	United States. Navy—Recruiting, enlistment, etc.
359.32	V750-995	Warships
359.32	V799-800	Armored vessels
359.32	V890	Floating batteries
359.32	VF440	Warships—Turrets
359.32092	VK221	Ships—Manning
359.3220948	V46	Viking ships
359.3220973	V880	United States. Navy—Boats
359.3253	V820-.5	Battle cruisers
359.3254	V825-.5	Destroyers (Warships)
359.3258	V830-840	Torpedo-boats
359.331	VB190	Admirals
359.332	VB310-315	Navies—Officers
359.3320973	V123	United States. Navy—Petty officers' handbooks
359.3320973	V133	United States. Navy—Officers' handbooks
359.3320973	VB308	United States—Armed Forces—Warrant officers
359.3320973	VB313-314	United States. Navy—Officers
359.3380973	V143-144	United States. Navy—Sailors' handbooks
359.3380973	VD150-155	United States. Navy—Sailors' handbooks
359.3380973	VG803	United States. Navy—Machinist's mates
359.3380973	VG903	United States. Navy—Yeomen
359.3380973	VG913	United States. Navy—Draftsmen
359.3380973	VG953	United States. Navy—Boatswains
359.34	VG60-65	Postal service
359.340973	VG63	United States. Navy—Postal service
359.342	VG500-505	Journalism, Military
359.3420973	VG503	Journalism, Military—United States
359.3432	VB230-250	Intelligence service
359.3432092	VB250	Spies
359.34320973	VG1020	United States. Navy—Intelligence specialists
359.345	VG	Medicine, Naval
359.345	VG100-475	Medicine, Naval
359.345	VG270-275	Pharmacy, Military
359.345	VG280-285	Dentistry, Naval
359.345	VG470-475	Naval hygiene
359.345071	VG230-235	Medicine, Naval—Study and teaching
359.34509(4-9)	VG121-224	Medicine, Naval—[By region or country]
359.345092	VG226-228	Medicine, Naval—Biography
359.345094	VG155-196	Medicine, Naval—Europe
359.3450941	VG157-164	Medicine, Naval—Great Britain
359.3450943	VG173-174.5	Medicine, Naval—Germany
359.3450944	VG171-172	Medicine, Naval—France
359.3450945	VG179-180	Medicine, Naval—Italy
359.3450946	VG187-188	Medicine, Naval—Spain
359.3450948	VG186.5	Medicine, Naval—Scandinavia
359.345095	VG199-213	Medicine, Naval—Asia
359.3450952	VG205-206	Medicine, Naval—Japan
359.345096	VG215-219	Medicine, Naval—Africa
359.3450971	VG126-127	Medicine, Naval—Canada
359.3450972	VG128-129	Medicine, Naval—Mexico
359.34509728	VG130-131	Medicine, Naval—Central America
359.3450973	VG123-125	Medicine, Naval—United States
359.345098	VG134-154	Medicine, Naval—South America
359.3450993	VG222.5	Medicine, Naval—New Zealand
359.3450994	VG221-222	Medicine, Naval—Australia
359.347	VG20-25	Chaplains, Military
359.3470973	VG23	United States. Navy—Chaplains
359.350973	V175	United States. Navy—Field service
359.37	VA45	Naval reserves
359.370941	VA460	Navy-yards and naval stations—Great Britain
359.370971	VA402	Naval militia—Canada
359.4	D27	Naval battles
359.41	V215	Warships—Camouflage
359.41	V215	Camouflage (Military science)
359.41	V245	Naval maneuvers

Dewey	LC	Subject Heading	Dewey	LC	Subject Heading
359.410973	V245	United States. Navy— Maneuvers	359.60982	VB36-37	Naval art and science— Argentina
359.411	V179	Logistics, Naval	359.60983	VB43-44	Naval art and science— Chile
359.413	V190	Naval reconnaissance			
359.42	V160-165	Naval strategy	359.609861	VB45-46	Naval art and science— Colombia
359.42	V167-178	Naval tactics			
359.422	VF520-530	Fire control (Naval gunnery)	359.6099(5-6)	VB123-124	Naval art and science— Oceania
359.422	VF550	Range-finding			
359.450947	VG185-186	Medicine, Naval—Russia	359.60994	VB121-122	Naval art and science— Australia
359.4509729	VG132-133	Medicine, Naval—West Indies	359.610973	VB258	United States. Navy— Personnel management
359.48	V250	War games, Naval			
359.48	V253	Imaginary wars and battles	359.62120973	VC260-267	United States. Navy— Procurement
359.50973	V263	United States. Navy— Physical training	359.6220973	VA53	United States. Navy— Appropriations and expenditures
359.50973	V435-436	Training-ships			
359.547	VF310-315	Target practice	359.6220973	VC503	United States. Navy— Accounting
359.6	VB	Naval art and science	359.6229	VA20-25	Navies, Cost of
359.609(4-9)	VB21-124	Naval art and science—[By region or country]	359.6850973	VB223	United States. Navy— Inspection
359.6094	VB55-96	Naval art and science— Europe	359.7	V230	Navy-yards and naval stations
359.60941	VB57-64	Naval art and science— Great Britain	359.70973	VA66	Navy-yards and naval stations—United States
359.60943	VB73-74.5	Naval art and science— Germany	359.710973	VC423	United States. Navy— Barracks and quarters
359.60944	VB71-72	Naval art and science— France	359.72	VG410-450	Hospitals, Naval and marine
359.60945	VB79-80	Naval art and science—Italy	359.8	V396-.5	Military oceanography
359.60946	VB87-88	Naval art and science— Spain	359.80287	VF540	Ordnance testing
			359.80941	VC184-187	Great Britain. Royal Navy
359.609469	VB83-84	Naval art and science— Portugal	359.80973	VC20-65	United States. Navy
359.60947	VB85-86	Naval art and science— Russia	359.80973	VC50-65	United States. Navy— Pay, allowances, etc.
359.609495	VB75-76	Naval art and science— Greece	359.80973	VC263	United States. Navy— Supplies and stores
359.6095	VB99-113	Naval art and science—Asia	359.80973	VF353-420	United States. Navy—Ordnance and ordnance stores
359.60951	VB101-102	Naval art and science— China			
359.60952	VB105-106	Naval art and science— Japan	359.80975	VA393-395	Confederate States of America. Navy—-Ordnance and ordnance stores
359.6096	VB115-119	Naval art and science— Africa	359.81	VC300-345	Military uniforms
359.60971	VB26-27	Naval art and science— Canada	359.82	V880	Steel boats
			359.82	VF	Ordnance, Naval
359.60972	VB28-29	Naval art and science— Mexico	359.8206	VF1	Ordnance, Naval—Societies, etc.
359.609728	VB30-31	Naval art and science— Central America	359.82074	VF6	Naval museums
			359.8209	VF15	Ordnance, Naval—History
359.609729	VB32-33	Naval art and science— West Indies	359.8209(4-9)	VF21-124	Ordnance, Naval—[By region or country]
359.60973	VB23-25	Naval art and science— United States	359.82094	VF55-96	Ordnance, Naval—Europe
			359.820941	VF57-64	Ordnance, Naval—Great Britain
359.6098	VB34-54	Naval art and science— South America	359.820943	VF73-74.5	Ordnance, Naval—Germany
			359.820944	VF71-72	Ordnance, Naval—France

Dewey	LC	Subject Heading	Dewey	LC	Subject Heading
359.820945	VF79-80	Ordnance, Naval—Italy	359.9383	V857-859	Submarine boats
359.820946	VF87-88	Ordnance, Naval—Spain	359.93834	V857.5	Nuclear submarines
359.8209469	VF83-84	Ordnance, Naval—Portugal	359.94	VG	Naval aviation
359.820947	VF85-86	Ordnance, Naval—Russia	359.94	VG90-95	Naval aviation
359.820948	VF86.5	Ordnance, Naval—Scandinavia	359.940973	VG93	United States. Navy—Aviation
359.82095	VF101-113	Ordnance, Naval—Asia	359.9435	V874-875	Aircraft carriers
359.820952	VF105-106	Ordnance, Naval—Japan	359.94834	VG90-95	Airplanes, Military—Turrets
359.8209561	VF111-112	Ordnance, Naval—Turkey	359.96	VE	Marines
359.82096	VF115-119	Ordnance, Naval—Africa	359.9609	VE15	Marines—History
359.820971	VF26-27	Ordnance, Naval—Canada	359.961342	VE345	Marines—Insignia
359.820972	VF28-29	Ordnance, Naval—Mexico	359.9614	VE400-405	Marines—Uniforms
359.8209728	VF30-31	Ordnance, Naval—Central America	359.96309(4-9)	VE21-124	Marines—[By region or country]
359.8209729	VF32-33	Ordnance, Naval—West Indies	359.963094	VE55-96	Marines—Europe
			359.9630941	VE57-64	Marines—Great Britain
359.820973	VF23-25	Ordnance, Naval—United States	359.9630943	VE73-74.5	Marines—Germany
			359.9630944	VE71-72	Marines—France
359.820973	VF347	United States. Navy—Weapons systems	359.9630945	VE79-80	Marines—Italy
			359.9630946	VE87-88	Marines—Spain
359.820973	VF440	Ridgway's revolving battery	359.9630947	VE85-86	Marines—Russia
359.82098	VF34-54	Ordnance, Naval—South America	359.9630948	VE86.5	Marines—Scandinavia
			359.963095	VE99-113	Marines—Asia
359.820982	VF36-37	Ordnance, Naval—Argentina	359.9630952	VE105-106	Marines—Japan
			359.963096	VE115-119	Marines—Africa
359.820983	VF43-44	Ordnance, Naval—Chile	359.9630971	VE26-27	Marines—Canada
359.8209861	VF45-46	Ordnance, Naval—Colombia	359.9630972	VE28-29	Marines—Mexico
359.820993	VF122.5	Ordnance, Naval—New Zealand	359.96309728	VE30-31	Marines—Central America
			359.96309729	VE32-33	Marines—West Indies
359.820994	VF121-122	Ordnance, Naval—Australia	359.9630973	VE23-25	United States. Marine Corps
359.824	VD360-390	Firearms	359.963098	VE34-54	Marines—South America
359.8240973	VD360-390	United States. Navy—Firearms	359.9630993	VE122.5	Marines—New Zealand
			359.9630994	VE121-122	Marines—Australia
359.8240973	VF350-420	United States. Navy—Firearms	359.9633	VE150-155	Marines—Handbooks, manuals, etc.
359.82424	VF410	Machine-guns	359.965	VE430-435	Military training camps
359.82424	VF410.G2-.G24	Gardner machine-gun	359.9650973	VE160-162	United States. Marine Corps—Drill and tactics
359.82424	VF410.G3-.G34	Gatling guns			
359.82425	VD370	Rifles	359.9671	VE420-425	Marines—Barracks and quarters
359.82432	VD390	Pistols			
359.82436	VD390	Revolvers	359.96824	VE350-390	Marines—Firearms
359.8251	VF480-500	Projectiles	359.9709073	V437	United States. Coast Guard
359.8251	VF509	Depth charges	359.970973	VG53	United States. Coast Guard
359.82517	V850-855	Torpedoes	359.98170973	VF347	AEGIS (Weapons system)
359.83	V880	Motor vehicles, Amphibious	359.98170973	VF347	United States. Navy— Fire control technicians (Missile)
359.83	VC	Transportation, Military			
359.83	VK	Ships	359.981782	V990-995	Fleet ballistic missile weapons systems
359.8352	V815-.5	Battleships			
359.88	VG290-295	Medical supplies	359.9830973	VG73	United States. Navy—Communication systems
359.93	V210-214.5	Submarine warfare			
359.93	V214.5	Submarine boat combat	359.984	VG50-55	Coastal surveillance
359.93	V214-.5	Anti-submarine warfare	359.984	VG86-88	Underwater demolition teams
359.933	V857-859	Submarines (Ships)			
359.9330973	V858	United States. Navy—Submarine forces	359.9840973	VG87	Underwater demolition teams—United States

Dewey	LC	Subject Heading	Dewey	LC	Subject Heading
359.985	V865	Naval auxiliary vessels	362.104258	RA413-.7	Health maintenance organizations
359.985	VC530-535	Military sealift	362.104258	RA413-.5	Managed care plans (Medical care)
359.985	VC550-580	Transportation, Military			
359.9850973	VC553	United States. Navy—Transportation	362.108697	UB368-369.5	Veterans—Medical care
			362.108996073	RA448.5.N4	Afro-Americans—Medical care
360	HN29.5	Applied sociology			
361	HV1-696	Social service	362.11	RA960-996	Hospitals
361.006	HV6	Social service—Societies, etc.	362.11	RA960-996	Public hospitals
			362.11	RA975.D57	Disaster hospitals
361.025	HV7	Social service—Directories	362.11	RD705-706	Orthopedic hospitals
361.05	HV59-63	Institutional care	362.11	RF5-6	Hospitals, Ophthalmic and aural
361.1	HN	Social problems			
361.105	HN1	Social problems—Periodicals	362.11	RG12-16	Hospitals, Gynecologic and obstetric
			362.11	RK3-.5	Dental clinics
361.106	HN3	Social problems—Congresses	362.11	RX6-.5	Homeopathy—Hospitals and dispensaries
361.10723	HN29	Social surveys			
361.109	HN8-19	Social problems—History	362.11	RZ302-304	Osteopathic hospitals
361.3	HV7428	Social work with criminals	362.11068	RA971-.8	Hospitals—Administration
361.3023	HV10.5	Social service—Vocational guidance	362.11072	RA964.5	Hospitals—Research
			362.110902	RA964	Hospitals, Medieval
361.3071	HV11-.8	Social work education	362.11091734	RA975.R87	Rural hospitals
361.308664	HV1449	Social work with gays	362.1109174927	RA990.5	Hospitals—Arab countries
361.3092	HV40.54	Social workers—Supervision of	362.1109(4-9)	RA980-993	Hospitals—[By region or country]
361.322	H61.28	Focused group interviewing	362.1109(4-9)	RF6	Hospitals, Ophthalmic and aural—[By region or country]
361.4	HV45	Social group work			
361.4	HV547	Self-help groups			
361.6	HV	Public welfare	362.1109(4-9)	RK3.5	Dental clinics—[By region or country]
361.7	HV1-4959	Charities			
361.7	HV40-69	Charity organization	362.11094	RA985-989	Hospitals—Europe
361.7	HV544	Bazaars (Charities)	362.110941	RA986-988	Hospitals—Great Britain
361.7	HV687-694	Charities, Medical	362.11095	RA990	Hospitals—Asia
361.70681	HV41.2-.9	Fund raising	362.11096	RA991	Hospitals—Africa
361.709	HV16-25	Social service—History	362.110971	RA983	Hospitals—Canada
361.75	HV530	Church charities	362.110973	RA981-982	Hospitals—United States
361.77	UH535-537	Red Cross	362.110973	RD705.5	Orthopedic hospitals—United States
361.77	VG457	Red Cross			
361.77	HV560-583	Red Cross	362.110973	RJ27.2-.3	Pediatric clinics—United States
361.7709(4-9)	HV575-580	Red Cross—[By region or country]			
			362.110993	RA992.5-.7	Hospitals—New Zealand
361.91734	HV67	Social service, Rural	362.110994	RA992-.3	Hospitals—Australia
361.9(4-9)	HV85-520.5	Social service—[By region or country]	362.11099(5-6)	RA993	Hospitals—Oceania
			362.12	RA960-993	Dispensaries
361.973	HV85-99	Social service—United States	362.12	RA966	Clinics
			362.12	RA974-.5	Hospitals—Outpatient services
361.97(4-9)	HV98-99	Social service—[United States, By state or city]			
			362.12	RA974-.5	Public hospitals—Outpatient services
361.9(4-9)	HV101-520.5	Social service—[Other countries]			
			362.12	RC660.7	Diabetes clinics
362.0425	HD7255-7256	Rehabilitation counselors	362.12	RJ27-28	Pediatric clinics
362.1	HV687-694	Sick	362.12	RZ242	Chiropractic clinics
362.1	RA390-392	Missions, Medical	362.14	RA645.3-.37	Home care services
362.10425	HV687-688	Medical social work	362.16	HV1454-.2	Old age homes
			362.16	RA960-993	Sanatoriums

Dewey	LC	Subject Heading	Dewey	LC	Subject Heading
362.16	RA997-999	Long-term care facilities	362.29209(4-9)	HV5301-5722	Alcoholism—[Other countries]
362.16	RA997-999	Nursing homes			
362.16092	RA997-998	Volunteer workers in long-term care facilities	362.2923	HV5132	Children of alcoholics
			362.2923	HV5132	Alcoholics' spouses
362.172	R727.5	Medical referral	362.2923	HV5132	Alcoholics—Family relationships
362.172	RC455.2.R43	Psychiatric referral			
362.174	RA975.5.I56	Intensive care units	362.2923	HV5132	Adult children of alcoholics
362.1756	R726.8	Hospices (Terminal care)	362.2926	HV5001-5720	Temperance
362.177	RA427.5-.6	Medical screening	362.292606	HV5006	Temperance—Societies, etc.
362.1783	RD127-128.5	Tissue banks			
362.1783	RD128	Musculoskeletal banks	362.292609	HV5020-5025	Temperance—History
362.1783	RD129.5	Donation of organs, tissues, etc.	362.29286	HV5275-5283	Alcoholism counseling
			362.29(3-8)	HV5800-5840	Drug abuse
362.1783	RE89	Eye banks	362.29(3-8) 09 + (4-9)	HV5825-5840	Drug abuse—[By region or country]
362.1783092	RD129.5	Organ donors			
362.1784	RM172	Blood banks	362.29(3-8) 09 + (4-9)	HV5840	Drug abuse—[Other countries]
362.18	RA645.5-.9	Emergency medical services			
362.18	RA975.5.E5	Hospitals—Emergency service	362.29(3-8)0973	HV5825-5833	Drug abuse—United States
			362.29(3-8)7	HV5800-5840	Drug abuse—Prevention
362.18	RA975.5.T83	Trauma centers	362.293	HV5800-5840	Narcotic habit
362.188	RA995-996	Ambulance service	362.293	HV5813	Morphine habit
362.188	RA996.5	Airplane ambulances	362.293	HV5816	Opium habit
362.1961204	RA975.5.C6	Coronary care units	362.293	HV5822.H4	Heroin
362.1968	HV891-901	Developmentally disabled children	362.29363	HV5823-.5	Drug testing
			362.294	HV5822.5.L9	LSD (Drug)
362.1968	HV1570-.5	Developmentally disabled	362.295	HV5822.M3	Marihuana
362.1969792	P96.A39	AIDS (Disease) in mass media	362.296	HV5725-5770	Smoking
			362.296	HV5725-5770	Ex-smokers
362.196995	RC309-.5	Tuberculosis—Hospitals	362.296	HV5725-5770	Tobacco habit
362.2	HV4975-4977	Insanity	362.296	HV5740-5745	Cigarette habit
362.2	RA790-.95	Mental health services	362.29609(4-9)	HV5755-5770	Smoking—[By region or country]
362.2	RA790-.95	Mental health			
362.20425	HV689-690	Psychiatric social work	362.2960973	HV5755-5768	Smoking—United States
362.20846	RC451.4.A5	Aged—Mental health services	362.29609(4-9)	HV5770	Smoking—[Other countries]
			362.298	HV5810	Cocaine habit
362.21	RC439.4	Violence in psychiatric hospitals	362.298	HV5810	Crack (Drug)
			362.299	HV5822.G5	Glue-sniffing
362.22	RA790.55	Community psychology	362.299	RC567.5	Caffeine habit
362.22	RC455	Community psychiatry	362.(3-4)	HV1551-3024	Handicapped
362.28021	HB1323.S8	Suicide—Statistics	362.(3-4)	HV888-907	Handicapped children—Services for
362.2881	RC480.6	Psychiatric hospitals—Emergency service			
			362.3	HV3004-3009	Mental retardation
362.29	HV4997-5840	Substance abuse	362.30973	HV3006-3008	Mentally handicapped—[By region or country]
362.29083	HV4999.Y68	Youth—Substance use			
362.290834	HV4999.C45	School children—Substance use	362.385	HV3004-3008	Mental retardation facilities
			362.4072	HV1568.2-.25	Disability studies
362.2909(4-9)	HV4999.2-5000	Substance abuse—[By region or country]	362.4083	HV903-907	Disfigured children
			362.408697	UB360-366	Veterans, Disabled
362.292	HV5001-5722	Alcoholism	362.41	HV1571-2349	Blind
362.292	HV5053-5055	Alcoholism and crime	362.41	HV1597-.2	Blind-deaf—Services for
362.29201	B105.D78	Drunkenness (Philosophy)	362.4109(4-9)	HV1783-2220.5	Blind—[By region or country]
362.29205	HV5001-5002	Alcoholism—Periodicals			
362.29209(4-9)	HV5285-5722	Alcoholism—[By region or country]	362.410973	HV1783-1796	Blind—United States
			362.4109(4-9)	HV1801-2220.5	Blind—[Other regions or places]
362.2920973	HV5285-5298	Alcoholism—United States			

Dewey	LC	Subject Heading	Dewey	LC	Subject Heading
362.418	HV1631.5	Visually handicapped—Means of communication	362.609(4-9)	HV1457-1494	Aged—[By region or country]
362.418	HV1701	Blind, Apparatus for the	362.68	HV1455-.2	Day care centers for the aged
362.418071	HV1780-.6	Guide dog schools			
362.42	HV2350-2990.5	Deaf	362.7	HV701-1420.5	Child welfare
362.42	HV2350-2990.5	Hearing impaired	362.705	HV701	Child welfare—Periodicals
362.4209(4-9)	HV2510-2990.5	Deaf—[By region or country]	362.7083	HV1423	Young men
			362.7083	HV1425	Young women
362.420973	HV2510-2561	Deaf—United States	362.70869	HV873-887	Street children
362.4283	HV2402	Interpreters for the deaf	362.709(4-9)	HV741-804	Child welfare—[By region or country]
362.4283	HV2503	Video recordings for the hearing impaired	362.70973	HV741-743	Child welfare—United States
362.48	HV1568.7-.8	Day care centers for the handicapped	362.709(4-9)	HV745-804	Child welfare—[Other countries]
362.48	HV3011-3024	Physically handicapped—Services for	362.712	HQ778.5-.7	Day care centers
362.4809(4-9)	HV3023-3024	Physically handicapped—[By region or country]	362.713	HV697-700	Aid to families with dependent children
362.480973	HV3023	Physically handicapped—United States	362.73	HV835-847	Foundlings
			362.73	HV873-875.7	Abandoned children
362.4809(4-9)	HV3024	Physically handicapped—[Other countries]	362.73	HV959-1420.5	Orphans
362.5	HV1-4630	Poverty	362.7309(4-9)	HV880-887	Abandoned children—[By region or country]
362.5	HV4023-4470.7	Poor	362.730973	HV880-885	Abandoned children—United States
362.5	HV4480-4630	Tramps			
362.5091724	HV4173	Poor—Developing countries	362.732	HV862-866	Group homes for children
362.5091732	HV4023-4470.7	Urban poor	362.732	HV959-1420.5	Orphanages
362.509(4-9)	HV4041-4173	Poor—[By region or country]	362.73209(4-9)	HV971-1420.5	Orphanages—[By region or country]
362.5094	HV4084-4131.84	Poor—Europe	362.7320973	HV971-995	Orphanages—United States
362.50941	HV4085-4087.5	Poor—Great Britain	362.734	HV874.8-875.7	Adoption
362.50943	HV4097-4100.5	Poor—Germany	362.734	HV875.5	Intercountry adoption
362.50944	HV4093-4096	Poor—France	362.809(4-9)	HQ301-440.7	Church work with prostitutes
362.50945	HV4102-4105	Poor—Italy			
362.50946	HV4125-4128	Poor—Spain	362.8292	HV697-700.5	Abused wives—Services for
362.50947	HV4114-4117	Poor—Russia	362.829209(4-9)	HV699-700	Abused wives—Services for—[By region or country]
362.509492	HV4105.5-4113.5	Poor—Benelux countries			
362.5095	HV4131.85-4156.5	Poor—Asia	362.8294	HV700.7	Unmarried fathers
362.50951	HV4150	Poor—China	362.83	HV697-700	Maternal and infant welfare
362.50952	HV4147	Poor—Japan	362.83	HV1442-1448	Women—Services for
362.50954	HV4137-4140	Poor—India	362.8394	HV700.5	Unmarried mothers
362.5096	HV4157-4169.3	Poor—Africa	362.8496073	HV3181-3185	Afro-Americans—Services for
362.50971	HV4047-4050	Poor—Canada			
362.50972	HV4051	Poor—Mexico	362.858	HV3025-3163	Sailors—Services for
362.509728	HV4053-4059	Poor—Central America	362.86	VB280-285	Military pensions
362.509729	HV4060-4065.9	Poor—West Indies	362.87	HV640-.5	Refugees
362.50973	HV4043-4046	Poor—United States	362.87	HV640-.5	Refugees, Political
362.5098	HV4066-4083	Poor—South America	362.87	HV6322-.7	Disappeared persons
362.50994	HV4170	Poor—Australia	362.88	HV6250-.4	Victims of crimes
362.585	HV61	Almshouses	362.880723	HV6250	Victims of crimes surveys
362.6	HV1450-1494	Aged	362.88082	HV6250.4.W65	Women—Crimes against
362.6	HV1450-1493	Old age	362.88083	HV6250.4.Y68	Youth—Crimes against
362.6	HV1597.5	Blind aged	362.880846	HV6250.4.A34	Aged—Crimes against
362.6091734	HV1450-1494	Rural aged	362.88088375	HV6250.4.S78	Students—Crimes against
			362.8808996 + 073	HV6250.4.E75	Afro-Americans—Crimes against

Dewey	LC	Subject Heading	Dewey	LC	Subject Heading
362.883	RC560.R36	Rape victims	363.20954	HV8247-8250	Police—India
363	HD3840-4420.8	Public works	363.20956	HV8241.9-8242.56	Police—Middle East
363.107	HD7273	Safety appliances	363.209599	HV8255	Police—Philippines
363.107	HV675-677	Accidents—Prevention	363.2096	HV8267-8279.3	Police—Africa
363.11	HD7262-.5	Industrial accidents	363.20971	HV8157-8160	Police—Canada
363.11	T54	Hazardous occupations	363.20972	HV8161	Police—Mexico
363.11	T55-.3	Industrial safety	363.209728	HV8163-8169	Police—Central America
363.1172	HD7395.C5	Protective clothing	363.209729	HV8170-8175.9	Police—West Indies
363.119371	LB2864.6.A25	School accidents	363.20973	HV8130-8148	Police—United States
363.122	HE1779-1795	Railroad accidents	363.2098	HV8176-8193	Police—South America
363.123	VK1250-1299	Steamboat disasters	363.20994	HV8280	Police—Australia
363.123	VK1250-1299	Shipwrecks	363.22	HV7936.P75	Police psychiatrists
363.123	VK1265	Submarine disasters	363.22	HV7936.P75	Police psychologists
363.12309(4-9)	VK1270-1294	Shipwrecks—[By region or country]	363.22	HV8012	Police chiefs
			363.22	HV8079.2-.3	Police social work
363.124	TL553.5	Aircraft accidents	363.22	HV8080.D54	Police divers
363.124	TL867	Space vehicle accidents	363.22019	HV7936.J63	Police—Job stress
363.125	HE5613.5-5614.6	Traffic safety	363.22082	HV8023	Policewomen
363.125	RA772.T7	Traffic accidents	363.232	HV8080.A6	Arrest (Police methods)
363.12514	HE5620.D7	Drinking and traffic accidents	363.232	HV8080.P2	Police patrol—Field interrogation
363.1257	LB2865	School safety patrols	363.232	HV8080.P2	Police patrol—Surveillance operations
363.19	HF5415.9	Product recall			
363.192	HD9000.9	Food adulteration and inspection	363.2332	HV8079.5-.55	Traffic police
			363.23320284	HV8079.5	Radar in speed limit enforcement
363.192064	TX501-597	Food adulteration and inspection	363.24	HV6071	Legal photography
			363.24	HV6074	Fingerprints
363.1929064	SH335	Fish inspection	363.24	HV7936.C8	Police communication systems
363.2	HV7551-8280.7	Police			
363.2	HV7936.D78	Police—Drug testing	363.24	HV7936.E85	Evidence preservation
363.2	HV7981	Constables	363.24	HV7936.R53	Police reports
363.2025	HV7900	Police—Directories	363.25	HV8073-8079.3	Criminal investigation
363.20284	HV7936.E7	Handcuffs	363.25	HV8073-8077.5	Chemistry, Forensic
363.20284	HV7936.E7	Riot helmets	363.25092	HV7551-8077	Detectives
363.20284	HV7936.E7	Nonlethal weapons	363.25092	P96.D4	Detectives in mass media
363.20284	HV7936.E7	Tear gas munitions	363.254	HV8078-.5	Lie detectors and detection
363.20284	HV7936.E7	Truncheons	363.254092	HV8078	Polygraph operators
363.2071	HV7923	Police—Study and teaching	363.256	HV7936.C88	Crime analysis
363.209	HV7903-7909	Police—History	363.2562	HV8077	Forensic ballistics
363.2091734	HV7965-7985	Police, Rural	363.2562	HV8077.5.F6	Footprints
363.209(4-9)	HV8130-8280.7	Police—[By region or country]	363.2565	HV8074-8076	Writing—Identification
			363.2565	HV8077	Firearms—Identification
363.2094	HV8194-8261.84	Police—Europe	363.258	HV6065-6079	Criminals—Identification
363.20941	HV8195-8197.5	Police—Great Britain	363.258	HV8073-.8	Identification
363.20943	HV8207-8210	Police—Germany	363.258	HV8073.4	Police artists
363.20944	HV8203-8206	Police—France	363.25906	HV8079.O73	Organized crime investigation
363.20945	HV8212-8215	Police—Italy			
363.20946	HV8235-8238	Police—Spain	363.25947	HV8079.D76	Drunk driving—Investigation
363.209469	HV8239	Police—Portugal	363.25953	HV8079.S48	Sex crimes—Investigation
363.20947	HV8224-8227	Police—Russia	363.259532	HV8079.R35	Rape—Investigation
363.209492	HV8215.5-8223.5	Police—Benelux countries	363.259552	HV8079.R62	Robbery investigation
363.209495	HV8241.83	Police—Greece	363.2595553	HV8079.S67	Wife abuse—Investigation
363.2095	HV8241.85-8263	Police—Asia	363.2595554	HV8079.C46	Child abuse—Investigation
363.20951	HV8260	Police—China			
363.20952	HV8257	Police—Japan			

Dewey	LC	Subject Heading	Dewey	LC	Subject Heading
363.2595554	HV8079.C48	Child sexual abuse—Investigation	363.50943	HD7339-.5	Housing—Germany
			363.50944	HD7338	Housing—France
363.25962	HV8079.A98	Automobile theft investigation	363.50945	HD7341	Housing—Italy
			363.50946	HD7351	Housing—Spain
363.25963	HV8079.F7	Fraud investigation	363.50947	HD7345	Housing—Russia
363.25968	HV8079.C65	Computer crimes—Investigation	363.509492	HD7342-7344.5	Housing—Benelux countries
363.25968	HV8079.W47	White collar crime investigation	363.509494	HD7353	Housing—Switzerland
			363.509495	HD7357.5	Housing—Greece
363.25977	HV8079.N3	Drug traffic—Investigation	363.5095	HD7359.6	Housing—Asia
363.283	HV7961	Secret service	363.50951	HD7368	Housing—China
363.289	HV8081-8099	Private investigators	363.50952	HD7367	Housing—Japan
363.289	HV8290-8291	Police, Private	363.50954	HD7361	Housing—India
363.289	HV8290-8291	Campus police	363.50955	HD7359.2	Housing—Iran
363.289	HV8290-8291	Private security services	363.509561	HD7358.25	Housing—Turkey
363.289	HV8290-8291	Watchmen	363.509567	HD7359	Housing—Iraq
363.32	HV6431	Terrorism—Prevention	363.5095694	HD7358.45	Housing—Israel
363.320973	HV6432.7	War on Terrorism, 2001-	363.509599	HD7366	Housing—Philippines
363.33	HV7435-7439	Gun control	363.5096	HD7372-7378.4	Housing—Africa
363.34068	HV551.2-639	Emergency management	363.50971	HD7305	Housing—Canada
363.348	HV553-639	Disaster relief	363.50972	HD7306	Housing—Mexico
363.34809(4-9)	HV555	Disaster relief—[By region or country]	363.509728	HD7307-7313	Housing—Central America
			363.509729	HD7314-7319.9	Housing—West Indies
363.3481	TL553.8	Search and rescue operations	363.50973	HD7293-7304	Housing—United States
			363.5098	HD7320-7331	Housing—South America
363.3481	VK1259	Refloating of ships	363.50994	HD7379	Housing—Australia
363.34810973	UG854.A4	Search and rescue operations—United States	363.51	HD7288.75-.76	Discrimination in housing
			363.5908996 + 073	HD7288.72U	Afro-Americans—Housing
363.3492	HV635.5-636	Storms	363.6	HD2763-2768	Public utilities
363.34929	HV625-626	Droughts	363.68	SB481-485	Parks
363.34938	HV609-610	Floods	363.68	SB481-484	National parks and reserves
363.3495	HV599-600	Earthquakes	363.68068	SB481-485	Parks—Management
363.34988	HV639	War relief	363.680973	SB482-483	Parks—United States
363.35	UA926-929	Civil defense	363.6809(4-9)	SB484-485	Parks—[Other countries or regions]
363.37	HV620	Fires			
363.37092	TH9128	Fire fighters—Physical training	363.7	TD194.5-.58	Environmental impact statements
363.46	HQ767-.52	Abortion	363.7	TD194.6	Environmental impact analysis
363.46	PN4784.A18	Abortion in the press			
363.46	RG734-.5	Abortion services	363.7	TD194.7	Environmental auditing
363.460973	PN4888.A2	Abortion in the press	363.7	GE	Environmental sciences
363.47	HQ471-472	Pornography	363.7	GE140-160	Environmental degradation
363.47	HQ471	Pornography—Social aspects	363.7	GE140-160	Environmental indicators
			363.7	GE140-160	Environmental quality
363.5	HD7285-7391	Housing	363.7063	QH541.15.M64	Environmental monitoring
363.5	HD7287.8-.82	Home ownership	363.7064	GE45.S25	Environmental sampling
363.506	HD7287.8-.82	Homeowners' associations	363.7064	TA171	Environmental testing
363.5091724	HD7391	Housing—Developing countries	363.728	TD796.5	Compost
			363.7288	TS214	Scrap metals
363.5091732	HD7289.4-.42	Urban homesteading	363.7386	QC926.5-.57	Acid rain
363.5091734	HD7289	Housing, Rural	363.7392	QC882	Smaze
363.509(4-9)	HD7291-7391	Housing—[By region or country]	363.7392	QC882.4-.46	Aerosols
			363.7392	QC882.6	Smoke plumes
363.5094	HD7332-7357.7	Housing—Europe	363.7394	GC1080-1581	Marine pollution
363.50941	HD7333-7335.5	Housing—Great Britain			

Dewey	LC	Subject Heading	Dewey	LC	Subject Heading
363.7396	TD878-880	Soil pollution	364.098021	HV7330-7341	Criminal statistics—South America
363.75	HD9999(.U5-.U54)	Undertakers and undertaking	364.0994021	HV7389	Criminal statistics—Australia
363.75	RA622-623.6	Undertakers and undertaking	364.0995021	HV7368-7381	Criminal statistics—Asia
363.75	RA626-630	Cemeteries	364.1	HV6053	Crimes of passion
363.75	RA636-.7	Crematoriums	364.1	HV6275	Conspiracies
363.8	HC79.F3	Famines	364.1	HV6705-6738	Crimes without victims
363.8	HD9000-9019	Food supply	364.106	HV6437-6439	Gangs
363.8	HV630-635	Famines	364.106	HV6441-6453	Mafia
363.8	TX341-641	Nutrition	364.10660973	HV6448	Black Hand (United States)
363.8071	TX364-365	Nutrition—Study and teaching	364.130947	HV9715.15	Prisoners—Russia (Federation)
363.83	HV868	Milk programs	364.131	HV6254-6322.7	Political crimes and offenses
363.882	HV696.F6	Food stamps			
363.883	HV694	Diet kitchens	364.131	HV6275	Treason
363.883	HV696.F6	Food relief	364.131	HV6285	Sedition
363.9	HB883.5	Population policy	364.1323	HV6301-6321	Bribery
363.92	HQ750-755.5	Eugenics	364.132309(4-9)	HV6303-6321	Bribery—[By region or country]
363.96	HQ766.2-.4	Birth control—Moral and ethical aspects			
			364.13230973	HV6306-6316	Bribery—United States
363.96091724	HB884.5	Population assistance	364.133	HJ6619	Smugglers
364	HV	Criminology	364.1330973	HJ6690-6710	Smugglers—United States
364	HV6001-7220.5	Criminology	364.134	HV6326	Perjury
364	HV6001-7220.5	Crime	364.134	HV6455-6471	Lynching
364	HV8067	Vice control	364.1340973	JK1543	Contempt of court
364	P96.C74	Crime in mass media	t364.135	HV6252	Transnational crime
364.05	HV6001-6006	Criminology—Periodicals	364.13809041	D625-626	War crimes
364.071	HV6024	Criminology—Study and teaching	364.142	HV6419-6433	Offenses against public safety
364.072	HV6024.5	Criminology—Research	364.143	HV6474-6485	Riots
364.09	HV6021-6023	Criminology—History	364.143	HV6474-6485	Mobs
364.09(4-9)021	HV7245-7400	Criminal statistics—[By region or country]	364.143	HV6486-6491	Disorderly conduct
			364.147	HE5620.D65	Drugged driving
364.094021	HV7342-7367.7	Criminal statistics—Europe	364.147	HE5620.D7	Drunk driving
364.0941021	HV7343-7345.5	Criminal statistics—Great Britain	364.147	HV6422-6425	Traffic violations
			364.148	HV4480-4630.7	Vagrancy
364.0943021	HV7349-.5	Criminal statistics—Germany	364.15	HV6493-6633	Offenses against the person
			364.151	HV6322.7	Genocide
364.0944021	HV7348	Criminal statistics—France	364.1522	HV6543-6548	Suicide
364.0945021	HV7351	Criminal statistics—Italy	364.1522	HV6547	Mass suicide
364.0946021	HV7361	Criminal statistics—Spain	364.1523	HV6499-6542	Murder
364.0947021	HV7355	Criminal statistics—Russia	364.1523	HV6537-6541	Infanticide
364.0951021	HV7378	Criminal statistics—China	364.152309(4-9)	HV6518-6535	Murder—[By region or country]
364.0952021	HV7377	Criminal statistics—Japan			
364.0954021	HV7371	Criminal statistics—India	364.15230973	HV6518-6534	Murder—United States
364.096021	HV7382-7388.4	Criminal statistics—Africa	364.152309(4-9)	HV6535	Murder—[Other regions or countries]
364.0971021	HV7315	Criminal statistics—Canada			
364.0972021	HV7316	Criminal statistics—Mexico	364.1524	HV6278	Assassination
364.09728021	HV7317-7323	Criminal statistics—Central America	364.1524	HV6499-6535	Assassination
			364.153	HQ71-72	Sex offenders
364.09729021	HV7324-7329.9	Criminal statistics—West Indies	364.153	HQ71-72	Sex crimes
			364.153	HV6558-6569	Sex crimes
364.0973021	HV7245-7300	Criminal statistics—United States	364.153	HV6584-6589	Seduction
			364.1532	HV6558-6569	Gang rape

Dewey	LC	Subject Heading	Dewey	LC	Subject Heading
364.1532	HV6558-6569	Rape	364.3	HV6001-7220.5	Criminals
364.154	HV6571-6574	Abduction	364.309(4-9)	HV6774-7220.5	Criminals—[By region or country]
364.154	HV6595-6604	Kidnapping	364.30973	HV6774-6795	Criminals—United States
364.154092273	HV6432	Victims of terrorism—United States—Biography	364.309(4-9)	HV6801-7220.5	Criminals—[Other countries]
364.1552	HV6441-6453	Brigands and robbers	364.36	HV9051-9230.7	Juvenile delinquency
364.1552	HV6646-6665	Cattle stealing	364.36	HV9051-9230.7	Juvenile delinquents
364.1552	HV6646-6665	Mugging	364.36071	HV9068	Juvenile delinquency—Study and teaching
364.1555	HV6618	Assault and battery	364.3609(4-9)	HV9101-9230.7	Juvenile delinquency—[By region or country]
364.1555(3-4)	HV6626-.23	Family violence			
364.15553	HV6626-.23	Wife abuse	364.360973	HV9103-9106	Juvenile delinquency—United States
364.15554	HV6626.5-.54	Child abuse			
364.156	HV6631	Libel and slander	364.3609(4-9)	HV9107-9230.7	Juvenile delinquency—[Other countries]
364.16	HV6635-6700	Offenses against property			
364.162	HV6646-6665	Burglary	364.4	HV7431	Crime prevention
364.162	HV6653	Thieves	364.4	HV7936.C58	Crime stoppers programs
364.162	HV6675-6685	Embezzlement	364.6	HV7231-9960	Punishment
364.162	N8795	Art thieves	364.6	HV9051-9230.7	Social work with juvenile delinquents
364.163	CC140	Forgery of antiquities			
364.163	HV6675-6685	Forgery	364.601	HV9261-9430.7	Criminals—Rehabilitation
364.163	HV6691-6699	Fraud	364.63	HV9278	Parole
364.1630973	HV6679	Identification cards—Forgeries—United States	364.63	HV9278	Probation
			364.65	HV8692	Pardon
364.164	HV6640	Bombings	364.66	HV8551-8586	Executions and executioners
364.164	HV6666-6669	Vandalism			
364.164	HV6638-.5	Arson	364.66	HV8552-8555	Beheading
364.16409(4-9)	HV6638.5	Arson—[By region or country]	364.66	HV8555	Guillotine
			364.66	HV8569	Crucifixion
364.165	HV6688	Extortion	364.66	HV8579-8581	Hanging
364.168	HV6763-6771	Corporations—Corrupt practices	364.66	HV8696	Electrocution
			364.67	HQ770.4	Corporal punishment
364.168	HV6763-6771	Insurance crimes	364.67	HV8593-8599	Torture
364.168	HV6763-6771	Securities theft	364.67	HV8609	Branding (Punishment)
364.168	HV6763-6771	Securities fraud	364.67	HV8609-8621	Corporal punishment
364.168	HV6772-6773.3	Computer crimes	364.67	HV8613-8621	Flagellation
364.172	HV6708-6722	Gambling	364.68	HV9276.5	Alternatives to imprisonment
364.17206	HV6711	Casinos			
364.1791	HV6549-6555	Poisoning	364.68	HV9277	Fines (Penalties)
364.187	HV4749-4755	Horses	364.68	HV9277.5	Community service (Punishment)
364.2	HV6001-6197	Criminal anthropology			
364.2	HV6189	War and crime	365	HV8301-9960	Prisons
364.22	HV6177	Cities and towns	365	HV8705-8749	Imprisonment
364.24	HV6047	Criminal behavior—Genetic aspects	365	HV8708-8719	Prison sentences
			365.021	HV8482-8488	Prisons—Statistics
364.24	HV6121-6125	Heredity	365.068	HV8756-8763	Prison administration
364.24	HV6133	Insane, Criminal and dangerous	365.09	HV8497-8654	Prisons—History
			365.3	HV8647-8649	Galleys
364.24	HV6163	Crime and age	365.34	HV8748-8749	Workhouses
364.25	HV6166	Education and crime	365.34	HV8935-8962	Penal colonies
364.25	HV6166	Reading disability and crime	365.34	HV9051-9230.7	Reformatories
364.256	HV6174	Begging	365.34	HV9279	Community-based corrections
364.256	HV6441-6453	Vendetta			
364.3	HV6441-6453	Outlaws	365.34082	HV8738	Reformatories for women
364.3	HV6049	Recidivism			
364.3	HV6080-6113	Criminal psychology			

Dewey	LC	Subject Heading	Dewey	LC	Subject Heading
365.48	UB800-805	Military prisons	366.(1-5)03	HS121-123	Secret societies—Directories
365.48	VB890-895	Military prisons	366.(1-5)05	HS101-106	Secret societies—Periodicals
365.480973	UB803	Prisoners of war—United States	366.(1-5)06	HS110	Secret societies—Congresses
365.6	HV8884	Prison visits			
365.6	HV9025	Prison violence	366.(1-5)09	HS125-148	Secret societies—History
365.6	HV9051-9230.7	Status offenders	366.(1-5)09(4-9)	HS201-330.7	Secret societies—[By region or country]
365.64	HV8935-8962	Prisoners, Transportation of	366.(1-5)09(4-9)	HS207-330.7	Secret societies—[Other countries]
365.64	HV9025	Prison homicide			
365.641	HV8657-8658	Escapes	366.(1-5)0973	HS203-206	Secret societies—United States
365.643	HV8766-8778	Prison discipline			
365.65	HV8888-8931	Convict labor	366.1025	HS381-390	Freemasons—Directories
365.65	HV8888-8931	Prison industries	366.105	HS351-359	Freemasons—Periodicals
365.66	HV8833-8844	Prison physicians	366.108996073	HS875-895	Afro-American freemasonry
365.66	HV8833-8844	Prison nurses	366.109	HS403-420	Freemasons—History
365.7	HV8971-8978	Prison reformers	366.109(4-9)	HS501-680.7	Freemasons—[By region or country]
365.9(4-9)	HV9441-9649	Prisons—[By region or country]	366.10973	HS503-539	Freemasons—United States
365.94	HV9636-9775.7	Prisons—Europe	366.109(4-9)	HS557-680.7	Freemasons—[Other countries]
365.941	HV9641-9650	Prisons—Great Britain			
365.943	HV9671-9680.5	Prisons—Germany	366.12	HS455-459	Freemasonry—Rituals
365.9438	HV9715.7	Prisons—Social aspects—Poland	366.3	HS951-1179	Independent Order of Odd Fellows
365.944	HV9661-9670	Prisons—France	366.3	HS1019-1021	Independent Order of Odd Fellows—Rituals
365.945	HV9686-9695	Prisons—Italy			
365.946	HV9741-9745	Prisons—Spain	366.3025	HS963-975	Independent Order of Odd Fellows—Directories
365.947	HV9711-9715	Prisons—Russia			
365.9492	HV9696-9710.5	Prisons—Benelux countries	366.305	HS951-953	Independent Order of Odd Fellows—Periodicals
365.9495	HV9776-831	Prisons—Greece			
365.951	HV9816-9820	Prisons—China	366.309	HS987-991	Independent Order of Odd Fellows—History
365.952	HV9811-9815	Prisons—Japan			
365.954	HV9791-9795	Prisons—India	366.309(4-9)	HS1041-1051	Independent Order of Odd Fellows—[By region or country]
365.956	HV9776.5-9785.2	Prisons—Middle East			
365.9599	HV9806-9810	Prisons—Philippines	366.30973	HS1041-1045	Independent Order of Odd Fellows—United States
365.96	HV9836-9868.5	Prisons—Africa			
365.971	HV9501-9510	Prisons—Canada	366.46	U260	Unified operations (Military science)
365.972	HV9511-9515	Prisons—Mexico			
365.9728	HV9516-9550	Prisons—Central America	366.6027	HS159-160	Insignia
365.9729	HV9551-9575.95	Prisons—West Indies	367	HS2501-3371	Clubs
365.973	HV9456-9481	Prisons—United States	367.025	HS2507-2515	Clubs—Directories
365.98	HV9576-9635	Prisons—South America	367.05	HS2501-2503	Clubs—Periodicals
365.994	HV9871-9875	Prisons—Australia	367.082	HQ1871-2030.7	Women—Societies and clubs
366	HS	Societies			
366.0025	HS17	Societies—Directories	367.4	HS3250-3270	Youth—Societies and clubs
366.003	HS12	Societies—Encyclopedias	367.9(4-9)	HS2721-3200	Clubs—[By region or country]
366.005	HS1	Societies—Periodicals			
366.006	HS5	Societies—Congresses	367.973	HS2721-2725	Clubs—United States
366.009	HS25-35	Societies—History, organization, etc.	367.9(4-9)	HS2731-3200	Clubs—[Other regions or countries]
366.1	HS351-929	Freemasons	368	HG8011-9999	Insurance
366.1	HS351-929	Freemasonry	368	HG8054.5	Risk (Insurance)
366.(1-5)	GN495.2	Secret societies	368	HG8082	Self-insurance
366.(1-5)	HS101-330.7	Secret societies			
366.(1-5)	HS155-158	Secret societies—Rituals			

Dewey	LC	Subject Heading	Dewey	LC	Subject Heading
368	HG9997	Insurance, Surety and fidelity	368.5728	HG9970.A4-.A68	Insurance, No-fault automobile
368.0065	HG8075-8107	Insurance companies	368.852	HG9992	Mortgage guarantee insurance
368.092	HG9970	Insurance, Automobile			
368.093	HG9972	Insurance, Aviation	368.854	HG1662	Deposit insurance
368.094	HG8059	Insurance, Business	368.88	HG9999	Insurance, Title
368.096	HG9986	Homeowner's insurance	368.9(4-9)	HG8501-8745	Insurance—[By region or country]
368.11	HG9651-9899	Insurance, Fire			
368.110021	HG9663	Insurance, Fire—Statistics	368.973	HG8501-8540	Insurance—United States
368.11009	HG9660	Insurance, Fire—History	368.9(4-9)	HG8550-8740.5	Insurance—[Other regions or countries]
368.11009(4-9)	HG9751-9899	Insurance, Fire—[By region or country]			
			369	HS2301-2460.7	Patriotic societies
368.1100973	HG9751-9780	Insurance, Fire—United States	369.1	HS2321-2330	Patriotic societies—United States
368.11009(4-9)	HG9781-9866	Insurance, Fire—[Other countries]	369.42	HS3301-3325	Boys—Societies and clubs
			369.42	HV877-878	Boys
368.11014	HG9711-9715	Fire insurance claims adjusters	369.42	HV878	Boys—Societies and clubs
			369.43	HS3312-3316	Boy Scouts
368.121	HG9966-9969	Insurance, Agricultural	369.46	HV879-887	Girls
368.121	HG9968	Crop insurance	369.463	HS3353.G5	Girl Scouts
368.122	HG9979	Insurance, Disaster	369.463	HS3359	Daisy Girl Scouts
368.1222	HG9983	Insurance, Flood	370	L	Education
368.1226	HG9981	Insurance, Earthquake	370	LB	Education
368.22	HE961-971	Insurance, Marine	370	LC1035-.8	Basic education
368.23	HE961-971	Insurance, Marine	370	P96.E29	Education in mass media
368.23	HG9903-9905	Insurance, Inland marine	370.1	LB41	Education—Aims and objectives
368.3	HG8058	Insurance, Group			
368.32	HG8751-9271	Insurance, Life	370.1	LB125-875	Education—Philosophy
368.32	HG9271	Insurance, Child	370.111	LC213-.3	Compensatory education
368.3200151	HG8779-8793	Insurance, Life—Mathematics	370.111	LC5161-5163	Fundamental education
			370.112	LB41.5	Education—Forecasting
368.32009(4-9)	HG8941-9200.5	Insurance, Life—[By region or country]	370.112	LC1001-1024	Education, Humanistic
			370.11209024	LA106-108	Education, Humanistic
368.3201	HG8783-8785	Mortality—Tables	370.113	HD5715-.5	Occupational training
368.362	HG9251-9262	Industrial life insurance	370.113	LC1037-.8	Career education
368.366	HG9466-9479	Insurance, Burial	370.113	LC1041-1047	Vocational education
368.37	HG8790-8793	Annuities	370.113	LC1041-1047	Technical education
368.382	HD7105.2-.25	Insurance, Disability	370.113082	LC1500-1506	Women—Vocational education
368.382	HG9371-9399	Insurance, Health			
368.3827	HG9389	Insurance, Hospitalization	370.113087	LC4219.7	Physically handicapped children—Vocational education
368.384	HG9301-9343	Insurance, Accident			
368.4	HD7088-7250.7	Social security			
368.4	HG8205-8220	Insurance, Government	370.11308996 + 073	LC2780	Afro-Americans—Vocational education
368.4009	HD7121-7250.7	Social security—[By region or country]			
			370.114	LC251-301	Character
368.400973	HD7123-7126	Social security—United States	370.114	LC251-318	Moral education
			370.116	LB2283-2286	Educational exchanges
368.424	HG9291-9295	Insurance, Maternity	370.1163	LB2283-2285	Teacher exchange programs
368.5	HG9956-9969	Insurance, Casualty	370.117	LC201.5-.7	Native language and education
368.5	HG9990	Insurance, Liability			
368.562	HG9995	Insurance, Products liability	370.117	LC1099-.5	Multicultural education
368.564	HG8053.5 -8054.45	Insurance, Malpractice	370.1175	LC3701-3743	Education, Bilingual
			370.14	LB1033.5	Nonverbal communication in education
368.5642	HG8054	Insurance, Physicians' liability			
			370.15	LB1051-1091	Educational psychology

Dewey	LC	Subject Heading	Dewey	LC	Subject Heading
370.1522	LB1063-1064	Memory	370.9492	L441-446	Education—Netherlands
370.1528	LB1060.2	Behavior modification	370.9493	L431-436	Education—Belgium
370.157	LB1062	Creative thinking	370.9494	L531-536	Education—Switzerland
370.158	LB1139.S88	Student adjustment	370.9495	L411-416	Education—Greece
370.207	LA23	Humor in education	370.9497	L549-550	Education—Yugoslavia
370.21	LB2846	Educational statistics	370.9498	L545-546	Education—Romania
370.25	L900-991	Education—Directories	370.9499	L541-542	Education—Bulgaria
370.5	L7-101	Education—Periodicals	ht370.95	L561-642	Education—Asia
370.6	L106-107	Education—Congresses	370.951	L571-573	Education—China
370.71	LB2157	Student teachers	370.9519	L613-614	Education—Korea
370.711	LB1705-2286	Teachers—Training of	370.952	L611-612	Education—Japan
370.711	LB1731	Teachers—In-service training	370.954	L577-578	Education—India
			370.95491	L578.5-.6	Education—Pakistan
370.711	LB1762-1765	Examinations	370.955	L615-616	Education—Iran
370.711	LB1805-2151	Teachers colleges	370.9561	L539-540	Education—Turkey
370.72	LB1028-.25	Education—Research	370.9567	L627-628	Education—Iraq
370.72	LB1028.24	Action research in education	370.95694	L631-632	Education—Israel
			370.957	L617-620	Education—Siberia
370.723	LB2823	Educational surveys	370.959(4-7)	L585-586	Education—Indochina
370.74	L797-898	Education—Museums	370.9598	L597-598	Education—Indonesia
370.8968073	LC2667-2688	Hispanic Americans—Education	370.96	L651-742	Education—Africa
			370.971	L221-223	Education—Canada
370.9	LA	Education—History	370.972	L227-229	Education—Mexico
370.9(1-5)	LA190-2284	Education—History	370.9728	L231-249	Education—Central America
370.901	LA31-81	Education, Ancient	370.9729	L251-267	Education—West Indies
370.902	LA91-98	Education, Medieval	370.973	L111-219	Education—United States
370.91724	LC2601-2611	Education—Developing countries	370.97(4-9)	L116-219	Education—[United States, By state]
370.91732	LC5101-5143	Education, Urban	370.98	L291-335	Education—South America
370.91732	LC5101-5143	Urban schools	370.993	L754-755	Education—New Zealand
370.91734	LC5146-5148	Education, Rural	370.994	L750-792, 757-775	Education—Australia
370.92	LA2301-2397	Educators			
370.92	LA2301-2397	Teachers	370.99(5-6)	L777-791	Education—Oceania
370.92	LB51-875	Educators	371	L	Schools
370.932	LA37	Education, Egyptian	371	LB	Schools
370.938	LA75	Education, Greek	371.00973	LD	Schools—United States
370.938	LA77	Education, Minoan	371.01	LC	Public schools
370.9(4-9)	L111-791	Education—[By region or country]	371.02	LC47-57	Private schools
			371.04	LB1029.F7	Free schools
370.94	L341-551	Education—Europe	371.04	LC46-.8	Alternative schools
370.941	L341-359	Education—Great Britain	371.042	LC40	Home schooling
370.9415	L346-348	Education—Ireland	371.071	BV1580-1583	Week-day church schools
370.943	L401-410	Education—Germany	371.071	LC427-629	Church schools
370.9436	L361-366	Education—Austria	371.1	LB1025-1050.7	Teaching
370.9437	L385-387	Education—Czechoslovakia	371.1	LB1775-1785	Teaching
370.9439	L381-383	Education—Hungary	371.1	LB2832-2844.47	Teachers
370.944	L391-396	Education—France	371.100882971	LC905.T42	Muslim teachers
370.945	L421-426	Education—Italy	371.102	LB	Teaching
370.946	L511-516	Education—Spain	371.1023	LB1033	Teacher-student relationships
370.9469	L521-526	Education—Portugal			
370.947	L451-466	Education—Russia	371.1024	LB3013	Classroom management
370.9481	L491-496	Education—Norway	371.103	LC225.5	Parent-teacher conferences
370.9485	L501-506	Education—Sweden	371.104	LB2836	Teachers—Tenure
370.9489	L471-476	Education—Denmark			
370.94912	L481	Education—Iceland			

Dewey	LC	Subject Heading	Dewey	LC	Subject Heading
371.104	LB2843.L4	Teachers—Leaves of absence	371.2913	LC142-145	Dropouts
			371.2914	LB3064	Students, Transfer of
371.104	LC72-.5	Academic freedom	371.294	LB3081-3087	School attendance
371.104	LC72-.5	Teaching, Freedom of	371.294	LC142-148.5	School attendance
371.11	LB1755-1779	Teachers	371.3	LB1027	Educational innovations
371.12	LB1771-1773	Teachers—Certification	371.3	LB1027.25	Creative activities and seat work
371.14	LB2844.1	Teachers, Part-time			
371.1412	LB2844.1.W6	Teachers—Workload	371.3	LB1027.3	Education—Experimental methods
371.144	LB2844.1.P7	Teachers, Probationary			
371.148	LB1032	Team learning approach in education	371.3	LB1140.35.C74	Creative activities and seat work
371.19206	LC230-235	Parents' and teachers' associations	371.3	LB1537	Creative activities and seat work
371.2	LB2806.3	School management teams	371.30281	LB1048	Homework
371.2	LB3011-3095	School management and organization	371.32	LB3045-3048	Textbooks
			371.32	LB3045.6	Textbook bias
371.201	LB2831.5-2844.4	School personnel management	371.32	LT	Textbooks
			371.33	LB1028.4	Media programs (Education)
371.201	LB2831.5-.585	School employees			
371.2011	LB2831.7-.776	School superintendents	371.33	LB1043.6	Displays in education
371.2011	LB2831.8-.876	School administrators	371.3331	LB1044.5-.6	Radio in education
371.2012	LB2831.9-.976	School principals	371.334	LB1028.43	Education—Data processing
371.203	LB2806.4	School supervision			
371.206	LB2824-2830	Education—Finance	371.334	LB1028.5-.7	Computer-assisted instruction
371.206	LC241-245	Educational fund raising			
371.207	LC71.2	Educational planning	371.334	LB1028.5	Programmed instruction
371.219	LC130-139	School enrollment	371.334	LB1028.75	Interactive video
371.223	LB2848-2849	Scholarships	371.334	LB1029.A85	Teaching machines
371.22308996 + 073	LC2707	Afro-Americans—Scholarships, fellowships, etc.	371.335	LB1043-1044.9	Audio-visual education
			371.335	LB1043.5-1044	Visual aids
371.23	LB3034	School year	371.335	LB1043.5	Overhead projection
371.232	LC5701-5760	Summer schools	371.3352	LB1043.67	Pictures in education
371.25	LB3061.8	Track system (Education)	371.3352	LB1043.8	Filmstrips in education
371.251	LB3013.2	Class size	371.33523	LB1044.75	Video tapes in education
371.254	LB3061	Ability grouping in education	371.33523	LB1044.75	Video tapes
371.255	LB1029.N6	Nongraded schools	371.3358	LB1044.7	Television in education
371.256	LB1029.06	Open plan schools	371.337	LB1029.G3	Educational games
371.27	LB3060.57	Examinations—Study guides	371.337	LB1029.T6	Educational toys
			371.35	LC5800-5808	Distance education
371.27	LB3060.65	Examinations—Design and construction	371.36	LB1029.U6	Unit method of teaching
			371.37	LB1039	Recitation (Education)
371.27	LB3060.77	Examinations—Scoring	371.382	LB1029.L3	Dalton laboratory plan
371.271	LB3050-3060	Examinations	371.384	LB1047	School field trips
371.271	LB3051-3059	Examinations—Questions	371.384	LB1047	Outdoor education
371.271	LB3051-3060.87	Educational tests and measurements	371.39	LB1029.M7	Monitorial system of education
371.271	LB3060.3	Achievement tests	371.392	LB1029.M75	Montessori method of education
371.271	LB3060.32.D65	Domain-referenced tests			
371.271	LB3060.32.M85	Multiple-choice examinations	371.393	LB2806.2	Performance contracts in education
371.271	LB3060.32.N67	Norm-referenced tests	371.394	LC41	Tutors and tutoring
371.271	LB3060.32.035	Objective tests	371.3943	LB1049	Independent study
371.272	LB3051-3063	Grading and marking (Students)	371.396	LC6501-6560	Forums (Discussion and debate)
371.28	LC1049-.8	Educational acceleration			

Dewey	LC	Subject Heading	Dewey	LC	Subject Heading
371.397	LB1029.S5	Simulated environment (Teaching method)	371.9	LC3950-3990.4	Special education
			371.9	LC4704-4706	Learning disabilities
371.397	LB1029.S53	Education—Simulation methods	371.9	LC4818-.53	Learning disabled
			371.91	LC4001-4100	Handicapped children—Education
371.4	LB1027.5-.8	Educational counseling			
371.4	LB2341	Deans (Education)	371.91	LC4201-4580	Physically handicapped children—Education
371.4047	LB1027.5	Peer counseling of students			
371.46	LB3013.4	School social work	371.911	HV1618-1782	Blind—Education
371.46	LB3013.5	Visiting teachers	371.912	HV2417-2500	Deaf—Education
371.5	LB3011-3095	School discipline	371.9144	LB1050.5	Dyslexia
371.5	LB3025	Discipline of children	371.9144	LC4708-4710	Dyslexic children
371.543	LB3089-.4	Student suspension	371.92	LC4601-4700	Mentally handicapped children—Education
371.58	LB3249	School vandalism			
371.59	LB3092-3095	Student government	371.926	LC4661-4700.4	Slow learning children
371.6	LB3205-3295	School buildings	371.94	LC4165-4184	Mentally ill children—Education
371.6	LB3205-3325	School facilities			
371.61	LB3251	School grounds	371.9573	LC4604	Mentally handicapped children—Education (Secondary)
371.61	LB3253	Campus parking			
371.63	LB3261-3281	Schools—Furniture, equipment, etc.			
			372	LB1501-1547	Education, Primary
371.71	LB3401-3495	School hygiene	372	LB1555-1601	Education, Elementary
371.71	LB3401-3495	School health services	372.11	LB1537	Education, Primary—Activity programs
371.713	LB1027.55	School psychology			
371.716	LB3473-3479	School children—Food	372.11	LB1775.6	Early childhood educators
371.716	LB473-3479	School milk programs	372.11	LB1776	Elementary school teachers
371.716	LB3473-3479	School breakfast programs	372.12	LB2822.5	Elementary school administration
371.78	LB3013.3	School violence			
371.8	LB3602-3618	Students	372.12012	LB2831.9-.976	Elementary school principals
371.8	LB3604-3615	Hazing			
371.8	LB3604	Students—Language	372.12913	LC145.5-.8	Elementary school dropouts
371.8	LB3605	Student activities	372.182996073	LC2771	Afro-Americans—Education (Elementary)
371.8	LB3618	Class reunions			
371.81	LA186	Student movements	372.21	LB1139.2-.4	Early childhood education
371.822	LC1401-2571	Women—Education	372.21	LB1140-.5	Education, Preschool
371.82621	JC393	Education of princes	372.21	LB1775.5	Preschool teachers
371.82623	LC5001-5060	Working class—Education	372.218	LB1141-1499	Kindergarten
371.82655	LB3613.M3	Married students	372.4	LB1050	Reading
371.82694	LC4051-4100	Socially handicapped children—Education	372.4	LB1140.5.R4	Reading (Preschool)
			372.4	LB1181.2	Reading (Kindergarten)
371.826942	LC5144-.3	Homeless students	372.4	LB1525-.8	Reading (Primary)
371.82697	UB356-359	Veterans—Education	372.4	LB1525	Reading (Elementary)
371.8279	LC3991-4000	Gifted children	372.4	LB1573	Reading (Elementary)
371.829	LC3701-3740	Minorities—Education	372.40284	LB1050.37	Reading machines
371.829	LC3800-3806	Ethnic schools	372.414	LB1050.43	Reading readiness
371.82991497	LC3503-3520	Gypsies—Education	372.43	LB1050.5	Reading—Remedial teaching
371.82995	LC3001-3501	Asians—Education			
371.82996073	LC2699-2913	Blacks—Education	372.452	LB1573.5	Oral reading
371.82996073	LC2701-2853	Afro-Americans—Education	372.462	LB1573.37	Reading (Elementary)—Whole-word method
371.85	LJ	Greek letter societies			
371.871	LB3226-3228	Student housing	372.465	LB1573.3	Reading—Phonetic method
371.871	LB3226-3229	Dormitories	372.47	LB1050.45	Reading comprehension
371.872	LB2864	School children—Transportation	372.48	LB1050.46	Reading—Ability testing
			372.5	LB1595-1599	Manual training
371.897	LB3621	Student publications	372.6	LB1576	Language arts (Elementary)
371.897	TR818	School photography	372.632	LB1574	Spelling ability

Dewey	LC	Subject Heading	Dewey	LC	Subject Heading
372.634	LB1536	Penmanship	378.1	LB2801-2997	School management and organization
372.634	LB1590	Penmanship			
372.677	LB1042	Storytelling	378.104	LB2331.5	University cooperation
373.11	LB1777-.4	High school teachers	378.106	LB2335.95-2337	Educational fund raising
373.12012	LB2831.9-.976	High school principals	378.106	LB2336-2337	Endowments
373.1219	LC146	High school enrollment	378.106	LB2342	Universities and colleges—Finance
373.12913	LC146.5-.8	High school dropouts			
373.182996073	LC2779	Afro-Americans—Education (Secondary)	378.111	LB2341	College administrators
			378.12	LB1778	College teachers
373.222	LC58-.7	Preparatory schools	378.12	LB2331.7-.74	Universities and colleges—Faculty
373.236	LB1623	Middle schools			
373.236	LB1623	Junior high schools	378.1543	LB2328	Junior colleges
373.238	LB1603-1694	High schools	378.1543	LB2328	Community colleges
373.238	LB1627.7	High school equivalency certificates	378.15430973	LD6501	Junior colleges—United States
373.241	LB2818	Magnet schools	378.155	LB2371	Universities and colleges—Graduate work
373.242	LC1001-1021	Classical education			
373.246	TT161-170.7	Manual training	378.155	LB2372.E3	Education—Graduate work
373.73	LD7501	High schools—United States	378.161	LB2341	Student registration
			378.161	LB2351-2359	Universities and colleges—Admission
374	LC5451-5493	Aged—Education			
374	LC5201-6660	Adult education	378.1616	LB2351.5-.52	College applications
374	LC5201-6660	Continuing education	378.1617	LB2351-2360	Universities and colleges—Entrance requirements
374	LC5225.L42	Adult learning			
374.012	LB1029.R4	Remedial teaching			
374.1822	LC1660-1666	Adult education of women	378.1618	LB2359.5	College credits
374.8	LC5501-5560	Evening and continuation schools	378.1662	LB2353	Universities and colleges—Examinations
375	LB1570-1571	Education—Curricula	378.1662	LB2367	Universities and colleges—Examinations
302.2308996 + 073	P94.5.A37	Afro-Americans and mass media	378.170281	LB2395	Note-taking
302.2308996 + 073	P94.5.A37	Afro-Americans in mass media	378.175	LC6201-6401	University extension
			378.177	LB2393.5	Seminars
302.2308996 + 073	P94.5.A37	Afro-American mass media	378.1796	LB2393	Lecture method in teaching
			378.194	LB2343	Faculty advisors
378	LB2300-2411	Universities and colleges	378.19822	LC1551-1651	Women—Education (Higher)
378	LF	Universities and colleges—Europe	378.1982996073	LC2781	Afro-Americans—Education (Higher)
378.009	LA173-186	Education, Higher			
378.00902	LA177	Education, Medieval	378.199	LB2361-2365	Universities and colleges—Curricula
378.013	LC1051-1071	Professional education			
378.013076	LC1070-1071	Examinations	378.2	LB2381-2391	Degrees, Academic
378.01308996 + 073	L2785	Afro-Americans—Professional education	378.2	LB2383	Bachelor of arts degree
			378.2	LB2385	Master of arts degree
378.016	LB2375-2378	Student exchange programs	378.2	LB2386	Doctor of philosophy degree
378.016	LB2375-2378	Educational exchanges	378.241	LB2366-2367	Examinations
378.052	LB2328.4	Urban universities and colleges	378.242	LB2369	Dissertations, Academic
			378.28	LB2389	Academic costume
378.052	LB2329	Municipal universities and colleges	378.3	LB2337.2-2340.8	Student aid
			378.34	LB2338-2339	Scholarships
378.053	LB2329.5	State universities and colleges	378.362	LB2340-.4	Student loan funds
			378.38	LB2342-.2	College costs
378.071	LC427-629	Church colleges	378.5	LG21-320	Universities and colleges—Asia
378.07122	LC487	Catholic universities and colleges	378.56	LG331-370	Universities and colleges—Middle East

Dewey	LC	Subject Heading	Dewey	LC	Subject Heading
378.6	LG401-690	Universities and colleges—Africa	381.025	HF54	Commerce—Directories
378.7	LE3-5	Universities and colleges—Canada	381.03	HF1001-1002.5	Commerce—Encyclopedias
			381.05	HF1-53	Commerce—Periodicals
378.72	LE7-9	Universities and colleges—Mexico	381.06	HF294-343	Commercial associations
			381.06	HF294-343	Boards of trade
378.728	LE11-13	Universities and colleges—Central America	381.0609	HF351-499	Boards of trade—History
			381.09	HF1021-1027	Commercial geography
378.729	LE15-17	Universities and colleges—Caribbean Area	381.092	HF5439.25-.8	Sales executives
			381.092	HF5439.25-.8	Sales personnel
378.73	LD13-7251	Universities and colleges—United States	381.092	HF5441-5444	Traveling sales personnel
			381.092	HF5457-5459	Peddlers and peddling
378.8	LE21-78	Universities and colleges—South America	381.093944	HF370	Phoenicians
			381.094	HF3491-3750.7	Europe—Commerce
378.93	LG741-745	Universities and colleges—New Zealand	381.0941	HF3501-3530.5	Great Britain—Commerce
			381.0943	HF3561-3570.5	Germany—Commerce
378.94	LG715-720	Universities and colleges—Australia	381.0944	HF3551-3560	France—Commerce
			381.0945	HF3581-3590	Italy—Commerce
378.9(5-6)	LG961	Universities and colleges—Oceania	381.0946	HF3681-3690	Spain—Commerce
			381.0947	HF3621-3630	Russia—Commerce
379	LC71-188	Education and state	381.09492	HF3591-3620.5	Benelux countries—Commerce
379.111	LB1027.9	School choice			
379.121	LB2825-2826.6	Federal aid to education	381.09494	HF3701-3710	Switzerland—Commerce
379.123	LB2813	County school systems	381.09495	HF3750.5	Greece—Commerce
379.13	LB2824-2830	School bonds	381.0951	HF3831-3840	China—Commerce
379.130973	HG4951-4953	School bonds	381.0952	HF3821-3830	Japan—Commerce
379.152	LB2809	State departments of education	381.0954	HF3781-3790	India—Commerce
			381.0955	HF3770.2	Iran—Commerce
379.1531	LB2831	School boards	381.0956	HF3756-3770.2	Middle East—Commerce
379.1535	LB2817-.5	School districts	381.09567	HF3770	Iraq—Commerce
379.1535	LB2823.2	School closings	381.095694	HF3760	Israel—Commerce
379.1535	LB2832.2	Public school closings	381.0958	HF3770.22-.27	Asia, Central—Commerce
379.1535	LB2861	Schools—Centralization	381.09599	HF3811-3820	Philippines—Commerce
379.1535	LB2862	Schools—Decentralization	381.096	HF3871-3937	Africa—Commerce
379.156	LB3045.66	Sexism in textbooks	381.0971	HF3221-3230	Canada—Commerce
379.158	LB2806.22	Educational accountability	381.0972	HF3231-3240	Mexico—Commerce
379.158	LB2810-.5	Accreditation (Education)	381.09728	HF3241-3310	Central America—Commerce
379.158	LB2822.75	Educational evaluation			
379.23	LC129-139	Education, Compulsory	381.09729	HF3311-3369	West Indies—Commerce
379.24	LC149-160	Literacy	381.0973	HF3000-3163	United States—Commerce
379.26	LC212-.863	Discrimination in education	381.098	HF3371-3480	South America—Commerce
379.26	LC212.5-.73	Segregation in education	381.0994	HF3941-3950	Australia—Commerce
379.26	LC212.8-.83	Sex discrimination in education	381.1	HF5410-5417.5	Marketing
			381.1	HF5415.126	Direct marketing
379.26	LC213-.3	Educational equalization	381.1	HF5415.126	Database marketing
379.263	LC212.6-.63	De facto school segregation	381.1	HF5415.126	Multilevel marketing
379.263	LC214-.3	School integration	381.1	HF5415.6-.9	Physical distribution of goods
379.263	LC214.5-.53	Busing for school integration	381.1	HF5428-5429.6	Retail trade
379.28	LC107-120	Religion in the public schools	381.1	HF5438-5439	Selling
			381.1	HF5469.7-5481	Fairs
379.32	LB2828	State aid to private schools	381.1	HF5481	Fairs
381	HF	Commerce	381.1	HF5495	Stores or stock-room keeping
381	HF5416	Product coding			
381	HF5446-5456	Canvassing	381.1092	HD8039.M39	Clerks (Retail trade)
381	HF5484-5495	Warehouses			

Dewey	LC	Subject Heading	Dewey	LC	Subject Heading
381.11	HF5429.7-5430.6	Shopping centers	382	HF1371-1385	International trade
381.11	HF5429.7-5430.6	Shopping malls	382	HF1417.5	Foreign trade promotion
381.12	HF5468	Chain stores	382	HF4050	East-West trade
381.141	HF5460-5469.5	Department stores	382.17	HF1014	Balance of trade
381.142	HF5415.1265	Telemarketing	382.5	HF1419-1420	Imports
381.142	HF5465.5-5467	Mail-order business	382.6	HF1414.4-1417.3	Exports
381.147	HF5469.25-.55	Convenience stores	382.6	HF1425	Dumping (International trade)
381.149	HF5429.2-.215	Discount houses (Retail trade)	382.63	HF2701	Export subsidies
381.15	HF5429.2-.215	Outlet stores	382.64	HF1414.5-.55	Export controls
381.17	HF5476-5477	Auctions	382.7	HF1715-1718	Drawbacks
381.18	HF5469.7-5481	Markets	382.7	HF1701-2701	Tariff
381.192	HF5482.15	Flea markets	382.7	HF1721-1733	Tariff preferences
381.195	HF5482.3	Garage sales	382.709(4-9)	HF1745-2580.9	Tariff—[By region or country]
381.2	HF5419-5422	Wholesale trade			
381.2092	HF5419-5422	Brokers	382.70973	HF1750-1757	Tariff—United States
381.2092	HF5422	Commission merchants	382.709(4-9)	HF1761-2580.9	Tariff—[Other regions or countries]
381.3	HF1410-1411	Commercial policy			
381.3	HF5415	Rationing	382.9	HF1430	Nontariff trade barriers
381.3	HF5415.5	Consumer affairs departments	382.9	HF1721-1733	Reciprocity
			383.1	HE5999	Mail receiving and forwarding services
381.4	HF1040-1054	Primary commodities			
381.4	HF1040-1044	Commercial products	383.1	HE6000-7500	Postal service
381.41	HD9000-9019	Farm produce—Marketing	383.1	HE6149	Postal service—Unclaimed mail
381.41	S571-.5	Farm produce—Marketing			
381.41	S571.5	Roadside marketing	383.1	HE6182-6228	Postmarks
381.4131	HD9030-9049	Grain trade	383.1025	HE6031	Postal service—Directories
381.41331	HF2651.G8	Grain trade	383.1071	HE6036	Postal service—Study and teaching
381.41351	HD9070-9089	Cotton trade			
381.41351	HD9870-9889	Cotton trade	383.1202	HE6148	Franking privilege
381.41383	HD9210-9211	Spice trade	383.12020973	HE6448	Franking privilege—United States
381.415	HD9220-9235	Vegetable trade			
381.4159092	SB442.8-445	Florists	383.122	HE6184.P65	Postcards
381.4162	HD9433	Cattle trade	383.125	HE6171-6173	Parcel post
381.4167	SF434.5-435	Dog industry	383.1250973	HE6471-6473	Parcel post—United States
381.41670833	SF427.55	Dog grooming industry	383.143	HE6175-.5	Railway mail service
381.417	HD9275-9283.7	Dairy products—Marketing	383.1430973	HE6475-.3	Railway mail service—United States
381.417	SF261	Dairy products—Marketing			
381.422	HD9540-9559	Coal trade	383.144	HE6184.A35	Aerogrammes
381.424	HD9506-9624	Metal trade	383.144	HE6238	Air mail service
381.43	HF1051-1054	Raw materials	383.1450973	HE6455-6456	Rural free delivery—United States
381.44	HT975-1445	Slave-trade			
381.45002	Z278-550	Booksellers and bookselling	383.23	HE6125-6148	Postal rates
381.45004	HF5468.2	Computer stores	383.23	HE6182-6228	Postage stamps
381.45388342	HD9710-.37	Automobiles—Marketing	383.49	HE6041-6055	Postal service—History
381.45388342	HF5439.A8	Selling—Automobiles	383.492	HE6061	Postal service—Biography
381.45391	HD9940-9949.5	Fashion merchandising	383.49(4-9)	HE6300-7496	Postal service—[By region or country]
381.456151	HF5439.D75	Selling—Drugs			
381.456213121	HD9697	Electric industries	383.4973	HE6300-6500	Postal service—United States
381.457(3-6)	N8610-8660	Art dealers			
381.45769	NE62	Prints—Marketing	383.49(4-9)	HE6651-7496	Postal service—[Other countries]
381.45808	PN161	Authorship—Marketing			
381.45808	PN161	Queries (Authorship)	384	HE9723-9737	Signals and signaling
381.7021	HF1016-1017	Commercial statistics	384.1	TK5601-5681	Cables, Submarine
			384.1	HE7709-7741	Cables, Submarine

Dewey	LC	Subject Heading	Dewey	LC	Subject Heading
384.1	HE7601-8635	Telegraph	385.09438	HE3060.5	Railroads—Poland
384.1025	HE7621	Telegraph—Directories	385.09439	HE3059.5	Railroads—Hungary
384.106	HE7603	Telegraph—Societies, etc.	385.0944	HE3061-3070	Railroads—France
384.109(4-9)	HE7761-8630.7	Telegraph—[By region or country]	385.0945	HE3091-3100	Railroads—Italy
			385.0946	HE3191-3200	Railroads—Spain
384.10973	HE7761-7798	Telegraph—United States	385.09469	HE3201-3210	Railroads—Portugal
384.13	HE7681-7691	Telegraph—Rates	385.0947	HE3131-3140.2	Railroads—Russia
384.14	HE7669-7679	Cipher and telegraph codes	385.09481	HE3171-3180	Railroads—Norway
384.15	TK5301-5481	Telegraph lines	385.09485	HE3181-3190	Railroads—Sweden
384.34	HE7551	Electronic mail systems	385.09489	HE3151-3160	Railroads—Denmark
384.51	HE9719-9721	Artificial satellites	385.094912	HE3161-3170	Railroads—Iceland
384.52	HE8660-8688	Telegraph, Wireless	385.09492	HE3121-3130	Railroads—Netherlands
384.53	HE9713-9715	Cellular radio	385.09493	HE3111-3120	Railroads—Belgium
384.54	HE8689.7.F34	Fairness doctrine (Broadcasting)	385.09494	HE3211-3220	Railroads—Switzerland
			385.09497	HE3241-3245	Railroads—Yugoslavia
384.54	HE8690-8699	Radio broadcasting	385.09498	HE3251-3260	Railroads—Romania
384.54	HE8697.P57	Pirate radio broadcasting	385.09499	HE3231-3240	Railroads—Bulgaria
384.54	PN1990-1992.92	Broadcasting	385.0951	HE3281-3290	Railroads—China
384.54089	PN1991.8.E84	Ethnic radio broadcasting	385.09519	HE3360.5	Railroads—Korea
384.55	HE8700-.95	Television broadcasting	385.0952	HE3351-3360	Railroads—Japan
384.55	HE8700.7-.72	Low power television	385.09538	HE3380.3	Railroads—Saudi Arabia
384.552	TK6677	Direct broadcast satellite television	385.0954	HE3291-3300	Railroads—India
			385.095491	HE3300.5	Railroads—Pakistan
384.5532	HE8700.65-.66	Television programs—Rating	385.095492	HE3300.6	Railroads—Bangladesh
			385.095493	HE3300.3	Railroads—Sri Lanka
384.5532	PN1992-.92	Television programs	385.09594	HE3320.4	Railroads—Laos
384.555	HE8700.7-.72	Satellite master antenna television	385.09595	HE3321-3330	Railroads—Malaysia
			385.09597	HE3320.3	Railroads—Vietnam
384.556	TK6680	Closed-circuit television	385.09598	HE3331-3340	Railroads—Indonesia
384.558	TK6685	Videodisc players	385.09599	HE3341-3350	Railroads—Philippines
384.558	TR882.3	Camcorders	385.09611	HE3413	Railroads—Tunisia
384.6	HE8701-9685	Telephone companies	385.09612	HE3414	Railroads—Libya
384.6	HE8701-9685	Telephone	385.0962	HE3401-3410	Railroads—Egypt
384.609(4-9)	HE8801-9685	Telephone companies—[By region or country]	385.09624	HE3415	Railroads—Sudan
			385.0963	HE3416	Railroads—Ethiopia
384.60973	HE8801-8846	Telephone companies—United States	385.0964	HE3411	Railroads—Morocco
			385.09648	HE3458.2	Railroads—Western Sahara
384.609(4-9)	HE8861-9685	Telephone companies—[Other countries]	385.0965	HE3412	Railroads—Algeria
			385.09661	HE3452	Railroads—Mauritania
385	HE1001-5600	Railroads	385.096623	HE3449	Railroads—Mali
385.021	HE2271-2273	Railroads—Statistics	385.096625	HE3450	Railroads—Burkina Faso
385.025	HE1009	Railroads—Directories	385.096626	HE3446	Railroads—Niger
385.05	HE1001	Railroads—Periodicals	385.09663	HE3451	Railroads—Senegal
385.06	HE1003	Railroads—Societies, etc.	385.09664	HE3455	Railroads—Sierra Leone
385.068	HE1621-1813	Railroads—Management	385.096651	HE3456	Railroads—Gambia
385.09	HE1021	Railroads—History	385.096652	HE3448	Railroads—Guinea
385.092	HD8039.R1-.R45	Railroads—Employees	385.096657	HE3458	Railroads—Guinea-Bissau
385.092	HE1811	Railroad conductors	385.096662	HE3457	Railroads—Liberia
385.09(4-9)	HE2701-3560	Railroads—[By region or country]	385.096668	HE3447	Railroads—Cote d'Ivoire
385.0941	HE3011-3040	Railroads—Great Britain	385.09667	HE3454	Railroads—Ghana
385.09415	HE3041-3050	Railroads—Ireland	385.096681	HE3445	Railroads—Togo
385.0943	HE3071-3080.5	Railroads—Germany	385.096683	HE3444	Railroads—Benin
385.09436	HE3051-3059.2	Railroads—Austria	385.09669	HE3453	Railroads—Nigeria
385.09437	HE3059.3	Railroads—Czechoslovakia	385.096711	HE3442	Railroads—Cameroon

Dewey	LC	Subject Heading	Dewey	LC	Subject Heading
385.096715	HE3436	Railroads—Sao Tome and Principe	385.0994	HE3461-3550	Railroads—Australia
			385.1	HE2231-2261	Railroads—Finance
385.096718	HE3435	Railroads—Equatorial Guinea	385.2	HE1821-2591	Railroads—Traffic
			385.22	HE1826	Demurrage (Car service)
385.096721	HE3438	Railroads—Gabon	385.22	HE1951-2100	Railroads—Fares
385.096724	HE3439	Railroads—Congo (Brazzaville)	385.22	HE2556	Railroads—Baggage handling
385.09673	HE3433	Railroads—Angola	385.22	HE2561-2591	Railroads—Passenger traffic
385.096743	HE3441	Railroads—Chad	385.22	TF653	Railroads—Passenger traffic
385.096751	HE3434	Railroads—Zaire	385.24	TF970	Electric railroads—Freight
385.0967571	HE3421	Railroads—Rwanda	385.24	HE2301-2547	Freight and freightage
385.0967572	HE3422	Railroads—Burundi	385.24	HE2301-2547	Railroads—Freight
385.096761	HE3420	Railroads—Uganda	385.24	HE2321.E8	Explosives—Transportation
385.096762	HE3419	Railroads—Kenya	385.24	HE2321.L7	Railroads—Livestock transportation
385.096773	HE3417	Railroads—Somalia			
385.09678	HE3423	Railroads—Tanzania	385.24	HE2321.L7	Cattle—Transportation
385.09679	HE3424	Railroads—Mozambique	385.312	HE1617-1618	Railroads—Crossings
385.0968	HE3426	Railroads—South Africa	385.314	HE1613-1614	Railroad stations
385.096881	HE3432.3	Railroads—Namibia	385.37	HE1830	Railroads—Cars
385.096883	HE3431	Railroads—Botswana	385.4183	UG1240	Stealth aircraft
385.096885	HE3429	Railroads—Lesotho	385.52	TF675	Railroads, Narrow-gage
385.096887	HE3430	Railroads—Swaziland	385.54	TF677	Railroads, Industrial
385.096894	HE3428	Railroads—Zambia	385.6	HE4051-4071	Mountain railroads
385.096897	HE3432	Railroads—Malawi	386	HE380.8-560	Waterways
385.09691	HE3425	Railroads—Madagascar	386.0971	HE399-401.25	Waterways—Canada
385.0971	HE2801-2810	Railroads—Canada	386.0973	HE392.8-398	Waterways—United States
385.0972	HE2811-2820	Railroads—Mexico	386.098	HE401.5-402	Waterways—Latin America
385.097281	HE2836-2840	Railroads—Guatemala	386.09(4-9)	HE403.5-520.9	Waterways—[Other countries]
385.097282	HE2825.5	Railroads—Belize			
385.097283	HE2841-2845	Railroads—Honduras	386.229	GN440.2	Outrigger canoes
385.097284	HE2851-2855	Railroads—El Salvador	386.229	GN440.2	Dugout canoes
385.097285	HE2846-2850	Railroads—Nicaragua	386.229	GN440.2	Canoes and canoeing
385.097286	HE2831-2835	Railroads—Costa Rica	386.4	HE526	Canals
385.09729	HE2856-2889	Railroads—West Indies	386.42	HE528-545	Canals, Interoceanic
385.0973	HE2704-2791	Railroads—United States	386.6	HE5751-5870	Ferries
385.0979	HE1062	Pacific railroads	387.1	SH337.5	Fishing ports
385.0979	HE2763	Pacific railroads—Early projects	387.1	HE550-560	Harbors
			387.1	TC203-327	Harbors
385.0979	HE2763	Pacific railroads	387.1	VK321-369.8	Harbors
385.098	HE2891-3000	Railroads—South America	387.1	VK369-.8	Harbors of refuge
385.0981	HE2921-2930	Railroads—Brazil	387.12	VK321	Roadsteads
385.0982	HE2901-2910	Railroads—Argentina	387.13	HF1418-.5	Free ports and zones
385.0983	HE2931-2940	Railroads—Chile	387.15	HE550-560	Docks
385.0984	HE2911-2920	Railroads—Bolivia	387.15	HE951-953	Docks
385.0985	HE2971-2980	Railroads—Peru	387.15	VK361-365	Docks
385.09861	HE2941-2950	Railroads—Colombia	387.15	VK369-.8	Marinas
385.09866	HE2951-2960	Railroads—Ecuador	387.155	VK381-397	Aids to navigation
385.0987	HE2991-3000	Railroads—Venezuela	387.155	VK1000-1249	Aids to navigation
385.09881	HE2962	Railroads—Guyana	387.2	GN440.1	Ships
385.09882	HE2964	Railroads—French Guiana	387.2	HE565	Tonnage
385.09883	HE2963	Railroads—Surinam	387.20216	HE565-566	Ship registers
385.09892	HE2966-2970	Railroads—Paraguay	387.2044	HE566.P3	Paddle steamers
385.09895	HE2981-2990	Railroads—Uruguay	387.2044	HE599-601	Steamboats—Passenger accommodation
385.0993	HE3550.5	Railroads—New Zealand			

Dewey	LC	Subject Heading	Dewey	LC	Subject Heading
387.2044	HE945	Steamboat lines	387.55	HE971	Salvage
387.2045	GC67	Oceanographic submersibles	387.7	HE9761-9900	Aeronautics, Commercial
			387.7	HE9761-9990	Airlines
387.245	VK235-237	Ships—Cargo	387.7	HE9785	Local service airlines
387.245	HE566.T3	Tankers	387.7	HE9795-9796	Airplanes, Company
387.29	VK1473	Life-boats	387.705	HE9761-.9	Aeronautics, Commercial—Periodicals
387.5	HE561-971	Shipping			
387.5	VK	Merchant marine	387.709	HE9774-9775	Aeronautics, Commercial—History
387.5	HE730-943	Merchant marine			
387.5023	VK160	Merchant marine—Vocational guidance	387.709(4-9)	HE9801-9900	Aeronautics, Commercial—[By region or country]
387.505	VK1-4	Merchant marine—Periodicals	387.7094	HE9842-9867.7	Aeronautics, Commercial—Europe
387.505	HE561	Shipping—Periodicals	387.70941	HE9843-9845.5	Aeronautics, Commercial—Great Britain
387.506	VK5	Merchant marine—Congresses	387.70943	HE9849-.5	Aeronautics, Commercial—Germany
387.506	HE562	Shipping—Congresses			
387.506	HE564	Shipping—Societies, etc.	387.70944	HE9848	Aeronautics, Commercial—France
387.50681	HE740-743	Shipping bounties and subsidies	387.70945	HE9851	Aeronautics, Commercial—Italy
387.509	VK15-20	Merchant marine—History			
387.5091724	HE943	Merchant marine—Developing countries	387.70946	HE9861	Aeronautics, Commercial—Spain
387.5092	HD8039.L8	Stevedores	387.70947	HE9855	Aeronautics, Commercial—Russia
387.5092	HD8039.S4	Sailors			
387.5092	VK205	Ship captains	387.709494	HE9863	Aeronautics, Commercial—Switzerland
387.5092	VK139-140	Merchant mariners—Biography	387.709495	HE9867.5	Aeronautics, Commercial—Greece
387.5092	VK221	Merchant marine—Officers			
387.509(4-9)	HE745-943	Merchant marine—[By region or country]	387.7095	HE9869.22-.27	Aeronautics, Commercial—Asia
387.509(4-9)	VK21-124	Merchant marine—[By region or country]	387.70951	HE9878	Aeronautics, Commercial—China
387.50973	HE745-767	Merchant marine—United States	387.70952	HE9877	Aeronautics, Commercial—Japan
387.50973	VK23-25	Merchant marine—United States	387.70954	HE9871	Aeronautics, Commercial—India
387.509(4-9)	HE769-937	Merchant marine—[Other countries]	387.70955	HE9869.2	Aeronautics, Commercial—Iran
387.52	VK570	Optimum ship routing	387.70956	HE9868.2-.95	Aeronautics, Commercial—Middle East
387.52	VK571	Great circle sailing			
387.524	HE730-943	Coastwise shipping	387.709567	HE9869	Aeronautics, Commercial—Iraq
387.54	VK381-397	Merchant marine—Signaling	387.7095694	HE9868.45	Aeronautics, Commercial—Israel
387.54	HE594	Shipping—Rates	387.709599	HE9876	Aeronautics, Commercial—Philippines
387.54	HE603-605	Shipping—Finance			
387.54044	VK149	Seafaring life	387.7096	HE9882-9888.4	Aeronautics, Commercial—Africa
387.54044	VK361-365	Mooring of ships	387.70971	HE9815	Aeronautics, Commercial—Canada
387.54044	VK361	Coaling			
387.544	VK235	Cargo handling	387.70972	HE9816	Aeronautics, Commercial—Mexico
387.544	VK235	Stowage			
387.544	VK237	Load-line	387.709728	HE9817-9823	Aeronautics, Commercial—Central America
387.544	HE593-597	Freight and freightage			
387.5442	HE566.R64	Roll-on/roll-off ships	387.709729	HE9824-9829.9	Aeronautics, Commercial—West Indies
387.5448	HE595.L7	Cattle—Transportation			
387.55	VK1491	Salvage			

Dewey	LC	Subject Heading	Dewey	LC	Subject Heading
387.70973	HE9803-9814	Aeronautics, Commercial—United States	388.341	HD9709.5	Wagons
387.7098	HE9830-9841	Aeronautics, Commercial—South America	388.341	SF304.5-307	Driving of horse-drawn vehicles
387.70994	HE9889	Aeronautics, Commercial—Australia	388.341	SF304.5-307	Coaching
387.712	HE9783-.75	Airlines—Rates	388.34232	HE5601-5725	Taxicabs
387.72	TL725-733	Airways	388.3472	HE5736-5739	Bicycles
387.736	HE9797-.5	Airports	388.4	HE305-311	Urban transportation
387.7364	HE9797.4.S56	Airport slot allocation	388.4	TA1205-1207	Urban transportation
387.742	HE9787-.5	Aeronautics, Commercial—Passenger traffic	388.411	HE331-380	Streets
			388.413212	HE5620.C3	Car pools
387.744	TL720.7	Aeronautics, Commercial—Freight	388.413212	HE5620.R53	Ridesharing
			388.413214	HE5601-5725	Cab and omnibus service
388	HE	Transportation	388.42	HE3601-4043	Railroads, Local and light
388.01	HE147.5-149	Transportation—Theory	388.42	HE5351-5600	Electric railroads
388.021	HE191.4-.5	Transportation—Statistics	388.4205	HE3601	Railroads, Local and light—Periodicals
388.042	HE1831-2220	Transportation—Rates			
388.044	HE199-.5	Freight and freightage	388.4209(4-9)	HE3651-4043	Railroads, Local and light—[By region or country]
388.044	HE5880-5990	Express service			
388.04409(4-9)	HE5893-5990	Express service—[By region or country]	388.44	HE4201-5300	Railroads, Elevated
			388.4409(4-9)	HE4401-5260	Railroads, Elevated—[By region or country]
388.0440973	HE5893-5904.5	Express service—United States			
			388.440973	HE4401-4491	Railroads, Elevated—United States
388.04409(4-9)	HE5905-5990	Express service—[Other countries]			
			388.4409(4-9)	HE4500-5260	Railroads, Elevated—[Other countries]
388.049	HE195.4-.5	Transportation—Rates	388.46	HE4341-4345	Street-railroads—Fares
388.05	HE1-8	Transportation—Periodicals	388.46	HE4351	Street-railroads—Finance
388.06	HE11	Transportation—Congresses	388.47	TA1225	Terminals (Transportation)
388.071	HE191.9-192	Transportation—Study and teaching	388.57	TJ898.5	Coal slurry pipelines
			390	GN494	Taboo
388.09	HE159-181	Transportation—History	390	GT	Manners and customs
388.092	HE151.4-.5	Transportation—Biography	390.082	GT2520-2540	Women
388.1	HE331-380	Roads	390.08342	GT2540	Girls
388.1	HE336.R68	Route choice	390.089 + (96073)	E185.86	Afro-Americans—Social life and customs
388.10937	DG28-29	Roads, Roman			
388.12	HE336.B8	Bus lanes	390.08997	E98.S7	Indians of North America—Social life and customs
388.12	HE336.B8	High occupancy vehicle lanes			
			390.09143	GT3490	Mountain life
388.12091734	HE336.R85	Rural roads	390.091734	GT3470	Country life
388.122	HE336.E94	Beltways	390.0952	GT3412	Geishas
388.122	HE336.E94	Express highways	390.23	GT3510-3530	Courts and courtiers
388.122	HE336.T64	Toll roads	390.23	GT5010-5090	Nobility—Social life and customs
388.132	HE374-377	Bridges			
388.228	HE5746-5749	Coaching	390.23	GT5350-5490	Nobility—Social life and customs
388.310723	HE369-373	Traffic surveys			
388.312	HE369-373	Traffic regulations	390.24	GT5650-5680	Peasantry—Social life and customs
388.314	HE336.C64	Traffic congestion			
388.314	HE336.H48	Highway capacity	390.406927	GT6550-6710	Criminals
388.322	HE5601-5725	Bus lines	390.463	GT5810-5856.995	Harvesting
388.324	HE5601-5725	Trucking	390.463	S521	Farm life
388.32409(4-9)	HE5623-5725	Trucking—[By region or country]	390.478	GT3650	Minstrels
			390.478	GT3650	Troubadours
388.33	HE5620.B87	Bus stops	391	GN418-419	Clothing and dress
388.34	TL235.6-.7	All terrain vehicles	391	GT49	Beauty, Personal

Dewey	LC	Subject Heading	Dewey	LC	Subject Heading
391	GT500-2350	Clothing and dress	391.5	GT2320	Beard
391	GT500-2370	Fashion	391.63	GT2340-2341	Cosmetics
391	GT500-2370	Costume	391.63	GT2340	Perfumes
391	GT525	Clothing and dress—Social aspects	391.65	GN419.15	Body marking
			391.65	GN419.2	Mutilation
391	GT529	Cold weather clothing	391.7	GN419.25	Body piercing
391	GT1747-1748	Disguise	391.7	GT2250-2281	Jewelry
391.0088296	GT540	Costume, Jewish	391.7	GT2250-2280	Gems
391.0090(1-5)	GT530-596	Costume—History	391.7	GT2260	Necklaces
391.00901	GT530-560	Costume—History—To 500	391.7	GT2265	Earrings
391.00902	GT575	Costume—History—Medieval, 500-1500	391.7	GT2270	Rings
			392	GT2420	Family
391.009031	GT585	Costume—History—16th century	392	GT3000.3-.5	Sleeping customs
			392	GT3005.3-.4	Sitting customs
391.009032	GT585	Costume—History—17th century	392.1	GN484	Circumcision
			392.12	GN482.1	Birth customs
391.009033	GT585	Costume—History—18th century	392.12	GT2460-2465	Birth customs
			392.3	GT2420	Home
391.009(4-9)	GT601-1605	Costume—[By region or country]	392.3	GT5870-5899	Domestication
			392.36	GR490-497	Dwellings
391.0094	GT720-1330	Costume—Europe	392.36	GT165-476	Dwellings
391.0095	GT1370-1570	Costume—Asia	392.36	GT170	Dwellings—Social aspects
391.00952	GT1560	Kimonos	392.36	GT420-425	Heating
391.0096	GT1580-1589	Costume—Africa	392.36	GT440-445	Lighting
391.0097	GT603-648	Costume—North America	392.36	GT445	Lanterns
391.0098	GT675-716	Costume—South America	392.36	GT445	Lamps
391.00993	GT1590-1593	Costume—Australia	392.36	GT450	Furniture
391.00994	GT1595	Costume—New Zealand	392.36	GT472	Sanitation, Household
391.00996	GT1597-1599	Costume—Oceania	392.36	GT476	Toilets
391.024	GT1850	Peasantry	392.3609(4-9)	GT201-384	Dwellings—[By region or country]
391.04204	BV167	Church vestments			
391.04282	BX1925	Church vestments	392.360941	GT285-294	Dwellings—Great Britain
391.04282	BX2790	Church vestments	392.3609415	GT294.5-.6	Dwellings—Ireland
391.04283	BX5180	Church vestments	392.360943	GT298.9-300.5	Dwellings—Germany
391.08997	E59.C6	Indians—Costume	392.3609436	GT295-296	Dwellings—Austria
391.412	GT2170	Gloves	392.3609439	GT296.5-.6	Dwellings—Hungary
391.412	GT2190	Muffs	392.360944	GT297-298	Dwellings—France
391.413	GT2128	Hosiery	392.360945	GT303-304	Dwellings—Italy
391.413008997	E98.C8	Moccasins	392.360946	GT323-324	Dwellings—Spain
391.42	GT2073	Underwear	392.3609469	GT325-326	Dwellings—Portugal
391.42	GT2075	Crinolines	392.360947	GT311-312	Dwellings—Russia
391.42	GT2075	Corsets	392.3609481	GT319-320	Dwellings—Norway
391.43	GT2110	Head-gear	392.3609485	GT321-322	Dwellings—Sweden
391.43	GT2110	Hats	392.3609489	GT315-316	Dwellings—Denmark
391.43	GT2112	Veils	392.36094912	GT317-318	Dwellings—Iceland
391.434	GN419.5	Masks	392.3609492	GT307-308	Dwellings—Netherlands
391.434	GT1747-1748	Masks	392.3609494	GT327-328	Dwellings—Switzerland
391.44	GT2120	Neckties	392.3609495	GT301-302	Dwellings—Greece
391.44	GT2150	Fans	392.3609496	GT331-341	Dwellings—Balkan Peninsula
391.44	GT2210	Umbrellas and parasols			
391.44	GT2220	Staffs (Sticks, canes, etc.)	392.36095	GT343-372	Dwellings—Asia
391.44	GT2280	Pins and needles	392.36095	GT349-350	Dwellings—Asia
391.44	GT2370	Eyeglasses	392.360951	GT365-366	Dwellings—China
391.5	GT2310	Wigs	392.3609519	GT369-370	Dwellings—Korea
391.5	GT2318	Mustache			

Dewey	LC	Subject Heading	Dewey	LC	Subject Heading
392.360952	GT367-368	Dwellings—Japan	392.5	HQ745	Marriage service
392.360954	GT351-352	Dwellings—India	392.50882971	GT2695.M8	Marriage customs and rites, Islamic
392.36095493	GT352.5-.6	Dwellings—Sri Lanka			
392.360955	GT347-348	Dwellings—Iran	392.50902	GT2680	Marriage customs and rites, Medieval
392.3609561	GT345-346	Dwellings—Turkey			
392.3609567	GT346.5-.6	Dwellings—Iraq	392.509(4-9)	GT2701-2796	Marriage customs and rites—[By country]
392.36095691	GT344-.2	Dwellings—Syria			
392.3609593	GT355-356	Dwellings—Thailand	392.6	GN484.3	Sex customs
392.3609595	GT357-358	Dwellings—Malaysia	393	GN486	Funeral rites and ceremonies
392.3609598	GT359-360	Dwellings—Indonesia			
392.3609599	GT361-362	Dwellings—Philippines	393	GR455	Dead
392.36096	GT373-377	Dwellings—Africa	393	GR455	Death
392.360962	GT375-376	Dwellings—Egypt	393	GT3150-3390.5	Death
392.360971	GT228-229	Dwellings—Canada	393	GT3150-3390.5	Funeral rites and ceremonies
392.360972	GT231-232	Dwellings—Mexico			
392.36097281	GT239-240	Dwellings—Guatemala	393	GT3150-3390	Dead
392.36097282	GT235-236	Dwellings—Belize	393	GT3353	Body snatching
392.36097283	GT241-242	Dwellings—Honduras	393.0901	GT3170	Funeral rites and ceremonies, Ancient
392.36097284	GT246-.5	Dwellings—El Salvador			
392.36097285	GT243-244	Dwellings—Nicaragua	393.1	GN486	Burial
392.36097286	GT237-238	Dwellings—Costa Rica	393.1	GT3150-3390.5	Burial
392.36097287	GT245-.5	Dwellings—Panama	393.1	GT3320	Cemeteries
392.36097291	GT251-252	Dwellings—Cuba	393.1	GT3380	Ship burial
392.36097292	GT255-256	Dwellings—Jamaica	393.2	GT3330	Cremation
392.36097294	GT253-254	Dwellings—Haiti	393.3	GT3340	Embalming
392.36097295	GT257-.5	Dwellings—Puerto Rico	393.4	GT3350	Scaffold burial
392.36097296	GT249-250	Dwellings—Bahamas	393.9	GT3370	Sati
392.360973	GT205-227	Dwellings—United States	393.9	GT3370	Widow suicide
392.360981	GT265-266	Dwellings—Brazil	394	GT2640	Kissing
392.360982	GT261-262	Dwellings—Argentina	394	GT3050	Salutations
392.360983	GT267-268	Dwellings—Chile	394	GT3050	Gifts
392.360984	GT263-264	Dwellings—Bolivia	394	GT3080	Swearing
392.360985	GT277-278	Dwellings—Peru	394	GT3085	Oaths
392.3609861	GT269-270	Dwellings—Colombia	394.1	GT2850-2960	Food habits
392.3609866	GT271-272	Dwellings—Ecuador	394.1	GT2850-2930	Drinking customs
392.360987	GT281-282	Dwellings—Venezuela	394.12	GT2865-2866	Food of animal origin
392.3609892	GT275-276	Dwellings—Paraguay	394.12	GT2870	Condiments
392.3609895	GT279-280	Dwellings—Uruguay	394.12	GT2870	Salt
392.360993	GT381-382	Dwellings—New Zealand	394.12	GT2870	Spices
392.360994	GT379-380	Dwellings—Australia	394.12	GT2905-2916	Tea
392.36099(5-6)	GT383-384	Dwellings—Oceania	394.12	GT2918	Coffee
392.4	B105.E5	Engagement (Philosophy)	394.12	GT2940-2947	Drinking cups
392.4	GN480.1	Bridal price	394.12	GT2952	Toothpicks
392.4	GN484.43	Betrothal	394.12	GT2995	Lying down position
392.4	GT2600-2640	Love	394.120952	GT2910-2916	Japanese tea ceremony
392.4	GT2620	Courtly love	394.13	GT2940-2947	Drinking cups
392.4	GT2650	Betrothal	394.14	GT3010	Narcotics
392.4	HQ1017	Dowry	394.14	GT3020-3030	Tobacco
392.5	GR465	Marriage	394.14	GT3020	Smoking
392.5	GT2660-2800	Marriage customs and rites	394.14	GT3030	Snuff
392.5	GT2797	Wedding cakes	394.15	GT2955	Picnicking
392.5	GT2810	Chastity belts	394.2	GT2800	Wedding anniversaries
392.5	GV1462.7.B33	Bachelorette parties	394.2	GT3920-4995	Fasts and feasts
392.5	GV1472.7.B33	Bachelor parties	394.23	GT5020	Heralds
			394.26	GT3930-4995	Festivals

Dewey	LC	Subject Heading	Dewey	LC	Subject Heading
394.26	GT3930-4995	Holidays	395.22	BJ2051-2065	Wedding etiquette
394.26	GT4180-4299	Carnivals	395.23	BJ2071-2075	Mourning etiquette
394.26	GT4380-4499	Harvest festivals	395.3	BJ2021-2028	Hospitality
394.26	GT4403	Kwanzaa	395.3	BJ2021-2078	Entertaining
394.2608997	E98.P86	Powwows	395.4	BJ2100-2115	Letter writing
394.261	GT4995.G	Groundhog Day	395.5	BJ2137-2156	Travel etiquette
394.2614	GT4905-4908	New Year	395.5	GT5810-5895	Hunting
394.262	GT4504-.995	Spring festivals	395.52	GT6010-6070	Commerce
394.262	GT4995.A6	April Fools' Day	395.52	GT6110-6390	Professions
394.262	GT4995.P3	Saint Patrick's Day	395.52	HF5389	Business etiquette
394.2627	GT4945	May Day	395.53	BJ2018-2019	Church etiquette
394.2627	GT4945	May-pole	395.53	BJ2018-2019	Church etiquette
394.2628	HQ759.2	Mother's Day	395.53	GT3770-3896	Hotels
394.2635	DC167	Bastille Day	395.54	BJ2041	Table etiquette
394.264	E120	Columbus Day	395.54	BJ2041	Table etiquette
394.264	GT4995.A4	All Souls' Day	395.59	BJ2120-2128	Conversation
394.2646	GT4965	Halloween	395.59	BJ2195	Telephone etiquette
394.2649	GT4975	Thanksgiving Day	396.70944	DC611.P961	Courts of love
394.266	GT4995.A8	Ascension Day	398	GR	Folklore
394.266	GT4995.P45	Pentecost Festival	398	GR72.3	Folklore—Performance
394.2663	GT4985	Christmas	398.08997	E59.F6	Indians—Folklore
394.2663	GT4989	Christmas trees	398.092	GR50	Folklorists
394.2667	GT4930	Holy Week	398.09(4-9)	GR100-390	Folklore—[By region or
394.2667	GT4935	Easter			country]
394.2667	GT4987.5	Advent calendars	398.094	GR135-263	Folklore—Europe
394.268	AS7	Anniversaries	398.095	GR265-345	Folklore—Asia
394.26973	E231	Patriots' Day	398.096	GR350-360	Folklore—Africa
394.26973	E312.6	Washington's Birthday	398.097	GR101-118	Folklore—North America
394.26973	E642	Memorial Day	398.098	GR130-133	Folklore—South America
394.26973	JK1761	Flag Day	398.0993	GR365-370	Folklore—Australia
394.26975	E645	Confederate Memorial Day	398.0994	GR375-376	Folklore—New Zealand
394.3	GN454-456	Toys	398.0996	GR380-385	Folklore—Oceania
394.3	GN454.8-455	Games	398.2	GR72-390	Folk literature
394.3	GR480-485	Games	398.2	GR74-76	Tales
394.3	GT5810-5850	Hunting customs	398.2	GR550-552	Fairy tales
394.3	GT5904-5905	Fishing	398.2	PN1341-1347	Folk poetry
394.308996073	GR103	Afro-American children's games	398.2	PZ8	Fairy tales
			398.2042	PR951-981	Folk literature, English
394.4	D127	Coronations	398.20431	PT881-951	Folk literature, German
394.4	GT5050	Coronations	398.2043931	PT5351-5395	Folk literature, Dutch
394.40973	JK536	Inauguration Day	398.2043931	PT6200-6230	Folk literature, Flemish
394.5	GT3980-4096	Parades	398.2043936	PT6540-6545	Folk literature, Afrikaans
394.5	GT3980-4099	Processions	398.204394	PT4829-4830	Folk literature, Low German
394.5	GT3980-4099	Pageants	398.204395	PT7088-7089	Folk literature, Scandinavian
394.53	GT5220-5285	Travel			
394.53	GT5220	Transportation	398.20439691	PT7420-7438	Folk literature, Icelandic
394.6	GT4580-4699	Fairs	398.204397	PT9509-9542	Folk literature, Swedish
394.8	CR4571-4595	Dueling	398.2043981	PT7900-7930	Folk literature, Danish
395	BJ1801-2195	Etiquette	398.2043982	PT8600-8635	Folk literature, Norwegian
395.03	BJ1815	Etiquette—Dictionaries	398.20441	PQ781-841	Folk literature, French
395.05	BJ1801	Etiquette—Periodicals	398.20451	PQ4186-4199	Folk literature, Italian
395.09	BJ1821	Etiquette—History	398.20461	PQ6155-6167	Folk literature, Spanish
395.142	BJ1855	Etiquette for men	398.20469	PQ9121-9128	Folk literature, Portuguese
395.144	BJ1856	Etiquette for women	398.2048	PA3285	Folk literature, Greek

Dewey	LC	Subject Heading
398.2049155	PK6426	Folk literature, Persian
398.204924	PJ5048	Folk literature, Hebrew
398.204927	PJ7580	Folk literature, Arabic
398.204927	PJ7680	Folk literature, Arabic
398.204951	PL2445-2446	Folk literature, Chinese
398.204956	PL748-749	Folk literature, Japanese
398.204957	PL968.2-.4	Folk literature, Korean
398.209	PN905-1008	Folk literature—History and criticism
398.20902	PN683-687	Legends
398.20973	PS451-478	Folk literature, American
398.21	BF1552	Fairies
398.21	GR75.S6	Snow White (Tale)
398.245	GR75.L56	Little Red Riding Hood (Tale)
398.27	GN492.3	Political customs and rites
398.32	GR650-690	Geographical myths
398.32	GR940-941	Geographical myths
398.3209143	GR660	Mountains
398.32091693	GR680	Rivers
398.33	GR930	Days
398.33	GR930	Seasons
398.354	GR462	Sex—Folklore
398.355	GR890-910	Occupations—Folklore
398.355	GR950.L4	Lanterns
398.362	GR625	Sun
398.362	GR625	Stars
398.363	GR630	Lightning
398.363	GR630	Thunderstorms
398.364	GR690	Springs—Folklore
398.364	GR690	Wells
398.365	GR800	Rocks
398.368	GR780	Botany—Folklore
398.368	GR780-790	Plants
398.368216	GR785	Trees—Folklore
398.369	GR820-830	Animals, Mythical
398.36957	GR750	Insects
398.3697	GR745	Fishes—Folklore
398.36979	GR740	Reptiles
398.3699772	GR720	Dogs
398.41	GR81	Superstition
398.41	GR933	Thirteen (The number)
398.45	GR500-510	Supernatural
398.45	GR525	Ghouls and ogres
398.45	GR530	Witchcraft
398.45	GR540	Demonology
398.45	GR540	Exorcism
398.45	GR540	Incantations
398.45	GR549-552	Fairies
398.45	GR555	Trolls
398.45	GR560	Ghouls and ogres
398.45	GR600	Amulets
398.45	GR600	Charms
398.45	GR600	Talismans
398.45	GR825-830	Monsters
398.45	GR830.V3	Vampires
398.45	GR910	Mermaids
398.469	GR830.D7	Dragons
398.469	GR830.U6	Unicorns
398.47	GR580	Ghosts
398.8	GR485	Counting-out rhymes
398.8	PN6110.C4	Nursery rhymes
398.8	PZ8.3	Nursery rhymes
398.9	PN6269-6278	Aphorisms and apothegms
398.9	PN6299-6308	Maxims
398.9	PN6400-6525	Proverbs
399.08997	E98.W2	Scalping
400	P	Philology
400	P1-410	Language and languages
401.3	PM7801-7895	Lingua francas
401.3	PM8008	Language, Universal
401.4	P305-.18	Vocabulary
401.409	P326	Historical lexicology
401.41	P99-.4	Semiotics
401.41	P302-.87	Discourse analysis
401.43	P325-.5	Semantics
401.4309	P325.5.H57	Semantics, Historical
401.9	P37	Psycholinguistics
401.9	P99.4.P72	Pragmatics
401.93	P118-.7	Language acquisition
401.93	P118.2	Second language acquisition
403	P29	Language and languages—Dictionaries
405	P1-10	Language and languages—Periodicals
407.1	P51-59	Language and languages—Study and teaching
407.1	P53.44	Immersion method (Language teaching)
409	P375-381	Linguistic geography
410	P121-143.3	Linguistics
410	P123	Comparative linguistics
410	P501-769	Indo-European languages
410	P501-769	Indo-European philology
410.1	P128.M48	Metalanguage
410.18	P147	Functionalism (Linguistics)
410.6	P505	Indo-European languages—Congresses
410.92	P121-149	Linguists
411	P211-214	Alphabets
411	P226	Transliteration
411.7	CN	Inscriptions
411.7	CN120-730	Inscriptions, Ancient
411.7	Z105-115.5	Paleography
411.701	CN40-42	Inscriptions—Philosophy
411.703	CN70	Inscriptions—Dictionaries
411.705	CN1	Inscriptions—Periodicals

Dewey	LC	Subject Heading	Dewey	LC	Subject Heading
411.706	CN15	Inscriptions—Congresses	415	P631-663	Indo-European languages—Parts of speech
411.7071	CN50	Inscriptions—Study and teaching	415	P671-675	Indo-European languages—Syntax
411.7074	CN25-30	Inscriptions—Collectors and collecting	417.2	P409-410	Slang
			417.2	P409	Jargon (Terminology)
411.709	CN55	Inscriptions—History	417.2	PM9001-9021	Languages, Secret
411.709	CN870-1355	Inscriptions—[By region or country]	417.22	PM7801-7895	Pidgin languages
			417.24	P128.E94	Linguistics, Experimental
411.7094	CN900-1130	Inscriptions—Europe	417.7	P35	Linguistic paleontology
411.70941	CN960-997	Inscriptions—Great Britain	417.7	P140	Historical linguistics
411.70943	CN950-957	Inscriptions—Germany	418	P408	Colloquial language
411.709436	CN910-915	Inscriptions—Austria	418	PB73	Polyglot glossaries, phrase books, etc.
411.70944	CN945-948	Inscriptions—France			
411.70945	CN1010-1015	Inscriptions—Italy	418.020285	P307-310	Machine translating
411.70946	CN1090-1095	Inscriptions—Spain			
411.70947	CN1060-1065	Inscriptions—Russia			
411.7095	CN1150-1230	Inscriptions—Asia	418.4	LB1050.53	Developmental reading
411.70951	CN1160-1161	Inscriptions—China	418.4	LB1050.55	Silent reading
411.70952	CN1180-1181	Inscriptions—Japan	419	E98.S5	Sign language
411.70954	CN1170-1175	Inscriptions—India	419	HV2477-2480	Finger spelling
411.7095694	CN1193-1194	Inscriptions—Israel	420	PE	English philology
411.7096	CN1300-1320	Inscriptions—Africa	420	PE1001-3729	English language
411.70972	CN877-878	Inscriptions—Mexico	420.71	PE1065-1069	English language—Study and teaching
411.709728	CN882-884	Inscriptions—Central America			
			421	PE1151	Phonetic alphabet
411.70973	CN870-872	Inscriptions—United States	421	PE1151	Phonetic spelling
411.7098	CN886-888	Inscriptions—South America	421.5	PE1133-1168	English language—Phonology
			421.509	PE1133	English language—Phonology, Historical
411.70994	CN1340-1345	Inscriptions—Australia			
412	P321-324.5	Language and languages—Etymology	422	PE1571-1599	English language—Etymology
412	P721-725	Indo-European languages—Etymology	423	PE1704	English language—Dictionaries
413	P361	Polyglot glossaries, phrase books, etc.	423.028	PE1601-1693	English language—Lexicography
413	P361	Dictionaries, Polyglot	423.1	PE1591	English language—Synonyms and antonyms
413	PB331	Dictionaries, Polyglot			
413.028	P501	Indo-European philology—Periodicals	425	PE1097-1105	English language—Grammar
413.028	P761-769	Indo-European languages—Lexicography	425	PE1112	English language—Grammar—1950-
414	P583-610	Indo-European languages—Phonology	425	PE1171	English language—Morphology
414.8	P221-232	Phonetics	425	PE1199-1359	English language—Parts of speech
414.8	P223	Tone (Phonetics)			
415	P151-299	Grammar, Comparative and general	427	PE1700-3601	English language—Dialects
415	P207	Language and languages—Grammars	427	PE3729.U	Pig Latin
			427.00903(1-2)	PE1079-1081	English language—Early modern, 1500-1700
415	P241-259	Morphemics			
415	P270-288	Parts of speech	427.009033	PE1083	English language—18th century
415	P575-769	Indo-European languages—Grammar, Comparative	427.009034	PE1085	English language—19th century
415	P611-627	Indo-European languages—Morphology			

Dewey	LC	Subject Heading	Dewey	LC	Subject Heading
427.02	PE501-685	English language— Middle English, 1100-1500	430.043028	PD601-660	Germanic languages— Lexicography
427.02	PE524-531	English language— Middle English, 1100-1500— Philology	430.045	PD99-321	Germanic languages— Grammar
427.022	PE561-569	English language— Middle English, 1100-1500— Etymology	430.047	PD700-777	Germanic languages— Dialects
			430.05	PD1-9	Germanic languages— Periodicals
427.023	PE575-585	English language— Middle English, 1100-1500— Dictionaries	430.071	PD65-69	Germanic languages— Study and teaching
427.023028	PE574-585	English language— Middle English, 1100-1500— Lexicography	430.71	PF3065-3069	German language—Study and teaching
427.025	PE29-531	English language— Middle English, 1100-1500— Grammar	431.5	PF3131-3168	German language— Phonology
			432	PF3571-3599	German language—E tymology
427.027	PE688	English language— Middle English, 1100-1500— Dialects	433	PF3620-3693	German language— Dictionaries
			433.028	PF3601-3693	German language— Lexicography
427.09	PE3701-3729	English language—Slang	435	PF3097-3400	German language— Grammar
427.73	PE2801-3102	English language—United States	435	PF3171-3197	German language— Morphology
427.9	PE1079-1087	English language—History	435	PF3199-3335	German language—Parts of speech
427.9	PM7875.G8	Sea Islands Creole dialect			
427.9	PM7891	Pidgin English	437	PD51-60	Germanic languages— History
427.9411	PE2101-2364	Scots language			
428.1	PE1144-1146	Spellers	437	PF3051-3060	German language—History
428.6	PE1117-1130	Readers	437	PF5000-5951	German language—Dialects
428.6	PE1417	Readers	437.01	PF3801-3991	German language— Old High German, 750-1050
429	PE101-299	English language— Old English, ca. 450-1100	437.01	PF3801-3823	German language—Old High German, 750-1050—Philology
429	PE101-123	English language—Old English, ca. 450-1100 –Philology	437.015	PF3831-3931	German language— Old High German, 750-1050—Grammar
429.2	PE261-269	English language—Old English, ca. 450-1100—Etymology	437.02	PF4043-4350	German language—Middle High German, 1050-1500
429.3	PE275-285	English language— Old English, ca. 450-1100—Dictionaries	437.023	PF4333-4345	German language—Middle High German, 1050-1500—Dictionaries
429.3028	PE274-285	English language— Old English, ca. 450-1100—Lexicography	437.023028	PF4327-4345	German language—Middle High German, 1050-1500—Lexicography
429.5	PE129-231	English language— Old English, ca. 450-1100 —Grammar	437.025	PF4061-4171	German language—Middle High German, 1050-1500—Grammar
429.7	PE287-299	English language— Old English, ca. 450-1100—Dialects	437.09	PF5971-5999	German language—Slang
430	PD	Germanic languages	437.090(1-2)	PF4501-4596	German language—Early modern, 1500-1700
430	PF	Germanic languages	439.1	PJ5111-5119	Yiddish language
430	PF3001-5999	German language	439.13	PJ5117	Yiddish language— Dictionaries
430.042	PD571-599	Germanic languages— Etymology			
430.043	PD625-660	Germanic languages— Dictionaries	439.15	PJ5115-5116.5	Yiddish language— Grammar

Dewey	LC	Subject Heading	Dewey	LC	Subject Heading
439.2	PF1401-1497	Frisian language	439.69	PD2401-2447	Icelandic language
439.2	PF1401-1411	Frisian language—Philology	439.69071	PD2407	Icelandic language—Study and teaching
439.31	PF1-979	Dutch language			
439.31	PF1-979	Dutch philology	439.692	PD2431	Icelandic language—Etymology
439.31	PF1001-1184	Dutch language			
439.31071	PF65-69	Dutch language—Study and teaching	439.693	PD2437	Icelandic language—Dictionaries
439.31071	PF1019	Dutch language—Study and teaching	439.695	PD2411-2423	Icelandic language—Grammar
439.3109	PF51-60	Dutch language—History	439.697	PD2447	Icelandic language—Slang
439.3109	PF1015	Dutch language—History	439.699	PD2483	Faroese language
439.3115	PF131-168	Dutch language—Phonology	439.7	PD5001-5929	Swedish language
			439.7	PD5001-5071	Swedish philology
439.312	PF1161-1167	Dutch language—Etymology	439.7071	PD5065	Swedish language—Study and teaching
439.313	PF620-693	Dutch language—Dictionaries			
439.313	PF1175-1184	Dutch language—Dictionaries	439.72	PD5571-5599	Swedish language—Etymology
439.313028	PF601-693	Dutch language—Lexicography	439.73	PD5625-5693	Swedish language—Dictionaries
439.315	PF97	Dutch language—Grammar	439.73028	PD5611-5693	Swedish language—Lexicography
439.315	PF171-197	Dutch language—Morphology	439.75	PD5101-5400	Swedish language—Grammar
439.315	PF199-335	Dutch language—Parts of speech	439.77	PD5700-5929	Swedish language—Dialects
439.315	PF1033-1125	Dutch language—Grammar	439.81	PD3001-3929	Danish language
439.317	PF700-979	Dutch language—Dialects	439.81	PD3001-3071	Danish philology
439.317	PF951-979	Dutch language—Slang	439.81071	PD3065	Danish language—Study and teaching
439.32	PF571-599	Dutch language—Etymology			
439.36	PF861-884	Afrikaans language	439.812	PD3571-3599	Danish language—Etymology
439.4	PF3992-4000	Old Saxon language	439.813	PD3625-3693	Danish language—Dictionaries
439.4	PF5601-5844	Low German language			
439.(5-6)	PD1501-5929	Scandinavian languages	439.813028	PD3601-3693	Danish language—Lexicography
439.(5-6)	PD1501-1541	Scandinavian philology			
439.(5-6)071	PD1535-1539	Scandinavian languages—Study and teaching	439.815	PD3101-3400	Danish language—Grammar
439.(5-6)5	PD1559-1701	Scandinavian languages—Grammar	439.817	PD3700-3929	Danish language—Dialects
			439.817	PD3901-3929	Danish language—Slang
439.(5-6)2	PD1801-1819	Scandinavian languages—Etymology	439.82	PD2501-2999	Norwegian philology
			439.82	PD2571-2699	Norwegian language
439.(5-6)3028	PD1823	Scandinavian languages—Lexicography	439.82071	PD2611-2612	Norwegian language—Study and teaching
439.(5-6)7	PD1850-1893	Scandinavian languages—Dialects	439.822	PD2683-2684	Norwegian language—Etymology
439.6	PD2201-2392	Old Norse language	439.823	PD2688-2695	Norwegian language—Dictionaries
439.6	PD2201-2392	Old Norse philology			
439.62	PD2361-2369	Old Norse language—Etymology	439.823028	PD2687-2695	Norwegian language—Lexicography
439.63028	PD2376-2385	Old Norse language—Lexicography	439.825	PD2619-2673	Norwegian language—Grammar
439.65	PD2229-2331	Old Norse language—Grammar	439.827	PD2696-2699	Norwegian language—Dialects
439.67	PD2387-2392	Old Norse language—Dialects	439.827	PD2699	Norwegian language—Slang
			439.9	PD1101-1211	Gothic language
439.67	PD2483-2489	Old Norse Language—Dialects	439.9	PD1270	Vandal language

Dewey	LC	Subject Heading	Dewey	LC	Subject Heading
439.93	PD1193	Gothic language—Dictionaries	449.95	PC3819-3873	Catalan language—Grammar
439.95	PD1119-1167	Gothic language—Grammar	450	PC1001-1977	Italian language
440	PC	Romance languages	450	PC1001-1977	Italian philology
440	PC2001-3761	French language	450.71	PC1065	Italian language—Study and teaching
440	PC2001-2071	French philology			
440.05	PC1-5	Romance languages—Periodicals	452	PC1571-1580	Italian language—Etymology
440.071	PC35-39	Romance languages—Study and teaching	453	PC1620-1645	Italian language—Dictionaries
			453.028	PC1620-1693	Italian language—Lexicography
440.71	PC2065	French language—Study and teaching	455	PC1099-1400	Italian language—Grammar
441.5	PC2131-2151	French language—Phonology	457	PC1700-1977	Italian language—Dialects
			457	PC1851-1874	Gallo-Italian dialects
442	PC2571-2591	French language—Etymology	457.09	PC1951-1977	Italian language—Slang
442	PC2761	French language—Etymology	457.994972	PC890	Dalmatian language (Romance)
443.028	PC2620-2693	French language—Lexicography	459	PC601-872	Romanian philology
			459	PC601-799	Romanian language
443.028	PC2766	French language—Lexicography	459.071	PC619	Romanian language—Study and teaching
445	PC2721-2746	French language—Grammar	459.11	PC785	Abbreviations, Romanian
445	PC2101-2400	French language—Grammar	459.2	PC761-767	Romanian language—Etymology
445	PC2171-2175	French language—Morphology			
445	PC2201-2321	French language—Parts of speech	459.3028	PC775-784	Romanian language—Lexicography
			459.5	PC631-725	Romanian language—Grammar
447	PC2700-3761	French language—Dialects			
447.0(1-2)	PC2801-2896	French language—To 1500	459.7	PC799	Romanian language—Slang
447.0(1-2)5	PC2821-2873	French language—To 1500—Grammar	459.9	PC901-949	Raeto-Romance language
447.01(1-2)2	PC2883-2886	French language—To 1500—Etymology	459.9071	PC907	Raeto-Romance language—Study and teaching
447.0(1-2)3028	PC2887-2895	French language—To 1500—Lexicography	459.92	PC931	Raeto-Romance language—Etymology
447.9	PM7831-7875	Creole dialects	459.93	PC937	Raeto-Romance language—Dictionaries
448.6	PC2113-2117	French language—Readers	459.95	PC911-923	Raeto-Romance language—Grammar
449	PC3081-3148	Franco-Provencal dialects			
449	PC3201-3299	Provencal language	459.97	PC941-949	Raeto-Romance language—Dialects
449	PC3371-3420	Langue d'oc			
449.2	PC3283-3286	Provencal language—Etymology	459.97	PC949	Raeto-Romance language—Slang
449.3028	PC3287-3295	Provencal language—Lexicography	460	PC4001-4977	Spanish language
			460	PC4001-4071	Spanish philology
449.5	PC3219-3273	Provencal language—Grammar	460.71	PC4065	Spanish language—Study and teaching
449.7	PC3299	Provencal language—Slang	462	PC4571-4580	Spanish language—Etymology
449.77	PC3296	Provencal language—Dialects	463	PC4620-4645	Spanish language—Dictionaries
449.9	PC3801-3899	Catalan language			
449.92	PC3883-3886	Catalan language—Etymology	463.028	PC4620-4693	Spanish language—Lexicography
449.93028	PC3887-3895	Catalan language—Lexicography	465	PC4099-4400	Spanish language—Grammar
			467	PC4700-4941	Spanish language—Dialects

Dewey	LC	Subject Heading	Dewey	LC	Subject Heading
467.09	PC4951-4977	Spanish language—Slang	481.10953	CN440-441	Inscriptions, Greek—Middle East
469	PC5001-5498	Portuguese language	481.109561	CN410-415	Inscriptions, Greek—Turkey
469	PC5001-5041	Portuguese philology	481.1095693	CN430	Inscriptions, Greek—Cyprus
469.0071	PC5035-5039	Portuguese language—Study and teaching	485	PA111	Classical languages—Grammar, Comparative
469.2	PC5301-5315	Portuguese language—Etymology	487.311	CN455	Inscriptions, Byzantine
469.3	PC5325-5348	Portuguese language—Dictionaries	487.4	CN750-753	Inscriptions, Christian
469.3028	PC5320-5348	Portuguese language—Lexicography	487.4	PA600-895	Greek language, Hellenistic (300 B.C.-600 A.D.)
469.5	PC5061-5231	Portuguese language—Grammar	487.4	PA695-895	Greek language, Biblical
469.7	PC5350-5498	Portuguese language—Dialects	487.43	PA881	Greek language, Biblical—Dictionaries
469.709	PC5498	Portuguese language—Slang	487.45	PA813-857	Greek language, Biblical—Grammar
469.794	PC5411-5414	Galician dialect	489	PA500-581	Greek language—Dialects
470	PA2001-2995	Latin language	489	PA1000-1179	Greek language, Medieval and late
470	PA2001-2067	Latin philology	489.3	PA201-1179	Greek language
470	PA2420-2915	Italic languages and dialects	489.3	PA1000-1179	Greek language, Modern
470.71	PA2061-2067	Latin language—Study and teaching	489.3071	PA231-241	Greek language—Study and teaching
471	CN510-740	Inscriptions, Latin	489.3071	PA1041-1049	Greek language, Modern—Study and teaching
472	PA2341-2350	Latin language—Etymology	489.315	PA265-281	Greek language—Phonology
473	PA2361-2390	Latin language—Dictionaries	489.315	PA1061-1072	Greek language, Modern—Phonology
473.028	PA2351-2390	Latin language—Lexicography	489.32	PA421-430	Greek language—Etymology
475	PA2071-2310	Latin language—Grammar	489.32	PA1111-1114.5	Greek language, Modern—Etymology
475	PA2111-2131	Latin language—Phonology	489.33	PA441-465	Greek language—Dictionaries
475	PA2133-2158	Latin language—Morphology	489.33	PA1031	Greek language, Modern—Dictionaries
475	PA2161-2281	Latin language—Parts of speech	489.33	PA1123-1145	Greek language, Modern—Dictionaries
475	PA2285-2297	Latin language—Syntax	489.33028	PA431-465	Greek language—Lexicography
477	PA2300-2309	Latin language, Postclassical	489.35	PA251-379	Greek language—Grammar
477	PA2510-2519	Latin language, Preclassical to ca. 100 B.C.	489.35	PA283-287	Greek language—Morphology
477	PA2600-2748	Latin language, Vulgar	489.35	PA303-361	Greek language—Parts of speech
480	PA	Classical languages	489.35	PA367-379	Greek language—Syntax
480	PA1-199	Classical philology	489.35	PA1051-1099	Greek language, Modern—Grammar
480	PA530-539	Doric Greek dialect	489.35	PA1076	Greek language, Modern—Morphology
480	PA550-554	Aeolic Greek dialect	489.35	PA1081-1089	Greek language, Modern—Parts of speech
480.03	PA31	Classical languages—Dictionaries	489.35	PA1091-1097	Greek language, Modern—Syntax
481.10932	CN440-441	Inscriptions, Greek—Egypt	489.37	PA1151-1159	Greek language, Modern—Dialects
481.1	CN350-455	Inscriptions, Greek	490	PJ	Oriental languages
481.1	CN1000-1005	Inscriptions, Greek			
481.109(3-9)	CN380-455	Inscriptions, Greek—[By region or country]			
481.1094959	CN420	Inscriptions, Greek—Crete			
481.1095	CN400	Inscriptions, Greek—Asia			

Dewey	LC	Subject Heading	Dewey	LC	Subject Heading
490	PL	Oriental languages	491.4	PK1501-2845	Indo-Aryan languages, Modern
490.071	PJ65-69	Oriental languages—Study and teaching	491.4(1-9)	PK1550-2899	Indo-Aryan languages, Modern—Dialects
490.2	PJ183	Oriental languages—Etymology	491.41	PK2781-2794	Sindhi language
			491.42	PK2631-2639	Panjabi language
490.3028	PJ187	Oriental languages—Lexicography	491.43	PK1931-1937	Hindustani language
			491.43	PK1931-1939	Hindi language
490.5	PJ120-171	Oriental languages—Grammar	491.439	PK1975-1987	Urdu language
491.1	PK	Indo-Iranian languages	491.44	PK1651-1695	Bengali language
491.1	PK1-9201	Indo-Iranian languages	491.45	PK2561-2569	Oriya language
491.1	PK1-17	Indo-Iranian philology	491.451	PK1550-1599	Assamese language
491.1	PK1231-1239	Maharashtri language	491.454	PK1821-1824	Magahi language
491.1071	PK11-13	Indo-Iranian philology—Study and teaching	491.46	PK2351-2378	Marathi language
			491.47	PK1841-1847	Gujarati language
491.13	PK14	Indo-Iranian languages—Dictionaries	491.479	PK2701-2709	Rajasthani language
			491.487	PK1836	Divehi language
491.13	PK75-77	Indo-Iranian languages—Dictionaries	491.49	PK2591-2610	Pahari languages
			491.495	PK2595-2599	Nepali language
491.13	PK1537	Indo-Aryan languages, Modern—Dictionaries	491.497	PK2896-2899	Romany language
			491.499	PK7001-7070	Dardic languages
491.15	PK21-41	Indo-Iranian languages—Grammar	491.499	PK7021-7029	Kashmiri language
			491.499	PK7045.M3	Maiya language
491.15	PK1511-1523	Indo-Aryan languages, Modern—Grammar	491.499	PK7070	Khowar language
491.2	PK401-976	Sanskrit language	491.5	PK6001-6996	Iranian languages
491.2	PK401-418	Sanskrit philology	491.5	PK6001-6996	Iranian philology
491.(2-4)	PK101-2899	Indo-Aryan languages	491.51	PK6121-6129	Old Persian language
491.(2-4)	PK101-119	Indo-Aryan philology	491.5111	PK6128	Old Persian inscriptions
491.(2-4)	PK119	Devanagari alphabet	491.52	PK6101-6109	Avestan language
491.22	PK901-919	Sanskrit language—Etymology	491.53	PK6135	Iranian languages, Middle
491.23	PK925-969	Sanskrit language—Dictionaries	491.55	PK6201-6399	Persian language
			491.5511	PK6395	Abbreviations, Persian
491.23028	PK920-969	Sanskrit language—Lexicography	491.56	PK6871-6879	Dari language
			491.6	PB	Celtic languages
491.25	PK501-811	Sanskrit language—Grammar	491.6	PB	Brythonic languages
			491.6	PB1001-1095	Celtic philology
491.29	PK201-379	Vedic language	491.6	PB1001-1095	Celtic languages
491.292	PK361-369	Vedic language—Etymology	491.6	PB2001-2060	Brythonic languages
491.293	PK375-379	Vedic language—Dictionaries	491.6	PB3001-3029	Gaulish language
			491.6071	PB1011	Celtic languages—Study and teaching
491.295	PK231-313	Vedic language—Grammar	491.62	PB	Irish language
491.3	PK1201-1429	Prakrit languages	491.62	PB1201-1299	Irish language
491.33	PK1223-1225	Prakrit languages—Dictionaries	491.6(2-3)	PB1501-1599	Gaelic language
			491.6(2-3)	PB1101-1113	Gaelic philology
491.35	PK1206-1215	Prakrit languages—Grammar	491.6(2-3)071	PB1111	Gaelic philology—Study and teaching
491.37	PK1001-1095	Pali language	491.6(2-3)071	PB1511	Gaelic language—Study and teaching
491.37	PK1001-1095	Pali philology			
491.372	PK1083-1086	Pali language—Etymology	491.6(2-3)2	PB1583-1584	Gaelic language—Etymology
491.373	PK1089-1095	Pali language—Dictionaries			
491.373028	PK1087-1093	Pali language—Lexicography	491.6(2-3)3028	PB1587-1595	Gaelic language—Lexicography
491.375	PK1017-1073	Pali language—Grammar	491.6(2-3)3028	PB1187-1189	Gaelic language—Lexicography

Dewey	LC	Subject Heading	Dewey	LC	Subject Heading
491.6(2-3)5	PB1521-1573	Gaelic language—Grammar	491.79	PG3801-3899	Ukrainian language
491.6(2-8)2	PB2021	Brythonic languages—Etymology	491.793	PG3888-3894.5	Ukrainian language—Dictionaries
491.6(2-8)2	PB1083-1085	Celtic languages—Etymology	491.793028	PG3887-3894.5	Ukrainian language—Lexicography
491.6(2-8)3028	PB2023	Brythonic languages—Lexicography	491.795	PG3819-3881	Ukrainian language—Grammar
491.6(2-8)3028	PB1087-1089	Celtic languages—Lexicography	491.8	PG	Slavic languages
			491.8	PG1-9198	Slavic languages
491.6(2-8)071	PB2005	Brythonic languages—Study and teaching	491.8	PG1-41	Slavic philology
491.6(2-8)5	PB1019-1071	Celtic languages—Grammar	491.8042	PG301-319	Slavic languages—Etymology
491.6(2-8)5	PB2009-2015	Brythonic languages—Grammar	491.8043028	PG320-335	Slavic languages—Lexicography
491.62071	PB1211	Irish language—Study and teaching	491.8045	PG59-97	Slavic languages—Grammar
491.622	PB1283-1284	Irish language—Etymology	491.8071	PG35-39	Slavic languages—Study and teaching
491.623028	PB1287-1295	Irish language—Lexicography	491.81	PG801-993	Bulgarian language
491.625	PB1221-1273	Irish language—Grammar	491.81	PG801-823	Bulgarian philology
491.627	PB1218	Irish language—To 1100	491.813	PG975-984	Bulgarian language—Dictionaries
491.627	PB1218	Irish language—Middle Irish, 1100-1550	491.815	PG831-925	Bulgarian language—Grammar
491.627	PB1299	Irish language—Slang	491.81701	PG601-698	Church Slavic language
491.64	PB1801-1847	Manx language	491.817015	PG661-698	Church Slavic language—Grammar
491.66	PB2101-2199	Welsh language			
491.67	PB	Cornish language	491.819	PG1161-1164	Macedonian language
491.67	PB2501-2549	Cornish language	491.82	PG1201-1223	Serbo-Croatian philology
491.67071	PB2507	Cornish language—Study and teaching	491.82	PG1224-1399	Serbo-Croatian language
491.675	PB2511-2547	Cornish language—Grammar	491.823	PG1374-1384	Serbo-Croatian language—Dictionaries
491.68	PB2800-2849	Breton language	491.825	PG1229-1313	Serbo-Croatian language—Grammar
491.68071	PB2807	Breton language—Study and teaching	491.827	PG1399	Serbo-Croatian language—Slang
491.685	PB2811-2847	Breton language—Grammar	491.83	PG331-335	Slavic languages—Dictionaries
491.7	PG2001-2847	Russian language			
491.7	PG2001-2069	Russian philology	491.84	PG1801-1899	Slovenian language
491.7071	PG2065-2069	Russian language—Study and teaching	491.84	PG1801-1813	Slovenian philology
491.715	PG2131-2161	Russian language—Phonology	491.843	PG1888-1894.5	Slovenian language—Dictionaries
491.72	PG2571-2591	Russian language—Etymology	491.843028	PG1887-1894.5	Slovenian language—Lexicography
491.73	PG2625-2693	Russian language—Dictionaries	491.845	PG1819-1881	Slovenian language—Grammar
491.73028	PG2601-2693	Russian language—Lexicography	491.85	PG6001-6790	Polish language
			491.85	PG6001-6790	Polish philology
491.75	PG2097-2127	Russian language—Grammar	491.853028	PG6625-6638	Polish language—Lexicography
491.75	PG2171-2197	Russian language—Morphology	491.857	PG6700-6790	Polish language—Dialects
491.75	PG2199-2321	Russian language—Parts of speech	491.86	PG4001-4771	Czech philology
			491.86	PG4601-4771	Czech language
491.77	PG2700-2850	Russian language—Dialects	491.863	PG4625-4693	Czech language—Dictionaries
491.7709	PG2850	Russian language—Slang	491.867	PG4700-4771	Czech language—Dialects

Dewey	LC	Subject Heading	Dewey	LC	Subject Heading
491.87	PG5201-5399	Slovak language	492.42	PJ4801-4819	Hebrew language—Etymology
491.87	PG5201-5223	Slovak philology	492.42	PJ4931-4933	Hebrew language—Etymology
491.873	PG5375-5384	Slovak language—Dictionaries	492.43	PJ4825-4847	Hebrew language—Dictionaries
491.875	PG5231-5325	Slovak language—Grammar	492.43	PJ4935-4937	Hebrew language—Dictionaries
491.877	PG350-400	Slavic languages—Dialects	492.43028	PJ4820-4847	Hebrew language—Lexicography
491.877	PG400	Slavic languages—Slang	492.43028	PJ4934-4937	Hebrew language—Lexicography
491.88	PG5631-5698	Sorbian languages			
491.91	PG8201-8208	Prussian language	492.45	PJ4553-4731	Hebrew language—Grammar
491.913	PG8206	Prussian language—Dictionaries	492.45	PJ4601-4677	Hebrew language—Morphology
491.92	PG8501-8693	Lithuanian language	492.47	PJ4855-4937	Hebrew language—Dialects
491.92	PG8501-8693	Lithuanian philology	492.47	PJ4901-4950	Hebrew language, Talmudic
491.93	PG8801-8993	Latvian language	492.475	PJ4911-4925	Hebrew language—Grammar
491.93	PG8801-8993	Latvian philology	492.6	PJ4171-4187	Phoenician language
491.991	PG9501-9599	Albanian language	492.67	PJ4150	Ugaritic language
491.991	PG9501-9513	Albanian philology	492.7	PJ6001-7144	Arabic language
491.992	PK8001-8454	Armenian language	492.7	PJ6001-6071	Arabic philology
491.9927	PK8451-8499	East Armenian dialect	492.7071	PJ6065-6069	Arabic language—Study and teaching
491.998	P945	Hittite language	492.71	CN1153	Inscriptions, Islamic
491.998	P1001	Anatolian languages	492.711	PJ6123	Arabic alphabet
492	PJ990	Afroasiatic languages	492.711	PJ7593-7600	Inscriptions, Arabic
492	PJ3001-9278	Semitic languages	492.72	PJ6172-6199	Arabic language—Etymology
492.04071	PJ3011-3013	Semitic languages—Study and teaching	492.73	PJ6031	Arabic language—Dictionaries
492.0411	PJ3081-3095	Inscriptions, Semitic	492.75	PJ6101-6599	Arabic language—Grammar
492.042	PJ3065	Semitic languages—Etymology	492.77	PJ6701-6901	Arabic language—Dialects
492.043	PJ3004	Semitic languages—Dictionaries	492.77	PJ6751-6760	Arabic language—Dialects—Spain
492.043028	PJ3071-3075	Semitic languages—Lexicography	492.77	PJ6771-6799	Arabic language—Dialects—Egypt
492.045	PJ3021-3041	Semitic languages—Grammar	492.77	PJ6805-6808	Arabic language—Dialects—Palestine
492.047	PJ4121-4129	Semitic languages, Northwest	492.77	PJ6810	Arabic language—Dialects—Lebanon
492.1	PJ3101	Akkadian language	492.77	PJ6811-6820	Arabic language—Dialects—Syria
492.111	PJ3191-3225	Cuneiform writing	492.77	PJ6821-6830	Arabic language—Dialects—Iraq
492.2	PJ5201-5329	Aramaic language			
492.211	PJ5208-5209	Inscriptions, Aramaic	492.77	PJ6841-6880	Arabic language—Dialects—Arabian Peninsula
492.29	PJ5271-5279	Samaritan Aramaic language	492.8	PJ8991-8999	Ethiopian languages
492.3	PJ5401-5411	Syriac philology	492.81	PJ9001-9087	Ethiopic language
492.3	PJ5701-5809	Syriac language	493.1	PJ1001-1479	Egyptian language
492.32	PJ5483	Syriac language—Etymology	493.1	PJ1001-1109	Egyptian philology
492.33	PJ5490-5493	Syriac language—Dictionaries	493.1	PJ1091	Hieroglyphics
492.35	PJ5419-5471	Syriac language—Grammar			
492.37	PJ5401	Mandailing dialect			
492.4	PJ4501-4937	Hebrew language			
492.4	PJ4501-4541	Hebrew philology			
492.411	CN745	Inscriptions, Jewish			
492.411	PJ5034.4-.9	Inscriptions, Hebrew			
492.415	PJ4576-4583	Hebrew language—Phonology			

Dewey	LC	Subject Heading	Dewey	LC	Subject Heading
493.1	PJ1801-1921	Egyptian language—Demotic, ca. 650 B.C.-450 A.D.	494.1	PL471-479	Manchu language
			494.1	PL481.E92	Even language
493.11	PJ1105	Egyptian language—Writing, Hieratic	494.23	PL400-431	Mongolian languages
			494.23	PL401-409	Mongolian language
493.111	PH1091-1097	Hieroglyphics	494.3	PL21-29	Turkic languages
493.111	PJ1051-1109	Egyptian language—Writing	494.31	PL31	Old Turkic language
493.111	PJ1091-1097	Egyptian language—Writing, Hieroglyphic	494.332	PL364.Z9.D	Dolgan dialect
			494.35	PL	Turkish language
493.111	PJ1107	Egyptian language—Writing, Demotic	494.35	PL101-199	Turkish language
			494.357	PL51-56	Turkic languages, Southeast
493.111	PJ1501-1921	Egyptian language—Papyri	494.361	PL311-314	Azerbaijani language
493.111	PJ1501-1819	Egyptian language—Inscriptions	494.364	PL331-334	Turkmen language
			494.37	PL41-45	Turkic languages, Northeast
493.12	PJ1350-1371	Egyptian language—Etymology	494.37	PL61-65	Turkic languages, Northwest
			494.38	PL65.B2	Karachay-Balkar language
493.13	PJ1031	Egyptian language—Dictionaries	494.387	PL65.T3	Tatar language
			494.388	PL65.C74	Crimean Tatar language
493.13	PJ1423-1439	Egyptian language—Dictionaries	494.5	PH	Finno-Ugric languages
			494.5	PH1-11	Finno-Ugric philology
493.13028	PJ1401-1439	Egyptian language—Lexicography	494.5071	PH11	Finno-Ugric languages—Study and teaching
493.15	PJ1121-1201	Egyptian language—Grammar	494.51	PH1251-1254	Ob-Ugric languages
			494.511	PH2001-2800	Hungarian language
493.2	PJ2001-2187	Coptic language	494.5113	PH2625-2693	Hungarian language—Dictionaries
493.2071	PJ2019	Coptic language—Study and teaching	494.5113028	PH2601-2693	Hungarian language—Lexicography
493.22	PJ2161	Coptic language—Etymology	494.5115	PH2097-2410	Hungarian language—Grammar
493.23028	PJ2181	Coptic language—Lexicography	494.5117	PH2800	Hungarian language—Slang
493.25	PJ2029-2113	Coptic language—Grammar	494.53	PH1001-1004	Permic languages
493.3	PJ2340-2349	Berber languages	494.54	PH91-98	Finnic languages
493.3	PJ2369-2399	Berber languages	494.54	PH501-509	Karelian language
493.3	PJ2377	Rif language	494.54	PH541-549	Veps language
493.32	PJ2347	Berber languages—Etymology	494.54	PH561-569	Votic language
			494.54	PH581-589	Livonian language
493.33	PJ2349	Berber languages—Dictionaries	494.541	PH101-293	Finnish language
			494.541	PH101-123	Finnish philology
493.35	PJ2345	Berber languages—Grammar	494.5415	PH131-225	Finnish language—Grammar
493.5	PJ2401-2413	Cushitic languages	494.545	PH601-629	Estonian language
493.5	PJ2465	Afar language	494.55	PH21-41	Finno-Ugric languages—Grammar
493.52	PJ2409	Cushitic languages—Etymology	494.55	PH701-729	Lapp language
493.53	PJ2413	Cushitic languages—Dictionaries	494.56	PH751-779	Mordvin language
			494.56	PH801-807	Mari language
493.54	PJ2531-2534	Somali language	494.6	PL495	Ainu language
493.55	PJ2405	Cushitic languages—Grammar	494.6	PM1-95	Hyperborean languages
			494.8	PL4601-4794	Dravidian languages
493.57	PJ2425-2594	Cushitic languages—Dialects	494.8	PL4601	Dravidian philology
			494.811	PL4751-4759	Tamil language
493.7	PL8117	Daba language	494.812	PL4711-4719	Malayalam language
494	PL1-9	Altaic languages	494.814	PL4641-4649	Kannada language
494.1	PL450	Tungus-Manchu languages	494.82	PL4627	Gadaba language (Dravidian)
494.1	PL451-459	Evenki language			

Dewey	LC	Subject Heading	Dewey	LC	Subject Heading
494.827	PL4771-4779	Telugu language	496.071	PL8004	African languages—Study and teaching
495	PL3521-3529	Sino-Tibetan languages			
495	PL4051-4054	Karen language	496.1	PL8541	Nama language
495.1	PL1001-2244	Chinese language	496.3	PL8026.N44	Niger-Congo languages
495.1	PL1891-1900	Mandarin dialects	496.32	PL8134	Diola language
495.115	PL1201-1219	Chinese language—Phonology	496.322	PL8181-8184	Fula language
			496.33	PL8221	Grebo language
495.12	PL1281-1315	Chinese language—Etymology	496.337	PL8164.Z9	Fon dialect
			496.3374	PL8161-8164	Ewe language
495.13	PL1420-1498	Chinese language—Dictionaries	496.3378	PL8191	Ga language
			496.3385	PL8046.A63	Akan language
495.13028	PL1401-1498	Chinese language—Lexicography	496.3385	PL8167.F4	Fanti language
			496.348	PL8204	Gbandi language
495.15	PL1099-1241	Chinese language—Grammar	496.35	PJ4149	Mossi languages
			496.361	PL8024.A33	Adamawa languages
495.17	PL1077	Chinese language—To 600	496.361	PL8205	Gbaya language
495.17	PL1079	Chinese language—Ancient Chinese, 600-1200	496.3642	PL8147	Efik language
			496.39	PL8025	Bantu languages
495.17	PL1081	Chinese language—Middle Chinese, 1200-1919	496.391	PL8025	Bisa language
			496.392	PL8701-8704	Swahili language
495.17	PL1083	Chinese language—Modern Chinese, 1919-	496.395	PL8207.G55	Gisu language
			496.3957	PL8201	Ganda language
495.17	PL1501-1940	Chinese language—Dialects	496.396	PL8167.F3	Fang language
495.172	PL1931-1940	Wu dialects	496.3962	PL8141	Duala language
495.17215	PL1861-1870	Hsiang dialects	496.397	PL8771	Venda language
495.1727	PL1731-1740	Cantonese dialects	496.397	PL8801-8804	Yao language
495.4	PL3551-4001	Tibeto-Burman languages	496.3977	PL8689	Sotho language
495.4	PL3601-3651	Tibetan language	496.3986	PL8841-8844	Zulu language
495.4	PL3651.D96	Dzongkha language	496.5	PL8008	African languages—Grammar
495.4	PL3881-3884	Naga languages			
495.4	PL4001.G2	Garo language	496.5	PL8041	Acoli language
495.6	PL501-700	Japanese language	496.5	PL8127	Daza language
495.611	PL750-751	Inscriptions, Japanese	496.5	PL8131	Dinka language
495.63	PL674.5-677.6	Japanese language—Dictionaries	496.5	PL8197	Gambai dialect
			496.5	PL8571-8574	Nubian languages
495.65	PL531.3-532.5	Japanese language—Grammar	497	E98.P6	Picture-writing, Indian
			497	PM	North American language
495.67	PL525-.6	Japanese language—Meiji period, 1868-1912	497	PM1-7356	Indians of North America—Languages
495.67	PL525.2	Japanese language—To 794	497	PM5071-5079	Indians of the West Indies—Languages
495.67	PL525.5	Japanese language—Edo period, 1600-1868	497.1	PM50-94	Eskimo languages
			497.12	PM50-64	Inuit language
495.7	PL901-949	Korean language	497.19	PM31-34	Aleut language
495.711	PL969.2-.4	Inscriptions, Korean	497.26	PM2006-2009	Navajo language
495.73	PL935-.6	Korean language—Dictionaries	497.3	PM600-609	Algonquian languages
			497.333	PM851-854	Ojibwa language
495.8	PL3921-3969	Burmese language	497.344	PM1885	Mohegan language
495.91	PL4111-4251	Thai language	497.354	PM635	Arapaho language
495.922	PL4371-4379	Vietnamese language	497.38	PM1971-1974	Muskogean languages
495.93	PL4281-4587	Austroasiatic languages	497.42	PM3961-3969	Mayan languages
495.93	PL4301-4309	Mon-Khmer languages	497.452	PM4061-4069	Nahuatl Language
495.95	PL4501-4509	Munda languages	497.45529	PM2175	Pima languages
496	PL	African languages	497.4574	PM2321	Shoshonean languages
496	PL8000-8008	African languages			

Dewey	LC	Subject Heading	Dewey	LC	Subject Heading
497.4576	PM2515	Ute language	499.99	PM	Languages, Artificial
497.458	PM1351	Hopi language	499.99	PM8001-9021	Languages, Artificial
497.5243	PM1021-1024	Dakota language	499.992	PM8201-8298	Esperanto
497.5272	PM1001	Crow language			
497.55	PM1381-1384	Iroquoian languages	500	Q	Science
497.5542	PM1881-1884	Mohawk language	500.2	Q	Physical sciences
497.557	PM781-784	Cherokee language	500.5	QB495-500.268	Space sciences
497.57	PM1343	Hokan-Coahuiltecan languages	501	Q174-175.32	Science—Philosophy
			501	Q174-175.32	Science—Methodology
497.9	PM3001-4566	Indians of Central America—Languages	501.4	Q179	Science—Terminology
			501.4	Q179	Science—Nomenclature
497.994	PM2711	Zuni language	502.2	Q222	Scientific illustration
498	PM5001-7356	Indians of South America—Languages	502.5	Q145	Scientists—Directories
			502.82	QH212.A25	Acoustic microscopy
498.3829	PM7171-7179	Tupi languages	502.84	Q184-185.7	Scientific apparatus and instruments
499.12	PL6601-6621	Papuan languages			
499.15	PL7001-7101	Australian languages	502.85	Q183.9	Science—Data processing
499.2	PL5021-6571	Austronesian languages	503	Q123	Science—Dictionaries
499.21	PL5501-6135	Philippine languages	505	Q1-9	Science—Periodicals
499.211	PL6051-6059	Tagalog language	506	Q10-99	Science—Societies, etc.
499.22	PL5221-5224	Balinese language	507.1	Q181-183.4	Science—Study and teaching
499.221	PL5071-5079	Indonesian language			
499.222	PL5161-5169	Javanese language	507.2	Q180	Research
499.28	PL5101-5129	Malay language	507.2	Q183-.4	Laboratories
499.4	PL6401-6551	Polynesian languages	507.4	Q105	Science—Exhibitions
499.442	PL6465	Maori language	507.8	Q182.3	Science projects
499.444	PL6515	Tahitian language	508	Q148-149	Scientific surveys
499.48	PL6531	Tonga language (Tonga Islands)	508	QH	Natural history
			508.014	QH83	Natural history—Terminology
499.5	PL6201-6209	Melanesian languages			
499.5	PL6235	Fijian language	508.022	QH46.5	Natural history illustration
499.52	PL6191-6195	Micronesian languages	508.0222	QH46	Natural history—Pictorial works
499.92	PH5001-5259	Basque language			
499.92	PH5001-5022	Basque philology	508.03	QH13	Natural history—Dictionaries
499.93	P943	Elamite language			
499.94	P1078	Etruscan language	508.06	QH1-7	Natural history—Periodicals
499.9411	CN479	Inscriptions, Etruscan	508.071	QH51-58	Natural history—Study and teaching
499.95	PJ4001-4041	Sumerian language			
499.9511	PJ4051-4075	Cuneiform inscriptions, Sumerian	508.071	QH51-58	Nature study
			508.072	QH75-77	Research natural areas
499.953	PJ4037	Sumerian language—Dictionaries	508.074	QH70	Natural history museums
			508.092	QH26-35	Naturalists
499.955	PJ4011-4025	Sumerian language—Grammar	509	Q124.6-127.2	Science—History
			509	Q180.55.D57	Discoveries in science
499.96	PK9001-9201	Caucasian languages	509.01	Q124.95	Science, Ancient
499.962	PK9051	Abkhazo-Adyghian languages	509.02	Q124.97	Science, Medieval
			509.0(24-31)	Q125.2	Science, Renaissance
499.962	PK9201.A2	Abazin language	509.2	Q141-143	Scientists—Biography
499.9623	PK9201.A3	Abkhaz language	509.(4-9)	Q127-.2	Science—[By region or country]
499.9624	PK9201.K3	Kabardian language			
499.964	PK9051	Daghestan languages	510	QA	Mathematics
499.964	PK9201.D3	Dargwa language	510.1	QA8-10.5	Mathematics—Philosophy
499.965	PK9106-9115	Georgian language—Grammar	510.1	QA9	Metamathematics
			510.284	QA71-90	Mathematical instruments
499.969	PK9101-9151	Georgian language	510.284	QA73	Slide-rule

Dewey	LC	Subject Heading	Dewey	LC	Subject Heading
510.284	QA75	Calculators	512.32	QA211	Galois theory
510.3	QA5	Mathematics—Dictionaries	512.32	QA214	Galois theory
510.5	QA1	Mathematics—Periodicals	512.4	QA171	Group extensions (Mathematics)
510.71	QA11-20	Mathematics—Study and teaching	512.4	QA247	Ideals (Algebra)
510.9	QA21-27	Mathematics—History	512.4	QA247	Rings (Algebra)
510.901	QA22	Mathematics, Ancient	512.4	QA251.3	Dedekind rings
510.902	QA23	Mathematics, Medieval	512.482	QA252.3	Lie algebras
510.902	QA32	Mathematics, Medieval	512.482	QA387	Lie groups
510.92	QA28-29	Mathematicians	512.5	QA184	Algebras, Linear
510.931	QA27.C	Mathematics, Chinese	512.5	QA190-201	Substitutions, Linear
510.935	QA22	Mathematics, Babylonian	512.5	QA199.5	Multilinear algebra
510.938	QA22	Mathematics, Greek	512.556	QA326	Operator algebras
510.9(4-9)	QA27	Mathematics—[By region or country]	512.56	QA247.4	Difference algebra
511.3	BC131-135	Logic, Symbolic and mathematical	512.56	QA372.5	Differential-algebraic equations
511.3	BC131-135	Logic, Symbolic and mathematical	512.7	QA141.15	Number concept
511.3	QA9-10.3	Logic, Symbolic and mathematical	512.7	QA171.5	Lattices, Distributive
511.3	QA9.65	Decidability (Mathematical logic)	512.7	QA241-247.5	Number theory
511.31	QA9.4-.5	Nonclassical mathematical logic	512.72	QA242	Diophantine equations
511.324	QA10-.3	Algebraic logic	512.72	QA242	Numbers, Divisibility of
511.324	QA10.3	Algebra, Boolean	512.72	QA242-244	Congruences and residues
511.33	QA171.5	Lattice theory	512.723	QA246	Numbers, Prime
511.34	QA9.A7	Forcing (Model theory)	512.73	QA165	Partitions (Mathematics)
511.34	QA9.7	Model theory	512.74	QA242	Diophantine analysis
511.35	QA9.5	Lambda calculus	512.74	QA244	Fermat's theorem
511.35	QA267-268.5	Machine theory	512.74	QA341	Algebraic functions
511.36	QA9.54	Proof theory	512.922	QA55-59	Logarithms
511.42	QA275	Least squares	512.923	QA161.F3	Factors (Algebra)
511.43	QA275	Error analysis (Mathematics)	512.923	QA242	Factors (Algebra)
511.5	QA166-.24	Graph theory	512.924	QA221-224	Approximation theory
511.6	QA164-167.2	Combinatorial analysis	512.94	QA211-218	Equations, Theory of
511.64	QA165	Combinations	512.94	QA211-218	Equations
511.64	QA165	Magic squares	512.9422	QA161.B5	Binomial theorem
511.64	QA165	Permutations	512.9422	QA215	Equations, Quartic
511.66	QA306	Maxima and minima	512.9422	QA215	Equations, Cubic
512	QA150-272.5	Algebra	512.9422	QA245	Equations, Binomial
512	QA246	Numerical functions	512.94222	QA161	Equations, Quadratic
512	QA251	Algebra, Universal	512.9432	QA191	Determinants
512.0071	QA159	Algebra—Study and teaching	512.9434	QA188-196	Matrices
512.02	QA162	Algebra, Abstract	512.944	QA201	Forms (Mathematics)
512.2	QA174-183	Group theory	512.944	QA243	Forms (Mathematics)
512.22	QA176	Representations of groups	513	GN476.1	Arithmetic
512.25	QA215	Equations, Abelian	513	QA101-141.8	Arithmetic
512.3	QA171	Infinite groups	513	QA248-.5	Arithmetic—Foundations
512.3	QA247-.45	Algebraic fields	513.0284	QA75	Abacus
512.3	QA247.45	Division algebras	513.211	QA113	Counting
512.32	QA171	Galois theory	513.211	QA115	Addition
			513.212	QA115	Subtraction
			513.213	QA115	Multiplication
			513.214	QA115	Division
			513.23	QA49	Square root
			513.23	QA119	Roots, Numerical
			513.23	QA119	Square root

Dewey	LC	Subject Heading	Dewey	LC	Subject Heading
513.23021	QA51	Factor tables	515.55	QA353.G44	Generating functions
513.26	QA117	Fractions	515.56	QA351	Functions, Zeta
513.26071	QA135-139	Fractions—Study and teaching	515.625	QA431	Difference equations
			515.63	QA433	Vector analysis
513.265	QA242	Decimal fractions	515.64	QA315-316	Calculus of variations
513.5	QA141-.8	Numeration	515.642	QA402.3-.37	Control theory
513.5	QA141.5	Duodecimal system	515.642	QA402.35	Nonlinear control theory
513.5	QA141.8.S4	Sexadecimal system	515.7	QA319-329.9	Functional analysis
513.6	QA247.35	Modular arithmetic	515.7	QA324	Theory of distributions (Functional analysis)
514	QA611-614.97	Topology			
514	QA611.5	Ergodic theory	515.723	QA432	Laplace transformation
514.23	QA612.3-.77	Homology theory	515.7242	QA329.42	Partial differential operators
514.3	QA611.234	Hewitt-Nachbin spaces	515.7248	QA321.5	Nonlinear functional analysis
514.3	QA689	Generalized spaces			
514.325	QA611.28	Metric spaces	515.73	QA322	Linear topological spaces, Ordered
514.72	QA613.6-.66	Differential topology			
514.72	QA613.62	Foliations (Mathematics)	515.73	QA331	Analytic functions
514.74	QA614-.97	Global analysis (Mathematics)	515.8	QA331.5	Functions of real variables
			515.9	QA360	Conformal mapping
514.74	QA614.92	Index theorems	515.9	QA646	Conformal mapping
515	QA299.82	Nonstandard mathematical analysis	515.92	QA331.7	Functions of complex variables
			515.93	QA333-337	Riemann surfaces
515	QA303-316	Calculus	515.983	QA343	Elliptic functions
515.24	QA9	Infinite	516	QA440-699	Geometry
515.24	QA295	Processes, Infinite	516.	QA481	Axioms
515.243	QA295	Partial sums (Series)	516.04	QA473-475	Geometry, Modern
515.243	QA295	Series, Infinite	516.04	QA473	Inversions (Geometry)
515.2433	QA403-.3	Harmonic analysis	516.1	QA601-608	Transformations (Mathematics)
515.2433	QA403.3	Wavelets (Mathematics)			
515.2433	QA403.5-404.5	Fourier analysis	516.15	QA465	Mensuration
515.25	QA331-355	Functions	516.152	QA484	Circle
515.26	QA295	Inequalities (Mathematics)	516.152	QA485	Parabola
515.35	QA370-380	Differential equations	516.154	QA482	Polygons
515.353	QA374-377	Differential equations, Partial	516.154	QA482	Triangle
			516.156	QA491	Prisms
515.354	QA372	Differential equations, Linear	516.183	QA608	Line geometry
			516.2	QA608	Congruences (Geometry)
515.37	QA381	Differential invariants	516.21	QA451-469	Euclid's Elements
515.37	QA381	Differential forms	516.22	QA451-485	Geometry, Plane
515.38	QA373	Differential-difference equations	516.23	QA457	Geometry, Solid
			516.23	QA491	Geometry, Solid
515.39	QA614.8	Differentiable dynamical systems	516.24	QA531-538	Trigonometry
			516.24021	QA55	Trigonometry—Tables
515.39	QA614.83	Hamiltonian systems	516.242	QA533	Plane trigonometry
515.392	QA871	Perturbation (Mathematics)	516.244	QA535	Spherical trigonometry
515.392	QA871	Stability	516.3	QA551-563	Geometry, Analytic
515.4	QA308-311	Integrals	516.35	QA564-609	Geometry, Algebraic
515.4	QA312	Integrals, Generalized	516.352	QA571-573	Surfaces
515.48	QA313	Ergodic theory	516.36	QA615-639	Geometry, Infinitesimal
515.52	QA246	Euler's numbers	516.36	QA631-638	Surfaces
515.52	QA353.G3	Gamma functions	516.36	QA641-672	Surfaces
515.53	QA405	Harmonic functions	516.36	QA641-672	Geometry, Differential
515.53	QA408	Hankel functions	516.375	QA689	Finsler spaces
515.54	QA405	Mathieu functions	516.375	QA689	G-spaces
515.55	QA164.8	Generating functions			

Dewey	LC	Subject Heading	Dewey	LC	Subject Heading
516.5	QA501-521	Projection	520.931	QB17	Astronomy, Chinese
516.6	QA501-521	Geometry, Descriptive	520.935	QB19	Astronomy, Assyro-Babylonian
518	QA297-299.4	Numerical analysis			
518	QA297	Numerical calculations	520.938	QB21	Astronomy, Greek
518	QA402.2	Decomposition method	521	QB349-421	Celestial mechanics
518.23	QA90	Nomography (Mathematics)	521.3	QB355-357	Orbits
518.53	QA355	Numerical differentiation	521.4	QB361-407	Perturbation (Astronomy)
518.54	QA299.3-.4	Numerical integration	521.4	QB362.F47	Few-body problem
519.2	QA273-274.8	Chance	521.4	QB362.M3	Many-body problem
519.2	QA273-274.8	Probabilities	521.4	QB362.T9	Two-body problem
519.23	QA274-.8	Stochastic processes	521.9	QB165	Nutation
519.233	QA274.7-.76	Markov processes	522	QB51.3.I45	Imaging systems in astronomy
519.233	QA274.75	Diffusion processes			
519.24	QA273.6	Distribution (Probability theory)	522	QB84.5-135	Lenses
			522	QB105	Solar compass
519.27	QA273	Games of chance (Mathematics)	522	QB807	Astrometry
			522.1	QB4-.9	Astronomy—Observations
519.3	QA269-272.5	Game theory	522.2	QB84.5-115	Astronomical instruments
519.3	T57.92	Game theory	522.2	QB88	Reflecting telescopes
519.5	QA276-280	Mathematical statistics	522.2	QB88	Telescopes
519.5	QA278.8	Nonparametric statistics	522.29	QB81-84	Astronomical observatories
519.52	QA276.6	Sampling (Statistics)	522.29	QB500.267-.268	Orbiting astronomical observatories
519.535	QA278.6	Latent structure analysis			
519.535	QA278.65	Discriminant analysis	522.4	QB105	Quadrant
519.5354	QA278.5	Factor analysis	522.5	QB107	Chronometers
519.537	QA273-281	Correlation (Statistics)	522.5	QB107	Astronomical clocks
519.538	QA279-.2	Analysis of variance	522.62	QB135	Astronomical photometry
519.542	QA279.4-.7	Decision-making	522.63	QB121-.5	Astronomical photography
519.544	QA276.8	Estimation theory	522.67	QB465	Astronomical spectroscopy
519.55	QA280	Time-series analysis	522.68	QB480	Radar in astronomy
519.7	QA402.5	Programming (Mathematics)	522.682	QB475-479.55	Radio astronomy
			522.682	QB479.2	Radio telescopes
519.72	T57.74-.79	Linear programming	522.683	QB470	Infrared astronomy
519.76	T57.8-.825	Nonlinear programming	522.6862	QB471.7.B85	Gamma ray bursts
519.82	QA274.8	Queuing theory	522.6863	QB472-473	X-ray astronomy
520	QB	Astronomy	522.7	QB140-237	Spherical astronomy
520	QB25-26	Astrology	522.9	QB155-156	Refraction, Astronomical
520	QB136	Space astronomy	522.9	QB163	Aberration
520.1	QB14.5	Astronomy—Philosophy	523	QB15-26	Zodiac
520.151	QB47	Astronomy—Mathematics	523	QB802	Zodiac
520.21	QB149	Statistical astronomy	523.01	QB460-466	Astrophysics
520.216	QB6	Astrographic catalog and chart	523.019	QB462.6	Molecular astrophysics
			523.019	QB462.7-.72	Plasma astrophysics
520.223	QB65	Stars—Atlases	523.019	QB463-464.2	Nuclear astrophysics
520.228	QB67	Astronomical models	523.02	QB450-.5	Cosmochemistry
520.3	QB14	Astronomy—Encyclopedias	523.1	QB63	Constellations
520.5	QB1	Astronomy—Periodicals	523.1	QB980-991	Cosmology
520.71	QB61-62.7	Astronomy—Study and teaching	523.112	QB856-858.8	Galaxies
			523.112	QB858	Dwarf Galaxies
520.9	QB15-34	Astronomy—History	523.112	QB858.3	Active galaxies
520.901	GN799.A8	Astronomy, Prehistoric	523.1125	QB790-792	Interstellar matter
520.901	QB16-22	Astronomy, Ancient	523.1125	QB791	Cosmic dust
520.902	QB23-26	Astronomy, Medieval	523.1126	QB791.3	Dark matter (Astronomy)
520.90(23-31)	QB29	Astronomy, Renaissance	523.1135	QB855.5	Planetary nebulae
520.92	QB35-36	Astronomers—Biography			

Dewey	LC	Subject Heading	Dewey	LC	Subject Heading
523.115	QB860	Quasars	523.72	QB539.N6	Solar noise storms
523.12	QB632	Earth—Origin	523.73	QB523	Sun—Rotation
523.12	QB980-991	Cosmogony	523.73	QB526.C9	Solar cycle
523.18	QB991.B54	Big bang theory	523.73	QB551	Sun—Rotation
523.18	QB991.I54	Inflationary universe	523.75	QB516.F6	Solar flares
523.19	QB991.E53	End of the universe	523.75	QB525	Sunspots
523.2	QB500.5-785	Solar system	523.75	QB529	Sun—Corona
523.3	QB391-399	Lunar theory	523.76	QB539.I5	Sun—Internal structure
523.3	QB580-595	Moon	523.78	QB541-545	Solar eclipses
523.3	QB591	Moon—Surface	523.8	QB6	Stars—Observations
523.3	QB592	Lunar geology	523.8	QB799-903	Stars
523.3	QB592	Lunar soil	523.8	QB843.A12	A stars
523.3021	QB399	Moon—Tables	523.8	QB843.B12	B stars
523.3021	VK563-567	Moon—Tables	523.80216	QB6	Stars—Catalogs
523.38	QB579	Lunar eclipses	523.81	QB814	Stars—Masses
523.4	QB361-389	Planetary theory	523.82	QB817	Stars—Radiation
523.4	QB600-701	Planets	523.83	QB810	Stars—Rotation
523.4	QB603.R55	Planetary rings	523.83	QB812	Stellar oscillations
523.41	QB371	Mercury (Planet)	523.841	QB421	Double stars
523.41	QB611	Mercury (Planet)	523.841	QB821-830	Multiple stars
523.42	QB372	Venus (Planet)	523.841	QB821-830	Double stars
523.42	QB621	Venus (Planet)—Surface	523.844	QB833-841	Variable stars
523.42	QB621	Venus (Planet)	523.8444	QB835.E4	Eclipsing binaries—Orbits
523.423	QB372	Venus (Planet)—Orbit	523.8446	QB843.D85	Dwarf Novae
523.423	QB509-513	Venus (Planet), Transit of	523.85	QB851-855.9	Stars—Clusters
523.43	QB376	Mars (Planet)	523.87	QB121	Stars—Photographic measurements
523.43	QB641	Mars (Planet)			
523.44	QB377-379	Asteroids	523.88	QB806	Stars—Formation
523.44	QB516	Asteroids	523.88	QB806	Stars—Evolution
523.44	QB651	Asteroids	523.88	QB841	Stars, New
523.45	QB384	Jupiter (Planet)	523.88	QB843.D9	Dwarf stars
523.45	QB661	Jupiter (Planet)	523.88	QB843.E2	Early stars
523.46	QB384	Saturn (Planet)	523.88	QB843.N12	N stars
523.46	QB671	Saturn (Planet)	523.88	QB843.R4	Red dwarfs
523.47	QB387	Uranus (Planet)	523.88	QB843.R42	Red giants
523.47	QB681	Uranus (Planet)	523.88	QB895	Stars, New
523.481	QB388	Neptune (Planet)	523.887	QB843.W5	White dwarfs
523.481	QB691	Neptune (Planet)	523.8874	QB843.N4	Neutron stars
523.482	QB701	Pluto (Planet)	523.8875	QB843.B55	Black holes (Astronomy)
523.51	QB738	Meteoroids	523.8875	QB843.B55	Kerr black holes
523.51	QB740-753	Meteors	523.9	QB175-185	Transits
523.51	QB754.8-759	Meteorites	523.98	QB401-407	Satellites
523.58	QB529	Solar wind	523.986	QB405	Saturn (Planet)—Ring system
523.6	QB717-732	Comets			
523.6	QB723.B5	Biela's comet	523.9881	QB407	Neptune (Planet)—Satellites
523.6	QB723.D	Donati's Comet			
523.6	QB723.E3	Encke's comet	523.99	QB175-185	Eclipses
523.63	QB357	Comets—Orbits	525	QB630-638.8	Earth
523.642	QB723.H2	Halley's comet	525	QB630-638.8	Astronomical geography
523.7	QB520-545	Sun	525.317	QB216	Sun—Rising and setting
523.7021	QB374	Sun—Tables	525.35	QB633	Earth—Rotation
523.72	QB524-526	Solar activity	525.5	QB637.2-.8	Seasons
523.72	QB531	Solar radiation	526	GA	Mathematical geography
523.72	QB539.M23	Solar magnetic fields	526	GA	Cartography

Dewey	LC	Subject Heading	Dewey	LC	Subject Heading
526	GA1-87	Mathematical geography	528	QB8	Nautical almanacs
526	GA101-1999	Cartography	529	CE	Chronology
526	GA130	Map drawing	529	QB209-224	Time
526.021	GA4	Mathematical geography—Tables	529.0218	QB223	Time—Systems and standards
526.0284	QB331	Gravimeters (Geophysical instruments)	529.03	CE4	Chronology—Dictionaries
			529.05	CE1	Chronology—Periodicals
526.0285	GA139	Digital mapping	529.06	CE1.5	Chronology—Congresses
526.09	GA201-246	Cartography—History	529.09	CE6	Chronology—History
526.0973	GA405	Cartography—United States	529.0935	CE33	Calendar, Assyro-Babylonian
526.097(4-9)	GA409-460	Cartography—[United States, By state]	529.1	QB217	Time, Equation of
526.1	QB275-343	Geodesy	529.223	QB65	Astronomy—Charts, diagrams, etc.
526.10285	QB297	Geodesy—Computer programs	529.3	CE73	Calendars
526.103	QB279	Geodesy—Encyclopedias	529.3	CE91-92	Perpetual calendars
526.109	QB280.5	Geodesy—History	529.30935	CE33	Chronology, Assyro-Babylonian
526.3	GA23	Area measurement			
526.3	QB301-328	Surveys	529.309376	CE46	Calendar, Roman
526.3	QB303	Base measuring	529.30938	CE42	Chronology, Greek
526.3	TA590	Topographical surveying	529.325	CE31-39.5	Chronology, Oriental
526.30287	QB291	Arc measures	529.326	CE35	Calendar, Jewish
526.33	QB311	Triangulation	529.327	CE59	Calendar, Islamic
526.33	TA583	Triangulation	529.42	CE75	Calendar, Julian
526.6	QB201-205	Geodetic astronomy	529.44	CE81-83	Church calendar
526.61	QB231-237	Latitude	529.44	CE83	Easter
526.62	QB225-229.5	Longitude	529.7	QB213	Time measurements
526.63	QB207	Azimuth	529.7	QB214	Hour-glasses
526.63	TA597	Azimuth	529.7	QB215	Dialing
526.7	QB330-339	Gravity	529.7	QB215	Sundials
526.7	QB341	Gravitation	530	QC	Physics
526.8	GA110-115	Map projection	530	QC120-168.86	Mechanics
526.9	GA51-87	Surveys	530	QC170-197	Matter
526.9	TA501-625	Surveying	530.01	QC5.56-6.4	Physics—Philosophy
526.9	TA515-531	Surveyors	530.03	QC5	Physics—Encyclopedias
526.9	TA611	Surveys—Plotting	530.06	QC1	Physics—Congresses
526.9	TA625	Route surveying	530.071	QC29	Physics—Vocational guidance
526.90284	TA562-581	Surveying—Instruments	530.071	QC30-48	Physics—Study and teaching
526.90284	TA579-581	Measuring-tapes			
526.90284	TA579	Surveyors' chains	530.072	QC51	Physical laboratories
526.9071	TA535-538	Surveying—Study and teaching	530.078	QC35-37	Physics—Laboratory manuals
526.98	TA616	Topographical drawing	530.09	QC6.9-9	Physics—History
526.982	TA592-593.9	Photographic surveying	530.092	QC15-16	Physicists
526.982	TA593	Photogrammetry	530.11	QC173.5-.65	Relativity (Physics)
526.982	TR693-696	Photogrammetry	530.11	QC173.59.S65	Space and time
527	VK549-587	Nautical astronomy	530.12	QC173.96-174.52	Quantum theory
527	VK563	Azimuth	530.12	QC174.17.B6	Bound states (Quantum mechanics)
527.015308	VK572	Mile, Nautical			
527.021	VK563-567	Navigation—Tables	530.122	QC174.17.D44	Density matrices
527.0284	VK584.A7	Artificial horizons (Nautical instruments)	530.122	QC174.17.H4	Heisenberg uncertainty principle
527.1	VK565	Latitude	530.122	QC174.3-.35	Matrix mechanics
527.2	VK565-567	Longitude			
528	QB7-9	Ephemerides	530.124	QC174.2-.26	Wave mechanics

Dewey	LC	Subject Heading	Dewey	LC	Subject Heading
530.13	QC174.7-175.36	Statistical mechanics	531.112	QA841-842	Kinematics
530.133	QC174.4-.43	Quantum statistics	531.1134	QC189-.2	Viscosity
530.138	QC175.2-.25	Transport theory	531.1134	QC197	Friction
530.14	QC173.68-.75	Field theory (Physics)	531.12	QA821-835	Statics
530.14	QC174.17.P7	Few-body problem	531.12	QA821-835	Equilibrium
530.142	QC794.6.G7	Grand unified theories (Nuclear physics)	531.12	QA839	Moments of inertia
			531.14	QC111-114	Specific gravity
530.1423	QC174.17.S9	Supergravity	531.14	QC178	Gravitational fields
530.143	QC174.45-.52	Quantum field theory	531.14	QC178	Gravitation
530.143	QC174.52.D43	Degree of freedom	531.16	QA851-855	Dynamics of a particle
530.1433	QC679-680.5	Quantum electrodynamics	531.32	QA865-867.5	Oscillations
530.1435	QC793.3.F5	Gauge fields (Physics)	531.32	QA935-939	Vibration
530.144	QC174.17.P7	Many-body problem	531.324	QA862.P4	Pendulum
530.15	QC19.2-20.85	Mathematical physics	531.33	QA935	Wave-motion, Theory of
530.15071	QC20.8-.82	Mathematical physics—Study and teaching	531.34	QA862.G9	Gyroscopes
			531.381	QA931-939	Strains and stresses
530.41	QC173.45-.458.U54	Condensed matter	531.382	QA931-939	Elasticity
			531.382	QA935	Elastic solids
530.411	QC176.8.L3	Lattice dynamics	531.382	QA935	Elastic plates and shells
530.416	QC174.1	Tunneling (Physics)	531.382	QA935	Elastic waves
530.416	QC176.8.E9	Exciton theory	531.382	QC191	Elastic solids
530.4175	QC176.82-.9.R37	Thin films	531.382	QC191	Elasticity
530.42	QA911-930	Fluid dynamics	531.382	QC191	Elastic waves
530.42	QC175.4-.47	Superfluidity	531.385	QA931-939	Plasticity
530.427	QC183	Surface tension	531.385	QC191	Plasticity
530.44	QC702-721	Ionization of gases	531.6	QC72-73.8	Force and energy
530.44	QC717-.8	Plasma (Ionized gases)	531.62	QC73.8.C6	Energy conservation
530.444	QC701.7-702.7	Ionization	532	QA901-930	Fluids
530.474	QC173.4.C74	Critical phenomena (Physics)	532	QC138-168.86	Fluids
530.474	QC175.16.P5	Phase transformations (Statistical physics)	532	QC141-159	Liquids
			532	TC160-179	Hydraulics
530.475	QC183	Brownian movements	532.051	QA913	Boundary layer
530.475	QC185	Diffusion	532.0525	QA929	Laminar flow
530.475	QC318.M3	Mass transfer	532.25	QA907	Floating bodies
530.7	QC53-55	Physical instruments	532.25	QC147	Floating bodies
530.7	QC53	Recording instruments	532.5	QA911-930	Hydrodynamics
530.7	QC100.5-.8	Measuring instruments	532.5	QA913	Kinematics
530.7	QC107	Scales (Weighing instruments)	532.5	QA913	Rotating masses of fluid
			532.5	QC150-159	Fluid dynamics
530.7	QC107	Weighing-machines	532.5	QC150-159	Hydrodynamics
530.8	G86	Mile, Roman	532.5	QC175.3-.36	Kinetic theory of liquids
530.8	QC100-111	Testing	532.5	TC171-179	Hydrodynamics
530.8	T50-51	Mensuration	532.510284	TC177	Flow meters
530.81	QC81-114	Weights and measures	532.52	TC173	Water jets
530.8109	QC83-86	Weights and measures—History	532.52	TC173	Nozzles
			532.54	TC175-.2	Channels (Hydraulic engineering)
530.812	QC90.8-94	Metric system			
530.812	QC90.8-94	Decimal system	532.59	QA913	Turbulence
531	QC176-.9	Solid state physics	532.59	QA925	Vortex-motion
531.01515	QA801-871	Mechanics, Analytic	532.59	QA927	Gravity waves
531.11	QA801-935	Motion	532.59	TC172	Wave makers
531.11	QA845-871	Dynamics	532.59	TC172	Water waves
531.11	QA861-863	Dynamics, Rigid	532.593	QA913	Wakes (Fluid dynamics)
531.11	QC122-168	Motion	532.593	QA927	Nonlinear wave equations
531.11	QC131	Equilibrium			

Dewey	LC	Subject Heading	Dewey	LC	Subject Heading
532.593	QA927	Wave-motion, Theory of	535.6019	BF789.C7	Color—Psychological aspects
532.593	QC157	Waves			
532.593	QC168.85.D46	Detonation waves	535.6019	BF789.C7	Color—Psychological aspects
532.595	QC159	Vortex-motion			
533	QC161-166.5	Pneumatics	535.84	QC454.A8	Atomic absorption spectroscopy
533	QC161-166.5	Gases			
533.2	QA930	Gas dynamics	535.84	QC454.E46	Emission spectroscopy
533.2	QC167.5-168.86	Gas dynamics	535.84	QC465	Spectroscope
533.5	QC166-.5	Vacuum	535.840284	QC451	Spectrum analysis—Instruments
533.50284	QC166	Vacuum-gages			
533.6	QC161-166.5	Air	535.842	QC457	Infrared spectra
533.61	QC168	Aerostatics	535.842	QC457	Infrared spectroscopy
533.62	QA930	Aerodynamics	535.843	QC454.L63	Light beating spectroscopy
533.7	QC175-.16	Kinetic theory of gases	535.844	QC459-.5	Ultraviolet spectroscopy
534	QC220-246	Sound	535.846	QC454.R36	Raman effect
534.0284	QC228.3	Sound—Equipment and supplies	536	QC251-338.5	Heat
			536.2	QC319.8-338.5	Heat—Transmission
534.0287	QC243	Sound—Measurement	536.4	QC284	Compressibility
534.204	QC233	Echo	536.41	QC281.5.E9	Expansion (Heat)
534.208	QC233	Absorption of sound	536.412	QC164	Expansion of gases
534.208	QC235	Sound-waves—Damping	536.42	QC303	Fusion
534.208	QC243	Sound-waves—Damping	536.42	QC303	Solidification
534.23	QC242-.5	Underwater acoustics	536.44	QC304	Evaporation
534.5	QC231	Kinematics	536.50287	QC270-278.6	Temperature measurements
534.5	QC235-241	Vibration	536.50287	QC270-278.6	Thermometers
534.55	QC244	Ultrasonic waves	536.520287	QC277	Pyrometers
535	QC350-467	Light	536.56072	QC277.9-278.6	Low temperature research
535	QC350-467	Optics	536.57	QC276-277	High temperatures
535.014	QC459-.5	Ultraviolet radiation	536.6	QC290-297	Calorimeters
535.014	QC459.5	Far ultraviolet radiation	536.7	QC310.15-319	Thermodynamics
535.028	QC370.5-379	Optical instruments	537	QC501-721	Electricity
535.0284	QC367	Optical measurements	537	QC669-675.8	Electromagnetic theory
535.12	QC402	Light, Corpuscular theory of	537	QC759.6-761.3	Electromagnetism
535.13	QC403	Light, Wave theory of	537.0284	QC543-544	Electric apparatus and appliances
535.2	QC392-449.5	Physical optics			
535.2	QC403	Coherence (Optics)	537.0284	QC544.C3	Cathode ray tubes
535.2	QC446.15-.3	Nonlinear optics	537.0287	QC535-537	Electric measurements
535.220287	QC391	Photometry	537.072	QC541	Electric laboratories
535.323	QC385	Reflection (Optics)	537.0724	QC527	Electricity—Experiments
535.323	QC425	Reflection (Optics)	537.0724	QC533-534	Electricity—Experiments
535.324	QC385	Lenses	537.092	QC514-515	Electricians
535.324	QC425	Refraction, Double	537.2	QC570-596.9	Electrostatics
535.326	QC437	Absorption of light	537.21	QC581.E4	Electric charge and distribution
535.35	QC476.4-480.2	Luminescence			
535.352	QC477-.4	Fluorescence	537.24	QC584-585.8	Dielectrics
535.357	QC480	Electroluminescence	537.240287	QC584	Dielectric measurements
535.4	QC414.8-417	Diffraction	537.2448	QC596-.9	Ferroelectricity
535.4	QC431-435	Dispersion	537.5	QC685-689.55	Quantum electronics
535.420284	QC425	Prisms	537.5	QC703.7	Exploding wire phenomena
535.47	QC411	Interference (Light)	537.52	QC705	Electric arc
535.52	QC440-446	Polarization (Light)	537.534	QC660.5-665	Electric waves
535.6	QC494-496.9	Colors	537.534	QC665.P6	Radio waves—Polarization
535.6	QC494-496.9	Color	537.534	QC676-678.6	Radio waves
			537.5352	QC482.S6	X-ray spectroscopy
			537.54	QC611	Photoelectricity

Dewey	LC	Subject Heading	Dewey	LC	Subject Heading
537.54	QC612.P5	Photoconductivity	539.2	QC665.T7	Electromagnetic waves—Transmission
537.54	QC715.15	Photoemission			
537.56	QC793.5.E62-.E629	Electron optics	539.6	QC173	Molecules
537.6	QC601-641	Electric currents	539.6	QC179	Molecules
537.6	QC612.H3	Hall effect	539.7	QC173	Atoms
537.6	QC623	Electric currents—Heating effects	539.7	QC770-798	Nuclear physics
			539.7	QC791.9-792.8	Nuclear energy
537.6	QC630-648	Electrodynamics	539.72	QC793-.5	Particles (Nuclear physics)
537.6	QC641	Electric currents, Alternating	539.721	QC793.5.F42-.F429	Fermions
537.62	QC610.3-635	Electric conductivity			
537.62	QC611	Electric resistance	539.7211	QC793.5.L42-.L429	Leptons (Nuclear physics)
537.6223	QC611.8.D66	Doped semiconductors			
537.6223	QC611.8.M25	Diluted magnetic semiconductors	539.72112	QC793.5.E462-.E4629	Electrons
537.6223	QC611.8.N35	Narrow gap semiconductors	539.72112	QC793.5.E628	Electrons—Polarization
537.6223	QC611.8.O7	Organic semiconductors	539.72123	QC793.5.P72-.P729	Antiprotons
537.6223	QC611.8.W53	Wide gap semiconductors	539.7213	QC793.5.N462-.N4622	Neutrons
537.6226	QC610.9-611.8	Semiconductors			
537.623	QC611.9-.98	Superconductivity	539.7213	QC793.5.N4629	Neutron sources
537.65	QC621-625	Thermoelectricity	539.7215	QC793.5.N42-.N429	Neutrinos
538	QC750-776	Magnetism			
538	QC760-.3	Electromagnets	539.7216	QC793.5.H32-.H329	Hadrons
538.0287	QC761	Magnetic measurements			
538.0287	QC818-849	Magnetic measurements	539.7216	QC793.5.S72-.S729	Strange particles
538.362	QC762	Nuclear magnetic resonance	539.72162	QC793.5.M42-.M429	Mesons
538.362	QC762	Deuteron magnetic resonance spectroscopy	539.72162	QC793.5.M42-.M429	Kaons
538.362	QC762.6.A25	Acoustic nuclear magnetic resonance	539.72167	QC793.5.Q252-.Q2529	Quarks
538.364	QC763	Electron paramagnetic resonance	539.7217	QC173	Photon beams
538.4	QC754.2.M33	Magnetic induction	539.7217	QC793.5.P42-.P429	Photons
538.4	QC757	Magnets			
538.42	QC771	Diamagnetism	539.7222	QC480-482.3	X-rays
538.6	QC718.5.M36	Magnetohydrodynamics	539.7222	QC484.3	Bremsstrahlung
538.6	QC809.M3	Magnetohydrodynamics	539.7222	QC793.5.G322	Gamma ray sources
538.7	QC809.M25	Cosmic magnetic fields	539.7223	QC484.8-485.9	Cosmic rays
538.7	QC811-849	Geomagnetism	539.7223	QC485	Solar cosmic rays
538.70223	QC822	Geomagnetism—Maps	539.7223	QC485.8.S5	Cosmic ray showers
538.727	QE501.4.P35	Paleomagnetism	539.7232	QC793.5.A22-.A229	Alpha rays
538.744	QC835	Magnetic storms			
538.748	QC845	Earth currents	539.7234	QC702.7.H42	Heavy ions
538.766	QC809.M35	Magnetosphere	539.725	Q172.5.S95	Symmetry
538.766	QC809.V3	Van Allen radiation belts	539.725	QC174.17.S9	Symmetry (Physics)
538.7672	QC881.2.D2	D region	539.725	QC793.3.S9	Symmetry (Physics)
538.768	QC970-972.5	Auroras	539.725	QC794.6.E9	Spin excitations
538.79	QC818	Geomagnetic observatories	539.725	QC795.8.E5	Energy levels (Quantum mechanics)
539.14	QC173.4.A87	Atomic structure			
539.2	QC474-492	Radiation	539.73	QC787.E39	Electron accelerators
539.2	QC476.S6	Radiation sources	539.73	QC787.P3	Particle accelerators
539.2	QC665.D5	Electromagnetic waves—Diffraction	539.73	QC793.3.B4	Particle beams
			539.73	TK9340	Particle accelerators
539.2	QC665.E4	Electromagnetic fields	539.732	QC787.E4	Electrostatic accelerators
			539.733	QC787.L5	Linear accelerators

Dewey	LC	Subject Heading	Dewey	LC	Subject Heading
539.735	QC787.S9	Synchrotrons	541.22	QD461	Molecular structure
539.736	QC787.S83	Superconducting Super Collider	541.222	QD463-464	Molecular weights
			541.224	QD471	Radicals (Chemistry)
539.74	QC793.3.S8	Nuclear structure	541.224	QD471	Free radicals (Chemistry)
539.75	QC794	Annihilation reactions	541.224	QP527	Free radicals (Chemistry)
539.752	QC793.3.D4	Decay schemes (Radioactivity)	541.224	RB170	Free radicals (Chemicals)
			541.2252	QD471	Tautomerism
539.752	QC794.95-798	Radioactivity	541.242	QC173	Atomic mass
539.752	QC795.8.D4	Decay schemes (Radioactivity)	541.242	QD463-464	Atomic weights
			541.242	QD466	Atomic mass
539.752	QC795.8.H3	Half-life (Nuclear physics)	541.28	QD462-464	Quantum chemistry
539.7523	QC793.5.B425	Beta decay	541.33	QC183	Adhesion
539.7544	QC794.8.W4	Weak interactions (Nuclear physics)	541.33	QC183	Cohesion
			541.33	QD506-509	Surface chemistry
539.7546	QC794.8.E4	Electromagnetic interactions	541.34	QD541-549	Solution (Chemistry)
			541.34	QD541-543	Activity coefficients
539.756	QC794.8.P4	Photonuclear reactions	541.3415	QD543	Osmosis
539.757	QC794.6.C6	Collisions (Nuclear physics)	541.342	QD543	Solubility
539.758	QC794.6.S3	Scattering amplitude (Nuclear physics)	541.35	QD701-731	Photochemistry
			541.36	QD510-536	Thermochemistry
539.758	QC794.6.S3	Scattering (Physics)	541.361	QD516	Combustion
539.76	QC794.8.D57	Direct reactions (Nuclear physics)	541.361	QD516	Explosions
			541.361	QD516	Flame
539.762	QC789.7-790.8	Nuclear fission	541.364	QD517	Dissociation
539.764	QC790.95-791.8	Nuclear fusion	541.3686	QD515	Cryochemistry
539.764	QC791.7-.775	Controlled fusion	541.3686072	QD536	Low temperature research
539.77	QC787.C6	Neutron counters	541.37	QD273	Electrochemistry
539.77	QC787.C6	Nuclear counters	541.37	QD551-575	Electrochemistry
539.770284	QC785.5-787	Radioactivity—Instruments	541.370284	QD277	Electric furnaces
539.772	QC787.I6	Ionization chambers	541.372	QC541-543	Electrolytes
539.774	QC787.G4	Geiger-Muller counters	541.372	QD79.E44	Electrophoresis
539.775	QC787.S34	Scintillation counters	541.372	QD117.E45	Electrophoresis
540	QD	Chemistry	541.372	QD272.E43	Electrophoresis
540	QD466-467	Chemical elements	541.372	QD549	Electrolytes
540.112	QD13	Alchemy	541.372	QD553-585	Electrolytes
540.112	QD23.3-26.5	Alchemy	541.372	QD561-562	Ions
540.14	QD7	Chemistry—Nomenclature	541.372	QD565	Electrolytes—Conductivity
540.3	QD4-5	Chemistry—Dictionaries	541.3722	QD561-562	Ionization
540.6	QD1	Chemistry—Societies, etc.	541.3722	QD562.I65	Dissociation
540.71	QD40-49	Chemistry—Study and teaching	541.3723	QD562.I63	Ion exchange
			541.3724	QD571-572	Electrodes
540.72	QD51-64	Chemical laboratories	541.38	QD601-608	Nuclear chemistry
540.724	QD43	Chemistry—Experiments	541.38	QD601-608	Radiochemistry
540.9	QD11-18	Chemistry—History	541.382	QD625-655	Radiation chemistry
540.92	QD21-22	Chemists	541.388	QD466.5	Isotopes
541	QD450-801	Chemistry, Physical and theoretical	541.39	QD501-505.5	Chemical reaction, Conditions and law of
541.0421	QD478	Organic solid state chemistry	541.392	QD501	Chemical equilibrium
541.0421	QD478	Solid state chemistry	541.392	QD503	Phase rule and equilibrium
541.0424	QD581	Plasma chemistry	541.393	QD63.O9	Electrolytic oxidation
541.06	QD450	Chemistry, Physical and theoretical—Societies, etc.	541.393	QD63.R4	Electrolytic reduction
			541.393	QD63.R4	Reduction (Chemistry)
541.2	QD461	Atomic theory	541.395	QD501	Catalysts
541.2	QD461	Molecular theory	541.395	QD505	Phase-transfer catalysts

Dewey	LC	Subject Heading	Dewey	LC	Subject Heading
541.395	QD505	Catalysis	546.734	QD181.I1	Iodine
542	QD53-54	Chemical apparatus	546.751	QD181.H4	Helium
542	QD54.C4	Centrifuges	546.752	QD181.N5	Neon
542	QD535	Dewar flasks	546.753	QD181.A6	Argon
542.4	QD63.D6	Distillation	546.755	QD181.X1	Xenon
542.4	QD87	Blowpipe	546.756	QD181.R2	Radon
542.6	QD63.F5	Filters and filtration	546.8	QD467	Periodic law
543	QD71-142	Chemistry, Analytic	547	QD241-441	Chemistry, Organic
543	QD81-98	Chemistry, Analytic—Qualitative	547.005	QD241	Chemistry, Organic—Periodicals
543	QD171-172	Metals	547.05	QD410-412.5	Organometallic compounds
543.05	QD71	Chemistry, Analytic—Periodicals	547.2	QD262	Organic compounds—Synthesis
543.1	QD101-117	Chemistry, Analytic—Quantitative	547.2	QD341	Condensation products (Chemistry)
543.24	QD111	Volumetric analysis	547.23	QD281.O9	Electrolytic oxidation
543.26	QD79.T38	Thermal analysis	547.23	QD281.O9	Oxidation
543.26	QD117.T4	Thermal analysis	547.23	QD281.R4	Electrolytic reduction
543.4	QC115-116	Electrochemical analysis	547.28	QD281.P6	Addition polymerization
543.5	QC450-467	Spectrum analysis	547.28	QD281.P6	Polymerization
543.5	QD95-96	Spectrum analysis	547.41	QD305.H5-.H9	Hydrocarbons
543.85	QD79.C45	Gas chromatography	547.413	QD305.H8	Acetylene compounds
543.85	QD117.C515	Gas chromatography	547.413	QD305.H8	Acetylene
546	QD146-197	Chemistry, Inorganic	547.59	QD399-406	Heterocyclic compounds
546.0284	QD157	Electric furnaces	547.6	QD330-341	Aromatic compounds
546.06	QD146	Chemistry, Inorganic—Societies, etc.	547.61	QD341.H9	Hydrocarbons
			547.611	QD341.H9	Benzene
546.2	QD181.H1	Hydrogen	547.62	QD412	Halogen compounds
546.212	QD181.H1	Deuterium	547.632	QD341.P5	Phenols
546.22	GB855	Water chemistry	547.7	QD380-388	Polymers
546.22	QD142	Water—Analysis	547.7	QD421-.7	Alkaloids
546.22	QD169.W3	Water	547.75	QD431-.7	Proteins
546.24	QD167	Inorganic acids	547.75	QD431-.7	Amino acids
546.34	QD189-193	Salts	547.756	QD431-.7	Peptides
546.34	QD191	Double salts	547.78	QD320-327	Carbohydrates
546.38	QD172.A4	Alkalies	547.78	QD320-327	Sugars
546.385	QD181.C8	Cesium	547.78	QD321	Fructose
546.41	QD172.R2	Earths, Rare	547.78	QD321	Dextrose
546.41	QD172.R2	Rare earth metals	547.78	QD321	Glucose
546.431	QD181.U7	Uranium	547.8434	QD419-.7	Gums and resins
546.6	QD172.T6	Transition metal compounds	548	QD901-999	Crystallography
			548.5	QD901-999	Crystallization
546.621	QE391.I7	Iron	548.5	QD921-926	Crystal growth
546.663	QD181.H6	Mercury	548.7	QD911-919	Crystallography, Mathematical
546.678	QD181.T7	Thallium			
546.6812	QD181.C1	Carbon dioxide	548.7	QD911-919	Lattice theory
546.7	QD161-169	Nonmetals	548.842	QD945	Dislocations in crystals
546.711	QD181.N1	Nitrogen	549	QE351-399.2	Mineralogy
546.7112	QD181.N1	Ammonia	549.012	QE388	Minerals—Classification
546.712	QD181.P1	Phosphorus	549.05	QE351	Mineralogy—Periodicals
546.716	QD181.S3	Antimony	549.1	QE367-369	Mineralogy, Determinative
546.721	QD181.O1	Oxygen	549.13	QE371	Mineralogical chemistry
546.721	QD181.O1	Active oxygen	549.2	QE389.1	Native element minerals
546.73	QD165	Halogen compounds	549.27	QE393	Diamonds
546.731	QD181.F1	Fluorine			

Dewey	LC	Subject Heading	Dewey	LC	Subject Heading
549.4	QE389.4	Halide minerals	551.31	GB2401-2598	Ice sheets
549.528	QE364.2.R3	Radioactive substances	551.31	GB2401-2597	Ice
549.62	QE391.G37	Garnet	551.31028	GB2401.72.A37	Aerial photography in glaciology
549.62	QE391.T6	Topaz			
549.68	QE391.F3	Feldspar	551.312	GB641-648	Rock glaciers
549.68	QE391.Q2	Quartz	551.312	GB2401-2598	Glaciers
549.68	QE394.07	Opals	551.313	QE575-579	Glacial erosion
549.72	QE389.64	Phosphate minerals	551.315	GB581-588	Glacial landforms
549.72	QE394.T8	Turquoise	551.342	GB2401-2597	Icebergs
549.74	QE390.2.T85	Tungsten ores	551.343	GB2401-2598	Sea ice drift
549.782	QE391.D6	Dolomite	551.353	TC175.2	Sediment transport
550	QC801-809	Cosmic physics	551.372	QE597	Wind erosion
550	QC801-809	Geophysics	551.375	GB631-638	Sand dunes
550	QE500-511.7	Geophysics	551.375	GB649.S3	Sand waves
550.284	QE49.5	Earth science instruments	551.38	QC929.H6	Frost
551	QE	Geology	551.397	QB754.8-759	Meteorite craters
551	QE28.2	Physical geology	551.41	GB400-649	Geomorphology
551.014	QE7	Geology—Terminology	551.41	GB400-649	Landforms
551.0223	QE36	Geology—Maps	551.41	GB621-628	Bogs
551.0228	QE43	Geological modeling	551.41	GB621-628	Swamps
551.0285	QE48.8	Geology—Computer programs	551.41028	GB400.42.A35	Aerial photography in geomorphology
551.06	QE1	Geology—Societies, etc.	551.415	GB611-618	Arid regions
551.071	QE40-48	Geology—Study and teaching	551.415	GB611-618	Desertification
			551.415	GB611-618	Desertification—Control
551.0723	QE61-350.62	Geological surveys	551.415	GB611-618	Deserts
551.0723	QE61-350	Surveys	551.42	GB471-478	Islands
551.074	QE51	Geological museums	551.424	GB461-468	Reefs
551.09	QE11-13	Geology—History	551.424	GB461-468	Coral reefs and islands
551.09	QE28.3	Historical geology	551.424	QE565-566	Coral reefs and islands
551.092	QE21-22	Geologists	551.43	GB448	Slopes (Physical geography)
551.11	QE509	Earth—Internal structure	551.432	GB501-555	Mountains
551.12	QE509	Earth temperature	551.434	GB571-578	Plateaus
551.136	QE511.7	Sea-floor spreading	551.434	GB571-578	Mesas
551.(2-3)	QE500-639.5	Geodynamics	551.44	GB454.F5	Fjords
551.21	QE521.5-527.5	Volcanoes	551.44	GB454.I54	Inlets
551.22	QE531-541	Seismology	551.442	GB561-568	Arroyos
551.22	QE531-541	Earthquakes	551.442	GB561-568	Floodplains
551.22	QE539	Elastic waves	551.442	GB561-568	Valleys
551.220287	QE541	Seismometry	551.447	GB599-609.2	Karst
551.23	GB1198-.4	Hot springs	551.447	GB601-608	Caves
551.23	GB1198.5-.8	Geysers	551.447	GB609.2	Sinkholes
551.23	QE528	Hot springs	551.45	GB561-568	Watersheds
551.23	QE545	Volcanic gases	551.453	GB561-568	Savannas
551.302	QE570	Weathering	551.453	GB571-578	Prairies
551.302	QE571-597	Erosion	551.453	GB571-578	Plains
551.303	QE571-597	Sedimentation and deposition	551.453	GB571-578	Steppes
			551.453	GB591-598	Alluvial plains
551.307	QC929.A8	Avalanches	551.456	GB591-598	Deltas
551.307	QE598-600.3	Earth movements	551.457	GB450-460	Coasts
551.307	QE598-600.3	Mass-wasting	551.458	GB451-460	Seashore
551.307	QE599	Debris avalanches	551.46	GC	Oceanography
551.307	QE599	Landslides	551.460284	GC41	Oceanographic instruments
551.307	QE599	Rockslides	551.4607	GC65-78	Underwater exploration

Dewey	LC	Subject Heading	Dewey	LC	Subject Heading
551.4607	VK588-597	Hydrographic surveying	551.5	QC851-999	Meteorology
551.46072	GC57-59	Oceanography—Research	551.5	QC880-.4	Dynamic meteorology
551.46072	GC66	Manned undersea research stations	551.5	QC880	Atmospheric density
			551.5	QC883-.2	Weather, Influence of the moon on
551.4613	GC481-711	Oceanography—Atlantic Ocean	551.5014	QC854.2	Meteorology—Terminology
551.46132	GC401-455	Oceanography—Arctic Ocean	551.50284	QC875.5-876.7	Meteorological instruments
			551.50284	QC880	Densitometer (Meteorological instrument)
551.4614	GC771-871	Oceanography—Pacific Ocean	551.505	QC851	Meteorology—Periodicals
551.4615	GC721-761	Oceanography—Indian Ocean	551.509	QC855-857	Meteorology—History
			551.5092	QC858	Meteorologists—Biography
551.4617	GC461-462	Oceanography—Antarctic Ocean	551.51	QC973.4.R35	Atmospheric radio refractivity
551.4618	GC96-97.8	Estuarine oceanography	551.511	QC879.6-.85	Atmospheric chemistry
551.4618	GC96-97.8	Estuaries	551.5113	QC882.5	Dust
551.462	GC228.5-.6	Ocean circulation	551.513	QC881.2.T75	Troposphere
551.462	GC229-299	Ocean currents	551.514	QC879-.59	Atmosphere, Upper
551.462	GC296.8.E	El Nino Current	551.514	QC879	Atmosphere, Upper—Rocket observations
551.462	GC296.G9	Gulf Stream			
551.463	GC205-226	Ocean waves	551.514	QC973.4.M33	Magnetospheric radio wave propagation
551.463	GC211-222	Waves			
551.463	GC211.2	Waves	551.5142	QC881.2.09	Ozone layer
551.463	GC225-226	Storm surges	551.5145	QC879	F region
551.464	GC300-376	Tides	551.5145	QC881.2.E2	E region
551.464	GC308-309	Tidal currents	551.5145	QC881.2.I6	Ionosphere
551.464	GC376	Bores (Tidal phenomena)	551.515	QC880.4.D5	Divergence (Meteorology)
551.464	QC883.2.A8	Atmospheric tides	551.517	QC880.4.A8	Atmospheric circulation
551.465	GC100-103	Seawater	551.518	QC930.5-959	Winds
551.465	GC109-149	Chemical oceanography	551.518	QC935	Winds aloft
551.4653	GC160-177	Ocean temperature	551.5183	QC935	Jet stream
551.4653	GC175	Deep-sea temperature	551.5183	QC939.T7	Trade winds
551.4664	GC121-127	Salinity	551.5184	QC939.M7	Monsoons
551.468	GC87.6	Submarine trenches	551.5185	QC939.F6	Chinook winds
551.468	QE39	Submarine geology	551.5185	QC939.L37	Sea breeze
551.4683	GC83-87.6	Submarine topography	551.5185	QC939.M8	Mountain wave
551.4683	GC87-.6	Ocean bottom	551.52	QC880.4.T5	Atmospheric thermodynamics
551.4686	GC380-399	Marine sediments			
551.48	GB651-2998	Hydrology	551.5246	GC190-.5	Ocean-atmosphere interaction
551.48	GB651-2998	Water			
551.48	GB651-2998	Water-supply	551.525	QC901-912.2	Atmospheric temperature
551.48028	GB656.2.A37	Aerial photography in hydrology	551.5253	QC981.8.C5	Climatic changes
			551.5253	QC981.8.G56	Global warming
551.482	GB1601-1798.9	Lakes	551.5253	QC982.8-994.9	Climatic changes
551.482	GB2201-2398	Lagoons	551.5271	QC910.2-913.2	Sunshine
551.483	GB1201-1399.5	Rivers	551.5271	QC910.2-911.82	Solar radiation
551.483	GB1207	Streamflow	551.5272	QC809.T4	Terrestrial radiation
551.4830287	GB1201-1398	Stream measurements	551.5273	QC912.3	Atmospheric radiation
551.484	GB1401-1597	Waterfalls	551.5276	QC809.C6	Cosmic noise
551.489	GB1203	Flood routing	551.5276	QC883.2.S6	Cosmic physics
551.489	GB1399-.5	Floods	551.5276	QC913-.2	Atmospheric radioactivity
551.4890112	GB1399.2	Flood forecasting	551.54	QC885-896	Atmospheric pressure
551.49	GB1001-1199.8	Groundwater	551.540284	QC886-887	Barometers
551.498	GB1198-.4	Springs	551.55	QC880.4.S65	Squall lines
551.5	QC851-999	Atmosphere	551.55	QC880.4.S65	Squalls

Dewey	LC	Subject Heading	Dewey	LC	Subject Heading
551.55	QC880.4.T8	Atmospheric turbulence	551.634	QC996	Numerical weather forecasting
551.55	QC940.6-959	Storms	551.635	QC972.6-973.8	Radio meteorology
551.5512	QC880.4.A5	Air masses	551.6353	QC973.45-.8	Radar meteorology
551.5512	QC880.4.F7	Fronts (Meteorology)	551.6353	QC973.8.W	Weather radar networks
551.5512	QC880.4.F7	Occluded fronts (Meteorology)	551.6362	QC997.75	Nowcasting (Meteorology)
551.5512	QC981.8.A5	Cold waves (Meteorology)	551.6365	QC997	Long-range weather forecasting
551.5513	QC940.6-959	Cyclones	551.6365	QC999	Almanacs
551.552	QC944-948	Hurricanes	551.6418	QC931	Wind forecasting
551.552	QC948	Typhoons	551.64513	QC951	Cyclone forecasting
551.553	QC955-.5	Tornadoes	551.64773	QC929.2-.28	Drought forecasting
551.553	QC957	Waterspouts	551.65162	QC993.83-994.9	Marine meteorology
551.554	QC929.H15	Hailstorms	551.66	QC883.7-.86	Micrometeorology
551.554	QC968-.2	Thunderstorms	551.68	QC926.6-928.74	Weather control
551.559	QC958-959	Dust storms	551.68	QC928.6	Rain-making
551.56	QC974.5-976	Meteorological optics	551.68	QC948	Typhoon modification
551.561	QC966.7.A84	Atmospheric ionization	551.69	QC884-.2	Paleoclimatology
551.563	QC960.5-969	Atmospheric electricity	551.6913	QC993.5	Tropics—Climate
551.5632	QC966-.7	Lightning	551.69143	QC993.6	Mountain climate
551.567	QC976.R2	Rainbow	551.69154	QC993.7	Arid regions climate
551.57	GB2801-2998	Hydrometeorology	551.691732	QC981.7.U7	Urban climatology
551.57	QC915-929	Moisture	551.694	QC989	Europe—Climate
551.57	QC915	Moisture index	551.695	QC990	Asia—Climate
551.57	QC920	Water	551.696	QC991	Africa—Climate
551.571	QC915-917	Humidity	551.6971	QC985-.5	Canada—Climate
551.572	QC915-917	Evaporation (Meteorology)	551.6972	QC986	Mexico—Climate
551.572	QC915.5-.7	Evapotranspiration	551.69729	QC987	West Indies—Climate
551.574	QC921.6.C6	Condensation (Meteorology)	551.6973	QC983-984	United States—Climate
551.5741	QC921.6.C6	Atmospheric nucleation	551.698	QC988	South America—Climate
551.5744	QC929.D5	Dew	551.6994	QC992	Australia—Climate
551.575	QC929.F7	Ice fog	551.7	QE501.4.P3	Paleogeography
551.575	QC929.F7	Fog	551.7	QE640-699	Geology, Stratigraphic
551.576	QC920.7-924	Clouds	551.701	QE508	Earth—Age
551.577	QC924.5-926.2	Rain and rainfall	551.701	QE508	Geological time
551.577	QC929	Precipitation (Meteorology)	551.701	QE508	Radioactive dating
551.5770284	QC926	Rain gauges	551.72	QE654-674	Geology, Stratigraphic—Paleozoic
551.5770284	QC926	Precipitation gauges			
551.5771	QC926.5-.57	Acid precipitation (Meteorology)	551.76	QE675-688	Geology, Stratigraphic—Mesozoic
551.5773	QC929.2-.28	Droughts	551.78	QE690-699	Geology, Stratigraphic—Cenozoic
551.5784	QC929.S7	Snow			
551.5787	QC929.H15	Hail	551.792	QE697-698	Glacial epoch
551.6	QC851-999	Climatology	551.8	QE511.4-.48	Plate tectonics
551.6	QC980-999	Weather	551.8	QE604	Rock deformation
551.605	QC980	Weather—Periodicals	551.872	QE606-.5	Faults (Geology)
551.63	QC875	Automatic meteorological stations	551.875	QE606-.5	Folds (Geology)
			551.88	QE611-.5	Dikes (Geology)
551.63	QC875	Meteorological stations	551.88	QE611-.5	Necks (Geology)
551.63	QC994.95-999	Weather forecasting	551.88	QE611-.5	Intrusions (Geology)
551.632	QC877.5	Weather reporting, Radio	551.88	QE611-.5	Veins (Geology)
551.632	QC877.5	Weather broadcasting	551.9	QE514-516.5	Geochemistry
551.632	QC877.5	Television weathercasting	552	QE420-499	Petrology
551.633	QC996.5	Statistical weather forecasting	552	QE420-499	Rocks
			552.005	QE420	Petrology—Periodicals

Dewey	LC	Subject Heading	Dewey	LC	Subject Heading
552.0094	QE451	Petrology—Europe	560.1766	QE733	Paleontology—Jurassic
552.00971	QE445.5-446	Petrology—Canada	560.177	QE734	Paleontology—Cretaceous
552.00972	QE446.5-.6	Petrology—Mexico	560.178	QE735-741.3	Paleontology—Cenozoic
552.00973	QE444-445	Petrology—United States	560.1784	QE737	Paleontology—Eocene
552.095	QE452	Petrology—Asia	560.1785	QE738	Paleontology—Oligocene
552.096	QE453	Petrology—Africa	560.1787	QE739	Paleontology—Miocene
552.09728	QE447	Petrology—Central America	560.5	QE701	Paleontology—Periodicals
552.09729	QE448	Petrology—West Indies	560.75	QE718	Fossils—Collection and preservation
552.098	QE449	Petrology—South America			
552.0993	QE454.5-.6	Petrology—New Zealand	560.94	QE753-755	Paleontology—Europe
552.0994	QE453.5-454	Petrology—Australia	560.95	QE756	Paleontology—Asia
552.099(5-6)	QE455	Petrology—Oceania	560.96	QE757	Paleontology—Africa
552.09981	QE456	Petrology—Arctic regions	560.971	QE748	Paleontology—Canada
552.09989	QE456.5	Petrology—Antarctic regions	560.972	QE749	Paleontology—Mexico
552.1	QE461-462	Rocks, Igneous	560.9728	QE751	Paleontology—Central America
552.22	QE461	Lava			
552.23	QE461-462	Volcanic ash, tuff, etc.	560.9729(9)	QE750	Paleontology—West Indies
552.3	QE462.D56	Diorite	560.973	QE746-747	Paleontology—United States
552.3	QE462.G7	Granite			
552.4	QE475	Rocks, Metamorphic	560.98	QE752	Paleontology—South America
552.4	QE475.A2	Metamorphism (Geology)			
552.5	QE471-.15	Rocks, Sedimentary	560.994	QE758	Paleontology—Australia
552.5	QE471-.15	Sedimentology	560.9981	QE744	Paleontology—Arctic regions
552.5	QE471.15.S25	Sandstone			
552.5	QE471.15.S5	Shale	560.9989	QE760	Paleontology—Antarctic regions
552.5	QE471.3	Clay			
552.5	QE472	Sedimentary structures	561	QE980-983	Angiosperms, Fossil
552.58	QE471.15.C3	Rocks, Carbonate	561.16	QE991	Petrified forests
552.58	QE471.15.D6	Dolomite	561.194	QE943-945	Paleobotany—Europe
553	TN260	Geology, Economic	561.195	QE946	Paleobotany—Asia
553.6	QD181.B1	Boron	561.196	QE947	Paleobotany—Africa
554	QE260-288	Geology—Europe	561.1971	QE938	Paleobotany—Canada
555	QE289-319	Geology—Asia	561.1972	QE939	Paleobotany—Mexico
556	QE320-339	Geology—Africa	561.19728	QE941	Paleobotany—Central America
557	QE71-217	Geology—North America			
557.1	QE185-199	Geology—Canada	561.19729	QE940	Paleobotany—West Indies
557.2	QE201-203	Geology—Mexico	561.1973	QE936-937	Paleobotany—United States
557.28	QE210-217	Geology—Central America	561.198	QE942	Paleobotany—South America
557.29	QE220-226	Geology—West Indies			
557.3	QE72-182	Geology—United States	561.1993	QE948.2	Paleobotany—New Zealand
557.(4-9)	QE81-182	Geology—[United States, By state]	561.1994	QE948	Paleobotany—Australia
			561.199(5-6)	QE949	Paleobotany—Oceania
558	QE230-251	Geology—South America	561.1998(1-8)	QE934	Paleobotany—Arctic regions
559.4	QE340-348	Geology—Australia	561.19989	QE950	Paleobotany—Antarctic regions
559.8(1-2)	QE70	Geology—Arctic regions			
559.89	QE350	Geology—Antarctica	561.3	QE983	Dicetyledons, Fossil
560	QE701-996.5	Paleontology	561.5	QE975-978	Gymnosperms, Fossil
560	QE760.8-899.2	Animals, Fossil	562	QE770-832	Invertebrates, Fossil
560	QL88-.15	Extinct animals	565	QE815-832	Arthropoda, Fossil
560.171	QE724	Paleontology—Precambrian	566	QE841-899	Vertebrates, Fossil
560.172	QE725-730	Paleontology—Paleozoic	567.9	P96.M6	Dinosaurs in mass media
560.1723	QE726	Paleontology—Cambrian	567.9	QE862.D5	Dinosaurs
560.174	QE728	Paleontology—Devonian	569	QE881-882	Mammals, Fossil
560.176	QE731-734	Paleontology—Mesozoic	569	QL707	Extinct mammals
			569.5	QE882.C5	Dolphins, Fossil

Dewey	LC	Subject Heading	Dewey	LC	Subject Heading
569.78	QE882.C15	Cave bear	571.45	QP82.2.N64	Nonionizing radiation
569.8	QE882.P7	Primates, Fossil	571.464	QP82.2.C6	Cold—Physiological effect
569.9	GN282-286.7	Fossil man	571.4645	QH324.9.C7	Cryobiology
569.9	GN282.5	Missing link	571.49	QP82.2.A4	Altitude, Influence of
569.9	GN283.9	Homo habilis	571.49	QP82.2.C5	Weather—Physiological
569.9	GN284.4	Solo man			effect
569.9	GN307-499	Man, Primitive	571.49	QP82.2.P6	Pollution—Physiological
569.9	GN700-890	Man, Prehistoric			effect
569.9	GN785-786	Lake-dwellers and	571.49	QP801.P38	Pesticides—Physiological
		lake-dwellings			effect
569.9	GN799.W66	Women, Prehistoric	571.5	QL807	Histology
569.97	GN284-.7	Homo erectus	571.6	QH573-671	Cytology
569.97	GN284.6	Java man	571.6	QH573-671	Cells
569.97	GN284.7	Peking man	571.6	QH631-647	Cell physiology
569.98	GN286.3	Cro-Magnon man	571.6072	QH583-.2	Cytology—Research
569.986	GN285	Neanderthals	571.629	QR77.35	Bacteria cell surfaces
570	QH301-705	Biology	571.63435	QH657	Gravity
570.1	QH325-349	Life (Biology)	571.6345	QH652-.7	Cells—Effect of radiation on
570.1	QH331	Biology—Philosophy	571.63455	QH651	Light—Physiological effect
570.1	QP81-87	Life (Biology)	571.638	QH585.2-.45	Cell culture
570.151	QH323.5	Biomathematics	571.64	QH509	Biological transport
570.228	QH324.8	Biological models	571.64	QH601-602	Cell membranes
570.282	QH201-278.5	Microscopy	571.658	QH603.R5	Ribosomes
570.282	QH211-212	Microscopes	571.66	QH595	Cell nuclei
570.2825	QH212.E4	Electron microscopy	571.672	QR78	Flagella (Microbiology)
570.2825	QH212.E4	Electron microscopes	571.7	QH508	Biological control systems
570.2827	QH236.2	Freeze fracturing	571.7236	QK725	Plant cells and tissues
570.2827	QH237	Stains and staining	571.7236	QK725	Plant cell development
		(Microscopy)	571.72366	QK725	Plant chromosomes
570.284	QH324	Biological apparatus and	571.742	QK898.H67	Plant hormones
		supplies	571.75	QP90.4	Homeostasis
570.285	QH324.2	Biology—Data processing	571.77	QH527	Biological rhythms
570.71	QH315-320	Biology—Study and	571.77	QP84.6	Biological rhythms
		teaching	571.77	QP84.6	Sleep-wake cycle
570.72	QH315-320	Biology—Research	571.772	QK761	Biological rhythms in plants
570.72	QH321-323.2	Biological laboratories	571.782	QK761	Dormancy in plants
570.9	QH305-.2	Biology—History	571.8	QH471-489	Reproduction
570.92	QH26-31	Biologists	571.8	QH511	Growth
571	QP	Physiology	571.82	QK731-745	Growth (Plants)
571.014	QP13	Physiology—Terminology	571.835	QH607	Cell differentiation
571.0284	QP55	Physiological apparatus	571.844	QH605-.3	Cell division
571.05	QP1	Physiology—Periodicals	571.844	QH605.2	Mitosis
571.071	QP39-47	Physiology—Study and	571.845	QH605	Meiosis
		teaching	571.845	QK658	Pollen
571.0919	QH327-328	Space biology	571.847	QK929	Spores (Botany)—Dispersal
571.1	QP31-33	Physiology, Comparative	571.86	QL951-991	Embryology
571.3	QH351	Morphology	571.86	QL975	Amniotic liquid
571.3	QL799-.5	Morphology (Animals)	571.860724	QL961	Embryology, Experimental
571.3	QL801-950.9	Anatomy, Comparative	571.862	QK740	Germination
571.4	QH505	Biophysics	571.864	QH485	Fertilization (Biology)
571.43	QH513	Biomechanics	571.8642	QK828	Fertilization of plants
571.435	QP82.2.G7	Gravity	571.8642	QK926	Fertilization of plants by
571.437	QP82.2.P7	Atmospheric pressure—			insects
		Physiological effect	571.8642	QK926	Pollination
571.444	QP82.2.N6	Noise—Physiological effect			

Dewey	LC	Subject Heading	Dewey	LC	Subject Heading
571.876	QL981	Metamorphosis	572.46	QK882	Photosynthesis
571.878	QH529	Aging	572.47	QH633	Cell respiration
571.884	QH489	Generations, Alterating	572.472	QK891	Plants—Respiration
571.889	QH499	Regeneration (Biology)	572.51	QP531-535	Bioinorganic chemistry
571.8892	QK840	Regeneration (Botany)	572.51	QP533	Minerals in the body
571.89	QH475-479	Reproduction, Asexual	572.515	QP534	Trace elements in the body
571.9	RB113	Physiology, Pathological	572.516	QP535.C2	Calcium in the body
571.936	QH671	Death	572.516	QP535.C2	Calcium
571.9379	RB131-.5	Suppuration	572.516	RB138	Calcification
571.939	QH671	Cell death	572.52	QP532	Metals in the body
571.939	QP87	Death	572.5238224	QP913.N2	Salt—Physiological effect
571.96	QR180-189.5	Immunology	572.53	QP535.01	Active oxygen in the body
571.96	QR185.2	Natural immunity	572.53	QP913.01	Oxygen—Physiological effect
571.960724	QR180-183.5	Experimental immunology			
571.9638	QR184.5	Developmental immunology	572.539	QP535.H1	Water in the body
571.964	QR186-.3	Immune response	572.54	QP535.N1	Nitrogen in the body
571.9644	QR187.5	Interferon inducers	572.548	QP801.A48	Amines in the body
571.9644	QR187.5	Interferon	572.56	QP701-702	Carbohydrates
571.9645	QR186.5-.6	Antigens	572.565	QP702.S85	Sugar in the body
571.9645	QR186.6.B33	Bacterial antigens	572.565	QP702.S85	Sugars
571.9648	QR184-.4	Immunogenetics	572.57	QP751-752	Lipids
571.966	QR185.8.T2	T cells	572.57	QP752.E84	Essential fatty acids
571.967	QR186.7-.85	Immunoglobulins	572.57	QP752.F35	Fatty acids in human nutrition
571.9677	QR187-.3	Antigen-antibody reactions			
571.9688	QR185.8.C6	Complement (Immunology)	572.57	QP752.F35	Fatty acids
571.972	QR188	Allergy	572.5795	QP752.C5	Cholesterol
571.973	QR186.82-.83	Autoantibodies	572.59	QP670-671	Pigments (Biology)
571.973	QR188.3	Autoimmunity	572.592	QK898.P7	Plant pigments
571.974	QR188.35	Immunodeficiency	572.633	QP551	Amino acid sequence
571.992	QR201.E75	Epstein-Barr virus diseases	572.645	QH450.5	Genetic translation
571.992445	QR201.P26	Papillomavirus diseases	572.65	QP552.P4	Peptides
571.99247	QR201.P33	Parvovirus infections	572.65	QP561-563	Amino acids
571.992562	QR201.A72	Arbovirus infections	572.65	QP572.P4	Peptide hormones
571.993	QR201.B34	Bacterial diseases	572.65	QP572.V28	Vasoactive intestinal peptides
571.99327	QR353.5.R4	Rickettsia			
571.99353	QR201.S68	Staphylococcal infections	572.696	QP552.C34	Carrier proteins
571.995	QR245-248	Pathogenic fungi	572.7	QP601-619	Enzymes
572	QD415-436	Biochemistry	572.72	QK898.E58	Plant enzymes
572	QH345	Biochemistry	572.8	QH506	Molecular biology
572	QH613	Histochemistry	572.8	QP620-625	Nucleic acids
572	QP501-801	Biochemistry	572.82	QK728	Plant molecular biology
572	QP550-801	Bioorganic chemistry	572.86	QH447-.8	Genes
572.2	QK861-899	Botanical chemistry	572.86	QH447	Genomes
572.36	QP519.7-.9	Analytical biochemistry	572.86	QP616.D56	DNA topoisomerase I
572.4	QH521	Metabolism	572.86	QP616.D56	DNA topoisomerase II
572.4	QH634.5	Cell metabolism	572.86	QP619.D53	DNA Ligases
572.42	QK867-898	Plants—Nutrition	572.86	QP624-.75	DNA
572.42	QK881-897	Plants—Metabolism	572.86	QP624.5.C57	Circular DNA
572.43	QP176	Energy metabolism	572.8633	QH445.2	Gene mapping
572.435	QP517.P45	Photobiochemistry	572.8633	QP625.N89	Nucleotide sequence
572.4358	QH641	Bioluminescence	572.865	QH450-.6	Genetic regulation
572.437	QH517	Electrophysiology	572.87	QH600-.6	Chromosomes
572.437	QP341	Electrophysiology	572.877	QH443-450.6	Genetic recombination
572.4372	QK845	Electrophysiology of plants	572.88	QP623-.5	RNA

Dewey	LC	Subject Heading	Dewey	LC	Subject Heading
572.88	QP623.5.M47	Messenger RNA	573.667	QL881	Uterus
572.8845	QH450.2	Genetic transcription	573.679	QL944	Mammary glands
572.886	QP623.5.T73	Transfer RNA	573.7	QL821-831	Musculoskeletal system
573.1	QL835-841	Cardiovascular system	573.701	B105.M65	Movement (Philosophy)
573.1555	QL868	Spleen	573.75	QL831	Muscles
573.16	QL841	Lymphatics	573.76	QL821-827	Skeleton
573.17	QL838	Heart—Anatomy	573.76	QL821	Bones
573.18	QL835	Blood-vessels	573.78	QL825	Joints
573.185	QL835	Arteries	573.78356	QL827	Ligaments
573.186	QL835	Veins	573.79	QL950.7	Leg
573.187	QP106.6	Capillaries	573.798	QP310.F5	Animal flight
573.2	QL845-855	Respiratory organs	573.8	QL921-939	Nervous system
573.22	QL848	Lungs	573.85	QL939	Nerves
573.26	QL851	Diaphragm	573.85	QL939	Sympathetic nervous system
573.3	QL856-867	Digestive organs			
573.347	QP609.D52	Digestive enzymes	573.86	QL933-937	Medulla oblongata
573.35	QL857	Mouth	573.86	QL933-937	Meninges
573.355	QL857	Lips	573.86	QL937	Cerebellum
573.356	QL858	Teeth	573.86	QL938.H56	Hippocampus (Brain)
573.357	QL946	Tongue	573.869	QL938.S6	Spinal cord
573.359	QL861	Esophagus	573.87	QL698.8	Bird navigation
573.36	QL862	Stomach	573.87	QL782	Animal navigation
573.37	QL863	Intestines	573.87	QL945-949	Sense organs
573.377	QL866	Pancreas	573.88	QL949	Eye
573.378	QL863	Duodenum	573.88	QL949	Eyelids
573.38	QL867	Gallbladder	573.88	QL949	Optic nerve
573.38	QL867	Bile ducts	573.88	QL949	Pupil (Eye)
573.38	QL867	Liver	573.88	QL949	Retina
573.38	QM351	Bile ducts	573.89	QL948	Ear, External
573.38379	QP197	Bile	573.89	QL948	Ear
573.38379	QP752.B54	Bile acids	573.89	QL948	Eustachian tube
573.4	QL865-868	Glands	573.89	QL948	Middle ear
573.4	QL868	Endocrinology, Comparative	575	QK641-707	Botany—Anatomy
573.4	QL868	Endocrine glands	575	QK710-899	Plant physiology
573.44	QP801.H7	Hormones	575.49	QK645-650	Shoots (Botany)
573.45	QL868	Pituitary gland	575.54	QK644	Roots (Botany)
573.46	QP572.A27	Adrenaline	575.57	QK649	Leaves
573.49	QL872-881	Urinary organs	575.6	QK653	Double flowers
573.49	QL872-875	Excretory organs	575.6	QK658-659	Plants, Sex in
573.49	QL872	Bladder	575.6	QK825-830	Plants—Reproduction
573.496	QL873	Kidneys	575.6	QK827-830	Plants, Sex in
573.5	QL941-943	Dermis	575.6	QK830	Plants, Flowering of
573.5	QL941-943	Epidermis	575.6	QK830	Double flowers
573.5	QL941-943	Skin	575.633	QK653-661	Flowers—Anatomy
573.5	QP88.5	Dermis	575.633	QK653-661	Flowers—Morphology
573.5	QP88.5	Epidermis	575.65	QK828	Pollination
573.58	QL942	Hair	575.75	QK871	Plants, Motion of fluids in
573.59	QL942	Nails (Anatomy)	575.76	QK871	Plants—Absorption of water
573.59	QL942	Toenails	575.8	QK873	Evapotranspiration
573.6	QL876-881	Generative organs	575.8	QK876	Gases from plants
573.65	QL878	Generative organs, Male	576.15	QR100-130	Microbial ecology
573.658	QL878	Prostate	576.5	QH426-470	Genetics
573.66	QL881	Generative organs, Female	576.54	QH401-411	Variation (Biology)
573.665	QL881	Ovaries	576.549	QH460-468	Mutation (Biology)

Dewey	LC	Subject Heading	Dewey	LC	Subject Heading
576.549	QH465-.5	Mutagens	577.64	QH541.5.S7	Stream ecology
576.58	QH455	Population genetics	577.68	QH541.5.M3	Wetland ecology
576.8	QH359-425	Evolution (Biology)	577.68	QH541.5.S9	Swamp ecology
576.82	QH375	Natural selection	577.687	QH541.5.B63	Bog ecology
576.83	QH325	Spontaneous generation	577.69	QH541.5.C65	Coastal ecology
576.84	QE721.2.E97	Extinction (Biology)	577.69	QH541.5.S35	Seashore ecology
576.84	QH78	Extinction (Biology)	577.69	QH541.5.S35	Tide pool ecology
576.87	QH372	Coevolution	577.7	QH541.5.D35	Deep-sea ecology
577	QH514.15.E27	Ecotones	577.78	QH541.5.S87	Sublittoral ecology
577	QH540-549.5	Ecology	577.786	QH541.5.E8	Estuarine ecology
577	QH541.15.E24	Ecological heterogeneity	577.789	QH541.5.C7	Coral reef ecology
577	QK900-938	Plants—Habitat	577.83	QH546.3	Competition (Biology)
577.071	QH541.2-.264	Environmental education	577.83	QK911	Plant competition
577.0723	QH541.15.S95	Ecological surveys	577.852	QH548.3	Mutualism (Biology)
577.14	QH343.7-344	Biogeochemistry	577.88	QH352	Population biology
577.14	TD193-.5	Environmental chemistry	578.09	QH84-198	Biogeography
577.15	QH541.3	Biological productivity	578.09(4-9)	QH101-199	Natural history—[By region or country]
577.18	QH353	Biological invasions			
577.22	QH543-.2	Bioclimatology	578.094	QH135-178	Natural history—Europe
577.27	QK750-751	Plants, Effect of pollution on	578.095	QH179-193	Natural history—Asia
			578.096	QH194-195	Natural history—Africa
577.273	TD195.A34	Agricultural pollution	578.0971	QH106-.2	Natural history—Canada
577.2752	QK751	Plants, Effect of acid precipitation on	578.0972	QH107	Natural history—Mexico
			578.09728	QH108	Natural history—Central America
577.276	QK751	Plants, Effect of air pollution on	578.09729	QH109	Natural history—West Indies
577.277	QH543.5-.6	Radioecology	578.0973	QH104-105	Natural history—United States
577.3	QH541.5.F6	Forest ecology			
577.34	QH101-198	Cloud forest ecology	580.97(4-9)	QK145-195	Botany—[United States, By state]
577.34	QH541.5.C63	Cloud forest ecology	578.098	QH111-130	Natural history—South America
577.34	QH541.5.R27	Rain forest ecology			
577.38	QH541.5.C5	Chaparral ecology	578.0994	QH197	Natural history—Australia
577.38	QH541.5.M6	Moor ecology	578.4	QH546	Adaptation (Biology)
577.38	QH541.5.S55	Shrubland ecology	578.4	QP82-.2	Adaptation (Physiology)
577.4	QH541.5.P7	Grasslands	578.42	QH543.2	Acclimatization
577.4	QH541.5.P7	Grassland ecology	578.42	QH544	Phenology
577.4	QH541.5.R3	Range ecology	578.68	QH75-77	Endangered species
577.44	QH541.5.P7	Prairie ecology	578.68	QH75-77	Endangered ecosystems
577.46	QH541.5.M4	Meadow ecology	578.68	QL81.5-84.77	Endangered species
577.48	QH541.5.P7	Savanna ecology	578.738	QH87.5	Moors and heaths
577.54	QH541.5.D4	Desert ecology	578.738	SD397.C47	Chaparral
577.55	QH541.5.R62	Roadside ecology	578.748	QH87.7	Savannas
577.55	S441-482	Agricultural ecology	578.754	QH88	Desert biology
577.554	QH541.5.G37	Garden ecology	578.754	QH88	Deserts
577.554	QH541.5.H67	Household ecology	578.757	QH84.8	Soil biology
577.56	HT241-243	Urban ecology	578.76	QH90-100	Aquatic biology
577.56	QH541.5.C6	Urban ecology (Biology)	578.76	QH96-100	Freshwater biology
577.57	QH541.5.S6	Soil ecology	578.763	QH98	Lakes
577.583	QH541.5.S26	Sand dune ecology	578.768	QH87.3	Wetlands
577.6	QH541.5.F7	Freshwater ecology	578.768	QH87.3	Marshes
577.6	QH541.5.W3	Aquatic ecology	578.768	QH87.3	Swamps
577.63	QH541.5.L27	Lagoon ecology	578.77	QH91-95.59	Marine biology
577.63	QH541.5.L3	Lake ecology	578.77	QH91.75	Marine parks and reserves
577.639	QH541.5.S22	Salt lake ecology			

Dewey	LC	Subject Heading	Dewey	LC	Subject Heading
578.77	QH95.9	Brackish water biology	579.562	QR151	Yeast
578.77072	QH91.6-.65	Marine laboratories	579.6	QK600-635	Mushrooms, Hallucinogenic
578.773	QH92-93.9	Marine biology—Atlantic Ocean	579.6	QK617	Mushrooms, Edible
			579.7	QK580.7-597.7	Lichens
578.774	QH95-.55	Marine biology—Pacific Ocean	579.8	QK564-580.5	Algae
			579.82	QL368.F5	Flagellata
578.775	QH94-.7	Marine biology—Indian Ocean	579.88	QK569.P5	Brown algae
			579.89	QL948	Labyrinth (Ear)
578.776	QH90.8.P5	Plankton	580	QK	Botany
578.777	QH95.58	Marine biology—Antarctic Ocean	580	QK495.A1	Angiosperms
			580.12	QK91-97	Botany—Classification
578.7789	QH95.8	Coral reef biology	580.14	QK10	Botany—Terminology
579	QR	Microbiology	580.14	QK96	Botany—Nomenclature
579.012	QR12	Microbiology—Classification	580.222	QK98	Botany—Pictorial works
579.014	QR11	Microbiology—Terminology	580.223	QK63	Vegetation mapping
579.0222	QR54	Microbiology—Pictorial works	580.3	QK9	Botany—Dictionaries
			580.6	QK1	Botany—Societies, etc.
579.028	QR65-69	Microbiology—Technique	580.71	QK51-57	Botany—Study and teaching
579.05	QR1	Microbiology—Periodicals			
579.072	QR61-63	Microbiology—Research	580.723	QK62	Vegetation surveys
579.09	QR21-22	Microbiology—History	580.73	QK71-73	Botanical gardens
579.092	QR30-31	Microbiologists	580.74	QK75-77	Herbaria
579.138	QR13	Microorganisms—Evolution	580.74	QK79-.5	Botany—Exhibitions
579.165	QR201	Pathogenic microorganisms	580.75	QK61	Plants—Collection and preservation
579.17	QR130	Space microbiology			
579.1757	QR111-113	Soil microbiology	580.92	QK26-31	Botanists
579.176	QR105.5	Freshwater microbiology	580.94	QK281-339	Botany—Europe
579.177	QR106-.5	Marine microbiology	580.95	QK341-379	Botany—Asia
579.2	QR355-502	Viruses	580.956	QK353	Botany—Middle East
579.24	QR394.5	DNA viruses	580.959	QK360-368	Botany—Asia, Southeastern
579.2445	QR406-.2	Papovaviruses	580.96	QK381-424	Botany—Africa
579.247	QR408-.2	Parvoviruses	580.971	QK201-203	Botany—Canada
579.25	QR395	RNA viruses	580.972	QK211	Botany—Mexico
579.2562	QR398	Arboviruses	580.9728	QK215-222	Botany—Central America
579.2569	QR372.058	Oncogenic DNA viruses	580.9729	QK225-231	Botany—West Indies
579.2569	QR414.5-.6	Retroviruses	580.973	QK115-195	Botany—United States
579.26	QR342-.2	Bacteriophages	580.98	QK241-274	Botany—South America
579.27	QR343	Fungal viruses	580.994	QK431-461	Botany—Australia
579.28	QR351	Plant viruses	580.998	QK474-.3	Botany—Arctic regions
579.3	QR	Bacteriology	580.9989	QK474.4	Botany—Antarctica
579.3	QR75-99.5	Bacteria	581.35	QK981.3	Plant biochemical genetics
579.3	QR201	Pathogenic bacteria	581.35	QK981.4	Plant genetic regulation
579.3028	QR65-69	Bacteriology—Technique	581.38	QK980-989	Plants—Evolution
579.3072	QR64-.8	Bacteriological laboratories	581.47	QK648	Bark
579.3138	QR81.7	Bacteria—Evolution	581.498	QK776	Roots (Botany)
579.3149	QR89.5	Anaerobic bacteria	581.63	QK98.4	Plants, Useful
579.31755	QR111	Bacteriology, Agricultural	581.632	QK98.5	Wild plants, Edible
579.31755	QR351	Bacteriology, Agricultural	581.632	QK98.5	Plants, Edible
579.332	QR82.P78	Pseudomonas	581.634	QK99	Botany, Medical
579.355	QR82.S78	Streptococcus	581.634	QK99	Medicinal plants
579.362	QR82.B3	Bacillus (Bacteria)	581.636	QK98.7	Dye plants
579.4	QL366-369.2	Protozoa	581.659	QK100	Poisonous plants
579.432	QL368.A5	Amoeba	581.659	QK617	Mushrooms, Poisonous
579.5	QK600-635	Fungi	581.68	QK86	Endangered plants
579.5135	QK602	Fungi—Genetics			

Dewey	LC	Subject Heading	Dewey	LC	Subject Heading
581.7	QK900-938	Plant ecology	584.9	QK495.G74	Deepwater rice
581.73	QK108-474.5	Forest plants	584.9	QK495.G74	Durum wheat
581.73	QK938.F6	Timberline	584.9	QK495.G74	Fescue
581.73	QK938.F6	Forest ecology	584.9	QK495.G74	Grasses
581.73	QK938.F6	Forest plants	584.9	QK495.G74	Bamboo
581.74	QK938.P7	Grasslands	584.92	QK495.G74	Corn
581.744	QK938.P7	Prairies	584.92	QK495.G74	Crabgrass
581.746	QK938.M4	Meadow plants	585	QK494-.5	Gymnosperms
581.748	QK936	Tropical plants	585	QK494	Conifers
581.7538	QK937	Mountain plants	585.2	QK494.5.P66	Douglas fir
581.754	QK922	Desert plants	585.2	QK494.5.P66	Eastern hemlock
581.754	QK938.D4	Desert plants	585.2	QK494.5.P66	Fir
581.76	QK102-105	Aquatic plants	585.4	QK494.5.C975	Eastern red cedar
581.76	QK105	Freshwater plants	585.5	QK494.5.T3	Dawn redwood
581.76	QK930-935	Aquatic plants	586	QK504-635	Cryptogams
581.76	QK932-.7	Freshwater plants	587	QK520-532	Pteridophyta
581.7786	QK108-474.5	Estuarine plants	588	QK532.4-563.87	Bryophytes
581.7786	QK938.E	Estuarine plants	590	QL	Zoology
581.9	QK101-474.5	Phytogeography	590.14	QL10	Zoology—Terminology
581.9561	QK376	Botany—Turkey	590.222	QL46	Zoology—Pictorial works
582.16	QK474.8-494	Trees	590.6	QL1	Zoology—Societies, etc.
583	QK108-474.5	Dicotyledons	590.71	QL51-58	Zoology—Study and teaching
583	QK495.A12	Dicotyledons			
583.45	QK495.M73	Fig	590.72309676	QL337.E25	Wildlife watching—Africa, Eastern
583.46	QK495.F14	Durmast oak			
583.46	QK495.F14	English oak	590.724	HV4905-4959	Animal experimentation
583.53	QK495.N9	Bougainvillea	590.724	QL52.6	Zoology—Experiments
583.627	QK495.B4	Begonias	590.73	QL73	Menageries
583.64	QK495.C9	Bok choy	590.73	QL76-77.5	Petting zoos
583.685	QK495.M27	Hibiscus	590.73	QL76-77.5	Zoos
583.73	QK495.R78	Apples	590.74	QL71	Zoological museums
583.75	QK917	Carnivorous plants	590.752	QL63	Taxidermy
583.76	QK495.L9	Crape myrtle, Common	590.92	QL26-31	Ethologist
583.765	QK495.M9	Guava	590.9(4-9)	QL101-345	Zoogeography
583.766	QK495.M9	Eucalyptus	590.9(4-9)	QL155-339	Zoology—[By region or country]
583.77	QK495.R98	Citrus			
583.79	QK495.E92	Coca	590.98	QL105	Zoology—Arctic regions
583.84	QK495.A6853	Ginseng	591.35	QH432	Animal genetics
583.849	QK495.U48	Dill	591.47	QL759	Animal defenses
583.86	QK495.V84	Grapes	591.47	QL940	Animal weapons
583.94	QK495.C98	Dodder	591.472	QL767	Protective coloration (Biology)
583.95	QK495.G4	African violets			
583.952	QK495.S7	Eggplant	591.477	QL401-432	Shells
583.952	QK495.S7	Belladonna (Plant)	591.479	QL768	Animal tracks
583.99	QK495.C74	Dandelions	591.5	QL750-795	Animal behavior
583.99	QK495.C74	Daisies	591.5	QL785-.27	Animal psychology
583.99	QK495.C74	Big sagebrush	591.5	QL785.3	Extrasensory perception in animals
584.32	QK495.L72	Daylilies			
584.32	QK495.L72	Easter lily	591.5092	QL26-31	Zoologists
584.34	QK495.A484	Daffodils	591.512	QL781	Instinct
584.352	QK495.A26	Agave	591.513	QL785	Cognition in animals
584.38	QK495.I75	Dwarf irises	591.513	QL785	Animal intelligence
584.39	QK495.M98	Bananas	591.53	QL756.57	Cannibalism in animals
584.5	QK495.P17	Date palm	591.5(3-4)	QL756.5-.57	Animals—Food
			591.56	QL775	Social hierarchy in animals

Dewey	LC	Subject Heading
591.562	QL761	Sexual behavior in animals
591.562	QL761	Sexual selection in animals
591.563	QL761.5	Familial behavior in animals
591.563	QL762	Parental behavior in animals
591.563	QL763.2	Imprinting (Psychology)
591.563	QL763.5	Play behavior in animals
591.564	QL756-.15	Animals—Habitations
591.5648	QL756.15	Animal burrowing
591.565	QL755	Hibernation
591.59	QL776	Animal communication
591.59	QL776	Human-animal communication
591.594	QL765	Animal sounds
591.594	QL765	Sound production by animals
591.594	QL765	Voice
591.6	SB922-998	Zoology, Economic
591.609(4-9)	SB993.3-.34	Zoology, Economic—[By region or country]
591.60973	SB993.3-32	Zoology, Economic—United States
591.609(4-9)	SB993.34	Zoology, Economic—[Other countries]
591.65	QL100	Dangerous animals
591.65	QL100	Poisonous animals
591.65	QL757	Parasitology
591.65	QL757	Parasites
591.6509162	QL100	Dangerous marine animals
591.7	QH540-549.5	Animal ecology
591.73	QL112	Forest animals
591.74	QL115.3-.5	Grassland fauna
591.754	QL116	Desert animals
591.7584	QL117	Cave animals
591.76	QL141-149	Freshwater animals
591.77	QL120-149	Aquatic animals
591.773	QL127-135	Aquatic animals—Atlantic Ocean
591.7732	QL126	Aquatic animals—Arctic Ocean
591.774	QL138	Aquatic animals—Pacific Ocean
591.775	QL137	Aquatic animals—Indian Ocean
591.777	QL126.5	Aquatic animals—Antarctic Ocean
591.788	QL752	Animal populations
592	QL360-599	Invertebrates
592.3	QL386-394	Worms
592.64	QL391.A6	Earthworms
593.4	QL370.7-374.2	Sponges
593.5	QL375-379	Coelenterata
593.8	QL380-.8	Ctenophora
593.9	QL381-385.2	Echinodermata
594	QL401-445.2	Shellfish
594	QL401-432	Mollusks
594.32	QL430.5.H34	Abalones
594.4	QL430.6-.7	Clams
594.4	TC201	Shipworms
595	QL434-599.82	Arthropoda
595.3	QL435-445.2	Crustacea
595.35	QL444.C58	Barnacles
595.38	QL444.M33	Decapoda (Crustacea)
595.384	QL444.M33	Crayfish
595.386	QL444.M33	Blue crab
595.386	QL444.M33	Crabs
595.4	QL451-459.2	Arachnida
595.62	QL449.5-.55	Centipedes
595.66	QL449.6-.65	Millipedes
595.7	QL461-599.82	Insects
595.7072	QL468.5	Entomology—Research
595.726	QL508.A2	Desert locust
595.726	QL508.A2	Migratory locust
595.726	QL508.G8	Crickets
595.728	QL505.5-.82	Cockroaches
595.733	QL520-.42	Damselflies
595.733	QL520-.42	Dragonflies
595.76	QL571-597.2	Beetles
595.76	QL596.S35	Douglas fir beetle
595.7649	QL596.S3	Dung beetles
595.78	QL561.S2	Ailanthus moth
595.78	QL561.T55	Clothes moths
595.78139	QL561.L3	Eastern tent caterpillar
595.789	QL541-562.4	Butterflies
595.796	QL568.F7	Army ants
595.796	QL568.F7	Ants
595.796	QL568.F7	Fire ants
595.799	QL563-569.4	Bees
595.799	QL568.A6	Honeybee
595.799	QL568.A6	Africanized honeybee
595.799	QL568.A6	Bumblebees
596	QL605-739.8	Vertebrates
596	QL605-739.8	Chordata
597	QL614-639.8	Fishes
597.012	QL618	Fishes—Classification
597.072	QL618.5-.55	Fishes—Research
597.073	QL78-79	Aquariums, Public
597.073	QL78.5	Marine aquariums, Public
597.073	SF456-458.83	Aquariums
597.09(4-9)	QL619-637	Fishes—Geographical distribution
597.135	QL638.99	Fishes—Genetics
597.1477	QL639	Scales (Fishes)
597.1479	QL639	Fins
597.1479	QL639.4	Fishes—Locomotion
597.1568	QL639.5	Fishes—Migration
597.165	QL618.7	Dangerous fishes
597.165	QL618.7	Poisonous fishes
597.168	QL676.7	Rare birds

Dewey	LC	Subject Heading	Dewey	LC	Subject Heading
597.168	QL676.8	Extinct birds	598.94	QL696.F3	Buzzards
597.177073	SF457.1	Marine aquariums	598.942	QL696.F32	African fish eagle
597.1788	QL618.3	Fish populations	598.942	QL696.F32	Eagles
597.3	QL638.95.S7	Hammerhead sharks	598.943	QL696.F32	Bald eagle
597.36	QL638.9	Dogfish	598.96	QL696.F34	Falcons
597.43	QL637.9.A5	Eels	599	QL700-739.8	Mammals
597.554	QL638.S2	Brook trout	599.168	QL706.8-.83	Rare mammals
597.56	QL638.S2	Chinook salmon	599.1788	QL708.6	Mammal populations
597.56	QL638.S2	Coho salmon	599.31	QL737.T8	Aardvark
597.562	QL639.2	Fishes—Spawning	599.336	QL737.M242	Elephant shrews
597.6798	QL638.S9	Dwarf sea horse	599.35	QL737.R6	Dancing mice
597.75	QL638.P4	Darters (Fishes)	599.356	QL737.R666	Hamsters
597.8	QL641-669.3	Amphibians	599.356	QL737.R638	Dwarf hamsters
597.89	QL668.E2-.E275	Frogs	599.3592	QL737.R634	Guinea pigs
597.9	QL641-669	Reptiles	599.3596	QL737.R656	Dormice
597.9165	QL645.7	Dangerous reptiles	599.3596	QL737.R656	Edible dormouse
597.92	QL666.C584	Desert tortoise	599.35987	QL737.R66	Desert kangaroo rat
597.956	QL666.L23	Chameleons	599.36	QL737.R68	Abent squirrel
597.96	QL666.06-.694	Snakes	599.364	QL737.R68	Eastern chipmunk
597.96	QL666.064	Cobras	599.37	QL737.R632	American beaver
597.96	QL666.069	Broad-banded copperhead	599.5276	QL737.C423	Bowhead whale
597.96	QL666.069	Eastern diamondback rattlesnake	599.53	QL737.C432	Dolphins
597.963	QL666.069	Copperhead	599.53	QL737.C434	Dall Porpoise
597.9644	QL666.064	Coral snakes	599.6362	QL737.U54	Camels
597.982	QL666.C925	Crocodiles	599.638	QL737.U56	Giraffe
597.984	QL666.C925	Alligators	599.64	QL737.U53	Antelopes
598	QL671-699	Ornithology	599.642	QL737.U5	Elands
598	QL671-699	Birds	599.642	QL737.U5	Buffaloes
598.073	QL677.8	Aviaries	599.642	QL737.U53	African buffalo
598.09(4-9)	QL678-695.5	Birds—Geographical distribution	599.643	QL737.U53	American bison
598.147	QL697	Feathers	599.65	QL737.U55	Deer
598.1479	QL698.7	Birds—Flight	599.657	QL737.U55	Elk
598.1594	QL698.5	Birdsongs	599.665	QL737.U62	African wild ass
598.165	QL677.75	Dangerous birds	599.665	QL737.U62	Asses
598.41	QL696.A52	Ducks	599.665	QL737.U62	Equus
598.415	QL696.A52	Eider	599.67	QL737.P98	Elephants
598.47	QL696.S473	Adelie penguin	599.674	QL737.P98	African elephant
598.47	QL696.S473	Emperor penguin	599.7	QL737.C2	Carnivora
598.53	QL696.C34	Emus	599.756	QL737.C23	Tigers
598.625	QL696.G27	Pheasants	599.77	QL737.C2	Dogs
598.65	QL696.C63	Eared dove	599.775	QL737.C22	Foxes
598.65	QL696.C67	Dodo	599.78	QL737.C27	Bears
598.71	QL696.P7	African gray parrot	599.784	QL737.C27	Brown bear
598.71	QL696.P7	Cockatoos	599.79	QL737.P63	Eared seals
598.82	QL696.P23	Creepers (Birds)	599.794	QL737.P64	Elephant seals
598.832	QL696.P235	Dippers (Birds)	599.8	QL737.P9-.P968	Primates
598.842	QL696.P288	Eastern bluebird	599.83	QL737.P93	Demidoff's galago
598.864	QL696.P2367	Crows	599.85	QL737.P925	Capuchin monkeys
598.874	QL696.P2475	Cowbirds	599.88	QL737.P96	Apes
598.883	QL696.P2438	Dusky seaside sparrow	599.884	QL737.P96	Gorilla
598.883	QL696.P2438	Cardinals (Birds)	599.885	QL737.P96	Chimpanzees
598.92	QL696.F33	Andean condor	599.9	GN49-298	Physical anthropology
			599.90835	GN63	Adolescence
			599.938	GN281-289	Human evolution

Dewey	LC	Subject Heading	Dewey	LC	Subject Heading
599.938	GN281-.4	Man—Origin	608.0228	T324	Models (Patents)
599.94	GN51-59	Anthropometry	608.7	T221-323.7	Patents—History
599.940846	GN59.A35	Aged—Anthropometry	609	T14.7-33	Technology—History
599.943	GN209	Dental anthropology	609	T15-31	Inventions—History
599.943	GN209	Teeth	609.2	T39-40	Inventors
599.945	GN191-199	Skin	610	R	Medicine
599.945	GN192	Dermatoglyphics	610.089927	R143	Medicine, Arab
599.945	GN192	Fingerprints	610.1	R723-.5	Medicine—Philosophy
599.945	GN197	Color of man	610.14	R123	Medicine—Terminology
599.945	GN199	Albinos and albinism	610.21	RA407-409.5	Medical statistics
599.947	GN70	Skeleton	610.222	R120	Medicine—Pictorial works
599.947	GN70	Ribs	610.28	R856-857	Biomedical engineering
599.947	GN231-232	Posture	610.284	R856-858	Medical instruments and apparatus
599.948	GN71-131	Craniology	610.284	RC75	Medical thermometers
599.948	GN71-131	Skull	610.284	RM889	Electric apparatus and appliances
599.948	GN131	Eye-sockets			
599.948	GN181-190.5	Brain	610.285	R858-859.7	Medical informatics
599.949	GN66-69	Proportion (Anthropometry)	610.3	R121	Medicine—Dictionaries
599.949	GN66	Somatotypes	610.5	R5-101	Medicine—Periodicals
599.949	GN69.3-.5	Midgets	610.6	R10-99.7	Medicine—Societies, etc.
599.949	GN69.3-.5	Dwarfs	610.6	R106	Medicine—Congresses
599.949083	HQ773.65	Dwarf children	610.6	R729.5	Medicine—Practice
			610.6	R728	Medical offices
600	T	Technology	610.695	R707-.4	Physicians
601	T14	Technology—Philosophy	610.695	RA972	Interns (Medicine)
601.12	T174	Technological forecasting	610.695	RA972	Residents (Medicine)
601.4	T9-10	Technology—Terminology	610.695025	R711-713.97	Physicians—Directories
601.4	T11-.3	Technology—Language	610.696	R727.3-.45	Physician and patient
601.48	T8	Technology—Abbreviations	610.71	R735-845	Medicine—Study and teaching
601.9	R726.5-.8	Medicine and psychology			
602.2	T11.8	Technical illustration	610.711	R735-845	Medical colleges
602.75	T325	Trademarks	610.72	R860-862	Medical laboratories
603	T9-10	Technology—Dictionaries	610.73	RT	Nursing
604.2	T351-385	Mechanical drawing	610.7301	RT84.5	Nursing—Philosophy
604.2	T355	Structural drawing	610.73019	RT86	Nursing—Psychological aspects
604.2	T359	Freehand technical sketching			
			610.73025	RT25	Nurses—Directories
604.20284	T375-377	Drawing instruments	610.73028	RT90.5	Team nursing
604.2068	T352	Drawing-room management	610.730285	RT50.5	Nursing—Data processing
604.24	T352	Drawing-room practice	610.7306	RT1	Nursing—Societies, etc.
604.245	T362-369	Projection	610.7306	RT3	Nursing—Congresses
604.245	T369	Perspective	610.73069	RT48-.6	Nursing assessment
604.25	T379	Blueprints	610.73069	RT48.6	Nursing diagnosis
604.7	T55.3.H3	Hazardous substances	610.73069	RT86.7-.75	Nursing—Practice
605	T1-5	Technology—Periodicals	610.730692	RT82.8	Nurse practitioners
606	T6	Technology—Congresses	610.730693	RT62	Practical nursing
607.1	T61-173	Technical education	610.730698	RT84	Nurses' aides
607.10(4-9)	T71-170	Technical education—[By region or country]	610.730699	RT86.3	Nurse and patient
			610.730699	RT86.4	Nurse and physician
607.2	T65	Research	610.73071	RT71-81	Nursing—Study and teaching
607.2	T175-178	Research, Industrial			
607.34	T391-999	Exhibitions	610.730711	RT71-81	Nursing schools
608	T201-342	Patents	610.73072	RT81.5	Nursing—Research
608	T201-339	Inventions	610.7309	RT31	Nursing—History

Dewey	LC	Subject Heading	Dewey	LC	Subject Heading
610.73092	RT34-37	Nurses	610.9599	R618-621	Medicine—Philippines
610.7309(4-9)	RT4-17	Nursing—[By region or country]	610.96	R651-654	Medicine—Africa
			610.971	R461-464	Medicine—Canada
610.732	RT104	Private duty nursing	610.972	R465-468	Medicine—Mexico
610.733	RT90.7	Primary nursing	610.9728	R469-472	Medicine—Central America
610.734	RT97	Public health nursing	610.9729	R473-476	Medicine—West Indies
610.7343	RT98	Visiting nurses	610.973	R151-363	Medicine—United States
610.7343	RT98	Community health nursing	610.97(4-9)	R155-363	Medicine—[United States, By state]
610.7349	RT108	Disaster nursing			
610.7368	RD596	Neurological nursing	610.98	R480-483	Medicine—South America
610.737	R697.A4	Allied health personnel	610.993	R675-678	Medicine—New Zealand
610.737	R728.8	Medical assistants	610.994	R671-674	Medicine—Australia
610.82	R692	Women physicians	610.99(5-6)	R681-684	Medicine—Oceania
610.8996073	R695	Afro-Americans in medicine	611	QM	Human anatomy
610.8996073	R695	Blacks in medicine	611	QM24	Human anatomy—Variation
610.9	R131-684	Medicine—History	611.0022	QM25	Human anatomy—Atlases
610.901	R135-138.5	Medicine, Ancient	611.0074	QM51	Anatomical museums
610.902	R141-144	Medicine, Medieval	611.0078	QM34	Human anatomy—Laboratory manuals
610.92	R134-.5	Physicians—Biography			
610.935	R135	Medicine, Persian	611.013	QM601-695	Embryology, Human
610.94	R484-575	Medicine—Europe	611.013	QM611	Amniotic liquid
610.941	R486-498.4	Medicine—Great Britain	611.018	QM550-577.8	Histology
610.9415	R498.6-.9	Medicine—Ireland	611.018	QM551-575	Tissues
610.943	R509-512.5	Medicine—Germany	611.018	QP88-.6	Tissues
610.9436	R499-502	Medicine—Austria	611.0182	QM563	Elastic tissue
610.9438	R535-538	Medicine—Poland	611.01827	QM565	Adipose tissues
610.944	R504-507	Medicine—France	611.0183	QM567	Cartilage
610.945	R517-520	Medicine—Italy	611.0188	QM575	Nerve tissue
610.946	R555-558	Medicine—Spain	611.1	QM178-197	Cardiovascular system
610.9469	R559-562	Medicine—Portugal	611.11	QM181	Pericardium
610.947	R531-534	Medicine—Russia	611.12	QM181	Heart—Anatomy
610.9481	R547-550	Medicine—Norway	611.12	QM181	Myocardium
610.9485	R551-554	Medicine—Sweden	611.13	QM191	Aorta
610.9489	R539-542	Medicine—Denmark	611.13	QM191	Blood-vessels
610.94912	R543-546	Medicine—Iceland	611.13	QM191	Arteries
610.9492	R526-529	Medicine—Netherlands	611.13	QM191	Pulmonary artery
610.9493	R521-524	Medicine—Belgium	611.14	QM191	Veins
610.9494	R563-566	Medicine—Switzerland	611.2	QM251-265	Respiratory organs
610.9495	R513-516	Medicine—Greece	611.21	QM505	Frontal sinus
610.95	R581-644	Medicine—Asia	611.21	QM505	Nasopharynx
610.95	R581	Medicine, Oriental	611.22	QM255	Epiglottis
610.951	R601-604	Medicine—China	611.22	QM255	Glottis
610.951	R603.T5	Medicine, Tibetan	611.22	QM255	Larynx
610.9519	R627-630	Medicine—Korea	611.24	QM261	Lungs
610.952	R623-626	Medicine—Japan	611.26	QM265	Diaphragm
610.9538	R591-594	Medicine—Saudi Arabia	611.3	QM301-367	Alimentary canal
610.954	R605-608	Medicine—India	611.3	QM301-367	Digestive organs
610.95491	R604.2-.5	Medicine—Pakistan	611.3	QM301-367	Gastrointestinal system
610.95493	R608.2-.5	Medicine—Sri Lanka	611.31	QM306	Mouth
610.955	R631-634	Medicine—Iran	611.313	QM503	Tongue
610.9561	R640-643	Medicine—Turkey	611.314	QM311	Teeth
610.957	R635-638	Medicine—Asiatic Russia	611.316	QM325-371	Salivary glands
610.959(3-7)	R609-612	Medicine—Indochina	611.317	QM306	Lips
610.9598	R614-617	Medicine—Indonesia	611.32	QM331	Esophagus

Dewey	LC	Subject Heading	Dewey	LC	Subject Heading
611.32	QM331	Pharynx	611.74	QM563	Connective tissues
611.32	QM331	Tonsils	611.74	QM563	Fasciae (Anatomy)
611.32	QM535	Throat	611.77	QM481-484	Skin
611.33	QM341	Stomach	611.77	QM484	Dermis
611.34	QM345	Intestines	611.77	QM484	Epidermis
611.341	QM345	Duodenum	611.77	QM561	Epidermis
611.345	QM345	Appendix (Anatomy)	611.78	QM488	Eyelashes
611.347	QM345	Colon (Anatomy)	611.78	QM488	Hair
611.36	QM351	Liver	611.78	QM488	Nails (Anatomy)
611.36	QM352	Gallbladder	611.8	QM451-471	Nervous system
611.37	QM353	Pancreas	611.8	QM501-511	Sense organs
611.38	QM367	Peritoneum	611.81	QM455	Cerebellum
611.4	QM325-371	Glands	611.81	QM455	Hippocampus (Brain)
611.4	QM371	Endocrine glands	611.81	QM455	Hypothalamus
611.4	QM576	Endocrine glands	611.81	QM455	Medulla oblongata
611.41	QM371	Spleen	611.81	QM469	Meninges
611.41	QM569	Bone marrow	611.82	QM465	Spinal cord
611.42	QM197	Lymphatics	611.83	QM471	Nerves
611.44	QM371	Thyroid gland	611.83	QM471	Sympathetic nervous system
611.45	QM371	Adrenal glands			
611.47	QM371	Pituitary gland	611.84	QM511	Eye
611.49	QM495	Breast	611.84	QM511	Eyelids
611.49	QM495	Mammary glands	611.84	QM511	Optic nerve
611.6	QM416-421	Generative organs	611.84	QM511	Pupil (Eye)
611.61	QM401-413	Urinary organs	611.84	QM511	Retina
611.61	QM404	Kidneys	611.85	QM507	Ear
611.62	QM411	Bladder	611.85	QM507	Ear, External
611.63	QM416	Prostate	611.85	QM507	Eustachian tube
611.63	QM416	Generative organs, Male	611.85	QM507	Middle ear
611.64	QM416	Penis	611.85	QM507	Labyrinth (Ear)
611.65	QM421	Fallopian tubes	611.9	QM531-549	Anatomy, Surgical and topographical
611.65	QM421	Generative organs, Female			
611.65	QM421	Ovaries	611.91	QM535	Head
611.66	QM421	Uterus	611.92	QM535	Chin
611.7	QM100-170	Musculoskeletal system	611.92	QM535	Face
611.71	QM101-117	Human skeleton	611.92	QM535	Cheek
611.71	QM101-117	Skeleton	611.93	QM535	Neck
611.71	QM101-117	Bones	611.95	QM543	Abdomen
611.711	QM111	Spinal canal	611.97	QM548	Arm
611.711	QM111	Cervical vertebrae	611.97	QM548	Hand
611.711	QM111	Vertebrae	611.97	QM548	Forearm
611.711	QM111	Spine	611.97	QM548	Fingers
611.712	QM113	Ribs	611.9(7-8)	QM548-549	Extremities (Anatomy)
611.715	QM105	Skull	611.98	QM549	Toes
611.716	QM105	Jaws	611.98	QM549	Foot
611.717	QM101	Clavicle	611.98	QM549	Leg
611.718	CC400	Fibula (Archaeology)	612	QP34-38	Human physiology
611.718	QM117	Femur	612	QP34-38	Human biology
611.72	QM131-142	Joints	612	RC1151.B54	Biological rhythms—Effect of space flight on
611.72	QM141	Ligaments			
611.72	QM563	Ligaments	612.0083	RJ125-137	Children—Physiology
611.73	QM151-170	Muscles	612.01426	QP135	Body temperature
611.73	QM571	Muscles	612.0145	RC1150-1151	Space flight—Physiological effect
611.74	QM170	Tendons			

134

Dewey	LC	Subject Heading	Dewey	LC	Subject Heading
612.02	QP572.M44	Melatonin	612.405	QP572.P74	Prolactin
612.044	QP301-310	Exercise—Physiological aspects	612.405	QP572.S4	Hormones, Sex
			612.405	QP572.T4	Testosterone
612.11	QP91-99.5	Blood	612.41	QP187	Spleen
612.1111	QP96.5	Hemoglobin	612.42	QP115	Lymphatics
612.115	QP91	Fibrin	612.44	QP188.P3	Parathyroid glands
612.115	QP93.5-.7	Blood—Coagulation	612.45	QP188.A28	Adrenal cortex
612.115	QP93.5-.7	Blood coagulation factors	612.45	QP188.A3	Adrenal glands
612.116	QP99	Blood plasma	612.46	QP159	Excretion
612.11825	QP98	Blood groups	612.46	QP211	Excretion
612.14	QP101	Pulse	612.46	QP247-250.8	Urinary organs
612.14	QP105-.4	Blood pressure	612.463	QP249	Kidneys
612.17	QP108	Coronary circulation	612.492	QP188.P58	Pituitary gland
612.17	QP111-114	Heart	612.6	QP84	Human growth
612.17	QP113.2	Myocardium	612.6	QP84	Growth
612.18	QP109	Vasomotor system	612.6	QP251-285	Generative organs
612.2	QP107	Pulmonary circulation	612.6	QP251-285	Reproduction
612.2	QP121-125	Lungs	612.6	QP251-285	Human reproduction
612.2	QP121-125	Respiratory organs	612.61	QP253-257	Generative organs, Male
612.2	QP121-125	Respiration	612.61	QP255	Semen
612.2	QP121	Diaphragm	612.61	QP572.A5	Androgens
612.2	QP306	Larynx	612.62	QP259-281	Generative organs, Female
612.22	QP913.C1	Carbon dioxide—Physiological effect	612.63	QP251-281	Conception
			612.647	RG610-621	Fetus—Physiology
612.3	QP141-185.3	Nutrition	612.647	RG613	Fetus—Growth
612.3	QP145-159	Digestion	612.65	GN63	Child development
612.3	QP151-156	Gastrointestinal system	612.65	RJ131-137	Child development
612.3	RJ206-235	Children—Nutrition	612.65	RJ131-137	Children—Growth
612.312	QP146	Tonsils	612.654	RJ134	Infants—Development
612.313	QP191	Saliva	612.661	QP84.4	Puberty
612.313	QP188.S2	Salivary glands	612.661	RJ140-145	Youth—Physiology
612.315	QP146	Esophagus	612.661	RJ140	Teenagers—Growth
612.32	QP151	Stomach	612.662	RJ145	Menarche
612.32	QP193	Gastric juice	612.664	QP188.M3	Mammary glands
612.32	QP193	Stomach—Secretions	612.664	QP246	Lactation
612.33	QP156	Duodenum	612.67	QP86	Old age
612.33	QP156	Intestines	612.68	QP85	Longevity
612.34	QP188.P26	Pancreas	612.68	RA776.75	Longevity
612.34	QP195	Pancreas—Secretions	612.7	QP301-336	Musculoskeletal system
612.34	QP572.I5	Insulin	612.74	QP321-322	Muscles
612.35	QP185	Gallbladder	612.744	QP321	Fatigue
612.35	QP185	Liver	612.76	QP301-336	Human mechanics
612.38	QP165	Absorption (Physiology)	612.76	QP301-336	Locomotion
612.38	QP165	Intestinal absorption	612.76	QP301-310	Animal locomotion
612.39	QP171-177	Metabolism	612.78	QP306	Voice
612.391	QP139	Thirst	612.78	QP306	Speech
612.391	QP141	Hunger	612.7921	QP221	Perspiration
612.4	QP187-.6	Endocrinology, Comparative	612.8	QP431-495	Senses and sensation
612.4	QP187-.6	Endocrinology	612.8042	QP356.3	Neurochemistry
612.4	QP187-.6	Endocrine glands	612.81	QP351-430	Nervous system
612.4	QP187.7	Exocrine glands	612.81	QP361-375.5	Nerves
612.4	QP186-246	Glands	612.82	QP376-430	Brain
612.4	QP190-246.5	Secretion	612.82	QP406	Memory
612.405	QP572.P7	Progesterone	612.821	QP425-427	Sleep

Dewey	LC	Subject Heading	Dewey	LC	Subject Heading
612.825	QP383-.17	Cerebral cortex	613.26	RM237.85	Sugar-free diet
612.8262	QP572.H9	Hypothalamic hormones	613.26	RM237.87	Wheat-free diet
612.827	QP379	Cerebellum	613.262	RM236	Vegetarianism
612.828	QP377	Medulla oblongata	613.262	TX392-.8	Vegetarianism
612.83	QP330	Spine	613.263	TX553.F53	Fiber in human nutrition
612.83	QP370-375	Spinal cord	613.263	RM237.6	High-fiber diet
612.84	QP474-495	Vision	613.269	RJ216	Breast feeding
612.84	QP475-495	Eye	613.282	QP551	Amino acids in nutrition
612.84	QP476	Pupil (Eye)	613.282	QP561	Amino acids in human nutrition
612.843	QP479	Retina			
612.846	QP477.5	Eye—Movements	613.282	RM237.65	High-protein diet
612.85	QP460-471.2	Ear	613.283	RM237.58	Complex carbohydrate diet
612.85	QP460-469.3	Hearing	613.283	RM237.59	High-carbohydrate diet
612.85	RF294-.5	Audiometry	613.283	RM237.73	Low-carbohydrate diet
612.854	QP461	Eustachian tube	613.283	TX553.C28	Food—Carbohydrate content
612.854	QP461	Middle ear			
612.858	QP471-.2	Labyrinth (Ear)	613.283	TX553.S8	Sugars in human nutrition
612.858	QP471	Vestibular apparatus	613.284	TX553.C43	Food—Cholesterol content
612.86	QP455-458	Chemical senses	613.284	RM237.7	Low-fat diet
612.86	QP458	Odors	613.284	RM237.75	Low-Cholesterol diet
612.86	QP458	Nose	613.285	RM237.56	High-calcium diet
612.86	QP458	Smell	613.285	RM237.8	Salt-free diet
612.87	QP456	Taste	613.286	TX553.V5	Vitamins
612.88	QP401	Pain	613.287	RA793-954	Mineral waters
612.88	QP451	Touch	613.4	RL87	Skin—Care and hygiene
612.9	QM540	Back	613.41	RA780	Baths
612.92	QP311	Jaws	613.6	RC88.9.T47	Bioterrorism
613	RA421-790	Medicine, Preventive	613.62	RC967	Industrial hygiene
613	RA427.8	Health promotion	613.62	RC968-969	Occupational health services
613	RA770.5	Hygiene			
613	RA773-790	Health	613.62092	RC963	Industrial hygienists
613	RA780	Hygiene	613.6209(4-9)	HD7651-7780.8	Industrial hygiene—[By region or country]
613.04	RA418.5.F3	Family—Health and hygiene			
613.0432	RJ240	Immunization of children	613.66	GV1111	Self-defense
613.08996073	RA448.5.N4	Afro-Americans—Health and hygiene	613.68	RA783.5	Travel—Health aspects
			613.69	RC1040-1045	Traffic accidents
613.091732	RA566.7	Urban health	613.69	TL553.7	Survival after airplane accidents, shipwrecks, etc.
613.091734	RA771-.7	Rural health			
613.092	RA424.4-.5	Hygienists	613.7	QP303	Kinesiology
613.1	RA571	Soil pollution	613.70287	GV436	Physical fitness—Testing
613.122	RA794-954	Health resorts	613.7042	GV443	Physical education for children
613.192	RA782	Breathing exercises			
613.193	RM843	Sun-baths	613.706	GV428-433	Physical fitness centers
613.194	GV450	Nudism	613.71	GV460-548	Exercise
613.19406	GV451-.4	Nudist camps	613.71	GV501.5	Step aerobics
613.2	RA784	Diet	613.71	QP301-336	Exercise
613.2	RA784	Nutrition	613.71	RA781-.85	Exercise
613.23	TX551	Food—Caloric content	613.71	RA781.15	Aerobic exercises
613.25	RM222.2	Low-calorie diet	613.71	RA781.15	Low impact aerobic exercises
613.25	RM222.2	Reducing diets			
613.25	RM226-228	Fasting	613.71	RA781.17	Aquatic exercises
613.26	RM232	Egg-free diet	613.71081	GV482.5	Exercise for men
613.26	RM234.5	Milk-free diet	613.713	GV546.3	Weight lifting
613.26	RM237.5	Raw food diet	613.713	GV546.5-.56	Bodybuilding
			613.7130284	GV547.4	Dumbbells

Dewey	LC	Subject Heading	Dewey	LC	Subject Heading
613.714	GV464	Musico-callisthenics	614.109	RA1021-1022	Medical jurisprudence—History
613.714	GV481-510	Calisthenics	614.12	RA1057	Chemistry, Forensic
613.714	GV536	Uneven parallel bars	614.15	RA1148	Psychology, Forensic
613.714	GV539	Rings (Gymnastics)	614.15	RA1151-1152	Forensic psychiatry
613.716	GV838.53.E94	Aquatic exercises	614.18	RA1062	Dental jurisprudence
613.716	GV838.53.E94	Aquatic exercises	614.4	RA404	Diseases—Reporting
613.78	RA781.5	Posture	614.4	RA648.5-654	Epidemics
613.79	RA785	Rest	614.4	RA648.5-653.5	Epidemiology
613.792	RA785	Relaxation	614.42	RA407.3-408	Health surveys
613.794	RA786-.3	Sleep	614.42	RA652.2.P82	Public health surveillance
613.9071	HQ51	Sex instruction for girls	614.42	RA791-954	Medical geography
613.9071	HQ53	Sex instruction for children	614.42(4-9)	RA801-954	Medical geography—[By region or country]
613.9071	HQ41	Sex instruction for boys	614.42(4-9)	RA650.9	Epidemics—[By region or country]
613.9071	HQ54-.4	Sex instruction for the handicapped	614.424	RA650.6	Epidemics—Europe
613.9071	HQ55	Sex instruction for the aged	614.424	RA845-887	Medical geography—Europe
613.9071	HQ56-59	Sex instruction	614.425	RA650.7	Epidemics—Asia
613.9072	HQ60	Sexology—Research	614.425	RA891-934	Medical geography—Asia
613.94	RG136-137.6	Contraception	614.426	RA650.8	Epidemics—Africa
613.9432	RG136.85	Antifertility vaccines	614.426	RA943-949	Medical geography—Africa
613.9432	RG137-.6	Contraceptives	614.42(7-8)	RA650-.55	Epidemics—America
613.9432	RG137.2	Spermicides	614.4271	RA809-810	Medical geography—Canada
613.9432	RG137.4-.6	Contraceptive drugs	614.4272	RA811-812	Medical geography—Mexico
613.94322	RG137.5	Oral contraceptives	614.42728	RA813-814	Medical geography—Central America
613.9434	RG136.5	Natural family planning			
613.9435	RG137.2	Contraceptives, Vaginal	614.42729	RA815-816	Medical geography—West Indies
613.9435	RG137.3	Intrauterine contraceptives	0614.4273	RA804-807	Medical geography—United States
613.95	RA788	Hygiene, Sexual			
614	RA	Public health	614.428	RA817-844	Medical geography—South America
614.072	RA440.85-.87	Public health—Research			
614.091724	RA441.5	Public health—Developing countries	614.4293	RA952.5	Medical geography—New Zealand
614.09(4-9)	RA442-558	Public health—[By region or country]	614.4294	RA650.9.A8	Epidemics—Australia
			614.4294	RA951-952	Medical geography—Australia
614.094	RA483-523	Public health—Europe			
614.095	RA525-541	Public health—Asia	614.429(5-6)	RA953-954	Medical geography—Oceania
614.096	RA545-552	Public health—Africa			
614.097	RA443-450	Public health—North America	614.43	RA639-641	Animals as carriers of disease
614.0971	RA449-450	Public health—Canada	614.43	RA639.3	Vector control
614.0972	RA451-452	Public health—Mexico	614.432	RA639.5	Insects as carriers of disease
614.09728	RA453-454	Public health—Central America	614.432	RC641.C6	Cockroaches as carriers of disease
614.09729	RA455-456	Public health—West Indies	614.4322	RA641.T7	Tsetse-flies
614.0973	RA445-448.5	Public health—United States	614.4323	RA640	Mosquitoes as carriers of disease
614.098	RA457-482	Public health—South America	614.4323	RA640	Mosquitoes—Control
614.1	RA1063.4	Forensic pathology	614.433	RA641.M5	Mites as carriers of disease
614.1	RA1063.4	Autopsy	614.433	RA641.T5	Tick-borne diseases
614.1	RA1001-1171	Medical jurisprudence	614.45	RA975	Isolation (Hospital care)
614.1021	RA1018.5-.56	Medical jurisprudence—Statistics	614.46	RA655-758	Quarantine
614.107	RA1027-.5	Medical jurisprudence—Study and teaching			

Dewey	LC	Subject Heading
614.4609(4-9)	RA664-758	Quarantine—[By region or country]
614.46094	RA700-737	Quarantine—Europe
614.46095	RA738-751	Quarantine—Asia
614.46096	RA753-755	Quarantine—Africa
614.46097	RA664-677	Quarantine—North America
614.460971	RA671	Quarantine—Canada
614.460972	RA673	Quarantine—Mexico
614.4609728	RA675	Quarantine—Central America
614.4609729	RA677	Quarantine—West Indies
614.460973	RA665-667	Quarantine—United States
614.46098	RA678-699	Quarantine—South America
614.460994	RA756	Quarantine—Australia
614.46099(5-6)	RA758	Quarantine—Oceania
614.47	RA638	Vaccination
614.48	RA761-767	Fumigation
614.48	RA761-767	Disinfection and disinfectants
614.48	RA766.G6	Glycerin
614.48	RA766.H9	Hydrogen peroxide
614.48	RA766.R2	Radiation sterilization
614.48	RA766.S8	Steam as a disinfectant
614.5	RA601.5	Foodborne diseases
614.5	RA643-644	Communicable diseases
614.5112	RA644.T8	Typhoid fever
614.5112	RA644.T8	Typhoid fever—Vaccination
614.5123	RA644.D6	Diphtheria—Prevention
614.514	RA644.C3	Cholera
614.516	RA644.A57	Amebiasis
614.518	RA644.I6	Influenza
614.523	RA644.M5	Measles
614.524	RA644.R8	Rubella
614.532	RA644.M2	Malaria
614.541	RA644.Y4	Yellow fever
614.542	RA644.T7	Tuberculosis
614.542	RA644.T7	Tuberculosis—Vaccination
614.543	RA644.W6	Whooping cough
614.547	RA644.H45	Herpes genitalis
614.547	RA644.V4	Sexually transmitted diseases
614.547	RA644.V4	Sexually transmitted diseases—Prevention
614.55	RA643-644	Parasitic diseases
614.5552	RA644.F5	Filariasis
614.56	RA639-641	Zoonoses
614.56	RA641.D6	Dogs as carriers of disease
614.5610947	RA644.A6	Anthrax—Russia (Federation)—Epidemiology
614.563	RA644.R3	Rabies
614.57	RA644.V55	Virus diseases
614.5732	RA644.P7	Plague—Vaccination
614.58852	RA644.D4	Dengue
614.59	RA576	Smog
614.59	TD884	Smoke
614.5939	RA645.N87	Nutrition disorders
614.5939	RA645.N87	Nutritionally induced diseases
614.5939	RA645.N87	Malnutrition
614.59462	RA645.D5	Diabetes
614.59832	RA644.E52	Epidemic encephalitis
614.59834	RA645.M82	Multiple sclerosis
614.59836	RA645.C47	Cerebral palsy
614.5993	RA645.A44	Allergy
614.599392	RA644.A25	AIDS-related complex
614.5996	RK52-.45	Dental public health
614.6	RA619-640	Dead
614.6	RA625-630	Burial
614.6	RA631-636.7	Cremation
614.832	RC141.E6	Epidemic encephalitis
615	RM301.28	Clinical pharmacology
615.025	RC87	Resuscitation
615.1	RM300-671.5	Pharmacology
615.1	RM300-671.5	Drugs
615.1	RM671-.5	Drugs, Nonprescription
615.1	RM671-.5	Patent medicines
615.1	RS	Pharmacy
615.1	RS153-185	Materia medica
615.1	RS424	Drug stability
615.10128	RS189	Drugs—Standards
615.1014	RS55	Pharmacy—Terminology
615.10151	RS57	Pharmaceutical arithmetic
615.1025	RS74-76	Pharmacists—Directories
615.105	RS21	Pharmacy—Periodicals
615.106	RS1	Pharmacy—Societies, etc.
615.106	RS3	Pharmacy—Congresses
615.1068	RS100-.4	Pharmacy management
615.1071	RS101-121	Pharmacy—Study and teaching
615.10710(4-9)	RS110-121	Pharmacy—Study and teaching—[By region or country]
615.10724	RM301.25-.27	Pharmacology, Experimental
615.10724	RS122	Pharmacy—Research
615.1074	RS123	Pharmaceutical museums
615.1078	RS93	Pharmacy—Laboratory manuals
615.1083(2-4)	RJ560-570	Pediatric pharmacology
615.10846	RC953.7	Geriatric pharmacology
615.108996073	RS122.5	Afro-American pharmacists
615.109	RS61-68	Pharmacy—History
615.1092	HD8039.D7	Drugstore employees
615.1092	RS71-73	Pharmacists
615.1092	RS122.95	Pharmacy technicians
615.11	RS139-141.9	Pharmacopoeias
615.13	RS125-131.9	Medicine— Formulae, receipts, prescriptions
615.13	RS151.2-.9	Dispensatories
615.14	RM138	Drugs—Prescribing
615.14	RM139	Prescription writing

Dewey	LC	Subject Heading	Dewey	LC	Subject Heading
615.14	RS200-201	Drugs—Dosage forms	615.372	RM281	Vaccination
615.18	RS159	Drugs—Preservation	615.39	RM171-174	Blood—Transfusion
615.18	RS159.5	Drugs—Packaging	615.39	RM171.4-.45	Blood products
615.19	RM301.25	Drug development	615.39	RM171.4	Recombinant blood proteins
615.19	RS192-210	Pharmaceutical technology	615.39	RM171.5	Blood coagulation factors
615.19	RS199.5-210	Drug delivery systems	615.39	RM175-176	Plasma exchange (Therapeutics)
615.19	RS201.B54	Bioadhesive drug delivery systems	615.39	RM177	Blood platelets—Transfusion
615.19	RS201.C3	Capsules (Pharmacy)	615.39	RM298.P5	Placental extracts
615.19	RS201.C64	Drugs—Controlled release	615.399	RM171.7	Blood plasma substitutes
615.19	RS201.E4	Elixirs	615.399	RM171.7	Blood substitutes
615.19	RS201.E5	Emulsions (Pharmacy)	615.5	R727.43	Patient compliance
615.19	RS201.O3	Ointments	615.5	R733	Alternative medicine
615.19	RS201.P37	Parenteral solutions	615.5	RC90	Iatrogenic diseases
615.19	RS201.P5	Pills	615.5	RM	Therapeutics
615.19	RS201.P8	Powders (Pharmacy)	615.5014	RM38	Therapeutics—Terminology
615.19	RS201.S6	Solutions (Pharmacy)	615.505	RM16	Therapeutics—Periodicals
615.19	RS201.S8	Syrups	615.506	RM1	Therapeutics—Societies, etc.
615.19	RS201.T2	Tablets (Medicine)			
615.19	RS201.V43	Drugs—Vehicles	615.506	RM21	Therapeutics—Congresses
615.19	RS210	Drug delivery devices	615.507	RT90-.3	Patient education
615.19	RS400-431	Pharmaceutical chemistry	615.5071	RM108-.5	Therapeutics—Study and teaching
615.1901	RM301.27	Drugs—Testing			
615.1901	RS189-190	Drugs—Analysis	615.5072	RM111	Therapeutics, Experimental
615.3137	RM666.A82	Aspirin	615.50724	R853.C55	Clinical trials
615.321	RM666.A4	Alkaloids	615.50724	R853.H8	Human experimentation in medicine
615.321	RM666.H33	Herbs—Therapeutic use			
615.321	RS160-167	Pharmacognosy	615.509	RM41-47	Therapeutics—History
615.321	RS431.E73	Exgot alkaloids	615.53	RV	Medicine, Eclectic
615.32103	RS164	Medicinal plants—Encyclopedias	615.53	RV1-9	Medicine, Botanic
			615.53	RV11-431	Medicine, Eclectic
615.3219	RM666.A68	Aromatherapy	615.53	RV431	Dispensatories, Eclectic
615.32369	RM666.C375	Castor oil	615.53	RZ414	Medicine, Chronothermal
615.32379	RS165.C5	Coca	615.5305	RV15	Medicine, Eclectic—Periodicals
615.323952	RM666.B4	Belladonna (Drug)			
615.328	RM259	Vitamin therapy	615.5306	RV21	Medicine, Eclectic—Congresses
615.329	RM265-267	Antibiotics			
615.329	RM409	Antibacterial agents	615.53071	RV100-181	Medicine, Eclectic—Study and teaching
615.329	RM666.B2	Bacitracin			
615.3295654	RM666.P35	Penicillin	615.5309	RV61	Medicine, Eclectic—History
615.3295654	RS165.P38	Penicillin	615.532	RX	Homeopathy
615.36	RM283-298	Hormone therapy	615.532	RX81	Homeopathy—Attenuations, dilutions, and potencies
615.36	RM666.B375	Bee pollen			
615.37	RM270-282	Immunotherapy	615.532	RX601-675	Homeopathy—Materia medica and therapeutics
615.37	RM270-282	Serotherapy			
615.37	RM278	Antitoxins	615.532	RX671-675	Pharmacy, Homeopathic
615.37	RM282.T7	Transfer factor (Immunology)	615.532	RZ420	Electrohomeopathy
			615.532025	RX46	Homeopathic physicians—Directories
615.37	RM370-373	Immunopharmacology			
615.37	RM373	Immunosuppressive agents	615.53205	RX11	Homeopathy—Periodicals
615.372	QR189-.5	Vaccines	615.53206	RX1	Homeopathy—Societies, etc.
615.372	QR189.5.A33	AIDS vaccines			
615.372	QR189.5.B33	Bacterial vaccines	615.53206	RX21	Homeopathy—Congresses
615.372	QR189.5.E53	Enterobacterial vaccines	615.532071	RX91-101	Homeopathy—Study and teaching

Dewey	LC	Subject Heading	Dewey	LC	Subject Heading
615.53209	RX51	Homeopathy—History	615.716	RM347	Myocardial depressants
615.532092	RX61-66	Homeopathic physicians—Biography	615.72	RM388-.7	Pulmonary pharmacology
			615.72	RM388-.7	Respiratory agents
615.533	RZ	Osteopathic medicine	615.72	RM390	Expectorants
615.533	RZ301-397.5	Osteopathic medicine	615.73	RM355-365	Gastrointestinal agents
615.533023	RZ336	Osteopathic medicine—Vocational guidance	615.73	RM359	Emetics
			615.73	RM365	Antacids
615.533025	RZ333	Osteopathic physicians—Directories	615.73	RM666.T2	Tartar emetic
			615.7308996073	RT83.5	Afro-American nurses
615.53305	RZ311	Osteopathic medicine—Periodicals	615.732	RM357	Laxatives
615.53306	RZ301	Osteopathic medicine—Societies, etc.	615.761	RM377	Diuretics
			615.761	RS431.D58	Diuretics
615.53306	RZ313	Osteopathic medicine—Congresses	615.7669	RM386	Aphrodisiacs
615.533071	RZ337-338	Osteopathic medicine—Study and teaching	615.773	RM312	Musculoskeletal system—Effect of drugs on
615.5330711	RZ337-338	Osteopathic schools	615.773	RM312	Neuromuscular blocking agents
615.53309	RZ321-325	Osteopathic medicine—History	615.78	RM315-334	Neuropsychopharmacology
			615.78	RM315-334	Psychopharmacology
615.533092	RZ331-332	Osteopathic physicians—Biography	615.78	RM315-334	Neuropharmacology
			615.78	RM316	Drugs of abuse
615.534	RZ	Chiropractic	615.78	RM332-.3	Antidepressants
615.534	RZ201-275	Chiropractic	615.78	RS190.D77	Drugs of abuse
615.534	RZ237-238	Chiropractic schools	615.781	RD78.3-87.3	Anesthesia
615.534	RZ260-275	Diseases—Chiropractic treatment	615.781	RD78.3-87.3	Anesthetics
			615.781	RD86.C5	Chloroform
615.534025	RZ233	Chiropractors—Directories	615.782	RM325	Hypnotics
615.53405	RZ211	Chiropractic—Periodicals	615.782	RM325	Sedatives
615.53406	RZ201	Chiropractic—Societies, etc.	615.782	RM330	Central nervous system depressants
615.53406	RZ213	Chiropractic—Congresses	615.7821	RM325	Barbiturates
615.534071	RZ237-238	Chiropractic—Study and teaching	615.7822	RM328	Narcotics
			615.7822	RM666.M8	Morphine
615.53409	RZ221-225	Chiropractic—History	615.7827	RM666.C266	Cannabis
615.534092	RZ231-232	Chiropractors—Biography	615.783	RM319	Analgesics
615.535	RZ433-445	Naturopathy	615.785	RM332-.3	Stimulants
615.535092	RZ440	Naturopaths	615.788	RM315-334	Psychotropic drugs
615.542	RJ52-53	Children—Diseases—Treatment	615.788	RM666.L88	LSD (Drug)
			615.7882	RM333	Tranquilizing drugs
615.542	RJ434	Respiratory therapy for children	615.7883	RM324.8	Hallucinogenic drugs
			615.82	RD736.M25	Manipulation (Therapeutics)
615.58	RM260-263	Chemotherapy	615.82	RM695-951	Medicine, Physical
615.6	RM147-180	Drugs—Administration	615.82	RM695-931	Therapeutics, Physiological
615.6	RM162	Oral medication	615.82	RM695-893	Physical therapy
615.6	RM163-176	Injections	615.82	RM719-727	Mechanotherapy
615.6	RM169	Injections, Hypodermic	615.82	RM724	Manipulation (Therapeutics)
615.7	RM301.5	Pharmacokinetics	615.82	RM725-727	Exercise therapy
615.7042	RM302.5	Drugs—Side effects	615.82025	RM697	Physical therapists—Directories
615.7045	RM301.56	Drug activation			
615.7045	RM302-.4	Drug interactions	615.8206	RM695	Physical therapy—Societies, etc.
615.71	RM345-349	Cardiovascular agents			
615.71	RM345-349	Cardiovascular pharmacology	615.8206	RM696	Physical therapy—Congresses
615.71	RM349	Cardiotonic agents			
615.711	RM666.D5	Digitalis	615.82071	RM706-707	Physical therapy—Study and teaching
615.711	RS165.D5	Digitalis			

Dewey	LC	Subject Heading	Dewey	LC	Subject Heading
615.820846	RC953.8.E93	Exercise therapy for the aged	615.9	RA1190-1270	Toxicology
615.82092	RM699.5-.7	Physical therapists	615.9	RA1190-1270	Poisoning
615.822	RA780.5	Massage	615.90071	RA1198-.3	Toxicology—Study and teaching
615.822	RM721-723	Massage	615.90072	RA1199-.5	Toxicology—Research
615.8222	RM723.A27	Acupressure	615.90083	RA1225	Poisoning, Accidental, in children
615.8222083	RJ53.A27	Acupressure for children	615.902	RA1226	Environmental toxicology
615.83	RM862.7	Ultrasonic waves—Therapeutic use	615.902	RA1229-.5	Industrial toxicology
615.831	RM835-844	Phototherapy	615.907	RA1199-.5	Toxicity testing
615.831	RM835-844	Light, Colored	615.907	RA1199.4.A38	Acute toxicity testing
615.831	RM838	Light—Physiological effect	615.907	RA1221-1223	Analytical toxicology
615.8312	RM840	Color—Therapeutic use	615.908	RA1224.5	Toxicological emergencies
615.8312	RZ414.6	Color—Therapeutic use	615.91	RA577	Gases, Asphyxiating and poisonous
615.832	RM865-868.5	Thermotherapy	615.91	RA1245-1247	Gases, Asphyxiating and poisonous
615.832	RM868-.5	Fever therapy			
615.8323	RM874	Diathermy	615.91	RA1247.C17	Carbon monoxide
615.836	RC735.I5	Respiratory therapy	615.91	RA1247.M8	Mustard gas
615.836	RM161	Respiratory therapy	615.942	RA1242.S53	Poisonous snakes—Venom
615.836	RM666.08	Oxygen therapy	615.954	RA1242.S48	Seafood poisoning
615.836	RM824-827	Aerotherapy	615.954	RA1258-1260	Food—Toxicology
615.836	RM827	Compressed air—Therapeutic use	615.954	SH177.R4	Paralytic shellfish poisoning
615.842	RM845-862.5	Radiotherapy	616	RC	Internal medicine
615.842	RM845-862.5	Radiation—Dosage	616	RC31-80	Clinical medicine
615.8423	RM859	Radium—Therapeutic use	616.003	RC41	Internal medicine—Dictionaries
615.845	RM862.E4	Electron beams—Therapeutic use	616.00835	RJ550	Adolescent medicine
615.845	RM869-890	Electrotherapeutics	616.0088791	RC965.P46	Entertainers—Diseases
615.845	RM886	Electrolysis in medicine	616.009	R702	Diseases and history
615.8454	RZ422	Magnetic healing	616.025	RA645.5-.7	Emergency medical technicians
615.851	RZ400-408	Mental healing	616.025	RA645.5-.8	Emergency medical personnel
615.851	RZ403.S56	Silva Mind Control			
615.851092	RZ407-408	Healers	616.025	RC86-88.9	Emergency medicine
615.8515	RM735-.7	Occupational therapy	616.025	RC86-88.9	Medical emergencies
615.85153	RM736.7	Recreational therapy	616.025	RT120.E4	Emergency nursing
615.85154	ML3919-3920	Music therapy	616.0252	RC86-88.9	First aid in illness and injury
615.85155083	RJ505.D3	Dance therapy for children	616.027	R850-854	Medicine, Experimental
615.85156	RM735.7.H35	Handicraft—Therapeutic use	616.028	RC86-88.9	Critical care medicine
615.8516	RC489.B48	Bibliotherapy	616.028	RT120.I5	Intensive care nursing
615.853	RM801-822	Hydrotherapy	616.029	R726.8	Terminally ill
615.854	RD52.F59	Electrolyte therapy	616.029	R726.8	Terminal care
615.854	RM214-258	Dietetics	616.029	RT87.T45	Hospice care
615.854	RM214-258	Diet therapy	616.029	RT87.T45	Terminal care
615.854	RM214-258	Diet in disease	616.042	RB155-.8	Medical genetics
615.855	RM149	Parenteral therapy	616.042	RB155.5-.8	Human chromosome abnormalities
615.855	RM149	Parenteral solutions	616.042	RB155.5-.8	Genetic disorders
615.855	RM170-180	Intravenous therapy	616.042	RB155.8	Gene therapy
615.88	GN477-.7	Traditional medicine	616.044	RB156	Chronic diseases
615.88	GR880	Traditional medicine	616.044	RC108	Chronic diseases
615.892	RC73.2	Acupuncture points	616.047	RB48.5	Endocrine manifestations of general diseases
615.892	RM184-.5	Acupuncture			
615.892083	RJ53.A27	Acupuncture for children	616.047	RB129	Fever
615.9	RA1190-1270	Poisons			

Dewey	LC	Subject Heading	Dewey	LC	Subject Heading
616.047	RB144-.5	Edema	616.078	RA1063	Death, Apparent
616.047	RB150.S5	Shock	616.078	RA1063.3	Brain death
616.047	RC69	Symptomatology	616.0796	QR184.2	Human immunogenetics
616.047	RC144.G3	Gas gangrene	616.08	RC49-52	Medicine, Psychosomatic
616.047	RD153	Gangrene	616.1	RB144-.5	Blood circulation disorders
616.047	RD628	Gangrene	616.1	RC666-701	Cardiovascular system—Diseases
616.047	RD641	Abscess			
616.04706	RV211	Fever—Eclectic treatment	616.10092	RC666.7-.72	Cardiologists
616.04706	RX211	Fever—Homeopathic treatment	616.10231	RC674	Cardiovascular system—Diseases—Nursing
616.0472	RB127	Pain	616.1025	RC87.9	CPR (First aid)
616.0472	RC73-.2	Pain	616.1043	RC701	Cardiovascular system—Abnormalities
616.0478	RB150.F37	Chronic fatigue syndrome	616.106	RV251-256	Cardiovascular system—Diseases—Eclectic treatment
616.07	RB	Pathology			
616.0705	RB1	Pathology—Periodicals			
616.0706	RB3	Pathology—Congresses	616.106	RX311-316	Cardiovascular system—Diseases—Homeopathic treatment
616.07071	RB123-124	Pathology—Study and teaching			
616.0709	RB15-.2	Pathology—History	616.1075	RC670-.5	Cardiovascular system—Diagnosis
616.075	R837.E9	Medicine—Examinations			
616.075	RA1055.5	Disability evaluations	616.11	RC685.E5	Endocarditis
616.075	RB37-56.5	Diagnosis, Laboratory	616.11	RC685.P5	Pericardium
616.075	RC71-78.7	Diagnosis	616.12	RC681-688	Heart—Diseases
616.075	RC71.5	Diagnosis, Differential	616.12	RC685.C18	Cardiogenic shock
616.075	RC71.6	Diagnosis, Noninvasive	616.12028	RC684.C36	Cardiac intensive care
616.075	RC80	Prognosis	616.12043	RC687	Congenital heart disease
616.075	RC963.4	Disability evaluations	616.1206	RC634	Adrenergic alpha blockers
616.0751	RC65	Medical history taking	616.1206	RC684.A35	Adrenergic beta blockers
616.0754	RC75	Body temperature	616.120645	RC684.E4	Electric countershock
616.0754	RC76-.5	Physical diagnosis	616.12075	RC683.5.B63	Body surface mapping
616.0754	RC78.7.D53	Diagnostic imaging	616.12075	RC683.5.E94	Treadmill exercise tests
616.0754028	RC76.3	Stethoscopes	616.1207543	RC683.5.U5	Doppler echocardiography
616.07543	R857.U48	Ultrasonics in medicine	616.1207543	RC683.5.U5	Two-dimensional echocardiography
616.07543	RC78.7.D86	Duplex ultrasonography—Diagnostic use			
			616.1207543	RC683.5.U5	Echocardiography
616.07543	RC78.7.U4	Diagnosis, Ultrasonic	616.1207547	RC683.5.A45	Ambulatory electrocardiography
616.07545	RC78.7.E5	Endoscopy			
616.07547	RC77-.5	Electrodiagnosis	616.1207547	RC683.5.E5	Electrocardiography
616.07548	RC78.7.N83	Magnetic resonance imaging	616.1207572	RC683.5.A5	Angiocardiography
			616.122	RC685.A6	Angina pectoris
616.0756	RB52	Body fluids—Analysis	616.123	RC685.C6	Coronary heart disease
616.0756	RB112.5	Clinical biochemistry	616.123025	RC685.C173	Cardiac arrest
616.0756	RM40	Clinical chemistry	616.1237	RC685.I6	Myocardial infarction
616.07561	RB45-15	Blood—Analysis	616.124	RC685.M9	Myocardium—Diseases
616.0757	RC78-.5	Diagnosis, Radioscopic	616.124	RC685.M92	Myocarditis
616.0757	RC78.7.T6	Tomography	616.125	RC685.V2	Heart valves—Diseases
616.07572	RC78-.5	Radiography, Medical	616.125	RC685.V2	Mitral valve insufficiency
616.07572	RC78.7.F5	Diagnosis, Fluoroscopic	616.128	RC685.A65	Arrhythmia
616.07575	R895-920	Nuclear medicine	616.128	RC685.A65	Palpitation
616.0758	RB43-.6	Medical microscopy	616.128	RC685.V43	Ventricular fibrillation
616.0758	RB46.7	Electron microscopic immunocytochemistry	616.13	RC685.H93	Hypotension
			616.13	RC691-701	Blood-vessels—Diseases
616.0759	RB57	Autopsy	616.13	RC691-697	Arteries—Diseases
616.078	RA1063-.5	Death	616.13	RC694.5.I53	Arteritis
616.078	RA1063	Death—Causes			

Dewey	LC	Subject Heading	Dewey	LC	Subject Heading
616.13075	RC691.5-.6	Blood-vessels—Diseases—Diagnosis	616.22	RF526	Vocal cords—Diseases
			616.2207545	RF514-.5	Laryngoscopy
616.1307543	RC691.6.D87	Duplex ultrasonography—Diagnostic use	616.23	RC778	Bronchi—Diseases
			616.234	RC778	Bronchitis
616.1307572	RC691.6.A53	Angiography	616.238	RB150.A87	Asthma
616.131	RC694	Peripheral vascular diseases	616.238	RC591	Asthma
616.131	RC694.5.I53	Vasculitis	616.24	RC756-776	Lungs-Diseases
616.132	RC685.H8	Hypertension	616.24	RC776.F33	Farmer's lung
616.132	RC685.H8	Essential hypertension	616.24	RC776.O3	Respiratory organs—Obstructions
616.132	RC918.R38	Renal hypertension			
616.132075	RC683.5.A43	Ambulatory blood pressure monitoring	616.241	RA644.P8	Pneumonia
			616.241	RC771-772	Pneumonia
616.133	RC693	Aneurysms	616.244	RD137	Respiratory organs—Foreign bodies
616.135	RC691	Embolism			
616.138	RC691	Aorta—Diseases	616.248	RC776.E5	Emphysema, Pulmonary
616.138	RC693	Aortic aneurysms	616.249	RC776.P85	Pulmonary embolism
616.14	RC695-697	Veins—Diseases	616.25	RC751	Pleurisy
616.142	RC696	Phlebitis	616.3	RC799-869	Digestive organs—Diseases
616.143	RC695-697	Varicose veins	616.306	RV271-276	Digestive organs—Diseases—Eclectic treatment
616.15	RC633-647.5	Blood—Diseases			
616.15	RC647.B5	Blood platelet disorders			
616.15027	RB145	Hematology, Experimental	616.306	RX331-336	Digestive organs—Diseases—Homeopathic treatment
616.15027	RC636	Hematology, Experimental			
616.152	RC641-.7	Anemia			
616.152	RC641.7.F36	Fanconi's anemia	616.306	RX336.D5	Diarrhea—Homeopathic treatment
616.152	RC641.7.R44	Renal anemia			
616.157	RB144-.5	Hemorrhage	616.307572	RC804.A5	Digestive organs—Radiography
616.157	RC647.C55	Blood coagulation disorders			
616.157	RC647.D5	Disseminated intravascular coagulation	616.31	RC811	Gastrointestinal system—Motility—Disorders
			616.31	RC815-.6	Mouth—Diseases
616.1572	RC642	Hemophilia	616.31	RC815-.6	Oral medicine
616.2	RC705-779	Respiratory organs—Diseases	616.31	RF460-547	Throat—Diseases
			616.31075	RF476	Throat—Examination
616.2	RC740	Respiratory infections	616.313	RC168.M8	Mumps
616.201	RC746	Croup	616.314	RF491	Tonsillitis
616.202	RC589-596	Respiratory allergy	616.32	RC815.2	Deglutition disorders
616.202	RC590	Hay fever	616.32	RC815.7	Esophagus—Diseases
616.20231	RC735.5	Respiratory organs—Diseases—Nursing	616.32	RC815.7	Esophageal varices
			616.32	RF481-499	Tonsils—Diseases
616.203	RC150-.9	Influenza	616.32	RF481-499	Pharnyx—Diseases
616.203	RC150	Asian flu	616.32	RF485	Pharyngitis
616.204	RC204	Whooping cough	616.32	RF545	Esophagus—Foreign bodies
616.205	RF361	Cold (Disease)	616.32043	RC815.7	Esophagus—Abnormalities
616.206	RC735.H54	High-frequency ventilation (Therapy)	616.33	RC799-869	Gastrointestinal system
			616.33	RC816-840	Stomach—Diseases
616.206	RV261-266	Respiratory organs—Diseases—Eclectic treatment	616.33	RC840.G3	Gastroenteritis
			616.3307545	RC804.G3	Gastroscopy
616.206	RX321-326	Respiratory organs—Diseases—Homeopathic treatment	616.332	RC815.2	Indigestion disorders
			616.332	RC827	Indigestion
			616.333	RC831	Gastritis
616.2075	RC734.P84	Pulmonary function tests	616.34	RC860-862	Colon—Diseases
616.209	RC737-.5	Apnea	616.3407545	RC804.D79	Duodenoscopy
616.21	RF341-437	Nose—Diseases	616.3407572	RC804.R6	Duodenum—Radiography
616.21207545	RF345	Nasoscopy	616.342	RC866.D43	Fecal incontinence

Dewey	LC	Subject Heading	Dewey	LC	Subject Heading
616.342	RC866.D43	Defecation disorders	616.5	RL242-249	Atopic dermatitis
616.3427	RC862.D5	Diarrhea	616.5	RL247	Photosensitivity disorders
616.3428	RC861	Constipation	616.5	RL701-751	Neurocutaneous disorders
616.343	RC821	Peptic ulcer	616.50014	RL39	Dermatology—Terminology
616.344	RC862.E5	Enteritis	616.50025	RL43	Dermatologists—Directories
616.3447	RC862.C6	Colitis	616.500284	RL55	Dermatology—Apparatus
616.35	RC864-866	Proctology			and instruments
616.352	RC865	Hemorrhoids	616.5005	RL26	Dermatology—Periodicals
616.362	RC845-848	Liver—Diseases	616.5006	RL1	Dermatology—Societies,
616.362075	RC847-.5	Liver function tests			etc.
616.3623	RC848.C4	Chronic active hepatitis	616.5006	RL31	Dermatology—Congresses
616.3623	RC848.H42	Hepatitis	616.50071	RL77	Dermatology—Study and
616.3624	RC848.A42	Alcoholic liver diseases			teaching
616.3625	RC851	Jaundice	616.5009	RL46	Dermatology—History
616.365	RC849-853	Gallbladder—Diseases	616.50092	RL46.2-.3	Dermatologists
616.37	RC857-858	Pancreas—Diseases	616.50231	RL125	Dermatologic nursing
616.37	RC858.C95	Cystic fibrosis	616.5027	RL79	Dermatology, Experimental
616.39	RA1116	Starvation	616.506	RV381-391	Dermatology
616.39	RB147	Metabolism—Disorders	616.506	RX561-581	Dermatology
616.39	RC620-627	Nutrition disorders	616.51	RL244	Contact dermatitis
616.39	RC622	Nutritionally induced	616.51	RL251	Eczema
		diseases	616.523	RL221	Carbuncle
616.39	RC623	Malnutrition	616.523	RL221	Furuncle
616.39	RC623.5-627	Deficiency diseases	616.523	RL283	Impetigo
616.39	RC623.7	Avitaminosis	616.526	RL321	Psoriasis
616.39	RC627.5-632	Metabolism—Disorders	616.53	RL131	Acne
616.39043	RC627.8	Metabolism, Inborn errors	616.544	RL435	Keratosis
		of	616.544	RL435	Ichthyosis
616.398	RC628-.5	Obesity	616.544	RL451	Scleroderma (Disease)
616.399	RC862.M3	Malabsorption syndromes	616.544	RL471	Warts
616.3992	RB147	Acidosis	616.545	RL675	Bedsores
616.3992	RC630	Water-electrolyte	616.546	RL91	Dandruff
		imbalances	616.546	RL91	Beard
616.3998	RC632.L33	Lactose intolerance	616.546	RL155-.5	Baldness
616.3999	RC629-.5	Gout	616.546	RL431	Hupertrichosis
616.4	RC648-665	Endocrine glands—	616.547	RD563	Nails, Ingrowing
		Diseases	616.55	RL793	Mole (Dermatology)
616.4	RC648-665	Endocrinology	616.57	RL764.S28	Scabies
616.44	RC655-657	Thyroid gland—Diseases	616.57	RL780	Ringworm
616.442	RC656-.3	Goiter	616.6	RC870-923	Urology
616.443	RC657.5.G7	Graves' disease	616.6	RC900-923	Urinary organs—Diseases
616.444	RC657	Hypothyroidism	616.6	RC901.75	Urination disorders
616.45	RC659	Adrenal glands—Diseases	616.6	RC901.8	Urinary tract infections
616.45	RC659	Addison's disease	616.6075	RC901	Urinary organs—
616.462	RC658.5	Diabetes			Examination
616.462	RC660-662.18	Non-insulin-dependent	616.61	RC902-918	Kidneys—Diseases
		diabetes	616.61	RC902	Nephrology
616.462	RC660-662.4	Diabetes	616.61075	RC904-.5	Kidneys—Diseases—
616.46200835	RJ420.D5	Diabetes in adolescence			Diagnosis
616.47	RB140-.5	Growth disorders	616.612	RC907	Bright's disease
616.47	RC658-.7	Pituitary gland—Diseases	616.614	RC918.R4	Chronic renal failure
616.47	RC658.3	Acromegaly	616.62	RC892	Urethra—Diseases
616.5	RL	Dermatology	616.62	RC919-921	Bladder—Diseases
616.5	RL231-241	Skin—Inflammation	616.62	RG484-485	Bladder—Diseases
616.5	RL241	Occupational dermatitis	616.622	RC916	Urinary organs—Calculi

Dewey	LC	Subject Heading	Dewey	LC	Subject Heading
616.635	RC915	Uremia	616.8047547	RC386.6.A45	Ambulatory electroencephalography
616.65	RC875-899.5	Andrology	616.8047547	RC386.6.E43	Electroencephalography
616.65	RC899	Prostate—Diseases	616.806	RC350.N48	Neural stimulation
616.65043	RC881.5-883.5	Generative organs—Abnormalities	616.806	RV241-246	Nervous system—Diseases—Eclectic treatment
616.66	RC896	Penis—Diseases			
616.67	RC897	Scrotum—Diseases	616.806	RX281-301	Nervous system—Diseases—Homeopathic treatment
616.692	RC889	Infertility			
616.6921	RC889	Infertility, Male			
616.6922	RC889	Impotence	616.8(1-4)	RC346-429	Neurology
616.693	RC884	Climacteric, Male	616.8(1-4)	RC346-429	Nervous system—Diseases
616.694	RC883	Hermaphroditism	616.8(1-4)	RC386-395	Brain—Diseases
616.7	RC925-935	Muscles—Diseases	616.81	RC388.5	Cerebrovascular disease
616.7	RD701-811	Orthopedics	616.81	RC394.I5	Cerebral infarction
616.7	RD762	Posture disorders	616.82	RC124	Meningitis
616.700284	RE73	Optical instruments	616.82	RC376	Meningitis
616.7005	RD711	Orthopedics—Periodicals	616.83	RC394.M46	Memory disorders
616.70231	RD753	Orthopedic nursing	616.83	RC521-524	Dementia
616.70232	RD727-728	Orthopedists	616.83	RC524	Senile dementia
616.7025	RD750	Orthopedic emergencies	616.831	RC523-.2	Alzheimer's disease
616.70284	RD757.S45	Orthopedic shoes	616.832	RC390	Chronic encephalitis
616.70754	RD734-.5	Orthopedics—Diagnosis	616.833	RC382	Parkinsonism
616.709	RD725-726	Orthopedics—History	616.833	RC382	Parkinsonism, Symptomatic
616.71	RC930-931	Bones—Diseases	616.834	RC377	Multiple sclerosis
616.71	RC931.F5	Fibrous dysplasia of bone	616.835	RC180-181	Poliomyelitis
616.71043	RD763	Skull—Abnormalities	616.8350231	RC180.8	Poliomyelitis—Nursing
616.71043	RD775-789	Extremities (Anatomy)—Abnormalities	616.836	RC388	Cerebral palsied
			616.845	RC394.C77	Convulsions
616.71043	RD779-789	Leg—Abnormalities	616.849	RB150.C6	Coma
616.712	RC931.064	Osteitis	616.849	RC569.5.E5	Enuresis
616.716	RC931.073	Osteoporosis	616.8491	RB128	Headache
616.722	RC933	Arthritis	616.8491	RC392	Headache
616.7223	RC931.067	Osteoarthritis	616.84913	RC392	Cluster headache
616.7227	RC933	Rheumatoid arthritis	616.84914	RB128	Tension headache
616.723	RC927-.5	Rheumatism	616.8498	RC547-549	Sleep disorders
616.723	RC927.3	Fibromyalgia	616.8498	RC549	Narcolepsy
616.723	RC927.5.N65	Nonarticular rheumatism	616.84982	RC548-.5	Insomnia
616.73	RC422.C4	Cervical syndrome	616.852	RC530-552	Neuroses
616.73	RD771.I58	Spine—Instability	616.8521	RC550	War neuroses
616.73043	RD768-771	Spine—Abnormalities	616.8521	RC552.03	Occupational neuroses
616.73062	RZ265.S64	Spinal adjustment	616.8521	RC552.P67	Post-traumatic stress disorder
616.74	RC935.A8	Muscular atrophy			
616.74	RD688	Muscles—Diseases	616.8521	RC560.R36	Rape trauma syndrome
616.74	RD925-927	Muscles—Diseases	616.85212	RC550	Combat—Psychological aspects
616.76	RC935.B8	Bursitis			
616.76	RC935.T4	Tendinitis	616.8522	RC531	Anxiety
616.77	RC924-.5	Connective tissues—Diseases	616.85223	RC535	Panic disorders
			616.85225	RC535	Phobias
616.8	RC394.D35	Brain—Degeneration	616.85225	RC552.A43	Acrophobia
616.8028	RC350.N49	Neurological intensive care	616.85225	RC552.A44	Agoraphobia
616.804075	RC348-349	Neurologic examination	616.85227	RC533	Obsessive-compulsive disorders
616.804231	RC350.5	Neurological nursing			
616.8047543	RC386.6.U45	Ultrasonic encephalography	616.8523	RC553.D5	Dissociative disorders
			616.85232	RC394.A5	Amnesia

Dewey	LC	Subject Heading	Dewey	LC	Subject Heading
616.85236	RC569.5.M8	Multiple personality	616.85835	RC553.M36	Masochism
616.8524	RC532	Hysteria	616.85835	RC560.S23	Sadomasochism
616.8524	RC552.S66	Somatization disorder	616.85836	RC560.C46	Child sexual abuse
616.8526	RC552.C65	Compulsive eating	616.85836	RC560.I53	Incest
616.8526	RC552.E18	Eating disorders	616.85836	RJ506.C48	Child sexual abuse
616.8526	RC567.5	Coffee habit	616.8584	RC533	Compulsive behavior
616.852600835	RJ506.E18	Eating disorders in adolescence	616.8584	RC569.5.I46	Impulsive personality
			616.85841	RC569.5.G35	Compulsive gambling
616.85262	RB150.A65	Anorexia	616.85843	RC569.5.P9	Pyromania
616.85262	RC552.A5	Anorexia nervosa	616.858445	RA1136-1137	Suicide
616.85263	RC552.B84	Bulimia	616.858445	RC569	Suicide
616.8527	RC537-545	Affective disorders	616.858445	RC569	Suicidal behavior
616.8527	RC537-545	Depression, Mental	616.85852	RC569.5.B67	Borderline personality disorder
616.852700835	RJ506.D4	Depression in adolescence			
616.852700846	RC537.5	Depression in old age	616.85854	RC553.N36	Narcissism
616.8528	RC552.N5	Neurasthenia	616.8588	RC569.7-571	Mental retardation
616.853	RC372-374.5	Epilepsy	616.85882	RC553.A88	Autism
616.853	RC374.5	Petit mal epilepsy	616.858842	RC571	Down's syndrome
616.85300835	RJ496.E6	Epilepsy in adolescence	616.858843	RC391	Hydrocephalus
616.855	RC423-428.8	Speech disorders	616.858848043	RC657	Cretinism
616.855	RC423-428.8	Communicative disorders	616.86	RC563-568	Substance abuse
616.855	RC423-428.5	Language disorders	616.86	RM316	Designer drugs
616.855	RC424.7	Articulation disorders	616.861	RC525-527	Alcoholic psychoses
616.855	RF510-540	Voice disorders	616.861	RC526	Delirium tremens
616.85506	RC423-428.8	Speech therapy	616.861	RC564.7-565.9	Alcoholism
616.8552	RC425-.7	Aphasia	616.8610019	HV5045	Alcoholism—Psychological aspects
616.8552	RC425.5	Agrammatism			
616.8553	RC394.W6	Dyslexia	616.8619	RC569.5.C63	Codependency
616.8554	RC424	Stuttering	616.8632	RC566	Narcotic habit
616.856	RC400-406	Spinal cord—Diseases	616.8632	RC568.O58	Opioid habit
616.856	RC416	Neuritis	616.8632	RC568.06	Morphine habit
616.856	RC420	Sciatica	616.8632	RC568.06	Opium habit
616.856	RC422.C26	Carpal tunnel syndrome	616.8634	RC553.H3	Hallucinations and illusions
616.856	RF341	Smell disorders	616.8635	RC568.C2	Hashish
616.858	RC554-569.5	Personality disorders	616.8635	RC568.C2	Cannabis
616.858	RC555	Antisocial personality disorders	616.8647	RC568.C6	Cocaine habit
			616.8647	RC568.C6	Crack (Drug)
616.8582	RA1146	Self-mutilation	616.865	RC567	Tobacco—Physiological effect
616.8582	RC552.S4	Self-mutilation			
616.8582	RC569.5.S45	Self-destructive behavior	616.865	RC567	Nicotine
616.8582	RC569.5.S48	Self-injurious behavior	616.865	RC567	Smoking
616.8582	RC569.5.V55	Violence	616.865	RC567	Tobacco habit
616.85822	RC569.5.F3	Family violence	616.865	RM666.T6	Tobacco—Physiological effect
616.85822	RC569.5.F3	Wife abuse			
616.858223	RC569.5.C55	Child abuse	616.89	RC435-571	Psychology, Pathological
616.858223	RC569.5.P75	Psychological child abuse	616.89	RC440.7	Mental health care teams
616.8583	RC556-560	Psychosexual disorders	616.89	RC455.4.C6	Psychiatry, Comparative
616.8583	RC558-.5	Homosexuality	616.89	RC466.8-467.95	Clinical psychology
616.8583	RC558.5	Lesbianism	616.89	RC512-528	Psychoses
616.8583	RC560.A97	Autoerotic asphyxia	616.89001	RC455.2.M4	Psychiatry—Methodology
616.8583	RC560.S43	Sex addition	616.890028	RC473.P7	Projective techniques
616.8583	RC560.S45	Sexual aversion disorders	616.8900835	RJ502.3	Adolescent psychiatric nursing
616.8583	RC560.V68	Voyeurism			
616.85832	RC560.I45	Impotence	616.8900835	RJ503	Adolescent psychopathology
			616.8900835	RJ503	Adolescent psychiatry

Dewey	LC	Subject Heading	Dewey	LC	Subject Heading
616.89008996 + 073	RC451.5.N4	Afro-Americans—Mental health	616.89165	RC487	Occupational therapy
616.890092	RC440.5	Psychiatric aides	616.891653	RC489.R4	Recreational therapy
616.890231	RC440	Psychiatric nursing	616.891655	RC489.D3	Dance therapy
616.89025	RC480.6	Psychiatric emergencies	616.891656	RC489.A7	Art therapy
616.89075	RC455.2.C4	Mental illness—Classification	616.8917	RC489.O24	Object constancy (Psychoanalysis)
616.89075	RC469-473	Psychodiagnostics	616.8917	RC489.O25	Object relations (Psychoanalysis)
616.89075	RC469	Mental illness—Diagnosis	616.8917	RC500-510	Psychoanalysis
616.89075	RC473.M5	Minnesota Multiphasic Personality Inventory	616.8917	RC510	Group psychoanalysis
616.89075	RC473.R6	Rorschach Test	616.8918	RC489.N3	Narcotherapy
616.890932	RJ502.5	Infant psychiatry	616.895	RC516	Manic-depressive psychoses
616.891	RC439.2	Psychiatric day treatment	616.898	RC514	Schizophrenia
616.891	RC480.52	Psychiatry—Differential therapeutics	616.898	RC514	Paranoid schizophrenia
			616.9	RA642.A5	Airborne infection
616.8910028	RC480.7	Interviewing in psychiatry	616.9	RB153-154	Infection
616.89122	RC485	Electroconvulsive therapy	616.9	RC106	Exanthemata
616.8914	RC455.2.E8	Psychotherapy—Moral and ethical aspects	616.9(01-6)	RC109-216	Communicable diseases
616.8914	RC475-489	Psychotherapy	616.9041	QR46-48	Body, Human—Microbiology
616.8914	RC480.55	Single-session psychotherapy	616.9041	QR46	Medical microbiology
616.8914	RC480.55	Brief psychotherapy	616.9041	QR177	Drug resistance in microorganisms
616.8914	RC481	Client-centered psychotherapy	616.91	RC114-.7	Virus diseases
616.8914	RC489.C68	Countertransference (Psychology)	616.91	RC114.6	Slow virus diseases
616.8914	RC489.D45	Desensitization (Psychotherapy)	616.91	RC141.5	Epstein-Barr virus diseases
			616.91122	RC147.G6	Mononucleosis
616.8914	RC489.E24	Eclectic psychotherapy	616.912	RC183-.9	Smallpox
616.8914	RC489.E93	Existential psychotherapy	616.914	RC125	Chickenpox
616.8914	RC489.F27	Psychotherapy—Failure	616.915	RC168.M4	Measles
616.8914	RC489.I45	Impasse (Psychotherapy)	616.916	RC182.R8	Rubella
616.8914	RC489.M85	Multiple psychotherapy	616.91852	RC137	Dengue
616.8914	RC489.P68	Problem-solving therapy	616.91854	RC206-216	Yellow fever
616.8914	RC489.S86	Supportive psychotherapy	616.92	RC115-116	Bacterial diseases
616.8914	RC489.T45	Psychotherapy—Termination	616.92	RC116.M8	Mycobacterial diseases
			616.92	RC116.S8	Staphylococcal infections
616.891400835	RJ503	Adolescent psychotherapy	616.9201	QR46	Medical bacteriology
616.891400835	RJ505.T47	Adolescent psychotherapy—Termination	616.9222	RC199-.9	Typhus fever
			616.9232	RC171-179	Black death
			616.9232	RC171-179	Plague
			616.9244	RC182.R3	Relapsing fever
616.89140092	RC455.2.A28	Psychotherapy patients—Abuse of	616.927	RC182.S12	Salmonellosis
			616.9272	RC187-197	Typhoid fever
616.89142	RC489.B4	Behavior therapy	616.92987	RC182.S2	Scarlatina
616.89142	RC489.B4	Aversion therapy	616.9313	RC138-.9	Diphtheria
616.89142	RC489.C6	Cognitive-analytic therapy	616.9318	RC185	Tetanus
616.89142	RC489.C63	Cognitive therapy	616.932	RC126-134	Cholera
616.89145	RC489.T7	Transactional analysis	616.935	RC140	Dysentery
616.89152	RC488-.6	Group psychotherapy	616.936	RC118.7	Protozoan diseases
616.891523	RC489.P7	Psychodrama	616.936	RC121.A5	Amebiasis
616.89156	RC488.5-.6	Marital psychotherapy	616.936	RC156-166	Malaria
616.89156	RC488.5-.6	Family psychotherapy	616.9363	RC186.T82	African trypanosomiasis
616.89156	RC488.6	Divorce therapy	616.94	RA642.B56	Bloodborne infections
616.89162	RC490-499	Therapeutics, Suggestive			

Dewey	LC	Subject Heading	Dewey	LC	Subject Heading
616.951	RC200-203	Sexually transmitted diseases	616.9940072	RC267	Cancer—Research
			616.9940231	RC266	Cancer—Nursing
616.9513	RC201-.9	Syphilis	616.994042	RC268.4-.44	Cancer—Genetic aspects
616.9518	RC203.H45	Herpes genitalis	616.99405	RC268-.15	Cancer—Prevention
616.953	RC148	Rabies	616.994059	RD651-678	Cancer—Surgery
616.956	RC121.A6	Anthrax	616.99406	RC270.8-271	Cancer—Treatment
616.959	RC113.5	Zoonoses	616.99406	RX261.C3	Cancer—Homeopathic treatment
616.96	QR251-255	Medical parasitology			
616.96	RC119-.7	Parasitic diseases	616.99406	RC271.H55	Cancer—Hormone therapy
616.96	RC226-248	Blood—Parasites	616.99406	RC271.I45	Cancer—Immunotherapy
616.964	RC184.T6	Echinococcosis	616.99406	RC271.P54	Plasma exchange (Therapeutics)
616.9652	RC142.5	Elephantiasis			
616.9652	RC142.5	Filariasis	616.99406	RC271.C5	Antineoplastic agents
616.968	RC119.5	Ectoparasitic infestations	616.994061	RC271.D68	Doxorubicin
616.969	RC117	Mycoses	616.9940642	RC271.R3	Cancer—Radiotherapy
616.97	RC583-598	Allergy	616.994071	RC268.48	Cancer—Etiology
616.97	RC588.C45	Antiallergic agents	616.994071	RC268.5-.7	Carcinogenesis
616.975	RC596	Food allergy	616.994071	RC268.57	Viral carcinogenesis
616.9750654	RC588.D53	Food allergy—Diet therapy	616.994071	RC268.6-.7	Carcinogens
616.9758	RC598.D7	Drug allergy	616.99419	RC280.H47	Hematological oncology
616.978	RC600	Autoimmune diseases	616.99419	RC643	Acute leukemia
616.979	RC606-607	Immunological deficiency syndromes	616.99419	RC643	Chronic lymphocytic leukemia
616.9792	RA644.A25	AIDS (Disease)	616.99419	RC643	Leukemia
616.9792	RC607.A26	AIDS (Disease)	616.99419	RC643	Lymphocytic leukemia
616.979200835	RJ387.A25	AIDS (Disease) in adolescence	616.99424	RC280.L8	Lungs—Cancer
			616.99431	RC280.M6	Mouth—Cancer
616.979201	QR414.6.H58	HIV (Viruses)	616.99432	RC280.E8	Esophagus—Cancer
616.98	RB152	Environmentally induced diseases	616.99432	RC280.E8	Esophagus—Tumors
			616.99434	RC280.D5	Digestive organs—Cancer
616.98	RC88.9.O95	Outdoor medical emergencies	616.994347	RC280.C6	Colon—Cancer
			616.99446	RC644	Hodgkin's disease
616.9802	RC1030-1035	Transportation medicine	616.99449059	RD667.5	Mastectomy
616.980213	RC1050-1097	Aviation medicine	616.9947	RC280.B6	Osteosarcoma
616.980213	RC1076.J48	Jet lag	616.99477	RC280.M37	Melanoma
616.980214	RC1120-1160	Space medicine	616.99477	RC280.S5	Basal cell carcinoma
616.98022	RC1000-1020	Submarine medicine	616.99477	RC280.S5	Skin—Cancer
616.98023	RC970-971	Medicine, Military	616.9948	RC280.N4	Neuroblastoma
616.98024	RC981-986	Medicine, Naval	616.9948	RD663	Nervous system—Tumors
616.9803	RC963-969	Work environment	616.99481	RC280.B7	Brain—Cancer
616.9803	RC963-969	Medicine, Industrial	616.99481	RD663	Brain—Tumors
616.988	RA791-954	Medical climatology	616.99485	RC280.E2	Ear—Tumors
616.9881	RC955-958	Circumpolar medicine	616.99495	RC280.A2	Abdomen—Tumors
616.9883	RC960-962	Tropical medicine	616.99495	RC280.A2	Abdomen—Cancer
616.9892	RC103.M6	Motion sickness	616.995	RC306-320.5	Tuberculosis
616.9893	RC103.A4	Mountain sickness	616.995061	RC311.3.C45	Tuberculosis—Chemotherapy
616.9894	RC103.C3	Decompression sickness			
616.9897	RA1231.R2	Radioactive substances—Toxicology	616.9950654	RC311.D5	Tuberculosis—Diet therapy
			616.995075	RC311.2	Tuberculin test
616.991	RC182.R4	Rheumatic fever	616.998	RC154-.9	Leprosy
616.994	RC254-282	Tumors	617	RD	Surgery
616.994	RD651-678	Tumors	617	RX366-376	Surgery, Homeopathic
616.994	RC254-282	Oncology	617.0231	RD99-.35	Surgical nursing
616.994	RC261-282	Cancer	617.024	RD110-.5	Ambulatory surgery
616.994	RC268.55	Radiation carcinogenesis			

Dewey	LC	Subject Heading	Dewey	LC	Subject Heading
617.024	RD111-114	Surgery, Minor	617.414059	RM182-190	Veins—Puncture
617.03	RM930-950	Medical rehabilitation	617.44	RD599.5.A37	Adrenalectomy
617.03	RM950	Rehabilitation technology	617.440592	RD599.5.P58	Pituitary gland—Transplantation
617.044	RD156	War wounds	617.4410592	RD123.5	Bone marrow—Transplantation
617.05	RD33.5	Electrolysis in surgery			
617.057	RD33.53	Endoscopic surgery	617.462059	RD580-581	Bladder—Surgery
617.0901	GN477.5-.7	Surgery, Primitive	617.463	RD585.5	Sterilization reversal
617.0901	GN477.5-.7	Surgery, Primitive	617.463	RD585.5	Vasectomy
617.1	RA1121	Wounds and injuries	617.463	RD590	Circumcision
617.1	RC87	Wounds and injuries	617.463059	RD572	Castration
617.1	RD96.15	Blunt trauma	617.47	RD701-789	Orthopedic surgery
617.1027	RC1200-1245	Sports medicine	617.47044	RD680-688	Musculoskeletal system—Wounds and injuries
617.1062	RZ270-275	Wounds and injuries—Chiropractic treatment			
			617.470592	RD755.5-.7	Orthopedic implants
617.11	RA1085	Fires—Casualties	617.471	RD103.B65	Bone wiring (Orthopedics)
617.11	RD96.4-.55	Burn care teams	617.471059	RD103.E88	External skeletal fixation (Surgery)
617.11	RD96.4-.55	Burns and scalds			
617.11	RD96.45	Chemical burns	617.471059	RD684	Bones—Surgery
617.12	RA1091	Electrical injuries	617.4710592	RD123	Bone-grafting
617.12	RD96.5	Electrical burns	617.4720592	RD549	Artificial hip joints
617.145	RD96.3	Gunshot wounds	617.4720592	RD549	Total hip replacement
617.15	RD101-104	Fractures	617.4770592	RD121	Skin-grafting
617.15	RD101	Fractures, Spontaneous	617.48044	RD592.5-596	Nervous system—Wounds and injuries
617.15	RD104.A95	Avulsion fractures			
617.15	RD104.S77	Stress fractures (Orthopedics)	617.48059	RD592.5-596	Nervous system—Surgery
			617.481	RD594-.15	Psychosurgery
617.155	RD529	Skull—Fractures	617.481044	RD594-.15	Brain—Wounds and injuries
617.157	RD558	Elbow—Fractures	617.481059	RD594-.15	Brain—Surgery
617.158	RD549-.5	Pelvic bones—Fractures	617.482044	RD533	Spine—Wounds and injuries
617.158	RD551-563	Extremities (Anatomy)—Fractures			
			617.482059	RD594.3	Spinal cord—Surgery
617.16	RD106	Dislocations	617.51	RC936	Head—Diseases
617.16	RD557.5	Shoulder joint—Dislocation	617.51	RF	Otolaryngology
617.18	RA1071-1082	Asphyxia	617.510025	RF28	Otolaryngologists—Directories
617.18	RA1076	Drowning			
617.18	RC87.3	Asphyxia	617.51005	RF11	Otolaryngology—Periodicals
617.1806	RC87.9	Artificial respiration	617.51006	RF1	Otolaryngology—Societies, etc.
617.300222	RD733.2	Orthopedics—Pictorial works			
			617.51006	RF16	Otolaryngology—Congresses
617.41	RD597-598.7	Cardiovascular system—Surgery	617.51044	RF50	Otolaryngology—Wounds and injuries
617.412	RD598-.35	Heart—Surgery			
617.412	RD598.35.C35	Cardiac catheterization	617.51059	RF51-52	Otolaryngology, Operative
617.412	RD598.35.C37	Cardiomyoplasty	617.5106	RV291	Head—Diseases—Eclectic treatment
617.4120592	RD598.35.A78	Heart, Artificial			
617.4120592	RD598.35.T7	Heart—Transplantation	617.51075	RF48-.5	Otolaryngology—Diagnosis
617.4120645	RC684.P3	Cardiac pacing	617.51075	RF48-.5	Otolaryngologic examination
617.4120645	RC684.P3	Pacemaker, Artificial (Heart)	617.5109	RF25-26	Otolaryngology—History
617.4120645	RC684.P3	Cardiac pacemakers	617.51092	RF37-38	Otolaryngologists
617.413	RD598.35.C67	Coronary artery bypass	617.514	RD529	Craniotomy
617.413	RD598.5-.7	Blood-vessels—Surgery	617.52044	RD523	Face—Wounds and injuries
617.413	RD598.5	Angioplasty	617.52059	RD523-527	Face—Surgery
617.413	RD598.5	Arterial catheterization	617.520592	RD119.5.F33	Facelift
617.413	RD598.5	Dissecting aortic aneurysms	617.522	RD524	Cleft lip
617.413059	RC693	Dissecting aortic aneurysms			

Dewey	LC	Subject Heading	Dewey	LC	Subject Heading
617.52306	RV341-347	Nose—Diseases—Eclectic treatment	617.584059	RD562	Excision of ankle
617.52306	RX451	Nose—Diseases—Homeopathic treatment	617.585	RC951	Foot—Diseases
			617.585	RD563	Podiatry
617.531044	RF547	Throat—Wounds and injuries	617.585043	RD781-789	Foot—Abnormalities
			617.585043	RD786-789	Toes—Abnormalities
617.531059	RF484.5	Tonsillectomy	617.585044	RD563	Foot—Wounds and injuries
617.533059	RF516-517	Larynx—Surgery	617.585044	RD781	Foot—Dislocation
617.533059	RF517	Tracheotomy	617.585059	RD563	Foot—Surgery
617.5330592	RF538	Artificial larynx	617.5850592	RD563	Foot—Amputation
617.54	RC941	Chest pain	617.5850592	RD563	Foot—Reimplantation
617.54	RC941	Chest—Diseases	617.585075	RD563	Foot—Examination
617.5406	RV293	Chest—Diseases—Eclectic treatment	617.6	RK	Dentistry
			617.6	RK328	Dental calculus
617.5406	RX360	Chest—Diseases—Homeopathic treatment	617.6	RK328	Dental plaque
			617.6	RK328	Dental deposits
617.548	RD539.5	Esophagectomy	617.60014	RK28	Dentistry—Terminology
617.548044	RD539.5	Esophagus—Wounds and injuries	617.60019	RK53	Dentistry—Psychological aspects
617.548059	RD539.5	Esophagus—Surgery	617.60023	RK60-.5	Dentistry—Vocational guidance
617.55	RC944	Abdomen—Diseases	617.60025	RK37	Dentists—Directories
617.55	RC946	Pelvis—Diseases	617.600284	RK681-686	Dental instruments and apparatus
617.55	RD540-548	Acute abdomen			
617.55044	RD540-548	Abdomen—Wounds and injuries	617.6005	RK16	Dentistry—Periodicals
			617.6006	RK1	Dentistry—Societies, etc.
617.55059	RD540-548	Abdomen—Surgery	617.6006	RK21	Dentistry—Congresses
617.55059	RD540-547	Digestive organs—Surgery	617.60071	RK60.8	Dental health education
617.5506	RV297	Pelvis—Diseases—Eclectic treatment	617.60071	RK71-231	Dentistry—Study and teaching
617.553059	RD540.5-.57	Gastrectomy	617.600710(4-9)	RK86-231	Dentistry—Study and teaching—[By region or country]
617.553059	RD540.5-.57	Stomach—Surgery			
617.553059	RD540.5	Gastrostomy			
617.5545	RD542	Appendectomy	617.60072	RK80	Dentistry—Research
617.5565	RD546-547	Gallbladder—Surgery	617.600723	RK52-.45	Dental surveys
617.5567	RD546-547	Bile ducts—Surgery	617.60076	RK57	Dentistry—Examinations, questions, etc.
617.559059	RD621-626	Hernia			
617.564	RD771.B217	Backache	617.6008996073	RK60.45	Afro-Americans in dentistry
617.574	RD756.2-.22	Artificial arms	617.601	RK60.7-.8	Dental prophylaxis
617.574059	RD557	Arm—Amputation	617.601	RK60.7-.8	Preventive dentistry
617.575059	RD778-.5	Hand—Surgery	617.601	RK60.7	Teeth—Polishing
617.58	RC406.P3	Paraplegics	617.601	RK61	Teeth—Care and hygiene
617.58	RC951	Extremities (Anatomy)—Diseases	617.6023	RK58-59.3	Dentistry—Practice
			617.60233	RK60.5	Dental auxiliary personnel
617.58	RD553	Phantom limb	617.6044	RK490-493	Teeth—Wounds and injuries
617.58	RD756-.42	Artificial limbs	617.605	RK501-519	Dentistry, Operative
617.58	RD756.4-.42	Artificial legs	617.605	RK503	Dentistry, Operative—Positioning
617.58044	RD551-563	Extremities (Anatomy)—Wounds and injuries	617.605	RK513	Dentistry, Operative—Complications
617.58059	RD551-563	Extremities (Anatomy)—Surgery			
			617.605	RK529-535	Mouth—Surgery
617.58059	RD553	Amputation	617.60592	RK533	Teeth—Transplantation
617.580592	RD551-563	Extremities (Anatomy)—Transplantation	617.606	RK318-320	Dental therapeutics
			617.606	RK701-715	Dentistry—Formulae, receipts, prescriptions
617.5820592	RD561	Artificial knee			
617.5820592	RD561	Total knee replacement			

Dewey	LC	Subject Heading	Dewey	LC	Subject Heading
617.6071073	RK91-97	Dentistry—Study and teaching—United States	617.7005	RE6	Ophthalmology—Periodicals
617.60901	RK29-34	Dentistry—History	617.7006	RE1	Ophthalmology—Societies, etc.
617.60901	RK31	Dentistry, Ancient	617.7006	RE11	Ophthalmology—Congresses
617.63	RK301-493	Teeth—Diseases			
617.63	RK305	Focal infection, Dental	617.70071	RE56	Ophthalmology—Study and teaching
617.63	RK351	Focal infection, Dental	617.70231	RE88	Ophthalmic nursing
617.630754	RK308-310	Teeth—Diseases—Diagnosis	617.70232	RE31-36	Ophthalmologists
617.632	RK361-450	Periodontal disease	617.7026	RE48	Ophthalmologic emergencies
617.632	RK401-410	Gums—Diseases			
617.632	RK410	Gingivitis	617.7043	RE906	Eye—Abnormalities
617.632	RK450.P4	Periodontitis	617.7059	RE80-87	Eye—Surgery
617.634	RK320.E53	Dental enamel microabrasion	617.706	RV321-331	Eye—Diseases—Eclectic treatment
617.634	RK340-341	Dental enamel—Diseases	617.706	RX410-431	Eye—Diseases—Homeopathic treatment
617.6342	RK351-356	Endodontics			
617.643	RK520-528	Orthodontics	617.7061	RE994	Ophthalmic drugs
617.643	RK523	Malocclusion	617.7061	RE994	Ocular pharmacology
617.643	RK527-528	Orthodontics, Corrective	617.7075	RE75-79	Eye—Examination
617.64300284	RK527-528	Orthodonic appliances	617.707547	RE79.E39	Electroculography
617.645	RK55.C5	Pedodontics	617.707547	RE79.E4	Electroretinography
617.645	RK361-450	Periodontics	617.707572	RE79.R3	Eye—Radiography
617.66	RK531-.5	Teeth—Extraction	617.709	RE26-30	Ophthalmology—History
617.67	RK331	Dental caries	617.71043	RD772	Hip joint—Dislocation, Congenital
617.672	RK515	Dental drilling			
617.672	RK515	Dental cavity preparation	617.712	RE91-95	Blindness
617.675	RK517-519	Fillings (Dentistry)	617.712	RE91	Low vision
617.675	RK519.A4	Dental amalgams	617.712	RE95	Vision, Monocular
617.675	RK653	Dental metallurgy	617.713	RE831-840	Eye—Wounds and injuries
617.675	RK653	Gold alloys	617.719	RE328	Sclera—Diseases
617.675	RK653.5	Dental ceramic metals	617.719	RE336-340	Cornea—Diseases
617.675	RK655	Dental ceramics	617.7190592	RE336	Artificial corneas
617.69	RK641-667	Prosthodontics	617.72	RE350-355	Uvea—Diseases
617.69	RK652.7-.8	Dental bonding	617.732	RE725-780	Neuroophthalmology
617.69	RK656	Denture attachments	617.735	RE551-661	Retina—Diseases
617.69	RK667.T57	Tissue-integrated prostheses	617.735	RE603	Retinal detachment
			617.735	RE661.D5	Diabetic retinopathy
617.692	RK656-666	Dentures, Immediate	617.74	RE96	Eye—Infections
617.692	RK656-666	Overlay dentures	617.74	RE96	Eye—Inflammation
617.692	RK656-666	Dentures	617.74	RE651	Thrombosis
617.692	RK664-666	Partial dentures	617.74	RE835	Eye—Foreign bodies
617.692	RK665	Partial dentures, Removable	617.741	RE871	Glaucoma
617.692	RK666	Bridges (Dentistry)	617.742	RE401-461	Crystalline lens—Diseases
617.6922	RK666	Crowns (Dentistry)	617.742	RE451	Cataract
617.693	RK667.I45	Implant dentures	617.746	RE501	Vitreous body—Diseases
617.695	RK652.5-655	Dental materials	617.75	RE51	Eyestrain
617.695	RK652.7-.8	Dental cements	617.75	RE91-95	Vision disorders
617.695	RK652.7-.8	Dental adhesives	617.75	RE940-981	Optometry
617.7	RE	Ophthalmology	617.7522	RE940-981	Eyeglasses
617.70014	RE20	Ophthalmology—Terminology	617.7522	RE961-962	Ophthalmic lenses
			617.7523	RE977.C6	Contact lenses
617.70025	RE22	Ophthalmologists—Directories	617.7524	RE988	Intraocular lenses
			617.755	RE48	Eyestrain
617.700284	RE73	Ophthalmology—Instruments	617.755	RE925-939	Eye—Refractive errors

Dewey	LC	Subject Heading	Dewey	LC	Subject Heading
617.755	RE925-939	Eye—Accommodation and refraction	617.9676	RK510-512	Anesthesia in dentistry
617.755	RE932	Astigmatism	617.9682	RG732-733	Anesthesia in obstetrics
617.759	RE921	Color blindness	617.97	RD145	Aged—Surgery
617.759075	RE918-921	Color vision—Testing	617.98	RD137-139	Children—Surgery
617.762	RE731-780	Eye—Muscles	617.99	RD151-498	Surgery, Military
617.762	RE731-780	Eye—Movement disorders	617.99	RD151-498	Surgery, Naval
617.762	RE738	Diplopia	617.99094	RD268-441	Surgery, Military—Europe
617.762	RE760	Eye—Paralysis	617.99095	RD445-476	Surgery, Military—Asia
617.764	RE201-216	Lacrimal apparatus—Diseases	617.99096	RD481-489	Surgery, Military—Africa
			617.990971	RD216	Surgery, Military—Canada
617.771	RE121-155	Eyelids—Diseases	617.990972	RD221	Surgery, Military—Mexico
617.773	RE310-326	Conjunctiva—Diseases	617.9909728	RD224-225	Surgery, Military—Central America
617.773	RE320	Acute hemorrhagic conjunctivitis	617.9909729	RD231-232	Surgery, Military—West Indies
617.773	RE321	Conjunctivitis	617.990973	RD200-214	Surgery, Military—United States
617.78	RE711	Eye-sockets—Diseases			
617.79	RE986-988	Eyes, Artificial	617.99098	RD235-267	Surgery, Military—South America
617.8	RF110-320	Ear—Diseases			
617.8	RF110-320	Otology	617.990993	RD493.5	Surgery, Military—New Zealand
617.8	RF286-320	Audiology			
617.8	RF286-320	Deafness	617.990994	RD493	Surgery, Military—Australia
617.8	RF286-320	Hearing disorders	617.99099(5-6)	RD498	Surgery, Military—Oceania
617.8	RF293.5	Deafness, Noise induced	618	RC48.6	Women—Diseases
617.800284	RF298-310	Audiology—Instruments	618	RG831	Puerperal convulsions
617.8006	RF286	Audiology—Societies, etc.	618.07	RG77	Gynecologic pathology
617.80071	RF62	Otolaryngology—Study and teaching	618.1	RG	Gynecology
			618.1	RG316	Endometrium—Diseases
617.80231	RF52.5	Otolaryngological nursing	618.1	RG483.P44	Pelvic pain
617.8059	RF126-127	Ear—Surgery	618.10014	RG47	Gynecology—Terminology
617.84	RF220-229	Middle ear—Diseases	618.10019	RG103.5	Gynecology—Psychological aspects
617.85	RF210	Tympanic membrane—Diseases	618.10025	RG32-33	Gynecologists—Directories
617.86	RF230	Eustachian tube—Diseases	618.1005	RG26	Gynecology—Periodicals
617.87	RF235	Mastoid process—Diseases	618.1006	RG1	Gynecology—Societies, etc.
617.882	RF260-275	Labyrinth (Ear)—Diseases	618.1006	RG31	Gynecology—Congresses
617.8820592	RF305	Cochlear implants	618.1009	RG51-67	Gynecology—History
617.89	RF300-310	Hearing aids	618.10231	RG105	Gynecologic nursing
617.9	RD130	Prosthesis	618.1025	RG158	Gynecologic emergencies
617.9	RD736.T7	Orthopedic traction	618.1059	RG104.5	Gynoplasty
617.9	RD755-757	Orthopedic apparatus	618.1075	RG107-.5	Gynecologic examination
617.9	RD756	Crutches	618.1075	RG304-.5	Uterus—Diseases—Diagnosis
617.9	RD757.S5	Orthopedic slings			
617.9	RD757.W4	Wheelchairs	618.107543	RG107.5.E48	Endoscopic ultrasonography
617.919	RD98-.4	Surgery—Complications	618.107545	RG107.5.L34	Laparoscopy
617.919	RD98.3	Surgical wound infections	618.1092	RG71-76	Gynecologists
617.919	RD98.4	Postoperative pain	618.12	RG421-433	Fallopian tubes—Diseases
617.93	RD113-.4	Bandages and bandaging	618.12059	RG138	Sterilization of women
617.93	RD113-.4	Surgical dressings	618.12059	RG138	Sterilization reversal
617.952	RD118-120.5	Surgery, Plastic	618.14	RG301-391	Uterus—Diseases
617.954	RD120.6-129.8	Transplantation of organs, tissues, etc.	618.14	RG310-315	Cervix uteri—Diseases
			618.14	RG314	Cervix erosion
617.96	RD79-86	Ether (Anesthetic)	618.14	RG361	Uterus—Rupture
617.960083	RD139	Pediatric anesthesia	618.142	RG411	Pelvic inflammatory disease
617.9600846	RD145	Geriatric anesthesia	618.145	RD585	Sterilization reversal

Dewey	LC	Subject Heading	Dewey	LC	Subject Heading
618.145	RG104-.7	Generative organs, Female—Surgery	618.32	RG600-650	Perinatology
			618.32	RG613.7	Fetus—Immunology
618.1453	RG391	Hysterectomy	618.32	RG626-629	Fetus—Diseases
618.15	RG268-272	Vagina—Diseases	618.32	RG627.6.D79	Fetus—Effect of drugs on
618.16	RG261-266	Vulva—Diseases	618.32	RG627.6.M34	Fetal malnutrition
618.17	RG159-208	Endocrine gynecology	618.32	RG629.G75	Fetal growth disorders
618.172	RG161-186	Menstrual cycle	618.32	RG629.G76	Fetal growth retardation
618.172	RG161-186	Menstruation disorders	618.32	RG631-633	Perinatal death
618.172	RG165	Premenstrual syndrome	618.32	RG631-633	Fetal death
618.172	RG181	Dysmenorrhea	618.3204275	RG628.3.A48	Amniocentesis
618.172	RG734	Menstrual regulation	618.32043	RG626-629	Fetus—Abnormalities
618.175	RG186	Menopause	618.32043	RG626-629	Abnormalities, Human
618.178	RG133.5-135	Human reproductive technology	618.32075	RG628-.3	Prenatal diagnosis
			618.32075	RG628-.3	Fetal monitoring
618.178	RG134	Artificial insemination, Human	618.3207543	RG628.3.U58	Fetus—Ultrasonic imaging
			618.326	RG580.D5	Diabetes in pregnancy
618.178	RG201-205	Infertility, Female	618.326	RG615	Fetus—Metabolism
618.178059	RG135	Fertilization in vitro, Human	618.3261	RG580.H47	Blood diseases in pregnancy
618.19	RG491-499	Breast—Diseases	618.3261	RG618	Perinatal cardiology
618.19059	RD539.8	Mammaplasty	618.3261043	RJ269	Fetal heart—Abnormalities
618.190592	RD539.8	Augmentation mammaplasty	618.3261075	RG628.3.H42	Fetal heart rate monitoring
618.2	RG	Obstetrics	618.326107543	RG628.3.E34	Echocardiography
618.2	RG133	Conception	618.3268	RG580.D76	Drug abuse in pregnancy
618.2	RG519-520	Uterus, Pregnant	618.3268	RG580.E64	Epilepsy in pregnancy
618.2	RG551-591	Pregnancy	618.3268	RG580.S75	Substance abuse in pregnancy
618.2	RG950	Midwives			
618.20019	RG560	Pregnancy—Psychological aspects	618.34	RG591	Placenta
			618.392	RG648	Miscarriage
618.20025	RG504-505	Obstetricians—Directories	618.397	RG649	Labor, Premature
618.200284	RG545	Obstetrics—Apparatus and instruments	618.4	RG620	Fetus—Respiration and cry
			618.4	RG631-633	Stillbirth
618.20072	RG155	Obstetrics—Research	618.4	RG651-791	Labor (Obstetrics)
618.200835	RG556.5	Teenage pregnancy	618.4	RG661.5	Childbirth at home
618.20231	RG951	Maternity nursing	618.4	RG662	Active childbirth
618.20284	RG739	Obstetrical forceps	618.4	RG663	Underwater childbirth
618.206	RV361-365	Obstetrics, Eclectic	618.4	RG734	Labor, Induced (Obstetrics)
618.206	RX476	Obstetrics, Homeopathic	618.42	RG671-693	Fetal presentation
618.2075	RG563-564	Pregnancy—Signs and diagnosis	618.45	RG661-662	Natural childbirth
			618.5	RG701-721	Labor (Obstetrics)—Complications
618.207543	RG527.5.U48	Ultrasonics in obstetrics			
618.209	RG511-518	Obstetrics—History	618.5	RG715	Placenta praevia
618.209	RG529	Obstetrics—Case studies	618.5	RG719	Umbilical cord—Prolapse
618.2092	RG509-510	Obstetricians	618.54	RG580.H5	Uterine hemorrhage
618.24	RG559	Pregnancy—Nutritional aspects	618.54	RG711	Uterine hemorrhage
			618.54	RG821	Uterine hemorrhage
618.24	RJ91	Prenatal influences	618.7	RC867.5	Peritonitis
618.25	RG567	Multiple pregnancy	618.7	RG575-576	Toxemia of pregnancy
618.25	RG696-698	Multiple birth	618.7	RG576	Eclampsia
618.3	RG580.A44	AIDS (Disease) in pregnancy	618.7	RG801-871	Puerperal disorders
			618.7	RG801-871	Postnatal care
618.3	RG580.M34	Malnutrition in pregnancy	618.71	RG861-866	Lactation disorders
618.3025	RG571-591	Obstetrical emergencies	618.76	RG850-852	Postpartum psychiatric disorders
618.31	RG586	Ectopic pregnancy			
618.32	RG600-650	Fetus			

Dewey	LC	Subject Heading	Dewey	LC	Subject Heading
618.76	RG851	Puerperal psychoses	618.922	RJ431-436	Pediatric respiratory diseases
618.76	RG852	Postpartum depression			
618.8	RG725-791	Obstetrics—Surgery	618.92238	RJ436.A8	Asthma in children
618.82	RG741	Obstetrical extraction	618.9231	RJ460-463	Pediatric oral medicine
618.86	RG761	Cesarean section	618.9232	RJ456.E83	Esophagus—Atresia
618.88	RG781	Craniotomy	618.9233	RJ267	Colic
618.92	RJ	Pediatrics	618.9233	RJ446-456	Pediatric gastroenterology
618.92	RJ	Children—Diseases	618.92342	RJ456.F43	Fecal incontinence in children
618.92	RJ135	Failure to thrive syndrome			
618.92	RJ320.S93	Sudden infant death syndrome	618.923427	RJ456.D5	Diarrhea Infantile
			618.923623	RJ272	Hepatitis, Neonatal
618.9200019	RJ47.5-.53	Pediatrics—Psychosomatic aspects	618.923625	RJ276	Jaundice, Neonatal
			618.9239	RJ399.M26	Malnutrition in children
618.9200025	RJ29	Pediatricians—Directories	618.92395	RJ396	Rickets
618.920005	RJ16	Pediatrics—Periodicals	618.924	RJ418-420	Pediatric endocrinology
618.920006	RJ1	Pediatricians—Societies, etc	618.92442	RJ420.G65	Endemic goiter in children
			618.9245	RJ420.A27	Adrenal glands
618.920006	RJ21	Pediatrics—Congresses	618.92462083	RJ420.D5	Diabetes in youth
618.920009	RJ36-42	Pediatrics—History	618.92462083	RJ420.D5	Diabetes in children
618.9200092	RJ43	Pediatricians	618.9247	RJ420.P58	Dwarfism, Pituitary
618.9200231	RJ245-247	Pediatric nursing	618.92521	RJ516.E35	Eczema in children
618.920025	RJ370	Pediatric emergencies	618.926	RJ466-478.5	Pediatric urology
618.920028	RJ370	Pediatric intensive care	618.92614	RJ476.R46	Acute renal failure in children
618.920042	RJ47.3-.4	Genetic disorders in children			
			618.9271	RJ482.B65	Bone diseases in children
618.920062	RJ53.E95	Exercise therapy for children	618.92716	RJ128	Children—Metabolism
618.9200653	RJ53.F5	Fluid therapy for children	618.92748	RJ482.D78	Duchenne muscular dystrophy
618.9200654	RJ53.D53	Diet therapy for children			
618.9201	RJ61	Infants—Care	618.9277	RJ482.C65	Connective tissue diseases in children
618.9201	RJ251-325	Neonatology			
618.9201	RJ253.5	Neonatal emergencies	618.9277	RJ520.C64	Collagen diseases in children
618.9201	RJ253.5	Neonatal intensive care			
618.9201	RJ268.8	Neonatal gastroenterology	618.928	RJ486-496	Pediatric neurology
618.9201	R281	Birth weight, Low	618.928043	RJ290-.5	Nervous system—Abnormalities
618.92011	RJ250-.3	Infants (Premature)			
618.920232	RJ33.5-.8	Pediatrics—Practice	618.928043	RJ496.B7	Brain-damaged children
618.9206	RV375-377	Children—Diseases—Eclectic treatment	618.92836	RJ496.C4	Cerebral palsied children
			618.92842	RJ301	Paralysis
618.9206	RX501-531	Children—Diseases—Homeopathic treatment	618.92842	RJ496.P2	Paralysis
			618.92845	RJ496.C7	Febrile convulsions
618.920977	RE48.2.C5	Pediatric ophthalmology	618.92849	RJ476.E6	Enuresis
618.92097773	RJ296	Conjunctivitis, Infantile	618.9285223	RJ506.A58	Anxiety in children
618.92098	RJ476.5-478.5	Sexual disorders in children	618.9285225	RJ506.P38	Phobias in children
618.92098	RJ478-.5	Adolescent gynecology	618.928527	RJ506.D4	Depression in infants
618.92107572	RJ423.5.D54	Digital subtraction angiography	618.928527	RJ506.D4	Depression in children
			618.928527	RJ506.D4	Affective disorders in children
618.9212	RJ421-426	Pediatric cardiology			
618.921207543	RJ423.5.U46	Echocardiography	618.92853	RJ496.E6	Epilepsy in children
618.9215	RJ269.5-271	Neonatal hematology	618.928553	RJ496.A5	Dyslexic children
618.9215	RJ411-416	Pediatric hematology	618.928554	RJ496.S8	Stuttering in children
618.922	RJ256	Asphyxia neonatorum	618.92858	RJ506.B44	Behavior disorders in children
618.922	RJ274	Hyaline membrane disease			
618.922	RJ312	Respiratory insufficiency in children	618.928582	RJ506.S39	Self-destructive behavior in children
			618.9285836	RC560.I53	Incest victims

Dewey	LC	Subject Heading	Dewey	LC	Subject Heading
618.9285836	RJ507.S49	Sexually abused children	620.006	TA157	Engineering firms
618.928588	RJ506.F73	Fragile X syndrome	620.006	TA216-217	Engineering firms
618.9285884	RJ506.M4	Mental retardation	620.0068	TA190-194	Engineering—Management
618.92858842	RJ506.D68	Down's syndrome	620.00681	TA177.4-185	Engineering economy
618.928589	RJ506.H9	Attention-deficit hyperactivity disorder	620.0072	TA160-.6	Engineering—Research
			620.0072	TA416-417	Engineering experiment stations
618.9289	RJ499-520	Child psychiatry			
618.9289	RJ499-520	Child psychopathology	620.0072	TA416-417	Engineering laboratories
618.9289	RJ499-507	Child mental health	620.00727	TA340	Engineering—Statistical methods
618.9289	RJ506.C65	Conduct disorders in children			
			620.00728	TA337-338	Engineering—Graphic methods
618.9289027	RJ500.2	Child psychopathology— Research			
			620.008996073	TA157	Afro-American engineers
618.928914	RJ504-505	Child psychotherapy	620.009	TA15-19	Engineering—History
618.928917	RJ503	Adolescent analysis	620.0092	TA139-140	Engineers—Biography
618.928917	RJ504.2	Child analysis	620.009(4-9)	TA21-127	Engineering—[By region or country]
618.928982	RJ506.A9	Autism in children			
618.929	RJ275	Neonatal infections	620.00941	TA57-64	Engineering—Great Britain
618.9292	RJ406.B32	Bacterial diseases in children	620.00943	TA73-74.5	Engineering—Germany
			620.009436	TA65-.2	Engineering—Austria
618.92925	RJ401-406	Virus diseases in children	620.009437	TA65.3-.4	Engineering—Czechoslovakia
618.9297	RJ386-.5	Allergy in children	620.009439	TA65.5-66	Engineering—Hungary
618.92975	RJ386.5	Food allergy in children	620.00944	TA71-72.5	Engineering—France
618.92975	RJ386.5	Food allergy in infants	620.00945	TA79-80	Engineering—Italy
618.929792	RJ387.A25	AIDS (Disease) in children	620.00946	TA87-88	Engineering—Spain
618.929792	RJ387.A25	AIDS (Disease) in infants	620.009469	TA83-84.5	Engineering—Portugal
618.9299419	RJ416.A25	Acute myelocytic leukemia in children	620.00947	TA85-86	Engineering—Russia
			620.00948	TA88.5	Engineering—Scandinavia
618.97	RC952-954.6	Aged—Diseases	620.009481	TA81-82	Engineering—Norway
618.97	RC952-954.6	Geriatrics	620.009485	TA89-90	Engineering—Sweden
618.970231	RC954	Geriatric nursing	620.009489	TA69-70	Engineering—Denmark
618.9789	RC451.4.A5	Geriatric psychiatry	620.0094897	TA95.F5	Engineering—Finland
620	TA	Engineering	620.009492	TA77-78	Engineering—Netherlands
620.001171	TA168	Systems engineering	620.009493	TA67-68	Engineering—Belgium
620.00148	TA11	Engineering—Notation	620.009494	TA91-92	Engineering—Switzerland
620.00151	TA329-348	Engineering mathematics	620.009495	TA75-76	Engineering—Greece
620.00151	TA347.D45	Differential equations	620.009496	TA95.A2	Engineering—Balkan Peninsula
620.00151535	TA347.F5	Finite element method			
620.00212	TA180-182	Engineering—Specifications	620.009497	TA95.Y8	Engineering—Yugoslavia
620.00212	TA180-181	Specifications	620.00951	TA101-102	Engineering—China
620.00218	TA368	Standards, Engineering	620.00952	TA105-106	Engineering—Japan
620.00228	TA177	Engineering models	620.00954	TA103-104	Engineering—India
620.0023	TA157-158.3	Engineers	620.0095491	TA104.5-.6	Engineering—Pakistan
620.0025	TA12	Engineering firms— Directories	620.0095493	TA104.7-.8	Engineering—Sri Lanka
			620.00955	TA107-108	Engineering—Iran
620.00284	T13	Engineering—Supplies	620.009561	TA111-112	Engineering—Turkey
620.00284	TA165	Engineering instruments	620.009567	TA113.I7	Engineering—Iraq
620.00284	TA213-215	Engineering—Equipment and supplies	620.0095694	TA113.I75	Engineering—Israel
			620.00957	TA109-110	Engineering—Asiatic Russia
620.003	TA9	Engineering—Dictionaries	620.009598	TA113.I55	Engineering—Indonesia
620.0042	TA174	Engineering design	620.009599	TA113.P6	Engineering—Philippines
620.00420285	TA345	Computer-aided engineering	620.0096	TA115-119	Engineering—Africa
620.0044	TA191	Engineering inspection	620.00962	TA117-118	Engineering—Egypt
620.005	TA1-4	Engineering—Periodicals	620.00971	TA26-27	Engineering—Canada
620.006	TA5	Engineering—Congresses	620.00972	TA28-29	Engineering—Mexico

Dewey	LC	Subject Heading	Dewey	LC	Subject Heading
620.009728	TA30-31	Engineering—Central America	620.11274	TA417.4	Ultrasonic testing
			620.11295	TA418.12	Photoelasticity
620.009729	TA32-33	Engineering—West Indies	620.118	TA418.9.C6	Composite materials
620.00973	TA23-25	Engineering—United States	620.1(2-9)	TA401-492	Building materials
620.00981	TA41-42	Engineering—Brazil	620.12	TA419-424.6	Timber
620.00982	TA36-37	Engineering—Argentina	620.136	TA439	Expansive concrete
620.00983	TA43-44	Engineering—Chile	620.136	TA439-446	Concrete
620.00984	TA38-39	Engineering—Bolivia	620.14	TA447	Drain-tiles
620.00985	TA52	Engineering—Peru	620.143	TA455.F5	Fire-clay
620.009861	TA45-46	Engineering—Colombia	620.144	TA450	Glass
620.009866	TA47	Engineering—Ecuador	620.16	TA479.S7	Steel, Stainless
620.00987	TA54	Engineering—Venezuela	620.16	TA486	Corrosion resistant alloys
620.009881	TA48	Engineering—Guyana	620.160287	TA459-492	Metals—Testing
620.009882	TA50	Engineering—French Guiana	620.166	TA460	Metals—Fatigue
			620.17	TA472-473	Steel, Galvanized
620.009883	TA49	Engineering—Surinam	620.17	TA474-475	Cast-iron
620.009892	TA51	Engineering—Paraguay	620.17	TA479.C37	Carbon steel
620.009895	TA53	Engineering—Uruguay	620.176	TA473	Steel—Fatigue
620.00993	TA122.5-.6	Engineering—New Zealand	620.18	TA478	Nonmetallic steel
620.00994	TA121-122	Engineering—Australia	620.18	TA479.3	Nonferrous metals
620.0099(5-6)	TA123-124	Engineering—Oceania	620.182	TA480.C7	Copper
620.00998	TA125-.5	Engineering—Arctic regions	620.185	TA480.T5	Tin
620.1	TA350-359	Mechanics, Applied	620.186	TA480.A6	Aluminum, Structural
620.106	TA357-359	Fluid dynamics	620.186	TA480.A6	Aluminum alloys
620.1064	TA357.5.C38	Cavitation	620.188	TA480.N6	Nickel
620.1064	TA357.5.M59	Mixing	620.18923	TA480.S5	Silver
620.1064	TA357.5.M84	Multiphase flow	620.18932	TA480.T54	Titanium
620.1064	TA357.5.U57	Unsteady flow (Fluid dynamics)	620.192	TA455.P58	Polymers
			620.1923	TA455.P5-.P55	Plastics
620.1064	TC174	Water hammer	620.2	TA365-367	Acoustical engineering
620.10640287	TA357.5.M43	Fluid dynamic measurements	620.23	TD891-893.6	Noise pollution
			620.23	TD891-893	City noise
620.11	TA401-492	Materials	620.23	TD892	Noise barriers
620.110287	TA401-492	Testing	620.23	TD893.6.T7	Transportation noise
620.1103	TA402	Materials—Dictionaries	620.4162	TC1501-1800	Ocean engineering
620.1105	TA401	Materials—Periodicals	620.416205	TC1501	Ocean engineering—Periodicals
620.11072	TA404.2	Materials—Research			
620.112	TA405	Strength of materials	620.416206	TC1505	Ocean engineering—Congresses
620.112	TA410-417.7	Strength of materials			
620.112	TA410	Buckling (Mechanics)	620.5	T174.7	Nanotechnology
620.1121	TA418.58	Thermal stresses	620.86	TH7694	Clean rooms
620.11223	TA418.74-.76	Corrosion and anti-corrosives	621	TJ	Mechanical engineering
			621	TJ163.6-.95	Power (Mechanics)
620.11232	TA417.6	Deformations (Mechanics)	621.01	TJ14	Mechanical engineering—Philosophy
620.11233	TA418.22	Materials—Creep			
620.11233	TA652	Plastic analysis (Engineering)	621.025	TJ11-13	Mechanical engineers—Directories
620.1126	TA354.5	Penetration mechanics	621.042	TJ807-830	Renewable energy sources
620.1126	TA409	Fracture mechanics	621.05	TJ1-4	Mechanical engineering—Periodicals
620.1126	TA418.16	Brittleness			
620.1126	TA418.42	Hardness	621.06	TJ5	Mechanical engineering—Congresses
620.1126	TA418.45	Hard materials			
620.11260287	TA413-.5	Fatigue testing machines	621.071	TJ158-159	Mechanical engineering—Study and teaching
620.11260287	TA413-.5	Testing-machines			
620.1127	TA417.2-.55	Non-destructive testing			

Dewey	LC	Subject Heading	Dewey	LC	Subject Heading
621.09	TJ15-20	Mechanical engineering—History	621.3071	TK165-213	Electric engineering—Study and teaching
621.092	TJ139-140	Mechanical engineers—Biography	621.3074	TK6	Electric engineering—Museums
621.09(4-9)	TJ21-127	Mechanical engineering—[By region or country]	621.309	TK15-18	Electric engineering—History
621.1	TJ268-748	Steam engineering	621.309(4-9)	TK21-127	Electric engineering—[By region or country]
621.1	TJ268-280.7	Steam			
621.1	TJ461-740	Steam-engines	621.31	TK153	Electric power factor
621.1071	TC157-.5	Hydraulic engineering—Study and teaching	621.31	TK1001-1841	Electric power
			621.31	TK3001-3511	Electric power
621.109(4-9)	TC21-127	Hydraulic engineering—[By region or country]	621.31	TK4001-9971	Electric power
			621.31042	TK2000-2891	Electric machinery
621.165	TJ735-740	Steam-turbines	621.31042	TK2271	Eddy currents (Electric)
621.183	TJ281-393	Steam-boilers	621.3121	TJ164	Power-plants
621.183	TJ320-358	Furnaces	621.3121	TK1001-1841	Electric power production
621.1830289	TJ350-357	Steam-boilers—Safety appliances	621.3121	TK1041-1078	Cogeneration of electric power and heat
621.185	TJ370-372	Pressure gages	621.3121	TK1191-1841	Electric power-plants
621.185	TJ415-444	Steam-pipes	621.31210287	TK1831	Electric power-plants—Testing
621.185	TJ427	Steam-pipe coverings			
621.194	TJ290-291	Boiler-plates	621.312132	TJ395-444	Steam power plants
621.197	TJ557-565	Condensers (Steam)	621.312134	TK1081-1083	Hydroelectric power plants
621.197	TJ563	Cooling towers	621.312134	TK1081	Tidal power-plants
621.2	TC	Hydraulic engineering	621.3124	TK2896	Direct energy conversion
621.2	TJ836-935	Hydraulic machinery	621.31242	TK2896-2986	Electric batteries
621.2	TJ855-857	Hydraulic motors	621.31242	TK2941	Storage batteries
621.2	TJ1435	Hydraulic jacks	621.312429	TK2931	Fuel cells
621.203	TC9	Hydraulic engineering—Dictionaries	621.31244	TK1085-1087	Solar power plants
			621.31244	TK1545	Solar power plants
621.20422	TC147	Tidal power	621.31244	TK2960	Solar cells
621.20422	TC147	Ocean wave power	621.3126	TK1751	Electric substations
621.20422	TC147	Water-power	621.313	TK2411-2491	Electric generators
621.20424	TJ843	Oil hydraulic machinery	621.313	TK2796	Electric current converters
621.20424	TJ844	Hydraulic fluids	621.313	TK2796	Rotary converters
621.205	TC1	Hydraulic engineering—Periodicals	621.3132	TK2441	Gramme dynamos
			621.3132	TK2611-2699	Electric machinery—Direct current
621.2072	TC158	Hydraulic laboratories			
621.209	TC15-20	Hydraulic engineering—History	621.3133	TK2711-2799	Electric machinery—Alternating current
621.2092	TC139-140	Hydraulic engineers—Biography	621.3137	TK7872.R35	Electric current rectifiers
621.21	TJ840-890	Water-power	621.314	TK2551	Electric transformers
621.21	TJ859	Water mills	621.314	TK7872.T7	Electronic transformers
621.21	TJ860-880	Water-wheels	621.316	TK2477	Armatures
621.3	TK	Electric engineering	621.316	TK2484	Brushes, Carbon
621.30221	TK431	Electric drafting	621.317	TK2821-2846	Electric switchgear
621.3025	TK12	Electric engineering—Directories	621.317	TK2842	Electric circuit-breakers
			621.317	TK2851	Electric rheostats
621.303	TK9	Electric engineering—Dictionaries	621.317	TK2861	Electric contactors
			621.317	TK2861	Differential relays
621.305	TK1-4	Electric engineering—Periodicals	621.319	TK3001-3521	Electric power distribution
			621.319	TK3001-3521	Electric power transmission
621.306	TK5	Electric engineering—Congresses	621.319	TK3091	Electric power failures
			621.31912	TK3111	Electric power distribution—Direct current

Dewey	LC	Subject Heading	Dewey	LC	Subject Heading
621.31913	TK1141-1168	Electric currents, Alternating	621.3309(4-9)	TF1021-1127	Electric railroads—[By region or country]
621.31913	TK3141-3171	Electric power transmission—Alternating current	621.36	TA1501-1820	Photonics
			621.362	TA1570	Infrared technology
621.31913	TK3141-3171	Electric power distribution—Alternating current	621.362	TA1570	Infrared sources
			621.366	TA1671-1715	Lasers
621.31913	TK3144	Electric power distribution—High tension	621.366	TA1693	Free electron lasers
			621.366	TA1705	Ruby lasers
621.3192	TK454.2	Electric networks, Active	621.3663	TA1695	Gas lasers
621.3192	TK454.2	Electric network topology	621.3664	TA1690	Dye lasers
621.3192	TK454.2	Electric networks, Passive	621.367	TA1637	Image processing
621.3192	TK3001-3521	Electric circuits	621.3692	QC447.9-448.2	Fiber optics
621.3192	TK3201-3261	Electric lines	621.3693	TA1660	Integrated optics
621.3192	TK3226	Electric networks	621.37	TK275-399	Electric measurements
621.3192	TK3242-3243	Electric lines—Poles and towers	621.37	TK401	Electric testing
			621.373	TK301-399	Electric meters
621.31921	TK3226	Transients (Electricity)	621.373	TK393	Recording instruments
621.31923	TK3251-3261	Underground electric lines	621.3743	QC615	Voltameter
621.31924092	TK139-140	Electricians	621.3743	TK321	Voltmeter
621.3193	TK3301-3351	Electric conductors	621.3744	TK331	Voltameter
621.31933	TK3201-3285	Electric wiring	621.381	TK7800-8360	Electronics
621.31933	TK3271-3285	Electric wiring, Interior	621.381	TK7870	Electronic systems
621.31933	TK3301-3351	Electric wire	621.3810221	TK7866	Electronic drafting
621.31934	TK3301-3351	Electric cables	621.3810223	TK7866	Electronics—Charts, diagrams, etc.
621.31937	TK3331-3441	Electric insulators and insulation	621.3810228	TK7870	Miniature electronic equipment
621.32	TH7700-7975	Lighting	621.3810284	TK7869-7872	Electronic apparatus and appliances
621.32	TK4125-4399	Electric lighting			
621.32	TK4310-4399	Electric lamps	621.3810284	TK7870	Electronic instruments
621.320284	TK4198	Electric light fixtures	621.3810287	TK7878-7879.4	Electronic measurements
621.3209(4-9)	TK4134-4156	Electric lighting—[By region or country]	621.38105	TK7800	Electronics—Periodicals
			621.38106	TK7801	Electronics—Congresses
621.3229	SB476	Garden lighting	621.381072	TK7855	Electronics—Research
621.3229	TK4188	Exterior lighting	621.3810728	TK7825	Electronics—Graphic methods
621.3229	TK4399.S6	Electric signs			
621.324	TH7910-7970	Gas-lighting	621.3813	TK7876	Microwave devices
621.3240284	TH7960-7967	Gas-fixtures	621.38131	TK7876	Microwave transmission lines
621.325	TK4311-4335	Electric lighting, Arc			
621.325	TK4321-4335	Electric lamps, Arc	621.381331	QC661	Wave guides
621.326	TK4341-4367	Electric lighting, Incandescent	621.381334	TK7871.75	Magnetrons
			621.3815	TK7867-7868	Electronic circuits
621.326	TK4351-4367	Incandescent lamps	621.3815	TK7872.F44	Ferroelectric devices
621.3273	TK4386	Fluorescent lamps	621.38151	TK7871.7-.84	Electron Tubes
621.3275	TK4383	Neon tubes	621.381512	TK7872.V3	Vacuum-tubes
621.3275	TK4383	Neon lamps	621.381513	TK7871.8-.84	Gas tubes
621.33	TF858-859	Railroads—Electrification	621.38152	TK7871.85-.99	Semiconductor wafers
621.33	TF863-952	Electric railroads—Design and construction	621.38152	TK7871.99.M4	Metal insulator semiconductors
621.33	TF880-900	Electric railroads—Wires and wiring	621.381522	TK7871.89.A94	Diodes, IMPATT
			621.381522	TK7871.89.S95	Diodes, Switching
621.33	TF930	Electric controllers	621.381528	TK7871.96.B55	Bipolar transistors
621.33	TF935	Electric railway motors	621.3815282	TK7871.92	Junction transistors
621.330284	TF920-952	Electric railroads—Equipment and supplies	621.381531	TK7868.P7	Printed circuits
			621.3815322	TK2699	Electric inverters

Dewey	LC	Subject Heading	Dewey	LC	Subject Heading
621.3815322	TK7872.I65	Electric inverters	621.38483	TK6587	Radar transmitters
621.381533	TK7872.O7	Feedback oscillators	621.385	TK6001-6571.5	Telephone
621.381535	TK7871.2-.58	Transistor amplifiers	621.385	TK6391-6397	Telephone switchboards
621.381535	TK7871.2-.58	Amplifiers (Electronics)	621.385025	TK6011	Telephone—Directories
621.381535	TK7871.58.B74	Broadband amplifiers	621.38505	TK6001	Telephone—Periodicals
621.381535	TK7871.58.D5	Direct current amplifiers	621.3857	TK6397	Telephone switching systems, Electronic
621.381537	TK7868.S9	Switching circuits			
621.381542	TK8300-8360	Photoelectric cells	621.387	TK6401-6505	Telephone systems
621.381542	TK8314	Photoelectric multipliers	621.38784	TK6201-6285	Telephone lines
621.3815422	TK7872.L56	Liquid crystal displays	621.38784	TK6381-6383	Telephone wire
621.381548	TK7872.S5	Signal generators	621.38784	TK6381-6383	Telephone cables
621.3815483	TK7878.7	Cathode ray oscilloscope	621.388	TK6630-6720	Television
621.382	TK5101-5105.9	Telecommunication	621.38800284	TK6650-6655	Television—Equipment and supplies
621.382	TK5103.7-.8	Digital communications			
621.38216	TK5105-.42	Data transmission systems	621.388005	TK6630.A1	Television—Periodicals
621.38216	TK5105	Packet switching (Data transmission)	621.38804	TK6670	Color television
			621.38807	TK6678	Digital television
621.38224	TK5101	Random noise theory	621.3883	TK7881.65	Digital audiotape recorders and recording
621.38234	TK5984	Magnetic tapes			
621.38235	TK6710-7620	Facsimile transmission	621.38833	TK6655.V5	Videocassette recorders
621.3824	TK7871.6	Antennas (Electronics)	621.388332	TK6680.5-6687	Digital video
621.3825	TK5104-.2	Artificial satellites in telecommunication	621.38835	TK6676	Television, Master antenna
			621.38928	TK7241	Electric alarms
621.3827	TK5103.59	Optical communications	621.38928	TK7882.E2	Electronic surveillance
621.3828	TA1770	Acoustooptical devices	621.38932	TK7881.6	Magnetic recorders and recording
621.3828	TK5981-5990	Electro-acoustics			
621.38284	TK5986	Electrostatic microphone	621.38932	TK7881.75	Compact disc players
621.383	TK5105-5865	Telegraph	621.39	TK7885-7895	Computer engineering
621.38305	TK5107	Telegraph—Periodicals	621.39	TK7885-7895	Computers
621.38405	TK6540	Radio—Periodicals	621.39	TK7888.3-.4	Electronic digital computers
621.384(1-5)	TK6540-6571.5	Radio	621.390288	TK7887	Computers—Maintenance and repair
621.384 (1-5) + 0288	TK6553	Radio—Repairing			
			621.3919	TK7888	Electronic analog computers
621.384 (1-5) + 0284	TK6560-6565	Radio—Equipment and supplies	621.395	TK7872.L64	Logic devices
621.38411	TK6553	Radio—Interference	621.395	TK7874-.8	Digital integrated circuits
621.38412	TK6565.A55	Amplifiers (Electronics)	621.395	TK7874	Linear integrated circuits
621.38412	TK6565.O7	Oscillators, Electric	621.395	TK7888.4	Electronic digital computers—Circuits
621.384131	TK6561-6562	Radio—Transmitters and transmission			
			621.395	TK7888.4	Logic circuits
621.384132	TK6565.V3	Vacuum-tubes	621.397	TK7895.M4	Cache memory
621.384133	TK6565.R426	Electric resistors	621.3973	TK7895.M4	Random access memory
621.384135	TK6565.A6	Radio—Antennas	621.3973	TK7895.M4	Read-only memory
621.38416	TK9956	Amateur radio stations	621.39732	TK7895.M4	Semiconductor storage devices
621.38418	TK6563-6564	Radio—Receivers and reception			
			621.3976	TK7882.C56	Compact discs
621.384191	TL696.B4	Radio beacons	621.3976	TK7887.55	Data tape drives
621.3842	TK5700-5865	Telegraph, Wireless	621.39763	TK7872.M25	Magnetic bubble devices
621.3842	TK5811-5865	Telegraph, Wireless—Marconi system	621.39767	TK7895.C39	CD-ROMs
			621.39767	TK7895.M4	Optical storage devices
621.38454	TK6570.C5	Citizens band radio	621.398	TK7887.5	Computer interfaces
621.3848	TK6573-6595	Radar	621.3981	TK7868.I58	Interface circuits
621.3848	TK6592.D6	Doppler radar	621.39814	TK7887.6	Analog-to-digital converters
621.3848	TK6592.M67	Moving target indicator radar	621.39814	TK7887.8.M63	Modems
			621.3984	TA167	Man-machine systems

Dewey	LC	Subject Heading	Dewey	LC	Subject Heading
621.3985	TK7887.8.T4	Computer terminals	621.48336	TK9212	Nuclear reactors—Cooling
621.399	TK7882.S65	Speech synthesis	621.4834	TK9203.B6	Boiling water reactors
621.4	TJ250-255	Engines	621.4834	TK9203.B7	Liquid metal fast breeder reactors
621.402	TK4601-4661	Electric heating			
621.4021	TJ265	Thermodynamics	621.4834	TK9203.H4	Heavy water reactors
621.4024	TH1715-1718	Insulation (Heat)	621.4834	TK9203.S65	Solid fuel reactors
621.4025	TJ255-265	Heat-engines	621.4834	TK9203.S86	Superheating reactors
621.4025	TJ262	Heat pumps	621.4835	TK9151.6-.7	Remote handling (Radioactive substances)
621.4028	TK4601	Induction heating			
621.4028	TK4601	Microwave heating	621.4838	TK9360	Reactor fuel reprocessing
621.4028	TK4661	Electric furnaces	621.484	TK9204	Fusion reactors
621.406	TJ266-267.5	Turbines	621.484	TK9360	Thermonuclear fuels
621.406	TJ266-267.5	Turbomachines	621.485	TK9230	Nuclear propulsion
621.43	TJ254.7	Combustion chambers	621.51	TJ950-1030	Pneumatic machinery
621.43	TJ751-805	Internal combustion engines	621.51	TJ981-1009	Compressed air
			621.51	TJ990-992	Air-compressors
621.433	TJ778	Gas-turbines	621.51	TJ990-992	Compressors
621.4335	TJ779	Free piston engines	621.55	TJ940-.5	Vacuum technology
621.43560228	TL844	Rockets (Aeronautics)—Models	621.55	TJ940.5	Vacuum pumps
			621.56	TP480-482	Low temperature engineering
621.436	TJ795	Diesel motor			
621.437	TJ787	Carburetors	621.56	TP490-497	Refrigeration and refrigerating machinery
621.45	TJ820-828	Wind power			
621.453	TJ823-828	Windmills	621.57	TP496-497	Refrigerators
621.46	TK2435	Electric motors—Design and construction	621.6	TJ901	Ejector pumps
			621.65	TJ915	Reciprocating pumps
621.46	TK2511-2541	Electric motors	621.66	TJ917	Rotary pumps
621.46	TK2681	Electric motors	621.69	TJ899-927	Pumping machinery
621.46	TK2781-2789	Electric motors, Alternating current	621.8	TJ	Machinery
			621.80287	TJ148	Machinery—Testing
621.46	TK2781-2789	Electric motors	621.81	TJ177	Machinery—Vibration
621.47	TJ809-812.8	Solar energy	621.81	TJ181-210	Mechanical movements
621.47072	TJ811-.5	Solar energy—Research	621.81	TJ181.5	Wheels
621.472	TJ812	Solar collectors	621.815	TJ227-240	Machine design
621.473	TJ812.5	Solar engines	621.822	TJ1061-1073.7	Bearings (Machinery)
621.48	TK9001-9401	Nuclear engineering	621.822	TJ1071-1073	Ball-bearings
621.48	TK9001-9401	Nuclear energy	621.822	TJ1071	Roller bearings
621.480284	TK9178-9183	Nuclear power plants—Instruments	621.822	TJ1073.R8	Rubber bearings
			621.824	TJ210	Springs (Mechanism)
621.480289	TK9152-.16	Radiation—Safety measures	621.825	TJ183	Couplings
			621.833	TJ184-204	Gearing
621.480289	TK9152-.16	Nuclear engineering—Safety measures	621.8332	TJ193-196	Gearing, Bevel
			621.8333	TJ192	Gearing, Spiral
621.4805	TK9001	Nuclear engineering—Periodicals	621.8333	TJ200	Gearing, Worm
			621.84	TJ533	Pistons
621.483	QC786.4-786.8	Nuclear reactors	621.85	TJ1045-1119	Power transmission
621.483	TK1078	Nuclear power plants	621.85	TJ1103	Pulleys
621.483	TK9202-9230	Nuclear reactors	621.852	TJ1100-1119	Belts and belting
621.483	TK9203.H4	Steam generating heavy water reactors	621.862	TJ1350-1383	Hoisting machinery
			621.864	VM811	Windlasses
621.4830285	QC783.3-.4	Nuclear reactors—Computer programs	621.864	VM811	Capstan
			621.865	TA735-747	Excavating machinery
621.4833	TK9207	Nuclear fuel rods	621.867	TJ1385-1418	Conveying machinery
621.4833	TK9360	Nuclear fuels	621.8672	TJ930-934	Pipelines
621.48335	TK9360	Spent reactor fuels			

Dewey	LC	Subject Heading	Dewey	LC	Subject Heading
621.8676	TJ1376	Escalators	622.0947	TN85-86	Mines and mineral resources—Russia
621.87	TJ1363-1365	Cranes, derricks, etc.	622.0948	TN88.5	Mines and mineral resources—Scandinavia
621.873	TJ1363-1365	Electric cranes			
621.873	TJ1365	Gantry cranes	622.09481	TN81-82	Mines and mineral resources—Norway
621.877	TJ1370-1380	Elevators			
621.88	TJ1320-1340	Fasteners	622.09485	TN89-90	Mines and mineral resources—Sweden
621.882	TJ1330-1333	Bolts and nuts			
621.882	TJ1338-1340	Screws	622.09489	TN69-70	Mines and mineral resources—Denmark
621.89	TJ1075-1081	Lubrication and lubricants			
621.890284	TJ1081	Oil filters	622.094897	TN95.F5	Mines and mineral resources—Finland
621.9	GN436.8-437	Tools			
621.9	TJ1180-1313	Tools	622.09492	TN77-78	Mines and mineral resources—Netherlands
621.9	TJ1193	Diamonds, Industrial			
621.902	TJ1180-1313	Machine-tools	622.09494	TN91-92	Mines and mineral resources—Switzerland
621.904	TJ1005-1007	Pneumatic tools			
621.91	TJ1205-1210	Planing-machines	622.09495	TN75-76	Mines and mineral resources—Greece
621.91	TJ1225-1227	Milling-machines			
621.914	TJ1345	Crushing machinery	622.09496	TN95.A2	Mines and mineral resources—Balkan Peninsula
621.92	TJ1280-1298	Grinding and polishing			
621.923	TJ1290	Emery-wheels	622.09497	TN95.Y8	Mines and mineral resources—Yugoslavia
621.93	TJ1230-1240	Cutting machines			
621.93	TJ1233	Hacksaws	622.0951	TN101-102	Mines and mineral resources—China
621.934	TJ1233-1255	Saws			
621.942	TJ1218-1222	Lathes	622.0952	TN105-106	Mines and mineral resources—Japan
621.952	TA745-747	Rock-drills			
621.952	TJ1260-1270	Drilling and boring	622.0954	TN103-104	Mines and mineral resources—India
621.952	TJ1260	Drill presses			
621.973	TJ1201.H3	Hammers	622.095491	TN104.5-.6	Mines and mineral resources—Pakistan
621.98	TJ1465	Pneumatic presses			
621.984	TJ1335	Taps and dies	622.095493	TN104.7-.8	Mines and mineral resources—Sri Lanka
621.984	TS253	Dies (Metal-working)			
622	TN	Mining engineering	622.0955	TN107-108	Mines and mineral resources—Iran
622.0284	TN345-347	Mining machinery			
622.071	TN165-213	Mining schools and education	622.09561	TN111-112	Mines and mineral resources—Turkey
622.092	TN139-140	Mining engineers	622.09567	TN113.I7	Mines and mineral resources—Iraq
622.0941	TN57-64	Mines and mineral resources—Great Britain	622.095694	TN113.I75	Mines and mineral resources—Israel
622.0943	TN73-74.5	Mines and mineral resources—Germany	622.0957	TN109-110	Mines and mineral resources—Asiatic Russia
622.09436	TN65-.2	Mines and mineral resources—Austria	622.09598	TN113.I55	Mines and mineral resources—Indonesia
622.09437	TN65.3-.4	Mines and mineral resources—Czechoslovakia	622.09599	TN113.P6	Mines and mineral resources—Philippines
622.09439	TN65.5-66	Mines and mineral resources—Hungary	622.096	TN115-119	Mines and mineral resources—Africa
622.0944	TN71-72.5	Mines and mineral resources—France	622.0962	TN117-118	Mines and mineral resources—Egypt
622.0945	TN79-80	Mines and mineral resources—Italy	622.0971	TN26-27	Mines and mineral resources—Canada
622.0946	TN87-88	Mines and mineral resources—Spain	622.0972	TN28-29	Mines and mineral resources—Mexico
622.09469	TN83-84.5	Mines and mineral resources—Portugal	622.09728	TN30-31	Mines and mineral resources—Central America

Dewey	LC	Subject Heading	Dewey	LC	Subject Heading
622.09729	TN32-33	Mines and mineral resources—West Indies	622.337	TN853	Asphalt
622.0973	TN23-25	Mines and mineral resources—United States	622.338	TN870	Oil fields—Production methods
622.0981	TN41-42	Mines and mineral resources—Brazil	622.3381	TN871.2-.3	Oil well drilling
			622.3381	TN871.27	Drilling muds
			622.3381	TN871.5	Oil well drilling rigs
622.0982	TN36-37	Mines and mineral resources—Argentina	622.33819	TN871.3	Oil well drilling, Submarine
622.0983	TN43-44	Mines and mineral resources—Chile	622.3382	TN860-879	Petroleum
			622.3382	TN871	Gushers
622.0984	TN38-39	Mines and mineral resources—Bolivia	622.3382	TN871	Oil reservoir engineering
			622.3382	TN871.37	Secondary recovery of oil
622.0985	TN52	Mines and mineral resources—Peru	622.3385	TN880-884	Gas wells
			622.3385	TN880-884	Gas engineering
622.09861	TN45-46	Mines and mineral resources—Colombia	622.3385	TN880-884	Natural gas
			622.339	TN885	Amber
622.09866	TN47	Mines and mineral resources—Ecuador	622.34	TN400-580	Metals
			622.34	TN400-580	Ores
622.0987	TN54	Mines and mineral resources—Venezuela	622.341	TN400-409	Iron mines and mining
			622.342	TN410-439	Precious metals
622.09881	TN48	Mines and mineral resources—Guyana	622.3422	TN410-429	Gold mines and mining
			622.3422	TN420-429	Gold ores
622.09882	TN50	Mines and mineral resources—French Guiana	622.3422	TN422	Gold dredging
			622.3423	TN430-439	Silver mines and mining
622.09883	TN49	Mines and mineral resources—Surinam	622.343	TN440-449	Copper mines and mining
			622.344	TN450-459	Lead ores
622.09892	TN51	Mines and mineral resources—Paraguay	622.3453	TN470-479	Tin mines and mining
			622.3453	TN470-479	Tin ores
622.09895	TN53	Mines and mineral resources—Uruguay	622.347	TN490.B6	Bismuth ores
			622.3483	TN490.C6	Cobalt ores
622.0993	TN122.5-.6	Mines and mineral resources—New Zealand	622.35	TN950-997	Stone
			622.3516	TN967	Dolomite
622.0994	TN121-122	Mines and mineral resources—Australia	622.352	TN970	Granite
			622.353	TN957	Sandstone
622.0998	TN125-.5	Mines and mineral resources—Arctic regions	622.36	TN948.D5	Diatomaceous earth
			622.361	TN941-943	Clay
622.14	TN273	Mine surveying	622.3622	TN939	Sand and gravel plants
622.18	TN270-271	Prospecting	622.3622	TN939	Sand
622.1828	TN271.P4	Petroleum—Prospecting	622.3632	TN900-909	Salt mines and mining
622.2	TN	Mines and mineral resources	622.3632	TN900-909	Salt
622.23	TN279-281	Rock-drills	622.3633	TN917	Borax
622.23	TN279	Percussion drilling	622.3635	TN946	Gypsum
622.23	TN279	Blasting	622.3636	TN919	Potassium salts
622.23	TN281.5	Rotary drilling	622.364	TN911	Nitrates
622.24	TN281	Boring	622.364	TN913-914	Phosphate mines and mining
622.25	TN283	Shaft sinking			
622.26	TN285	Tunneling	622.3662	TN948.P5	Pigments
622.28	TN289	Mine timbering	622.3668	TN890	Sulphur
622.292	TN277	Quarries and quarrying	622.367	TN941-943	Fire-clay
622.292	TN291	Strip mining	622.3672	TN930	Asbestos
622.2927	TN278	Hydraulic mining	622.3674	TN933	Mica
622.33	TN850	Bitumen	622.368	TN945	Cement
622.334	TN799.9-844.7	Coal	622.373	TN923-929.7	Mineral waters
622.334	TN799.9-844.7	Coal mines and mining	622.38	TN980-997	Precious stones
622.335	TN820-823	Anthracite coal	622.382	TN990-994	Diamonds

Dewey	LC	Subject Heading	Dewey	LC	Subject Heading
622.384	TN997.S24	Sapphires	623.452	TP268-299	Explosives, Military
622.386	TN997.E5	Emeralds	623.46	UF850-857	Range-finding
622.387	TN997.A35	Agates	623.46	UF853	Position-finders
622.387	TN997.G3	Garnet	623.46	UF854	Firearms—Sights
622.42	TN301-306	Mine ventilation	623.46	UF855	Telescopic sights
622.47	TN306.5-309	Mine lighting	623.51	UF820-840	Ballistics
622.473	TN307	Safety-lamps	623.51021	UF820	Ballistics—Tables
622.473	TN307	Electric lamps, Portable	623.51021	VF550	Ballistics—Tables
622.48	TN343	Electricity in mining	623.510284	UF830	Ballistic instruments
622.5	TN318	Mine water	623.55	UF800-805	Gunnery
622.6	TN342	Shuttle cars (Mine haulage)	623.558	UF848-856	Fire control (Gunnery)
622.66	TN336	Mine railroads	623.5580284	UF849	Fire control (Gunnery)— Optical equipment
622.66	TN338	Gasoline locomotives			
622.77	TN530	Magnetic separation of ores	623.62	UG330	Military roads
622.8	TN277	Quarries and quarrying— Safety measures	623.63	UG345	Armored trains
			623.63	UG345	Military railroads
622.8	TN295	Coal mines and mining— Safety measures	623.67	UG335	Military bridges
			623.67	UG335	Pontoon bridges
622.8	TN311-320	Coal mine accidents	623.68	UG340	Tunneling
622.8	TN311-320	Mine accidents	623.71	UG470-474	Maps, Military
622.80284	TN297	Gas masks	623.72	UG476	Photographic interpretation (Military science)
622.82	TN305-306	Firedamp			
622.82	TN305-306	Mine gases	623.72	TR785	Photography, Military
622.82	TN313-315	Combustion, Spontaneous	623.7312	UG582.H4	Heliograph
622.82	TN313	Mine explosions	623.7314	TA1750	Electrooptical devices
622.82	TN315	Mine fires	623.73 (2-3)	UG590-610.5	Military telecommunication
622.89	TN297	Mine rescue work	623.732	UG590-613.5	Military telegraph
623.042	UG487	Infrared radiation—Military applications	623.7341	UG611-.5	Radio, Military
			623.7348	UG612-.5	Radar—Military applications
623.043	UG485	Electronic counter-countermeasures	623.746	TL685.3	Airplanes, Military
			623.7464	TL685.3	Fighter planes
623.043	UG485	Electronic countermeasures	623.746	UG630-635	Airplanes, Military—Turrets
623.043	UG485	Electronics in military engineering	623.7465	TL685.7	Jet transports
			623.7465	TL685.7	Supersonic transport planes
623.1	UG400-442	Fortification	623.7469	UG1242.D7	Drone aircraft
623.1	UG403	Fortification, Field	623.7472	UG615-620	Automobiles, Military
623.1	UG403	Intrenchments	623.7472	UG615-620	Tracked landing vehicles
623.1	UG405.15	Bunkers (Fortification)	623.76	UG480	Electricity in military engineering
623.26	V856-.5	Mines and minelaying			
623.263	QB384	Saturn (Planet)—Orbit	623.8071	VM725-728	Marine engineering—Study and teaching
623.4409	U800-897	Armor			
623.441	U872	Lances	623.809	VM615-619	Marine engineering— History
623.441	TL732	Catapults (Aeronautics)			
623.441	GN498	Spears	623.809(4-9)	VM621-724	Marine engineering—[By region or country]
623.441	GN498.B78	Arrowheads			
623.441	GN498.B78	Bow and arrow	623.81	VM	Ships
623.441	GN498.S5	Shields	623.81	VM	Naval architecture
623.441	GN498.S55	Slings	623.81	VM157	Displacement (Ships)
623.441	GN799.W3	Weapons, Prehistoric	623.81	VM159	Stability of ships
623.441074	U804	Armor—Exhibitions	623.81	VM340-349	Motorboats
623.44109(4-9)	U818-823.5	Armor—[By region or country]	623.81	VM340-349	Launches
			623.810287	VM155	Ships—Measurement
623.4410901	U805	Armor, Ancient	623.81071	VM165-276	Naval architecture—Study and teaching
623.45115	UG490	Mines (Military explosives)			
623.452	UF860-880	Military fireworks	623.810951	VM101	Junks

Dewey	LC	Subject Heading	Dewey	LC	Subject Heading
623.81821	VM146-147	Ships, Iron and steel	623.8504	VM325	Boats and boating—Electronic equipment
623.81821	VM146	Marine steel			
623.81833	VM148	Ships, Concrete	623.8504	VM480-.5	Ships—Electronic equipment
623.8184	VM142-144	Ships, Wooden			
623.82	VM320-361	Boatbuilding	623.852	VM491-493	Ships—Lighting
623.8201	VM298	Ship models	623.852	VM493	Search-lights
623.8201043	VM298	Sailing ships—Models	623.852	VM815	Ships' lights
623.8202	VM352	Rafts	623.853	VM481-482	Ships—Heating and ventilation
623.8202	VM353	Dugout canoes			
623.82023	VM331-333	Yachts	623.8535	VM485	Marine refrigeration
623.8203	VM311.C33	Catboats	623.8535	VM485	Cold storage on shipboard
623.8204	VM362	Hydrofoil boats	623.854	VM505	Seawater—Distillation
623.8205	TC1662	Remote submersibles	623.854	VM505	Distilled water
623.820681	VM299.5-.7	Shipbuilding subsidies	623.8542	VM503-505	Ships—Water-supply
623.821	VM17	Ships, Medieval	623.8561	V280-285	Signals and signaling
623.821	VM311.C27	Caravels	623.8561	VK381-397	Signals and signaling
623.821	GN799.B62	Boats, Prehistoric	623.85641	VM325	Radio on boats
623.822	VM311.C3	Catamarans	623.85642	VK397	Telegraph, Wireless—Installation on ships
623.8223	VM351-361	Sailboats			
623.8226	VM331	Skipjacks	623.8567	VG70-85	Communications, Military
623.8226	VM371	Dhows	623.86	VM781-861	Ships—Equipment and supplies
623.8226	VM453	Oceanographic research ships			
			623.86	VM781	Deck machinery
623.8231	VM341	Cigarette boats	623.86	VM801	Davits
623.8232	VM464	Tugboats	623.86	VM831	Davits
623.8232	VM464	Towboats	623.862	VM531-533	Masts and rigging
623.8243	VM381-383	Passenger ships	623.862	VM532	Sails
623.82436	VM396	Inland waterway vessels	623.862	VM791	Anchors
623.82436	VM460	Lake steamers	623.862	VM841-845	Steering-gear
623.82436	VM461-.5	River boats	623.8620901	GN799.C49	Cordage, Prehistoric
623.82436	VM461-.5	River steamers	623.865	VK1477	Life-preservers
623.8245	VM391-395	Cargo ships	623.865	VK1479	Line-throwing rockets
623.8245	VM393.B7	Bulk carrier cargo ships	623.865	VK1481.L55	Line-throwing guns
623.8245	VM393.R64	Roll-on/roll-off ships	623.87	VM595-989	Marine engineering
623.8245	VM455	Tankers	623.87	VM731-779	Marine engines
623.8245	VM455.3	Chemical carriers (Tankers)	623.8722	VM741-750	Steam-boilers, Marine
623.8245	VM457	Ore carriers	623.87236	VM770	Marine diesel motors
623.8245	VM459	Refrigerator ships	623.8726	VM345-347	Electric boats
623.8257	VM365-367	Submarines (Ships)	623.8728	VM317	Nuclear ships
623.826	VM466.035	Offshore support vessels	623.8728	VM774-777	Nuclear ships
623.827	VM987	Diving bells	623.8728	VM774-777	Marine nuclear reactor plants
623.828	VM451	Ice-breaking vessels			
623.828	VM453	Deep-sea drilling ships	623.873	VM753-757	Propellers
623.829	VM466.B3	Barges	623.874	VM779	Ships—Fuel
623.829	TC765	Canal-boats	623.88	VK541-547	Seamanship
623.83	TC363	Floating harbors	623.88	VM531-533	Marlin spike seamanship
623.84	VM308	Figureheads of ships	623.880971	VK525-529	Nautical training-schools
623.84	VM341-349	Planing hulls	623.88203	VK543	Sailing
623.843	VM320-361	Steel boats	623.888	V810	Damage control (Warships)
623.8432	VM965	Underwater welding and cutting	623.888	VK200	Merchant marine—Safety measures
			623.8882	VM533	Knots and splices
623.8501	VM821	Marine compressors	623.8884	VK371-378	Collisions at sea—Prevention
623.8503	VM471-479	Ships—Electric equipment			
			623.8884	VK371	Rule of the road at sea

Dewey	LC	Subject Heading	Dewey	LC	Subject Heading
623.8886	VK1250-1294	Ships—Fires and fire prevention	623.8932	VK577	Radio compass
			623.8932	VK577	Gyro compass
623.8887	VK1300-1481	Life-saving	623.8932	VK577	Compass
623.8887	VK1460-1481	Life-saving apparatus	623.8938	VK388	Sonar
623.888709	VK1315	Life-saving—History	623.8938	VK560	Sonar
623.888709(4-9)	VK1321-1424	Life-saving—[By region or country]	623.8938	VK584.S6	Echo sounding
			623.8938	VK584.S6	Sounding and soundings
623.89	VK560	Hyperbolic navigation	623.8942	VK1000-1246	Lighthouses
623.89	VK560	Decca navigation	623.894209	VK1015	Lighthouses—History
623.89	VK583.5	Inertial navigation systems	623.894209 + 6347	VK1025.D	Drum Point Lighthouse (Md.)
623.89	SH343.8	Fisheries navigation			
623.890284	VK581	Logs (Nautical instruments)	623.894209(4-9)	VK1021-1124	Lighthouses—[By region or country]
623.890284	VK583	Sextant			
623.890284	VK583	Quadrant	623.89420971	VK1026-1027	Lighthouses—Canada
623.890289	VK200	Navigation—Safety measures	623.89420973	VK1023-1025	Lighthouses—United States
			623.894209751	VK1025.H	Harbor of Refuge Lighthouse
623.89071	VK401-529	Navigation—Study and teaching			
			623.8943	VK1000-1246	Lightships
623.89(2-3)	VK573-587	Nautical instruments	623.8944	VK1000-1249	Beacons
623.892(2-9) + (4-9)	VK1521-1624	Pilots and pilotage—[By region or country]	623.8944	VK1000-1246	Buoys
			623.8944	VK1150-1246	Buoys—[By region or country]
623.8922	VK798-997	Pilot guides			
623.8922	VK798	Notices to mariners	624	TA	Civil engineering
623.8922	VK1500-1661	Pilots and pilotage	624.1	TA630-901	Structural engineering
623.892209	VK1515	Pilots and pilotage—History	624.10285	TA641	Structural engineering—Computer programs
623.892216(3-7)	VK804-997	Pilot guides—[By place]			
623.89223	VK810-880	Pilot guides—Atlantic Ocean	624.10289	TA656.5	Safety factor in engineering
			624.105	TA630	Structural engineering—Periodicals
623.8922334	VK819-821.8	Pilot guides—Baltic Sea			
623.8922336	VK815-818	Pilot guides—North Sea	624.1072	TA638.2	Structural engineering—Research
623.8922336	VK839-844	Pilot guides—English Channel			
			624.15	TA775-787	Foundations
623.89223(4/6)	VK947-948	Pilot guides—United States	624.151	TA703-705.4	Engineering geology
623.892238	VK853-874	Pilot guides—Mediterranean Sea	624.15109(3-4)	TA705.2-.4	Engineering geology—[By region or country]
			624.15136	TA710-711.5	Soil mechanics
623.89224	VK915-956	Pilot guides—Pacific Ocean	624.152	TA715-772	Earthwork
623.892244	VK917	Pilot guides—North Pacific Ocean	624.152	TA730-748	Excavation
			624.152	TA740-747	Rock excavation
623.892248	VK925	Pilot guides—South Pacific Ocean	624.152	TH5101	Excavation
			624.152	TH5281	Shoring and underpinning
623.89225	VK885-901	Pilot guides—Indian Ocean	624.1520284	TA725	Earthmoving machinery
623.89229	HE617-720	Inland navigation	624.1520284	TA725	Scrapers (Earthmoving machinery)
623.89229	TC601-791	Inland navigation			
623.89229	TC769	Canals—Steam-navigation	624.1526	TA748	Blasting
623.89229(4-9)	HE623-720	Inland navigation—[By region or country]	624.154	TA780-787	Piling (Civil engineering)
			624.157	TC198	Coffer-dams
623.8922973	HE623-633	Inland navigation—United States	624.162	TA760-772	Embankments
			624.164	TA760-772	Retaining walls
623.89229(4-9)	HE635-720	Inland navigation—[Other countries]	624.171	TA645-656.5	Structural analysis (Engineering)
			624.172	TA648.2	Dead loads (Mechanics)
623.893	VK560	Electronics in navigation	624.172	TA654.4	Snow loads
623.893	VK562	Artificial satellites in navigation	624.176	TA654-656.5	Structural dynamics
623.8932	VK397	Radio—Installation on ships			
623.8932	VK397	Radio in navigation			
623.8932	VK560-561	Loran			

Dewey	LC	Subject Heading	Dewey	LC	Subject Heading
624.1762	TA654.6	Earthquake engineering	624.252	TG304	Snow loads
624.1762	TA658.44	Earthquake resistant design	624.257	TG260	Structural frames
624.1771	TA658-.8	Structural design	624.257	TG325	Retaining walls
624.1772	TA660.S6	Slabs	624.28	TG325	Bridges—Abutments
624.17723	TA492.G5	Girders	624.283	TG325.6	Bridges—Floors
624.17723	TA660.S67	Steel I-beams	624.284	TG320	Bridges—Foundations and piers
624.1773	TA660.F7-.F73	Structural frames	625.1	TF	Railroad engineering/Railroads
624.1773	TA660.T8	Trusses			
624.1779	TA492.S25	Sandwich construction	625.1	TF16	Horse railroads
624.182	TA684-695	Building, Iron and steel	625.1	TF200-320	Railroads—Design and construction
624.1821	TA684-695	Steel, Structural			
624.183	TA670-683.94	Masonry	625.10021	TF205	Railroad engineering—Tables
624.1833	TA680-683.94	Portland cement			
624.1834	TA680-683.94	Concrete construction	625.100212	TF195	Railroads—Specifications
624.1834	TA683.5.S4	Shells, Concrete	625.10025	TF12	Railroads—Directories
624.1834	TA683.5.W34	Concrete walls	625.100284	TF340-499	Railroads—Equipment and supplies
624.18341	TA683-683.94	Reinforced concrete construction			
			625.100288	TF530-548	Railroads—Maintenance and repair
624.183412	TA665	Prestressed construction			
624.183412	TA683.9-.94	Prestressed concrete construction	625.100288	TF542	Railroads—Snow-plows
			625.100289	TF610	Railroads—Safety measures
624.18923	TA668	Plastics in building	625.1005	TF1-4	Railroads—Periodicals
624.19	TA712	Underground construction	625.1006	TF5	Railroads—Congresses
624.19	TA800-820	Tunneling	625.10072	TF171-183	Railroads—Research
624.2	TG	Bridges	625.10074	TF6	Railroad museums
624.2	TG365-370	Trestles	625.1009	TF15-20	Railroads—History
624.20288	TG315	Bridges—Maintenance and repair	625.10092	TF139-140	Railroad engineers
			625.1009(4-9)	TF21-127	Railroads—[By region or country]
624.205	TG1-4	Bridges—Periodicals			
624.206	TG5	Bridges—Congresses	625.103	TF694	Monorail railroads
624.209	TG15-20	Bridges—History	625.11	TF210-217	Railroads—Surveying
624.209(4-9)	TG21-127	Bridges—[By region or country]	625.11299	TF193	Railroads—Design and construction—Costs
624.21	TG350-362	Girders	625.12	TF220-226	Railroads—Earthwork
624.21	TG355	Girders, Continuous	625.14	TF240-268	Railroads—Track
624.21	TG413-416	Bridges, Continuous	625.15	TF258-262	Railroads—Rails
624.217	TG375-380	Bridges, Truss	625.15	TF262	Railroads—Continuous rails
624.218	TG365	Bridges, Wooden	625.15	TF872	Electric railroads—Rails
624.218	TG375	Bridges, Wooden	625.15	TF890	Electric railroads—Third rail
624.219	TG385	Bridges, Cantilever	625.163	TF263	Railroads—Crossings
624.22	TG335-340	Bridges, Concrete	625.163	TF592	Railroads—Switching
624.225	TG327-340	Bridges, Arched	625.165	TF615-640	Railroads—Signaling
624.225	TG330	Bridges, Brick	625.18	TF300-308	Railroad terminals
624.225	TG330	Bridges, Stone	625.18	TF590-593	Railroads—Yards
624.23	TG400	Suspension bridges	625.19	TF197	Railroads—Models
624.24	TG420	Drawbridges	625.19	TF857	Electric railroads, Miniature
624.24	TG450	Pontoon bridges	625.2	TF371-499	Railroads—Cars
624.25	TG260-270	Structural analysis (Engineering)	625.2	TF920-952	Electric railroads—Cars
			625.21	TF413	Draft-gear
624.25	TG265-267	Moments of inertia	625.22	TF485	Cabooses (Railroads)
624.25	TG300-304	Bridges—Design and construction	625.22	TF542	Snow removal
			625.23	TF455-461	Railroads—Passenger-cars
624.252	TG265-267	Strains and stresses	625.23	TF457	Pullman cars
624.252	TG265	Flexure	625.23	TF459	Sleeping-cars (Railroads)
624.252	TG265	Buckling (Mechanics)			

Dewey	LC	Subject Heading	Dewey	LC	Subject Heading
625.23	TF656	Railroads—Baggage handling	625.84	TE278-.8	Pavements, Concrete
			625.84	TE278-.8	Roads, Concrete
625.24	TF470-481	Railroads—Freight-cars	625.85	TE210.5.B5	Bitumen
625.24	TF477	Refrigerator cars	625.85	TE221	Bituminous materials
625.24	TF662-667	Railroads—Freight	625.85	TE266-276	Pavements, Asphalt
625.25	TF420-430	Air-brakes	625.86	TE243	Roads, Macadamized
625.25	TF949.B7	Electric railroads—Brakes	625.88	TE280-295	Sidewalks
625.26	TJ603-695	Locomotives	625.88	TE301	Bicycle trails
625.263	TF975	Electric locomotives	625.88	TE303	Trails
625.263	TF980	Electro-diesel locomotive	625.88	TE304	Trails
625.266	TJ619-.7	Diesel locomotives	625.888	TE298	Curbs
625.39	TC771-772	Ship-railroads	625.889	TE279.3	Driveways
625.(4-6)	TF670-1124	Railroads, Local and light	627	TC401-558	Water resources development
625.4	TF1600	Magnetic levitation vehicles			
625.42	TF845-851	Subways	627.1	TC601-791	Canals, Interoceanic
625.44	TF840-841	Railroads, Elevated	627.109(4-9)	TC615-727	Inland navigation—[By region or country]
625.5	TF835	Railroads, Cable			
625.66	TF701-1124	Street-railroads	627.13	TC601-791	Canals
625.66	TF830	Horse railroads	627.133	TC759	Embankments
625.7	TE	Highway engineering	627.1353	TC763	Canals—Lifts
625.7	TE176.5	Traffic circles	627.1370962	TC791	Suez Canal (Egypt)
625.7	TE206-209.5	Roads—Location	627.2	TC353-365	Harbors
625.70212	TE180	Roads—Specifications	627.24	TC330-340	Shore protection
625.70284	TE223-227	Road machinery	627.24	TC333	Breakwaters
625.70284	TE223-227	Road-rollers	627.24	TC335	Sea-walls
625.705	TE1-4	Roads—Periodicals	627.24	TC337	Dikes (Engineering)
625.706	TE5	Roads—Congresses	627.24	TC337	Levees
625.7071	TE191	Roads—Study and teaching	627.24	TC337	Embankments
625.709	TE15-19	Roads—History	627.31	TC355-365	Docks
625.709(4-9)	TE21-127	Roads—[By region or country]	627.31	TC357	Piers
			627.31	TC357	Wharves
625.709143	TE229.8	Mountain roads	627.31	TC361	Dry docks
625.709152	TE229.5	Forest roads	627.38	TC328	Marinas
625.7091734	TE229-.9	Rural roads	627.4	TC167	Flood dams and reservoirs
625.723	TE209-.5	Roads—Surveying	627.42	TC533	Embankments
625.725	TE175	Roads—Design and construction	627.42	TC533	Levees
			627.5	TC801-937	Reclamation of land
625.732	TE208-.5	Soil surveys	627.5	TC970-978	Reclamation of land
625.733	TE210-212	Roads—Foundations	627.509(4-9)	TC815-927	Reclamation of land—[By region or country]
625.734	TE215	Road drainage			
625.7342	TE213	Culverts	627.52	TC930-933	Irrigation canals and flumes
625.74	TE230	Roads, Earth	627.52	TC933	Flumes
625.76	TE220-.63	Roads—Maintenance and repair	627.54	TC343-345	Reclamation of land
			627.54	TC970-978	Drainage
625.763	TD868-870	Snow removal	627.54	TC970	Ditches
625.77	TE177	Roadside improvement	627.54	TC975	Marshes
625.77	TE178.8	Roadside rest areas	627.7	TC195-201	Underwater construction
625.794	TE228	Electronic traffic controls	627.7	TC1800	Underwater pipelines
625.8	TE200-205	Road materials	627.73	TC187-188	Dredging
625.8	TE250-278.8	Pavements	627.73	TC187	Dredging spoil
625.82	TE233	Roads, Gravel	627.73	TC188	Dredges
625.82	TE255	Roads, Brick	627.75	TC193	Underwater drilling
625.83	TE245	Roads, Plank	627.8	TC540-558	Dams
625.83	TE253	Pavements, Wooden	627.8	TC540-558	Flood dams and reservoirs

Dewey	LC	Subject Heading	Dewey	LC	Subject Heading
627.8	TC540	Dams—Design and construction	628.167	TD478-480.7	Saline water conversion
627.8	TC542.5	Dams—Earthquake effects	628.16723	TD479.6	Nuclear saline water conversion plants
627.8	TC547	Arch dams	628.16725	TD479.7	Solar saline water conversion plants
627.80684	TC550	Dam safety			
627.82	TC547	Concrete dams	628.1674	TD480.5	Saline water conversion—Electrodialysis process
627.83	TC543	Earth dams			
627.86	TC167	Reservoirs			
627.882	TC553	Sluice gates	628.16744	TD480.4	Saline water conversion—Reverse osmosis process
627.883	TC555	Spillways			
627.922	TC375-381	Lighthouses			
628	TD	Sanitary engineering	628.168	TD419-428	Water—Pollution
628	TD159-168	Municipal engineering	628.168	TD426-.8	Groundwater—Pollution
628	TD169-171.8	Environmental protection	628.168	TD427.V55	Viral pollution of water
628.025	TD12	Sanitary engineers—Directories	628.1682	TD427.D4	Detergent pollution of rivers, lakes, etc.
628.05	TD1-4	Sanitary engineering—Periodicals	628.1682	TD427.07	Organic water pollutants
			628.16833	TD427.P4	Oil pollution of water
628.09	TD15-20	Sanitary engineering—History	628.16836	TD196.C45	Chemical spills
			628.16836	TD899.P4	Petroleum waste
628.092	TD139-140	Sanitary engineers—Biography	628.16837	TD800	Petroleum waste
			628.16846	TD930.2	Feedlot runoff
628.09(4-9)	TD21-127	Sanitary engineering—[By region or country]	628.1685	TD427.R3	Radioactive substances in rivers, lakes, etc.
628.1	TD201-500	Municipal water supply	628.1685	TD427.R3	Radioactive pollution of water
628.1	TD201-500	Water-supply			
628.109	TD215-220	Water-supply—History	628.2	TD678-688	Sewer design
628.109(4-9)	TC415-527	River engineering—[By region or country]	628.2	TD682	Sewers, Concrete
			628.21	TD657-.5	Urban runoff
628.109(4-9)	TD221-327	Water-supply—[By region or country]	628.212	TD665	Storm sewers
			628.3	TD511-780	Sewerage
628.11	TD418	Rain-water (Water-supply)	628.3	TD730-737	Sewage
628.112	TC401-558	River engineering	628.3	TD745-758.5	Sewage—Purification
628.112	TC401-558	Rivers	628.309	TD515-520	Sewerage—History
628.114	TD405-414	Wells	628.309(4-9)	TD521-627	Sewerage—[By region or country]
628.114	TD412	Boring			
628.114	TD412	Percussion drilling	628.351	TD746.5	Sewage lagoons
628.13	TD388-.5	Water conservation	628.36	TD741-780	Sewage disposal
628.13	TD388-.5	Water conservation projects	628.3623	TD760	Sewage irrigation
628.13	TD395	Dew-ponds	628.364	TD769.7	Sewage sludge—Conditioning
628.13	TD489	Water towers			
628.132	TD395-397	Reservoirs	628.37	TD770-.3	Sewage sludge—Incineration
628.132	TD396	Reservoir sedimentation			
628.144	TD481-493	Water—Distribution	628.42	TD812-.4	Radioactive waste disposal
628.144	TD485-487	Pumping stations	628.42	TD899.M5	Acid mine drainage
628.15	TD398	Aqueducts	628.44	TD785-812.5	Refuse and refuse disposal
628.15	TD491	Water-pipes	628.44	TD793.95	Source reduction (Waste management)
628.15	TD491	Electrolytic corrosion			
628.16	TD365-.5	Water quality management	628.44	TD813-870	Litter (Trash)
628.16	TD370-375	Water quality	628.44072	TD793.3	Refuse and refuse disposal—Research
628.162	TD429	Water reuse			
628.162	TD429.5-477	Water—Purification	628.440973	TD788-.4	Refuse collection—United States
628.162	TD434	Water treatment plants			
628.164	TD441-449	Filters and filtration	628.4409(4-9)	TD789	Refuse collection—[Other countries]
628.165	TD458	Water—Aeration	628.442	TD794	Refuse collection

Dewey	LC	Subject Heading	Dewey	LC	Subject Heading
628.44564	TD795-.7	Sanitary landfills	628.9252	TH9365	Hydrants
628.4457	TD796-.2	Incineration	628.9254	TH9338	Fire extinction—Chemical systems
628.4458	TD794.5	Recycling (Waste, etc.)	628.9254	TH9362	Fire extinguishers
628.46	TD813-870	Street cleaning	628.9259	TH9371-9377	Fire engines
628.460284	TD860	Street cleaning—Equipment and supplies	628.9259	TH9375	Chemical fire engines
628.4609(4-9)	TD815-849	Street cleaning—[By region or country]	628.9259	TH9391	Fireboats
			629.04	TA1001-1280	Transportation engineering
628.5	TD172-193.5	Pollution	629.040289	TA1250	Signal lights
628.5	TD878-880	Soil protection	629.0405	TA1001-1004	Transportation engineering—Periodicals
628.5028	TD192	Pollution control equipment			
628.5072	TD178.5-.7	Pollution—Research	629.04071	TA1163	Transportation engineering—Study and teaching
628.509	TD179	Pollution—History			
628.509(4-9)	TD179.5-191	Pollution—[By region or country]	629.0409	TA1015	Transportation engineering—History
628.5094	TD186-.5	Pollution—Europe	629.0409(4-9)	TA1021-1127	Transportation engineering—[By region or country]
628.5095	TD187-.5	Pollution—Asia			
628.5096	TD188-.5	Pollution—Africa			
628.50971	TD182-.4	Pollution—Canada	629.040973	TA1023-1025	Transportation engineering—United States
628.50972	TD182.6-.7	Pollution—Mexico			
628.50973	TD180-181	Pollution—United States	629.1	TL500-4050	Aerospace engineering
628.5098	TD185-.5	Pollution—South America	629.13	TL500-830	Aeronautics
628.50993	TD189.5.N4	Pollution—New Zealand	629.13	TL570-578	Flight
628.50994	TD189.5.A8	Pollution—Australia	629.13	TL721	Aeronautics—Flights
628.50998	TD190-.5	Pollution—Arctic regions	629.1300148	TL509	Aeronautics—Abbreviations
628.51	TD895	Factory sanitation	629.1300222	TL549	Aeronautics—Pictorial works
628.51	TD896-899	Factory and trade waste			
628.53	TD881-890	Air—Pollution	629.1300272	TL513	Aeronautics—Patents
628.53	TD883	Air quality	629.1300289	TL553.5	Aeronautics—Safety measures
628.532	TD884	Smoke prevention			
628.532	TD885	Flue gases	629.13006	TL500-504	Aeronautics—Societies, etc.
628.532	TD885.5.G73	Greenhouse gases			
628.532	TD887.H3	Halocarbons	629.13006	TL505	Aeronautics—Congresses
628.535	TD887.R3	Radioactive pollution of the atmosphere	629.130072	TL566-568	Aeronautical laboratories
			629.130072	TL567.R47	Research aircraft
628.55	TD879.P37	Soils—Pesticide content	629.130074	TL506	Aeronautical museums
628.55	TD879.P4	Oil pollution of soils	629.13009	TL515-532	Aeronautics—History
628.7	TD920-931	Sanitation, Rural	629.130092	TL539-540	Aeronautics—Biography
628.72	TD927	Water-supply, Rural	629.1323	TL570-574	Aerodynamics
628.742	TD778	Septic tanks	629.1323	TL574.N6	Aerodynamic noise
628.742	TD929-930.4	Sewerage, Rural	629.13230287	TL573	Aerodynamic measurements
628.742	TD929-930.4	Sewage disposal, Rural			
628.742	TD929	Drainage, House	629.132306	TL571.5	Aerodynamics, Hypersonic
628.744	TD929-930.4	Refuse and refuse disposal, Rural	629.13232	TL574.U5	Unsteady flow (Aerodynamics)
			629.13236	TL574.S7	Stability of airplanes
628.92	TH9448-9449	Fires	629.132362	TL574.F6	Flutter (Aerodynamics)
628.922	TH2274	Fire-escapes	629.132362	TL574.V5	Vibration (Aeronautics)
628.922072	TH9120	Fire prevention—Research	629.132364	TL574.M6	Rolling (Aerodynamics)
628.9225	TH9271-9275	Fire alarms	629.132364	TL574.M6	Yawing (Aerodynamics)
628.9225	TH9271	Fire detectors	629.13237	TL574.B6	Boundary layer
628.925	TH9111-9599	Fire extinction	629.1324	TL556-558	Meteorology in aeronautics
628.9252	TH9311-9334	Fire extinction—Water-supply	629.1324	TL557.F6	Fog—Control
			629.1325071	TL711.S8	Student flying
628.9252	TH9332-9334	Water towers	629.1325071	TL712-.8	Flight training
628.9252	TH9336	Fire sprinklers			

Dewey	LC	Subject Heading	Dewey	LC	Subject Heading
629.13251	TL586-589	Navigation (Aeronautics)	629.13445	TL681.C3	Aircraft cabins
629.13252	TL710-713.5	Airplanes—Piloting	629.13452	TL671.7	Airplanes—Inspection
629.13252	TL711.H65	Holding patterns (Aeronautics)	629.13453	TL671.7	Airplanes—Flight testing
			629.135	TL589-.5	Aeronautical instruments
629.13252	TL712	Air pilots	629.135	TL692-696	Aeronautics—Communication systems
629.1325212	TL711.T3	Airplanes—Take-off			
629.1325213	TL696.L33	Ground controlled approach	629.135	TL695-696	Avionics
629.1325213	TL711.L3	Airplanes—Landing	629.1351	TL695-696	Aids to air navigation
629.1325214	TL711.B6	Instrument flying	629.1351	TL696.L3	Landing aids (Aeronautics)
629.1325214	TL711.N5	Night flying	629.1352	TL589.2.A3	Accelerometers
629.1326	TL589.5	Automatic pilot (Airplanes)	629.1352	TL589.2.C58	Gyro compass
629.13322	TL609-639	Balloons	629.1352	TL589.2.D7	Drift indicator
629.13322	TL620	Balloon ascensions	629.1352	TL589.2.O6	Optical gyroscopes
629.13322	TL638	Hot air balloons	629.1352	TL696.C7	Radio compass
629.13324	TL650-668.1	Airships	629.1352	TL696.D5	Radio direction finders
629.13332	TL759-.7	Kites	629.1354	TL690-691	Electricity in aeronautics
629.13333	TL760-769	Gliders (Aeronautics)	629.1355	TL693.R2	Airplanes—Radio equipment
629.13334	TL670-724	Flying-machines			
629.13334	TL670-723	Airplanes	629.1355	TL693-696	Airplanes—Electronic equipment
629.13334	TL686.B36	Beechcraft (Airplanes)			
629.13334	TL686.D65	Douglas airplanes	629.1355	TL693-696	Radio in aeronautics
629.13334	TL686.D65	Douglas transport planes	629.136	TL557.V5	Airports—Visibility
629.133340422	TL686.G	Lear jet aircraft	629.136	TL725-733	Airports
629.133343	TL684.4	Biplanes	629.136	TL725.3.B8	Airport buildings
629.133347	TL684-.3	Seaplanes	629.136	TL726.15	International airports
629.13335	TL685	Vertically rising aircraft	629.1361	TL725.6	Seaplane bases
629.133352	TL716-.9	Helicopters	629.1363	TL725.3.R8	Runways (Aeronautics)
629.13431	TL671.6	Airframes	629.1366	TL725.3.C64	Airport control towers
629.13432	TL672-673	Airplanes—Wings	629.1366	TL725.3.T7	Air traffic control
629.13432	TL673.S9	Airplanes—Wings, Swept-back	629.1366092	HD8039.A425	Air traffic controllers
			629.2	TL	Motor vehicles
629.13433	TL673.F6	Flaps (Airplanes)	629.221	TL237-.2	Automobiles—Models
629.13433	TL677.E6	Elevators (Airplanes)	629.222	TL1-230.5	Automobiles
629.13435	TL701-704.7	Airplanes—Motors	629.222	TL236.7	Dune buggies
629.134351	TL704.7	Airplanes—Fuel	629.2220294	TL12	Automobiles—Catalogs
629.134353	TL709-.5	Airplanes—Jet propulsion	629.22203	TL9	Automobiles—Encyclopedias
629.134353	TL709.5.C55	Aircraft gas-turbines—Combustion chambers			
			629.22205	TL1-5	Automobiles—Periodicals
629.134353	TL709.5.I5	Airplanes—Turbojet engines—Air intakes	629.22206	TL6	Automobiles—Congresses
			629.222074	TL7	Automobiles—Museums
629.1343532	TL709.3.T8	Airplanes—Turbine-propeller engines	629.22209	TL15	Automobiles—History
			629.222092	TL139-140	Automobile engineers—Biography
629.1343533	TL709.3.T83	Airplanes—Turbojet engines			
629.134355	TL708	Airplanes—Nuclear power plants	629.2220941	TL57-64	Automobiles—Great Britain
			629.2220943	TL73-74.5	Automobiles—Germany
629.13436	TL705-708	Propellers, Aerial	629.2220944	TL71-72.5	Automobiles—France
629.134381	TL682-683	Airplanes—Landing gear	629.2220947	TL85-86	Automobiles—Russia
629.134386	TL750-758	Parachuting	629.2220952	TL105-106	Automobiles—Japan
629.134386	TL750-758	Parachutes	629.2220973	TL23-25	Automobiles—United States
629.134386	TL753	Parachutes—Rigging	629.22233	TL232	Trolley buses
629.1344	TL697.O8	Airplanes—Oxygen equipment	629.22233092	TL232.3	Bus drivers
			629.22234	TL235.8	Ambulances
629.1344	RA615.2	Aeronautics—Sanitation	629.2234	TL230	Vans
629.13442	TL681.A5	Airplanes—Air conditioning	629.224	TL230-.5	Trucks
629.13442	TL681.P7	Airplanes—Pressurization	629.224	TL230	Dump trucks

Dewey	LC	Subject Heading	Dewey	LC	Subject Heading
629.224092	TL230.3	Truck drivers	629.453	TL1070	Astronautical charts
629.2252	TL233-.8	Traction-engines	629.454	TL799.M6	Space flight to the moon
629.2252	TL233-.8	Farm tractors	629.455	TL789-790	Interplanetary voyages
629.2272	TL410-438	Bicycles	629.455	TL943	Planetary quarantine
629.2275	TL439-448	Motorcycles	629.4552	TL799.V45	Space flight to Venus
629.2275	TL443	Minibikes	629.4553	TL799.M3	Space flight to Mars
629.228	TL236	Automobiles, Racing	629.4555	TL799.J8	Space flight to Jupiter
629.2292	TL200	Automobiles, Steam	629.457	TL4030	Space vehicles—Tracking
629.2293	TK4058-4059	Electric driving	629.458	TL1090-1095	Space vehicles—Piloting
629.23	TL240-278	Automobiles—Design and construction	629.46	TL796-798	Artificial satellites
			629.46	TL798.G4	Geodetic satellites
629.231	TL245	Automobiles—Aerodynamics	629.47	TL795-.5	Space ships
			629.470284	TL784.E4	Electronics in rocketry
629.25	TL214.P6	Automobiles—Pollution control devices	629.472	TL950-954	Space vehicles—Materials
			629.474	TL1082	Astronautical instruments
629.25	TL214.P6	Motor vehicles—Pollution control devices	629.474	TL1100-1102	Space vehicles—Electric equipment
629.252	TL210-.7	Automobiles—Motors	629.474	TL3000-3285	Space vehicles—Electronic equipment
629.2548	TL272	Automobiles—Electric equipment	629.47445	TL1102.B3	Space vehicles—Batteries
629.2549	TL272.5-.55	Motor vehicles—Electronic equipment	629.475	TL780-785.8	Rockets (Aeronautics)
			629.47522	TL784.C63	Liquid propellant rocket—Control systems
629.26	TL255-256.5	Automobiles—Bodies	629.47524	TL785	Solid propellants
629.276	TL159.5	Air bag restraint systems	629.4753	TL783.5	Nuclear rockets
629.2772	TL271-.5	Automobiles—Heating and ventilation	629.4754	TL783.57	Photon rockets
			629.4755	TL783.54-.63	Electric rocket engines
629.282	TL285-295	Automobiles—Testing	629.4755	TL783.6	Plasma rockets
629.283	TL152.5-.55	Automobile driving	629.4755	TL783.63	Ion rockets
629.283	TL154	Automobile parking	629.477	TL1500-1575	Life support systems (Space environment)
629.283092	TL152.5-.55	Automobile drivers			
629.286	TL153	Service stations	629.477	TL1530	Space cabin atmospheres
629.287	TL152-.2	Automobiles—Maintenance and repair	629.4772	TL1550	Space suits
			629.4773	TL1565	Space vehicles—Water-supply
629.287	TL152.2	Automobiles—Conservation and restoration	629.4774	TL945	Space vehicles—Sterilization
629.295	TL475-480	Roving vehicles (Astronautics)	629.478	TL4000-4050	Ground support systems (Astronautics)
629.295	TL480	Lunar surface vehicles	629.8	TA165	Automatic control
629.4	TL787-4050	Astronautics	629.8	TJ212.2-225	Automatic machinery
629.4	TL1050-1060	Astrodynamics	629.8043	TK2851	Electric controllers
629.40212	TL869	Space vehicles—Specifications	629.82	TJ1560	Vending machines
			629.83	TJ216	Feedback control systems
629.4071	TL845-848	Astronautics—Study and teaching	629.89	TJ217.5	Intelligent control systems
			629.892	TJ210.2-211.49	Robots
629.40724	TL794.3	Astronautics—Experiments	629.892	TJ210.2-211.49	Robotics
629.41	TL790	Space flight	630	GN407.4-.8	Traditional farming
629.433	TL784.C63	Rockets (Aeronautics)—Guidance systems	630	S494.5.A47	Agropastoral systems
			630	S560-575	Farms
629.434	TL796.5.U6D	Discoverer (Artificial satellite)	630	SB	Crops
629.437	TL694.T35	Aerospace telemetry	630	SB45.65	Crop science literature
629.437	TL4030	Space vehicles—Tracking	630-638	S	Agriculture
629.442	TL795.7	Space colonies	630-638	S1-954	Agriculture
629.442	TL797	Space stations	630.11	S439-481	Agricultural systems
629.450284	TL1098	Space tools			
629.45071	TL1085	Space flight training			
629.453	TL1065-1080	Navigation (Astronautics)			

Dewey	LC	Subject Heading	Dewey	LC	Subject Heading
630.23	S494.5.A4	Agriculture—Vocational guidance	631.37	S715.C64	Cotton-picking machinery
			631.372	S711-713	Power transmission
630.2515	S600	Meteorology, Agricultural	631.372	S711-713	Farm tractors
630.289	S565	Agriculture—Safety measures	631.373	S711-713	Farm trucks
			631.4	S589.8-.85	Potting soils
630.5	S1-19	Agriculture—Periodicals	631.4	S589.8	Plant growing media
630.5	SB1-13	Crops—Periodicals	631.4	S590-599.9	Soils
630.6	S20	Agriculture—Societies, etc.	631.4	S590-599.9	Soil science
630.6	S533.F66	4-H clubs	631.4	S590-599.9	Land capability for agriculture
630.6	SB16	Crops—Congresses			
630.68	S560-572	Farm management	631.4	S590-592	Soil management
630.7	S530-539	Agricultural education	631.4	S593	Soils—Analysis
630.71	S531-539	Agriculture—Study and teaching	631.41	S583-587.5	Agricultural chemistry
			631.41	S592.5-.6	Soil chemistry
630.711	S537-539	Agricultural colleges	631.41	S592.6.A34	Soils—Agricultural chemical content
630.715	S544-545	Agricultural extension work			
630.715092	S533-534	County agricultural agents	631.417	S592.7-.85	Soil biochemistry
630.72	S539.5-542	Agriculture—Research	631.42	S592.367	Clay soils
630.72	SB51-56	Crops—Research	631.42	S592.57-.575	Acid soils
630.723	S441-451	Agricultural surveys	631.42	S592.575	Acid sulphate soils
630.723	S494.5.E8	Agricultural surveys	631.42	S592.575	Soil acidity
630.724	S541-543	Agricultural experimental stations	631.42	S595	Alkali lands
			631.43	S589-.6	Agricultural physics
630.74	S549	Agricultural museums	631.432	S594	Moisture index
630.74	S550-559	Agricultural exhibitions	631.432	S594	Soil moisture
630.9	S419-481	Agriculture—History	631.45	S622-627	Soil conservation
630.901	GN799.A4	Agriculture—Origin	631.45	S627.P55	Plants for soil conservation
630.901	GN799.A4	Agricultural implements, Prehistoric	631.45	S627.P76	Soil conservation projects
			631.451	S604.5-.64	Agricultural conservation
630.901	S421-431	Agriculture, Prehistoric	631.451	S661.5	Mulching
630.911	S604.33	Cold regions agriculture	631.455	S627.H5	Hillside planting
630.911	SB109.7	Cold regions agriculture	631.47	S592.14-.147	Soil surveys
630.9154	S612-619	Arid regions agriculture	631.49154	S592.17.A73	Arid soils
630.91732	S494.5.U72	Urban agriculture	631.49154	S592.17.D47	Desert soils
630.92	HD8039.P496	Plantation workers	631.49154	S599-.9	Desert soils
630.9(4-9)	S439-481	Agricultural geography	631.51	S604	Tillage
630.945632	S431	Agriculture—Rome	631.510284	TJ1482	Cultivators
631	S671-760	Agricultural engineering	631.52	SB106.I47	Crop improvement
631.27	NA8390-8392	Fences	631.52	SB106.O74	Crops—Evolution
631.27	S723	Gates	631.52	SB119-124	Plant propagation
631.27	S790-.3	Fences	631.52	SB123-.25	Selection (Plant breeding)
631.3	S671-760	Agricultural machinery	631.52	SB123-.5	Plant breeding
631.3	TJ1480-1496	Agricultural machinery	631.521	SB113.2-118.45	Seeds
631.3	S671-760	Farm equipment	631.521	SB113.2-118.45	Seed technology
631.3	S675.3	Agricultural mechanics	631.521	SB114	Seed adulteration and inspection
631.3	S676-.3	Agricultural implements			
631.3	S676.5	Agricultural instruments	631.523	SB108-109	Plant introduction
631.3	S683-685	Plows	631.5233	SB106.B56	Plant biotechnology
631.3	S683-685	Cultivators	631.5233	SB123.57	Crops—Genetic engineering
631.3	S687-689	Drill (Agricultural implement)	631.5233	SB123.57	Transgenic plants
			631.5233	SB123.57	Plant genetic engineering
631.3	S695-697	Sickles	631.53	S600.7.P53	Planting time
631.3	S695-697	Mowing machines	631.53	SB121	Planting (Plant culture)
631.3	S699-701	Threshing machines	631.53	SB123.65	Budding (Plant propagation)
631.37	S494.5.E5	Agriculture and energy			

Dewey	LC	Subject Heading	Dewey	LC	Subject Heading
631.53	SB185.8	Planting time	632.11	QK756	Plants—Frost resistance
631.531	SB121	Sowing	632.19	SB745	Crops—Effect of air pollution on
631.536	SB121	Seedlings—Transplanting	632.19	SB745	Crops—Effect of acid precipitation on
631.54	SB123.65	Grafting	632.19	SB745	Plants, Effect of air pollution on
631.54	SB125	Disbudding	632.19	SB745	Plants, Effect of acid precipitation on
631.55	S600.7.H37	Harvesting time			
631.55	SB129	Harvesting	632.2	SB767	Galls (Botany)
631.55	SB185.8	Harvesting time	632.3	SB599-989	Plant diseases
631.58	S494.5.P47	Permaculture	632.4	SB733	Fungal diseases of plants
631.58	S603.5	Intercropping	632.4	SB733	Fungi in agriculture
631.58	S603.7	Double cropping	632.43	SB741.M65	Mildew
631.58	S603.7	Multiple cropping	632.446	SB741.D68	Downy mildew diseases
631.5814	S604	No-tillage	632.5	SB610-615	Weeds
631.5818	S602.87	Shifting cultivation	632.5	SB610-615	Weeds—Control
631.582	S603	Crop rotation	632.52	SB610-615	Parasitic plants
631.583	SB415-416.3	Greenhouses	632.6	SB950-.5	Agricultural pests—Control
631.583	SB415-416.3	Solar greenhouses	632.(6-7)	SB599-1100	Pests
631.584	S605.5	Organic farming	632.(6-7)	SB599-999	Agricultural pests
631.585	SB126.5-.57	Hydroponics	632.(6-7)06	SB599.2	Agricultural pests—Congresses
631.586	SB110	Dry farming			
631.587	S599-.9	Soils, Irrigated	632.68	SB995	Bird pests
631.587	S612-619	Irrigation	632.69	SB993.5-994	Mammal pests
631.587	S612-619	Irrigation farming	632.7	SB818-945	Insect pests
631.6	S604.8-621.5	Reclamation of land	632.752	SB939	Scale insects
631.6	S612-619	Desert reclamation	632.9	SB950-989	Pests—Control
631.61	S607	Clearing of land	632.9	SB950-989	Plants, Protection of
631.62	S594	Drain-gages	632.9	SB951.145.B68	Botanical pesticides
631.62	S621	Drainage	632.93	SB979.5-985	Plant quarantine
631.64	S621.5.P59	Plants for land reclamation	632.94	SB952.8-955	Pesticides—Application
631.64	S621.5.S3	Sand dune planting	632.94	SB953	Spraying and dusting in agriculture
631.8	S631-667	Fertilizers			
631.8	S633	Garden fertilizers	632.94	SB955	Fumigation
631.8	S662-.5	Liquid fertilizers	632.95	SB950.9-970.4	Pesticides
631.826	S592.85	Peat soils	632.95	SB951.145.N37	Natural pesticides
631.84	S587.5.N5	Nitrogen in agriculture	632.95	SB952.B7	Bromides
631.84	S651-.3	Nitrogen fertilizers	632.95042	SB750	Plants—Disease and pest resistance
631.842	S651-.3	Nitrates			
631.847	S654.5	Biofertilizers	632.95042	SB957	Pesticide resistance
631.85	S647	Phosphatic fertilizers	632.9517	SB951.5-.54	Insecticides
631.85	S659	Bone-meal	632.952	SB951.3	Fungicides
631.86	S587.45	Natural products in agriculture	632.954	SB951.4	Herbicides
			632.96	SB975-989	Pests—Biological control
631.86	S654	Organic fertilizers	632.96	SB975	Biological pest control agents
631.86	S654	Organic wastes as fertilizer			
631.861	S655	Manures	632.96	SB995-996	Beneficial birds
631.861	S655	Farm manure	633	SB183-187	Seed crops
631.869	S657	Sewage	633.1	SB188-192	Winter grain
631.87	S661.2.M3	Marine algae as fertilizer	633.1	SB189-192	Grain
631.874	S661	Green manuring	633.11	SB191.W5	Durum wheat
631.875	S661	Compost	633.15	SB191.M2	Corn
631.913	SB111	Tropical crops	633. 16	SB191.B2	Barley
632	SB601	Plant parasites	633.2	SB193-207	Forage plants
632.09(4-9)	SB605	Garden pests—[By region or country]			

Dewey	LC	Subject Heading	Dewey	LC	Subject Heading
633.2	SB195	Silage	634.9	SD	Forests and forestry
633.2	SB197-202	Grasses	634.9	SD391-535	Trees
633.202	SB193-.55	Rangelands	634.9	SD411-428	Forest conservation
633.202	SB199	Meadows	634.90284	SD388	Forest machinery
633.202	SB199	Pastures	634.906	SD1	Forests and forestry—Societies, etc.
633.21	SB201.K4	Kentucky bluegrass	634.9071	SD250-381.5	Forestry schools and education
633.255	SF99.C59	Corn as feed			
633.28	SB413.R43	Red fescue	634.9072	SD356-.54	Forests and forestry—Research
633.3	SB203-205	Legumes			
633.3	SB205.F3	Fava bean	634.909(4-9)	SD11-115	Forests and forestry—[By region or country]
633.31	SB205.A4	Alfalfa			
633.5	SB241-261	Fiber plants	634.90973	SD11-12	Forests and forestry—United States
633.571	SB261.M3	Abaca (Fiber)			
633.58	SB281-283	Matwork plants	634.9097(4-9)	SD12	Forests and forestry—[United States, By state]
633.6	SB215-239	Sugar			
633.71	SB273-278	Tobacco	634.92	SD387.C58	Clearcutting
633.73	SB269	Coffee	634.92	SD387.S52	Short rotation forestry
633.74	SB267	Cacao	634.93	SD411-428	Forest protection
633.75	SB295.06	Opium	634.93	SD411	Forests and forestry—Safety measures
633.75	SB295.065	Opium poppy			
633.79	RS165.H3	Hashish	634.93	SD421.375	Fire lookout stations
633.81	SB301-303	Aromatic plants	634.95	SD392	Silvicultural systems
633.8(3-4)	SB305-307	Spice plants	634.953	SD396.5	Forest thinning
633.85	SB298-299	Oilseed plants	634.956	SD399.5	Forest genetics
633.86	SB285-287	Dye plants	634.956	SD409	Afforestation
633.88	SB293-295	Mushrooms, Hallucinogenic	634.956	SD409	Reforestation
633.88	SB293-295	Medicinal plants	634.9565	SD391	Tree planting
633.88	SB295.A45	Aloe	634.96	SB761	Forest insects
633.88384	SB295.G5	Ginseng	634.9617	SD425	Floods
633.88393	RS165.C3	Quinine	634.9618	SD420.5-421.5	Forest fires
633.8858	SB295.E63	Ephedra	634.9618	SD421	Forest fire detection
633.895	SB289-291	Gums and resins	634.9618	SD421	Forest fires—Prevention and control
633.8952	SB289-291	Rubber plants			
633.898	SB292	Pesticidal plants	634.9618	SD421.43	Aeronautics in wildfire control
634	SB354-399	Fruit			
634	SB354-402	Orchards	634.9721	SD397.D87	Durmast oak
634.11	SB363-.6	Apples	634.9721	SD397.E54	English oak
634.3	SB369	Citrus fruits	634.973766	SD397.E8	Eucalyptus
634.304	SB369-370	Citrus	634.974	SD397.C7	Conifers
634.32	SB370.G7	Grapefruit	634.9753	SD397.E27	Eastern hemlock
634.37	SB365	Fig	634.9754	SD397.D7	Douglas fir
634.5	SB401	Nuts	634.9754	SD397.F5	Fir
634.5	SB401.M32	Macadamia nut	634.9758	SD397.D37	Dawn redwood
634.57	SB401	Cashew nut	634.9758	SD397.R3	Redwood
634.61	SB401	Coconut	634.98	SD537-538.83	Logging
634.61	SB401	Copra	634.98	SD538-557	Lumbering
634.62	SB364	Date	634.9870973	SD543.3.U6	Non-timber forest products—United States
634.62	SB364	Date palm			
634.7	SB381-386	Berries	634.99	S494.5.A45	Agroforestry
634.713	SB386.B6	Blackberries	634.99	SB170-171	Tree crops
634.737	SB386.B7	Blueberries	634.99	SB172	Multipurpose trees
634.772	SB379.B2	Bananas	634.99	SD387.W6	Woodlots
634.775	SB317.C2	Cactus	635	SB118.48-.75	Nurseries (Horticulture)
634.8	SB387-399	Grapes	635	SB175-177	Food crops

Dewey	LC	Subject Heading	Dewey	LC	Subject Heading
635	SB317.5-319.77	Horticultural crops	635.9543	SB434.7	Gardening in the shade
635	SB320-353.5	Vegetable gardening	635.9543	SB434.7	Shade-tolerant plants
635	SB320-353.5	Vegetables	635.9642	SB433-.34	Turfgrasses
635	SB423.7-.75	Beds (Gardens)	635.9647	SB433-.34	Lawns
635	SB450.9-467.8	Gardening	635.965	SB419-.3	Indoor gardening
635	SB450.9-467	Gardens	635.965	SB419-.3	Indoor gardens
635	SB473	Backyard gardens	635.965	SB419-.3	House plants
635.0284	SB454.8	Garden tools	635.9671	SB419.5	Balcony gardening
635.043	SB454.3.P7	Planting time	635.9671	SB419.5	Roof gardening
635.0484	SB453.5	Organic gardening	635.9671	SB473.2	Patio gardening
635.1	SB209-211	Root crops	635.9672	SB459	Rock gardens
635.1	SB351.R65	Root crops	635.9674	SB423	Water gardens
635.25	SB341	Onions	635.9678	SB419-.3	Window gardening
635.3	SB351.C53	Bok choy	635.973	SBS428.5	Everlasting flowers
635.31	SB325	Asparagus	635.973	SB447	Everlasting flowers
635.61	SB339	Melons	635.975	SB431	Foliage plants
635.642	SB349	Tomatoes	635.976	SB437	Hedges
635.646	SB351.E5	Eggplant	635.977	SB435-437	Ornamental trees
635.677	SB191.P64	Popcorn	635.977	SB435-437	Tree planting
635.7	SB351.H5	Herb gardens	635.977	SB436	Trees in cities
635.7	SB351.H5	Herbs	635.97713	SB435-437	Flowering woody plants
635.8	SB353-.5	Fungi, Edible	635.97715	SB435	Ornamental evergreens
635.9	SB403-450.87	Flower gardening	635.9772	SB433.5	Bonsai
635.9	SB403-450.87	Floriculture	635.9772	SB433.5	Gardens, Miniature
635.9	SB403-450.87	Plants, Ornamental	635.9772	SB435-.8	Dwarf trees
635.9	SB403-450	Flowers	635.9775	SB435	Evergreens
635.9	SB431.7	Ornamental grasses	635.97752	SB413.E27	Eastern hemlock
635.9074	SB441-.75	Flower shows	635.9823	SB414.6-416.3	Greenhouse plants
635.92	SB603.5	Garden pests	635.9823	SB415	Greenhouse gardening
635.9312	SB422	Annuals (Plants)	635.9824	QH68	Terrariums
635.932	SB434	Perennials	635.986	SB415	Plants, Potted
635.93334	SB413.D4	Delphinium	635.986	SB418-.4	Container gardening
635.93353	SB413.B65	Bougainvillea	635.986	SB418-.4	Hanging baskets
635.93353	SB413.C3	Carnations	636	GN407.6-.7	Domestic animals
635.93356	SB438-.34	Cactus	636	SF	Animal culture
635.933627	SB413.B4	Begonias	636	SF1-140	Livestock
635.933685	SB413.H6	Hibiscus	636.0811	SF411.5	Pet shows
635.933734	SB410.9-411.7	Roses	636.082	S494	Breeding
635.933734	SB411	Rose gardens	636.082	S494	Inbreeding
635.93375	SB432.7	Carnivorous plants	636.082	SF41	Domestication
635.93379	SB413.G35	Dwarf pelargoniums	636.082	SF105-109	Animal breeding
635.93399	SB299.S9	Sunflowers	636.082	SF105	Inbreeding
635.93399	SB413.D2	Daisies	636.082	SF105.27-.275	Rare breeds
635.93399	SB413.D13	Dahlias	636.0821	SF140.B54	Animal biotechnology
635.93434	SB413.D12	Daffodils	636.0821	SF756.5	Domestic animals—Genetic engineering
635.93438	SB413.I8	Dwarf irises	636.0821	SF756.5	Veterinary genetics
635.9344	SB409	Dendrobium	636.08245	SF105.5	Artificial insemination
635.9345	SB413.P17	Palms	636.0832	HV4701-4959	Animal welfare
635.9373	SB429	Ferns, Ornamental	636.0832	HV4746	Dog rescue
635.951	SB439-.26	Native plant gardening	636.0832	QL83.2	Wildlife rescue
635.9525	SB427.5	Desert gardening	636.0839	SK341.C65	Coyote trapping
635.9525	SB427.5	Desert plants	636.084	SF94.5-99	Animal feeding
635.9525	SB439.8	Drought-tolerant plants	636.0845	SF84.82-85.6	Rangelands
635.9528	SB459	Alpine gardens			

Dewey	LC	Subject Heading	Dewey	LC	Subject Heading
636.0845	SF84.82-98	Range management	636.0896	SF600-1100	Domestic animals—Diseases
636.0845	SF140.P38	Pastoral systems			
636.085	SF94.5-99	Animal nutrition	636.0896	SF600-1100	Animals—Diseases
636.0852	SF98.F	Fiber in animal nutrition	636.0896	SF600-1100	Livestock—Diseases
636.0855	SF94.5-99	Feeds	636.0896014	SF780.3	Veterinary bacteriology
636.0855	SF97.7	Feeds—Flavor and odor	636.08960194	SF780.4	Veterinary virology
636.0855	SF98.F	Feeds—Fiber content	636.0896025	SF778	Veterinary emergencies
636.0855	SF98.P46	Pesticide residues in feeds	636.08960252	SF914.3	First aid for animals
636.0855	SF99.A5	Alfalfa as feed	636.0896028	SF778	Veterinary critical care
636.0855	SF99.D5	Distillers feeds	636.0896075	SF771-774	Veterinary medicine—Diagnosis
636.0855	SF99.F37	Feathers as feed			
636.0855	SF99.F5	Fish meal as feed	636.08960759	SF769	Veterinary autopsy
636.0855	SF99.M33	Marine algae as feed	636.089612	SF811	Veterinary cardiology
636.0855	SF99.W34	Organic wastes as feed	636.089639	SF851-855	Nutrition disorders in animals
636.0855	SF99.Y4	Yeast as feed			
636.08556	SF99.A37	Agricultural wastes as feed	636.08967	SF910.5	Veterinary orthopedics
636.08557	SF98.A2	Feed additives	636.089682	SF799	Meningitis
636.08557	SF98.A5	Antibiotics in animal nutrition	636.08969	SF781-809	Communicable diseases in animals
636.08557	SF98.M4	Medicated feeds	636.0896956	SF787	Anthrax
636.0882	SF180	Draft animals	636.0896959	SF740	Zoonoses
636.0885	SF405.5-407	Laboratory animals	636.089696	SF810	Domestic animals—Parasites
636.0886	SF170-180	Working animals			
636.0887	SF411-459	Pets	636.0896964	SF810.H8	Echinococcosis
636.0887	SF414.2	Pets—Housing	636.0896992	SF910.T8	Veterinary oncology
636.0887	SF414.3	Pet boarding facilities	636.0897	SF911-914.4	Veterinary surgery
636.089	SF600-1100	Veterinary medicine	636.089715	SF914.4	Fractures in animals
636.089	SF604.4-.7	Veterinary hospitals	636.089796	SF914	Veterinary anesthesia
636.089014	SF610	Veterinary medicine—Terminology	636.08982	SF887	Veterinary obstetrics
			636.1	SF277-359.7	Horses
636.089025	SF611	Veterinarians—Directories	636.1	SF290-291	Horse farms
636.08906	SF600-604	Veterinary medicine—Societies, etc.	636.1	SF360.6-361.75	Domestic asses
			636.101	SF277-359.7	Foals
636.08906	SF605	Veterinary medicine—Congresses	636.10811	SF294.5-297.7	Horse shows
			636.10811	SF295.185-.187	Show horses
636.0890711	SF756.3-.37	Veterinary colleges	636.10811	SF295.7	Event horses
636.089073	SF774.5	Veterinary nursing	636.10837	SF309.9	Bits (Bridles)
636.08909	SF615-724	Veterinary medicine—History	636.10837	SF309.9	Bridles
			636.1089755	SF959.C6	Colic in horses
636.089092	SF612-613	Veterinarians	636.109	SF293.M56	Miniature horses
636.0891	SF761-767	Veterinary anatomy	636.12	SF343	Harness racehorses
636.0892	SF768-.2	Veterinary physiology	636.13	SF293.A5	American saddlebred horse
636.0893	SF600-1100	Animal health	636.13	SF293.P5	Pinto horse
636.0894	SF740	Veterinary public health	636.13	SF293.S72	Standardbred horse
636.08944	SF780.9	Veterinary epidemiology	636.13	SF309.65-.653	Dressage horses
636.089448	SF757.15	Veterinary disinfection	636.13037	SF309.9	English saddles
636.089456	SF740	Animals as carriers of disease	636.13037	SF309.9	Western saddle
			636.14	SF312	Coach horses
636.08951	SF915-918	Pharmacy	636.15	SF311-.3	Draft horses
636.08951	SF916.5	Veterinary prescriptions	636.16	SF315	Ponies
636.0895329	SF918.A5	Antibiotics in veterinary medicine	636.16	SF315.2.C4	Chincoteague pony
			636.182	SF361	Donkeys
636.0895372	SF918.V32	Veterinary vaccines	636.182092	SF361	Donkey breeders
636.0895892	SF914.5	Veterinary acupuncture	636.183	SF362	Mules
			636.2	SF191-219	Cattle

Dewey	LC	Subject Heading	Dewey	LC	Subject Heading
636.2	SF191-219	Cows	636.68	SF461	Cage birds
636.20812	SF101-103.5	Livestock brands	636.68625	SF463-.7	Canaries
636.20812	SF101-103.5	Cattle brands	636.6865	SF473.C63	Cockatoos
636.20886	SF961-967	Cattle—Diseases	636.7	SF421-440.2	Dogs
636.208969	SF961-967	Cattle—Infections	636.707	SF421-435	Puppies
636.208969	SF962	Blackleg in cattle	636.708	SF422.7-.82	Dog owners
636.208969	SF967.E3	East Coast fever	636.70811	SF425-.8	Dog shows
636.213	SF207	Beef cattle	636.70811	SF425.3	Show dogs
636.213092	F596	Cowboys	636.70811	SF425.7	Dogs—Obedience trials
636.213092	F596	Cowgirls	636.7082	SF422.7-.86	Dog breeders
636.2142	SF208	Dairy cattle	636.70822	SF423	Dogs—Pedigrees
636.2142	SF221-250	Dairy farming	636.7083	SF427.46	Dog walking
636.2142	SF221-250	Dairy farms	636.70831	SF428	Kennels
636.2142	SF221-250	Dairying	636.70833	SF427.55	Pet grooming salons
636.21420284	SF247	Dairying—Equipment and supplies	636.70835	SF431	Dogs—Training
			636.70837	SF427.15	Dog collars
636.21420681	SF261	Dairying—Accounting	636.70886	HV8025	Police dogs
636.2142071	SF241-245	Dairying—Study and teaching	636.70886	SF428.55	Rescue dogs
			636.70886	SF428.6	Livestock protection dogs
636.21420711	SF241-245	Dairy schools	636.70886	SF428.7	Sled dogs
636.2(2-8)	SF198-199	Cattle breeds	636.70886	SF428.73	Search dogs
636.224	SF199.G8	Guernsey cattle	636.70886	SF428.8	Watchdogs
636.225	SF199.D4	Dexter cattle	636.70896	SF991.D5	Distemper
636.226	SF199.D38	Devon cattle	636.70896	SF991-992	Dogs—Diseases
636.226	SF211	Dual-purpose cattle	636.72	SF429.D3	Dalmatian dog
636.23	SF199.E2	East Prussian cattle	636.73	SF428.2	Working dogs
636.28	SF199.A3	Africander cattle	636.73	SF429.B47	Bernese mountain dog
636.292	SF401.A45	American bison	636.73	SF429.B86	Bullmastiff
636.29401	SF401.D3	Deer farming	636.73	SF429.E8	Eskimo dogs
636.295	SF401.C2	Camels	636.73	SF429.G75	Great Pyrenees
636.3	SF371-379	Sheep	636.736	SF429.D6	Doberman pinschers
636.3	SF376.5	Lambs	636.752	SF428.5	Bird dogs
636.30833	SF379	Sheep-shearing	636.7524	SF429.B78	Brittany spaniel
636.308969	SF969.E	Epizootic catarrh in sheep	636.7524	SF429.E47	English cocker spaniel
636.39	SF380-388	Goats	636.7524	SF429.E7	English springer spaniels
636.4	SF391-397.4	Swine	636.7526	SF429.S5	Setters (Dogs)
636.408969	SF977.P5	Swine plague	636.753	SF429.H6	Hounds
636.483	SF393.D9	Duroc Jersey swine	636.7532	SF429.S39	Scottish deerhound
636.5	SF481-513	Chickens	636.7533	SF429.A4	Afghan hounds
636.5082	SF492-493	Poultry—Breeding	636.7538	SF429.D25	Dachshunds
636.5082	SF495	Eggs—Incubation	636.755	SF429.C3	Cairn terriers
636.5082	SF495-497	Poultry—Hatcheries	636.755	SF429.D33	Dandie Dinmont terrier
636.50831	QL676.5-.57	Birdhouses	636.8	SF441-450	Cats
636.508(4-5)	SF494	Poultry—Feeding and feeds	636.8	SF449	Cat breeds
636.50896	SF995-.4	Poultry—Diseases	636.8	SF449.C34	Calico cats
636.5142	SF490-.8	Eggs—Production	636.80822	SF443	Cats—Pedigrees
636.5142	SF490-.8	Eggs	636.80835	SF446.6	Cats—Training
636.5871	SF489.B2	Bantams	636.808696	SF986.C37	Cat flea
636.592	SF507	Turkeys	636.80896	SF985-986	Cats—Diseases
636.597	SF504.7-505.63	Ducks	636.826	SF449.A28	Abyssinian cat
636.6	SF461	Aviculture	636.832	SF449.P4	Persian cat
636.6	SF462.5	Captive wild birds	636.9	SF408-.6	Captive wild animals
636.63	SF502.8-503.52	Game fowl	636.9322	SF451-455	Rabbits
636.63082	SF508-510	Game bird culture	636.9322	SF455.D8	Dutch rabbits

Dewey	LC	Subject Heading	Dewey	LC	Subject Heading
636.9322	SF455.D85	Dwarf rabbits	639.209163	SH213-.77	Fisheries—Atlantic Ocean
636.93560887	SF459.H3	Dwarf hamsters as pets	639.209164	SH214-215	Fisheries—Pacific Ocean
636.93592	SF401.G85	Guinea pigs	639.209165	SH216-.55	Fisheries—Indian Ocean
636.965701	SF401.E4	Elk farming	639.2092	HD8039.F65	Fishers
636.97	SF403-405	Fur-bearing animals	639.2092	SH20	Fish culturists
636.9701	SF402-405	Fur farming	639.2094	SH253-293	Fisheries—Europe
636.97662701	SF405.M6	Mink farming	639.20941	SH255-260	Fisheries—Great Britain
637	SF250.5-275	Dairy products	639.209415	SH261-262	Fisheries—Ireland
637.12	SF255	Dairy inspection	639.20945	SH277-278	Fisheries—Italy
637.124	SF250	Milking	639.20946	SH285-286	Fisheries—Spain
637.1240284	SF247	Milking machines	639.209469	SH281-282	Fisheries—Portugal
637.14	SF250.5-275	Dairy processing	639.20947	SH283-284	Fisheries—Russia
637.141	SF251-262.5	Milk	639.209481	SH279-280	Fisheries—Norway
637.141	SF259	Milk—Pasteurization	639.209485	SH287-288	Fisheries—Sweden
637.141	SF259	Milk—Sterilization	639.209489	SH267-268	Fisheries—Denmark
637.141	SF259	Homogenized milk	639.209492	SH275-276	Fisheries—Netherlands
637.142	SF259	Condensed milk	639.209495	SH273-274	Fisheries—Greece
637.143	SF259	Dairy products—Drying	639.2095	SH295-307	Fisheries—Asia
637.143	SF259	Dried milk	639.20951	SH297-298	Fisheries—China
637.148	SF247	Cream-separators	639.209519	SH302.5-.7	Fisheries—Korea
637.148	SF266	Creameries	639.20952	SH301-302	Fisheries—Japan
637.2	SF263-269.5	Butter	639.209561	SH291-292	Fisheries—Turkey
637.3	SF270-274	Cheese	639.20971	SH223-229	Fisheries—Canada
637.354	SF272.C5	Cheddar cheese	639.20972	SH231	Fisheries—Mexico
637.354	SF272.P3	Parmesan cheese	639.209728	SH232	Fisheries—Central America
638	SF517-562	Beneficial insects	639.209729	SH233	Fisheries—West Indies
638	SF518	Insect rearing	639.20973	SH221-222	Fisheries—United States
638.1	SF521-539	Bee culture	639.2098	SH234-251	Fisheries—South America
638.12	SF521-539	Honeybee	639.20993	SH318.5	Fisheries—New Zealand
638.16	SF539	Honey	639.20994	SH317-318	Fisheries—Australia
638.16	SF539	Bee products	639.2099(5-6)	SH319	Fisheries—Oceania
638.16	SF539	Bee pollen	639.209982	SH268.G83	Fisheries—Greenland
638.17	TP678	Beeswax	639.22	SH400-.8	Seafood gathering
638.2	SF541-560	Sericulture	639.2743	SH351.E4	Eel fisheries
638.2	SF541-560	Silk	639.2745	SH351.S3	Sardine fisheries
638.2	SF541-560	Silkworms	639.28	SH381-385	Whaling
638.2	SF559.5-560	Silkworms, Non-mulberry	639.29	SH360-363	Sealing
638.5789	QL544.6	Butterfly gardens	639.3	SH151-179	Fish-culture
639.0901	GN799.H84	Hunting, Prehistoric	639.305	SH1	Fisheries—Periodicals
639.1	SK283.2	Animal traps	639.32	SH399.C6	Coral fisheries
639.2	SH	Fisheries	639.3789	SH185	Frog culture
639.2028	SH334.5-344.8	Fishery technology	639.392	SH399.T9	Turtle fisheries
639.20284	SH344-.8	Fisheries—Equipment and supplies	639.3956	SF459.C45	Chameleons as pets
			639.3984	SF515.5.A44	Alligator farming
639.20284	SH344.6.T67	Fish traps	639.4	SH365-380.92	Shellfish culture
639.20284	SH344.8.H6	Fishhooks	639.4	SH400.4-.8	Shellfish gathering
639.20284	SH344.8.N4	Fishing nets	639.409(4-9)	SH365-367	Shellfish culture—[By region or country]
639.20289	SH343.9	Fisheries—Safety measures			
639.206	SH3	Fisheries—Congresses	639.41	SH371	Oyster fisheries
639.2068	SH328-329	Fishery management	639.41	SH379.5	Oyster shell
639.2071	SH332-.2	Fishery schools	639.412	SH375-377	Pearl fisheries
639.2072	SH332-.2	Fishery research stations	639.412	SH377.5	Mother-of-pearl
639.2072	SH343.5	Exploratory fishing	639.42	SH371-374.52	Mussel fisheries
639.209	SH211	Fisheries—History	639.42	SH372.5-.52	Mussels

Dewey	LC	Subject Heading	Dewey	LC	Subject Heading
639.44	SH400.5.C53	Clamming	640.284	TX298-299	Home economics—Equipment and supplies
639.4832	SH371.5-.52	Abalone fisheries	640.3	TX11	Home economics—Encyclopedias
639.4832	SH371.5-.52	Abalone culture			
639.56	SH380.4-.45	Crab culture	640.46	TX331-334	Domestics
639.56	SH380.4-.45	Crab fisheries	640.46	HD6072-.2	Domestics
639.56	SH400.5.C7	Crabbing	640.46	HD8039.D5	Domestics
639.75	SF597.E3	Earthworm culture	640.5	TX1	Home economics—Periodicals
639.8	SH20.5-191	Aquaculture			
639.8	SH138	Mariculture	640.6	TX5	Home economics—Congresses
639.809	SH21	Aquaculture—History			
639.809(4-9)	SH34-133	Aquaculture—[By region or country]	640.71	TX165-286	Home economics—Study and teaching
639.89	SH393	Seagrasses	640.73	TX335	Consumer education
639.9	SK351-579	Wildlife management areas	640.9	TX15-19	Home economics—History
639.906	SK352	Wildlife management—Congresses	640.92	HQ756.6	Househusbands
			640.9(4-9)	TX21-127	Home economics—[By region or country]
639.9092	SK354	Wildlife managers	641	TX341-357	Groceries
639.909(4-9)	SK361-579	Wildlife management areas—[By region or country]	641.013	TX631-641	Gastronomy
			641.2	TX951	Beverages
639.9094	SK503-543	Wildlife management areas—Europe	641.3	TX341-641	Food
639.90941	SK505-511	Wildlife management areas—Great Britain	641.3	TX553.A3	Food additives
			641.302	TX369	Natural foods
639.9095	SK553-567	Wildlife management areas—Asia	641.303	SB175	Food crops
639.9096	SK571-575	Wildlife management areas—Africa	641.31	TX356	Marketing (Home economics)
639.90971	SK470-471	Wildlife management areas—Canada	641.331	TX393	Flour
			641.331	TX393	Cereals as food
639.90972	SK473	Wildlife management areas—Mexico	641.331	TX395	Cereals, Prepared
			641.3318	TX558.R5	Rice
639.909728	SK475	Wildlife management areas—Central America	641.33682	SB211.C3	Cassava
			641.3373	TX415	Coffee
639.909729	SK477	Wildlife management areas—West Indies	641.3382	TX819	Condiments
			641.3383	TX406-407	Spices
639.9097(3-9)	SK361-465	Wildlife management areas—United States	641.3384	TX407.C	Chili powder
			641.35	TX391	Vegetable juices
639.9098	SK479-501	Wildlife management areas—South America	641.35655	TX401.2.S69	Tofu
			641.357	TX415	Herbal teas
639.90994	SK577	Wildlife management areas—Australia	641.36	TX371-389	Meat
			641.36	TX555-556	Meat
639.92	SH153	Fishways	641.36	TX743-759.5	Food of animal origin
639.92	SH157.8-.85	Fish habitat improvement	641.362	TX556.B4	Beef
639.92	SH157.85.A7	Artificial reefs	641.36292	TX556.B8	Buffalo meat
639.95	SK357	Game reserves	641.37143	TX556.M5	Dried skim milk
639.96	SH171-179	Fish kills	641.38	TX560.H7	Honey
639.96	SH175	Fishes—Parasites	641.392	TX385-388	Seafood
639.964	SH171-179	Fishes—Pathogens	641.392	TX385	Fish as food
639.964	SH171-179	Fishes—Diseases	641.4	TX599-613	Food—Preservation
639.964	SH171-179	Fishes—Infections	641.4	TX599-612	Canning and preserving
639.964	SH177.R4	Red tide	641.4	TX599-612	Food preservatives
639.977	SH327.7	Fishery conservation	641.44	TX609	Drying apparatus—Food
639.978	QL676.5-.57	Bird attracting	641.44	TX609	Dried foods
640	TX	Home economics	641.44	TX609	Food—Drying
			641.453	TX610	Frozen foods

Dewey	LC	Subject Heading	Dewey	LC	Subject Heading
641.494	TX612.F5	Fishery products—Preservation	641.692	TX747	Cookery (Seafood)
641.5	TX151-162	Recipes	641.71	TX690	Roasting (Cookery)
641.5	TX642-840	Cookery	641.73	TX691	Steaming (Cookery)
641.5028	TX657.S3-.S8	Stoves	641.73	TX693	Stews
641.5071	TX661-669	Cookery—Study and teaching	641.731	TX685	Boiling (Cookery)
			641.76	TX687	Broiling
641.509	TX645	Cookery—History	641.77	TX686	Braising (Cookery)
641.5092	TX649	Cooks	641.774	TX689.5	Stir frying
641.52	TX733	Breakfasts	641.812	TX740	Appetizers
641.53	TX735	Luncheons	641.812	GN432	Tapa
641.54	TX737	Dinners and dining	641.814	TX819	Sauces
641.563	TX551-560	Diet	641.814	TX819.S27	Salad dressing
641.563	TX551-560	Dietaries	641.815	HD8039.B2	Bakers and bakeries
641.563	RM219	Cookery for the sick	641.815	TX769-770	Bread
641.5631	RM221.D4	Deglutition disorders	641.815	TX769	Crackers
641.5636	TX837-838	Vegetarian cookery	641.815	TX770.B55	Biscuits
641.5636	TX837-838	Vegetarianism	641.815	TX770.B55	Scones
641.5676435	TX739.2.H35	Hanukkah cookery	641.815	TX770.P34	Pancakes, waffles, etc.
641.5676437	TX739.2.P37	Passover cookery	641.815	TX770.P56	Pita bread
641.568	TX739-.2	Holiday cookery	641.8157	TX770.M83	Muffins
641.568	TX739.2.E37	Easter cookery	641.819	TX740.5	Garnishes (Cookery)
641.568	TX739.2.T45	Thanksgiving cookery	641.82	TX740	Entrees (Cookery)
641.5686	TX739.2.C45	Christmas cookery	641.821	TX693	Casserole cookery
641.57	TX820	Quantity cookery	641.822	TX394.5	Pasta products
641.57	UC720-735	Cookery, Military	641.822	TX809.M17	Cookery (Pasta)
641.57	VC370-375	Cookery, Marine	641.822	TX809.N65	Noodles
641.578	TX823	Outdoor cookery	641.83	TX740	Salads
641.5784	TX840.B3	Barbecue cookery	641.83	TX807	Salads
641.58	TX840.C65	Convection oven cookery	641.84	TX818	Sandwiches
641.585	TX825	Chafing dish cookery	641.853	TX783-793	Candy
641.586	TX827	Stoves, Electric	641.853	TX783-799	Confectionery
641.587	TX840.P7	Pressure cookery	641.86	TX773	Desserts
641.5882	TX657.O64	Microwave ovens	641.86(2-3)	TX795	Ice cream, ices, etc.
641.5882	TX832	Microwave cookery	641.8644	TX773	Puddings
641.589	TX657.E35	Eggbeaters	641.8653	TX771-.2	Cake
641.589	TX724.5.C	Wok cookery	641.8653	TX773	Cheesecake (Cookery)
641.589	TX825.5	Clay pot cookery	641.86539	TX771.2	Cake decorating
641.589	TX840.W65	Wok Cookery	641.8654	TX772	Cookies
641.5892	TX840.F6	Food processor cookery	641.8659	TX771	Coffee cakes
641.592	GN407-411.5	Food	641.8659	TX773	Pastry
641.5943	TX721	Cookery, German	641.87	TX815-817	Beverages
641.5944	TX719-.2	Cookery, French	641.874	TX951	Bartending
641.5952	TX724.5.J3	Cookery, Japanese	641.874	TX951	Cocktails
641.5972	TX716.M4	Cookery, Mexican	641.874	TX951	Martinis
641.612	TX552	Canned foods	641.877	TX817.C5	Cocoa
641.612	TX821	Cookery (Canned foods)	642	TX727-739.2	Menus
641.65	TX801-807	Cookery (Vegetables)	642	TX871-885	Table
641.6565	TX558.L4	Legumes as food	642.(6-8)	TX851-885	Entertaining
641.657	TX406-407	Herbs	642.4	TX731-739	Entertaining
641.66	TX749-.5	Cookery (Meat)	642.4	TX901-921	Caterers and catering
641.665	TX750-.5	Cookery (Poultry)	642.6	TX885	Carving (Meat, etc.)
641.675	TX813.C7	Cookery (Eggs)	642.7	TX871-885	Table setting and decoration
641.692	TX747	Cookery (Fish)	643.16	TH9701-9745	Burglary protection

Dewey	LC	Subject Heading	Dewey	LC	Subject Heading
643.16	TH9739	Burglar alarms	648.1	TT583	Pressing of garments
643.2	TH4819.P7	Prefabricated houses	648.1	TT980-999	Laundries
643.2	GV811.65	Sailboat living	648.5	TX324	House cleaning
643.2	GV777.7	Boat living	649.1	HQ768-777.95	Child rearing
643.29	TX1100-1105	Mobile home living	649.1	HQ778.5-.7	Child care
643.3	TX653-655	Kitchens	649.10248	HQ769.5	Babysitting
643.4	TX855-859	Dining rooms	649.122	RJ101-103	Infants—Care
643.5	TH3000	Attics	649.132	HQ775	Boys
643.5	TH3000.B36	Basements	649.155	HQ773.5	Gifted children
643.6	TK7018-7301	Household appliances, Electric	649.64	HQ770.4	Discipline of children
645	TX311-317	Interior decoration	650.01513	HF5691-5716	Business mathematics
645.4	GN415.C8	Cradles	650.071	HF1101-1186	Business education
645.4083	TS886.5.C74	Cribs (Children's furniture)	650.0710 (4-9)	HF1131-1186	Business education—[By region or country]
645.8	SB473.5	Garden ornaments and furniture	650.07104	HF1140-1165	Business education—Europe
646.05	TT490	Clothing trade—Periodicals	650.07105	HF1171	Business education—Asia
646.2	TT700-715	Sewing	650.07106	HF1176	Business education—Africa
646.2	TT720-730	Clothing and dress—Repairing	650.071073	HF1131-1134	Business education—United States
646.2040284	GN799.P5	Pins and needles, Prehistoric	650.07108	HF1135	Business education—Latin America
646.2044	TT713	Machine sewing	650.071094	HF1181-1182	Business education—Australia
646.2044	TJ1501-1519	Sewing machines			
646.21	TT390	Drapery	650.1	HF5381-5382.5	Career development
646.3	TX340	Clothing and dress	650.1	HF5384.5	Career plateaus
646.402	TT570-630	Men's furnishing goods	650.1	HF5386	Success in business
646.406	TT635-645	Children's clothing	650.14	HF5382.7-.75	Job hunting
646.4060832	TT637	Layettes	650.14	HF5383	Resumes (Employment)
646.40608341	TT603	Boy's clothing	650.14	HF5384	Career changes
646.408	TT550	Clothing and dress—Alteration	650.14	HF5549.5.R45	Employment references
			650.142	HF5383	Applications for positions
646.7042	TT950-979	Beauty culture	651	HF5735-5746	Filing systems
646.724	TT950-979	Barbering	651.2	HF5548-.115	Office equipment and supplies
646.724	TT967	Electric shavers			
646.724	TT970	Shaving	651.29	HF5371	Business—Forms
646.724	TT973	Hair—Dyeing and bleaching	651.3	HF5546-5548	Office Management
646.724	TT975	Hairweaving	651.3741	R728	Medical secretaries
646.7240284	TT967	Razors	651.3743	HE9751-9756	Messengers
646.7240284	TT969	Hair preparations	651.53	HF5735-5746	Card system in business
646.7240284	TT969	Shampoos	651.53	HF5738	Electronic filing systems
646.7247	TT975	Braids (Hairdressing)	651.7	HF5717-5734.7	Business communication
646.7248	TT975	Wigs	651.74	HF5548	Dictating machines
646.727	RL94	Manicuring	651.74	HF5548	Dictograph
646.76	BJ1609-1610	Charm	651.74	HF5718.3-5734	Business writing
647	TX147	Institution management	651.74	HF5719	Business report writing
647	TX955	Building management	651.75	HF5721-5734	Commercial correspondence
647.92	TX957-959	Apartment houses			
647.95	TX901-910	Coffeehouses	651.8	HF5548.125-.6	Office practice—Automation
647.95	TX945-.5	Restaurants	651.8	HF5548.33	Electronic data interchange
647.950683	TX911.3.P4	Restaurants—Personnel management	652.1	Z40-104.5	Writing
			652.1	Z43-45	Penmanship
648	TH6014-7696	Sanitation, Household	652.3	Z49-50.5	Typewriters
648	TH6025	Electronics in sanitary engineering	652.8	Z102.5-104.5	Cryptography
			653	Z53-104.5	Shorthand

Dewey	LC	Subject Heading
657	HF5601-5689.8	Accounting
657	HF5680-5681	Account books
657	HF5681.G55	Going concern (Accounting)
657.0284	HF5679	Accounting machines
657.071	HF5630	Accounting—Study and teaching (Internship)
657.2	HF5601-5689.8	Bookkeeping
657.3	HF5667.65	Financial statements, Unaudited
657.3	HF5681.B2	Funds-flow statements
657.3	HF5681.B2	Financial statements
657.42	HF5686.C8	Cost accounting
657.42	HF5686.C8	Direct costing
657.42	HF5686.C8	Activity-based costing
657.45	HF5667-5668.25	Auditing
657.458	HF5668-.25	Auditing, Internal
657.46	HF5681.D39	Deferred tax
657.61	HJ9701-9995	Finance, Public—Accounting
657.72	HF5681.A2	Accounts current
657.72	HF5681.A3	Accounts receivable
657.73	HF5681.D5	Depreciation
657.73	HF5681.V3	Valuation
657.74	HF5681.A27	Accounts payable
657.742	HF5681.N65	Employee fringe benefits—Accounting
657.8333	HG1706-1708	Banks and banking—Accounting
657.95	HF5686.C7	Corporations—Accounting
658	T55.4-60.8	Management science
658	HD28-70	Management
658.019	HD58.7	Organizational behavior
658.1	HD2747	Liquidation
658.1511	HF5657.4	Managerial accounting
658.152	HD39-40.7	Capital
658.15224	HG177-.5	Fund raising
658.15224	HG4028.S7	Going public (Securities)
658.15244	HG4028.C45	Cash management
658.155	HD61	Risk management
658.1552	HD47.3	Cost control
658.1554	HD47.25	Break-even analysis
658.1554	HD47.4	Cost effectiveness
658.164	HD2746.6	Corporate divestiture
658.3	HF5549-.5	Personnel management
658.3	HF5549.5.C35	Career development
658.3	HF5549.5.D39	Employer-supported day care
658.3008	HF5549.5.M5	Diversity in the workplace
658.301	HF5549.5.M3	Manpower planning
658.302	HF5549.12	Supervision of employees
658.306	HF5549.5.J6	Job analysis
658.306	HF5549.5.J613	Job descriptions
658.3111	HF5549.5.R44	Employees—Recruiting
658.3112	HF5549.5.D7	Employees—Drug testing
658.3112	HF5549.5.E5	Employment tests
658.3112	HF5549.5.S38	Employee selection
658.31124	HF5549.5.I6	Employment interviewing
658.312	HF5549.5.S4	Seniority, Employee
658.31242	HF5549.5.I53	Employee orientation
658.3125	HF5549.5.R3	Employees-Rating of
658.3128	HD2331-2336.35	Telecommuting
658.3134	HF5549.5.D55	Downsizing of organizations
658.314	HF5549.5.M6	Employee morale
658.314	HF5549.5.M63	Employee motivation
658.3142	HF5549.5.I5	Incentives in industry
658.31424	HF5549.5.P7	Promotions
658.3151	HF5549.5.C8	Employees—Counseling of
658.3155	HF5549.5.G7	Grievance procedures
658.32021	HF5705-5707	Wages—Tables
658.3822	HF5549.5.A4	Alcoholism and employment
658.3822	HF5549.5.D7	Drugs and employment
658.4	HD57.7	Leadership
658.4	HD2741-2749	Corporate governance
658.4012	HD30.28	Strategic planning
658.4013	HD62.15	Total quality management
658.4013	HD66-.2	Quality circles
658.402	HD50-.5	Delegation of authority
658.402	HD50	Decentralization in management
658.402	HD66-.2	Work groups
658.403	HD30.23	Decision-making
658.4032	T57.85	Network analysis (Planning)
658.4034	T57.9	Queuing theory
658.4052	HD58.6	Negotiation in business
658.4056	HD49-.6	Crisis management
658.406	HD58.8	Organizational change
658.406	HD58.85	Downsizing of organizations
658.408	HD60-.5	Social responsibility of business
658.409	HD38.2-.25	Executive ability
658.422	HD2745	Directors of corporations
658.456	HF5734.5	Business meetings
658.46	HD69.C6	Business consultants
658.47	HD38.7	Business intelligence
658.473	HF5549.5.E43	Employee theft
658.477068	HD49	Emergency management
658.5	HD38.5	Business logistics
658.5	HF5415.15-.157	Product management
658.5	T56	Production control
658.5036	T57.95	Decision-making
658.515	T58.8	Industrial efficiency
658.542	T60.7	Motion study
658.5421	T60.4-.47	Time study
658.544	T57.72	Fatigue
658.562	T59-.2	Standardization
658.562	TS156-.6	Quality control
658.562	HD62	Standardization
658.567	TP995-996	Waste products
658.568	HD3656-3790.9	Factory inspection

Dewey	LC	Subject Heading	Dewey	LC	Subject Heading
658.56809(4-9)	HD3661-3790.9	Factory inspection—[By region or country]	660.072	TP165-183	Chemical engineering laboratories
658.7	TS161	Materials management	660.072	TP187-197	Research, Industrial—Laboratories
658.72	HD39.5	Industrial procurement	660.09	TP15-20	Chemistry, Technical—History
658.788	HF5761-5780	Delivery of goods			
658.788	HF5761-5780	Shipment of goods	660.28	TP155.5-.6	Chemical plants
658.7884	HF5770	Cartons	660.2804	TP149	Chemicals—Safety measures
658.8106	HF5438.8.M4	Sales meetings			
658.812	HF5415.5-.55	Customer relations	660.281	TP155.7-.75	Chemical processes
658.812	HF5415.5	Consumer satisfaction	660.283	TP157-159	Chemical engineering—Equipment and supply
658.816	HF5416.5-5417	Pricing			
658.816	HF5417	Price maintenance	660.28424	TP248.25.M45	Membrane reactors
658.816	HF5417	Price fixing	660.28424	TP248.25.M46	Membrane separation
658.82	HF5438.8.P74	Sales presentations	660.284245	TP156.F5	Filters and filtration
658.82	HG3752	Cash discounts	660.284248	TP156.E8	Extraction (Chemistry)
658.83	HF5415.2-.34	Marketing research	660.28425	TP156.D5	Distillation
658.83	HF5415.3	Market surveys	660.284292	TP156.F65	Fluidization
659.1	HD59.3	Advocacy advertising	660.294514	TP156.E6	Emulsions
659.1	HF5801-6182	Advertising	660.2961	TP265-267	Fire
659.1025	HF5804-5808	Advertising—Directories	660.297	TP250-261	Electrochemistry, Industrial
659.103	HF5803	Advertising—Encyclopedias	660.2995	TP159.C3	Catalysts
659.105	HF5801-5802	Advertising—Periodicals	660.6	TP248.13-.65	Biotechnology
659.1071	HF5814-5815	Advertising—Study and teaching	660.6	TP248.27.M53	Microbial biotechnology
659.109	HF5811-5813	Advertising—History	660.62	QR53-.5	Industrial microbiology
659.111	HF5826.5	Advertising media planning	660.63	TP248.3	Biochemical engineering
659.1122	HF5804-5808	Advertising departments	660.65	TP248.6	Genetic engineering
659.1125	HF6178-6182	Advertising agencies	660.65	QH442-.6	Genetic engineering
659.132	HF5825	Advertising layout and typography	660.65	QH442.2	Cloning
			660.65	QH442.2	Molecular cloning
659.132	HF5843-.5	Posters	661	TP200-248	Chemicals
659.132	HF5851	Advertising cards	661.03	TP222-223	Alkalies
659.132	HF5871-6141	Advertising, Newspaper	661.0385	TP245.C25	Cesium
659.13209(4-9)	HF5901-6097	Advertising, Newspaper—[By region or country]	661.0431	TP245.U7	Uranium
			661.0681	TP245.C4	Carbon
659.133	HF5861-5863	Commercial catalogs	661.0721	TP245.O9	Oxygen
659.133	HF5861-5863	Advertising, Direct-mail	661.0731	TP245.F6	Fluorine
659.1342	HF5843	Billboards	661.2	TP213-217	Acids
659.143	HF6146.T42	Television advertising	661.2	TP213-217	Inorganic acids
659.152	HF5845-5849	Display of merchandise	661.63	TP240	Sulphites
659.157	HF5828	Advertising, Point-of-sale	661.65	TP237-238	Nitrates
659.157	HF5845-5849	Show-windows	661.8	TP247-248	Organic compounds
659.17	HF6146.P75	Prize contests in advertising	661.803	TP953	Coal-tar
659.19	HF6146.D75	Advertising drinking glasses	661.806	TP958-959	Essence and essential oils
659.193877	HF6161.A38	Advertising—Airlines	661.807	TP247.5	Solvents
659.19658311	HF6125.5	Help-wanted advertising	661.86	TP247.2	Organic acids
659.2	HD59-.6	Public relations	662.1	TP300-301	Firecrackers
660	TP	Chemistry, Technical	662.1	TP300-301	Fireworks
660	TP155-156	Chemical engineering	662.2	TP267.5-301	Explosives
660.03	TP9	Chemistry, Technical—Encyclopedias	662.20289	TP297	Explosives—Safety measures
660.05	TP1	Chemistry, Technical—Periodicals	662.26	TP272	Gunpowder
			662.26	TP276	Guncotton
660.06	TP5	Chemistry, Technical—Congresses	662.27	TP285	Dynamite
			662.3383	TN858-859	Oil-shales

Dewey	LC	Subject Heading	Dewey	LC	Subject Heading
662.5	TP310	Matches	664.94(1-8)	SH335-337	Fishery products—
662.6	TP315-360	Fuel			Preservation
662.65	TP323	Briquets (Fuel)	665.1	TP669-695	Waxes
662.65	TP324	Fuelwood	665.1	TP993	Candles
662.66	TP692.2	Gasoline, Synthetic	665.2	TP676	Fish oils
662.6692	TP358	Alcohol as fuel	665.3	TP680-684	Vegetable oils
662.6692	TP358	Gasohol	665.332	TP977-979.5	Turpentine
662.74	TP331	Charcoal	665.353	TP684.C275	Castor oil
663	TP500-660	Beverages	665.355	TP684.C7	Coconut oil
663	TP866	Bottling	665.4	TP685-699	Mineral oils
663.1	TP593	Alcohol	665.5	TP355	Petroleum as fuel
663.2	TP544-559	Wine and wine making	665.5	TP690-692.5	Petroleum
663.223	TP559.P8	Madeira wine	665.5	TP690-692.5	Petroleum products
663.223	TP559.P8	Port wine	665.53	TP690-692.5	Petroleum—Refining
663.224	TP555	Champagne (Wine)	665.533	TP690.4	Cracking process
663.3	TP568-587	Brewing	665.533	TP690.4	Catalytic cracking
663.3	TP569-587	Breweries	665.53827	TP692.2	Gasoline
663.42	TP568-587	Beer	665.5383	TP692.4.K4	Kerosene
663.5	TP589-618	Liquors	665.5384	TP343	Diesel fuels
663.52	TP605	Whiskey	665.542	TP692.5	Oil storage tanks
663.53	TP599	Brandy	665.542	TP692.5	Petroleum—Storage
663.55	TP611	Liqueurs	665.544	TN879.5-.6	Petroleum pipelines
663.59	TP607.R9	Rum	665.7	TP350	Natural gas
663.62	TP628-636	Carbonated beverages	665.7	TP700-764	Gas manufacture and works
663.93	TP645	Coffee	665.7	TP700	Gas
664.001579	QR115-129	Food—Bacteriology	665.7	TP751-764	Gas
664.02	TX761-799	Bakers and bakeries	665.744	TN880.5	Natural gas pipelines
664.02	TX761-778	Baking	665.744	TP757	Gas distribution
664.024	TP248.65.F66	Food—Biotechnology	665.744	TP757	Gas-pipes
664.024	TP371.44	Fermented foods	665.75	TP345-350	Gas as fuel
664.02852	TP372.2	Cold storage	665.772	TP759	Coal gasification
664.02853	TP372.3	Frozen foods	665.773	TP759	Oil gasification
664.0288	TP371.8	Radiation preservation of	665.776	TP359.B48	Biogas
		food	665.822	TP245.H4	Helium
664.1	TP375-414.5	Sugar—Manufacture and	666.1	TP845-869	Glass manufacture
		refining	666.1092	HD8039.G5	Glass-workers
664.1	TP375-414.5	Syrups	666.122	TP859	Glass blowing and working
664.123	TP390-391	Beet sugar	666.156	QC375	Glass, Optical
664.2	TP415-416	Starch	666.19	TP865-868	Glassware
664.3	TP669-699	Oils and fats	666.192	TP866	Bottles
664.32	TP684.M3	Margarine	666.3	TP785-842	Pottery
664.34	TP676	Lard oil	666.3	TP811	Clay
664.34	TS1980-1981	Lard	666.427	TP812	Glazes
664.7207	TS2120-2159	Flour-mills	666.427	TP823	Glazes
664.7207	TS2120-2159	Meal	666.43	TP841-842	Kilns
664.7207	TS2120-2159	Flour	666.733	TP839	Drain-tiles
664.724	TP435.C67	Corn products	666.737	TP826-833	Brickmaking
664.756	TP434-435	Cereals, Prepared	666.737	TP826-833	Bricks
664.76	TS2158	Feed mills	666.86	TP870	Artificial minerals
664.805	TP443-444	Vegetables—Drying	666.88	TP873-.5	Precious stones, Artificial
664.9	TS1950-1982	Animal products	666.88	TP873.5.D5	Diamonds, Artificial
664.9029	TS1960-1967	Slaughtering and	666.894	TP885	Concrete products
		slaughter-houses	666.894	TP885.C7	Concrete blocks
664.94	SH334.9-336.5	Fishery processing	667.0283	TT310	Paint mixing

Dewey	LC	Subject Heading	Dewey	LC	Subject Heading
667.1	TP990-992.5	Cleaning compounds	669.05	TN600-605	Metallurgy—Periodicals
667.12	TP932-.6	Dry cleaning	669.071	TN675.3	Metallurgy—Study and teaching
667.14	TP894-895	Bleaching	669.09	TN615-620	Metallurgy—History
667.2	TP890-929	Dyes and dyeing—Chemistry	669.141	TN756-757	Iron alloys
667.2	TP897-929	Dyes and dyeing	669.1413	TN710	Cast-iron
667.29	TP934-937.5	Pigments	669.1413	TN713-718	Blast furnaces
667.4	TP946-950	Ink	669.142	TN755	Steel-works
667.4	Z247	Printing ink	669.1422	TN740-742	Open-hearth furnaces
667.6	TP934-937.5	Paint	669.1423	TN736-738	Bessemer process
667.6	TT300-380	Painting, Industrial	669.22	TN760-769	Gold—Metallurgy
667.6	TT360	Sign painting	669.3	TN780	Copper—Metallurgy
667.72	TP940	Polishes	669.72	TS551-552	Light metals
667.9	TA418.76	Protective coatings	669.722	TN775	Aluminum—Metallurgy
667.9	TP156.C57	Coating processes	669.725	TN895-897	Alkalies
668.12	TP990-992.5	Soap	669.8	TN672	Precipitation hardening
668.2	TP973	Glycerin	669.9	TN690	Physical metallurgy
668.3	TP967-970	Glue	669.92	TN550-580	Assaying
668.3	TP967-970	Adhesives	669.92	HG325-329	Assaying
668.37	TP977-979.5	Gums and resins	669.92	TN565	Metallurgical analysis
668.374	TP977-979.5	Gums and resins, Synthetic	669.95	TN689-693	Metallography
668.374	TP1180.E6	Epoxy resins	669.95	TN690	Alloys
668.4	TP1101-1185	Plastics	670	T55.4-60.8	Industrial engineering
668.4027	TP1114	Plastics—Patents	670	TS	Manufactures
668.403	TP1110	Plastics—Encyclopedias	670.21	T57.35	Industrial engineering—Statistical methods
668.405	TP1103	Plastics—Periodicals			
668.406	TP1101	Plastics—Societies, etc.	670.288	TS192	Plant maintenance
668.406	TP1105	Plastics—Congresses	670.42	T58.7-.8	Industrial capacity
668.4071	TP1127-1129	Plastics—Study and teaching	670.420151	TJ1165	Shop mathematics
			670.427	T59.5	Automation
668.409	TP1116-1118	Plastics—History	670.9	T55.6	Industrial engineering—History
668.41	TP1135	Plastics machinery			
668.412	TP1150	Plastics—Molding	670.92	T56.3	Industrial engineers
668.413	TP1175.E9	Plastics—Extrusion	670.941	TS57-64	Great Britain—Manufactures
668.415	TP1160	Plastics—Welding			
668.4225	TP1180.P6	Polyesters	670.943	TS73-74.5	Germany—Manufactures
668.4227	TS1927.S55	Silicone rubber	670.9436	TS65-.2	Austria—Manufactures
668.423	TP1180.A33	Acetal resins	670.9437	TS65.3-.4	Czechoslovakia—Manufactures
668.423	TP1180.P57	Polycarbonates			
668.4233	TP1180.S7	Styrene	670.9439	TS65.5-66	Hungary—Manufactures
668.44	TP1180.C5	Celluloid	670.944	TS71-72.5	France—Manufactures
668.44	TP1180.C6	Cellulose	670.945	TS79-80	Italy—Manufactures
668.492	TP1183.L3	Laminated plastics	670.946	TS87-88	Spain—Manufactures
668.493	TP1183.F6	Plastic foams	670.9469	TS83-84.5	Portugal—Manufactures
668.55	TP983-986	Cosmetics	670.947	TS85-86	Russia—Manufactures
668.92	TP156.P6	Polymerization	670.948	TS88.5	Scandinavia—Manufactures
669	TN600-799	Metallurgy	670.9481	TS81-82	Norway—Manufactures
669.028	TN687	Electric furnaces	670.9485	TS89-90	Sweden—Manufactures
669.0282	TN677-.5	Smelting furnaces	670.9489	TS69-70	Denmark—Manufactures
669.0282	TN677-.5	Blast furnaces	670.94897	TS95.F5	Finland—Manufactures
669.0282	TN677-.5	Metallurgical furnaces	670.9492	TS77-78	Netherlands—Manufactures
669.0283	TN688	Hydrometallurgy	670.9493	TS67-68	Belgium—Manufactures
669.0284	TN681-687	Electrometallurgy	670.9494	TS91-92	Switzerland—Manufactures
669.0284	TN686.5.E4	Electroslag process	670.9495	TS75-76	Greece—Manufactures

Dewey	LC	Subject Heading	Dewey	LC	Subject Heading
670.9496	TS95.A2	Balkan Peninsula—Manufactures	671.529	TS228.9	Pressure welding
			671.7	TS653-719	Metals—Finishing
670.9497	TS95.Y8	Yugoslavia—Manufactures	671.732	TS213	Plating
670.951	TS101-102	China—Manufactures	671.732	TS662-693	Plating
670.952	TS105-106	Japan—Manufactures	671.732	TS670-693	Electroplating
670.954	TS103-104	India—Manufactures	671.823	TS250	Sheet-metal
670.95491	TS104.5-.6	Pakistan—Manufactures	672	TS300-360	Steel-works
670.95493	TS104.7-.8	Sri Lanka—Manufactures	673.3	TS564-589	Brass
670.955	TS107-108	Iran—Manufactures	673.3	TS570	Bronze
670.9561	TS111-112	Turkey—Manufactures	674	TS800-915	Lumber
670.9567	TS113.I7	Iraq—Manufactures	674.0284	TS850-851	Saws
670.95694	TS113.I75	Israel—Manufactures	674.2	TS850	Sawmills
670.957	TS109-110	Asiatic Russia—Manufactures	674.386	TS932-934	Wood—Chemistry
			674.82	TS890	Coopers and cooperage
670.9598	TS113.I55	Indonesia—Manufactures	674.82	TS900	Crates
670.9599	TS113.P6	Philippines—Manufactures	674.83	TS870	Veneers and veneering
670.96	TS115-119	Africa—Manufactures	674.834	TS870	Plywood
670.962	TS117-118	Egypt—Manufactures	674.835	TS869	Laminated wood
670.971	TS26-27	Canada—Manufactures	675	TS940-1047	Leather
670.972	TS28-29	Mexico—Manufactures	675.2	TS967	Hides and skins
670.9728	TS30-31	Central America—Manufactures	675.23	TS940-1047	Tanning
			675.3	TS1060-1070	Fur
670.9729	TS32-33	West Indies—Manufactures	676	TS1080-1268	Papermaking
670.973	TS23-25	United States—Manufactures	676	TS1080-1268	Paper
			676	TS1080-1268	Paper products
670.981	TS41-42	Brazil—Manufactures	676	Z247	Paper
670.982	TS36-37	Argentina—Manufactures	676.02821	TS1485-1487	Carding
670.983	TS43-44	Chile—Manufactures	676.09	TS1090-1096	Papermaking—History
670.984	TS38-39	Bolivia—Manufactures	676.12	TS1171-1177	Wood-pulp
670.985	TS52	Peru—Manufactures	676.234	TS1118.F5	Paper finishing
670.9861	TS45-46	Colombia—Manufactures	676.235	TS1118.F5	Paper coatings
670.9866	TS47	Ecuador—Manufactures	676.2823	TS1228-1268	Stationery
670.987	TS54	Venezuela—Manufactures	676.2848	TH8461-8463	Wallpaper
670.9881	TS48	Guyana—Manufactures	677	TP890-933	Textile chemistry
670.9882	TS50	French Guiana—Manufactures	677	TS1300-1865	Textile fabrics
670.9883	TS49	Surinam—Manufactures	677	TS1540-1549	Textile fibers
670.9892	TS51	Paraguay—Manufactures	677	TS1760-1770	Dry-goods
670.9895	TS53	Uruguay—Manufactures	677.028	TS1488	Sizing (Textile)
670.99(5-6)	TS123-124	Oceania—Manufactures	677.02822	TS1480-1487	Spinning
670.993	TS122.5-.6	New Zealand—Manufactures	677.02822	GN432	Spinning
			677.028242	TS1490-1500	Weaving
670.994	TS121-122	Australia—Manufactures	677.028242	GN432	Weaving
671	TS200-770	Metal-work	677.028242092	GN432	Weavers
671.0284	TS215	Metal-working machinery	677.028242092	HD8039.T4	Weavers
671.05	TS200	Metal-work—Periodicals	677.02825	TS1510	Textile finishing
671.2	TS228.97-239	Founding	677.02825	TP934-945	Finishes and finishing
671.2	TS228.99-240	Founding	677.02854	TS1493	Looms
671.32	TS340	Roll-mill	677.02862	TS1550-1590	Yarn
671.332	TS225	Forging	677.02862	TS1590	Thread
671.36	TS320	Tempering	677.02862	TS1600-1631	Yarn
671.37	TN695-697	Powder metallurgy	677.11	TS1700-1735	Flax
671.52	TS227-228.96	Welding	677.21	TS1542	Cotton
671.521	TK4660	Electroslag welding	677.3	TS1545-1548	Animal fibers
671.521	TK4660	Electric welding	677.31	TS1547	Wool

Dewey	LC	Subject Heading	Dewey	LC	Subject Heading
677.31	TS1600-1631	Woolen and worsted manufacture	684.104	TT194-199.4	Furniture
677.39	TS1546	Silk	684.13	TS880	Tables
677.39	TS1640-1688	Satin	684.13	TS880	Chairs
677.39	TS1640-1688	Silk	684.13	TT197.5.D5	Dining room furniture
677.4	TS1688	Synthetic fabrics	684.13	TT197.5.T3	Tables
677.46	TS1688	Rayon	684.130288	TT199	Chair caning
677.4743	TS1548.7.P58	Polyester fibers	684.14	TS880	Desks
677.6	TS1828	Nonwoven fabrics	684.14	TT197.5.D4	Desks
677.6(2-3)	TS1825	Felt	684.16	TT197	Cabinetwork
677.617	TS1675	Velvet	684.16	TT197	Chests
677.617	TS1680	Plush	684.18	TT197.5.09	Outdoor furniture
677.64	TS1780	Tapestry	685.1	TS1030-1035	Saddlery
677.643	TS1772-1779.5	Carpets	685.24	TT525	Fur garments
677.682	TS1520	Waterproofing of fabrics	685.31	TS989-1025	Shoes
677.71	TS1784-1787	Cordage	685.31	TS989-1025	Boots
677.71	TS1784-1787	Rope	685.310092	HD8039.B7-.B72	Shoemakers
677.77	TS1783	Embroidery	685.4	TS2160	Gloves
678.2	TS1870-1935	Rubber industry and trade	686.071	Z122-.5	Printing—Study and teaching
678.24	TS1891	Vulcanization	686.09	Z124-242	Printing—History
678.32	TS1912	Tires, Rubber	686.2	Z	Printing
678.35	TS1920	Rubber bands	686.2	Z116.A2-265.5.A5	Printing
678.72	TS1925-1927	Rubber, Artificial	686.2	Z244	Print finishing processes
679.6	TS2301.B8	Brooms and brushes	686.20278	Z235-236	Printers' marks
679.7	TS2220-2283	Tobacco industry	686.20284	Z249	Paper-cutting machines
679.7	TS2255	Nicotine	686.20284	Z256	Rollers (Printing)
679.72	TS2260	Cigars	686.20299	Z245	Printing industry—Estimates
681.11(3-4)	TS540-549	Horology	686.2092	Z231-234	Printers
681.11(3-4)	TS540-549	Clock and watch making	686.221	Z252	Electrotyping
681.11(3-4)	TS540-549	Clocks and watches	686.224	Z250	Printing—Specimens
681.145	HF5688-5689	Calculators	686.225	Z242.9-264	Printing
683.4	HV8059	Firearms ownership	686.2252	Z246	Printing—Layout
681.4092	RE940-981	Opticians	686.2252	Z253.5	Magazine design
681.4125	QC373.B55	Binoculars	686.22542	Z253	Monotype
681.428	TP867	Mirrors	686.22542	Z253	Linotype
681.6	TS1262-1266	Pens	686.22544	TR1010	Phototypesetting
681.62	Z249-.4	Printing-press	686.22544416	Z253.53-.532	Desktop publishing
681.76041	TS283	Pressure vessels	686.22544416	Z286.D47	Desktop publishing
683	TS400-455	Hardware	686.2255	Z254	Proofreading
683.3	TS519-531	Locksmithing	686.23042	Z258	Color-printing
683.32	TS519-531	Locks and keys	686.2316	TP901	Silk-printing
683.32	TH2279	Locks and keys	686.2316	TT273	Screen process printing
683.32	TH9735	Locks and keys	686.232	TR925-997	Photomechanical processes
683.4	TS532-537.5	Firearms	686.2325	TR930-937	Collotype
683.4	TS535-.4	Gunsmithing	686.2325	TR940-950	Photolithography
683.422	TS536.6.B6	Rifles, Bolt action	686.2327	TR970-977	Photoengraving
683.436	TS537	Revolvers	686.2327	TR975	Photoengraving—Halftone process
683.82	TS380-.4	Cutlery	686.2327	TR980	Photogravure
684	N8550-8553	Picture frames and framing	686.233	Z252.5.N46	Nonimpact printing
684.08	TT152-153.7	Workshops	686.3	Z266-276	Bookbinding
684.1	TS880-889	Furniture	686.3	Z272	Endpapers
684.1	TS880-889	Furniture making	686.30092	Z269-.3	Bookbinders
684.1	TT194-199.4	Furniture making			
684.100288	TT199	Furniture—Repairing			

Dewey	LC	Subject Heading	Dewey	LC	Subject Heading
686.4	TR920-923	Photographic reproduction of plans, drawings, etc.	690.11	TH2101	Foundations
			690.11	TH5201	Foundations
686.4	Z48	Copying processes	690.12	TH2201-2251.5	Walls
686.4	Z48	Fluid copying processes	690.12	TH2235-2238.7	Exterior walls
686.4	TR824-835	Photocopying	690.12	TH2243	Brick walls
686.42	TR415	Blueprinting	690.12	TH2245	Concrete walls
686.42	TR921	Blueprinting	690.12	TH2249	Stone walls
686.43	Z265-.5	Documents on microfilm	690.13	TH2252-2253	Columns
686.43	Z265	Micrographics	690.146	TH2170-.7	Domes
686.44	TR1035-1050	Electrophotography	690.15	TH2180	Towers
686.45	TR470	Photostat	690.15	TH2281-2288	Chimneys
687	TT490-695	Clothing trade	690.15	TH2391-2495	Roofs
687	TT498	Clothing factories	690.15	TH2409	Flat roofs
687	TT507	Clothing and dress	690.15	TH2416-2417	Roofs, Shell
687.043	TT520	Garment cutting	690.15	TH2431-2459	Roofing
687.043	TT590	Garment cutting	690.16	TH2521-2529	Flooring
687.044	TT570-630	Tailoring	690.17	TH2531-2533	Ceilings
687.112	TT500-560	Dressmaking	690.182	TH2276	Blinds
687.113	TT605	Trousers	690.1822	TH2278	Fire doors
687.141	TT595-600	Coats	690.1822	TH2278	Screen doors
687.142	TT530	Coats	690.1822	TH2278	Doors
687.147	TT530-535	Cloaks	690.1822	TH2279	Door fittings
687.16	TT626	Livery	690.1823	TH2261-2276	Windows
687.19	TT616	Neckties	690.1832	TH5667-5680	Staircases
687.19	TT657	Kerchiefs	690.21	TH845-895	Strains and stresses
687.2	TT669-678	Underwear	690.21	TH895	Snow loads
687.21	TT675	T-shirts	690.22	TH443	Building—Accidents
687.22	TT669-670	Lingerie	690.24	TH3351-3361	Buildings—Maintenance
687.22	TT677	Foundation garments	690.24	TH3401-3411	Buildings—Remodeling for other use
687.3	TT679-695	Hosiery			
687.42	TT650-665	Millinery	690.24	TH3401-3411	Buildings—Repair and reconstruction
688.1	TT154-.5	Models and modelmaking			
688.42	TS2270	Tobacco-pipes	690.24	TH4816.2	Buildings—Additions
688.6	TS2001-2035	Carriage and wagon-making	690.5	TH1097	Air raid shelters
688.7221	TS2301.T7	Dolls	690.52	TH4311-4315	Commercial buildings—Design and construction
688.752	TJ1570	Slot machines			
688.8	TS195-198.8	Packaging	690.53	TH4461	Granaries—Design and construction
688.8	TS197.5	Containers			
690	TH	Building	690.535	TH4451-4499	Warehouses—Design and construction
690	TH6057.T23	Tall buildings			
690.025	TH12-13	Building—Directories	690.54	TH4511-4591	Factories
690.0284	TH900-915	Construction equipment	690.54	TH4511-4591	Factories—Design and construction
690.0284	TH915	Building—Equipment and supplies			
			690.54	TH4532	Distilleries
690.05	TH1-4	Building—Periodicals	690.54	TH4541	Drug factories
690.06	TH5	Building—Congresses	690.54	TH4581-4591	Power-plants
690.071	TH165-213	Building—Study and teaching	690.61	TH4224	Pagodas—Design and construction
			690.8	TH4805-4890	House construction
690.09	TH15-19	Building—History	690.8	TH4805-4890	Dwellings
690.09(4-9)	TH21-127	Building—[By region or country]	690.8370473	TH1421	Earth construction
			690.8370473	TH4818.A3	Earth houses
690.0973	TH23-25	Building—United States	690.8370473	TH4819.E27	Earth sheltered houses
690.1	TH2025-3000	Building—Details	690.86	TH4920	Farmhouses
690.1	TH2060	Buildings—Joints	690.872	TH4835	Vacation homes

Dewey	LC	Subject Heading	Dewey	LC	Subject Heading
690.873	TH4840	Log cabins	696.2	TH6703-6729	Pipe fitting
690.892	TH4911-4935	Farm buildings	696.2	TH6880	Gas-burners
690.892	TH4935	Silos	696.2	TH6840	Gas-fitting
690.8922	TH4930	Dairy barns	696.6	TH6551-6568	Hot-water supply
690.893	TH4970	Decks (Architecture, Domestic)	696.6	TH6561	Water heaters, Gas
691.2	TA426-428	Building stones	697	TH6014-6085	Buildings—Environmental engineering
691.4	TA432-433	Bricks	697	TH7005-7699	Heating
692.3	TH425	Buildings—Specifications	697.03	TH7461	Heating plants
692.5	TH434-437	Building—Estimates	697.043	TH7453-7457	Gas—Heating and cooking
693.1	TH1199-1301	Masonry	697.043	TH7454-7457	Stoves, Gas
693.1	TH1201	Building, Stone	697.044	TH7466.06	Oil burners
693.1	TH5311-5701	Masonry	697.07	TH7140	Fluidized-bed furnaces
693.1	TH5401-5440	Stonemasonry	697.07	TH7400	Furnaces
693.1	TH5501	Bricklaying	697.07	TH7538	Boilers
693.21	TH1301	Building, Brick	697.1	TH7421-7434.7	Fireplaces
693.3	TH1077-1083	Tile construction	697.22	TH7435-7458	Stoves
693.5	TH1461-1501	Concrete construction	697.22	TH7437-7441	Stoves, Wood
693.5	TH1491	Concrete blocks	697.22	TH7443-7446	Stoves, Coal
693.54	TH1501	Reinforced concrete construction	697.24	TH7450.5	Kerosene heaters
			697.3	TH7601-7635	Hot-air heating
693.6	TH8135-8139	Plaster	697.3	TH7638	Heat pumps
693.71	TH1610-1635	Building, Iron and steel	697.4	TH7511-7549	Hot-water heating
693.82	TH1061-1093	Building, Fireproof	697.5	TH7561-7599	Steam-heating
693.82	TH1061-1093	Fireproofing	697.5	TH7570-7578	Steam-heating, Low pressure
693.82	TH1065	Fire resistant materials			
693.82	TH9111-9599	Fire prevention	697.507	TH7480-7495	Radiators
693.834	TH1725	Factories—Soundproofing	697.507	TH7588	Boilers
693.834	TH1725	Soundproofing	697.78	TH7413-7414	Solar heating
693.852	TH1095	Buildings—Earthquake effects	697.78	TH7414	Solar houses
			697.8	TH2281-2288	Flues
693.854	TH1097	Building, Bombproof	697.92	TH7647-7699	Ventilation
693.892	TH9031	Dampness in buildings	697.93	TH7687-7688	Air conditioning
693.892	TH9031	Waterproofing	697.9354	TH7684.F2-.F3	Factories—Air conditioning
693.898	TH9057-9092	Lightning protection	697.938	TH7688.H6	Dwellings—Air conditioning
693.898	TH9057-9092	Lightning-conductors	698.1	TT320-324	House painting
693.91	TH1431	Building, Ice and snow	698.5	TH8251-8275	Glazing
693.96	TH1560	Glass construction	698.6	TH8441	Paperhanging
693.97	TH1098	Modular construction	700	N	Art
693.97	TH1098	Buildings, Prefabricated	700	NX	Arts
694	TH5601-5695	Carpentry	700.08996073	N6538.N5	Afro-American artists
694.0284	TH5618	Miter-gages	700.105	N72.T4	Art and technology
694.1	TH5611	Carpentry drafting	700.284	N8530-8540	Artists' materials
694.2	TH2301-2311	Framing (Building)	700.3	NX70	Arts—Encyclopedias
694.6	TH5640-5695	Finish carpentry	700.3	NX80	Arts—Dictionaries
694.6	TH5662-5663	Joinery	700.411	BH301.A94	Avant-garde (Aesthetics)
696-697	TH6010-6013	Building fittings	700.411	BH301.A94	Avant-garde (Aesthetics)
696.1	TH6101-6729	Plumbing	700.4112	N6490	Modernism (Art)
696.10288	TH6681-6685	Plumbing—Repairing	700.4145	ND1267	Primitivism in art
696.13	TH6571-6675	Drainage, House	700.42	BH301.L3	Landscape
696.182	TH6485-6500	Bathrooms	700.421734	N8205	Pastoral art
696.182	TH6492	Showers (Plumbing fixtures)	700.4548	N7720	Dance of death
696.182	TH6493	Bathtubs	700.46	BH301.N3	Nature (Aesthetics)
696.182	TH6498	Toilets	700.5	NX1-9	Arts—Periodicals

Dewey	LC	Subject Heading	Dewey	LC	Subject Heading
700.79	NX700-750	Arts—Endowments	700.97283	NX519	Arts—Honduras
700.901	GN799.A	Art, Prehistoric	700.97284	NX522	Arts—El Salvador
700.92	N40	Artists	700.97285	NX520	Arts—Nicaragua
700.9(4-9)	NX501-596.3	Arts—[By region or country]	700.97286	NX517	Arts—Costa Rica
700.94	NX542-571	Arts—Europe	700.97287	NX521	Arts—Panama
700.941	NX543-547.6	Arts—Great Britain	700.9729	NX523-529	Arts—West Indies
700.943	NX550-.6	Arts—Germany	700.97291	NX525	Arts—Cuba
700.9436	NX548	Arts—Austria	700.97292	NX527	Arts—Jamaica
700.944	NX549	Arts—France	700.97294	NX526	Arts—Haiti
700.945	NX552	Arts—Italy	700.97295	NX528	Arts—Puerto Rico
700.946	NX562	Arts—Spain	700.97296	NX524	Arts—Bahamas
700.9469	NX563	Arts—Portugal	700.973	NX503-512.3	Arts—United States
700.947	NX556	Arts—Russia	700.98	NX530-541	Arts—South America
700.948	NX557-561	Arts—Scandinavia	700.981	NX533	Arts—Brazil
700.9481	NX560	Arts—Norway	700.982	NX531	Arts—Argentina
700.9485	NX561	Arts—Sweden	700.983	NX534	Arts—Chile
700.9489	NX558	Arts—Denmark	700.984	NX532	Arts—Bolivia
700.94912	NX559	Arts—Iceland	700.985	NX539	Arts—Peru
700.9492	NX554	Arts—Netherlands	700.9861	NX535	Arts—Colombia
700.9493	NX555	Arts—Belgium	700.9866	NX536	Arts—Ecuador
700.9494	NX564	Arts—Switzerland	700.987	NX541	Arts—Venezuela
700.9495	NX551	Arts—Greece	700.9892	NX538	Arts—Paraguay
700.9496	NX566-569	Arts—Balkan Peninsula	700.9895	NX540	Arts—Uruguay
700.95	NX572-586	Arts—Asia	700.993	NX593	Arts—New Zealand
700.951	NX583	Arts—China	700.994	NX590	Arts—Australia
700.9519	NX584.6-.7	Arts—Korea	700.99(5-6)	NX595-596	Arts—Oceania
700.952	NX584	Arts—Japan	701	N61-75	Art—Philosophy
700.954	NX576	Arts—India	701.15	N61-79	Imagination
700.95491	NX576.7	Arts—Pakistan	701.17	N61-79	Aesthetics
700.95493	NX576.6	Arts—Sri Lanka	701.170902	N61	Aesthetics, Medieval
700.955	NX574	Arts—Iran	701.1709031	N61	Aesthetics, Modern—16th century
700.956	NX573-.7	Arts—Middle East	701.1709032	N61	Aesthetics, Modern—17th Century
700.9561	NX565	Arts—Turkey			
700.95694	NX573.7	Arts—Israel	701.1709033	N61	Aesthetics, Modern—18th century
700.957	NX575.7	Arts—Asiatic Russia			
700.9581	NX575.6	Arts—Afghanistan	701.1709034	N61	Aesthetics, Modern—19th century
700.9593	NX578.7	Arts—Thailand			
700.9594	NX578.6.L3	Arts—Laos	701.170904	N61	Aesthetics, Modern—20th century
700.9595	NX579	Arts—Malaysia			
700.9596	NX578.6.C3	Arts—Cambodia	701.18	N7475-7485	Art criticism
700.9597	NX578.6.V5-.V55	Arts—Vietnam	701.8	BH301.H3	Harmony (Aesthetics)
700.9598	NX580	Arts—Indonesia	701.8	N7429.7-7433	Composition (Art)
700.9599	NX581	Arts—Philippines	702.5	N50-55	Art—Directories
700.96	NX587-589.8	Arts—Africa	702.8	N7429.7-7433	Art—Technique
700.961	NX587.6-588.6	Arts—Africa, North	702.8	N7574	Artists' models
700.962	NX588-.3	Arts—Egypt	702.84	N8543	Artists' tools
700.963	NX588.7	Arts—Ethiopia	702.872	N8580	Pictures—Copying
700.966	NX589-.6	Arts—Africa, West	702.874	NX636	Arts—Forgeries
700.9676	NX588.8-.9	Arts—Africa, East	702.88	N8554-8585	Art—Conservation and restoration
700.968	NX589.7-.8	Arts—Africa, Southern			
700.971	NX513-.3	Arts—Canada	703	N33	Art—Dictionaries
700.972	NX514	Arts—Mexico	704.942	N7575-7649	Portraits
700.9728	NX515-522	Arts—Central America	704.942	N7616	Portrait miniatures
700.97281	NX518	Arts—Guatemala	704.9421	N7572	Nude in art

Dewey	LC	Subject Heading	Dewey	LC	Subject Heading
704.9428	N8217.E6	Erotic art	709.04052	N6490	Art, Abstract
704.9428	NX650.E7	Pornography	709.04062	N6494.D3	Dadaism
704.946	N7740-7745	Symbolism in art	709.04062	NX600.D3	Dadaism
704.946	N7740	Emblems	709.04062	NX600.S9	Surrealism
704.947	N7760-7763	Art and mythology	709.2	N40-43	Art—Biography
704.9482	BV150-168	Christian art and symbolism	709.31	N5343-5345	Oriental antiquities
704.9482	N7810-8189.6	Christian art and symbolism	709.32	N5350-5351	Art, Egyptian
704.9482	N7832	Art, Early Christian	709.35	N5370	Art, Sumerian
704.9489	NX688	Arts, Islamic	709.37	N5760-5763	Art, Roman
704.9497928	N8217.D3	Dance in art	709.38	N5603-5896.3	Art, Classical
705	N1-9.9	Art—Periodicals	709.38	N5630-5720	Art, Greek
706	N10-17	Art—Societies, etc.	709.392	N5480-5560	Art, Turkish
706	N21	Art—Congresses	709.394	N5470	Art, Arab
707.1	N81-390	Art—Study and teaching	709.3943	N5460	Art, Syrian
707.1	N325-335	Art schools	709.436	N6805-6808.5	Art—Austria—History
707.104	N332	Art schools—Europe	709.437	N6828-6831.5	Art—Czechoslovakia—History
707.1073	N328-330	Art schools—United States			
707.4	N4390-5098	Art—Exhibitions	709.439	N6819-6820.5	Art—Hungary—History
707.4	N8665	Sidewalk art exhibitions	709.45	N6915-6923	Art—Italy—History
708	N400-3990	Art museums	709.46	N7105-7108.5	Art—Spain—History
708	N5198-5299	Art—Private collections	709.469	N7125-7128.5	Art—Portugal—History
708.1(3-9)	N510-880	Art museums—United States	709.48	N7007-7088	Art—Scandinavia—History
708.1(3-9)	N5215-5220	Art—Private collections—United States	709.493	N6967-6973	Art—Belgium—History
			709.495	N6897-6898.5	Art—Greece—History
708.(2-9)	N1010-3690	Art museums—Europe	709.5	N7260-7355.5	Art, Oriental
708.(2-8)	N5240-5280	Art—Private collections—Europe	709.71	N6540-6545.5	Art—Canada—History
708.2	N1020-1560	Art museums—Great Britain	709.72	N6555-.5	Art—Mexico—History
708.3	N2210-2406	Art museums—Germany	709.728	N6573.2-6582.5	Art—Central America—History
708.4	N2010-2180	Art museums—France			
708.5	N2510-3065	Art museums—Italy	709.8	N6635-6735.5	Art—South America—History
708.6	N3410-3499	Art museums—Spain			
708.7	N3310-3382	Art museums—Russia	711	NA9000-9284	City planning
708.92	N2450-2505	Art museums—Netherlands	711.09(4-9)	NA9101-9285	City planning—[By region or country]
708.93	N1750-1850	Art museums—Belgium			
708.95	N2410-2430	Art museums—Greece	711.3	NA9000-9428	Regional planning
709	N5300-7418	Art—History	711.41	NA9053.B58	Blocks (City planning)
709.01	N5315-5899	Art, Ancient	711.45	NA9053.N	New towns
709.011	N5310-5313	Art, Primitive	711.55	NA9070-9072	Plazas
709.011	N5310-5313	Art, Prehistoric	712	SB469-476.4	Landscape architecture
709.02	N5940-6320	Art, Medieval	712	SB472.45	Landscape design
709.0216	N6280	Art, Romanesque	714	NA9400-9425	Fountains
709.024	N6370-6375	Art, Renaissance	714	SB475.8	Water in landscape architecture
709.03	N6350-6494	Art, Modern			
709.032	N6410-6415	Art, Modern—17th century	719	SB439-.26	Natural landscaping
709.033	N6420-6425	Art, Modern—18th century	719.33	SB475.9.F67	Forest landscape design
709.0332	N6410	Art, Rococo	720	NA	Architecture
709.034	N6450-6465	Art, Modern—19th century	720.1	NA2500	Architecture—Aesthetics
709.0342	N70	Romanticism in art	720.22	NA2790	Architectural models
709.0345	N6465.N44	Neo-impressionism (Art)	720.222	NA2600-2635	Architecture—Designs and plans
709.04	N6480-6494	Art, Modern—20th century			
709.04012	N6494.A7	Art deco	720.222	NA2700-2780	Architectural drawing
709.04042	ND1265	Expressionism (Art)	720.25	NA50-60	Architecture—Directories
			720.288	NA105-112	Architecture—Conservation and restoration]

Dewey	LC	Subject Heading	Dewey	LC	Subject Heading
720.3	NA31	Architecture—Encyclopedias	720.95692	NA1476.6-.8	Architecture—Lebanon
			720.95694	NA1477-1479	Architecture—Israel
720.473	NA2542.7	Underground architecture	720.95695	NA1479.6-.8	Architecture—Jordan
720.483	NA6230-6234	Tall buildings	720.957	NA1492.6-1499	Architecture—Asiatic Russia
720.5	NA1-9	Architecture—Periodicals	720.9581	NA1492-.3	Architecture—Afghanistan
720.6	NA10-17	Architecture—Societies, etc.	720.9591	NA1512-.3	Architecture—Burma
			720.9593	NA1521-1523	Architecture—Thailand
720.71	NA2000-2320	Architecture—Study and teaching	720.9594	NA1516-.3	Architecture—Laos
			720.9595	NA1525-.8	Architecture—Malaysia
720.79	NA2335-2360	Architecture—Competitions	720.9596	NA1515-.3	Architecture—Cambodia
720.87	NA2545	Architecture and the handicapped	720.9597	NA1514-.63	Architecture—Vietnam
			720.9598	NA1526-.8	Architecture—Indonesia
720.9154	NA2542.A73	Architecture—Arid regions	720.9599	NA1527-1529	Architecture—Philippines
720.92	NA40	Architecture—Biography	720.96	NA1580-1599	Architecture—Africa
720.94	NA950-1455	Architecture—Europe	720.9611	NA1591-.3	Architecture—Tunisia
720.941	NA961-981	Architecture—Great Britain	720.9612	NA1589-.3	Architecture—Libya
720.94209033	NA630	Architecture, Queen Anne	720.962	NA1581-1585.3	Architecture, Egyptian
720.943	NA1061-1089	Architecture—Germany	720.963	NA1586-.3	Architecture—Ethiopia
720.9436	NA1001-1011.6	Architecture—Austria	720.964	NA1590-.3	Architecture—Morocco
720.9437	NA1023-1034.5	Architecture—Czechoslovakia	720.965	NA1588-.3	Architecture—Algeria
			720.966	NA1598-1599	Architecture—Africa, West
720.9438	NA1466.P6	Architecture—Poland	720.9676	NA1597-.6	Architecture—Africa, East
720.9439	NA1012-1022	Architecture—Hungary	720.968	NA1591.7-1596.6	Architecture—Southern Africa
720.944	NA1041-1059	Architecture—France			
720.945	NA1111-1123.3	Architecture—Italy	720.9(7-8)	NA702.5-939	Architecture, American
720.946	NA1301-1313.3	Architecture, Spanish	720.971	NA740-749.5	Architecture—Canada
720.946	NA1301-1313.3	Architecture—Spain	720.972	NA750-759	Architecture—Mexico
720.9469	NA1321-1333.3	Architecture—Portugal	720.9728	NA760-790	Architecture—Central America
720.947	NA1181-1199	Architecture—Russia			
720.948	NA1201-1293.3	Architecture—Scandinavia	720.97281	NA776-778	Architecture—Guatemala
720.9481	NA1261-1273.3	Architecture—Norway	720.97283	NA779-781	Architecture—Honduras
720.9485	NA1281-1293.3	Architecture—Sweden	720.97284	NA788-790	Architecture—El Salvador
720.9489	NA1211-1223.3	Architecture—Denmark	720.97285	NA782-784	Architecture—Nicaragua
720.94897	NA1455.F5	Architecture—Finland	720.97286	NA773-775	Architecture—Costa Rica
720.94912	NA1241-1253.3	Architecture—Iceland	720.97287	NA785-787	Architecture—Panama
720.9492	NA1141-1153.3	Architecture—Netherlands	720.9729	NA791-815	Architecture—West Indies
720.9493	NA1161-1173.3	Architecture—Belgium	720.97291	NA803-805	Architecture—Cuba
720.9494	NA1341-1353.3	Architecture—Switzerland	720.97292	NA809-811	Architecture—Jamaica
720.9495	NA1091-1103	Architecture—Greece	720.97294	NA806-808	Architecture—Haiti
720.9497	NA1441-1453.3	Architecture—Yugoslavia	720.97295	NA812-814	Architecture—Puerto Rico
720.9498	NA1421-1433.3	Architecture—Romania	720.97296	NA800-802	Architecture—Bahamas
720.9499	NA1381-1393.3	Architecture—Bulgaria	720.973	NA705-738	Architecture—United States
720.95	NA1460-1579	Architecture, Oriental	720.98	NA820-939	Architecture—South America
720.951	NA1540-1549.6	Architecture—China			
720.951	NA1540-1547	Pagodas	720.981	NA850-859	Architecture—Brazil
720.9519	NA1560-1570.3	Architecture—Korea	720.982	NA830-839	Architecture—Argentina
720.952	NA1550-1559.6	Architecture—Japan	720.983	NA860-869	Architecture—Chile
720.9538	NA1470-1472	Architecture—Saudi Arabia	720.984	NA840-849	Architecture—Bolivia
720.954	NA1501-1510.3	Architecture—India	720.985	NA910-919	Architecture—Peru
720.95491	NA1510.7-.73	Architecture—Pakistan	720.9861	NA870-879	Architecture—Colombia
720.95493	NA1510.6-.63	Architecture—Sri Lanka	720.9866	NA880-889	Architecture—Ecuador
720.955	NA1480-1489	Architecture—Iran	720.987	NA930-939	Architecture—Venezuela
720.9561	NA1361-1375	Architecture—Turkey	720.9881	NA895	Architecture—Guyana
720.9567	NA1467-1469	Architecture—Iraq			
720.95691	NA1489.6-.8	Architecture—Syria			

Dewey	LC	Subject Heading	Dewey	LC	Subject Heading
720.9882	NA897	Architecture—French Guiana	724.19	NA627-640	Architecture, Modern—18th century
720.9883	NA896	Architecture—Surinam	724.19	NA640	Architecture, Georgian
720.9892	NA900-909	Architecture—Paraguay	724.2	NA600	Neoclassicism (Architecture)
720.9895	NA920-929	Architecture—Uruguay			
720.993	NA1606-1608	Architecture—New Zealand	724.5	NA645-670	Architecture, Modern—19th century
720.994	NA1600-1605.3	Architecture—Australia	724.6	NA673-682	Architecture, Modern—20th century
720.99(5-6)	NA1610-1613	Architecture—Oceania			
721	NA2750-2793	Architectural design	725	NA4170-5095	Public buildings
721	NA2835-3060	Architecture—Details	725	NA9050.5	Public architecture
721.04422	NA4145.A35	Building, Adobe	725.087	NA2545.P5	Public buildings—Access for the physically handicapped
721.0443	NA3705	Tiles			
721.0445	NA4125	Concrete construction	725.09(4-9)	NA4201-4385	Public buildings—[By region or country]
721.04496	NA4140	Glass construction			
721.04497	NA8480	Buildings, Prefabricated	725.0973	NA4205-4228.3	Public buildings—United States
721.2	NA2940-2942	Walls			
721.3	NA2860-2875	Columns, Corinthian	725.11	NA4410-4417	Capitols
721.3	NA2860	Columns, Ionic	725.110973	NA4411-4413	United States—Capital and capitol
721.41	NA2880	Arches			
721.46	NA2890	Domes	725.1109(4-9)	NA4415	[Other countries]—Capital and capitol
721.5	NA2900	Roofs, Open-timbered			
721.5	NA2920	Gables	725.13	NA4430-4437	City halls
721.5	NA2930	Spires	725.13	NA4430-4437	Municipal buildings
721.5	NA2930	Towers	725.15	CD981-986.5	Archive buildings
721.5	NA3040	Chimneys	725.15	NA4470-4477	Courthouses
721.6	NA2970	Floors	725.16	NA4450-4457	Post office buildings
721.7	NA2950	Ceilings	725.17	NA4440-4447	Embassy buildings
721.8	NA3050-3055	Fireplaces	725.18	NA490-497	Military architecture
721.822	NA3010	Doorways	725.18	NA4490-4497	Police stations
721.823	NA3000-3030	Windows	725.2	NA6210-6280	Commercial buildings
721.832	NA3060	Stairs	725.21	NA6225	Shop fronts
721.84	NA3070	Balconies	725.23	NA6230-6234	Office buildings
721.84	NA7125	Porches	725.24	NA6240-6245	Bank buildings
722	GN414	Architecture, Primitive	725.35	NA6340-6343	Warehouses
722	NA205-207	Architecture, Primitive	725.38	NA8348	Garages
722	NA210-340	Architecture, Ancient	725.39	NA6300-6307	Airport buildings
722-724	NA190-1555.5	Architecture—History	725.4	NA6396-6589	Industrial buildings
722.2	NA215-216	Architecture, Egyptian	725.4	NA6396-6589	Factories
722.51	NA220-221	Architecture, Assyro-Babylonian	725.4	NA6400-6589	Architecture, Industrial
			725.4	NA6598	Employees' buildings and facilities
722.62	NA300-301	Architecture, Etruscan			
722.7	NA310-340	Architecture, Roman	725.822	NA6820-6846	Theater architecture
722.70937	NA295-340	Architecture, Italian	725.822	NA6820-6845	Theaters
722.8	NA270-290	Architecture, Greek	725.823	NA6845-6846	Motion picture theaters
723	NA350-497	Architecture, Medieval	725.827	NA313	Amphitheaters
723.4	NA390-419	Architecture, Romanesque	725.827	NA6860-7010	Stadiums
723.4	NA423-429	Architecture, Norman	725.83	NA6815	Auditoriums
723.5	NA440-489	Architecture, Gothic	725.83	PN1585-1589	Centers for the performing arts
724	NA500-680	Architecture, Modern			
724.1	NA707	Architecture, Colonial	725.91	NA6750-6751	Exhibition buildings
724.12	NA510-575	Architecture, Renaissance	725.91	NA6880-.5	Convention facilities
724.16	NA590	Architecture, Baroque	725.94	NA9325-9355	Soldiers' monuments
724.19	NA590	Architecture, Rococo	725.94	NA9325-9330	War memorials
			725.94	NA9335-9355	Monuments

Dewey	LC	Subject Heading	Dewey	LC	Subject Heading
725.96	NA9360-9380	Triumphal arches	729.1	NA2840-2841	Facades
726.1	NA4610-4710	Temples	729.11	NA2760	Architecture—Composition, proportion, etc.
726.2	NA4670	Mosques			
726.3	NA4690	Synagogue architecture	729.24	NA2850-2856	Interior architecture
726.4	NA4910	Baptisteries	729.28	NA2794	Daylighting
726.5	NA4790-6113	Church architecture	729.28	TH7703	Lighting, Architectural and decorative
726.5	NA4790-5095	Church buildings			
726.5	NA4870	Chapels	729.29	NA2800	Architectural acoustics
726.51	NA5000	Church decoration and ornament	729.7	NA3750-3860	Pavements, Mosaic
			729.7	NA3750-3860	Mosaics
726.5291	NA5060	Altars	730	NB	Sculpture
726.5291	NA5070	Fonts	730.11	NB1142.5	Sculpture—Appreciation
726.58(1-9)	NA4828.5	Protestant church buildings	730.216	NB35	Sculpture—Catalogs
726.6	NA4830	Cathedrals	730.5	NB1	Sculpture—Periodicals
726.7	NA4800-6113	Abbeys	730.74	NB16-17	Sculpture—Exhibitions
726.7	NA4850	Monasteries	730.9	NB60-615	Sculpture—History
726.8	NA6120-6199	Tombs	730.92	NB1115	Sculptors
726.809	NA6149-6199	Tombs—[By region or country]	730.9(4-9)	NB201-1114	Sculpture—[By region or country]
727.3	NA6600-6605	College buildings	730.94	NB450-955	Sculpture—Europe
728	NA7100-7882	Architecture, Domestic	730.941	NB461-481	Sculpture—Great Britain
728	NA7100-7884	Dwellings	730.943	NB561-589	Sculpture—Germany
728.0222	NA7127-7135	Architecture, Domestic—Designs and plans	730.9436	NB501-511.6	Sculpture—Austria
			730.9437	NB523-534.5	Sculpture—Czechoslovakia
728	NA7150	Brick houses	730.9438	NB955.P6	Sculpture—Poland
728	NA7160	Concrete houses	730.9439	NB512-522.6	Sculpture—Hungary
728	NA7160	Stucco	730.944	NB541-553.3	Sculpture—France
728	NA7175	Half-timbered houses	730.945	NB611-623.3	Sculpture—Italy
728	NA7180	Steel houses	730.946	NB801-813.3	Sculpture—Spain
728.0846	NA7195.A4	Aged—Dwellings	730.9469	NB821-833.3	Sculpture—Portugal
728.091733	NA7570-7572.5	Suburban homes	730.947	NB681-699	Sculpture—Russia
728.09(4-9)	NA7201-7333	Architecture, Domestic—[By region and country]	730.948	NB701-793.3	Sculpture—Scandinavia
			730.9481	NB761-773.3	Sculpture—Norway
728.312	NA7520	Row houses	730.9485	NB781-793.3	Sculpture—Sweden
728.314	NA7860-7863	Apartment houses	730.9489	NB711-723.3	Sculpture—Denmark
728.37	NA7551-7555	Cottages	730.94897	NB955.F5	Sculpture—Finland
728.370473	NA7531	Earth sheltered houses	730.94912	NB741-753.3	Sculpture—Iceland
728.4	NA7910-7977	Clubhouses	730.9492	NB641-653.3	Sculpture—Netherlands
728.5	NA7800-7853	Hotels	730.9493	NB661-673.3	Sculpture—Belgium
728.6	NA8208-8210	Farmhouses	730.9494	NB841-853.3	Sculpture—Switzerland
728.7	NA7574-7579	Vacation homes	730.9495	NB591-603	Sculpture—Greece
728.73	NA8470	Log cabins	730.9497	NB941-953.3	Sculpture—Yugoslavia
728.78	VM335	Houseboats	730.9498	NB921-933.3	Sculpture—Romania
728.81	NA7710-7786	Castles	730.95	NB960-1070.3	Sculpture—Asia
728.82	NA7710-7786	Palaces	730.951	NB1040-1049.6	Sculpture, Chinese
728.8209376	NA320	Palaces	730.9519	NB1060-1070.6	Sculpture—Korea
728.820938	NA277	Palaces	730.952	NB1050-1059.6	Sculpture, Japanese
728.92	NA8200-8260	Farm buildings	730.9538	NB970-972	Sculpture—Saudi Arabia
728.92	NA8240	Granaries	730.954	NB1001-1010.3	Sculpture—India
728.922	NA8230	Barns	730.95491	NB1010.7-.73	Sculpture—Pakistan
728.922	NA8280	Dairy barns	730.95493	NB1010.6-.63	Sculpture—Sri Lanka
728.927	NA8370	Dovecotes	730.955	NB980-989	Sculpture—Iran
728.93	NA8375	Patios	730.9561	NB861-873.3	Sculpture—Turkey
729	NA3310-4050	Decoration and ornament, Architectural	730.9567	NB967-969	Sculpture—Iraq

Dewey	LC	Subject Heading	Dewey	LC	Subject Heading
730.95691	NB989.6-.8	Sculpture—Syria	730.9895	NB420-429	Sculpture—Uruguay
730.95692	NB976.6-.8	Sculpture—Lebanon	730.993	NB1106-1108	Sculpture—New Zealand
730.95694	NB977-979	Sculpture—Israel	730.994	NB1100-1105.3	Sculpture—Australia
730.95695	NB979.6-.8	Sculpture—Jordan	730.99(5-6)	NB1110-1113	Sculpture—Oceania
730.957	NB992.4-999	Sculpture—Asiatic Russia	731.028	NB1170-1195	Sculpture—Technique
730.9581	NB992-.3	Sculpture—Afghanistan	731.2	NB145-159	Terra-cotta sculpture
730.9591	NB1012-.3	Sculpture—Burma	731.2	NB1215	Concrete sculpture
730.9593	NB1021-1023	Sculpture—Thailand	731.2	NB1218	Marble sculpture
730.9594	NB1016-.3	Sculpture—Laos	731.2	NB1220	Metal sculpture
730.9595	NB1025-.8	Sculpture—Malaysia	731.2	NB1240.I75	Iron sculpture
730.9596	NB1015-.3	Sculpture—Cambodia	731.2	NB1250	Driftwood sculpture
730.9597	NB1014-.63	Sculpture—Vietnam	731.2	NB1265	Terra-cotta sculpture
730.9598	NB1026-.8	Sculpture—Indonesia	731.2	NB1270.G4	Glass sculpture
730.9599	NB1027-1029	Sculpture—Philippines	731.2	NB1270.G5	Fiberglass craft
730.96	NB1080-1099	Sculpture—Africa	731.2	NB1270.P3	Paper sculpture
730.9611	NB1091.6	Sculpture—Tunisia	731.2	NB1270.P5	Plastic sculpture
730.9612	NB1089.3	Sculpture—Libya	731.42	NB1180-1185	Modeling
730.962	NB1081-1085.3	Sculpture—Egypt	731.452	NB1190	Plaster casts
730.963	NB1086.3	Sculpture—Ethiopia	731.456	NB135-143	Bronze sculpture
730.964	NB1090.3	Sculpture—Morocco	731.463	NB1208-1210	Stone carving
730.965	NB1088.3	Sculpture—Algeria	731.48	NB1199	Sculpture—Conservation and restoration
730.966	NB1098-1099	Sculpture—Africa, West			
730.9676	NB1097-.6	Sculpture—Africa, East	731.54	NB1280-1291	Bas-relief
730.968	NB1091.7-1096.6	Sculpture—Africa, Southern	731.55	NB1315	Mobiles (Sculpture)
			731.74	NB1300	Busts
730.971	NB240-249.5	Sculpture—Canada	731.75	NB1310	Masks (Sculpture)
730.972	NB250-259	Sculpture—Mexico	731.76	NB1330-1685	Monuments
730.9728	NB260-290	Sculpture—Central America	731.7609(4-9)	NB1501-1685	Monuments—[By region or country]
730.97281	NB276-278	Sculpture—Guatemala			
730.97283	NB279-281	Sculpture—Honduras	731.81	NB1312-1313	Equestrian statues
730.97284	NB288-290	Sculpture—El Salvador	731.82	NB1293-1310	Portrait sculpture
730.97285	NB282-284	Sculpture—Nicaragua	731.82	NB1930-1936	Figure sculpture
730.97286	NB273-275	Sculpture—Costa Rica	731.832	NB1940-1942	Animal sculpture
730.97287	NB285-287	Sculpture—Panama	732	GN799.S4	Sculpture, Prehistoric
730.9729	NB291-315	Sculpture—West Indies	732.2	NB62-64	Sculpture, Primitive
730.97291	NB303-305	Sculpture—Cuba	732.2	NB69-169	Sculpture, Ancient
730.97292	NB309-311	Sculpture—Jamaica	732.2	NB69-169	Marble sculpture, Ancient
730.97294	NB306-308	Sculpture—Haiti	733.3	NB90-105	Sculpture, Greek
730.97295	NB312-314	Sculpture—Puerto Rico	733.3	NB144	Marble sculpture, Classical
730.97296	NB300-302	Sculpture—Bahamas	733.5	NB115-120	Sculpture, Roman
730.973	NB205-238	Sculpture—United States	734	NB170-180	Sculpture, Medieval
730.98	NB320-439	Sculpture—South America	734.224	NB172	Sculpture, Byzantine
730.981	NB350-359	Sculpture—Brazil	734.25	NB180	Sculpture, Gothic
730.982	NB330-339	Sculpture—Argentina	735	NB185-198.5	Sculpture, Modern
730.983	NB360-369	Sculpture—Chile	735.21	NB190	Sculpture, Renaissance
730.984	NB340-349	Sculpture—Bolivia	735.21	NB193	Sculpture, Rococo
730.985	NB410-419	Sculpture—Peru	736.20932	NK5561	Scarabs
730.9861	NB370-379	Sculpture—Colombia	736.222	NK5720-5722	Cameos
730.9866	NB380-389	Sculpture—Ecuador	736.4	NK9700-9799	Wood-carving
730.987	NB430-439	Sculpture—Venezuela	736.5	NB1800-1895	Sepulchral monuments
730.9881	NB395	Sculpture—Guyana	736.6	NK6020-6022	Bone carving
730.9882	NB397	Sculpture—French Guiana	736.982	TT870	Origami
730.9883	NB396	Sculpture—Surinam	737	CJ	Numismatics
730.9892	NB400-409	Sculpture—Paraguay	737.22	CJ5501-6661	Medals

Dewey	LC	Subject Heading	Dewey	LC	Subject Heading
737.2205	CJ5501	Medals—Periodicals	737.4946	CJ3189	Piece of eight
737.22071	CJ5525	Medals—Study and teaching	737.495	CJ3370-3893	Coins, Oriental
			737.496	CJ1071-1085	Coins, Ancient—Africa
737.22093	CJ5581-5690	Medals, Ancient	737.496	CJ3920-4389	Coins, African
737.220937	CJ5641-5685	Medals, Roman	737.4968	CJ3948	Krugerrand (Coin)
737.220938	CJ5625	Medals, Greek	737.4971	CJ1860-1879	Coins, Canadian
737.2209(4-9)	CJ5795-6661	Medals—[By Region or country]	737.4973	CJ1800-2449	Coins, American
			737.4973	CJ1835	Half-dollar
737.22094	CJ6091-6380	Medals—Europe	737.498	CJ1889-2449	Coins, Latin American
737.22095	CJ6381-6485	Medals—Asia	737.4994	CJ4400-4419	Coins, Australian
737.22096	CJ6491-6559	Medals—Africa	737.6	CD	Seals
737.2209728	CJ5841-5905	Medals—Central America	737.6	CD5001-6471	Seals (Numismatics)
737.220973	CJ5801-5812	Medals—United States	737.6028	CD5085-5175	Seals (Numismatics)—Techniques
737.220994	CJ6561-6569	Medals—Australia			
737.223	CJ5806	Campaign insignia	737.605	CD5001	Seals (Numismatics)—Periodicals
737.224	CJ5793.R34	Religious medals			
737.3	CJ4801-5450	Tokens	737.606	CD5005	Seals (Numismatics)—Societies, etc.
737.305	CJ4801	Tokens—Periodicals			
737.3074	CJ4805-4808	Tokens—Exhibitions	737.606	CD5009	Seals (Numismatics)—Congresses
737.3074	CJ4805-4806	Tokens—Museums			
737.309(4-9)	CJ4901-5336	Tokens—[By region or country]	737.6071	CD5045	Seals (Numismatics)—Study and teaching
			737.6074	CD5017-5018	Seals (Numismatics)—Exhibitions
737.30973	CJ4901-4906	Tokens—United States			
737.4	CJ1-4625	Coins	737.609	CD5049	Seals (Numismatics)—History
737.4	CJ101	Coins—Grading			
737.4	CJ125	Coins—Errors	737.6092	CD5051-5052	Seals (Numismatics)—Biography
737.4	CJ161.F3	Facing heads (Numismatics)			
			737.609(4-9)	CD5592-6471	Seals (Numismatics)—[By region or country]
737.401	CJ53	Coins—Philosophy			
737.405	CJ1-9	Coins—Periodicals	737.60971	CD5619	Seals (Numismatics)—Canada
737.406	CJ14-23	Coins—Societies, etc.			
737.406	CJ27	Coins—Congresses	737.60972	CD5620	Seals (Numismatics)—Mexico
737.4074	CJ39-41	Coins—Exhibitions			
737.409	CJ59	Coins—History	737.609728	CD5621-5700	Seals (Numismatics)—Central America
737.40902	CJ1601-1715	Coins, Medieval			
737.49(4-9)	CJ1800-4625	Coins, Medieval—[By region or country]	737.60973	CD5601-5617	Seals (Numismatics)—United States
			737.60973	CD5610	United States—Seal
737.493	CJ201-1397	Coins, Ancient	738	NK3700-4695	Pottery
737.493	CJ1021-1144	Coins, Ancient [By region or country]	738.075	NK4230	Pottery—Collectors and collecting
			738.0901	NK3800-3855	Pottery, Ancient
737.4936	CJ1101-1147	Coins, Ancient—Europe	738.0902	NK3870-3885	Pottery, Medieval
737.4937	CJ517-542	Coins, Italian	738.092	NK4200-4210	Potters
737.4937	CJ801-1147	Coins, Roman	738.09(4-9)	NK4001-4184	Pottery—[By region or country]
737.4937	CJ937	AS (Coin)			
737.4937	CJ1021-1070	Coins, Ancient—Italy	738.2	NK4370-4584	Porcelain
737.4938	CJ301-763	Coins, Greek	738.27	NK4277	Blue and white transfer ware
737.4938	CJ359	Decadrachma			
737.4938	CJ425-763	Coins, Greek	738.27	NK4399.B58	Blue and white ware
737.49396	CJ1087-1099	Coins, Ancient—Asian	738.3	NK4360-4367	Stoneware
737.49396	CJ1301-1397	Coins, Oriental	738.37	NK4295-.5	Delftware
737.49398	CJ1101-1147	Coins, Ancient—Europe	738.38	NK4695.T33	Ceramic tableware
737.49398	CJ1201-1291	Coins, Byzantine	738.4	NK4997-5024	Enamel and enameling
737.494	CJ2450-3369	Coins, European	738.5	NK8500	Mosaics
737.4941	CJ2484	Guinea (Coin)			
737.4946	CJ3188	Doubloons			

Dewey	LC	Subject Heading	Dewey	LC	Subject Heading
738.8	NK4695.F6	Food warmers	741.095	NC315-359	Drawing—Asia
738.82	NK4660	Hummel figurines	741.0951	NC348-350	Drawing—China
739	NK6400-8459	Art metal-work	741.09519	NC353.6-.7	Drawing—Korea
739	NK6400-8459	Metal-work	741.0952	NC351-353	Drawing—Japan
739.2282	NK7215-7230	Chalices	741.0954	NC327-329	Drawing—India
739.23	NK7100-7695	Silverwork	741.095491	NC331	Drawing—Pakistan
739.2383	NK7234-7235	Silver flatware	741.095493	NC330	Drawing—Sri Lanka
739.27	NK7300-7695	Jewelry	741.0955	NC321-323	Drawing—Iran
739.27	NK7650-7690	Precious stones	741.0956	NC318-320	Drawing—Middle East
739.27	NK7658-7663	Diamonds	741.09561	NC294-296	Drawing—Turkey
739.27	TS740-770	Jewelry making	741.095694	NC320	Drawing—Israel
739.27	TS747-770	Gems	741.0957	NC325	Drawing—Asiatic Russia
739.27	TS753-.5	Diamonds	741.09581	NC324.6	Drawing—Afghanistan
739.2782	NK7440-7459	Rings	741.09593	NC335	Drawing—Thailand
739.2782	TS720-770	Rings	741.09594	NC334.L3	Drawing—Laos
739.3	NK7480-7499	Clocks and watches	741.09595	NC336-338	Drawing—Malaysia
739.533	NK8400-8420	Pewter	741.09596	NC334.C3	Drawing—Cambodia
739.7	NK6600-6999	Weapons	741.09597	NC334.V5-.V55	Drawing—Vietnam
739.70228	NK8475.A7	Miniature weapons	741.09598	NC339-341	Drawing—Indonesia
739.722	NK6700-6799	Swords	741.09599	NC342-344	Drawing—Philippines
739.752	NK6808	Shields	741.096	NC360-368.6	Drawing—Africa
741	NC	Drawing	741.0961	NC361-365.6	Drawing—Africa, North
741.018	NC745	Proportion (Art)	741.0962	NC363-.3	Drawing—Egypt
741.0294	NC37-38.5	Drawing—Catalogs	741.0963	NC365.7	Drawing—Ethiopia
741.05	NC1	Drawing—Periodicals	741.0966	NC367-.6	Drawing—Africa, West
741.071	NC390-670	Drawing—Study and teaching	741.09676	NC366-6	Drawing—Africa, East
			741.0968	NC368-.6	Drawing—Africa, Southern
741.074	NC15-17	Drawing—Exhibitions	741.0971	NC141-143.3	Drawing—Canada
741.074	NC30-33	Drawing—Private collections	741.0972	NC144-146	Drawing—Mexico
			741.09728	NC147-167	Drawing—Central America
741.0902	NC70-75	Drawing, Medieval	741.097281	NC156-158	Drawing—Guatemala
741.09024	NC85	Drawing, Renaissance	741.097283	NC159-161	Drawing—Honduras
741.09032	NC86	Drawing—17th century	741.097284	NC167	Drawing—El Salvador
741.09033	NC87-.5	Drawing—18th century	741.097285	NC162-164	Drawing—Nicaragua
741.09034	NC90-.5	Drawing—19th century	741.097286	NC153-155	Drawing—Costa Rica
741.0904	NC95-.5	Drawing—20th century	741.097287	NC165	Drawing—Panama
741.09(4-9)	NC101-377	Drawing—[By region or country]	741.09729	NC168-186	Drawing—West Indies
			741.097291	NC174-176	Drawing—Cuba
741.094	NC225-312	Drawing—Europe	741.097292	NC180-182	Drawing—Jamaica
741.0941	NC228-242	Drawing—Great Britain	741.097294	NC177-179	Drawing—Haiti
741.0943	NC249-251.6	Drawing—Germany	741.097295	NC183-185	Drawing—Puerto Rico
741.0944	NC246-248	Drawing—France	741.097296	NC171-173	Drawing—Bahamas
741.0945	NC255-257	Drawing—Italy	741.0973	NC105-139.3	Drawing—United States
741.0946	NC285	Drawing—Spain	741.098	NC189-224	Drawing—South America
741.09469	NC288-290	Drawing—Portugal	741.0981	NC198-200	Drawing—Brazil
741.0947	NC267-269	Drawing—Russia	741.0982	NC192-194	Drawing—Argentina
741.0948	NC270-284	Drawing—Scandinavia	741.0984	NC195-197	Drawing—Bolivia
741.09481	NC279-281	Drawing—Norway	741.0985	NC216-218	Drawing—Peru
741.09485	NC282-284	Drawing—Sweden	741.09861	NC204-206	Drawing—Colombia
741.09489	NC273-275	Drawing—Denmark	741.09866	NC207-209	Drawing—Ecuador
741.094912	NC276-278	Drawing—Iceland	741.0987	NC222-224	Drawing—Venezuela
741.09494	NC291-293	Drawing—Switzerland	741.09892	NC213-215	Drawing—Paraguay
741.09495	NC252-254	Drawing—Greece	741.09895	NC219-221	Drawing—Uruguay
741.09496	NC297-308	Drawing—Balkan Peninsula	741.0993	NC372-374	Drawing—New Zealand

Dewey	LC	Subject Heading	Dewey	LC	Subject Heading
741.0994	NC369-371	Drawing—Australia	745.0938	NK665-680	Art objects, Classical
741.099(5-6)	NC375-376	Drawing—Oceania	745.09(4-9)	NK801-1094.5	Art objects—[By region or country]
741.2	NC730-758	Drawing—Technique			
741.2	NC845-915	Drawing instruments	745.1	NK	Antiques
741.217	NC1920-1940	Drawing—Copying	745.102872	NK1128	Antiques—Reproduction
741.22	NC850	Charcoal drawing	745.103	NK28	Antiques—Encyclopedias
741.23	NC855-875	Crayon drawing	745.103	NK30	Antiques—Dictionaries
741.23	NC870	Crayons	745.105	NK1-9	Antiques—Periodicals
741.235	NC880	Pastel drawing	745.1071	NK50-440	Antiques—Study and teaching
741.24	NC890-895	Pencil drawing			
741.25	NC900-902	Silverpoint drawing	745.1074	NK512-520	Antiques—Exhibitions
741.26	NC905	Pen drawing	745.1074	NK530-570	Antiques—Private collections
741.26	ND2460	Brush drawing			
741.5	NC1300-1766	Caricatures and cartoons	745.4	NC703	Design
741.505	NC1300	Caricatures and cartoons—Periodicals	745.4	NK1160-1590	Design
			745.4	NK1160-1590	Decoration and ornament
741.5074	NC1310-1312	Caricatures and cartoons—Exhibitions	745.4071	NK1170	Design—Study and teaching
741.58	NC1765-1766	Animated films	745.40882943	NK1676	Decoration and ornament, Buddhist
741.58	PN1997.5	Animated films			
741.59(4-9)	NC1400-1762	Caricatures and cartoons—[By region or country]	745.441	NK1177	Decoration and ornament, Primitive
			745.442	NK1180-1250	Decoration and ornament, Ancient
741.6	NC960-995.8	Illustration of books			
741.6	NC965.85	Picture books	745.442	NK1260-1295	Decoration and ornament, Medieval
741.6	NC997-1003	Commercial art			
741.605	NC997.A1	Commercial art—Periodicals	745.442	NK1285	Decoration and ornament, Romanesque
741.6071	NC1000	Commercial art—Study and teaching	745.442	NK1295	Decoration and ornament, Gothic
741.66	NC1882-1883.3	Sound recordings—Album covers	745.442	NK1652.25	Decoration and ornament, Byzantine
741.672	TT509	Fashion drawing	745.442088297	NK1270-1275	Decoration and ornament, Islamic
741.674	NC1800-1850	Posters			
741.674	NC1849.T68	Travel posters	745.443	NK1330	Decoration and ornament, Renaissance
741.683	NC1870-1879	Postcards			
741.685	NE965-.3	Business cards	745.443	NK1345	Decoration and ornament, Baroque
741.7	NC910-.5	Silhouettes			
742	NC749-750	Perspective	745.443	NK1355	Decoration and ornament, Rococo
742	NC755	Shades and shadows			
743.4	NC765-778	Figure drawing	745.5	TT	Handicraft
743.4	NC775	Drapery in art	745.50288	TT151	Repairing
743.42	NC770	Face	745.503	TT9	Handicraft—Encyclopedias
743.49	NC760-783.8	Anatomy, Artistic	745.505	TT1	Handicraft—Periodicals
743.6	NC780-783.8	Animals in art	745.5074	TT6	Handicraft—Exhibitions
743.828	NC825.E76	Erotic drawing	745.509(4-9)	TT15-127	Handicraft—[By region or country]
743.836	NC790-800	Landscape drawing			
745	N5312-5313	Folk art	745.51	NK9600-9955	Woodwork
745	NK1135-1149.5	Arts and crafts movement	745.51	TT180-203.5	Woodwork
745.0228	NK8470-8475	Miniature objects	745.531	NK6200-6210	Leatherwork
745.0294	NK1133-.26	Art objects—Catalogs	745.531	TT290	Leatherwork
745.075	NK1125-1130	Art objects—Collectors and collecting	745.55	NK8643	Shellcraft
			745.55	TT862	Shellcraft
745.08996073	NK839.3.A35	Afro-American decorative arts	745.56	TT205-273	Metal-work
			745.56	TT267	Brazing
745.0901	NK610-685	Art objects, Ancient	745.572	TT297-.5	Plastics craft

Dewey	LC	Subject Heading	Dewey	LC	Subject Heading
745.58	TT288	Bone carving	746.3	NK2975-3049	Tapestry
745.582	NK3650-.5	Beadwork	746.3	TT850.2	Wall hangings
745.582	TT860	Beadwork	746.4	NK8800-9505.5	Needlework
745.592	TL778	Paper airplanes	746.4	TT700-845	Needlework
745.592	TT174-.5	Toys	746.4	TT740-897	Fancy work
745.5922	TT175.7	Doll clothes—Patterns	746.41	TT877.5	Palm frond weaving
745.59221	NK4891.3-4894.4	Dolls	746.412	GN431	Basket making
			746.412	NK3649.5-.55	Basketwork
745.59221	TT175-.7	Dolls	746.412	TT879.B3	Basket making
745.5923	NK4891.3-4894.4	Dollhouses	746.432	TT819-829	Knitting
			746.434	TT820-829	Crocheting
745.5923	TT175.3	Dollhouses	746.436	TT840.T38	Tatting
745.5923	TT175.5	Doll furniture	746.44	NK9200-9315	Embroidery
745.5928	NK492	Miniature objects	746.44	NK9206.4.H56	Embroidery, Hmong
745.5928	VM298.3	Ship models in bottles	746.44	TT769-778	Embroidery
745.5933	NK3685	Candlesticks	746.44	TT778.C24	Candlewicking (Embroidery)
745.5936	TT199.75	Decoys (Hunting)	746.44	TT840.S66	Smocking
745.594	NK4870	Fans	746.442	TT778.C3	Canvas embroidery
745.5941	TT900.P3	Party decorations	746.442	TT778.C65	Counted thread embroidery
745.5941	TT926	Balloon decorations	746.46	NK9100-9499	Patchwork
745.59416	TT900.E2	Easter decorations	746.46	TT835	Quilting
745.59416	TT900.V34	Valentine decorations	746.46	TT835	Coverlets
745.5942	NK4890.C67	Costume jewelry	746.6	TT853-854.5	Dyes and dyeing
745.5943	TT890-894	Artificial flowers	746.662	TT852.5	Batik
745.5944	TT896.7	Egg decoration	746.70882971	NK2809.I8	Rugs, Islamic
745.61	NK3600-3640	Lettering	746.73	TT850	Rugs, Braided
745.61	NK3600-3640	Calligraphy	746.75095	NK2808-2810	Rugs, Oriental
745.61	TT360	Lettering	746.92092	HD6073.M7	Models (Persons)
745.61	Z43-45	Calligraphy	746.94	NK3175-3296.3	Drapery
745.67	ND2889-3416	Illumination of books and manuscripts	747	NK1700-3505	Interior decoration
			747.074	NK2210-2211	Furniture—Exhibitions
745.67074	ND2893	Illumination of books and manuscripts—Exhibitions	747.09(4-9)	NK2000-2096.3	Interior decoration—[By region or country]
745.670901	ND2910	Illumination of books and manuscripts, Ancient	747.3	NK3375-3496.3	Wallpaper
745.670902	ND2920-2980	Illumination of books and manuscripts, Medieval	747.5	NK2115.5.D73	Drapery in interior decoration
745.6709024	ND2990	Illumination of books and manuscripts—Renaissance	747.5	NK2775-2898	Rugs
			747.5	NK2775-2898	Carpets
745.6709(4-9)	ND3001-3294.5	Illumination of books and manuscripts—[By region or country]	747.5074	NK2790	Rugs—Private collections
			747.75	NK2117.L5	Living room furniture
			747.76	NK2117.D5	Dining room furniture
745.726	NK9900-.7	Lacquer and lacquering	747.76	NK2117.D5	Dining rooms
745.73	TT270-273	Stencil work	747.77	NK2117.B4	Bedrooms
745.74	NK9510	Decalcomania	747.78	NK2117.B33	Bathrooms
745.8	N7436.5-.53	Panoramas	747.86	NK2190-2192	Church decoration and ornament
745.92	SB449-450.87	Flower arrangement			
745.92	SB449.3.D7	Dried flower arrangement	748	NK5100-5440	Glass
745.926	SB449.5.W4	Wedding decorations	748.2	NK5100-5440	Glassware
746	NK8800-9505.5	Textile design	748.50282	NK5300-5430	Glass painting and staining
746	TT699-854.5	Textile crafts	748.50285	NK5430	Mosaics
746.12	TT847	Hand spinning	748.6	NK5200-5205	Cut glass
746.14	TT848-849.2	Hand weaving	748.6	NK5439.E5	Enameled glass
746.22	TT800-810	Lace and lace making	748.62	NE2690	Glass engraving
746.3	NK2910	Wall hangings	748.8	NK5440.S49	Glass shoes

Dewey	LC	Subject Heading	Dewey	LC	Subject Heading
748.8	NK8440-.2	Mirrors	757.0904	ND1309.6	Portrait painting—20th century
748.83	NK4895	Drinking vessels			
748.83	NK5440.D75	Drinking glasses	757.094	ND1313-1324	Portrait painting—Europe
748.83	NK5440.D85	Dwarf ale glasses	757.0941	ND1314-.6	Portrait painting—Great Britain
748.84	NK5440.P3	Paperweights			
749	NK2200-2750	Furniture	757.0943	ND1317-.7	Portrait painting—Germany
749	NK2235	Furniture—Styles	757.0944	ND1316-.6	Portrait painting—France
749.074	NK2220	Furniture—Private collections	757.0945	ND1318-.6	Portrait painting—Italy
			757.0947	ND1320-.6	Portrait painting—Russia
749.09(4-9)	NK2401-2694.5	Furniture—[By region or country]	757.09492	ND1319-.6	Portrait painting—Netherlands
749.3	NK2740	Shelving (Furniture)	757.095	ND1325-1326.8	Portrait painting—Asia
749.3	NK2910	Screens	757.0956	ND1322-.6	Portrait painting—Spain
749.63	NK8360	Chandeliers	757.0973	ND1311-.9	Portrait painting—United States
750	ND	Painting			
750	ND1142-1146	Pictures	757.7	ND1329.8-1337	Portrait miniatures
750.294	ND40-45	Painting—Catalogs	758.1	ND1340-1367	Landscape painting
750.71	ND1115-1120	Painting—Study and teaching	758.109(4-9)	ND1351-1367	Landscape painting—[By region or country]
750.882971	ND146	Painting, Islamic	758.1094	ND1353-1364	Landscape painting—Europe
751.2	ND1510	Pigments			
751.4	ND1505	Brushwork	758.10941	ND1354-.6	Landscape painting—Great Britain
751.422	ND1700-2495	Watercolor painting			
751.422071	ND2110-2115	Watercolor painting—Study and teaching	758.10943	ND1357-.6	Landscape painting—Germany
751.42242	ND2190-2192	Figure painting	758.10944	ND1356-.6	Landscape painting—France
751.42242	ND2200-2202	Portrait painting	758.10945	ND1358-.6	Landscape painting—Italy
751.422435	ND2290-2305	Still-life painting	758.10946	ND1362-.6	Landscape painting—Spain
751.422436	ND2240-2243	Landscape painting	758.1095	ND1365-.96	Landscape painting—Asia
751.422437	ND2270-2272	Marine painting	758.109(71-8)	ND1352	Landscape painting—America
751.426	ND1535	Acrylic painting			
751.46	ND2480	Encaustic painting	758.10973	ND1351-.6	Landscape painting—United States
751.6	ND1630-1662	Painting—Conservation and restoration	758.2	ND1370-1375	Marine painting
751.73	ND2550-2877	Mural painting and decoration	758.3	ND1380-1383	Animals in art
			758.4	ND1390-1400	Still-life painting
751.7309(4-9)	ND2601-2877	Mural painting—[By region or country]	759	ND34-38	Painting—Biography
			759	ND49-813	Painting—History
751.74	ND2880-2881	Panoramas	759	ND1328-1329	Portrait painting—Biography
751.74	ND2880-.5	Diorama	759.01	ND70-130	Painting, Ancient
751.75	ND2885-2888	Scene painting	759.02	ND140-146	Painting, Medieval
751.77	ND1159	Small painting	759.03	ND170-172	Painting, Renaissance
754	ND1450-1452	Genre painting	759.04	ND180-182	Painting, Modern—17th century
757	ND1290-1293	Figure painting			
757	ND1300-1337	Portrait painting	759.04	ND186-188	Painting, Modern—18th century
757.090(24-31)	ND1308	Portrait painting—15th century	759.05	ND190-192	Painting, Modern—19th century
757.09031	ND1308	Portrait painting—16th century	759.06	ND160-196	Painting, Modern
757.09032	ND1309.3	Portrait painting—17th century	759.06	ND195-196	Painting, Modern—20th century
757.09033	ND1309.4	Portrait painting—18th century	759.(1-9)	ND204-1113	Painting—[By region or country]
757.09034	ND1309.5	Portrait painting—19th century	759.11	ND240-249.5	Painting—Canada
			759.13	ND205-238	Painting—United States

Dewey	LC	Subject Heading	Dewey	LC	Subject Heading
759.(2-8)	ND450-955	Painting—Europe	759.968	ND1091.7-1096.6	Painting—Africa, Southern
759.2	ND461-481	Painting—Great Britain	759.972	ND250-259	Painting—Mexico
759.3	ND568-589	Painting—Germany	759.9728	ND260-290	Painting—Central America
759.3	ND591-603.3	Painting—Greece	759.97281	ND276-278	Painting—Guatemala
759.36	ND501-511.6	Painting—Austria	759.97283	ND279-281	Painting—Honduras
759.38	ND999.P6	Painting—Poland	759.97284	ND288-290	Painting—El Salvador
759.39	ND512-522.6	Painting—Hungary	759.97285	ND282-284	Painting—Nicaragua
759.4	ND541-553.3	Painting—France	759.97286	ND273-275	Painting—Costa Rica
759.5	ND611-623.3	Painting—Italy	759.97287	ND285-287	Painting—Panama
759.6	ND801-813.3	Painting—Spain	759.9729	ND291-315	Painting—West Indies
759.69	ND821-833.3	Painting—Portugal	759.97291	ND303-305	Painting—Cuba
759.7	ND681-699	Painting—Russia	759.97292	ND309-311	Painting—Jamaica
759.8	ND701-793.3	Painting—Scandinavia	759.97294	ND306-308	Painting—Haiti
759.81	ND761-773.3	Painting—Norway	759.97295	ND312-314	Painting—Puerto Rico
759.85	ND781-793.3	Painting—Sweden	759.97296	ND300-302	Painting—Bahamas
759.89	ND711-723.3	Painting—Denmark	759.98	ND320-439	Painting—South America
759.897	ND955.F5	Painting—Finland	759.981	ND350-359	Painting—Brazil
759.95	ND960-1070.3	Painting—Asia	759.982	ND330-339	Painting—Argentina
759.951	ND1040-1049.6	Painting—China	759.983	ND360-369	Painting—Chile
759.9519	ND1060-1070.3	Painting—Korea	759.984	ND340-349	Painting—Bolivia
759.9519	ND1060-1070.3	Painting, Korean	759.985	ND410-419	Painting—Peru
759.952	ND1050-1059.6	Painting—Japan	759.9861	ND370-379	Painting—Colombia
759.952	ND1050-1059.6	Painting, Japanese	759.9866	ND380-389	Painting—Ecuador
759.9538	ND970-972	Painting—Saudi Arabia	759.987	ND430-439	Painting—Venezuela
759.954	ND1001-1010.3	Painting—India	759.9881	ND395	Painting—Guyana
759.95491	ND1010.7-.73	Painting—Pakistan	759.9882	ND397	Painting—French Guiana
759.95493	ND1010.6-.63	Painting—Sri Lanka	759.9883	ND396	Painting—Surinam
759.955	ND980-989	Painting—Iran	759.9892	ND400-409	Painting—Paraguay
759.9561	ND861-873.3	Painting—Turkey	759.9895	ND420-429	Painting—Uruguay
759.9567	ND967-969	Painting, Iraqi	759.993	ND1106-1108	Painting—New Zealand
759.95691	ND989.6-.8	Painting—Syria	759.994	ND1100-1105.3	Painting—Australia
759.95692	ND976.6-.8	Painting—Lebanon	759.99(5-6)	ND1110-1113	Painting—Oceania
759.95694	ND977-979	Painting—Israel	760	NC915.R8	Rubbing
759.95695	ND979-.8	Painting—Jordan	760	NE	Engraving
759.957	ND992.4-999	Painting—Asiatic Russia	760	NE2800-2890	Engraving—Printing
759.9581	ND992-.3	Painting—Afghanistan	760.04	NE886	Engraving—Themes, motives
759.9591	ND1012-.3	Painting—Burma	760.074	NE1410-1412	Engraving—Exhibitions
759.9593	ND1021-1023	Painting—Thailand	760.09023	NE1638	Engraving—14th century
759.9594	ND1016-.3	Painting—Laos	760.09024	NE1655-1656	Engraving—15th century
759.9595	ND1025-.8	Painting—Malaysia	760.09031	NE1665-1666	Engraving—16th century
759.9596	ND1015-.3	Painting—Cambodia	760.09032	NE1670-1690	Engraving—17th century
759.9597	ND1014-.63	Painting—Vietnam	760.09033	NE1710-1719	Engraving—18th century
759.9598	ND1026-.8	Painting—Indonesia	760.09034	NE1720.5-1739	Engraving—19th century
759.9599	ND1027-1029	Painting—Philippines	760.0904	NE1740-1749	Engraving—20th century
759.96	ND1080-1099	Painting—Africa	760.278	NE820	Engravers' marks
759.9611	ND1091-.3	Painting—Tunisia	760.28	NE830-835	Prints—Technique
759.9612	ND1089-.3	Painting—Libya	761.2	NE1000-1325	Wood-engraving
759.962	ND1081-1085.3	Painting—Egypt	761.205	NE1000	Wood-engraving—Periodicals
759.963	ND1086-.3	Painting—Ethiopia	761.2074	NE1010-1012	Wood-engraving—Exhibitions
759.964	ND1090-.3	Painting—Morocco	761.209	NE1030-1196.3	Wood-engraving—History
759.965	ND1088-.3	Painting—Algeria			
759.966	ND1098-1099	Painting—Africa, West			
759.9676	ND1097-.6	Painting—Africa, East			

201

Dewey	LC	Subject Heading	Dewey	LC	Subject Heading
761.209024	NE1050-1075	Wood-engraving—15th century	769.56	HE6184.F57	First day covers (Philately)
761.209031	NE1050-1075	Wood-engraving—16th century	769.56	HE6187-6230	Stamp collecting
			769.56075	HE6221	Postage-stamp albums
761.209032	NE1050-1075	Wood-engraving—17th century	769.9	NE400-773	Prints—History
			769.92	NE800	Engravers
761.209033	NE1085-1088	Wood-engraving—18th century	769.9(4-9)	NE501-794.5	Prints—[By region or country]
761.209034	NE1090-1093	Wood-engraving—19th century	770	N72.P5	Art and photography
			770	TR	Photography
761.20904	NE1095-1097	Wood-engraving—20th century	770	TR183	Photography, Artistic
			770	TR269	Instant photography
761.209(4-9)	NE1101-1196.3	Wood-engraving—[By region or country]	770	TR640-688	Photography, Artistic
			770.21	TR151	Photography—Tables
763	NE2250-2529	Lithography	770.288	TR465	Photographs—Conservation and restoration
763.0294	NE2280	Lithography—Catalogs			
763.074	NE2272-2275	Lithography—Exhibitions	770.3	TR9	Photography—Encyclopedias
763.09	NE2295-2396.3	Lithography—History			
763.09034	NE2297	Lithography—19th century	770.5	TR1	Photography—Periodicals
763.0904	NE2298	Lithography—20th century	770.6	TR5	Photography—Congresses
763.092	NE2410	Lithographers	770.71	TR161	Photography—Study and teaching
763.09(4-9)	NE2301-2396.3	Lithography—[By region or country]	770.74	TR6	Photography—Exhibitions
			770.9	TR15	Photography—History
764.2	NE2500-2529	Chromolithography	770.92	TR139-140	Photography—Biography
764.8	NE1843-1844	Serigraphy	770.92	TR139	Photographers
765	NE2700-2710	Engraving (Metal-work)	770.9(4-9)	TR21-127	Photography—[By region or country]
766.2	NE1815-1816.5	Mezzotint engraving			
766.3	NE2230	Aquatint	770.94	TR55-95	Photography—Europe
767.2	NE1940-2232.5	Etching	770.941	TR57-64	Photography—Great Britain
767.20294	NE1960	Etching—Catalogs	770.9415	TR59-60	Photography—Ireland
767.2074	NE1950-1955	Etching—Exhibitions	770.943	TR73-74.5	Photography—Germany
767.209	NE1980-2055.5	Etching—History	770.9436	TR65-.2	Photography—Austria
767.209033	NE1990-1992	Etching—18th century	770.944	TR71-72.5	Photography—France
767.209034	NE1994-1995	Etching—19th century	770.945	TR79-80	Photography—Italy
767.20904	NE1997-1998	Etching—20th century	770.946	TR87-88	Photography—Spain
767.2092	NE2110	Etchers	770.947	TR85-86	Photography—Russia
767.209(4-9)	NE2001-2096.3	Etching—[By region or country]	770.9481	TR81-82	Photography—Norway
			770.9485	TR89-90	Photography—Sweden
767.3	NE2220-2225	Dry-point	770.9492	TR77-78	Photography—Netherlands
769	NE	Prints	770.9494	TR91-92	Photography—Switzerland
769	NE1850-1879	Color prints	770.9495	TR75-76	Photography—Greece
769.0288	NE380	Prints—Conservation and restoration	770.95	TR99-113	Photography—Asia
			770.951	TR101-102	Photography—China
769.0294	NE63-75	Prints—Catalogs	770.952	TR105-106	Photography—Japan
769.03	NE20	Prints—Encyclopedias	770.954	TR103-104	Photography—India
769.05	NE1	Prints—Periodicals	770.955	TR107-108	Photography—Iran
769.08996073	NE539.3.A35	Afro-American prints	770.9561	TR111-112	Photography—Turkey
769.12	NE57-59	Prints—Private collections	770.957	TR109-110	Photography—Asiatic Russia
769.12	NE880-885	Prints—Collectors and collecting	770.96	TR115-119	Photography—Africa
			770.962	TR117-118	Photography—Egypt
769.437	NE957-.3	Naval prints	770.971	TR26-27	Photography—Canada
769.49796	NE960-.3	Sporting prints	770.972	TR28-29	Photography—Mexico
769.56	HE6184.D4	Essays and proofs (Philately)	770.9728	TR30-31	Photography—Central America
769.56	HE6184.D56	Disinfection markings (Philately)			

Dewey	LC	Subject Heading	Dewey	LC	Subject Heading
770.9729	TR32-33	Photography—West Indies	778.5345	TR858	Cinematography—Special effects
770.973	TR22-25	Photography—United States	778.5347	TR897.5-.75	Animation (Cinematography)
770.981	TR41-42	Photography—Brazil	778.535	TR899-.5	Motion pictures—Editing
770.982	TR36-37	Photography—Argentina	778.53859	TR893.5	Wildlife cinematography
770.983	TR43-44	Photography—Chile	778.6	TR510-545	Color photography
770.984	TR38-39	Photography—Bolivia	778.71	TR659.5	Outdoor photography
770.985	TR52	Photography—Peru	778.719	TR610	Night photography
770.9861	TR45-46	Photography—Colombia	778.72	TR590-620	Photography—Lighting
770.9866	TR47	Photography—Ecuador	778.72	TR600	Photography—Artificial light
770.987	TR54	Photography—Venezuela	778.73	TR800	Underwater photography
770.9892	TR51	Photography—Paraguay	778.8	TR148	Trick photography
770.9895	TR53	Photography—Uruguay	778.92	TR575-581	Portrait photography
770.993	TR122.5-.6	Photography—New Zealand	778.92	TR680-681	Portrait photography
770.994	TR121-122	Photography—Australia	778.93	TR721-733	Nature photography
770.99(5-6)	TR123-124	Photography—Oceania	778.932	TR729.W54	Wildlife photography
771	TR196-199	Photography—Equipment and supplies	778.935	TR656.5	Still-life photography
771	TR268	Photography, Pinhole	778.936	TR660-.5	Landscape photography
771.1	TR550-581	Photography—Studios and dark rooms	778.937	TR670-.5	Marine photography
			778.94	TR659	Architectural photography
771.3	TR250-265	Cameras	779.074	N4000-4042	Photograph collections
771.32	TR262	35mm cameras	780	M	Music
771.33	TR256	Digital cameras	780	ML48-49	Librettos
771.352	TR270-271	Photographic lenses	780	ML93-98	Music—Manuscripts
771.43	TR290-312	Photography—Negatives	780.0365	ML3920	Music in prisons
771.44	TR340	Photographs—Trimming, mounting, etc.	780.0398	ML3849	Music and mythology
771.44	TR475	Photography—Enlarging	780.1	ML3800-3920	Music—Philosophy and aesthetics
771.44	TR905	Photography—Enlarging	780.12	ML105-107	Music—Bio-bibliography
771.47	TR225	Photography—Wastes, Recovery of	780.14	ML108	Music—Terminology
			780.14	MT35	Musical dictation
771.49	TR295	Photography—Developing and developers	780.1407	MT35	Musical shorthand
			780.148	MT35	Musical notation
771.5	TR210-212	Photographic chemistry	780.262	ML93-98	Musicians—Autographs
771.5	TR212	Photographic chemicals	780.26609	ML1055	Phonograph
771.5322	TR281	Photography—Plates	780.3	ML100-110	Music—Dictionaries
771.5324	TR283	Photography—Films	780.6	ML25-28	Music—Societies, etc.
772.12	TR365	Daguerreotype	780.7	MT	Music—Instruction and study
772.16	TR400	Kallitype			
772.774	TR287-500	Photography—Processing	780.72	ML	Musicology
772.774	TR330-333	Photography—Printing processes	780.76	MT9	Music—Examinations, questions, etc.
774.0153	QC449-.3	Holography	780.7809	ML457	Music—Performance
775	TR267	Digital photography	780.79	ML35-38	Music festivals
776	N7433.8	Computer art	780.87107	MT38	Blind, Music for the
778.2	TR504-508	Slides (Photography)	780.89	ML3797.7-3799	Ethnomusicology
778.34	TR755	Infrared photography	780.9	ML159-3799	Music—History and criticism
778.35	TR713	Space photography			
778.35	TR810	Aerial photography	780.9	ML3800	Music, Origin of
778.36	TR661	Photography, Panoramic	780.9034	ML196	Romanticism in music
778.37	TR593	Photography, High-speed	780.92	ML385-403	Musicians
778.53	TR845-899.5	Cinematography	780.92	ML385-429	Music—Bio-bibliography
778.53	TR855	Wide-screen processes (Cinematography)	781	MT6-7	Music—Theory
			781.11	ML3830-3838	Music—Psychology

Dewey	LC	Subject Heading	Dewey	LC	Subject Heading
781.17	MT90-145	Music appreciation	782	M1495-5000	Vocal music
781.2207	MT42	Tempo (Music)	782.001	MT825-850	Singing—Methods
781.22(4 or 6)	ML3850	Musical Meter and rhythm	782.001	MT882	Singing—Methods
781.232	ML3807-3809	Musical pitch	782.009	ML1400-3275	Vocal music—History and criticism
781.24	ML3834	Melody			
781.24	ML3851	Melody	782.042307	MT870	Sight-singing
781.2407	MT47	Melody	782.0438	M1528-1529.5	Vocal ensembles
781.246	ML3809	Musical intervals and scales	782.1	M1500-1527.8	Dramatic music
781.247	MT80	Embellishment (Music)	782.1	M1500-1508	Operas
781.247	MT80	Embellishment (Vocal music)	782.1	ML3858	Opera
			782.109	ML1699-2100	Dramatic music
781.25	ML3815	Harmony	782.1209	ML1900	Operetta
781.25	ML3836	Harmony	782.14	M1500-1508	Musicals
781.25	ML3852	Harmony	782.14	M1500-1508	Revues
781.3	M1470	Chance compositions	782.1409	ML1700-1751	Musicals—History and criticism
781.307	MT40-67	Composition (Music)			
781.309	ML430-455	Composition (Music)	782.2209	ML2900-3275	Sacred vocal music
781.42307	MT236	Sight-reading (Music)	782.221438	M2018-2019.5	Sacred vocal ensembles
781.424	MT35	Ear training	782.23	M2000-2007	Oratorios
781.426	MT82	Music—Memorizing	782.24	M2020-2036	Cantatas, Sacred
781.4409	ML457	Performance practice (Music)	782.253	M1670-1671	Spirituals (Songs)
			782.254	M2198-2199	Gospel music
781.4507	MT85	Conducting	782.265	M2038-2099	Anthems
781.4707	MT68	Songs—Accompaniment	782.27	M2115-2145	Hymns
781.4707	MT68	Musical accompaniment	782.3	M1999-2199	Sacred vocal music
781.542	M176	Silent film music	782.3209	ML3001	Music in churches
781.54207	MT737	Silent films—Musical accompaniment	782.32215009	ML3060	Church music—Catholic Church (Byzantine rite)
781.544	M176.5	Radio music	782.3222009	ML3002-3051	Church music—Catholic Church
781.552	ML3857-3862	Dramatic music			
781.55409	ML3400-3451	Dance music—History and criticism	782.3223009	ML3166	Church music—Episcopal Church
781.55609	ML3460	Ballet	782.3223009	ML3166	Church music—Church of England
781.56	ML3855	Program music			
781.5609	ML3300-3354	Program music	782.3224009	ML3100-3188	Church music—Protestant churches
781.592	M1977.P75	Protest songs			
781.599	M1270	Military music	782.3238	M2010-2014	Requiems
781.599	M1627-1853	National music	782.42	M1977.C5	Songbooks
781.599	UH40-45	Music in the army	782.42083	GV1215	Children's songs
781.599	UH40-45	Military calls	782.42083	M1990-1998	Children's songs
781.599	UH40-45	Trumpet-calls	782.4209	ML2500-2862	Songs—History and criticism
781.599	VG30-35	Military music			
781.59909	ML3545	National music—History and criticism	782.421595	M1977.S2	Sea songs
			782.421599	VG33	United States. Navy—Songs and music
781.63	M1627-1844	Popular music			
781.6309	ML3469-3541	Popular music	782.42162	M1627	Folk songs
781.645	M1366	Ragtime music	782.43	M1627	Ballads
781.65	M1366	Jazz	782.43	PR1195.M2	Madrigals
781.653	M1366	Dixieland music	782.47	M1621.4	Song cycles
781.71009	ML3000-3190	Church music	782.48	M1530-1546.5	Cantatas, Secular
781.71017	ML3869	Church music	782.5	M1547-1610	Choruses, Secular
781.76	M2099.5	Synagogue music	782.5	M1609	Cantatas, Secular (Unison)
781.76	M2114.3	Synagogue music	782.507	MT88	Choirs (Music)
781.76	M2186-2187	Synagogue music	782.507	MT875	Choral singing
781.825	ML3845	Variation (Music)	782.509	ML1500-1554	Choral music

Dewey	LC	Subject Heading	Dewey	LC	Subject Heading
782.98	MT949.5	Whistling	784.19481	ML515	Musical instruments—Norway
783.1	M1578-1600	Part-songs			
783.14	M1580.4	Barbershop quartets	784.19485	ML516	Musical instruments—Sweden
783.14	M1594	Barbershop quartets			
783.14	M1604	Barbershop quartets	784.19489	ML514	Musical instruments—Denmark
783.14	M3516	Barbershop singing			
784	M5-1459	Instrumental music	784.19492	ML505	Musical instruments—Netherlands
784	M1200-1268	Band music			
784.09	ML1300-1354	Bands (Music)	784.19493	ML496	Musical instruments—Belgium
784.117	MT125	Band music—Analysis, appreciation	784.19494	ML520	Musical instruments—Switzerland
784.16309	ML3469-3541	Popular instrumental music	784.195	ML525-541	Musical instruments—Asia
784.16409	ML3541	Western swing (Music)	784.195	ML531	Musical instruments—China
784.164209	ML3519-3520	Bluegrass music	784.19519	ML537	Musical instruments—Korea
784.164209	ML3523-3524	Country music			
784.164309	ML3521	Blues (Music)	784.1952	ML535	Musical instruments—Japan
784.165309	ML3505.8-3509	Dixieland music			
784.16609	ML3533.8-3534	Rock music	784.19538	ML527	Musical instruments—Saudi Arabia
784.16609	ML3535	Rockabilly music			
784.18307	MT62	Sonata	784.1954	ML533	Musical instruments—India
784.184	M1001	Symphonies	784.1955	ML539	Musical instruments—Iran
784.185	ML1158	Suite (Music)	784.196	ML544	Musical instruments—Africa
784.185	ML1258	Suite (Music)	784.1971	ML478	Musical instruments—Canada
784.18926	M1004	Overtures			
784.1897	M1247	Marches (Band)	784.1972	ML482	Musical instruments—Mexico
784.1897	M1260	Marches (Band)			
784.1901	ML162-169	Musical instruments, Ancient	784.19728	ML484	Musical instruments—Central America
784.190294	ML155	Musical instruments—Catalogs, Manufacturers'	784.19729	ML480	Musical instruments—West Indies
784.1907	MT170-805	Musical instruments	784.1973	ML476	Musical instruments—United States
784.1909	ML459-1093	Musical instruments			
784.1928	ML3809	Musical temperament	784.198	ML486	Musical instruments—South America
784.19(4-9)	ML475-1354	Musical instruments—[By region or country]	784.1993	ML547	Musical instruments—New Zealand
784.194	ML489-522	Musical instruments—Europe	784.1994	ML547	Musical instruments—Australia
784.1941	ML501	Musical instruments—Great Britain	784.199(5-6)	ML547	Musical instruments—Oceania
784.1943	ML499-500	Musical instruments—Germany	784.2	M1000-1075	Orchestral music
			784.209	ML1200-1251	Orchestra
784.19436	ML491	Musical instruments—Austria	784.2117	MT125	Orchestral music—Analysis, appreciation
784.19437	ML493	Musical instruments—Czechoslovakia	784.4	M450-454	String quartets
784.19439	ML494	Musical instruments—Hungary	784.4	M1350	Salon-orchestra music
			784.48	M1356	Dance-orchestra music
784.1944	ML497	Musical instruments—France	784.48	M1366	Big band music
784.1945	ML503	Musical instruments—Italy	784.4809	ML3518	Dance-orchestra music
784.1946	ML518	Musical instruments—Spain	784.7	M1100-1160	String-orchestra music
784.19469	ML519	Musical instruments—Portugal	784.8307	MT733.4	Marching bands
			784.9	M1200-1269	Brass band music
784.1948	ML513-516	Musical instruments—Scandinavia	785	M175.5	Solo instrument music
			785	M177-990	Chamber music

Dewey	LC	Subject Heading	Dewey	LC	Subject Heading
785.009	ML1100-1165	Chamber music—History and criticism	786.848	M172	Chime music
			786.873	M146	Cymbal music
785.12	M177-298.5	Duets	786.873	M175.C35	Castanet music
785.13	M300-386	Trios	786.8842	M175.T	Triangle music
785.13	M349-353	String trios	786.8848	CC200-255	Bells
785.14	M400-486	Quartets	786.88485	M147	Handbell music
785.143807	MT728	Ensemble playing	786.8848507	MT710	Handbell ringing
785.15	M500-586	Quintets	786.88709	ML1087	Jew's harp
785.16	M600-686	Sextets	786.909	ML1035	Drum
785.17	M700-786	Septets	786.93	M146	Tabla music
785.18	M800-886	Octets	786.93	M146	Timpani music
785.19	M900-986	Nonets	786.94	M146	Snare drum music
785.43	M955-959	Wind ensembles	786.9409	ML1038.S	Snare drum
785.8	M955-959	Woodwind ensembles	786.95	M175.T	Tambourine music
785.9	M955-959	Brass ensembles	787	M59.5	String instrument music
786.07	MT180-258	Keyboard instruments	787.07	MT259-338	Stringed instruments
786.14707	MT190	Musical accompaniment	787.09	ML750-927	Stringed instruments
786.2	M20-39	Piano music	787.2	M40-44	Violin music
786.207	MT220-255	Piano—Instruction and study	787.209	ML800-897	Violin
			787.3	M45-49	Viola music
786.209	ML649.8-747	Piano	787.4	M50-54	Violoncello music
786.214707	MT239	Musical accompaniment	787.5	M55-58	Double-bass music
786.3	M20-39	Clavichord music	787.5107	MT320-334	Double bass
786.309	ML649.8-747	Clavichord	787.6	M59	Hardanger fiddle music
786.4	M20-39	Harpsichord music	787.6	M59	Baryton music
786.4	M20-32	Electronic harpsichord music	787.6	M59	Viol music
			787.66	M59.V	Violetta d'amore music
786.5	M6-14	Organ music	787.69	M175.H9	Hurdy-gurdy music
786.507	MT180	Organ—Instruction and study	787.7	M135-137	Zither music
			787.707	MT620-634	Zither—Instruction and study
786.509	ML550-649	Organ			
786.509	ML597	Hammond organ	787.74	M142.D8	Dulcimer music
786.55	M15-17	Reed-organ music	787.7409	ML1015-1018	Dulcimer
786.5507	MT208	Reed-organ—Methods—Self-instruction	787.75	M142.A7	Appalachian dulcimer music
			787.75	M175.A8	Autoharp music
786.5509	ML597	Reed-organ	787.82	M142.S5	Sitar music
786.59	M14.8	Electronic organ music	787.83	M140-141	Lute music
786.607	MT700	Musical instruments (Mechanical)	787.84	M130-134	Mandolin music
			787.87	M125-129	Guitar music
786.64	M172	Carillon music	787.87	M125-129	Bass guitar music
786.6509	ML1065-1066	Music box	787.87	M142.E4	Electric guitar music
786.66	M20-32	Player-piano music	787.8707	MT580-588	Guitar
786.6609	ML1058	Mechanical organs	787.875	M142.B2	Balalaika music
786.707	MT724	Musical instruments, Electronic	787.88	M120-122	Banjo Music
			787.8807	MT560-570	Banjo
786.74	M1473	Synthesizer music	787.89	M142.U5	Ukulele music
786.7409	ML1092	Electronic keyboard (Synthesizer)	787.9	M115-119	Harp music
			787.95	M142.C44	Celtic harp music
786.8	M146	Percussion music	788	M111	Wind instrument music
786.809	ML1030-1040	Percussion instruments	788.09	ML929-990	Wind instruments
786.83	M175.C44	Celesta music	788.3	M60-64	Flute music
786.843	M147	Glockenspiel music	788.307	MT340-348	Flute
786.843	M175.X6	Vibraphone music	788.33	M60-62	Fife music
786.843	M175.X6	Marimba music	788.33	M110.P5	Piccolo music
786.843	M175.X6	Xylophone music			

Dewey	LC	Subject Heading	Dewey	LC	Subject Heading
788.3307	MT356	Fife	790.134	GV1191-.75	Tournaments
788.3309	ML935-937	Piccolo	790.138	GV1493	Literary recreations
788.36	M110.R4	Recorder music	790.191	GV182.8	Family recreation
788.3609	ML1055	Music recorder	790.1926	GV184	Aged—Recreation
788.49	M145	Bagpipe music	790.2	PN1560-1590	Performing arts
788.4909	ML980	Gaita	790.209	PN1581	Performing arts—History
788.52	M65-69	Oboe music	791.068	GV1851-186	Amusement parks
788.5207	MT360-378	Oboe	791.1	GV1834.7-1835.56	Carnivals
788.53	M110.E5	English-horn music	791.1	GV1835	Carnivals
788.58	M75-79	Bassoon music	791.12	M1365	Minstrel music
788.5807	ML953	Bassoon	791.3	GV1800-1831	Circus
788.62	M70-74	Clarinet music	791.3	GV1838	Amateur circus
788.6207	MT380-388	Clarinet	791.32	GV1829-1831	Animal training
788.65	M70-74	Bass clarinet music	791.33	GV1811	Clowns
788.7	M105-109	Saxophone music	791.4092	PN1995.9.E77	Entertainers in motion pictures
788.82	M175.M8	Harmonica music			
788.8209	ML1088	Harmonica	791.43	PN1993-1999	Motion pictures
788.84	M154	Concertina music	791.43	PN1995.9.F67	Foreign films
788.84	M175.B2	Bandonion music	791.4302	TR886.7	Dubbing of motion pictures
788.86	M175.A4	Accordion music	791.43028092	PN1995.9.S7	Stunt performers
788.8609	ML1083	Accordion	791.4308996	PN1995.9.N4	Blacks in motion pictures
788.863	M175.M38	Melodeon music	+ 073		
788.9	M111	Brass instrument music	791.43655	PN1995.9.D78	Drugs in motion pictures
788.907	MT418	Brass instruments	791.43657	PN1995.9.M86	Musical films
788.92	M85-89	Trumpet music	791.43682	PN1995.5	Motion pictures—Religious aspects
788.92	M110	Alpenhorn music			
788.92	M1270	Trumpet-calls	791.437	PN1996-1997	Motion picture plays
788.93	M90-94	Trombone music	791.4375	PN1995	Motion pictures—Reviews
788.974	M90-94	Alto trombone music	791.44	PN1991-.9	Radio broadcasting
788.96	M85-89	Cornet music	791.446	PN1991.8.S4	Soap operas
788.9707	MT493	Flugelhorn	791.44617	PN1991.8.C65	Radio comedies
788.974	M110	Alto horn music	791.45	PN1992.95	Video recordings
788.975	M90-94	Baritone music	791.45028092	PN1992.4	Television actors and actresses
788.975	M110.B33	Euphonium music			
788.97509	ML99L0.E	Euphonium	791.456	PN1992.8.S4	Soap operas
788.98	M95-99	Tuba music	791.45617	PN1992.8.C66	Television comedies
790	GV	Recreation	791.53	PN1970-1979	Puppets
790	GV	Leisure	791.53	PN1979.S5	Shadow shows
790.01	B105.P54	Play (Philosophy)	791.62	PN3202-3299	Pageants
790.068	GV182-.5	Recreation centers	791.64	LB3635	Cheerleading
790.068	HN41-46	Community centers	791.82	GV1107-1108.6	Bullfights
790.068(4-9)	HN43-46	Community centers—[By region or country]	791.84	GV1834	Rodeos
			791.84	GV1834.45.B35	Barrel racing
790.06873	HN43-45	Community centers—United States	792	PN2000-3299	Theater
			792.022	PN2219.08	Theater, Open-air
790.092	GV14.5	Recreation leadership	792.0222	PN3151-3171	Amateur theater
790.1	GV1-200	Leisure	792.0222	PN6119.9	Amateur plays
790.1	GV1199-1570	Games	792.02230973	PN2267	Little theater movement
790.102022	GV1201.42	Games—Rules	792.023	PN2055	Acting—Vocational guidance
790.13	GV1201	Hobbies			
790.133	GV1219	Dolls	792.025	PN2091.S8	Theaters—Stage-setting and scenery
790.133	GV1220	Dollhouses			
790.133	GV1220.7	Teddy bears	792.028	PN2061-2071	Acting
790.1330901	GN799.T75	Toys	792.028	PN2071.I5	Improvisation (Acting)
			792.028	PN2091.A	Theaters—Accidents

Dewey	LC	Subject Heading	Dewey	LC	Subject Heading
792.028092	PN2205-2217	Actors	793.38	GV1746-1750	Balls (Parties)
792.028092	PN2205-2217	Actresses	793.38	GV1757	Balls (Parties)
792.08996073	PN2270.A35	Afro-American theater	793.38	GV1747	Court dances
792.09	PN2100-2193	Theater—History	793.73	GV1491-1507	Puzzles
792.0901	PN2131-2145	Theater—History—To 500	793.73	PN6366-6377	Acrostics
792.0902	PN2152-2160	Theater—History—Medieval, 500-1500	793.732	GV1507.C7	Crossword puzzles
			793.734	GV1507.A5	Anagrams
792.09033	PN2171-2179	Theater—History—18th century	793.8	GV1541-1561	Conjuring
			793.8	GV1541-1561	Tricks
792.09034	PN2181-2193	Theater—History—20th century	793.8	GV1559	Coin tricks
			793.8092	GV1545	Magicians
792.09495	PN2660-2668	Theater—Greece	793.85	GV1549	Card tricks
792.0951	PN2870-2878	Theater—China	793.89	GV1557	Ventriloquism
792.0952	PN2920-2928	Theater—Japan	794	GV1312-1469	Board games
792.0952	PN2924.5.K3	Kabuki	794.1	GV1313-1457	Chess
792.0973	PN2220-2298	Theater—United States	794.172	GV1449.3	Computer chess
792.16	PN3203-3299	Passion-plays	794.2	GV1461-1463	Checkers
792.3	PN2071.G4	Mime	794.3	GV1564-1565	Darts (Game)
792.3	PN6120.P3-.P4	Pantomines	794.6	GV901-909	Bowling
792.319969	GV1796.H8	Hula (Dance)	794.6	GV907	Bowling alleys
792.7	PN1960-1969	Music-halls (Variety-theaters, cabarets, etc.)	794.6	GV910.5.D8	Duckpin bowling
			794.72	GV891	Billiards
792.7	PN1960-1969	Vaudeville	794.733	GV891-899	Pool (Game)
792.7	PN6231.B84	Burlesques	794.8	GV1469.15-.25	Computer games
792.78	GV1794	Tap dancing	794.8	GV1469.2	Electronic games
792.8	GV1580-1799.4	Dance	794.8	GV1469.3	Video games
792.8	GV1783	Modern dance	795	GV1301-1311	Gambling
792.8026	GV1789.2	Ballet—Costume	795	GV1302	Gambling systems
792.8028	GV1789.2	Ballet slippers	795.1	GV1303	Dice
792.809	GV1600	Dance criticism	795.1	GV1303	Dice games
792.8092	GV1785	Dance—Biography	795.23	GV1309	Roulette
792.84	GV1787	Ballet	795.3	GV1311.B5	Bingo
792.84	GV1788	Ballet dancing	795.32	GV1467	Dominoes
793	GV1221-1229	Indoor games	795.34	GV1299.M3	Mah jong
793.083	GV1799	Dance for children	795.4	GV1232-1299	Card games
793.0846	GV1799.3	Dance for the aged	795.412	GV1251-1255	Poker
793.087	GV1799.2	Dance for the handicapped	795.413	GV1283	Duplicate whist
793.2	GV1470-1521	Entertaining	795.414	GV1282	Auction bridge
793.21	GV1205	Children's parties	795.415	GV1281	Bridge whist
793.24	PN6366-6377	Charades	795.415	GV1282.8.D86	Duplicate contract bridge
793.3	GV1763	Country-dance	795.416	GV1295.P6	Double pinochle
793.3	GV1796.B74	Break dancing	795.418	GV1295.R8	Rummy (Game)
793.3	GV1796.C68	Country swing (Dance)	796	GV1018	Racing
793.3	GV1796.M5	Minuet	796	GV561-1198.995	Sports
793.31	GV1580-1799	Folk dancing	796	GV561-749.5	Athletics
793.31	GV1796.P55	Polka (Dance)	796.0284	GV743-749	Sporting goods
793.33	GV1751	Ballroom dancing	796.0284	GV743-749	Athletics—Equipment and supplies
793.33	GV1761	Waltz			
793.33	GV1796.C2	Cha-cha (Dance)	796.0284	GV749.M6	Mouth protectors
793.33	GV1796.C4	Charleston (Dance)	796.042	GV346	School sports
793.33	GV1796.D57	Disco dancing	796.042	GV710	Intramural sports
793.33	GV1796.J6	Jitterbug (Dance)	796.043	GV346-350	College sports
793.33	GV1796.L5	Lindy (Dance)	796.043	GV350.5	College athletes—Recruiting
793.35	GV1796.S9	Sword-dance			

Dewey	LC	Subject Heading	Dewey	LC	Subject Heading
796.06	GV713	Sports administration	796.3578	GV881	Slow pitch softball
796.068	GV401-433	Sports facilities	796.3578	GV881-.4	Softball
796.068	GV403-405	Gymnasiums	796.3578	GV881.5	T-ball
796.068	GV411-416	Athletic fields	796.358	GV911-929.3	Cricket
796.068	GV415-416	Stadiums	796.42	GV1060.5-1098	Track-athletics
796.068	GV421-433	Playgrounds	796.42	GV1061-1069	Running
796.068	GV563	Athletic clubs	796.425	GV749.5	Endurance sports
796.0680284	GV426-.5	Playgrounds—Equipment and supplies	796.4252	GV1065-.23	Marathon running
796.0681	GV716	Sports—Economic aspects	796.428	GV1063	Cross-country running
796.07	GV201-555	Physical education and training	796.432	GV1077	Broad jump
			796.434	GV1079-1080	Vaulting
796.077	GV711	Coaching (Athletics)	796.44	GV461-475	Gymnastics
796.087	GV709.3	Sports for the handicapped	796.44	GV512	Balance beam
796.092	GV697	Athletes	796.47	GV551-553	Acrobatics
796.154	GV761.5	Model airplane racing	796.48	GV721.8	Olympics—Records
796.156	GV1570	Model car racing	796.5	GV191.2-200.56	Outdoor life
796.2	GV1099	Shuffleboard	796.5	GV200.5-.56	Wilderness survival
796.2	GV1213	Marbles (Game)	796.51	GV199-.5	Hiking
796.21	GV858.2-859.7	Roller-skating	796.51	GV199.6	Backpacking
796.3	GV861	Ball games	796.51	GV1071	Walking (Sports)
796.30284	GV749.B34	Balls (Sporting goods)	796.52	GV200.3	Snow and ice climbing
796.323	GV885	Basketball	796.522	GV199.8-200.3	Mountaineering
796.323092	GV884	Basketball players	796.522	GV200.19.R34	Rappelling
796.325	GV1015-.57	Volleyball	796.5223	GV200.2	Rock climbing
796.325	GV1015.5.B43	Beach volleyball	796.525	GB601.52.M34	Cave mapping
796.33	GV948	Canadian football	796.525	GV200.6-.66	Caving
796.332	GV937-960	Football	796.53	GV454.B3	Beaches
796.33202022	GV955	Football—Rules	796.54	GV191.68-198.9	Camping
796.332083	GV959.55.C45	Football for children	796.54	GV192-198	Camps
796.332092	GV939	Football players	796.54	GV198.9	Snow camping
796.3322	GV951.18	Football—Defense	796.54	GV198.95	Swamp camping
796.3322	GV951.25	End play (Football)	796.54	GV198.L3	Camp sites, facilities, etc.
796.3322	GV951.8	Football—Offense	796.54	GV199.7	Packhorse camping
796.333	GV945	Rugby football	796.542087	GV197.H3	Camps for the handicapped
796.334	GV943-944	Soccer	796.5422	BV1650	Church camps
796.3343	GV942.7	Soccer referees	796.5423	GV197.D3	Day camps
796.33464	GV943.45-.54	Soccer—Tournaments	796.56	GV198.945-.975	Dude ranches
796.33466	GV943.5	Europa Cup (Soccer)	796.58	GV200.4	Orienteering
796.34	GV1003.2	Paddleball	796.6	GV1029.7	Soap box derbies
796.342	GV990-1005	Tennis	796.6	GV1040-1059	Cycling
796.342	GV1003	Court tennis	796.62	GV1049	Bicycle racing
796.346	GV1005	Table tennis	796.6(2-4)	GV1040-1058	Bicycles
796.346	GV1006	Paddle tennis	796.6(2-4)	GV1040-1058	Tricycles
796.347	GV989	Lacrosse	796.63	GV1056	All terrain cycling
796.352	GV961-987	Golf	796.64	GV1044-1046	Bicycle touring
796.35206	GV975-.5	Driving ranges	796.7	GV1021-1025	Automobile travel
796.354	GV931-933	Croquet	796.72	GV1029.3	Drag racing
796.357	GV862-880.6	Baseball	796.72	GV1029.9.D8	Dune buggy racing
796.357	GV877	Baseball—Records	796.72068	TE305	Racetracks (Automobile racing)
796.357075	GV875.3	Baseball cards	796.72068759	GV1033.5.D	Daytona International Speedway Race
796.357083	GV880.5	Little League baseball			
796.357092	GV865	Baseball players	796.72092	GV1032	Automobile racing drivers
796.35724	GV870	Fielding (Baseball)	796.73	GV1029	Grand Prix racing

Dewey	LC	Subject Heading	Dewey	LC	Subject Heading
796.73	GV1029.2	Automobile rallies	797.21	GV838.52.C73	Swimming—Crawl stroke
796.75	GV1060.14	Sidecar motorcycle racing	797.21	GV838.53.L65	Long distance swimming
796.8092	GV35	Gladiators	797.21	GV838.68-.76	Life-saving
796.8092	GV1113	Martial artists	797.21	GV838.76	Survival swimming
796.81	GV1111-1141	Hand-to-hand fighting	797.23	GV840.S78	Deep diving
796.812	GV1195	Wrestling	797.23092	GV837.9-838	Skin divers
796.812	GV1196.5	Arm wrestling	797.24	GV837	Diving
796.8152	GV1114	Judo	797.24	GV838.65.J32	Diving—Jackknife dive
796.8153	GV1114.3	Karate	797.24	GV838.65.S84	Diving—Swan dive
796.8154	GV1114.35	Aikido	797.24	GV838.67.S65	Springboard diving
796.8159	GV1114.7	Kung fu	797.24081	GV838.62.M45	Diving for men
796.83	GV1115-1137	Boxing	797.24082	GV838.62.W65	Diving for women
796.86	GV1143-1150.6	Fencing	797.33	GV811.63.W56	Windsurfing
796.86	GV1143-1150.6	Swordplay	797.35	GV840.S5	Water skiing
796.86092	GV1144-.2	Fencers	797.5	GV750-770	Aeronautical sports
796.9	GV841-857	Winter sports	797.5	GV770.27	Bungee jumping
796.91	GV848.9-852	Skating	797.51	GV762-763	Ballooning
796.92	GV853	Snowshoes and snowshoeing	797.51	GV763	Balloon racing
796.93	GV854	Skis and skiing	797.55	GV764-766	Gliding and soaring
796.93	GV854.9.D78	Dry slope skiing	797.56	GV769.5-770	Skydiving
796.93068	GV854.35	Ski resorts	797.56	GV769.5-770.2	Parachuting
796.932	GV854.B5	Biathlon	798	GV33	Chariot racing
796.932	GV855-.5	Cross-country skiing	798	SF294.2-294.35	Horse sports
796.932	GV855.5.R33	Cross-country ski racing	798.2	SF309	Horsemanship
796.935	GV854-.87	Downhill skiing	798.2028	SF296.R4	Reining (Horsemanship)
796.935	GV854.9.R3	Downhill ski racing	798.23	SF296.T75	Trick riding
796.935	GV854.9.R3	Ski racing	798.23	SF309.27	Sidesaddle riding
796.94	GV857.S6	Snowmobiling	798.23	SF309.28	Trail riding
796.95	GV856	Bobsledding	798.23	SF309.3	Western riding
796.95	GV856	Tobogganing	798.23	SF309.48-.658	Dressage
796.95	GV857.S57	Snowboarding	798.2306	SF310-.5	Riding clubs
796.962	GV847	Hockey	798.23071	SF310.4	Riding schools
796.97	GV843	Ice-boats	798.24	SF295.2	Show riding
797	GV771-840	Aquatic sports	798.25	SF296.V37	Vaulting (Horsemanship)
797.1	GV771-836.15	Boats and boating	798.4	SF321-359.7	Horse racing
797.122	GV781-785	Canoes and canoeing	798.40068	SF324-.4	Racetracks (Horse-racing)
797.1224	GV781-790.3	Kayaking	798.400942	SF357.E67	Epsom Derby, England (Horse race)
797.1224	GV788.5	Sea kayaking	798.400976944	SF357.K4	Kentucky Derby, Louisville, Ky.
797.123	GV790.9-807.5	Rowing			
797.124	GV811	Sailing	798.45	SF359-.7	Steeplechasing
797.124	GV811	Sailing, Single-handed	798.450942753	SF359.7.G7	Grand National Handicap Steeplechase
797.1246	GV811.53-.58	Multihull sailboats			
797.1246	GV811.57	Catamarans	798.46	SF338.7-345	Harness racing
797.1246	GV811.8-833	Yachting	798.8	SF439.5-440.2	Dog racing
797.125	GV833.5-835.9	Motorboats	798.8	SF440.2	Dog race betting
797.125	GV835	Launches	798.83	SF440.15	Sled dog racing
797.129	GV836	Houseboats	799.1028	SH452.9.K6	Fishing knots
797.14	GV826.5-832	Yacht racing	799.10284	SH447-453	Fishing tackle
797.14	GV775	Regattas	799.10284	SH447-453	Fishing—Equipment and supplies
797.14	GV786	Canoe racing			
797.14091631	GV832	Fastnet Yacht Race	799.10284	SH448	Bait
797.21	GV837	Swimming	799.10284	SH451.3	Fish decoys
797.21	GV838.5	Swimming—Records	799.10284	SH452-.2	Fishing rods

Dewey	LC	Subject Heading	Dewey	LC	Subject Heading
799.10284	SH452.9.H	Fishhooks	799.258	SK319	Bird trapping
799.109	SH421	Fishing—History	799.259328	SK341.H3	Hare hunting
799.1092	SH414-415	Fishers	799.2597	SK283-.6	Fur-bearing animals
799.1097	SH462	Fishing—North America	799.259775	SK284-287	Fox hunting
799.10971	SH571-572	Fishing—Canada	799.26	SK295-305	Big game hunting
799.10973	SH463-565	Fishing—United States	799.27643	SK297	American bison hunting
799.12	SH401-691	Fishing	799.2765	SK301	Deer hunting
799.12	SH457.5	Big game fishing	799.27657	SK303	Elk hunting
799.1205	SH401	Fishing—Periodicals	799.2767	SK305.E3	Elephant hunting
799.1206	SH403	Hunting and fishing clubs	799.2778	SK295	Bear hunting
799.1209729	SH577-578	Fishing—West Indies	799.27984	SK305.A	Alligator hunting
799.122	SH455.4	Bait fishing	799.292025	SK12	Hunters—Directories
799.122	SH455.6	Bottom fishing	799.29(4-9)	SK40-267	Hunting—[By region or country]
799.124	SH454-.9	Casting (Fishing)			
799.124	SH454.2	Fly casting	799.296	SK251-255	Hunting—Africa
799.124	SH456-.2	Fly fishing	799.297	SK40-157	Hunting—North America
799.16	SH457-.5	Saltwater fishing	799.2973	SK41-145	Hunting—United States
799.1743	SH691.E4	Eel fishing	799.297(4-9)	SK47-145	Hunting—[United States, By state]
799.1755	SH684-686.7	Salmon fishing			
799.1755	SH687-688	Trout fishing	799.2975	SK43	Hunting—Southern States
799.1758	SH681	Bass fishing	799.2978	SK45	Hunting—West (U.S.)
799.2	SK	Hunting	799.31	GV1151-1181.3	Shooting
799.2	SK283-.6	Trapping	799.31	GV1167-1172	Shooting contests
799.2028	SK36.7	Poaching	799.31	GV1175	Pistol shooting
799.2028	SK273-275	Hunting—Equipment and supplies	799.31	GV1175.5	Fast draw pistol shooting
			799.31	GV1177	Rifle practice
799.2028	SK335	Decoys (Hunting)	799.3132	GV1181-.3	Trapshooting
799.20283	SK274	Hunting guns	799.3132	GV1181.3	Skeet shooting
799.20283	SK274	Sporting guns	799.32	GV1185-1189	Archery
799.202832	SK274.2-.4	Rifles	800	PN	Literature
799.202834	SK274.5	Shotguns	801	PN45	Literature—Philosophy
799.205	SK7	Hunting—Periodicals	801.93	PN45	Literature—Aesthetics
799.206	SK1	Hunting—Societies, etc.	801.959	P47	Criticism, Textual
799.206	SK3	Hunting and fishing clubs	805	PN1-9	Literature—Periodicals
799.206	SK317	Shooting preserves	806	PN20-29	Literature—Societies, etc.
799.2074	SK276	Hunting—Museums	807.1	PN59-72	Literature—Study and teaching
799.209	SK21	Hunting—History			
799.2092	SK15-17	Hunters	808	PN6010-6078	Literature—Collections
799.21	SK37-39.5	Shooting	808	P301-.5	Rhetoric
799.213	SK39.3	Handgun hunting	808	PN167-168	Plagiarism
799.215	SK36	Bowhunting	808	PN171.4-229	Rhetoric
799.23	SF295.65	Hunt riding	808	PN203	Style, Literary
799.23	SK293	Ferreting	808.80024	PN715-749	Renaissance
799.232	SK321	Falconry	808.800(3-4)	PN695-779	Literature, Modern
799.24	SK36.2	Game and game-birds, Dressing of	808.02	PN101-249	Authorship
			808.027	PN162	Editing
799.24	SK311-335	Fowling	808.042	PE1402-1497	English language—Rhetoric
799.244	SK331-335	Waterfowl	808.0431	PF3410-3497	German language—Rhetoric
799.244	SK333.D8	Duck shooting			
799.246	SK325.P5	Pheasant shooting	808.043931	PF410-497	Dutch language—Rhetoric
799.246	SK323-325	Upland game bird shooting	808.0481	PA3265	Rhetoric, Ancient
799.24609(4-9)	SK324	Upland game bird shooting—[By region or country]	808.066	BF76.7	Psychological literature
			808.066	BF76.7	Psychological literature
			808.066	PN205	Exposition (Rhetoric)

Dewey	LC	Subject Heading	Dewey	LC	Subject Heading
808.068	PZ5-90	Children's literature	808.8245	PN1530	Monologue
808.1	P311	Versification	808.8245	PN4305.M6	Monologues
808.1	PN1010-1525	Poetry	808.825232	PN1940-1949	Farce
808.1	PN1031-1035	Versification	808.825232	PN6120.F3	Farces
808.1	PN1039-1049	Poetics	808.82527	PN1910-1919	Melodrama
808.108	PN6099-6110	Poetry—Collections	808.82527	PN6120.M9	Detective and mystery plays
808.14	PN1351-1389	Lyric poetry	808.8387	PN6120.95.A38	Adventure stories
808.2	PN1600-1861	Drama	808.83872	PZ1-3	Detective and mystery stories
808.2	PN1660-1692	Drama—Technique			
808.20071	PN1701	Drama—Study and teaching	808.838762	P96.S34	Science fiction
			808.838762	PN3433-.8	Science fiction
808.222	PN1991.73	Radio plays—Technique	808.838762	PN6120.95.S33	Science fiction
808.3	PN3311-3503	Fiction	808.84	PN6141-6145	Essays
808.3	PN3355-3383	Fiction—Technique	808.85	PN4001-4355	Oratory
808.4	PN4500	Essay	808.85	PN6121-6129	Speeches, addresses, etc.
808.5	PN4142	Speechwriting	808.851	PN4121-4130	Public speaking
808.53	PN4177-4191	Debates and debating	808.851	PN6340-6348	Toasts
808.54	PN4145-4151	Oral interpretation	808.86	PN6130-6140	Letters
808.54	PN4199-4355	Recitations	808.87	PN6110.P3	Parodies
808.543	GR72.3	Storytelling	808.87	PN6147-6231	Wit and humor
808.54509	PN83	Reading	808.87	PN6149.P3	Parody
808.8	PN6010-6065	Anthologies	808.87	PN6231.S2	Satire
808.8002	PN665-694	Literature, Medieval	808.87092	PN6147	Humorists
808.801163	PN56.S87	Surrealism (Literature)	808.882	PN171.Q6	Quotation
808.8012	PN56.R3	Realism in literature	808.882	PN1441	Epigrams
808.8012	PN56.R3	Naturalism in literature	808.882	PN6080-6095	Quotations
808.8012	PN601	Naturalism in literature	808.882	PN6259-6268	Anecdotes
808.80142	PN56.C6	Classicism	808.882	PN6279-6288	Epigrams
808.80145	PN56.R7	Romanticism	808.882	PN6366-6377	Riddles
808.80145	PN603	Romanticism	809	PN75-99	Literature—History and criticism
808.80145	PN750-759	Romanticism			
808.80145	PN816	Romance fiction	809	PN441-595	Literature—History and criticism
808.8015	PN56.A5	Allegory			
808.8015	PN56.M94	Myth in literature	809	PN4096	Rhetorical criticism
808.8015	PN56.S9	Symbolism in literature	809.01	PN611-630	Literature, Ancient
808.8024	PN44	Literature—Stories, plots, etc.	809.1	PN1105-1279	Poetry—History and criticism
808.8026	PN1551	Dialogue	809.2	PN1707	Dramatic criticism
808.803538	PN6071.E7	Erotic literature	809.2	PN1720-1861	Drama—History and criticism
808.8036	PN48	Nature in literature			
808.8037	PN56.M95	Mythology in literature	809.2527	PN1761	Mysteries and miracle-plays
808.804291	PN49	Mysticism in literature	809.3	PN3329-3503	Fiction—History and criticism
808.81071	PN1101	Poetry—Study and teaching			
808.813	PN6110.N17	Narrative poetry	809.31	PN3373	Short story
808.8132	PN1301-1333	Epic poetry	809.381	PN3441	Historical fiction
808.8132	PN6110.E6	Epic poetry	809.387	PN3448.A3	Adventure stories
808.814	PN691	Lyric poetry	809.3872	PN3377.5.D4	Detective and mystery stories—Technique
808.8142	PN1514	Sonnet			
808.8143	PN6110.04	Odes	809.3872	PN3448.D4	Detective and mystery stories
808.8175	PN6231.L5	Limericks			
808.82	PN688-691	Poetry, Medieval	809.5	PN4021-4055	Oratory—History
808.82	PN6110.5-6120	Drama—Collections	809.6	PN4400	Letters
808.820512	PN6111-6120	Tragedy	809.91	PN597	Literary movements
808.8222	PN6120.R2	Radio plays	809.924	PN3378	Plots (Drama, novel, etc.)
			809.933538	HQ450-472	Erotic literature

Dewey	LC	Subject Heading	Dewey	LC	Subject Heading
809.93522	BS535-537	Bible as literature	817.09	PS430-438	American wit and humor
809.93592	CT21-22	Biography as a literary form	818.03	PS409	American diaries
810	PS	American literature	818.08	PS642-659.2	American prose literature
810.109	PS185-191	American literature—Colonial period, ca. 1600-1775	818.0809	PS360-379	American prose literature
			818.08109	PS366	American prose literature—Colonial period, ca. 1600-1775
810.209	PS193	American literature—Revolutionary period, 1775-1783	818.08209	PS367-369	American prose—Revolutionary period, 1775-1783
810.(2-3)09	PS208	American literature—1783-1850	818.3	PS669	American diaries
810.309	PS201-214	American literature—19th century	820	PN849.G	British literature
			820	PR	English literature
810.509	PS221-228	American literature—20th century	820	PR1-9680	English literature
			820	PR8631-8644	Scottish literature
810.80896073	PS508.N3	American literature—Afro-American authors	820	PR9320-.9	Guyanese literature
			820	PR9600-9619.3	Australian literature
810.809287	PS508.W7	American literature—Women authors	820.0202	PR87	English literature—Outlines, syllabi, etc.
810.9	PS153-490	American literature—History and criticism	820.(1-2)08	PR1119-1131	English literature—Middle English, 1100-1500
810.9896073	PS153.N5	Afro-American authors	820.(1-2)09	PR251-369	English literature—Middle English, 1100-1500
810.99287	PS147-151	American literature—Women authors	820.3	PR19	English literature—Dictionaries
811	PS	American poetry			
811.00809287	PS589	American poetry—Women authors	820.(2-4)08	PR1119-1131	English literature— Early modern, 1500-1700
811.071	PS306-.5	American poetry—Study and teaching	820.(2-4)09	PR401-439	English literature—Early modern, 1500-1700
811.109	PS312	American poetry—Colonial period, ca. 1600-1775	820.508	PR1134-1139	English literature—18th century
811.209	PS314	American poetry—Revolutionary period, 1775-1783	820.509	PR441-449	English literature—18th century
811.209	PS319	American poetry—1783-1850	820.71	PR31-55	English literature—Study and teaching
811.309	PS316-321	American poetry—19th century	820.802	PN6081-6084	Quotations, English
			820.8022	PE1427	Description (Rhetoric)
811.509	PS324	American poetry—20th century	820.8022	PR1285	Description (Rhetoric)
			820.8023	PE1425	Narration (Rhetoric)
812.051209	PS336.T7	American drama (Tragedy)	820.808	PR1143-1145	English literature—19th century
812.052309	PS336.C7	American drama (Comedy)			
812.071	PS335	American drama—Study and teaching	820.808	PR1301-1304	English literature—19th century
812.08	PS623-635	American drama	820.809	PR451-469	English literature—19th century
812.09	PS330-351	American drama			
813	PZ1	American fiction	820.809222	PR1110.C3	English literature—Catholic authors
813.09	PS371-379	American fiction	820.809287	PR1110.W6	English literature—Women authors
814.08	PS680-688	American essays			
814.09	PS420-428	American essays	820.809411	PR8631-8693	English literature—Scottish authors
815.08	PS660-668	Speeches, addresses, etc., American	820.809415	PR8831-8893	English literature—Irish authors
815.09	PS400-408	Speeches, addresses, etc., American	820.809429	PR8900-8997	English literature—Welsh authors
816.08	PS670-678	American letters			
816.09	PS410-418	American letters			
817.008	PN6157-6162	American wit and humor			

Dewey	LC	Subject Heading	Dewey	LC	Subject Heading
820.80952	PR9900.J	English literature—Japanese authors	821.9109	PR601-609	English poetry—20th century
820.9	PR1-978	English literature—History and criticism	822	PR9343	African drama (English)
			822.051208	PR1257	English drama (Tragedy)
820.9	PR57-78	English literature—Criticism, Textual	822.051209	PR633	English drama (Tragedy)
			822.052308	PR1248	English drama (Comedy)
820.9	PR8510-8553	Scottish literature	822.052309	PR631	English drama (Comedy)
820.9	PR9340-9408	African literature (English)	822.08	PR1241-1273	English drama
820.9108	PR1149	English literature—20th century	822.08	PR9347	African drama (English)
			822.09	PR621-739	English drama
820.909	PR471-479	English literature—20th century	822.09	PR635.D45	Domestic drama, English
			822.(1-2)08	PR1260	English drama—To 1500
820.99287	PR111-119	English literature—Women authors	822.(1- 2)09	PR641-644	English drama—To 1500
			822.(2-3)08	PR1262-1263	English drama—Early modern and Elizabethan, 1500-1600
820.99411	PR8500-8621	English literature—Scottish authors			
820.99415	PR8700-8821	English literature—Irish authors	822.(2-3)09	PR646-658	English drama—Early modern and Elizabethan, 1500-1600
821	PR1170-1227	English poetry			
821.00809287	PR1177	English poetry—Women authors	822.33	PR2750-3112	Shakespeare, William, 1564-1616
821.00809411	PR8649-8663	English poetry—Scottish authors	822.408	PR1265.3-1266	English drama—17th century
821.00809415	PR8848-8863	English poetry—Irish authors	822.409	PR671-698	English drama—17th century
821.00809429	PR8955-8969	English poetry—Welsh authors	822.508	PR1269	English drama—18th century
821.0089411	PR8561-8581	English poetry—Scottish authors	822.509	PR701-719	English drama—18th century
821.00909429	PR8926-8932	English poetry—Welsh authors	822.808	PR1271	English drama—19th century
821.0099287	PR111-119	English poetry—Women authors	822.809	PR721-734	English drama—19th century
821.03209	PR321-347	Epic poetry, English	822.909	PR736-739	English drama—20th century
821.08	PR9346-.5	African poetry (English)			
821.09	PR9342	African poetry (English)	822.9108	PR1272	English drama—20th century
821.(1-2)09	PR311-369	English poetry, Middle English, 1100-1500	823	PR9344	African fiction (English)
			823.00809287	PZ1	English fiction—Women authors
821.(3-4)08	PR1204-1213	English poetry—Early modern, 1500-1700	823.08	PR1281-1309	English fiction
821.(3-4)09	PR521-549	English poetry—Early modern, 1500-1700	823.09	PR821-888	English fiction
			823.09	PR9347.5	African fiction (English)
821.508	PR1215-1219	English poetry—18th century	823.9109	PR881-888	English fiction—20th century
821.509	PR551-579	English poetry—18th century	824.009	PR921-927	English essays
			824.08	PR1361-1369	English essays
821.808	PR1221-1224	English poetry—19th century	825.08	PR1321-1329	Speeches, addresses, etc., English
821.809	PR581-599	English poetry—19th century	825.09	PR901-907	Speeches, addresses, etc., English
821.9	PR500-611	English poetry			
821.9	PR500-609	English poetry—History and criticism	826.009	PR911-917	English letters
			826.08	PR1341-1349	English letters
821.9108	PR1224-1227	English poetry—20th century	827	PN931-937	English wit and humor
			827.008	PN6173-6175	English wit and humor
			827.009	PR931-937	English wit and humor

Dewey	LC	Subject Heading	Dewey	LC	Subject Heading
827.0222	NC1470-1479	English wit and humor, Pictorial	830.6	PT31	German literature—Congresses
828.03	PR908	English diaries	830.608	PT1131	German literature—18th century
828.03	PR1330	English diaries	830.609	PT285-321	German literature—18th century—History and criticism
828.08	PR750-888	English prose literature			
828.08	PR1281-1300	English prose literature	830.708	PT1136	German literature—19th century
828.08	PR8597-8607	English prose literature—Scottish authors	830.709	PT341-395	German literature—19th century—History and criticism
828.08	PR8672-8687	English prose literature—Scottish authors			
828.08	PR9632.2-.6	New Zealand prose literature	830.71	PT51-65	German literature—Study and teaching
828.08	PR9637.25-.92	New Zealand prose literature	830.8	PT1100-1479	German literature
0828.08(2-3)	PR1293-1295	English prose literature—Early modern and Elizabethan, 1500-1600	830.802	PN6090-6093	Quotations, German
			830.909	PT1141	German literature—20th century
828.08(2-3)09	PR767-769	English prose literature—Early modern, 1500-1700	831.009	PT500-597	German poetry
828.085	PR1297	English prose literature—18th century	831.08	PT1151-1241	German poetry
			831.(2-3)08	PT1391-1429	German poetry—Middle High German, 1050-1500
828.08509	PR769	English prose literature—18th century	831.(2-3)09	PT175-227	German poetry—Middle High German, 1050-1500
829.09	PR171-236	English literature—Old English, ca. 450-1100	831.03208	PT1411-1418	Epic poetry, German
829.1	PR1490-1508	English poetry—Old English, ca. 450-1100	831.(4-5)08	PT1163-1165	German poetry—Early modern, 1500-1700
829.109	PR201-217	English poetry—Old English, ca. 450-1100	831.(4-5)09	PT525-531	German poetry—Early modern, 1500-1700
829.80809	PR221-236	English prose literature—Old English, ca. 450-1100	831.608	PT1167-1169	German poetry—18th century
830	PT	German	831.609	PT533-535	German poetry—18th century
830	PT1-1021	German literature	831.708	PT1171-1173	German poetry—19th century
830	PT3808-3809	German literature—Foreign countries	831.709	PT541-547	German poetry—19th century
830	PT3830-3837.5	German literature—Czechoslovakia	831.908	PT1174-1175	German poetry—20th century
830	PT3840-3848	Hungarian literature (German)	831.909	PT551-553	German poetry—20th century
830	PT3860-3878	Swiss literature (German)	832.051208	PT1271-1273	German drama (Tragedy)
830	PT3900-3919	German American literature (German)	832.052308	PT1275-1277	German drama (Comedy)
			832.08	PT1251-1299	German drama
830.109	PT183	German literature—Old High German, 750-1050	832.09	PT605-709	German drama
830.1099	PT401-403	German literature—20th century	833.0108	PT1337-1340	Short stories, German
			833.08	PT1314-1340	German fiction
830.(2-3)	PT175-230	German literature—Middle High German, 1050-1500	833.09	PT741-772	German fiction
830.208	PT1375-1479	German literature—Middle High German, 1050-1500	833.(4-5)09	PT753-756	German fiction—Early modern, 1500-1700
830.3	PT41	German language dictionaries	833.608	PT1315	German fiction—18th century
830.(4-5)08	PT1121-1126	German literature—Early modern, 1500-1700	833.609	PT759	German fiction—18th century
830.(4-5)09	PT238-281	German literature—Early modern, 1500-1700	833.708	PT1332	German fiction—19th century

Dewey	LC	Subject Heading	Dewey	LC	Subject Heading
833.709	PT763-771	German fiction—19th century	839.36208	PT6570	Afrikaans drama
			839.36209	PT6520	Afrikaans drama
833.908	PT1334	German fiction—20th century	839.36308	PT6570	Afrikaans fiction
			839.36309	PT6525	Afrikaans fiction
833.909	PT772	German fiction—20th century	839.367	PN6222.S	Afrikaans wit and humor
			839.36808	PT6525	Afrikaans prose literature
834.09	PT831	German essays	839.36808	PT6590	Afrikaans prose literature
834.08	PT1354	German essays	839.36808	PT6570	Afrikaans prose literature
835.009	PT801	Speeches, addresses, etc., German	839.4	PT4801-4897	Low German literature
			839.4071	PT4803	Low German literature—Study and teaching
835.08	PT1344-1345	Speeches, addresses, etc., German	839.41008	PT4834-4836	Low German poetry
			839.4109	PT4813	Low German literature—To 1500
836.009	PT811	German letters			
836.08	PT1348-1352	German letters	839.4109	PT4817-4820	Low German poetry
838.08	PT711-871	German prose literature	839.42008	PT4837-4838	Low German drama
838.08	PT1301-1340	German prose literature	839.4209	PT4821	Low German drama
839	PF3985-3991	German literature—Old High German, 750-1050	839.5	PT	Scandinavian literatures
			839.5	PT7001-9999	Scandinavian literature
839.09	PJ5120-5192	Yiddish literature	839.5071	PT7035-7039	Scandinavian literature—Study and teaching
839.2	PF1501-1541	Frisian literature			
839.3009	PN836	Germanic fiction	839.6	PT7101-7338	Old Norse literature
839.31	PT	Dutch	839.6071	PT7135-7139	Old Norse literature—Study and teaching
839.31	PT5001-5980	Dutch literature			
839.31	PT6000-6466.36	Flemish literature	839.6108	PT7230-7252	Old Norse poetry
839.31071	PT5040-5044	Dutch literature—Study and teaching	839.6109	PT7170-7175	Old Norse Poetry
			839.6308	PT7261-7262	Sagas
839.31071	PT6040	Flemish literature—Study and teaching	839.6309	PT7181-7193	Sagas
			839.6808	PT7177-7211	Old Norse prose literature
839.3109	PT5121-5137	Dutch literature—To 1500	839.6808	PT7255-7262	Old Norse prose literature
839.31108	PT5470-5488	Dutch poetry	839.69	PT7351-7550	Icelandic literature
839.31108	PT6330-6348	Flemish poetry	839.69071	PT7370-7373	Icelandic literature—Study and teaching
839.31109	PT5201-5245	Dutch poetry			
839.31109	PT6140	Flemish poetry	839.69108	PT7465-7467	Icelandic poetry
839.31(2-4)09	PT5141-5165	Dutch literature—1500-1800	839.69208	PT7470-7477	Icelandic drama
			839.69209	PT7411	Icelandic drama
839.31208	PT5490-5515	Dutch drama	839.69308	PT7485-7487	Icelandic fiction
839.31208	PT6350-6360	Flemish drama	839.69309	PT7413	Icelandic fiction
839.31209	PT5250-5295	Dutch drama	839.69808	PT412-418	Icelandic prose literature
839.31308	PT5520-5530	Dutch fiction	839.69808	PT7480-7495	Icelandic prose literature
839.31309	PT5320-5336	Dutch fiction	839.7	PT9201-9999	Swedish literature
839.31408	PT5539	Dutch essays	839.7108	PT9580-9599	Swedish poetry
839.31509	PT5170-5175	Dutch literature—19th century	839.7109	PT9375-9405	Swedish poetry
			839.7208	PT9605-9625	Swedish drama
839.31609	PT5180-5185	Dutch literature—20th century	839.7209	PT9415-9449	Swedish drama
			839.7308	PT9627-9630	Swedish fiction
839.317008	PN6222.N	Dutch wit and humor	839.7309	PT9480-9492	Swedish fiction
839.31708	PT5541	Dutch wit and humor	839.7808	PT9460-9499	Swedish prose literature
839.31709	PT5346	Dutch wit and humor	839.7808	PT9626-9639	Swedish prose literature
839.31808	PT5300-5336	Dutch prose literature	839.81	PT7601-8260	Danish literature
839.31808	PT5517-5547	Dutch prose literature	839.81071	PT7640-7644	Danish literature—Study and teaching
839.31808	PT6365-6397	Flemish prose literature			
839.36	PT6500-6593.36	Afrikaans literature	839.811	PT7721-7737	Danish literature—To 1500
839.36108	PT6545	Afrikaans poetry	839.811	PT7770-7795	Danish poetry
839.36108	PT6560	Afrikaans poetry	839.81108	PT7975-7994	Danish poetry
839.36109	PT6515	Afrikaans poetry			

Dewey	LC	Subject Heading	Dewey	LC	Subject Heading
839.81208	PT7999-8020	Danish drama	840.708	PQ1136-1139	French literature—19th century
839.81209	PT7800-7832	Danish drama			
839.81308	PT8022-8024	Danish fiction	840.709	PQ281-299	French literature—19th century
839.81309	PT7835-7862	Danish fiction			
839.814	PT7741-7747	Danish literature—18th century	840.71	PQ51-65	French literature—Study and teaching
839.816	PT7751-7756	Danish literature—19th century	840.802	PN6086-6089	Quotations, French
			840.9108	PQ1141	French literature—20th century
839.81608	PT8030	Danish letters			
839.81609	PT7866	Danish letters	840.9109	PQ301-307	French literature—20th century
839.817	PT7760	Danish literature—20th century	841.03209	PQ201-205	Epic literature, French
839.81808	PT7835-7862	Danish prose literature	841.08	PQ1160-1193	French poetry
839.81808	PT8021-8024	Danish prose literature	841.09	PQ400-491	French poetry—History and criticism
839.82	PT8301-9155	Norwegian literature	841.(1-2)08	PQ1300-1391	French poetry—To 1500
839.82	PT9000-9094	Norwegian literature (Nynorsk)	841.309	PQ416-418	French poetry—16th century
839.82071	PT8340-8344	Norwegian literature—Study and teaching	841.409	PQ421-423	French poetry—17th century
839.82108	PT8675-8695	Norwegian poetry	841.509	PQ426-428	French poetry—18th century
839.82109	PT8460-8490	Norwegian poetry			
839.82208	PT8699-8718	Norwegian drama	841.709	PQ431-439	French poetry—19th century
839.82209	PT8500-8534	Norwegian drama			
839.82308	PT8720-8722	Norwegian fiction	841.910	PQ441-443	French poetry—20th century
839.82309	PT8555-8567	Norwegian fiction			
839.82808	PT8540-8567	Norwegian prose literature	842.08	PQ1211-1241	French drama
839.82808	PT8719-8722	Norwegian prose literature	842.(1-2)08	PQ1341-1385	French drama—To 1500
840	PQ	Romance literatures	843.009	PQ631-671	French fiction
840	PQ1-3999	French literature	843.08	PQ1261-1279	French fiction
840	PQ3809	French literature—Foreign countries	843.909	PQ671	French fiction—20th century
840	PQ3810-3858	Belgian literature (French)	845.08	PQ1281-1283	Speeches, addresses, etc., French
840	PQ3870-3888	Swiss literature (French)	848.02	PN6282	Epigrams, French
840	PQ3900-3919.2	French-Canadian literature	848.08	PQ601-657	French prose literature
840	PQ3940-3949	West Indian literature (French)	848.08	PQ1243-1279	French prose literature
840	PQ3960-3979	Vietnamese literature (French)	848.(1-2)08	PQ151-216	French prose literature—To 1500
840	PQ3980-3989.2	African literature (French)	849	PC3301-3359	Provencal literature
840	PQ3998.5.N	New Caledonian literature (French)	849	PC3381-3420.5	Langue d'oc literature
			849.104	PC3304-3330	Troubadours
840.(1-2)08	PQ1300-1595	French literature—To 1500	849.9	PC3900-3976	Catalan literature
840.(1-2)09	PQ151-221	French literature—To 1500	850	PQ4001-5999	Italian literature
840.308	PQ1121-1125	French literature—16th century	850.209	PQ4075	Italian literature—15th century
840.309	PQ230-239	French literature—16th century	850.409	PQ4079-4080	Italian literature—16th century
840.408	PQ1126-1130	French literature—17th century	850.509	PQ4081-4082	Italian literature—17th century
840.409	PQ241-251	French literature—17th century	850.609	PQ4083-4084	Italian literature—18th century
840.508	PQ1131-1135	French literature—18th century	850.709	PQ4085-4086	Italian literature—19th century
840.509	PQ261-276	French literature—18th century	850.71	PQ4013-4023	Italian literature—Study and teaching

Dewey	LC	Subject Heading	Dewey	LC	Subject Heading
850.9	PQ4001-4199	Italian literature—History and criticism	863.09	PQ6138-6147	Spanish fiction
850.9109	PQ4087	Italian literature—20th century	868.0808	PQ6247-6264	Spanish prose literature
			868.0809	PQ6131-6153	Spanish prose literature
851.09	PQ4091-4131	Italian poetry	869	PQ9000-9999	Portuguese literature
852.09	PQ4133-4160	Italian drama	869	PQ9421	Portuguese literature—Foreign countries
854.09	PQ4183.E8	Italian essays			
856.09	PQ4183.L4	Italian letters	869	PQ9450-9469.2	Galician literature
857.00222	PC1300-1766	Wit and humor, Pictorial	869	PQ9500-9699	Brazilian literature
858.0809	PQ4161-4185	Italian prose literature	869	PQ9900-9948	African literature (Portuguese)
859	PC800-872	Romanian literature			
859.9	PC951-986	Raeto-Romance literature	869.071	PQ9008-9009.5	Portuguese literature—Study and teaching
860	PQ6001-8929	Spanish literature			
860	PQ7020-8921	Spanish literature—Foreign countries	869.108	PQ9149-9163	Portuguese poetry
			869.109	PQ9061-9081	Portuguese poetry
860	PQ7100-7298.36	Mexican literature	869.208	PQ9164-9170	Portuguese drama
860	PQ7370-7390	Cuban literature	869.209	PQ9083-9095	Portuguese drama
860	PQ7400-7409.2	Dominican literature	869.80808	PQ9172-9188	Portuguese prose literature
860	PQ7420-7440	Puerto Rican literature	869.80809	PQ9097-9119	Portuguese prose literature
860	PQ7480-7489.2	Costa Rican literature	870.8001	PA6101-6139	Latin literature
860	PQ7490-7499.2	Guatemalan literature	870.9001	PA6001-6098	Latin literature—History and criticism
860	PQ7500-7509.2	Honduran literature			
860	PQ7510-7519.2	Nicaraguan literature	870.900(3-4)	PA8001-8595	Latin literature, Medieval and modern
860	PQ7520-7529.2	Panamanian literature			
860	PQ7530-7539.2	Salvadoran literature	871.032108	PA6125	Epic poetry, Latin
860	PQ7600-7798.36	Argentine literature	871.08	PA6121-6135	Latin poetry
860	PQ7801-7820	Bolivian literature	871.09	PA6045-6063	Latin poetry
860	PQ7900-8098.36	Chilean literature	871.(3-4)08	PA8120-8133	Latin poetry, Medieval and modern
860	PQ8160-8180.36	Colombian literature			
860	PQ8200-8220.36	Ecuadorian literature	871.(3-4)09	PA8050-8065	Latin poetry, Medieval and modern—History and criticism
860	PQ8250-8259	Paraguayan literature			
860	PQ8300-8498.36	Peruvian literature			
860	PQ8510-8519	Uruguayan literature	871.6	PA2329-2340	Latin language—Metrics and rhythmics
860	PQ8530-8550.36	Venezuelan literature			
860	PQ8700-8899	Philippine literature	872.08	PA6137	Latin drama
860.71	PQ6013-6020	Spanish literature—Study and teaching	872.09	PA6067-6075	Latin drama—History and criticism
			872.(3-4)08	PA8135-8140	Latin drama, Medieval and modern
860.9	PQ6022-6167	Spanish literature—History and criticism			
			872.(3-4)09	PA8073-8079	Latin drama, Medieval and modern
861	PQ7402	Dominican poetry			
861	PQ7406	Dominican poetry	878.08	PA6081-6095.5	Latin prose literature—History and criticism
861	PQ8210	Ecuadorian poetry			
861	PQ8214-.5	Ecuadorian poetry	878.08	PA6138-6139	Latin prose literature
861.08	PQ6174.95-6215	Spanish poetry	878.08	PA8081-8096	Latin prose literature, Medieval and modern—History and criticism
861.09	PQ6075-6098	Spanish poetry			
860.(1-2)09	PQ6057-6060	Spanish literature—To 1500			
			878.08	PA8145-8149	Latin prose literature, Medieval and modern
860.(2-3)09	PQ6063-6072	Spanish literature—Classical period, 1500-1700			
			880	PA3051-4505	Greek literature
862.08	PQ6217-6241	Spanish drama	880	PA3081-3084	Greek literature, Hellenistic
862.09	PQ6099-6129	Spanish drama	880.01	PA3013	Classical literature—Appreciation
863	PQ8212	Ecuadorian fiction			
863	PQ8216.F5	Ecuadorian fiction	880.09	PA3001-3045	Classical literature—History and criticism
863.08	PQ6251-6257	Spanish fiction			

Dewey	LC	Subject Heading	Dewey	LC	Subject Heading
880.8	PA3300-3516	Greek literature	891.29	PK2911	Vedic literature
880.8	PA3301-3671	Classical literature	891.308	PK5003-5009	Prakrit literature
880.8002	PA5170-5198	Byzantine literature	891.309	PK4990-5001.8	Prakrit literature
880.9	PA47	Criticism, Textual	891.37	PK4501-4681	Pali literature
880.9	PA3520-3564	Greek literature—Criticism, Textual	891.43	PK2030-2142	Hindustani literature
			891.439	PK2030-2058	Urdu literature
880.9	PA3527	Greek literature, Hellenistic—Criticism, Textual	891.47	PK1850-1888	Gujarati literature
			891.499	PK7031-7037	Kashmiri literature
880.9002	PA5101-5167	Byzantine literature	891.55	PK6400-6599	Persian literature
881	PA3431-3459	Classical poetry	891.551009	PK6416-6420	Persian poetry
881.009	PA3019-3022	Classical poetry	891.552009	PK6421-6422	Persian drama
881.009	PA3092-3125	Greek poetry	891.55808	PK6423	Persian prose literature
881.03208	PA3437-3439	Epic poetry, Greek	891.55808	PK6443	Persian prose literature
881.03209	PA3105-3107.5	Epic poetry, Greek	891.62	PB1306-1449	Irish literature
881.09	PA3537-3543	Greek literature, Hellenistic—Criticism, Textual	891.6208001	PB1321	Irish literature—To 1100
			891.6208002	PB1322	Irish literature—Middle Irish, 1100-1550
881.208	PA5180-5189	Byzantine poetry	891.621009	PB1321	Fili (Irish poets)
881.209	PA5150-5155	Byzantine poetry	891.63	PB1605-1709	Gaelic literature
882	PA3461-3468	Greek drama	891.64	PB1851-1867	Manx literature
882.008	PA3461-3466	Classical drama	891.66	PB2206-2499	Welsh literature
882.009	PA3024-3029	Classical drama—History and criticism	891.67	PB2551-2621	Cornish literature
			891.68	PB2856-2932	Breton literature
882.009	PA3131-3239	Greek drama	891.7	PG2900-3580	Russian literature
882.051208	PA3461-3463	Greek drama (Tragedy)	891.708004	PN849.R9-.R92	Soviet literature
882.051209	PA3131-3159	Greek drama (Tragedy)	891.79	PG3900-3987	Ukrainian literature
882.052308	PA3465-3466	Greek drama (Comedy)	891.8	PG500-585	Slavic literature
882.052309	PA3161-3199	Greek drama (Comedy)	891.81	PG700-716	Church Slavic literature
882.208	PA5190-5194	Byzantine drama	891.8109	PG1000-1146	Bulgarian literature
882.209	PA5160-5163	Byzantine drama	891.821008	PG1654-.5	Dalmatian poetry
811.0080896 + 073	PS591.N4	American poetry—Afro-American authors	891.821009	PG1650-.5	Dalmatian poetry
			891.84	PG1900-1962	Slovenian literature
885.008	PA3482	Funeral orations	891.85	PG7001-7446	Polish literature
885.108	PA3479-3842	Oratory, Ancient	891.86	PG5000-5146	Czech literature
888.08	PA3255-3273	Greek prose literature	891.87	PG5400-5546	Slovak literature
888.08	PA3473-3475	Greek prose literature	891.88	PG5661-5698	Sorbian literature
888.08	PA5165	Byzantine prose literature	891.92	PG8701-8772	Lithuanian literature
888.08	PA5195-5196	Byzantine prose literature	891.93	PG8998-9146	Latvian literature
888.08	PA5265	Greek prose literature, Modern	891.991	PG9601-9665	Albanian literature
			891.992	PK8501-8835	Armenian literature
889	PA5201-5660	Greek literature, Modern	891.992	PK8601-8661	Armenian literature—Europe
889.08001	PA5301-5395	Greek literature, Modern—1453-1800	891.992	PK8681-8689	Armenian literature—United States
889.09	PA5230-5269	Greek literature, Modern—History and criticism	892.009	PJ3097	Semitic literature
889.1008	PA5280-5289	Greek poetry, Modern	892.1	PJ3601-3953	Assyro-Babylonian literature
889.1009	PA5259-5255	Greek poetry, Modern	892.3	PJ5601-5695	Syriac literature
889.2008	PA5290-5294	Greek drama, Modern	892.4	PJ5001-5060	Hebrew literature
889.2009	PA5260-5263	Greek drama, Modern	892.4071	PJ5007	Hebrew literature—Study and teaching
889.309	PA401-407	Greek language—Style			
889.808	PA5295	Greek prose literature, Modern	892.408002	PJ5037	Hebrew literature, Medieval
			892.408003	PJ5038	Hebrew literature, Modern
891.1	PK80-85	Indo-Iranian literature	892.409002	PJ5016	Hebrew literature, Medieval
891.2	PK3591-4485	Sanskrit literature	892.409003	PJ5017-5021	Hebrew literature, Modern

Dewey	LC	Subject Heading	Dewey	LC	Subject Heading
892.7	PJ7501-8518	Arabic literature	895.1090048	PL2297	Chinese literature—Ch'ing dynasty, 1644-1912—History and criticism
892.7	PJ8025-8190	Arabic literature—Asia			
892.7	PJ8030-8129	Arabic literature—Middle East			
892.7	PJ8195-8390	Arabic literature—Africa	895.11008	PL2517-2565.8	Chinese poetry
892.7	PJ8395-8490	Arabic literature—Europe	895.11009	PL2306-2355.8	Chinese poetry
892.7	PJ8500-8517	Arabic literature—America	895.1109	PL2280	Chinese literature—To 221 B.C.—History and criticism
892.71008	PJ7631-7661	Arabic poetry			
892.71009	PJ7541-7561	Arabic poetry	895.12008	PL2566-2603	Chinese drama
892.72008	PJ7665	Arabic drama	895.12009	PL2356-2393	Chinese drama
892.72009	PJ7565	Arabic drama	895.13008	PL2625-2653	Chinese fiction
892.7808	PJ7571-7577	Arabic prose literature	895.13009	PL2415-2443	Chinese fiction
892.7808	PJ7671-7677	Arabic prose literature	895.14008	PL2606-2623	Chinese essays
892.81	PJ9090-9101	Ethiopic literature	895.14009	PL2395-2413	Chinese essays
893.1	PJ1481-1989	Egyptian literature	895.2008	PJ371	Oriental drama
893.12	PJ1571	Egyptian drama	895.4	PL3701-3775	Tibetan literature
893.13	PJ1487	Egyptian fiction	895.408	PL772-.83	Japanese essays
893.2	PJ2190-2199	Coptic literature	895.6	PL700-889	Japanese literature
894.23	PL410-419	Mongolian literature	895.6009	PL742-.83	Japanese essays
894.35	PL201-272	Turkish literature	895.608	PL755.12	Japanese literature
894.352008	PL237-238	Turkish drama	895.608002	PL790-792	Japanese literature—1185-1600
894.352009	PL221	Turkish drama			
894.387	PL65.T35-.T39	Tatar literature	895.608003	PL793-799	Japanese literature—Edo period, 1600-1868
894.511	PH3001-3445	Hungarian literature			
894.54109	PH300-405	Finnish literature	895.6080042	PL800-820	Japanese literature—Meiji period, 1868-1912
894.545	PH630-671	Estonian literature			
894.55	PH731-735	Lapp literature	895.609001	PL726.12	Japanese literature—To 794
894.56	PH781-785	Mordvin literature			
895	PJ306-489	Oriental literature	895.609001	PL726.1185-.1186	Japanese literature—To 1185
895	PL491-494	East Asian literature			
895.1	PL2250-3207	Chinese literature	895.61008	PL757-763	Japanese poetry
895.10900(2-3)	PL2283	Chinese literature—221 B.C.-960 A.D.—History and criticism	895.61009	PL727-733	Japanese poetry
			895.6108001	PL787-789	Japanese literature—Heian period, 794-1185
895.109002	PL2284.5	Chinese literature—220-589—History and criticism	895.62008	PL764-769	Japanese drama
			895.62009	PL734-739	Japanese drama
			895.63008	PL770-777	Japanese fiction
895.109002	PL2285	Chinese literature—Three kingdoms, 220-265—History and criticism	895.63009	PL740-747	Japanese fiction
			895.7	PL950-998	Korean literature
			895.71008	PL974-976.4	Korean poetry
895.109002	PL2286	Chinese literature—Chin dynasty, 265-419—History and criticism	895.71009	PL959-961.4	Korean poetry
			895.72008	PL977-979	Korean drama
			895.72009	PL962-964	Korean drama
895.109002	PL2287	Chinese literature—Liu Sung dynasty, 420-479—History and criticism	895.73008	PL980-981.5	Korean fiction
			895.73009	PL965-967	Korean fiction
			895.8	PL3970-3988	Burmese literature
895.1090024	PL2290	Chinese literature—Sui dynasty, 581-618—History and criticism	895.911	PL4200-4209	Thai literature
			895.922	PL4378	Vietnamese literature
			896	PL8010-8014	African literature
895.1090044	PL2294	Chinese literature—Yüan dynasty, 1260-1368—History and criticism	896.34	PL8123.5-.9	Dan literature
			899	PN849.026	Pacific Island literature
			899.21	PL5530-5547	Philippine literature
895.1090046	PL2296	Chinese literature—Ming dynasty, 1368-1644—History and criticism	899.211	PL6058	Tagalog literature
			899.222	PL5170-5179	Javanese literature
			899.92	PH5280-5490	Basque literature

Dewey	LC	Subject Heading	Dewey	LC	Subject Heading
899.95	PJ4045-4083	Sumerian literature	909.04927	DS36-39.2	Arab countries
899.9623	PK9201.A35-.A39	Abkhaz literature	909.04927	DS36.77-.88	Arab countries—Civilization
899.9624	PK9201.K35-.K39	Kabardian literature	909.04927	DS36.77-.88	Civilization, Arab
899.9625	PK9201.A45-.A49	Adygei literature	909.04927	DS37-39.2	Arab countries—History
899.964	PK9051.5-.8	Daghestan literature	909.04927082	DS36.88 .B36	Civilization, Arab—20th
899.964	PK9201.D35-.D39	Dargwa literature			century
899.969	PK9160-9169	Georgian literature	909.07	CB351-355	Civilization, Medieval
895.60800 + (44-5)	PL821-866	Japanese literature—Showa period, 1926-1989	909.07	CB351-355	Middle Ages
			909.07	CB351-355	Middle Ages
			909.08	CB351-369	Renaissance
808.8038291 + 216	PN57.D4	Devil in literature	909.08	CB357-430	Civilization, Modern
			909.08	D204-725	History, Modern
			909.08	D839-850	History, Modern—1945-
900	C	Auxiliary sciences of history	909.0803	D205	History, Modern—Dictionaries
900	CB	Civilization			
900	D	History	909.08072	D206	Historiography
900	D11-.5	Chronology, Historical	909.0971241	DA10-18.2	Commonwealth countries—History
901	CB19	Civilization—Philosophy			
901	D16-.18	History—Methodology	909.09724	D880-888	Developing countries—History
901	D16.7-.9	History—Philosophy			
901	D16.9	Historicism	909.09749270 (5-821)	DS38.8	Arab countries—History—1517-1918
901.9	D16.16	Psychohistory			
902.22	CB13	Civilization—Pictorial works	909.097492708	DS38.9	Arab countries—History—1798-
902.28	D16	Historical models			
903	CB9	Civilization—Dictionaries	909.09749270 + 82	DS39	Arab countries—History—20th century
903	D9	History—Dictionaries			
904	CT9970-9971	Adventure and adventurers	909.09749270 + 821	DS39	Arab countries—History—Arab Revolt, 1916-1918
904	G521-539	Adventure and adventurers			
904	GB5018	Natural disasters			
904	PN4784.D57	Disasters in the press	909.097645	DS423-425	Civilization, Hindu
905	C4	Auxiliary sciences of history—Periodicals	909.0976701	DS35.62	Civilization, Islamic
			909.09811	D890-893	Eastern Hemisphere—History
905	CB3	Civilization—Periodicals			
905	D1	History—Periodicals	909.09812	CB245	Civilization, Western
906	C2	Auxiliary sciences of history—Societies, etc.	909.1	CB353	Twelfth century
			909.1	D201.7-.8	Twelfth century
906	C3	Auxiliary sciences of history—Congresses	909.5	CB367-401	Sixteenth century
			909.5	D219-234	History, Modern—16th century
906	D3	History—Congresses			
907.1	CB20	Civilization—Study and teaching	909.6	D242-283.5	Seventeenth century
			909.6	D242-283.5	History, Modern—17th century
907.1	D16.2-.5	History—Study and teaching			
			909.81	CB415-417	Nineteenth century
907.2	CB15-18	Civilization—Historiography	909.81	D351-400	Nineteenth century
907.2	D13-15	Historiography	909.8(24-3)05	D839	History, Modern—1945-—Periodicals
907.202	D14-15	Historians			
907.201822	DE8-9	Mediterranean Region—Historiography	909.82	CB425-430	Twentieth century
			909.82	D410-893	Twentieth century
909	HM101	Civilization	909.82	D410-893	History, Modern—20th century
909	CB481	War and civilization			
909	D17-24.5	World history	910	G	Geography
909	D31-34	World politics	910	G128	Geography
909.04	CB195-281	Race	910	G149-922	Voyages and travels
909.0491497	DX	Gypsies	910	G149-180	Travel
909.0491497	DX135-145	Gypsies—History	910	GN476.4	Geography
909.04924	BS649.J5	Jews—Restoration	910.01	G70-.4	Geography—Methodology
			910.02	GB	Physical geography

Dewey	LC	Subject Heading	Dewey	LC	Subject Heading
910.0211	G575-597	Polar regions	912.19812	G1100-1779	Western Hemisphere—Maps
910.0213	G905-910	Tropics	912.19813	G1050	Northern Hemisphere—Maps
910.0216327	G640-665	Northwest Passage	912.19813	G3210-3212	Northern Hemisphere—Maps
910.021732	GF125	Urban geography			
910.021734	GF127	Rural geography	912.19814	G1052	Southern Hemisphere—Maps
910.021811	G680-700	Eastern Hemisphere	912.19814	G3220-3222	Southern Hemisphere—Maps
910.021813	G912-916	Northern Hemisphere			
910.021814	G918-922	Southern Hemisphere	912.4	G5700-7153	Europe—Maps
910.202	G153	Travel—Guidebooks	912.41	G1805-1829.24	Great Britain—Maps
910.21	G109-110	Distances—Tables	912.41	G5740-5814	Great Britain—Maps
910.41	G420-445	Voyages around the world	912.411	G5770-5774	Scotland—Maps
910.41	G445	Flights around the world	912.415	G5780-5784	Ireland—Maps
910.45	G540-550	Seafaring life	912.416	G5790-5794	Northern Ireland—Maps
910.45	G540-550	Ocean travel	912.42	G5750-5754	England—Maps
910.45	G545	Whaling	912.429	G5760-5764	Wales—Maps
910.45092	F2161	Buccaneers	912.43	G1907-1924	Germany—Maps
910.45092	G535-537	Buccaneers	912.43	G6080-6428	Germany—Maps
910.45092	G535-537	Pirates	912.436	G1935-1939	Austria—Maps
910.452	G521-539	Shipwrecks	912.436	G6490-6494	Austria—Maps
910.45209164	G530.H82	Shipwrecks—Pacific Ocean	912.43648	G6050-6054	Liechtenstein—Maps
910.46	TX901-946	Hotels	912.437	G1945-1949	Czechoslovakia—Maps
910.460683	TX911.3.P4	Hotels—Personnel management	912.437	G6510-6514	Czechoslovakia—Maps
910.466	TX901-941	Tourist camps, hostels, etc.	912.438	G1950-1954	Poland—Maps
910.466	TX907-910	Youth hostels	912.438	G6520-6524	Poland—Maps
910.6	G2-55	Geography—Societies, etc.	912.439	G1940-1944	Hungary—Maps
910.71	G72-76.5	Geography—Study and teaching	912.439	G6500-6504	Hungary—Maps
910.83	G156.5.Y6	Youth—Travel	912.44	G1837-1844.24	France—Maps
910.9	G80-99	Geography—History	912.44	G5830-5834	France—Maps
910.9	G200-336	Discoveries in geography	912.44949	G5980-5984	Monaco—Maps
910.92	G67-69	Geographers—Biography	912.45	G1983-1989.53	Italy—Maps
910.92	G200-336	Travelers	912.45	G6710-6714	Italy—Maps
911	G141	Historical geography	912.458	G6760-6763	Sicily (Italy)—Maps
911.0902	G89-95	Geography, Medieval	912.46	G1965-1969	Spain—Maps
911.4	G1791-1799	Europe—Historical geography—Maps	912.46	G6560-6564	Spain—Maps
911.41	G5741	Great Britain—Historical geography—Maps	912.469	G1975-1979	Portugal—Maps
			912.469	G6690-6694	Portugal—Maps
911.73	G3701	United States—Historical geography—Maps	912.4698	G9140-9144	Madeira Islands—Maps
			912.4699	G9130-9134	Azores—Maps
912	G1001-1046	World maps	912.47	G2110-2193	Russia—Maps
912	G3200-9980	Maps	912.47	G7060-7342	Russia—Maps
912	GA101-130	Outline maps	912.4796	G7040-7043	Latvia—Maps
912.191	G1054-1055	Polar regions—Maps	912.4798	G7030-7033	Estonia—Maps
912.191	G3260-3272	Polar regions—Maps	912.48	G6910-6963	Scandinavia—Maps
912.193	G1053	Tropics—Maps	912.481	G2065-2069	Norway—Maps
912.193	G3240-3241	Tropics—Maps	912.481	G6940-6944	Norway—Maps
912.1954	G1046.C813	Deserts—Maps	912.485	G2070-2074	Sweden—Maps
912.1962	G1059-1061	Nautical charts	912.485	G6950-6954	Sweden—Maps
912.1963	G2805-2839	Atlantic Ocean—Maps	912.489	G2055-2059	Denmark—Maps
912.19632	G3055-3064	Arctic Ocean—Maps	912.489	G6920-6924	Denmark—Maps
912.1964	G2860-2867	Pacific Ocean—Maps	912.4897	G2075-2079	Finland—Maps
912.19811	G1780-2799	Eastern Hemisphere—Maps	912.4897	G6960-6964	Finland—Maps
			912.4912	G2060-2064	Iceland—Maps

Dewey	LC	Subject Heading	Dewey	LC	Subject Heading
912.4912	G6930-6934	Iceland—Maps	912.55	G2255-2259	Iran—Maps
912.492	G1850-1874	Benelux countries	912.55	G7620-7624	Iran—Maps
912.492	G6000-6004	Netherlands—Maps	912.56	G7420-7624	Middle East—Maps
912.493	G6010-6014	Belgium—Maps	912.561	G2210-2214	Turkey—Maps
912.4935	G6020-6024	Luxembourg—Maps	912.561	G7430-7434	Turkey—Maps
912.494	G1895-1899	Switzerland—Maps	912.567	G2250-2254	Iraq—Maps
912.494	G6040-6044	Switzerland—Maps	912.567	G7610-7614	Iraq—Maps
912.4947	G6035-6036	Alps—Maps	912.5691	G2220-2224	Syria—Maps
912.495	G2000-2004	Greece—Maps	912.5691	G7460-7464	Syria—Maps
912.495	G6810-6814	Greece—Maps	912.5692	G2225-2229	Lebanon—Maps
912.497	G6840-6844	Yugoslavia—Maps	912.5692	G7470-7474	Lebanon—Maps
912.4971	G2015-2017	Serbia—Maps	912.5693	G2215-2219	Cyprus—Maps
912.4971	G6850-6853	Serbia—Maps	912.5693	G7450-7454	Cyprus—Maps
912.4972	G2025-2027	Dalmatia (Croatia)—Maps	912.5694	G2235-2239	Israel—Maps
912.4972	G2030-2032	Croatia—Maps	912.5694	G7500-7504	Israel—Maps
912.4972	G6870-6873	Croatia—Maps	912.5695	G2240-2244	Jordan—Maps
912.4973	G6875-6878	Slovenia—Maps	912.5695	G7510-7514	Jordan—Maps
912.49742	G6860-6863	Bosnia and Herzegovina—Maps	912.581	G2265-2269	Afghanistan—Maps
			912.581	G7630-7634	Afghanistan—Maps
912.49745	G2020-2022	Montenegro—Maps	912.59	G8000-8198.54	Indochina—Maps
912.498	G2035-2039	Romania—Maps	912.591	G2285-2289	Burma—Maps
912.498	G6880-6884	Romania—Maps	912.591	G7720-7724	Burma—Maps
912.499	G2040-2044	Bulgaria—Maps	912.593	G2375-2379	Thailand—Maps
912.499	G6890-6894	Bulgaria—Maps	912.593	G8025-8029	Thailand—Maps
912.5	G2200-2444	Asia—Maps	912.594	G2374.5-.54	Laos—Maps
912.5	G7400-8198.54	Asia—Maps	912.594	G8015-8019	Laos—Maps
912.51	G2305-2321	China—Maps	912.595	G8030-8034	Malaysia—Maps
912.51	G7820-7824	China—Maps	912.5957	G8040-8044	Singapore—Maps
912.51249	G2340-2344	Taiwan—Maps	912.596	G2374.3-.34	Cambodia—Maps
912.5125	G7940-7944	Hong Kong—Maps	912.596	G8010-8014	Cambodia—Maps
912.5126	G7945-7947	Macao—Maps	912.597	G2370-2374	Vietnam—Maps
912.517	G7895-7899	Mongolia—Maps	912.597	G8020-8024	Vietnam—Maps
912.519	G2330-2334.34	Korea—Maps	912.598	G8070-8074	Indonesia—Maps
912.52	G2355-2359	Japan—Maps	912.599	G8060-8064	Philippines—Maps
912.52	G7960-7964	Japan—Maps	912.6	G2445-2739	Africa—Maps
912.533	G7550-7554	Yemen—Maps	912.6	G8200-8202	Africa—Maps
912.5353	G7560-7564	Oman—Maps	912.61	G2455-2499	Africa, North—Maps
912.5363	G7580-7584	Qatar—Maps	912.61	G8220-8222	Africa, North—Maps
912.5365	G7590-7594	Bahrain—Maps	912.611	G8250-8254	Tunisia—Maps
912.5367	G7600-7604	Kuwait—Maps	912.612	G8260-8264	Libya—Maps
912.538	G2249.3-.34	Saudi Arabia—Maps	912.62	G8300-8304	Egypt—Maps
912.538	G7530-7534	Saudi Arabia—Maps	912.63	G8330-8334	Ethiopia—Maps
912.54	G2280-2284	India—Maps	912.64	G8230-8234	Morocco—Maps
912.54	G7650-7654	India—Maps	912.649	G9150-9154	Canary Islands—Maps
912.5491	G2270-2274	Pakistan—Maps	912.65	G8240-8244	Algeria—Maps
912.5491	G7640-7644	Pakistan—Maps	912.66	G2640-2714	Africa, West—Maps
912.5492	G2275-2279	Bangladesh—Maps	912.661	G8820-8824	Mauritania—Maps
912.5492	G7645-7649	Bangladesh—Maps	912.6623	G8800-8804	Mali—Maps
912.5493	G2290-2294	Sri Lanka—Maps	912.6625	G8805-8809	Burkina Faso—Maps
912.5493	G7750-7754	Sri Lanka—Maps	912.6626	G8770-8774	Niger—Maps
912.5495	G9215-9219	Maldives—Maps	912.663	G8810-8814	Senegal—Maps
912.5496	G2295-2299	Nepal—Maps	912.664	G8860-8864	Sierra Leone—Maps
912.5496	G7760-7764	Nepal—Maps	912.6651	G8870-8874	Gambia—Maps
912.5498	G7780-7784	Bhutan—Maps	912.6652	G8790-8794	Guinea—Maps

Dewey	LC	Subject Heading	Dewey	LC	Subject Heading
912.6657	G8890-8894	Guinea-Bissau—Maps	912.715	G3410-3444	Maritime Provinces—Maps
912.6658	G9160-9164	Cape Verde—Maps	912.7151	G3430-3434	New Brunswick—Maps
912.6662	G8880-8884	Liberia—Maps	912.716	G3420-3424	Nova Scotia—Maps
912.6668	G8780-8784	Cote d'Ivoire—Maps	912.717	G3440-3444	Prince Edward Island—
912.667	G8850-8854	Ghana—Maps			Maps
912.6681	G8760-8764	Togo—Maps	912.718	G3600-3604	Newfoundland—Maps
912.6683	G8750-8754	Benin—Maps	912.7182	G3610-3612	Labrador (Nfld.)—Maps
912.669	G8840-8844	Nigeria—Maps	912.7191	G3520-3524	Yukon Territory—Maps
912.67	G2590-2639	Africa, Central—Maps	912.7192	G3530-3564	Northwest Territories—
912.6711	G8730-8734	Cameroon—Maps			Maps
912.6715	G8675-8679	Sao Tome and Principe—	912.72	G1545-1549	Mexico—Maps
		Maps	912.72	G4410-4414	Mexico—Maps
912.6718	G8660-8664	Equatorial Guinea—Maps	912.728	G1550-1594	Central America—Maps
912.6721	G8690-8694	Gabon—Maps	912.728	G4800-4884	Central America—Maps
912.6724	G8700-8704	Congo (Brazzaville)—Maps	912.7281	G4810-4814	Guatemala—Maps
912.673	G8640-8644	Angola—Maps	912.7282	G4820-4824	Belize—Maps
912.6741	G8710-8714	Central African Republic—	912.7283	G4830-4834	Honduras—Maps
		Maps	912.7284	G4840-4844	El Salvador—Maps
912.6743	G8720-8724	Chad—Maps	912.7285	G4850-4854	Nicaragua—Maps
912.6751	G8650-8654	Zaire—Maps	912.7286	G4860-4864	Costa Rica—Maps
912.67571	G8430-8434	Rwanda—Maps	912.7287	G4870-4874	Panama—Maps
912.67572	G8435-8439	Burundi—Maps	912.729	G1535-1537	Caribbean Area—Maps
912.676	G2500-2559	Africa, East—Maps	912.729	G1600-1692	West Indies—Maps
912.6761	G8420-8424	Uganda—Maps	912.729	G4390-4392	Caribbean Area—Maps
912.6762	G8410-8414	Kenya—Maps	912.729	G4900-5184	West Indies—Maps
912.6773	G8350-8354	Somalia—Maps	912.7291	G4920-4924	Cuba—Maps
912.678	G8440-8444	Tanzania—Maps	912.7292	G4960-4964	Jamaica—Maps
912.679	G8450-8454	Mozambique—Maps	912.72921	G4965-4969	Cayman Islands—Maps
912.68	G8500-8504	South Africa—Maps	912.7293	G4950-4954	Dominican Republic—Maps
912.682	G8540-8543	Transvaal—Maps	912.7294	G4940-4944	Haiti—Maps
912.684	G8530-8533	Natal (South Africa)—Maps	912.7295	G4970-4974	Puerto Rico—Maps
912.6881	G8620-8624	Namibia—Maps	912.7296	G4980-4984	Bahamas—Maps
912.6883	G8600-8604	Botswana—Maps	912.7297	G5030-5059	Leeward Islands (West
912.6885	G8580-8584	Lesotho—Maps			Indies)—Maps
912.6887	G8590-8594	Swaziland—Maps	912.729722	G5010-5014	Virgin Islands of the United
912.6897	G8610-8614	Malawi—Maps			States—Maps
912.691	G8460-8464	Madagascar—Maps	912.729725	G5020-5024	British Virgin Islands—Maps
912.694	G9210-9214	Comoro Islands—Maps	912.72973	G5040-5044	Saint Kitts (Island)—Maps
912.696	G9200-9204	Seychelles—Maps	912.72973	G5045-5049	Anguilla—Maps
912.6981	G9190-9194	Reunion—Maps	912.72974	G5050-5054	Antigua—Maps
912.6982	G9185-9189	Mauritius—Maps	912.72975	G5055-5059	Montserrat—Maps
912.7	G1105-1692	North America—Maps	912.72976	G5070-5074	Guadeloupe—Maps
912.7	G3290-5669	America—Maps	912.7298	G5090-5184	Windward Islands—Maps
912.7	G3300-4884	North America—Maps	912.72981	G5140-5144	Barbados—Maps
912.7(4-5)	G3709.3-3933	Atlantic States—Maps	912.72982	G5080-5084	Martinique—Maps
912.71	G1115-1193	Canada—Maps	912.72983	G5150-5162	Trinidad and Tobago—Maps
912.71	G3400-3612	Canada—Maps	912.729841	G5100-5104	Dominica—Maps
912.711	G3510-3514	British Columbia—Maps	912.729843	G5110-5114	Saint Lucia—Maps
912.712	G3470-3504	Prairie Provinces—Maps	912.729844	G5120-5124	Saint Vincent—Maps
912.7123	G3500-3504	Alberta—Maps	912.729845	G5130-5134	Granada—Maps
912.7124	G3490-3494	Saskatchewan—Maps	912.72986	G5170-5174	Aruba—Maps
912.7127	G3480-3484	Manitoba—Maps	912.72986	G5175-5179	Bonaire—Maps
912.713	G3460-3464	Ontario—Maps	912.72986	G5180-5184	Curacao—Maps
912.714	G3450-3454	Quebec (Province)—Maps	912.73	G1200-1534.24	United States—Maps

Dewey	LC	Subject Heading	Dewey	LC	Subject Heading
912.73	G3690-3691	United States—Territories and possessions—Maps	912.793	G4350-4354	Nevada—Maps
912.73	G3690-4383	United States—Maps	912.794	G4360-4364	California—Maps
912.74	G3720-3784	New England—Maps	912.795	G4290-4294	Oregon—Maps
912.74	G3790-3854	Middle Atlantic States—Maps	912.796	G4270-4274	Idaho—Maps
912.741	G3730-3734	Maine—Maps	912.797	G4280-4284	Washington (State)—Maps
912.742	G3740-3744	New Hampshire—Maps	912.798	G4370-4374	Alaska—Maps
912.743	G3750-3754	Vermont—Maps	912.8	G1700-1779	South America—Maps
912.744	G3760-3764	Massachusetts—Maps	912.8	G5200-5668	South America—Maps
912.745	G3770-3774	Rhode Island—Maps	912.81	G5400-5404	Brazil—Maps
912.746	G3780-3784	Connecticut—Maps	912.82	G5350-5354	Argentina—Maps
912.747	G3800-3804	New York (State)—Maps	912.83	G5330-5334	Chile—Maps
912.748	G3820-3824	Pennsylvania—Maps	912.84	G5320-5324	Bolivia—Maps
912.749	G3810-3814	New Jersey—Maps	912.85	G5310-5314	Peru—Maps
912.75	G3870-3933	South Atlantic States—Maps	912.861	G5290-5294	Colombia—Maps
			912.866	G5300-5304	Ecuador—Maps
912.751	G3830-3834	Delaware—Maps	912.87	G5280-5284	Venezuela—Maps
912.752	G3840-3844	Maryland—Maps	912.881	G5250-5254	Guyana—Maps
912.753	G3850-3854	Washington (D.C.)—Maps	912.882	G5270-5274	French Guiana—Maps
912.754	G3890-3894	West Virginia—Maps	912.883	G5260-5264	Surinam—Maps
912.755	G3880-3884	Virginia—Maps	912.892	G5380-5384	Paraguay—Maps
912.756	G3900-3904	North Carolina—Maps	912.895	G5370-5374	Uruguay—Maps
912.757	G3910-3914	South Carolina—Maps	912.93	G2795-2799	New Zealand—Maps
912.758	G3920-3924	Georgia—Maps	912.93	G9080-9084	New Zealand—Maps
912.759	G3930-3934	Florida—Maps	912.94	G2750-2793	Australia—Maps
912.761	G3970-3974	Alabama—Maps	912.94	G8960-8964	Australia—Maps
912.762	G3980-3984	Mississippi—Maps	912.95	G2870-2894	Melanesia—Maps
912.763	G4010-4014	Louisiana—Maps	912.95	G8140-8142	New Guinea—Maps
912.764	G4030-4034	Texas—Maps	912.95	G9260-9262	Melanesia—Maps
912.766	G4020-4024	Oklahoma—Maps	912.9593	G9280-9284	Solomon Islands—Maps
912.767	G4000-4004	Arkansas—Maps	912.9595	G9295-9297	Vanuatu—Maps
912.768	G3960-3964	Tennessee—Maps	912.9597	G9340-9344	New Caledonia—Maps
912.769	G3950-3954	Kentucky—Maps	912.96	G2970-2984	Polynesia—Maps
912.771	G4080-4084	Ohio—Maps	912.96	G9500-9652	Polynesia—Maps
912.772	G4090-4094	Indiana—Maps	912.961(3-4)	G9555-9557	Samoan Islands—Maps
912.773	G4100-4104	Illinois—Maps	912.9611	G9380-9384	Fiji—Maps
912.774	G4110-4114	Michigan—Maps	912.9612	G9570-9574	Tonga—Maps
912.775	G4120-4124	Wisconsin—Maps	912.9615	G9550-9554	Tokelau—Maps
912.776	G4140-4144	Minnesota—Maps	912.9616	G9515-9517	Wallis and Futuna Islands—Maps
912.777	G4150-4154	Iowa—Maps			
912.778	G4160-4164	Missouri—Maps	912.9618	G9660-9664	Pitcairn Island—Maps
912.78	G4050-4052	West (U.S.)—Maps	912.9621	G9640-9644	Society Islands—Maps
912.781	G4200-4204	Kansas—Maps	912.9623	G9600-9604	Cook Islands—Maps
912.782	G4190-4194	Nebraska—Maps	912.9631	G9620-9624	Marquesas Islands—Maps
912.783	G4180-4184	South Dakota—Maps	912.964	G9530-9534	Line Islands—Maps
912.784	G4170-4174	North Dakota—Maps	912.965	G2905-2934	Micronesia—Maps
912.786	G4250-4254	Montana—Maps	912.965	G9400-9494	Micronesia—Maps
912.787	G4260-4264	Wyoming—Maps	912.966	G9420-9424	Caroline Islands—Maps
912.788	G4310-4314	Colorado—Maps	912.967	G9410-9414	Mariana Islands—Maps
912.789	G4320-4324	New Mexico—Maps	912.9681	G9480-9484	Kiribati—Maps
912.79	G4230-4232	Pacific States—Maps	912.9683	G9460-9464	Marshall Islands—Maps
912.791	G4330-4334	Arizona—Maps	912.969	G4380-4384	Hawaii—Maps
912.792	G4340-4344	Utah—Maps	912.9711	G9175-9179	Falkland Islands—Maps
			912.973	G9170-9174	Saint Helena—Maps
			912.982	G1110-1114	Greenland—Maps

Dewey	LC	Subject Heading	Dewey	LC	Subject Heading
912.982	G3380-3384	Greenland—Maps	913.6404	DH431-435	Belgium—Description and travel
912.989	G3100-3102	Antarctica—Maps			
912.989	G9800-9804	Antarctica—Maps	913.6404	DQ20-26	Switzerland—Description and travel
912.991	G1000.3-.5	Moon—Maps			
912.991	G3195-3199	Moon—Maps	913.66003	DP12	Spain—Gazetteers
913	G83-88	Geography, Ancient	913.66003	DP514	Portugal—Gazetteers
913.104	DS707-712	China—Description and travel	913.6604	DP27-43.2	Spain—Description and travel
913.104	DS799.15-.24	Taiwan—Description and travel	913.6604	DP520-526.5	Portugal—Description and travel
913.2003	DT45	Egypt—Gazetteers	913.(7-8)	DE23-31	Classical geography
913.204	DT49.98-56	Egypt—Description and travel	913.(7-8)	G87	Classical geography
			913.7	DG27-31	Rome—Geography
913.304	DS103-108.5	Israel—Description and travel	913.7003	DG415	Italy—Gazetteers
			913.704	DG421.5-430.2	Italy—Description and travel
913.304	DS153.2	Jordan—Description and travel	913.804	DF27-30	Greece—Description and travel
913.404	DS377	Pakistan—Description and travel	913.9204	DR421-429.4	Turkey—Description and travel
913.5003	DS67.8	Iraq—Gazetteers	913.93704	DS54.A4-Z	Cyprus—Description and travel
913.5003	DS253	Iran—Gazetteers			
913.504	DS255-259.2	Iran—Description and travel	913.94003	DS43	Middle East—Gazetteers
913.63003	DD14	Germany—Gazetteers	913.9404	DS44.98-49.7	Middle East—Description and travel
913.63003	DD308	Prussia (Germany)—Gazetteers	913.943003	DS92.6	Syria—Gazetteers
913.63003	DH14	Netherlands—Gazetteers	913.94304	DS94	Syria—Description and travel
913.63003	DJ14	Netherlands—Gazetteers			
913.63003	DL4	Scandinavia—Gazetteers	913.944003	DS80.A5	Lebanon—Gazetteers
913.63003	DL105	Denmark—Gazetteers	913.94404	DS80.2	Lebanon—Description and travel
913.63003	DL405	Norway—Gazetteers			
913.63003	DL605	Sweden—Gazetteers	913.94904	DS204.5-208	Saudi Arabia—Description and travel
913.6304	DD21.5-43	Germany—Description and travel	913.96003	DS351	Afghanistan—Gazetteers
913.6304	DD314-320	Prussia (Germany)—Description and travel	913.9604	DS352	Afghanistan—Description and travel
913.6304	DH31-40	Netherlands—Description and travel	913.9704	DT163-165.2	Africa, North—Description and travel
913.6304	DJ33-41	Netherlands—Description and travel	913.971003	DT274	Algeria—Gazetteers
			913.971003	DT304	Morocco—Gazetteers
913.6304	DL6.7-11.5	Scandinavia—Description and travel	913.97104	DT277.8-280.2	Algeria—Description and travel
913.6304	DL115-120	Denmark—Description and travel	913.97104	DT307-310.2	Morocco—Description and travel
913.6304	DL415-419.2	Norway—Description and travel	913.973003	DT244	Tunisia—Gazetteers
913.6304	DL614.55-619.5	Sweden—Description and travel	913.97304	DT248-250.2	Tunisia—Description and travel
913.6304	DB21-27.5	Austria—Description and travel	913.97404	DT218-220.2	Libya—Description and travel
913.6304	DB888	Liechtenstein—Description and travel	913.98003	DR53	Bulgaria—Gazetteers
			913.98003	DR907	Albania—Gazetteers
913.64003	DH414	Belgium—Gazetteers	913.98003	DR1209	Yugoslavia—Gazetteers
913.64003	DQ14	Switzerland—Gazetteers	913.98003	DB904	Hungary—Gazetteers
913.64003	DC14	France—Gazetteers	913.9804	DB906.9-917.3	Hungary—Description and travel
913.6404	DC21-29.3	France—Description and travel	913.9804	DR57-61	Bulgaria—Description and travel

Dewey	LC	Subject Heading	Dewey	LC	Subject Heading
913.9804	DR207-210	Romania—Description and travel	914.7(04)	DK19-29	Russia—Description and travel
913.9804	DR914-918	Albania—Description and travel	914.70003	DJK6	Europe, Eastern—Gazetteers
913.9804	DR1218-1224	Yugoslavia—Description and travel	914.7003	DK14	Russia—Gazetteers
914	D901-980	Europe—Description and travel	914.7004	DJK11-18	Europe, Eastern—Description and travel
914.1003	DA640	Great Britain—Gazetteers	914.75604	DS165	Armenia—Description and travel
914.1104	DA850-878	Scotland—Description and travel	914.78003	DK507.18	Belarus—Gazetteers
914.1504	DA969-988	Ireland—Description and travel	914.793003	DK505.18	Lithuania—Gazetteers
			914.796003	DK504.18	Latvia—Gazetteers
914.204	DA600-632	England—Description and travel	914.798003	DK503.18	Estonia—Gazetteers
914.2904	DA725-731.2	Wales—Description and travel	914.8003	DL4	Scandinavia—Gazetteers
			914.804	DL6.7-11.5	Scandinavia—Description and travel
914.3003	DD14	Germany—Gazetteers	914.81003	DL405	Norway—Gazetteers
914.3003	DD308	Prussia(Germany)—Gazetteers	914.8104	DL415-419.2	Norway—Description and travel
914.304	DD21.5-43	Germany—Description and travel	914.843	G778-787	Arctic regions—Norwegian
914.304	DD314-320	Prussia (Germany)—Description and travel	914.85003	DL605	Sweden—Gazetteers
914.304	DAW1014-1015	Europe, Central—Description and travel	914.8504	DL614.55-619.5	Sweden—Description and travel
914.36003	DB14	Austria—Gazetteers	914.89003	DL105	Denmark—Gazetteers
914.3604	DB21-27.5	Austria—Description and travel	914.8904	DL115-120	Denmark—Description and travel
914.364804	DB888	Liechtenstein—Description and travel	914.897003	DL1007	Finland—Gazetteers
			914.89704	DL1015-.4	Finland—Description and travel
914.37003	DB2007	Czechoslovakia—Gazetteers	914.912003	DL304	Iceland—Gazetteers
914.37(04)	DB2018-2022	Czechoslovakia—Description and travel	914.91204	DL309-315	Iceland—Description and travel
914.373003	DB2707	Slovakia—Gazetteers	914.92003	DH14	Netherlands—Gazetteers
914.37304	DB2718-2722	Slovakia—Description and travel	914.92003	DJ14	Netherlands—Gazetteers
914.38003	DK4030	Poland—Gazetteers	914.9204	DH31-40	Netherlands—Description and travel
914.3804	DK4047-4081	Poland—Description and travel	914.9204	DJ33-41	Netherlands—Description and travel
914.39003	DB904	Hungary—Gazetteers	914.93003	DH414	Belgium—Gazetteers
914.3904	DB906.9-917.3	Hungary—Description and travel	914.9304	DH431-435	Belgium—Description and travel
914.4003	DC14	France—Gazetteers	914.935003	DH903	Luxembourg—Gazetteers
914.404	DC21-29.3	France—Description and travel	914.93504	DH906-907	Luxembourg—Description and travel
914.4040904	DC29	France—Description and travel—1945-1974	914.94003	DQ14	Switzerland—Gazetteers
914.5003	DG415	Italy—Gazetteers	914.9404	DQ20-26	Switzerland—Description and travel
914.504	DG421.5-430.2	Italy—Description and travel	914.95	DF518	Byzantine Empire—Geography
914.6003	DP12	Spain—Gazetteers	914.9504	DF27-30	Greece—Description and travel
914.604	DP27-43.2	Spain—Description and travel	914.9504	DF721-728	Greece—Description and travel
914.69003	DP514	Portugal—Gazetteers	914.96003	DR5	Balkan Peninsula—Gazetteers
914.6904	DP520-526.5	Portugal—Description and travel			

Dewey	LC	Subject Heading	Dewey	LC	Subject Heading
914.9604	DR11-16	Balkan Peninsula—Description and travel	915.69104	DS94	Syria—Description and travel
914.965003	DR907	Albania—Gazetteers	915.692003	DS80.A5	Lebanon—Gazetteers
914.96504	DR914-918	Albania—Description and travel	915.69204	DS80.2	Lebanon—Description and travel
914.97003	DR1209	Yugoslavia—Gazetteers	915.69304	DS54.A4-Z	Cyprus—Description and travel
914.9704	DR1218-1224	Yugoslavia—Description and travel	915.69404	DS103-108.5	Israel—Description and travel
914.98003	DR204	Romania—Gazetteers			
914.9804	DR207-210	Romania—Description and travel	915.69504	DS153.2	Jordan—Description and travel
914.99003	DR53	Bulgaria—Gazetteers	915.7	G820-839	Arctic regions—Siberian
914.9904	DR57-61	Bulgaria—Description and travel	915.81003	DS351	Afghanistan—Gazetteers
			915.8104	DS352	Afghanistan—Description and travel
915.03	DS4	Asia—Gazetteers			
915.04	DS5.95-10	Asia—Description and travel	915.9104	DS527.5-.7	Burma—Description and travel
915.1003	DS705	China—Gazetteers			
915.104	DS707-712	China—Description and travel	915.93003	DS563	Thailand—Gazetteers
			915.9304	DS564-566.2	Thailand—Description and travel
915.1249003	DS798.96	Taiwan—Gazetteers			
915.124904	DS799.15-.24	Taiwan—Description and travel	915.94003	DS555.25	Laos—Gazetteers
			915.9404	DS555.34-.382	Laos—Description and travel
915.15	DS785	Tibet (China)—Description and travel			
			915.95003	DS591.5	Malaysia—Gazetteers
915.17304	DS793.G6	Gobi Desert (Mongolia and China)—	915.9504	DS592.4-.6	Malaysia—Description and travel
		Description and travel	915.955003	DS650.2	Brunei—Gazetteers
915.19003	DS901.8	Korea—Gazetteers	915.95504	DS650.35	Brunei—Description and travel
915.1904	DS902.2-.4	Korea—Description and travel			
			915.96003	DS554.25	Cambodia—Gazetteers
915.2003	DS805	Japan—Gazetteers	915.9604	DS554.34-.382	Cambodia—Description and travel
915.204	DS807-811	Japan—Description and travel			
			915.97003	DS556.25	Vietnam—Gazetteers
915.3804	DS204.5-208	Saudi Arabia—Description and travel	915.9704	DS556.34-.39	Vietnam—Description and travel
915.491003	DS376.8	Pakistan—Gazetteers	915.98003	DS614	Indonesia—Gazetteers
915.49104	DS377	Pakistan—Description and travel	915.9804	DS617-620	Indonesia—Description and travel
915.492003	DS393.3	Bangladesh—Gazetteers	915.99003	DS654	Philippines—Gazetteers
915.493003	DS488.9	Sri Lanka—Gazetteers	915.9904	DS658-660	Philippines—Description and travel
915.49304	DS489-.15	Sri Lanka—Description and travel			
			916.003	DT2	Africa—Gazetteers
915.496	DS493.3	Nepal—Gazetteers	916.04	DT6.5-12.25	Africa—Description and travel
915.49604	DS493.5-.53	Nepal—Description and travel			
			916.04	G516	Safaris
915.49804	DS491.5	Bhutan—Description and travel	916.104	DT163-165.2	Africa, North—Description and travel
915.5003	DS253	Iran—Gazetteers	916.11003	DT244	Tunisia—Gazetteers
915.504	DS255-259.2	Iran—Description and travel	916.1104	DT248-250.2	Tunisia—Description and travel
915.6003	DS43	Middle East—Gazetteers			
915.604	DS44.98-49.7	Middle East—Description and travel	916.1204	DT218-220.2	Libya—Description and travel
915.6104	DR421-429.4	Turkey—Description and travel	916.2003	DT45	Egypt—Gazetteers
			916.204	DT49.98-56	Egypt—Description and travel
915.67003	DS67.8	Iraq—Gazetteers			
915.691003	DS92.6	Syria—Gazetteers	916.24003	DT154.4	Sudan—Gazetteers

Dewey	LC	Subject Heading	Dewey	LC	Subject Heading
916.2404	DT154.7-.75	Sudan—Description and travel	916.718003	DT620.15	Equatorial Guinea—Gazetteers
916.3003	DT371.5	Ethiopia—Gazetteers	916.721003	DT546.115	Gabon—Gazetteers
916.304	DT375-378.3	Ethiopia—Description and travel	916.72104	DT546.127-.128	Gabon—Description and travel
916.4003	DT304	Morocco—Gazetteers	916.724003	DT546.215	Congo (Brazzaville)—Gazetteers
916.404	DT307-310.2	Morocco—Description and travel	916.73003	DT1264	Angola—Gazetteers
916.5003	DT274	Algeria—Gazetteers	916.7304	DT1282-1286	Angola—Description and travel
916.504	DT277.8-280.2	Algeria—Description and travel	916.741003	DT546.315	Central African Republic—Gazetteers
916.604	DT333	Sahara—Description and travel	916.74304	DT546.427	Chad—Description and travel
916.61003	DT554.15	Mauritania—Gazetteers	916.75104	DT639	Congo River—Description and travel
916.6104	DT554.27	Mauritania—Description and travel	916.75104	DT645-647.5	Zaire—Description and travel
916.623003	DT551.15	Mali—Gazetteers	916.7571003	DT450.115	Rwanda—Gazetteers
916.62304	DT551.27	Mali—Description and travel	916.757104	DT450.2	Rwanda—Description and travel
916.625003	DT555.15	Burkina Faso—Gazetteers	916.7572003	DT450.515	Burundi—Gazetteers
916.62504	DT555.27	Burkina Faso—Description and travel	916.757204	DT450.6	Burundi—Description and travel
916.62604	DT547.27	Niger—Description and travel	916.761003	DT433.215	Uganda—Gazetteers
916.63003	DT549.15	Senegal—Gazetteers	916.76104	DT433.227	Uganda—Description and travel
916.6304	DT549.27	Senegal—Description and travel	916.762003	DT433.515	Kenya—Gazetteers
916.64003	DT516.15	Sierra Leone—Gazetteers	916.76204	DT433.527	Kenya—Description and travel
916.6404	DT516.2	Sierra Leone—Description and travel	916.771003	DT411.15	Djibouti—Gazetteers
916.65104	DT509.27	Gambia—Description and travel	916.77104	DT411.27	Djibouti—Description and travel
916.65204	DT543.27	Guinea—Description and travel	916.773003	DT401.2	Somalia—Gazetteers
916.65704	DT613.2	Guinea-Bissau—Description and travel	916.77304	DT401.8	Somalia—Description and travel
916.65804	DT671.C22	Cape Verde—Description and travel	916.78003	DT437	Tanzania—Gazetteers
916.662003	DT623	Liberia—Gazetteers	916.7804	DT439-440.5	Tanzania—Description and travel
916.66204	DT625-627	Liberia—Description and travel	916.79003	DT3294	Mozambique—Gazetteers
916.668003	DT545.15	Cote d'Ivoire—Gazetteers	916.7904	DT3308-3312	Mozambique—Description and travel
916.66804	DT545.27	Cote d'Ivoire—Description and travel	916.8003	DT1714	South Africa—Gazetteers
916.6704	DT510.2	Ghana—Description and travel	916.804	DT1730-1738	South Africa—Description and travel
916.681003	DT582.15	Togo—Gazetteers	916.881003	DT1514	Namibia—Gazetteers
916.68104	DT582.27	Togo—Description and travel	916.88104	DT1532-1536	Namibia—Description and travel
916.68304	DT541.27	Benin—Description and travel	916.883003	DT2434	Botswana—Gazetteers
916.69003	DT515.15	Nigeria—Gazetteers	916.885003	DT2554	Lesotho—Gazetteers
916.6904	DT515.27	Nigeria—Description and travel	916.88504	DT2572	Lesotho—Description and travel
916.711003	DT563	Cameroon—Gazetteers	916.887003	DT2714	Swaziland—Gazetteers
916.71104	DT566-568	Cameroon—Description and travel	916.88704	DT2732	Swaziland—Description and travel
			916.891003	DT2884	Zimbabwe—Gazetteers

Dewey	LC	Subject Heading	Dewey	LC	Subject Heading
916.89104	DT2900-2904	Zimbabwe—Description and travel	917.28404	F1484-.3	El Salvador—Description and travel
916.8910451	DT2886	Zimbabwe—Guidebooks	917.285003	F1522	Nicaragua—Gazetteers
916.894003	DT3037	Zambia—Gazetteers	917.28504	F1524-.3	Nicaragua—Description and travel
916.89404	DT3050	Zambia—Description and travel	917.286003	F1542	Costa Rica—Gazetteers
916.897003	DT3169	Malawi—Gazetteers	917.28604	F1544	Costa Rica—Description and travel
916.89704	DT3182	Malawi—Description and travel	917.287003	F1562	Panama—Gazetteers
916.91003	DT469.M24	Madagascar—Gazetteers	917.28704	F1564-.3	Panama—Description and travel
916.96003	DT469.S415	Seychelles—Gazetteers	917.29003	F1604	West Indies—Gazetteers
916.9604	DT469.S427	Seychelles—Description and travel	917.2904	F1610-1613	West Indies—Description and travel
916.981003	DT469.R32	Reunion—Gazetteers	917.291003	F1754	Cuba—Gazetteers
916.98104	DT469.R35	Reunion—Description and travel	917.29104	F1761-1765.3	Cuba—Description and travel
916.982003	DT469.M415	Mauritius—Gazetteers	917.292003	F1864	Jamaica—Gazetteers
916.98204	DT469.M429	Mauritius—Description and travel	917.29204	F1870-1872.2	Jamaica—Description and travel
917.003	E14	America—Gazetteers	917.293003	F1932	Dominican Republic—Gazetteers
917.003	E35	North America—Gazetteers	917.29304	F1936-.3	Dominican Republic—Description and travel
917.04	E41	North America—Description and travel	917.294003	F1913	Haiti—Gazetteers
917.1003	F1004	Canada—Gazetteers	917.29404	F1917	Haiti—Description and travel
917.104	F1012-1017	Canada—Description and travel	917.295003	F1954	Puerto Rico—Gazetteers
917.11003	F1086.4	British Columbia—Gazetteers	917.29504	F1961-1965.3	Puerto Rico—Description and travel
917.123003	F1075.4	Alberta—Gazetteers	917.296003	F1650.7	Bahamas—Gazetteers
917.124003	F1070.4	Saskatchewan—Gazetteers	917.29604	F1651	Bahamas—Description and travel
917.127003	F1061.4	Manitoba—Gazetteers	917.299003	F1630.7	Bermuda Islands—Gazetteers
917.13003	F1056.4	Ontario—Gazetteers			
917.14003	F1051.4	Quebec (Province)—Gazetteers	917.29904	F1631	Bermuda Islands—Description and travel
917.151003	F1041.4	New Brunswick—Gazetteers	917.3003	E154	United States—Gazetteers
917.16003	F1036.4	Nova Scotia—Gazetteers	917.304	E161.5-169.04	United States—Description and travel
917.18003	F1121.4	Newfoundland—Gazetteers	917.4003	F2	New England—Gazetteers
917.182003	F1135.4	Labrador (Nfld.)—Gazetteers	917.41003	F17	Maine—Gazetteers
917.191003	F1092	Yukon Territory—Gazetteers	917.42003	F32	New Hampshire—Gazetteers
917.2003	F1204	Mexico—Gazetteers	917.43003	F47	Vermont—Gazetteers
917.204	F1211-1216.5	Mexico—Description and travel	917.44003	F62	Massachusetts—Gazetteers
917.28003	F1424	Central America—Gazetteers	917.45003	F77	Rhode Island—Gazetteers
			917.46003	F92	Connecticut—Gazetteers
917.2804	F1431-1433.2	Central America—Description and travel	917.47003	F117	New York (State)—Gazetteers
917.281003	F1462	Guatemala—Gazetteers	917.48003	F147	Pennsylvania—Gazetteers
917.28104	F1464-.3	Guatemala—Description and travel	917.49003	F132	New Jersey—Gazetteers
917.28204	F1444-.3	Belize—Description and travel	917.51003	F162	Delaware—Gazetteers
917.283003	F1502	Honduras—Gazetteers	917.52003	F179	Maryland—Gazetteers
917.28304	F1504	Honduras—Description and Travel	917.53003	F192	Washington (D.C.)—Gazetteers
917.284003	F1482	El Salvador—Gazetteers			

Dewey	LC	Subject Heading	Dewey	LC	Subject Heading
917.54003	F239	West Virginia—Gazetteers	918.404	F3311-3315	Bolivia—Description and travel
917.55003	F224	Virginia—Gazetteers			
917.56003	F252	North Carolina—Gazetteers	918.5003	F3404	Peru—Gazetteers
917.57003	F267	South Carolina—Gazetteers	918.504	F3410.5-3425	Peru—Description and travel
917.58003	F284	Georgia—Gazetteers			
917.59003	F309	Florida—Gazetteers	918.61003	F2254	Colombia—Gazetteers
917.61003	F324	Alabama—Gazetteers	918.6104	F2259.5	Colombia—Guidebooks
917.62003	F339	Mississippi—Gazetteers	918.6104	F2261-2264.2	Colombia—Description and travel
917.63003	F367	Louisiana—Gazetteers			
917.64003	F384	Texas—Gazetteers	918.66003	F3704	Ecuador—Gazetteers
917.66003	F692	Oklahoma—Gazetteers	918.6604	F3711-3716	Ecuador—Description and travel
917.67003	F409	Arkansas—Gazetteers			
917.68003	F434	Tennessee—Gazetteers	918.7003	F2304	Venezuela—Gazetteers
917.69003	F449	Kentucky—Gazetteers	918.704	F2311-2315	Venezuela—Description and travel
917.71003	F489	Ohio—Gazetteers			
917.72003	F524	Indiana—Gazetteers	918.81003	F2364	Guyana—Gazetteers
917.73003	F539	Illinois—Gazetteers	918.82003	F2444	French Guiana—Gazetteers
917.74003	F564	Michigan—Gazetteers	918.8204	F2450-2452	French Guiana—Description and travel
917.75003	F579	Wisconsin—Gazetteers			
917.76003	F604	Minnesota—Gazetteers	918.83003	F2404	Surinam—Gazetteers
917.77003	F619	Iowa—Gazetteers	918.8304	F2410-2413	Surinam—Description and travel
917.78003	F464	Missouri—Gazetteers			
917.81003	F679	Kansas—Gazetteers	918.92003	F2664	Paraguay—Gazetteers
917.82003	F664	Nebraska—Gazetteers	918.9204	F2671-2676	Paraguay—Description and travel
917.83003	F649	South Dakota—Gazetteers			
917.84003	F634	North Dakota—Gazetteers	918.95003	F2704	Uruguay—Gazetteers
917.86003	F729	Montana—Gazetteers	918.9504	F2711-2715	Uruguay—Description and travel
917.87003	F759	Wyoming—Gazetteers			
917.88003	F774	Colorado—Gazetteers	919.(5-6)003	DU10	Oceania—Gazetteers
917.89003	F794	New Mexico—Gazetteers	919.(5-6)04	DU19-23.5	Oceania—Description and travel
917.91003	F809	Arizona—Gazetteers			
917.92003	F824	Utah—Gazetteers	919.3003	DU405	New Zealand—Gazetteers
917.93003	F839	Nevada—Gazetteers	919.304	DU409-413	New Zealand—Description and travel
917.94003	F859	California—Gazetteers			
917.95003	F874	Oregon—Gazetteers	919.4003	DU90	Australia—Gazetteers
917.96003	F744	Idaho—Gazetteers	919.404	DU97-5-105.2	Australia—Description and travel
917.97003	F889	Washington (State)—Gazetteers			
			919.69003	DU622	Hawaii—Gazetteers
917.98(6-7)	G725-770	Arctic regions—American	919.8	G600-839	Arctic regions
917.98008	F902	Alaska—Gazetteers	919.89	G845-890	Antarctica
918.003	E14	America—Gazetteers	919.890409034	G850	Expedition antarctique belge, 1897-1899
918.003	F1406	Latin America—Gazetteers			
918.04	F1409-.3	Latin America—Description and travel	920	CT	Biography
			920	CT25	Autobiography
918.1003	F2504	Brazil—Gazetteers	920	CT101	Autobiographies
918.104	F2511-2517	Brazil—Description and travel	920.00901	D55	Biography—To 500
			920.00902	D107-110.5	Biography—Middle Ages, 500-1500
918.2003	F2804	Argentina—Gazetteers	920.00902	D107	Emperors
918.204	F2811-2817	Argentina—Description and travel	920.00902	D115	Biography—Middle Ages, 500-1500
918.3003	F3054	Chile—Gazetteers	920.00904	D1070-1075	Biography—20th century
918.304	F3061-3065	Chile—Description and travel	920.009291497	DX125-127	Gypsies—Biography
			920.009296073	E185.96-.97	Afro-Americans—Biography
918.4003	F3304	Bolivia—Gazetteers	920.0361	DA28-.9	Great Britain—Biography
			920.0363	DB36-.7	Austria—Biography

Dewey	LC	Subject Heading	Dewey	LC	Subject Heading
920.0363	DD85-.8	Germany—Biography	920.07	E36	North America—Biography
920.0363	DH103	Netherlands—Biography	920.071	CT280-310	Canada—Biography
920.0363	DJ103-106	Netherlands—Biography	920.072	CT550-558	Mexico—Biography
920.0363	DL444	Norway—Biography	920.0728	CT570-638	Central America—Biography
920.0363	DL644	Sweden—Biography	920.0729	CT329-448	West Indies—Biography
920.0364	DH513-516	Belgium—Biography	920.073	E176	United States—Biography
920.0364	DQ52-.7	Switzerland—Biography	920.08	E17	America—Biography
920.0364	DC36-.8	France—Biography	920.08	CT640-758	South America—Biography
920.0366	DP58	Spain—Biography	920.0937	DE7	Classical biography
920.0366	DP536	Portugal—Biography	920.0938	DE7	Classical biography
920.037	DG203-204	Rome—Biography	920.0993	CT2880-2888	New Zealand—Biography
920.037	DG463-.8	Italy—Biography	920.0994	CT2800-2808	Australia—Biography
920.0398	DR66	Bulgaria—Biography	920.099(5-6)	CT2900-3090	Oceania—Biography
920.0398	DR928-934	Albania—Biography	920.72	CT3200-3830	Women—Biography
920.0398	DR1233-1235	Yugoslavia—Biography	929.1	CS	Genealogy
920.0398	DB922	Hungary—Biography	929.1025	CS5	Genealogy—Directories
920.04	CT759-1495	Europe—Biography	929.103	CS6	Genealogy—Dictionaries
920.041	CT770-858	Great Britain—Biography	929.105	CS1	Genealogy—Periodicals
920.041	DA28-.9	Great Britain—Biography	929.106	CS2	Genealogy—Congresses
920.0429	DA710	Wales—Biography	929.10720(4-9)	CS42-2209	[By region or country]—Genealogy
920.043	CT1050-1099.8	Germany—Biography			
920.043	DD85-.8	Germany—Biography	929.107204	CS410-1059	Europe—Genealogy
920.043	DD343-.8	Prussia (Germany)—Biography	929.1072041	CS410-479.5	Great Britain—Genealogy
			929.1072043	CS610-699	Germany—Genealogy
920.0436	DB36-.7	Austria—Biography	929.1072047	CS840-869	Russia—Genealogy
920.0438	DK4130-4138.5	Poland—Biography	929.1072048	CS890-939	Scandinavia—Genealogy
920.0439	DB922	Hungary—Biography	929.10720492	CS780-839	Benelux countries—Genealogy
920.044	DC36-.8	France—Biography			
920.045	DG463-.8	Italy—Biography	929.107205	CS1080-1549.5	Asia—Genealogy
920.046	DP58	Spain—Biography	929.107206	CS1550-1779	Africa—Genealogy
920.0469	DP536	Portugal—Biography	929.1072071	CS80-90	Canada—Genealogy
920.047	DJK31	Europe, Eastern—Biography	929.1072072	CS100-110	Mexico—Genealogy
920.048	CT1240-1328	Scandinavia—Biography	929.10720728	CS120-199	Central America—Genealogy
920.0481	DL444	Norway—Biography			
920.0485	DL644	Sweden—Biography	929.10720729	CS200-261	West Indies—Genealogy
920.04897	DL1024	Finland—Biography	929.1072073	CS42-71	United States—Genealogy
920.0492	DH103	Netherlands—Biography	929.107208	CS270-409	South America—Genealogy
920.0492	DJ103-106	Netherlands—Biography	929.1072093	CS2170-2179	New Zealand—Genealogy
920.0493	DH513-516	Belgium—Biography	929.1072094	CS2000-2009	Australia—Genealogy
920.04935	DH904	Luxembourg—Biography	929.107209(5-6	CS2191-2209	Oceania—Genealogy
920.0494	DQ52-.7	Switzerland—Biography	929.4	CS2300-3090	Names, Personal
920.0495	DF506-.5	Byzantine Empire—Biography	929.409(4-9)	CS2395-3090	Names, Personal—[By region or country]
920.0496	DR33	Balkan Peninsula—Biography	929.44	CT108	Nicknames
920.0496	CT1399-1458	Balkan Peninsula—Biography	929.50937	CN528.E6	Epitaphs
			929.50938	CN375.E6	Epitaphs
920.04965	DR928-934	Albania—Biography	929.6	CR	Heraldry
920.0497	DR1233-1235	Yugoslavia—Biography	929.6	CR29-69	Heraldry, Ornamental
920.0499	DR66	Bulgaria—Biography	929.6	CR41.C5	Collars in heraldry
920.05	CT1498-1919	Asia—Biography	929.6	CR41.F6	Flowers in heraldry
920.056	CT1870-1919	Middle East—Biography	929.6	CR55-57	Crests
920.06	CT1920-2750	Africa—Biography	929.6	CR67-69	Badges
920.07	E17	America—Biography	929.6	CR67-69	Devices (Heraldry)
			929.6	CR73-75	Mottoes

Dewey	LC	Subject Heading	Dewey	LC	Subject Heading
929.6	CR91-93	Shields	930.05	D51	History, Ancient—Periodicals
929.6	CR183-185	Heralds			
929.6	CR4553	Tournaments	930.072	D56-.52	History, Ancient—Historiography
929.601	CR14-16	Heraldry—Philosophy			
929.6025	CR11	Heraldry—Directories	930.1	GN700-890	Archaeology
929.603	CR13	Heraldry—Dictionaries	930.1	GN783-784	Cave dwellings
929.605	CR1	Heraldry—Periodicals	930.1	GN783-.5	Caves
929.606	CR2	Heraldry—Congresses	930.1	GN795-796	Mounds
929.6074	CR9	Heraldry—Exhibitions	930.1	T37	Industrial archaeology
929.609	CR151-159	Heraldry—History	930.101	CC72-81	Archaeology—Philosophy
929.7	CR3499-4420	Titles of honor and nobility	930.101	CC73-75	Archaeology—Methodology
929.7	CR3575	Precedence	930.1025	CC120-125	Archaeology—Directories
929.7	CR4480.C7	Crowns	930.1028	CC73-75	Archaeological surveying
929.7	CR4485.07	Orbs	930.1028	CC77.5	Archaeological geology
929.71	CR4501-6305	Orders of knighthood and chivalry	930.1028	GN789	Earthworks (Archaeology)
			930.102804	CC77.U5	Underwater archaeology
929.7(2-9)	CR4801-6305	Orders of knighthood and chivalry—[By region or country]	930.10283	CC75	Excavations (Archaeology)
			930.10283	CC165	Excavations (Archaeology)
			930.10288	CC135-137	Antiquities—Collection and preservation
929.72	CR4801-4917	Orders of knighthood and chivalry—Great Britain			
			930.103	CC70	Archaeology—Dictionaries
929.73	CR5100-5475	Orders of knighthood and chivalry—Germany	930.105	CC1-15	Archaeology—Periodicals
			930.106	CC20-39	Archaeology—Societies, etc.
929.736	CR4951-5005	Orders of knighthood and chivalry—Austria			
			930.1092	CC110-115	Archaeologists
929.738	CR5713-5737	Orders of knighthood and chivalry—Poland	930.11	GN775-776	Eoliths
			930.1(2-4)	GN775-768	Stone age
929.74	CR5025-5085	Orders of knighthood and chivalry—France	930.12	GN771	Paleolithic period, Lower
			930.15	GN777-778	Bronze age
929.75	CR5500-5580	Orders of knighthood and chivalry—Italy	930.15	GN777-778	Copper age
			931	DS701-799.9	China
929.76	CR5819-5889	Orders of knighthood and chivalry—Spain	931	DS721-727	China—Civilization
			931	DS799.4	Taiwan—Civilization
929.769	CR5900-5925	Orders of knighthood and chivalry—Portugal	931	DS799.99-.833	Taiwan—History
			931	DS799.64-.66	Taiwan—History—To 1895
929.77	CR5657-5703	Orders of knighthood and chivalry—Russia	931.0(1-3)	DS741-747.23	China—History—To 221 B.C.
929.78	CR5745-5809	Orders of knighthood and chivalry—Scandinavia	931.003	DS705	China—Gazetteers
			931.003	DS798.96	Taiwan—Gazetteers
929.795	CR5485-5489	Orders of knighthood and chivalry—Greece	931.004	DS730-731	Ethnology—China
			931.004	DS799.42-.43	Ethnology—Taiwan
929.81	CR4501-6305	Decorations of honor	931.01	DS747.15	China—History—Spring and Autumn period, 722-481 B.C.
929.8143	CR5351	Iron Cross			
929.8173	CR6253.Y	Young American Medal for Bravery			
			931.01	DS747.2	China—History—Warring States, 403-221 B.C.
929.(82 or 92)	JC345-347	Seals (Numismatics)			
929.88	Z41-42	Signatures (Writing)	931.04	DS747.28-749.7	China—History—221 B.C.-960 A.D.
929.88	Z41-42.5	Autographs			
929.9	CR4480-4485	Insignia	931.04	DS747.5-.9	China—History—Ch'in dynasty, 221-207 B.C.
929.92	CR101-115	Flags			
930	CB305	Protohistory	931.04	DS748-.164	China—History—Han dynasty, 202 B.C.-220 A.D.
930	CB311	Civilization, Ancient			
930	CC	Archaeology	931.04	DS748.17-.76	China—History—220-589
930	D51-95	History, Ancient	931.04	DS748.2-.29	China—History—Three Kingdoms, 220-265
930.03	D54	History, Ancient—Dictionaries			

Dewey	LC	Subject Heading	Dewey	LC	Subject Heading
931.04	DS748.4-.44	China—History—Chin dynasty, 265-419	934	DS381.7-388.2	Pakistan—History
			934	DS393.8	Bangladesh—Civilization
931.04	DS748.45-.48	China—History—Five Hu and the Sixteen kingdoms, 304-439	934	DS394.5-395.7	Bangladesh—History
			934	DS421-486.8	India
			934	DS421-428.2	India—Civilization
931.04	DS748.7-.76	China—History—Northern Wei dynasty, 386-534	934	DS451-.9	India—History—324 B.C-1000 A.D.
932	DT43-154	Egypt—History	934.003	DS376.8	Pakistan—Gazetteers
932	DT57-154	Egyptology	934.003	DS393.3	Bangladesh—Gazetteers
932	DT70	Egypt—Civilization	934.004	DS380.A1-.A2	Ethnology—Pakistan
932	DT83-93	Egypt—History—To 640 A.D.	934.004	DS393.82-.83	Ethnology—Bangladesh
			934.004	DS430-432.5	Ethnology—India
932.0(1-2)	DT83-91	Egypt—History—To 332 B.C.	934.02	DS425	Indo-Aryans
			935	DS69-70.5	Iraq—Antiquities
932.004	DT71-72	Ethnology—Egypt	935	DS70.7	Iraq—Civilization
932.01	DT63-.5	Pyramids	935	DS70.7	Civilization, Assyro-Babylonian
932.014	DT87-.5	Egypt—History—Eighteenth dynasty, ca. 1570-1320 B.C.	935	DS70.82-79.66	Iraq—History
			935	DS251-326	Iran
			935	DS270-318.85	Iran—History
932.02	DT92-93	Egypt—History—Greco Roman period, 332 B.C.-640 A.D.	935	DS276	Iran—History—To 640
			935.004	DS70.8	Ethnology—Iraq
932.02(2-3)	DT93	Egypt—History—30 B.C.-640 A.D.	935.004	DS268-269	Ethnology—Iran
			935.01	DS72	Sumerians
932.021	DT92-.7	Egypt—History—332 - 30 B.C.	935.05	DS281-284.7	Achaemenid dynasty, 559-330 B.C.
932.021	DT92-.7	Alexandrine War, 48-47 B.C.	935.06	DS276	Iran—History—Macedonian Conquest, 334-325 B.C.
933	DS101-151	Jews			
933	DS101-151	Israel	936.1	DA28-690	Great Britain—History
933	DS109-.94	Jerusalem	936.1	DA110-115	Great Britain—Civilization
933	DS109.85-.94	Jerusalem—History	936.1	DA750-890	Scotland
933	DS110.S3	Samaria Region	936.1	DA900-995	Ireland—History
933	DS112-113	Jews—Civilization	936.1	DA930-932.6	Ireland—History—To 1172
933	DS114-128.19	Israel—History	936.1004	DA120-125	Ethnology—Great Britain
933	DS153-154.9	Jordan	936.1005	DA750	Scotland—Periodicals
933	DS153.4	Jordan—Civilization	936.1005	DA900	Ireland—Periodicals
933	DS153.7-154.55	Jordan—History	936.2	DA20-690	England
933.0(3-5)	DS109.912	Jews—History—586 B.C.-70 A.D.	936.2	DA134-162	Great Britain—History—To 1066
933.0(4-5)	DS121.7-.8	Jews—History—168 B.C.-135 A.D.	936.2005	DA20	England—Periodicals
			936.3	DB1-879	Austria
933.004	DS113.2-.8	Ethnology—Israel	936.3	DB30	Austria—Civilization
933.004	DS153.5-.55	Ethnology—Jordan	936.3	DB46-99.2	Austria—History
933.004926	DS121.4	Canaanites	936.3	DB51-57	Austria—History—To 1273
933.01	DS121.121	Jews—History—To 1200 B.C.	936.3	DB881-898	Liechtenstein
933.02	DS121.121	Jews—History—To 953 B.C.	936.3	DB891-894	Liechtenstein—History
933.02	DS121.55	Jews—History—1200-953 B.C.	936.3	DD60-68	Germany—Civilization
			936.3	DD84-257.4	Germany—History
933.03	DS121.65	Jews—History—Babylonian captivity, 598-515 B.C.	936.3	DD121-134.2	Germany—History—To 843
			936.3	DD301-491	Prussia (Germany)
933.03	DS121.6	Jews—History—953-586 B.C.	936.3	DD331	Prussia (Germany)—Civilization
933.05	DS122.8	Jews—History—Rebellion, 66-73	936.3	DD341-454	Prussia (Germany)—History
			936.3	DH71	Netherlands—Civilization
934	DS379	Pakistan—Civilization	936.3	DH95-207	Netherlands—History

Dewey	LC	Subject Heading	Dewey	LC	Subject Heading
936.3	DH141-162	Netherlands—History—To 1384	936.4005	DC1	France—Periodicals
			936.4005	DH401	Belgium—Periodicals
936.3	DJ71	Netherlands—Civilization	936.4005	DQ1	Switzerland—Periodicals
936.3	DJ95-292	Netherlands—History	936.4006	DQ2	Switzerland—Congresses
936.3	DJ151-152	Netherlands—History—To 1384	936.40072	DQ52.8-.95	Switzerland—Historiography
			936.402	DC62	Gergovie, Battle of, 52 B.C.
936.3	DL30-33	Scandinavia—Civilization	936.402	DC62	Gaul—History—Gallic Wars, 58-51 B.C.
936.3	DL43-87	Scandinavia—History			
936.3	DL101-291	Denmark—History	936.6	DP1-402	Spain
936.3	DL131-133	Denmark—Civilization	936.6	DP48-.9	Spain—Civilization
936.3	DL401-596	Norway—History	936.6	DP91-96	Spain—History—To 711
936.3	DL431-433	Norway—Civilization	936.6	DP501-900	Portugal—History
936.3	DL460-478	Norway—History—To 1030	936.6	DP532-.7	Portugal—Civilization
936.3	DL601-991	Sweden—History	936.6	DP558-618	Portugal—History—To 1385
936.3	DL631-635	Sweden—Civilization			
936.3	DL660-700.9	Sweden—History—To 1397	936.6004	DP52-53	Ethnology—Spain
936.3004	DH91-92	Ethnology—Netherlands	936.6004	DP533-534.5	Ethnology—Portugal
936.3004	DJ91-92	Ethnology—Netherlands	936.6005	DP1	Spain—Periodicals
936.3004	DL41-42	Ethnology—Scandinavia	936.6005	DP501	Portugal—Periodicals
936.3004	DL141-142	Ethnology—Denmark	936.6006	DP2	Spain—Congresses
936.3004	DL441-442	Ethnology—Norway	936.60072	DP63-.83	Spain—Historiography
936.3004	DL639-641	Ethnology—Sweden	936.60072	DP536.8-.96	Portugal—Historiography
936.3004	DB33-34.5	Ethnology—Austria	936.603	DP94-95	Spain—History—Roman period, 218 B.C.-414 A.D.
936.3005	DB1	Austria—Periodicals			
936.3005	DB881	Liechtenstein—Periodicals	937	DE	Classical antiquities
936.3005	DD301	Prussia (Germany)—Periodicals	937	DE46-61	Civilization, Classical
			937	DG11-365	Rome
936.3005	DH1	Netherlands—Periodicals	937	DG61-365	Rome—History
936.3005	DJ1	Netherlands—Periodicals	937	DG75-142	Rome—Civilization
936.3005	DL1	Scandinavia—Periodicals	937	DG401-583	Italy
936.3005	DL401-403	Norway—Periodicals	937	DG441-453	Italy—Civilization
936.3005	DL601	Sweden—Periodicals	937	DG461-583	Italy—History
936.3006	DL1.5	Scandinavia—Congresses	937.0(1-2)	DG221-233.9	Rome—History—To 510 B.C.
936.30072	DD86-.7	Germany—Historiography			
936.30072	DD345	Prussia (Germany)—Historiography	937.0(2-5)	DG235-269	Rome—History—Republic, 510-30 B.C.
936.30072	DL445	Norway—Historiography	937.0(8-9)	DG310-365	Rome—History—Empire, 284-476
936.30072	DL645	Sweden—Historiography	937.0(8-9)	DG330-338	Rome—History—Theodosians, 379-455
936.30072	DB36.8-.9	Austria—Historiography			
936.4	D70	Celts—History	937.001	DG465.8	Italy—Study and teaching
936.4	DC33-.9	France—Civilization	937.004	DG455-457	Ethnology—Italy
936.4	DC35-423	France—History	937.005	DE1	Classical antiquities—Periodicals
936.4	DC62-63	Gaul—History			
936.4	DH401-811	Belgium	937.005	DG11	Rome—Periodicals
936.4	DH471	Belgium—Civilization	937.005	DG401	Italy—Periodicals
936.4	DH571-584	Belgium—History—To 1555	937.006	DG12.5	Rome—Congresses
			937.0071	DE15-.5	Classical antiquities—Study and teaching
936.4	DQ36-39	Switzerland—Civilization			
936.4	DQ79-84	Switzerland—History—To 1648	937.0071	DG206.5	Rome—Study and teaching
			937.0072	DG205	Rome—Historiography
936.4	DQ85-87	Switzerland—History—To 1032	937.0072	DG465-.7	Italy—Historiography
			937.0099	DG124	Roman emperors
936.4004	DH491-492	Ethnology—Belgium	937.0099	DG270-365	Emperors—Rome
936.4004	DQ48-49	Ethnology—Switzerland			
936.4004	DC34-.5	Ethnology—France			

Dewey	LC	Subject Heading	Dewey	LC	Subject Heading
937.04	DG243-244	Punic War, 1st, 264-241 B.C.	937.07	DG307.5	Rome—History—Gallienus, 260-268
937.04	DG247-249.4	Punic War, 2nd, 218-201 B.C.	937.08	DG314	Rome—History—Conference of Carnuntum, 308
937.04	DG251	Macedonian War, 1st, 215-205 B.C.	937.08	DG315	Rome—History—Constantine I, the Great, 306-337
937.04	DG251	Macedonian War, 2nd, 200-196 B.C.			
937.04	DG251.6	Macedonian War, 3rd, 171-168 B.C.	937.08	DG315-317	Rome—History—Constantines, 306-363
937.04	DG252.6	Punic War, 3rd, 149-146 B.C.	937.09	DG365	Rome—History—Romulus Augustulus, 475-476
937.05	DG252.9	Rome—History—Servile Wars, 135-71 B.C.	937.6	DG807.4	Catacombs
			938	DE	Classical antiquities
937.05	DG263	Rome—History—First Triumvirate, 60-53 B.C.	938	DE46-61	Civilization, Classical
			938.0(1-8)	DF218-238.9	Greece—History—To 146 B.C.
937.05	DG264	Gaul—History—Gallic Wars, 58-51 B.C.	938.0(1-8)	DF233-238	Macedonia—History—To 168 B.C.
937.05	DG266	Durazzo, Battle of, 48 B.C.	938.0(1-8)	DF233.2	Corinthian League
937.05	DG268-269	Rome—History—Civil War, 43-31 B.C.	938.0(5-6)	DF231-232	Greece—History—Spartan & Theban Supremacies, 404-362 B.C.
937.05	DG269	Actium, Battle of, 31 B.C.			
937.06	DG269.5-365	Rome—History—Empire, 30 B.C.-476 A.D.	938.004	DF135	Ethnology—Greece
937.06	DG279	Rome—History—Augustus, 30 B.C.-14 A.D.	938.005	DE1	Classical antiquities—Periodicals
937.07	DG59.D3	Dacian War, 1st, 101-102	938.005	DF10	Greece—Periodicals
937.07	DG59.D3	Dacian War, 2nd, 105-106	938.0071	DE15-.5	Classical antiquities—Study and teaching
937.07	DG282.5	Rome—History—Tiberius, 14-37	938.01	DF221-.3	Greece—History—Dorian Invasions, ca. 1125-1025 B.C.
937.07	DG283	Rome—History—Caligula, 37-41			
937.07	DG284	Rome—History—Claudius, 41-54	938.01	DF221.5	Greece—History—Geometric period, ca. 900-700 B.C.
937.07	DG285	Rome—History—Nero, 54-68	938.01	DF222-224	Greece—History—Age of Tyrants, 7th-6th centuries, B.C.
937.07	DG286	Rome—History—Civil War, 68-69	938.01004	DF136.D6	Dorians
937.07	DG288	Rome—History—Revolt of Civilis, 69-70	938.03	DF225-226	Greece—History—Persian Wars, 500-449 B.C.
937.07	DG289	Rome—History—Vitellius, 69	938.03	DF225.3	Greece—History—Ionian Revolt, 499-494 B.C.
937.07	DG290	Rome—History—Titus, 79-81	938.03	DF225.4	Marathon, Battle of, 490 B.C.
937.07	DG291	Rome—History—Domitian, 81-96	938.04	DF227-228	Greece—History—Athenian supremacy, 479-431 B.C.
937.07	DG292-299	Rome—History—Antonines, 96-192	938.05	DF229-230	Greece—History—Peloponnesian War, 431-404 B.C.
937.07	DG294	Parthian War, 113-117			
937.07	DG294	Rome—History—Trajan, 98-117	938.05	DF231.32	Greece—History—Expedition of Cyrus, 401 B.C.
937.07	DG295	Rome—History—Hadrian, 117-138	938.07	DF232.5-234.9	Greece—History—Macedonian Expansion, 359-323 B.C
937.07	DG300-304	Rome—History—Severans, 193-235			
937.07	DG306	Rome—History—Maximimus, 235-238	938.07	DF233.4	Greece—History—Third Sacred War, 355-346 B.C.

Dewey	LC	Subject Heading	Dewey	LC	Subject Heading
938.07	DF234.5	Gaugamela, Battle of, 331 B.C.	939.71	DT288	Algeria—History—To 647
			939.71	DT301-330	Morocco
938.08	DF235.3-.85	Greece—History—Macedonian Hegemony, 323-281 B.C.	939.71	DT312	Morocco—Civilization
			939.71	DT313.7-325.92	Morocco—History
			939.71	DT318	Morocco—History—To 647
938.08	DF236-238.9	Greece—History—281-146 B.C.	939.71004	DT283-.6	Ethnology—Algeria
			939.71004	DT313-.6	Ethnology—Morocco
938.08	DF236.4	Greece—History—Galatian Invasion, 279-278 B.C.	939.73	DT241-269	Tunisia
			939.73	DT252	Tunisia—Civilization
938.08	DF236.5	Greece—History—Chremonidean War, 267-262 B.C.	939.73	DT253.4-264.49	Tunisia—History
			939.73	DT258	Tunisia—History—To 647
			939.73004	DT253-.2	Ethnology—Tunisia
938.09	DF239-241	Greece—History—146 B.C.-323 A.D.	939.74	DT211-239	Libya
			939.74	DT222	Libya—Civilization
938.3	DF261.A2	Aetolia (Greece)	939.74	DT223.2-236	Libya—History
938.8	DF261.05	Olympia (Greece: Ancient sanctuary)	939.74	DT228	Libya—History—To 642
939.2	DR432	Turkey—Civilization	939.8	DJK77	Pannonia Region
939.2	DR436-603	Turkey—History	939.8	DR51-98	Bulgaria
939.2	DR481	Turkey—History—To 1453	939.8	DR63	Bulgaria—Civilization
939.2003	DR414	Turkey—Gazetteers	939.8	DR65-93.34	Bulgaria—History
939.2004	DR434-435	Ethnology—Turkey	939.8	DR74.3	Bulgaria—History—To 681
939.20072	DR438.8-.95	Turkey—Historiography	939.8	DR201-296	Romania
939.37	DS54.35	Cyprus—Civilization	939.8	DR212	Romania—Civilization
939.37	DS54.5-.9	Cyprus—History	939.8	DR215-267.5	Romania—History
939.37004	DS54.4-.44	Ethnology—Cyprus	939.8	DR238-241	Romania—History—To 1711
939.4	DS38	Middle East—History—To 622	939.8	DR901-998	Albania
939.4	DS41-66	Middle East	939.8	DR922	Albania—Civilization
939.43	DS94.6	Syria—Civilization	939.8	DR927-977.25	Albania—History
939.43	DS94.9-98.3	Syria—History	939.8	DR954-960.5	Albania—History—To 1501
939.43004	DS94.7-.8	Ethnology—Syria	939.8	DR1202-2285	Yugoslavia
939.44	DS80.3	Phoenician antiquities	939.8	DR1228	Yugoslavia—Civilization
939.44	DS80.4	Lebanon—Civilization	939.8	DR1232-1321	Yugoslavia—History
939.44	DS80.7-87.53	Lebanon—History	939.8	DR1352-1485	Slovenia
939.44	DS81-89	Phoenicians	939.8	DR1376-1450	Slovenia—History
939.44	DS83	Lebanon—History—635-1516	939.8	DR1502-1645	Croatia
			939.8	DR1547-1598	Croatia—History
939.44004	DS80.5	Ethnology—Lebanon	939.8	DR1652-1785	Bosnia and Herzegovina
939.49	DS201-248	Saudi Arabia	939.8	DB901-999	Hungary
939.49	DS215	Saudi Arabia—Civilization	939.8	DB920.5	Hungary—Civilization
939.49	DS221-244.63	Saudi Arabia—History	939.8	DB927-928.9	Hungary—History—To 896
939.49004	DS218-219	Ethnology—Saudi Arabia	939.8004	DB919-.2	Ethnology—Hungary
939.6	DS327-329.4	Asia, Central	939.8004	DR64	Ethnology—Bulgaria
939.6	DS354	Afghanistan—Civilization	939.8004	DR213-214	Ethnology—Romania
939.6	DS355-371.2	Afghanistan—History	939.8004	DR923-925	Ethnology—Albania
939.6004	DS354.5-.6	Ethnology—Afghanistan	939.8004	DR1229-1230	Ethnology—Yugoslavia
939.7	DT160-177	Africa, North	939.8005	DR51	Bulgaria—Periodicals
939.7	DT160-176	Africa, North—History	939.8005	DR201	Romania—Periodicals
939.7	DT179.2-.9	Africa, Northwest	939.8005	DR901	Albania—Periodicals
939.701	DT168-171	Africa, North—History—To 647	939.8005	DR1202	Yugoslavia—Periodicals
			939.8005	DB901	Hungary—Periodicals
939.71	DT271-299	Algeria	939.8006	DR903.5	Albania—Congresses
939.71	DT282	Algeria—Civilization	939.8006	DR1205	Yugoslavia—Congresses
939.71	DT283-299	Algeria—History	939.80072	DR66.7-.97	Bulgaria—Historiography

Dewey	LC	Subject Heading	Dewey	LC	Subject Heading
939.80072	DR216.7-.92	Romania—Historiography	940.27	DC222.F6	Fleurus, Battle of, 1794
939.80072	DR1239-1243	Yugoslavia—Historiography	940.27	DC226.N5	Nile, Battle of the, 1798
940	D900-1075	Europe—History	940.27	DC227.5.D8	Durnstein, Battle of, 1805
940.1	D111-203	Middle Ages—History	940.27	DC227.5.E6	Elchingen, Battle of, 1805
940.18	D151-173	Crusades	940.27	DC231-233.5	Peninsular War, 1807-1814
940.18072	D156.58	Crusades—Historiography	940.27	DC234.65	Graz (Austria), Battle of, 1809
940.18092	D156-.5	Crusades—Biography			
940.182	D161-.5	Crusades—First, 1096-1099	940.27	DC236-238.5	Wars of Liberation, 1813-1814
940.182	D162-.5	Crusades—Second, 1147-1149	940.27	DC236.7.D8	Dresden, Battle of, 1813
940.182	D163-.5	Crusades—Third, 1189-1192	940.27	DC241-244.7	Waterloo, Battle of, 1815
940.184	D164-.5	Crusades—Fourth, 1202-1204	940.284	DD207-209	Germany—History—Revolution, 1848-1849
940.184	D165	Crusades—Fifth, 1218-1221	940.284	DD424	Prussia (Germany)—History—Revolution, 1848-1849
940.184	D166	Crusades—Sixth, 1228-1229	940.284	DF823.65	Greece—History—Revolution, 1848
940.184	D167	Crusades—Seventh, 1248-1250	940.284	DR244	Romania—History—Revolution, 1848
940.184	D168	Crusades—Eighth, 1270	940.284	DB83	Austria—History—Revolution, 1848-1849
940.19	D171-173	Crusades—Later 13th, 14th, and 15th centuries	940.(288-559)	CB203-231	Europe—Intellectual life—20th century
940.2	D101-110.5	History, Modern	940.288	D443	Triple Entente, 1907
940.24	D251-271	Thirty Years' War, 1618-1648	940.288	D511	Triple Entente, 1907
940.252	D274.5-.6	Anglo-French War, 1666-1667	940.3	D501-680	World War, 1914-1918
940.252	D277-278.5	Dutch War, 1672-1678	940.3092	D507	World War, 1914-1918—Biography
940.2525	D279-280.5	Grand Alliance, War of the, 1689-1697	940.3092	D507	Generals
940.2(526-7)	CB411	Europe—Civilization—18th century	940.31426	D650.T4-651	Mandates
940.2526	D281-283.5	Spanish Succession, War of, 1701-1714	940.405	D625-626	World War, 1914-1918—Atrocities
940.2526	DP196	Spanish Succession, War of, 1701-1714	940.4(2-3)	D529-578	World War, 1914-1918—Campaigns
940.253	D283.5	Hague, Treaty of, 1717	940.4(2-3)	D530-549.5	World War, 1914-1918—Campaigns—Western front
940.253	D287.5	Quadruple Alliance, 1718			
940.253	D295	Neutrality, Armed	940.4(2-3)	D531-538.5	World War, 1914-1918—Campaigns—Germany
940.2532	D291-294	Austrian Succession, War of, 1740-1748	940.4(2-3)	D541-542	World War, 1914-1918—Campaigns—Belgium
940.2532	DB72	Austrian Succession, War of, 1740-1748	940.4(2-3)	D544-545	World War, 1914-1918—Campaigns—France
940.2534	DD409-412.8	Seven Years' War, 1756-1763	940.4(2-3)	D545.C37	Champagne, Battles of, 1914-1917
940.2(7-87)	CB204	Europe—Civilization—19th century	940.4(2-3)	D548-549.5	World War, 1914-1918—Campaigns—France
940.2(7-87)	CB204	Europe—Intellectual life—19th century	940.4(2-3)	D550-569.5	World War, 1914-1918—Campaigns—Eastern front
940.27	D301-309	Europe—History—1789-1815	940.4(2-3)	D566-568.9	World War, 1914-1918—Campaigns—Turkey
940.27	DP204-208	Spain—History—Napoleonic Conquest, 1808-1813	940.4(2-3)	D569	World War, 1914-1918—Campaigns—Italy
940.27	D383	Quadruliance, 1815	940.421	D545.L3	Le Cateau, Battle of, 1914
			940.421	D545.V25	Verdun, Battle of, 1914

Dewey	LC	Subject Heading	Dewey	LC	Subject Heading
940.422	D552.B7	Brzeziny, Battle of, 1914	940.5317599	D805.P5	O'Donnell Camp (Philippines : Concentration camp)
940.422	D557.L5	Limanova, Battle of, 1914			
940.424	D545.A6	Argonne, Battle of the, 1915	940.5318	D810.J4	World War, 1939-1945—Jews
940.4272	D545.V3	Verdun, Battle of, 1916	940.5318092	D804.3	Holocaust, Jewish (1939-1945)—Personal narratives
940.431	D545.A5	Aisne, Battle of the, France, 1917			
940.431	D545.A7	Arras, Battle of, 1917	940.531853	D805.G3	Berga (Germany : Concentration Camp)
940.432	D569.C	Carzano, Battle of, 1917	940.531853	D805.G3	Flossenburg (Germany : Concentration camp)
940.433	D568.7	Gaza, Battles of, 1917			
940.434	D545.A5	Aisne, Battle of the, France, 1918	940.5318532241	D805.G3	Buchenwald (Germany : Concentration camp)
940.434	D545.A63	Argonne, Battle of the, 1918	940.53185336	D805.G3	Dachau (Germany : Concentration camp)
940.434	D545.B4	Belleau Wood, Battle of, 1918	940.531853515	D805.G3	Neuengamme (Hamburg, Germany : Concentration camp)
940.439	D613-614	World War, 1914-1918—Peace			
940.439	D642-651	World War, 1914-1918—Peace	940.5318535954	D805.G3	Bergen-Belsen (Germany : Concentration camp)
940.44	D600-607	World War, 1914-1918—Aerial operations	940.5318538	D805.P7	Auschwitz (Poland : Concentration camp)
940.45	D580	Freedom of the seas	940.532	D748-754	World War, 1939-1945—Diplomatic history
940.454	D580-589	World War, 1914-1918—Naval operations	940.5336	D802	World War, 1939-1945—Underground movements
940.454	D582.F2	Falkland Islands, Battle of the, 1914	940.5336	D802.A2	World War, 1939-1945—Occupied territories
940.455	D582.D6	Dogger Bank, Battle of the, 1915	940.53440922	D802.F8	World War, 1939-1945—Underground movements—France—Biography
940.458	D589.U7	Durazzo, Battle of, 1918			
940.467	D609	World War, 1914-1918—Registers of dead	940.5400222	D745-.7	World War, 1939-1945—Caricatures and cartoons
940.472	D627	World War, 1914-1918—Prisoners and prisons	940.5405	D803-804.35	World War, 1939-1945—Atrocities
940.47247	D627.R8	World War, 1914-1918—Prisoners and prisons, Russian	940.5405	D804.S65	Katyn Forest Massacre, 1940
940.5 (1-2)	D652-659	Reconstruction (1914-1939)	940.541	D793	World War, 1939-1945—Tank warfare
940.53	D731-838	World War, 1939-1945	940.541273	D769.346	United States. Army—Airborne troops
940.5300222	D743.2	World War, 1939-1945—Pictorial works	940.541273	D769.347	United States. Army—Parachute troops
940.5308691	D808-809	World War, 1939-1945—Refugees	940.542	D755-769.87	World War, 1939-1945—Campaigns
940.53092	D736	World War, 1939-1945—Biography	940.5421	D756-763	World War, 1939-1945—Campaigns—Western front
940.531	D753.2	Lend-lease operations (1941-1945)	940.5421	D756.3	Atlantic Wall (France and Belgium)
940.5311	D741	World War, 1939-1945—Causes	940.5421	D756.5.A78	Arras, Battle of, 1940
940.5312	D812	World War, 1939-1945—Armistice	940.54211	D759-760.8	World War, 1939-1945—Campaigns—Great Britain
940.531422	D818-819	World War, 1939-1945—Reparations	940.54213	D757-.9	World War, 1939-1945—Campaigns—Germany
940.53144	D824-829	Reconstruction (1939-1951)	940.542131	D756.5.A7	Ardennes, Battle of the, 1944-1945
			940.54213155	D757.9	Berlin, Battle of, 1945

Dewey	LC	Subject Heading	Dewey	LC	Subject Heading
940.542138	D765-.2	World War, 1939-1945—Campaigns—Poland	940.54265933	D774.M5	Midway, Battle of, 1942
940.5421384	D765.2.W3	Warsaw, Battle of, 1945	940.542665	D767.99.W3	Wake Island, Battle of, 1941
940.54214	D756.5.D5	Dieppe Raid, 1942	940.5428	D767.92	Pearl Harbor (Hawaii), Attack on, 1941
940.54214	D756.5.V3	Verdun, Battle of, 1940			
940.54214	D761-762	World War, 1939-1945—Campaigns—France	940.5428	D772.G7	Rio de la Plata, Battle of the, 1939
940.54214	D772.B	Bordeaux Raid, 1942	940.544	D785-792	World War, 1939-1945—Aerial operations
940.542142	D756.5.C	Calais, Battle of, 1940	940.545	D770-784	World War, 1939-1945—Naval operations
940.5421428	D756.5.D8	Dunkerque (France), Battle of, 1940	940.5451	D780-784	World War, 1939-1945—Naval operations—Submarine
940.5421495	D766.3-.32	World War, 1939-1945—Campaigns—Greece			
940.5421497	D766.6-.62	World War, 1939-1945—Campaigns—Yugoslavia	940.5452	D770-784	World War, 1939-1945—Blockades
940.54217	D764.3	Commander Islands (Russia), Battle of, 1943	940.5467	D797	World War, 1939-1945—Casualties
940.54217	D847-.2	Communist countries	940.5467	D797	World War, 1939-1945—Registers of dead
940.5421721	D764.3.S7	Stalingrad, Battle of, 1942-1943	940.547	D804.7.D43	Death marches
940.5421731	D764.3.M	Moscow, Battle of, 1941-1942	940.5472	D805	World War, 1939-1945—Prisoners and prisons
940.542177	D764.3.B73	Brody (Ukraine), Battle of, 1944	940.547252	D805.J3	World War, 1939-1945—Prisoners and prisons, Japanese
940.5421772	D764.3	Odessa (Ukraine), Battle of, 1941	940.547252092	D805.J3	Prisoners of war—Japan—Diaries
940.54219218	D763.N4	Arnhem, Battle of, 1944	940.5475	D806-807	World War, 1939-1945—Medical care
940.542193222	D763.B42.A	Antwerp, Battle of, 1944			
940.5423	D766.82	World War, 1939-1945—Campaigns—Africa, North	940.5477	D808-809	World War, 1939-1945—Civilian relief
940.5423	D766.9	El Alamein, Battle of, Egypt, 1942	940.548	D797	World War, 1939-1945—Casualties
940.5425	D764-766.7	World War, 1939-1945—Campaigns—Eastern front	940.548(1-2)	D811-.5	World War, 1939-1945—Personal narratives
940.5425	D767.6	World War, 1939-1945—Campaigns—Burma	940.548641	D810.S7	World War, 1939-1945—Secret service—Great Britain
940.54252	D767.2-.25	World War, 1939-1945—Campaigns—Japan			
940.5425229	D767.99.045	World War, 1939-1945—Campaigns—Japan—Okinawa Island	940.5488	D810.P6-.P7	World War, 1939-1945—Propaganda
			940.55004	D1056-.2	Ethnology—Europe
940.542598	D767.7	Biak Island (Indonesia), Battle of, 1944	940.(55-56)	D1050-1075	Europe—History—1945-
			940.(55-56)005	D1050	Europe—History—1945- —Periodicals
940.5425991	D767.4	Bataan, Battle of, Philippines, 1942	941	DA	Great Britain—History
940.5426	D767-.99	World War, 1939-1945—Campaigns—Pacific	941	DA28-690	Great Britain—History
			941	DA110-115	Great Britain—Civilization
			941.004	DA120-125	Ethnology—Great Britain
940.5426	D767.917	Tarawa, Battle of, 1943	941.0042	CB216-220	Anglo-Saxon race
940.5426	D767.99.I9	Iwo Jima, Battle of, 1945	941.01	DA134-162	Great Britain—History—To 1066
940.5426	D774.B57	Bismarck Sea, Battle of the, 1943			
940.5426	D774.C	Coral Sea, Battle of the, 1942	941.017	DA150-162	Saxons
			941.021	DA196	Hastings, Battle of, 1066
940.5426	D774.J	Java Sea, Battle of the, 1942	941.0(2-46)	DA170-260	Great Britain—History—To 1485

Dewey	LC	Subject Heading	Dewey	LC	Subject Heading
941.0(5-8)	DA300-591	Great Britain—History—Modern period, 1485-	941.1082	DA821-826	Scotland—History—20th century
941.05	DA310-360	Great Britain—History—Tudors, 1485-1603	941.5	DA900-995	Ireland—History
			941.5005	DA900	Ireland—Periodicals
941.052	DA331-339	Great Britain—History—History—Henry VIII, 1509-1547	941.50(1-2)	DA930-932.6	Ireland—History—To 1172
			941.50(3-5)	DA933-937.5	Ireland—History—1172-1603
941.055	DA86.22.D7	Lisbon Expedition, 1589	941.506	DA940-946	Ireland—History—17th century
941.055	DA350-360	Great Britain—History—Elizabeth, 1558-1603	941.507	DA947-949.5	Ireland—History—18th century
941.06	DA370-419.5	Great Britain—History—Early Stuarts, 1603-1649	941.5081	DA949.7-958	Ireland—History—19th century
941.061	DA392-.1	Gunpowder Plot, 1605	941.5082	DA959-965	Ireland—History—20th century
941.062	DA410-429	Great Britain—History—Civil War, 1642-1649	941.7081	DA954	Fenians
941.063	DA420-429	Fifth Monarchy Men	942	DA20-690	England
941.06(6-9)	DA430-463	Great Britain—History—1660-1714	942.005	DA20	England—Periodicals
			942.017	DA150-162	Anglo-Saxons
941.071	DA499	Great Britain—History—George I, 1714-1727	942.055	DA360	Armada, 1588
941.072	DA498-499	Anglo-Spanish War, 1718-1748	942.1	DA675-689	London (England)—History
			942.9	DA700-745	Wales
941.072	DA500	Great Britain—History—George II, 1727-1760	942.9	DA711.5	Wales—Civilization
			942.9	DA714-722.1	Wales—History
941.073	DA87.5 1794	First of June, 1794, Battle of	942.9005	DA700	Wales—Periodicals
941.073	DA87.7 1797	Spithead Mutiny, 1797	943	CB213-214	Civilization, Germanic
941.073	DA88.5 1805	Trafalgar, Battle of, 1805	943	DAW	Europe, Central
941.073	DA505-522	Great Britain—History—George III, 1760-1820	943	DAW1024	Europe, Central—Civilization
			943	DAW1031-1051	Europe, Central—History
941.073	DA505-512	Anglo-Spanish War, 1762-1763	943	DD	Germany
			943	DD60-68	Germany—Civilization
941.073	DA535	Luddites	943	DD84-257.4	Germany—History
941.074	DA537-538	Great Britain—History—George IV, 1820-1830	943	DD301-491	Prussia (Germany)
			943	DD331	Prussia (Germany)—Civilization
941.075	DA539-542	Great Britain—History—William IV, 1830-1837	943	DD341-454	Prussia (Germany)—History
941.081	DA550-565	Great Britain—History—Victoria, 1837-1901	943.0005	DAW1001	Europe, Central—Periodicals
941.082	DA566-592	Great Britain—History—20th century	943.0006	DAW1004	Europe, Central—Congresses
941.0892	DA150-162	Anglo-Saxons	943.0025	DD15.5	Germany—Directories
941.089916	DA140-143	Celts	943.004	DAW1026-1028	Ethnology—Europe, Central
941.1	DA750-890	Scotland	943.004	DD73-78	Ethnology—Germany
941.1005	DA750	Scotland—Periodicals	943.005	DD301	Prussia (Germany)—Periodicals
941.101	DA777-778.9	Scotland—History—To 1057	943.0072	DD86-.7	Germany—Historiography
941.10(2-5)	DA779-790	Scotland—History—1057-1603	943.0072	DD345	Prussia (Germany)—Historiography
941.104	DA784.6	Flodden, Battle of, 1513	943.01	DD121-134.2	Germany—History—To 843
941.1063	DA803.8	Scotland—History—1649-1660	943.0(13-25)	DD126.5	Donation of Pepin
			943.013	DD128	Merovingians
941.10(69-73)	DA809-814.5	Scotland—History—18th century	943.014	DD129-134.9	Carolingians
941.10(69-72)	DA813-814	Jacobites	943.02	DD125-198.7	Holy Roman Empire—History
941.1081	DA815-818	Scotland—History—19th century	943.02(6-9)	DD156-174.6	Germany—History—1273-1517

Dewey	LC	Subject Heading	Dewey	LC	Subject Heading
943.021	DD134.3-135	Germany—History—843-918	943.085	DD257.A2	Germany—History—Allied occupation, 1918-1930
943.022	DD136-140.7	Germany—History—Saxon House, 919-1024	943.085	DD248	Germany—History—Revolution, 1918
943.023	DD141-144	Germany—History—Franconian House, 1024-1125	943.085	DD249	Germany—History—Kapp Putsch, 1920
943.024	DD145-155	Germany—History—Hohenstaufen, 1138-1254	943.085	DD249	Germany—History—March Uprising, 1921
943.03	D220-271	Counter-Reformation	943.085	DD249	Germany—History—Beer Hall Putsch, 1923
943.03	DD176-189	Counter-Reformation			
943.041	DD188-.5	Germany—History—1618-1648	943.086	DD253-256.5	Germany—History—1933-1945
943.0(41-52)	DD394-399.8	Prussia (Germany)—History—1640-1740	943.086	DD247.R56	Germany—History—Night of the Long Knives, 1934
943.0(43-52)	DD190-.8	Germany—History—1648-1740	943.086	DS135.G3315	Germany—History—Kristallnacht, 1938
943.044	DD394.3	Fehrbellin, Battle of, 1675	943.086	DD253-256.5	National socialism
943.05	DD191-199	Germany—History—18th century	943.086	DD256.3-.4	Anti-Nazi movement
			943.087	DD258-262	Germany (West)
943.05(3-7)	DD406-413.2	Prussia (Germany)—History—1740-1789	943.087(4-5)	DD257-.4	Germany—History—1945-1955
943.052	DD399-.8	Prussia (Germany)—History—Frederick William I, 1713-1740	943.088	DD257.4	Germany—History—1990-
			943.0881	DD257-.4	Germany—History—Unification, 1990
943.053	DD401-413.2	Prussia (Germany)—History—Frederick II, 1740-1786	943.1087	DD280-289	Germany (East)
			943.155	DD851-900	Berlin (Germany)
			943.21	DD801.S31-.S59	Saxony (Germany)—History
943.054	DD407.5	Dresden, Peace of, 1745	943.3	DJK76.2-.8	Danube River Valley
943.0(57-84)	DD197-231	Germany—History—1789-1900	943.(6, 7, 9)	DB	Austria, Czechoslovakia, Hungary
943.06	DD414-416	Prussia (Germany)—History—Frederick William II, 1786-1797	943.6	DB1-879	Austria
			943.6	DB30	Austria—Civilization
			943.6	DB46-99.2	Austria—History
943.07	DD206-214	Germany—History—1815-1866	943.60(25-3)	BD57-59	Austria—History—1273-1519
943.07	DD424-.9	Prussia (Germany)—History—Frederick William IV, 1840-1861	943.60(25-31)	DB65.2-77	Austria—History—1519-1740
			943.6004	DB33-34.5	Ethnology—Austria
			943.6005	DB1	Austria—Periodicals
943.0(76-83)	DD425-446	Prussia (Germany)—History—William I, 1861-1888	943.60072	DB36.8-.9	Austria—Historiography
			943.602	DB51-57	Austria—History—To 1273
943.076	DD436-440	Austro-Prussian War, 1866	943.6051	DB96-99.2	Austria—History—1918-1938
943.08(2-8)	DD446-454	Prussia (Germany)—History—1870-	943.6052	DB99	Austria—History—1938-1945
943.08(3-4)	DD217-231	Germany—History—1871-1918	943.6053	DB99.2	Austria—History—1955-
			943.613	DB841-860	Vienna (Austria)
943.08(4-79)	DD232-257.4	Germany—History—20th century	943.648	DB881-898	Liechtenstein
			943.648	DB891-894	Liechtenstein—History
943.081	DD214-216	Germany—History—1866-1871	943.648005	DB881	Liechtenstein—Periodicals
			943.7	DB2000-3150	Czechoslovakia
943.083	DD223-.9	Germany—History—William I, 1871-1888	943.7	DB2035	Czechoslovakia—Civilization
			943.7	DB2044-2232	Czechoslovakia—History
943.084	DD228-231	Germany—History—William II, 1888-1918	943.7	DB2185-2232	Czechoslovakia—History
			943.70025	DB2009	Czechoslovakia—Directories
943.084	DD224-226	Germany—History—Frederick III, 1888	943.7004	DB2040-2043	Ethnology—Czechoslovakia

Dewey	LC	Subject Heading	Dewey	LC	Subject Heading
943.7005	DB2000	Czechoslovakia—Periodicals	943.8	DK4110-4115	Poland—Civilization
943.7006	DB2003	Czechoslovakia—Congresses	943.80(25-3)	DK4314.5	Poland—History—18th century
943.7032	DB2195-2202	Czechoslovakia—History—1918-1939	943.8004	DK4120-4122	Ethnology—Poland
943.7033	DB2205-2211	Czechoslovakia—History—1938-1945	943.8005	DK4010	Poland—Periodicals
			943.8006	DK4018	Poland—Congresses
943.704	DB2215-2232	Czechoslovakia—History—1945-1992	943.80072	DK4139-.25	Poland—Historiography
			943.802(2-3)	DK4186-4289	Poland—History—To 1572
943.7042	DB2222	Czechoslovakia—History—Coup d'etat, 1948	943.802(2-5)	DK4186-4348	Poland—History—To 1795
943.7042	DB2232	Czechoslovakia—History—Intervention, 1968	943.802(3-4)	DK4276	Poland—History—16th century
943.7043	DB2225-2232	Czechoslovakia—History—1968-1989	943.802(4-5)	DK4289.5-4328	Poland—History—Elective monarchy, 1572-1763
943.7102	DB2155-2162	Bohemia (Czech Republic)—History—1618-1848	943.8022	DK4210-.7	Poland—History—To 960 (ca.)
943.71023	DB2080-2133	Bohemia (Czech Republic)—History—To 1526	943.8022	DK4211-4249.5	Poland—History—Piast period, 960-1386
943.710232	DB2135-2151	Bohemia (Czech Republic)—History—1526-1618	943.8022	DK4222	Poland—History—Mieszko II, 1025-1034
			943.8022	DK4223	Poland—History—Casimir I, 1040-1058
943.71024	DB2165-2182	Bohemia (Czech Republic)—History—1848-1918	943.8022	DK4227-4246.5	Poland—History—1138-1305
			943.8022	DK4245.7	Poland—History—Mongol Invasion, 1241
943.712	DB2600-2650	Prague (Czech Republic)	943.8023	DK4249.7-4289	Poland—History—Jagellons, 1386-1572
943.72	DB2300-2421	Moravia (Czech Republic)	943.8025	DK4328.9-4348	Poland—History—Partition period, 1763-1796
943.72	DB2335	Moravia (Czech Republic)—Civilization	943.8025	DK4330-4348	Poland—History—Stanislaus II Augustus, 1764-1795
943.72	DB2345-2421	Moravia (Czech Republic)—History	943.8025	DK4338-4345	Poland—History—Revolution of 1794
943.72	DK4600.S46	Silesia, Upper (Poland and Czech Republic) History	943.8032	DK4359-4363	Poland—History—Revolution, 1830-1832
943.72004	DB2340-2342	Moravia (Czech Republic)—Ethnography	943.8032	DK4363.2	Poland—History—Partisan Campaign, 1833
943.72021	DB2385-2391	Moravia (Czech Republic)—History—To 906	943.8032	DK4364	Poland—History—Revolution, 1846
943.73	DB2700-3150	Slovakia	943.8033	DK4366-4378	Poland—History—Revolution, 1863-1864
943.73	DB2735	Slovakia—Civilization			
943.73	DB2744-3000	Slovakia—History	943.8033	DK4379.5-4395	Poland—History—1864-1918
943.730(3-5)	DB2805-2841	Slovakia—History—1918-1993	943.8033	DK4383-4389	Poland—History—Revolution, 1905-1907
943.73004	DB2740-2743	Ethnology—Slovakia			
943.7302	DB2795-2791	Slovakia—History—To 1526	943.8033	DK4390-4395	Poland—History—German occupation, 1914-1918
943.7302(34-4)	DB2795-2801	Slovakia—History—1800-1918	943.8033	DK4394-4395	Poland—History—Austrian occupation, 1915-1918
943.73023	DB2795-2801	Slovakia—History—1526-1800	943.804	DK4404-4409	Poland—History—Wars of 1918-1921
943.73033	DB2822	Slovakia—History—Uprising, 1944	943.804	DK4409.4	Poland—History—Coup d'etat, 1926
943.73042	DB2842	Slovakia—History—Intervention, 1968	943.804(4-53)	DK4397-4420	Poland—History—1918-1945
943.8	DK	Russia, Soviet Union, Poland	943.805(4-7)	DK4429-4442	Poland—History—1945-
943.8	DK4010-4800	Poland			

243

Dewey	LC	Subject Heading	Dewey	LC	Subject Heading
943.8053	DK4410-4415	Poland—History—Occupation, 1939-1945	944.026	DC101-.7	France—History—Charles VI, 1380-1422
943.8056	DK4443	Poland—History—1980-1989	944.026	DC101.5.C33	France—History—Cabochien Uprising, 1413
943.8057	DK4442	Poland—History—1989-	944.026	DC101.5.A2	Agincourt, Battle of, 1415
943.82	DK4650-4685	Gdansk (Poland)	944.026	DC102-105.9	France—History—Charles VII, 1422-1461
943.84	DK4610-4645	Warsaw (Poland)			
943.85	DK4600.S44	Silesia, Lower (Poland and Germany)	944.027	DC106-.9	France—History—Louis XI, 1461-1483
943.85	DK4600.S46	Silesia, Upper (Poland and Czech Republic) History	944.027	DC107-.2	France—History—Charles VIII, 1483-1498
943.86	DK4700-4735	Krakow (Poland)	944.027	DC108-109	France—History—Louis XII, 1498-1515
943.9	DB901-999	Hungary			
943.9	DB920.5	Hungary—Civilization	944.028	DC113-.5	France—History—Francis I, 1515-1547
943.90(43-54)	DB947-957	Hungary—History—20th century	944.028	DC114-.5	France—History—Henry II, 1547-1559
943.9004	DB919-.2	Ethnology—Hungary			
943.900494511	DB919	Magyars	944.028	DC115	France—History—Francis II, 1559-1560
943.9005	DB901	Hungary—Periodicals			
943.901	DB927-928.9	Hungary—History—To 896	944.029	DC116-118	France—History—Charles IX, 1560-1574
943.902	DB929-.9	Hungary—History—896-1301	944.029	DC118	Saint Bartholomew's Day, Massacre of, France, 1572
943.903	DB930.2	Hungary—History—Charles Robert, 1308-1342	944.029	DC119-120	France—History—Henry III, 1574-1589
943.903	DB930.4	Hungary—History—Sigismund, 1387-1437	944.03	DC120.8-138	France—History—Bourbons, 1589-1789
943.903	DB930.3	Hungary—History—Louis I, 1342-1382	944.03(2-3)	DC124.45	Franco-Spanish War, 1635-1659
943.9041	DB931.94-932.4	Hungary—History—Turkish occupation, 1529-1699	944.031	DC122-.9	France—History—Henry IV, 1589-1610
943.9042	DB940-953	Hungary—History—Francis Joseph, 1848-1916	944.032	DC123-.9	France—History—Louis XIII, 1610-1643
943.9043	DB932.3-934	Hungary—History—1699-1848	944.033	DC124.5-130	France—History—Louis XIV, 1643-1715
943.905(1-2)	DB955	Hungary—History—1918-1945	944.033	DC124.45	Dunes, Battle of the, 1658
943.905(3-4)	DB956-957	Hungary—History—1945-	944.034	DC133-135	France—History—Louis XV, 1715-1774
943.9052	DB957	Hungary—History—Revolution, 1956	944.035	DC136-137.5	France—History—Louis XVI, 1774-1793
943.912	DB981-999	Budapest (Hungary)	944.035	DC137.15	Diamond Necklace Affair, France, 1785
944	DC	France			
944	DC33-.9	France—Civilization	944.04(1-2)	DC139-190.8	France—History—Revolution, 1789-1799
944	DC35-423	France—History			
944.0(29-3)	DC116-118	France—History—War of the Huguenots, 1562-1598	944.05	DC256-260	France—History—Louis XVIII, 1814-1824
944.0(46-5)	DC191.2-249	France—History—Consulate and First Empire, 1799-1815	944.063	DC265-269	France—History—Louis Philip, 1830-1848
			944.063	DC261-262	France—History—July Revolution, 1830
944.0025	DC15	France—Directories			
944.004	DC34-.5	Ethnology—France	944.07	DC271.5-274.5	France—History—Second Republic, 1848-1852
944.005	DC1	France—Periodicals			
944.01	DC60-81.5	France—History—To 987	944.07	DC274-.5	France—History—Coup d'etat, 1851
944.02(4-6)	DC97.5-101.7	France—History—14th century	944.07	DC275-292	France—History—Second Empire, 1852-1870
944.025	DC96-105	Hundred Years War, 1339-1453	944.08(2-4)	DC398-423	France—History—1945-

Dewey	LC	Subject Heading	Dewey	LC	Subject Heading
944.081	DC342.8-396	France—History—Third Republic, 1870-1940	945.083	DG554.5.E96	Expedition of the Thousand, Italy, 1860
944.0812	DC281-326.5	Franco-Prussian War, 1870-1871	945.083	DG554.5	Italy—History—War of 1860-1861
944.0812	DC309.E8	Epinal (France), Battle of, 1870	945.084	DG558	Austro-Italian War, 1866
944.0812	DC305.22	Belfort, Battle of, 1871	945.09(1-24)	DG572	Italy—History—Allied occupation, 1943-1947
944.0814	DC385	France—History—German occupation, 1914-1918	945.09(1-27)	DG577.5-579	Italy—History—1945-1976
944.0816	DC397	France—History—German occupation, 1940-1945	945.091	DG570-572	Italy—History—1914-1945
944.083(6-7)	DC421	France—Politics and government—1969-1974	945.091	DG571	Fascism
			945.091	DG571.75	Italy—History—March on Rome, 1922
944.083(7-8)	DC422	France—Politics and government—1974-1981	945.091	DG572	Italy—History—German occupation, 1943-1945
944.0838	DC423	France—Politics and government—1981-	945.091	DG572	Italy—History—Grand Council, 1943
944.36	DC701-790	Paris (France)	945.092(7-9)	DG581-583	Italy—History—1976-
944.9	DC608.1-.9	Riviera (France)	945.18	DG975.R6	Riviera (Italy)
944.945	DC611.C8-.C839	Corsica (France)—History	945.182	DG631-645	Genoa (Italy)
944.949	DC941-947	Monaco	945.2	DG651-664.5	Lombardy (Italy)
945	DG	Italy	945.31	DG670-684.72	Venice (Italy)
945	DG401-583	Italy	945.5	DG731-759.3	Tuscany (Italy)
945	DG461-583	Italy—History	945.6	DG691-694	Italy, Central
945.(1-3)	DG600-609	Italy, Northern	945.6	DG791-800	Papal States
945.0(3-4)	DG520-529	Italy—History—Germanic rule, 962-1268	945.6	DG796-800	Papal States—History
945.0(4-5)	DG530-537.8	Italy—History—1268-1492	945.632	DG803-818	Rome (Italy)—History
945.0(5-84)	DG538-551.8	Italy—History—1492-1870	945.632	DG807.4	Catacombs
945.0(6-7)	DG539-541.8	Italy—History—16th century	945.7	DG819-831	Italy, Southern
945.0(7-8)	DG550.5-551.8	Italy—History—1789-1870	945.73	DG845.8-851	Naples (Kingdom)—History
945.0(7-83)	DG546-549	Italy—History—1789-1815	945.8	DG861-875	Sicily (Italy)—History
945.0(84-91)	DG555-569	Italy—History—1870-1915	945.85	DG987-999	Malta
945.0025	DG413	Italy—Directories	945.85	DG989.8-994.8	Malta—History
945.004	DG455-457	Ethnology—Italy	946	DP	Spain
945.005	DG401	Italy—Periodicals	946	DP1-402	Spain
945.006	DG441-453	Italy—Civilization	946	DP48-.9	Spain—Civilization
945.0071	DG465.8	Italy—Study and teaching	946.0(2-3)	DP97.3-160.8	Spain—History—711-1516
945.0072	DG465-.7	Italy—Historiography	946.0(58-7)	DP201-232.6	Spain—History—19th century
945.01	DG503-514.7	Italy—History—476-774	946.0025	DP11	Spain—Directories
945.01	DG511-514.7	Lombards	946.004	DP52-53	Ethnology—Spain
945.02	DG509	Italy—History—Gothic War, 535-555	946.005	DP1	Spain—Periodicals
			946.006	DP2	Spain—Congresses
945.02	DG515-517	Italy—History—Carolingian rule, 774-887	946.0072	DP63-.83	Spain—Historiography
945.02	DG515-519	Franks	946.01	DP91-96	Spain—History—To 711
945.02	DG517.5-518	Italy— History—Period of the Italian Kings, 887-962	946.01	DP96	Spain—History—Gothic period, 414-711
945.05	DG737.42	Medici, House of	946.03	DP161.5-166	Spain—History—Ferdinand and Isabella, 1479-1516
945.06	DG541	Fornovo, Battle of, 1495	946.04	DP170-189	Spain—History—House of Austria, 1516-1700
945.08(3-4)	DG552-554.5	Italy—History—1849-1870	946.042	DP172-175	Spain—History—Charles I, 1516-1556
945.083	DG551	Italy—History—Uprising, 1831	946.043	DP176-181	Spain—History—Philip II, 1556-1598
945.083	DG553-.5	Austro-Sardinian War, 1848-1849	946.051	DP182-183.9	Spain—History—Philip III, 1598-1621

Dewey	LC	Subject Heading	Dewey	LC	Subject Heading
946.052	DP184-185.9	Spain—History—Philip IV, 1621-1665	946.82	DP115-118	Granada (Kingdom)—History
946.053	DP186-189	Spain—History—Charles II, 1665-1700	946.9	DP	Portugal
			946.9	DP501-900	Portugal—History
946.054	DP192-200.8	Spain—History—Bourbons, 1700-	946.9	DP532-.7	Portugal—Civilization
			946.90(1-2)	DP558-618	Portugal—History—To 1385
946.054	DP194-200.8	Spain—History—18th century	946.90(1-2)	DP570	Portugal—History—Alfonso Henriques, 1139-1185
946.055	DP194	Anglo-Spanish War, 1718-1748	946.90(2-4)	DP620-682.2	Portugal—History—Modern, 1580-
946.055	DP195	Spain—History—Louis I, 1724	946.9004	DP533-534.5	Ethnology—Portugal
			946.9005	DP501	Portugal—Periodicals
946.056	DP198-.7	Spain—History—Ferdinand VI, 1746-1759	946.90072	DP536.8-.96	Portugal—Historiography
946.057	DP199-.9	Spain—History—Charles III, 1759-1788	946.902	DP571	Portugal—History—Sancho I, 1185-1211
946.057	DP199	Anglo-Spanish War, 1762-1763	946.902	DP572	Portugal—History—Alfonso II, 1211-1223
946.058	DP200-.8	Spain—History—Charles IV, 1788-1808	946.902	DP573	Portugal—History—Sancho II, 1223-1248
946.07(3-4)	DP228-231.5	Spain—History—Carlist War, 1873-1876	946.902	DP574	Portugal—History—Alfonso III, 1248-1279
946.072	DP214-215.9	Spain—History—Ferdinand VII, 1813-1833	946.902	DP575-.3	Portugal—History—Denis, 1279-1325
946.072	DP212-220	Spain—History—Bourbon Restoration, 1814-1868	946.902	DP576	Portugal—History—Alfonso IV, 1325-1357
946.072	DP215	Spain—History—Revolution, 1820-1823	946.902	DP577	Portugal—History—Pedro I, 1357-1367
946.072	DP216-220	Spain—History—Isabella II, 1833-1868	946.902	DP578	Portugal—History—Fernando, 1367-1383
946.072	DP219-.2	Spain—History—Carlist War, 1833-1840	946.902	DP580	Portugal—History—Interregnum, 1383-1385
946.072	DP217	Spain—History—Revolution, 1854	946.902	DP582-618	Portugal—History—Period of discoveries, 1385-1580
946.073	DP230-231.5	Spain—History—Republic, 1873-1875	946.902	DP585-590	Portugal—History—John I, 1385-1433
946.073	DP222-232.6	Spain—History—Revolutionary period, 1868-1875	946.902	DP592-594	Portugal—History—Edward, 1433-1438
946.074	DP232-.6	Spain—History—Alfonso XII, 1875-1885	946.902	DP596-598	Portugal—History—Alfonso V, 1438-1481
946.074	DP233-272.4	Spain—History—Alfonso XIII, 1886-1931	946.902	DP600-602	Portugal—History—John II, 1481-1495
946.074	DP247	Spain—History—Dictatorship, 1923-1930	946.902	DP604-606	Portugal—History—Manual, 1495-1521
946.08	DP250	Spain—History—Revolution, 1931	946.902	DP608-610	Portugal—History—John III, 1521-1557
946.081	DP250-269.9	Spain—History—Republic, 1931-1939	946.902	DP612-616	Portugal—History—Sebastian, 1557-1578
946.081	DP269.A1-.9	Spain—History—Civil War, 1936-1939	946.902	DP614	Kassr-el-Kebir, Battle of, 1578
946.082	DP270-271	Spain—History—1939-1975	946.902	DP618	Portugal—History—Henry I, 1578-1580
946.083	DP272-.4	Spain—History—1975-	946.902	DP622-629	Portugal—History—Spanish dynasty, 1580-1640
946.083	DP272	Spain—History—Coup d'etat, 1981	946.902	DP628	Portugal—History—Revolution, 1640
946.41	DP350-374	Madrid (Spain)			
946.79	DC921-930	Andorra			

Dewey	LC	Subject Heading	Dewey	LC	Subject Heading
946.903(3-4)	DP642-644.9	Portugal—History—Maria I, 1777-1816	947.0(1-42)	DK70-104	Russia—History—To 1533
946.903(4-5)	DP650-651	Portugal—History—John VI, 1816-1826	947.0(47-83)	DK112.8-264.8	Russia—History—1613-1917
946.903(5-6)	DP653-660	Portugal—History—1826-1853	947.0(72-83)	DK188-264.8	Russia—History—1801-1917
946.9032	DP634-.8	Portugal—History—John IV, 1640-1656	947.0004	DJK26-28	Ethnology—Europe, Eastern
946.9032	DP635	Portugal—History—Alfonso VI, 1656-1683	947.0005	DJK1	Europe, Eastern—Periodicals
946.9032	DP635	Elvas, Linhas de, Battle of, 1659	947.0006	DJK1.5	Europe, Eastern—Congresses
946.9032	DP636-.8	Portugal—History—Peter II, 1683-1706	947.00071	DJK35-36	Europe, Eastern—Study and teaching
946.9032	DP638	Portugal—History—John V, 1706-1750	947.00072	DJK32-34	Europe, Eastern—Historiography
946.9033	DP639-641.9	Portugal—History—Joseph I, 1750-1777	947.00090(44-5)	DJK50	Europe, Eastern—History—1945-
946.9034	DP650	Portugal—History—Conspiracy of 1817	947.00090(48-5)	DJK51	Europe, Eastern—History—1989-
946.9035	DP650	Portugal—History—Revolution, 1820	947.000904(1-4)	DJK49	Europe, Eastern—History—1918-1945
946.9035	DP659	Portugal—History—Civil War, 1846-1847	947.000904(4-8)	DJK50	Europe, Eastern—History—1945-1989
946.9035	DP659	Portugal—History—Uprising, 1846	947.004	DK33-35	Ethnology—Russia (Federation)
946.9036	DP665-.5	Portugal—History—Peter V, 1853-1861	947.005	DK1	Russia—Periodicals
			947.006	DK2.5	Russia—Congresses
946.9036	DP668-669	Portugal—History—Charles I, 1889-1908	947.02	DK511.G44	Didgora Mountain (Georgia), Battle of, 1121
946.9036	DP662	Portugal—History—Revolution, 1891	947.04(6-9)	DK112.8-126	Russia—History—1613-1689
946.904	DP670-682.2	Portugal—History—20th century	947.043	DK106-107	Russia—History—Ivan IV, 1533-1584
946.904(1-3)	DP675-680.5	Portugal—History—1910-1974	947.045	DK111-112	Russia—History—Time of Troubles, 1598-1613
946.9041	DP674-682.2	Portugal—History—Revolution, 1910	947.048	DK116-122.5	Russia—History—Aleksei Mikhailovich, 1645-1676
946.9042	DP680	Portugal—History—Revolution, 1926	947.048	DK118.5	Russia—History—Rebellion of Stenka Razin, 1667-1671
946.9044	DP680	Portugal—History—1974-	947.049	DK125	Russia—History—Sofia Alekseevna, 1682-1689
946.9044	DP681	Portugal—History—Revolution, 1974	947.05	DK128-148	Russia—History—Peter I, 1689-1725
946.9044	DP681	Portugal—History—Coup d'etat, 1975	947.05	DK133	Russia—History—Streltsy Revolt, 1698
946.9425	DP752-776	Lisbon (Portugal)	947.05	DL733-743	Northern War, 1700-1721
947	DJK	Europe, Eastern	947.063	DK168-183	Russia—History—Catherine II, 1762-1796
947	DJK24	Europe, Eastern—Civilization	947.063	DK183	Russia—History—Rebellion of Pugachev, 1773-1775
947	DK	Russia, Soviet Union, Poland	947.072	DK190-201	Russia—History—Alexander I, 1801-1825
947	DK1-290.3	Russia			
947	DK32-.7	Russia—Civilization	947.073	DK209-215.97	Russia—History—Nicholas I, 1825-1855
947	DK65-290.3	Russia—History			
947	DK510-651	Russia	947.073	DK212	Russia—History—December Uprising, 1825
947.(6-7)	DK509.1-.95	Bessarabia (Moldova and Ukraine)	947.0738	DK214-215	Crimean War, 1853-1856

Dewey	LC	Subject Heading	Dewey	LC	Subject Heading
947.081	DK219-223	Russia—History—Alexander II, 1855-1881	947.56	DS186-188	Armenia—History—Turkic Mongol Domination, 1045-1522
947.082	DK234-243	Russia—History—Alexander III, 1881-1894	947.560(7-83)	DS194-.5	Armenia—History—1801-1900
947.083	DK251-264.8	Russia—History—Nicholas II, 1894-1917	947.560(83-841)	DS195.5	Armenian massacres, 1915-1923
947.083	DK263-264.7	Russia—History—Revolution, 1905-1907	947.56004	DS172	Ethnology—Armenia
947.084	DK265.8.R85	Russia (Federation)—History—Revolution, 1917-1921	947.5607	DS191-193	Armenia—History—1522-1800
			947.5608(3-6)	DS195-.3	Armenia—History—1901-
947.084(1-2)	DK265-272.7	Soviet Union—History—1917-1936	947.560841	DS195.5	Armenia—History—Revolution, 1917-1920
947.084005	DK266.A2	Soviet Union—Periodicals	947.560841	DS195.5	Armenia (Republic)—History—Uprising, 1921
947.0840072	DK266.A33	Soviet Union—Historiography			
947.0841	DK265-.95	Soviet Union—History—Revolution, 1917-1921	947.58	DK670-679.5	Georgia (Republic)
			947.7	DJK61-66	Black Sea Coast
947.0841	DK265.19	Russia—History—February Revolution, 1917	947.7	DK508-.95	Ukraine
			947.77	DK508.92-.939	Kiev (Ukraine)
947.0841	DK265.42.F8	Black Sea Mutiny, 1919	947.79	DJK71-76	Carpathian Mountains
947.0841	DK266-.5	Soviet Union—History—Allied intervention, 1918-1920	947.8	DK507-.95	Belarus
			947.8	DK507.37-.78	Belarus—History
			947.9	DK502.3-.7	Baltic States
947.0842	DK267-273	Soviet Union—History—1925-1953	947.9	DK502.7	Baltic States—History
			947.93	DK505-.95	Lithuania
947.0842	DK511.B3	Baltic Entente, 1934-1940	947.93	DK505.37-.79	Lithuania—History
947.0842	DK273	Soviet Union—History—1939-1945	947.96	DK504-.95	Latvia
			947.96	DK504.37-.79	Latvia—History
947.0842	DK273	Soviet Union—History—German occupation, 1941-1944	947.98	DK503-.95	Estonia
			947.98	DK503.75-.77	Estonia—History—1944-1991
947.085	DK274-282	Soviet Union—History—1953-1985	947.9808	DK503.8-.85	Estonia—History—1991-
			948	DL	Scandinavia
947.0854	DK285-290.3	Soviet Union—History—1985-1991	948	DL30-33	Scandinavia—Civilization
			948	DL43-87	Scandinavia—History
947.086	DK285-290.3	Soviet Union—History—Attempted coup, 1991	948.004	DL41-42	Ethnology—Scandinavia
			948.005	DL1	Scandinavia—Periodicals
947.31	DK588-609	Moscow (Russia)	948.006	DL1.5	Scandinavia—Congresses
947.48	DK34.K14	Kalmyks	948.03	DL179	Kalmar, Union of, 1397
947.52004	DK34.K13	Kabardians	948.03	DL485	Kalmar, Union of, 1397
947.54	DK690-699.5	Azerbaijan	948.03	DL61-65	Scandinavia—History—15th century
947.56	DK680-689.5	Armenia (Republic)			
947.56	DS161-195.5	Armenia	948.04	DL75-81	Scandinavia—History—The Count's War, 1534-1536
947.56	DS171	Armenia—Civilization			
947.56	DS173-195.5	Armenia—History	948.08	DL83-87	Scandinavia—History—20th century
947.56	DS181-184	Armenia—History—To 428			
947.56	DS181-184	Armenia—History—Arsacid (Arshakuni) dynasty, 66-428	948.1	DL401-596	Norway—History
			948.1	DL431-433	Norway—Civilization
947.56	DS186-188	Armenia—History—428-1522	948.1004	DL441-442	Ethnology—Norway
			948.1005	DL401-403	Norway—Periodicals
947.56	DS186-188	Armenia—History—428-640	948.10072	DL445	Norway—Historiography
			948.10(1-2)	DL485-502	Norway—History—1397-1814
947.56	DS186-188	Armenia—History—Arab period, 640-885	948.101	DL460-478	Norway—History—To 1030

Dewey	LC	Subject Heading	Dewey	LC	Subject Heading
948.101	DL480-502	Norway—History—1030-1397	948.5032	DL704.8	Sweden—History—Charles IX, 1604-1611
948.10(2-3)	DL500-502	Norway—History—Christian Frederick, 1814	948.5034	DL705.A2-715	Sweden—History—Gustavus II, Adolphus, 1611-1632
948.102	DL490	Norway—History—Christian IV, 1588-1648	948.5034	DL710	Kalmar War, 1611-1613
948.102	DL490	Norway—History—Scottish Expedition, 1612	948.5034	DL725.7	Sweden—History—Charles X Gustavus, 1654-1660
948.102	DL490	Norway—History—Hannibal's War, 1644-1645	948.5034	DL727-729	Sweden—History—Charles XI, 1660-1697
948.102	DL490	Norway—History—Frederick III, 1648-1670	948.5036	DL753	Sweden—History—Ulrika Eleonora, 1718-1720
948.102	DL495-.8	Norway—History—Christian V, 1670-1699	948.5034	DL730-743	Sweden—History—Charles XII, 1697-1718
948.102	DL499	Norway—History—War of 1807-1814	948.5036	DL755-759	Sweden—History—Frederick I, 1720-1751
948.103	DL503-526	Norway—History—1814-1905	948.5036	DL757	Sweden—History—Insurrection, 1743
948.1041	DL530-532	Norway—History—1905-1940	948.505	DL860-879	Sweden—History—20th century
948.1041	DL525	Norway—History—Separation from Sweden, 1905	948.505(1-3)	DL867-870	Sweden—History—Gustavus V, 1907-1950
			948.505(3-4)	DL872-876	Sweden—History—Gustavus VI Adolphus, 1950-1973
948.1041	DL532	Norway—History—German Occupation, 1940-1945	948.5051	DL868	Sweden—History—Farmers' Demonstration, 1914
948.10(43-5)	DL533	Norway—History—1945-			
948.5	DL601-991	Sweden—History	948.73	DL976	Stockholm (Sweden)
948.5	DL631-635	Sweden—Civilization	948.9	DL131-133	Denmark—Civilization
948.50(3-4)	DL807-859	Sweden—History—1814-1905	948.90(1-2)	DL174-183.9	Denmark—History—1241-1397
948.50(36-4)	DL747-805	Sweden—History—1718-1814	948.90(2-3)	DL182-192.3	Denmark—History—1448-1660
948.50(54-6)	DL877-879	Sweden—History—Carl XVI Gustav, 1973-	948.90(4-6)	DL248-263	Denmark—History—1900-
948.5004	DL639-641	Ethnology—Sweden	948.9004	DL141-142	Ethnology—Denmark
948.5005	DL601	Sweden—Periodicals	948.9005	DL101	Denmark—Periodicals
948.50072	DL645	Sweden—Historiography	948.9015	DL162-173.8	Denmark—History—To 1241
948.501	DL660-700.9	Sweden—History—To 1397			
948.501	DL689	Sweden— History—Magnus II Ericsson, 1319-1363	948.9015	DL176	Denmark—History—Waldemar IV, 1340-1375
948.5014	DL65	Vikings	948.902	DL179-181.6	Denmark—History—1397-1448
948.5018	DL696-700.9	Sweden—History—1397-1523	948.903	DL185-192.8	Denmark—History—Frederick I, 1523-1533
948.5018	DL694	Kalmar, Union of, 1397	948.903	DL187	Denmark—History—Christian III, 1534-1559
948.503	DL704.6-.7	Sweden—History—17th century	948.903	DL187	Denmark— History—The Count's War, 1534-1536
948.503(2-4)	DL701-879	Sweden—History—1523-1718	948.903	DL187	Denmark—History—Coup d'etat, 1536
948.503(6-8)	DL766-770	Sweden—History—Gustavus III, 1771-1792	948.903	DL188-.8	Denmark—History—Frederick II, 1559-1588
948.503(6-8)	DL766	Sweden—History—Revolution, 1772	948.903	DL189-.5	Denmark—History—Christian IV, 1588-1648
948.5032	DL703	Sweden—History—Gustavus I Vasa, 1523-1560	948.903	DL191.8	Denmark—History—Frederick III, 1648-1670
948.5032	DL703.8	Sweden—History—Eric XIV, 1560-1568	948.903	DL192.3	Denmark—History—Coup d'etat, 1660

Dewey	LC	Subject Heading	Dewey	LC	Subject Heading
948.903	DL195-.8	Denmark—History—Christian V, 1670-1699	948.97032	DL1095-1105	Russo-Finnish War, 1939-1940
948.903	DL196-.8	Denmark—History—Fredrick IV, 1699-1730	948.971	DL1175-.95	Helsinki
948.903	DL197-199	Denmark—History—18th century	949.(2-3)	DH	Benelux countries
			949.12	DL301-398	Iceland
948.903	DL199-.8	Denmark—History—Coup d'etat, 1784	949.12	DL351-380	Iceland—History
			949.12004	DL331-334	Ethnology—Iceland
948.903	DL206	Denmark—History—War of 1807-1814	949.12005	DL301	Iceland—Periodicals
			949.1201	DL357-360	Iceland—History—To 1262
948.904	DL201-249	Denmark—History—19th century	949.1205	DL375	Iceland—History—1918-1945
948.904	DL205-208	Denmark—History—Frederick VI, 1808-1839	949.2	DH71	Netherlands—Civilization
			949.2	DH95-207	Netherlands—History
948.904	DL209-212	Denmark—History—Christian VIII, 1839-1848	949.2	DJ	Netherlands
			949.2	DJ71	Netherlands—Civilization
948.904	DL213-228	Denmark—History—Frederick VII, 1848-1863	949.2	DJ95-292	Netherlands—History
			949.20(2-3)	DH185-207	Netherlands—History—Wars of Independence, 1556-1648
948.904	DL217-241	Denmark—History—1849-1866			
948.904	DL234-249	Denmark—History—Christian IX, 1863-1906	949.2004	DH91-92	Ethnology—Netherlands
			949.2004	DJ91-92	Ethnology—Netherlands
948.9051	DL255-257	Denmark—History—Christian X, 1912-1947	949.2005	DH1	Netherlands—Periodicals
			949.2005	DJ1	Netherlands—Periodicals
948.9051	DL256.5-257	Denmark—History—German occupation, 1940-1945	949.201	DJ151-152	Netherlands—History—To 1384
			949.201	DH141-162	Netherlands—History—To 1384
948.913	DL276	Copenhagen (Denmark)			
948.97	DL1002-1180	Finland	949.201	DH171-177	Netherlands—History—House of Burgundy, 1384-1477
948.97	DL1017	Finland—Civilization			
948.970(2-3)	DL1066-1141.6	Finland—History—20th century	949.202	DJ151-152	Netherlands—History—House of Habsburg, 1477-1556
948.97004	DL1018-1020	Ethnology—Finland			
948.97005	DL1002	Finland—Periodicals	949.202	DH179-184	Netherlands—History—House of Habsburg, 1477-1556
948.97006	DL1004	Finland—Congresses			
948.970072	DL1025	Finland—Historiography	949.202	DH182	Netherlands—History—Charles V, 1506-1555
948.9701	DL1050-1052.9	Finland—History—To 1523			
948.9701	DL1055-1141.6	Finland—History—1523-1611	949.202	DJ151-152	Netherlands—History—Charles V, 1506-1555
948.9701	DL1058-1063	Finland—History—Gustavus II Adolphus, 1611-1632	949.203	DH199.D4	Deventer, Surrender of, 1587
948.9701	DL190	Dano-Swedish War, 1643-1645	949.203	DH201	Netherlands—History—Twelve Years' Truce, 1609-1621
948.9701	DL190	Fehmarn, Battle of, 1644			
948.9701	DL1060-.5	Finland—History—Charles X Gustavus, 1654-1660	949.203	DJ170	Netherlands—History—Twelve Years' Truce, 1609-1621
948.9701	DL192	Dano-Swedish Wars, 1657-1660	0949.204	DJ180-209	Netherlands—History—1648-1795
948.9701	DL1063-.9	Finland—History—18th century	949.204	DJ180-182	Anglo-Dutch War, 1664-1667
948.9702	DL1065-.8	Finland—History—1809-1917	949.204	DJ190-191	Dutch War, 1672-1678
948.9703(2-4)	DL1090-1105	Finland—History—1939-	949.204	DJ205-206	Anglo-Dutch War, 1780-1784
948.97031	DL1070-1075	Finland—History—Revolution, 1917-1918			
948.97031	DL1084	Finland—History—1918-1939			

Dewey	LC	Subject Heading	Dewey	LC	Subject Heading
949.205	DJ211	Netherlands—History—Batavian Republic, 1795-1806	949.3502	DH913	Luxembourg (Luxembourg)—History—Siege, 1684
949.205	DJ241	Netherlands—History—1815-1830	949.4	DQ	Switzerland
			949.4	DQ36-39	Switzerland—Civilization
949.206	DJ241-251	Netherlands—History—1830-1849	949.40(1-2)	DQ88-110	Switzerland—History—1032-1499
949.206	DJ251	Netherlands—History—William II, 1840-1849	949.40(1-3)	DQ79-84	Switzerland—History—To 1648
949.206	DJ261	Netherlands—History—William III, 1849-1890	949.40(4-5)	DQ131-151	Switzerland—History—1789-1815
949.207(1-3)	DJ288-292	Netherlands—History—1945-	949.40(5-6)	DQ124	Switzerland—History—19th century
949.2071	DJ281-287	Netherlands—History—Wilhelmina, 1898-1948	949.40(63-74)	DQ171-210	Switzerland—History—1848-
949.2071	DJ287	Netherlands—History—German occupation 1940-1945	949.40(6-74)	DQ154-191	Switzerland—History—1815-
			949.4004	DQ48-49	Ethnology—Switzerland
949.2072	DJ288-289	Netherlands—History—Juliana, 1948-1980	949.4005	DQ1	Switzerland—Periodicals
			949.4006	DQ2	Switzerland—Congresses
949.2073	DJ290-292	Netherlands—History—Beatrix, 1980-	949.40072	DQ52.8-.95	Switzerland—Historiography
			949.401	DQ85-87	Switzerland—History—To 1032
949.213	DJ401.F5-.F59	Frisians			
949.2352	DJ411.A5-59	Amsterdam (Netherlands)	949.401	DQ85-87	Carolingians
949.3	DH401-811	Belgium	949.402	DQ90-91	Switzerland—History—Perpetual League, 1291
949.3	DH471	Belgium—Civilization			
949.30(1-2)	DH571-584	Belgium—History—To 1555	949.403	DQ104-118	Switzerland—History—1499-1648
949.3004	DH491-492	Ethnology—Belgium	949.403	DQ107.S8	Dornach, Battle of, 1499
949.3005	DH401	Belgium—Periodicals	949.404	DQ111-123	Switzerland—History—1648-1798
949.302	DH584	Belgium—History—Charles V, 1506-1555			
949.302	DH585-606	Belgium—History—1555-1648	949.405	DQ131-151	Switzerland—History—Helvetic Republic, 1798-1803
949.302	DH607-619	Belgium—History—1648-1794	949.4062	DQ154	Switzerland—History—1815-1830
949.302	DH616-618.5	Belgium—History—Revolution, 1789-1790	949.4062	DQ156	Switzerland—History—1830-1848
949.302	DH620-631	Belgium—History—1794-1814	949.4062	DQ158-161	Switzerland—History—Sonderbund, 1845-1847
949.303	DH650-665	Belgium—History—Revolution, 1830-1839	949.407	DQ201-210	Switzerland—History—20th century
949.303	DH671-676	Belgium—History—Leopold II, 1865-1909	tbl949.451	DQ458	Geneva (Switzerland)—History—1536-1603
949.304(3-4)	DH690-692	Belgium—History—Baudoiun I, 1951-	949.47	DQ820-829	Alps
			949.5	DF	Greece
949.3041	DH681-685	Belgium—History—Albert I, 1909-1934	949.5(4-9)005	DF701	Greece—Periodicals
949.3041	DH682	Belgium—History—German occupation, 1914-1918	949.50 (13-3) + 0071	DF505.8-.82	Byzantine Empire—Study and teaching
949.3042	DH687	Belgium—History—German occupation, 1940-1945	949.50 (13-3) + 0072	DF505-.7	Byzantine Empire—Historiography
			949.50 (13-3) + 0099	DF506-.5	Emperors—Byzantine Empire
949.332	DH802-809.95	Brussels (Belgium)	949.50(13-3)	DF501-649	Byzantine Empire
949.35	DH901-925	Luxembourg	949.50(13-3)	DF550-649	Byzantine Empire—History
949.35	DH908-918.5	Luxembourg—History	949.50(13-3)004	DF542-.4	Ethnology—Byzantine Empire
949.35005	DH901	Luxembourg—Periodicals			

Dewey	LC	Subject Heading	Dewey	LC	Subject Heading
949.50(13-3)005	DF501	Byzantine Empire—Periodicals	949.502	DF594	Byzantine Empire—History—Romanus II, 959-963
949.50(13-3)006	DF501.5	Byzantine Empire—Congresses	949.503	DF605	Byzantine Empire—Alexius I Comnenus, 1081-1118
949.50(3-4)	DF604-649	Byzantine Empire—History—1081-1453	949.503	DF606	Byzantine Empire—History—John II Comnenus, 1118-1143
949.50(4-9)	DF701-854.32	Greece			
949.50(4-9)	DF750-854.32	Greece—History	949.503	DF607	Byzantine Empire—History—Manuel I Comnenus, 1143-1180
949.50(4-9)004	DF745-747	Ethnology—Greece			
949.50(6-76)	DF802-854.32	Greece—History—1821-	949.504	DF610-629	Latin Empire, 1204-1261
949.5004	DF135	Ethnology—Greece	949.504	DF625	Byzantine Empire—History—Lascarid dynasty, 1208-1259
949.5005	DF10	Greece—Periodicals			
949.501	DF239-241	Greece—History—146 B.C.-323 A.D.	949.504	DF638	Byzantine Empire—History—John V Palaeologus, 1341-1391
949.501	DF559	Adrianople, Battle of, 378			
949.5013	DF553.5-568	Byzantine Empire—History—To 527	949.505	DF801-.9	Greece—History—1453-1821
949.5013	DF561	Byzantine Empire—History—Arcadius, 395-408	949.5072	DF823-.7	Greece—History—Otho I, 1832-1862
			949.5072	DF823.6	Greece—History—Acarnanian Revolt, 1836
949.5013	DF562	Byzantine Empire—History—Theodosius II, 408-450	949.5072	DF825-832	Greece—History—George I, 1863-1913
949.5013	DF564	Byzantine Empire—History—Leo I, 457-474	949.5072	DF823.68	Greece—History—Arta Revolt, 1854
949.5013	DF565	Byzantine Empire—History—Leo II, 474	949.5072	DF831.5	Greece—History—Coup d'etat, 1909
949.5013	DF566	Byzantine Empire—History—Zeno, 474-491	949.5072	DF837-841	Greece—History—Constantine I, 1913-1917
949.5013	DF572-.8	Byzantine Empire—History—Justinian I, 527-565	949.5074	DF849.5-.58	Greece—History—Civil War, 1944-1949
949.5013	DF573	Byzantine Empire—History—Justine II, 565-578	949.5074	DF850-852.5	Greece—History—1950-1967
949.5013	DF573.2	Byzantine Empire—History—Tiberius II, 578-582	949.5075	DF853-.5	Greece—History—1967-1974
949.5013	DF573.5	Byzantine Empire—History—Maurice, 582-602	949.5075	DF853	Greece—History—Coup d'etat, 1967 (April 21)
949.5013	DF574	Byzantine Empire—History—Heraclius, 610-641	949.5075	DF853	Greece—History—Coup d'etat, 1967 (Dec. 13)
949.5013	DF575.3	Byzantine Empire—History—Constans II, 641-668	949.5075	DF853	Greece—History—Coup d'etat, 1973 (May 22-23)
949.502	DF582	Byzantine Empire—History—Leo III the Isaurian, 717-741	949.5076	DF854-.32	Greece—History—1974-
			949.512	DF915-936	Athens (Greece)
			949.53	DF261.E65	Epirus (Greece and Albania)
949.502	DF583	Byzantine Empire—History—Constantine V Copronymus, 741-775	949.55	DF901.I57-.I69	Ionian Islands (Greece)
			949.59	DF901.C78-.C89	Crete (Greece)—History
949.502	DF586	Byzantine Empire—History—Irene, 797-802	949.6	DR	Balkan Peninsula
949.502	DF589	Byzantine Empire—History—Basil I, 867-886	949.6	DR22-23	Balkan Peninsula—Civilization
			949.6	DR32-48.5	Balkan Peninsula—History
949.502	DF592	Byzantine Empire—History—Leo VI, 886-911	949.6004	DR24-27	Ethnology—Balkan Peninsula
			949.6005	DR1	Balkan Peninsula—Periodicals

Dewey	LC	Subject Heading	Dewey	LC	Subject Heading
949.6006	DR1.5	Balkan Peninsula—Congresses	949.71013	DR1977-1999.5	Serbia—History—To 1456
949.61	DR50-.84	Thrace	949.71013	DR2000-2005	Serbia—History—1456-1804
949.618	DR716-741	Istanbul (Turkey)—History	949.71013	DR2004.8	Serbia—History—Great Emigration, 1690
949.65	DR901-998	Albania			
949.65	DR922	Albania—Civilization	949.71013	DR2005	Serbia—History—Insurrection, 1788
949.65	DR927-977.25	Albania—History			
949.65004	DR923-925	Ethnology—Albania	949.71014	DR343	Serbia—History—Insurrection, 1804-1813
949.65005	DR901	Albania—Periodicals			
949.65006	DR903.5	Albania—Congresses	949.71014	DR2016	Serbia—History—Milos Obrenovic, 1814-1839
949.6501	DR954-960.5	Albania—History—To 1501			
949.6501	DR959-960.5	Albania—History—Turkish War, 15th century	949.71015	DR2026.8	Serbia—History—Revolt, 1883
949.6501	DR961-969	Albania—History—1501-1912	949.7102	DR2033-2040	Serbia—History—1918-1945
949.6501	DR965.9-969	Albania—History—1840-1912	949.7103	DR1306-1312	Yugoslavia—History—1992-
949.6501	DR966	Albania—History—1878-1912	949.7103	DR2047	Serbia—History—1992-
			949.72	DR1502-1645	Croatia
949.6502	DR970-975	Albania—History—1912-1944	949.72	DR1547-1598	Croatia—History
			949.73	DR1352-1485	Slovenia
949.6502	DR969	Albania—History—Uprising, 1912	949.73	DR1376-1450	Slovenia—History
			949.7302	DR1444-1450	Slovenia—History—1945-1990
949.6502	DR972	Albania—History—Peasant Uprising, 1914-1915			
			949.7303	DR1452-1457.5	Slovenia—History—1990-
949.6502	DR973	Albania—History—June Revolution, 1924	949.742	DR1652-1785	Bosnia and Herzegovina
			949.742	DR1697-1785	Bosnia and Hercegovina—History
949.6502	DR975	Albania—History—Axis occupation, 1939-1944			
			949.745	DR1802-1928	Montenegro
949.650(3-4)	DR976-977.25	Albania—History—1990-	949.745	DR1827-1928	Montenegro—History
949.6503	DR976-977.25	Albania—History—1944-1990	949.76	DR701.M13-.M14	Macedonia—History
			949.76	DR2152-2285	Macedonia
949.7	DR1202-2285	Yugoslavia	949.8	DR	Romania
949.7	DR1228	Yugoslavia—Civilization	949.8	DR201-296	Romania
949.7	DR1232-1321	Yugoslavia—History	949.8	DR212	Romania—Civilization
949.70(2-3)	DR1281-1312	Yugoslavia—History—1918-1945	949.8	DR215-267.5	Romania—History
			949.80(16-2)	DR244	Romania—History—1859-1866
949.7004	DR1229-1230	Ethnology—Yugoslavia			
949.7005	DR1202	Yugoslavia—Periodicals	949.80(2-31)	DR267	Romania—History—1944-1989
949.7006	DR1205	Yugoslavia—Congresses			
949.70072	DR1239-1243	Yugoslavia—Historiography	949.8004	D90.D	Dacians
949.7022	D802.Y8	Yugoslavia—History—Axis occupation, 1941-1945	949.8004	DR213-214	Ethnology—Romania
			949.8005	DR201	Romania—Periodicals
949.7022	DR1297-1298	Yugoslavia—History—Coup d'etat, 1941	949.80072	DR216.7-.92	Romania—Historiography
			949.801	DR238-241	Romania—History—To 1711
949.7023	DR1300	Yugoslavia—History—1945-1980			
			949.8015	DR241	Romania—History—1711-1821
949.7024	DR1306-1313.8	Yugoslavia—History—1980-1992			
			949.8016	DR242-250	Romania—History—1821-1859
949.71	DR343	Serbia—History			
949.71	DR1932-2125	Serbia	949.8016	DR241	Romania—History—Revolution, 1821
949.710(2-3)	DR2033-2047	Serbia—History—1918-			
949.710(2-3)	DR2041-2047	Serbia—History—1945-1992	949.802	DR248	Romania—History—War of Independence, 1876-1878
			949.802	DR250-266	Romania—History—Charles I, 1866-1914
949.7101(4-5)	DR2006-2032	Serbia—History—1804-1918			

Dewey	LC	Subject Heading	Dewey	LC	Subject Heading
949.802	DR256	Romania—History—Peasants' Uprising, 1888	951.0(18-24)	DS751.72.-.78	China—History—Liao dynasty, 947-1125
949.802	DR263	Romania—History—1914-1918	951.0(35-59)	DS774	China—History—20th century
949.802	DR264-266	Romania—History—Uprising, 1941	951.0(57-6)	DS779.15-.29	China—History—1976-
949.8032	DR267-.5	Romania—History—1989-	951.004	DS730-731	Ethnology—China
949.8032	DR269.5-.6	Romania—History—Revolution, 1989	951.01	DS747.28-749.7	China—History—221 B.C.-960 A.D.
949.84	DR279-280.74	Transylvania (Romania)	951.015	DS748.5-.76	China—History—Northern and Southern dynasties, 386-589
949.9	DR	Bulgaria			
949.9	DR51-98	Bulgaria			
949.9	DR63	Bulgaria—Civilization	951.015	DS748.7-.76	China—History—Northern Wei dynasty, 386-534
949.9	DR65-93.34	Bulgaria—History	951.015	DS748.6-.66	China—History—Liu Sung dynasty, 420-479
949.90(2-3)	DR89.9-93.34	Bulgaria—History—1944-			
949.90025	DR53.7	Bulgaria—Directories	951.015	DS748.6-.66	China—History—Ch'i dynasty, 479-502
949.9004	DR64	Ethnology—Bulgaria			
949.9005	DR51	Bulgaria—Periodicals	951.015	DS748.6-.66	China—History—Liang dynasty, 502-557
949.90072	DR66.7-.97	Bulgaria—Historiography			
949.9013	DR74.3	Bulgaria—History—To 681	951.015	DS748.7-.76	China—History—Northern Ch'i dynasty, 550-577
949.9013	DR74.5	Bulgaria—History—681-1018	951.015	DS748.7-.76	China—History—Ch'en dynasty, 557-589
949.9014	DR79	Bulgaria—History—1018-1185	951.015	DS748.7-.76	China—History—Northern Chou dynasty, 557-581
949.9015	DR82-.5	Bulgaria—History—1393-1878	951.017	DS749.46	China—History—An Lu shan Rebellion, 755-763
949.902	DR84.9-.8	Bulgaria—History—1878-1944	951.017	DS749.47	China—History—Huang Ch'ao Rebellion, 874-884
949.98	DR2211	Macedonia—Karpos Uprising, 1689	951.018	DS749.7-.76	China—History—Earlier Shu kingdom, 907-925
949.99	DR97	Sofia (Bulgaria)	951.018	DS749.7-.76	China—History—Later Shu kingdom, 934-965
950	CB253-256	Civilization, Oriental			
950	DS	Asia	951.024	DS751.82-.88	China—History—Hsi Hsia dynasty, 1038-1227
950	DS11	Oriental antiquities			
950	DS31-35.2	Asia—History	951.024	DS751.92-.98	China—History—Chin dynasty, 1115-1234
950	DS501-519	East Asia			
950.(3-41)	DS740.6-.63	Eastern question (Far East)	951.026	DS753.65	China—History—Li Tzu ch'eng Rebellion, 1628-1645
950.04	DS13-28	Ethnology—Asia			
950.04	DS25	Hsiung-nu			
950.04942	DS19-23	Mongols	951.03	DS753.82-773.6	Manchus
950.04942	DS22.7	Golden Horde	951.03(4-5)	DS763.65	China—History—Self-strengthening movement, 1861-1895
950.0494387	DS25	Tatars			
950.05	DS1	Asia—Periodicals	951.03(4-6)	DS763.5-773.6	China—History—1861-1912
950.4	DS35-.2	Asia—History—20th century			
950.4(2-3)	DS35.2	Asia—History—1945-	951.033	DS756.3-.37	China—History—White Lotus Rebellion, 1796-1804
950.4(2-3)	DS518.1	East Asia—History—1945-			
951	DS701-799.9	China	951.033	DS757.4-.7	China—History—Opium War, 1840-1842
951	DS721-727	China—Civilization			
951.0(18-24)	DS749.5-.76	China—History—Five dynasties and the Ten kingdoms, 907-979	951.034	DS758.7-759.4	China—History—Taiping Rebellion, 1850-1864
951.0(18-24)	DS749.7-.76	China—History—Southern Han kingdom, 917-971	0951.034	DS759.5	China—History—Nien Rebellion, 1853-1868
951.0(18-24)	DS749.7-.76	China—History—Southern T'ang kingdom, 937-975	951.035	DS764.4-767.6	Chinese-Japanese War, 1894-1895

Dewey	LC	Subject Heading	Dewey	LC	Subject Heading
951.035	DS770-772.3	China—History—Boxer Rebellion, 1899-1901	951.2490(2-3)	DS799.64-.66	Taiwan—History—To 1895
951.035	DS771.5	German Expedition to China, 1900-1901	951.2490(3-4)	DS799.69-.72	Taiwan—History—1895-1945
951.035	DS773-.6	China—History—Hsuan t'ung, 1908-1912	951.249004	DS799.42-.43	Ethnology—Taiwan
951.036	DS773.32-.6	China—History—Revolution, 1911-1912	951.24904	DS799.69	Taiwan—History—Insurrection, 1895
951.04	DS773.83-777.5	China—History—Republic, 1912-1949	951.24905	DS799.77-.833	Taiwan—History—1945-
951.041	DS776.4-777.46	China—History—1912-1928	951.24905	DS799.823	Taiwan—History—February Twenty Eighth Incident, 1947
951.041	DS777.2	China—History—Revolution, 1913	951.24905	DS799.83-.833	Taiwan—History—1975-
951.041	DS777.25	China—History—Revolution, 1915-1916	951.24905	DS799.834	Taiwan—History—Kaohsiung Incident, 1979
951.041	DS777.36	China—History—Warlord period, 1916-1928	951.8	DS781-784.2	Manchus
951.041	DS777.43	China—History—May Fourth movement, 1919	951.8	DS781-784.2	Manchuria (China)
951.041	DS777.45	China—History—May Thirtieth movement, 1925	951.9	DS904	Korea—Civilization
951.042	DS777.462	China—History—Tsinan Incident, 1928	951.90(2-4s)	DS915.56-922.4	Korea—History—20th century
951.042	DS777.47-.514	China—History—1928-1937	951.9004	DS904.5-.7	Ethnology—Korea
951.042	DS777.5132-.51	China—History—Long March, 1934-1935	951.901	DS911-.78	Korea—History—To 935
951.042	DS777.51393	China—History—December Ninth Movement, 1935	951.901	DS912-.43	Korea—History—Koryo period, 935-1392
951.042	DS775	China—History—December Ninth Movement, 1935	951.901	DS912.4-.43	Korea—History—Mongolian Invasions, 1231-1270
951.042	DS777.518-.531	China—History—1937-1945	951.902	DS913-915.5	Korea—History—Yi dynasty, 1392-1910
951.042	DS777.514	China—History—Sian Incident, 1936	951.902	DS913-.45	Korea—History—Japanese Invasions, 1592-1598
951.042	DS796.N2	Nanking Massacre, Nanjing, Jiangsu Sheng, China, 1937	951.902	DS913.615-.675	Korea—History—Manchu Invasions, 1627-1637
951.042	DS777.534	China—History—Southern Anhui Incident, 1941	951.902	DS915-.5	Korea—History—1864-1910
951.042	DS777.535-.544	China—History—Civil War, 1945-1949	951.903	DS916.525-.58	Korea—History—Japanese occupation, 1910-1945
951.05	DS777.545-779	China—History—1949-	951.904	DS916.6-922.42	Korea—History—1945-
951.05(5-7)	DS777.55	China—History—1949-1976	951.9041	DS917.5-.55	Korea—History—Allied occupation, 1945-1948
951.055	DS778.4	China—History—Hundred Flowers Campaign, 1956	951.9042	DS918-921.8	Korean War, 1950-1953
951.055	DS778.5	China—History—Antirightist Campaign, 1957-1958	951.9042092	DS921.6	Korean War, 1950-1953—Personal narratives, American
951.056	DS778.7	China—History—Cultural Revolution, 1966-1969	951.90422	DS921.7	Korean Demilitarized Zone (Korea)
951.058	DS779.32	China—History—Tiananmen Square Incident, 1989	951.90422	DS921.7	Korean War, 1950-1953—Armistices
951.156	DS795.23-.3	Beijing (China)—History	951.904242	DS918.2	Korean War, 1950-1953—Campaigns
951.249	DS799.4	Taiwan—Civilization	951.904242	DS918.2	Naktong River (Korea), Battle of, 1950
951.249	DS799.99-.833	Taiwan—History	951.904248	DS920.2	Korean War, 1950-1953—Aerial operations.
			951.90427	DS921-.2	Korean War, 1950-1953—History—Prisoners and prisons
			951.90427	DS921	Korean War, 1950-1953—Prisoners and prisons, American

Dewey	LC	Subject Heading	Dewey	LC	Subject Heading
951.90428	DS920.8-.9	Korean War, 1950-1953—Atrocities	952.025	DS871.5	Japan—History—Ako Vendetta, 1703
951.90428	DS921.5.S4	Korean War, 1950-1953—Search and rescue operations—Korea (North)	952.025	DS881-.84	Japan—History—19th century
			952.025	DS881.2-.84	Japan—History—Restoration, 1853-1870
951.93	DS930-937	Korea (North)			
951.95043	DS922-.42	Korea (South)—History—April Revolution, 1960	952.025	DS881.4	Japan—History—Sakai Incident, 1868
951.95043	DS922.44	Korea (South)—May Revolution, 1961	952.025	DS881.83-.84	Japan—History—Civil War, 1868
951.95043	DS922.445	Kwangju Uprising , Kwangju-si, Korea, 1980	952.0(31-49)	DS884.5-890.3	Japan—History—20th century
952	DS801-897	Japan	952.031	DS516-517.9	Russo-Japanese War, 1904-1905
952	DS820.8-827	Japan—Civilization			
952.0(3-5)	DS881.85-890.3	Japan—History—1868-	952.031	DS881.98-884	Japan—History—Meiji period, 1868-1912
952.0(48-5)	DS890.3	Japan—History—Heisei period, 1989-	952.031	DS881.4	Japan—History—Kobe Incident, 1868
952.004	DS830-832	Ethnology—Japan	952.031	DS882.5	Japan—History—Takehashi Incident, 1878
952.004946	DS832	Ainu			
952.01	DS850-856.72	Japan—History—To 1185	952.031	DS882.5	Japan—History—Kioizaka Incident, 1878
952.01	DS854	Japan—History—Earlier Nine Years' War, 1051-1062	952.032	DS885.8-888	Japan—History—Taisho period, 1912-1926
952.01	DS855-.73	Japan—History—To 794	952.0(33-5)	DS888.84-890.3	Japan—History—1945-
952.01	DS855.6	Japan—History—Taika Reform, 645-710	952.033	DS888.4-.5	Japan—History—1926-1945
952.01	DS855.7-.73	Japan—History—Nara period, 710-794	952.033	DS888.15-890.3	Japan—History—Showa period, 1926-1989
952.01	DS855.87-856.7	Japan—History—Heian period, 794-1185	952.033	DS888.4-.5	Japan—History—February Incident, 1936 (February 26)
952.01	DS856.3	Japan—History—Later Three Years' War, 1083-1087	952.033	DS888.5	Japan—History—March and October Incidents, 1931
952.02(1-4)	DS856.75-869.6	Japan—History—1185-1600	952.033	DS888.5	Japan—History—May Incident, 1932 (May 15)
952.02(1-2)	DS863	Japan—History—Kenmu Restoration, 1333-1336	952.04(4-5)	DS889.16	Japan—History—Allied occupation, 1945-1952
952.02(2-3)	DS863.75-869.6	Japan—History—Muromachi period, 1336-1573	952.29	DS895.R97	Ryukyu Islands—History
			953.8	DS201-248	Saudi Arabia
952.02(3-4)	DS868-869.6	Japan—History—Period of civil wars, 1480-1603	953.8	DS215	Saudi Arabia—Civilization
			953.8	DS221-244.63	Saudi Arabia—History
952.021	DS858-861	Japan—History—Kamakura period, 1185-1333	953.8004	DS218-219	Ethnology—Saudi Arabia
			953.80099	DS234-238	Abbasids
952.021	DS861	Japan—History—Jokyu Revolt, 1221	953.80099	DS234-238	Caliphs
			953.802	DS232	Ditch, Battle of the, 627
952.021	DS861	Japan—History—Attempted Mongol Invasions, 1274-1281	954	DS421-486.8	India
			954	DS421-428.2	India—Civilization
952.021	DS861	Japan—History—Genko Incident, 1331-1333	954.0(2-223)	DS451-.9	India—History—324 B.C-1000 A.D.
952.025	DS870-881.84	Japan—History—Tokugawa period, 1600-1868	954.0(296-4)	DS463-480.83	India—History—British occupation, 1765-1947
952.025	DS871.5	Japan—History—Keicho Peasant Uprising, 1614-1615	954.0(4-5)	DS480.832-481	India—History—1947-
			954.004	DS430-432.5	Ethnology—India
			954.0049144	DS432.B4	Bengali (South Asian people)
			954.02	DS451.8	Gurjara-Pratihara dynasty

Dewey	LC	Subject Heading	Dewey	LC	Subject Heading
954.02(23-96)	DS452-462.8	India—History—1000-1765	955.0(4-51)	DS298-316	Iran—History—Qajar dynasty, 1794-1925
954.02(23-45)	DS457-460	India—History—1000-1526	955.004	DS268-269	Ethnology—Iran
			955.02	DS288-290	Iran—History—640-1500
954.0234	DS459.2	Khilji dynasty	955.02	DS287.8-288.9	Iran—History—640-1256
954.025	DS461-.9	Mogul Empire	955.02	DS288.95-289.8	Iran—History—1256-1500
954.0298	DS473	Maratha War, 1775-1782	955.03	DS292-297	Iran—History—16th-18th centuries
954.0311	DS474.1	India—History—Mysore War, 1790-1792	955.04	DS307.5	Iran—History—War with Great Britain, 1856-1857
954.0312	DS475.3	India—History—Mysore War, 1799	955.051	DS313	Iran—History—1905-1911
954.0313	DS475.6	Maratha War, 1816-1818	955.05(2-3)	DS316.2-318.7	Iran—History—Pahlavi dynasty, 1925-1979
954.0313	DS485.N4	Nepalese War, 1814-1816			
954.0313	DS475.5	India—History—Mutiny, 1809	955.053	DS318-.7	Iran—History—Mohammed Reza Pahlavi, 1941-1979
954.0317	DS478-.3	India—History—Sepoy Rebellion, 1857-1858	955.054	DS318.72-.85	Iran—History—1979-
			955.054	DS318.72-.85	Iran—History—Revolution, 1979
954.0357	DS480.5	Massacres—India—Amritsar	955.0542	DS318.85	Iran-Iraq War, 1980-1988
954.0359	DS480.82	India—History—Quit India movement, 1942	956	DS41-66	Middle East
			956.004926	DS121.4	Canaanites
954.042	DS480.85	Sino-Indian Border Dispute, 1957-	956.01(3-4)	DS38.6	Islamic Empire—History—750-1258
954.9042	DS385.9	India-Pakistan Conflict, 1947-1949	956.01(4-5)	DS38.7	Islamic Empire—History—1258-1517
954.91	DS379	Pakistan—Civilization	956.013	DS38.5	Islamic Empire—History—661-750
954.91	DS381.7-388.2	Pakistan—History			
954.91004	DS380.A1-.A2	Ethnology—Pakistan	956.013	DS38.1	Dhat al-Sawari, Battle of, 655
954.92	DS393.8	Bangladesh—Civilization			
954.92	DS394.5-395.7	Bangladesh—History	956.04	DS119.7-.76	Arab-Israeli conflict
954.92004	DS393.82-.83	Ethnology—Bangladesh	956.042	DS126.9-.99	Israel-Arab War, 1948-1949
954.92051	DS395.5	Bangladesh—History—Revolution, 1971	956.046	DS127-.9	Israel-Arab War, 1967
954.93	DS488-490	Sri Lanka	956.048	DS128.1-.19	Israel-Arab War, 1973
954.93	DS489.5-490	Sri Lanka—History	956.1	DR	Turkey
954.930(1-2)	DS489.7-.73	Sri Lanka—History—1505-1948	956.1	DR432	Turkey—Civilization
			956.1	DR436-603	Turkey—History
954.93004	DS489.2-.25	Ethnology—Sri Lanka	956.10(23-36)	DR589-590	Turkey—History—1918-1960
954.9301	DS489.6-.63	Sri Lanka—History—To 1505			
			956.10(36-4)	DR593-603	Turkey—History—1960-
954.9302	DS489.7	Sri Lanka—History—Rebellion, 1848	956.1003	DR414	Turkey—Gazetteers
			956.1004	DR434-435	Ethnology—Turkey
954.9302	DS489.7	Sri Lanka—History—Rebellion, 1818	956.10072	DR438.8-.95	Turkey—Historiography
			956.101	DR481	Turkey—History—To 1453
954.9303	DS489.8-.86	Sri Lanka—History—1948-	956.101(4-5)	DR485-486	Turkey—History—Ottoman Empire, 1288-1918
954.93031	DS489.8	Sri Lanka—History—Rebellion, 1971	956.101(4-5)	DR493-502	Turkey—History—1288-1453
954.96	DS493.7	Nepal—Civilization			
954.96	DS494.4-495.59	Nepal—History	956.1015	DR496	Turkey—History—Bayezid I, 1389-1403
954.96	DS495	Nepal—History—To 1768			
954.96	DS495.3	Nepal—History—1768-1951	956.1015	DR496	Turkey—History—Invasion of Timur, 1402
954.96004	DS493.8-.9	Ethnology—Nepal	956.1015(2-3)	DR502-536	Turkey—History—1453-1683
955	DS251-326	Iran			
955	DS270-318.85	Iran—History	956.1015(3-4)	DR536-562	Turkey—History—1683-1829

Dewey	LC	Subject Heading	Dewey	LC	Subject Heading
956.10152	DR501-.7	Turkey—History—Mehmed II, 1451-1481	956.1038	DR601	Turkey—History—Coup d'etat, 1980
956.10152	DR503	Turkey—History—Bayezid II, 1481-1512	956.7	DS70.7	Iraq—Civilization
			956.7	DS70.82-79.66	Iraq—History
956.10152	DR505-506	Turkey—History—Suleyman I, 1520-1566	956.7004	DS70.8	Ethnology—Iraq
			956.70442	DS79.72	Persian Gulf War, 1991
956.10153	DR523	Turkey—History—Wars with Persia, 1576-1639	956.704427	DS79.74	Persian Gulf War, 1991—Prisoners and prisons
956.10153	DR525	Turkey—History—Mehmed III, 1595-1603	956.70443	DS79.76	Iraq War, 2003
956.10153	DR529	Turkey—History—Murad IV, 1623-1640	956.91	DS94.6	Syria—Civilization
			956.91	DS94.9-98.3	Syria—History
956.10153	DR534-536.5	Turkey—History—Mehmed IV, 1648-1687	956.91004	DS94.7-.8	Ethnology—Syria
			956.92	DS80.4	Lebanon—Civilization
956.10153	DR534.5.D3	Dardanelles, Battle of the, 1656	956.92	DS80.7-87.53	Lebanon—History
			956.92004	DS80.5	Ethnology—Lebanon
956.10153	DR537	Turkey—History—Suleyman II, 1687-1691	956.9203	DS83	Lebanon—History—635-1516
956.10153	DR541.3	Turkey—History—Mustafa II, 1695-1703	956.92034	DS84	Lebanon—History—1516-1918
956.10153	DR542-545	Turkey—History—Ahmed III, 1703-1730	956.92044	DS87.5	Lebanon—History—Civil War, 1975-
956.10153	DR542	Turkey—History—Rebellion, 1703	956.92044	DS87.53	Lebanon—History—Israeli intervention, 1982-1984
956.10153	DR545	Austro-Turkish War, 1716-1718	956.92044092	DS87.2.C4	Hostages—Lebanon—Biography
956.10153	DR547-548	Turkey—History—Mahmud I, 1730-1754	956.93	DS54.35	Cyprus—Civilization
			956.93	DS54.5-.9	Cyprus—History
956.10153	DR548	Austro-Turkish War, 1737-1739	956.93004	DS54.4-.44	Ethnology—Cyprus
			956.94	DS101-151	Jews
956.10153	DR551-553	Turkey—History—Mustafa III, 1757-1773	956.94	DS101-151	Israel
			956.94	DS112-113	Jews—Civilization
956.10154	DR555	Turkey—History—Abdul Hamid I, 1774-1789	956.94	DS114-128.19	Israel—History
956.10154	DR559-.5	Turkey—History—Selim III, 1789-1807	956.940(3-4)	DS124-126	Jews—History—1789-1945
956.10154	DR562-564	Turkey—History—Mahmud II, 1808-1839	956.94004	DS113.2-.8	Ethnology—Israel
			956.9402	DS122.8	Jews—History—Rebellion, 66-73
956.10154	DR564-573.7	Turkey—History—1829-1878	956.9402	DS123.5	Palestine—History—70-638
956.10154	DR565	Turkey—History—Tanzimat, 1839-1876	956.9402	DS123.5	Jews—History—70-638
956.10154	DR567	Crimean War, 1853-1856	956.9402	DS122.8	Jerusalem—History—Siege, 70 A.D.
956.10154	DR573.7-584.5	Turkey—History—1878-1909	956.9402	DS122.9	Jews—History—Bar Kokhba Rebellion, 132-135
956.10154	DR583-588	Turkey—History—Mehmed V, 1909-1918	956.9402	DS121.7-.8	Jews—History—168 B.C.-135 A.D.
956.10154	DR583	Turkey—History—Revolution, 1909	956.9403	DS124-125.5	Palestine—History—638-1917
956.1023	DR589	Turkey—History—Revolution, 1918-1923	956.94034	DS125	Palestine—History—1799-1917
956.1023	DR589	Turkey—History—Mehmed VI, 1918-1922	956.9404	DS125.5-126.4	Palestine—History—1917-1948
956.1036	DR593	Turkey—History—Revolution, 1960	956.9404	DS126-.4	Palestine—History—1929-1948
956.1037	DR600	Turkey—History—Coup d'etat, 1971			

Dewey	LC	Subject Heading	Dewey	LC	Subject Heading
956.9404	DS126	Palestine—History—Arab riots, 1920	959.104	DS530	Burma—History—Peasant Uprising, 1931
956.9404	DS126	Palestine—History—Arab riots, 1929	959.105	DS530.4	Burma—History—1948-
956.9404	DS126	Palestine—History—Arab rebellion, 1936-1939	959.3	DS568	Thailand—Civilization
			959.3	DS570.95-586	Thailand—History
956.9404	DS126	Palestine—History—Proposed partition, 1937	959.3004	DS569-570	Ethnology—Thailand
			959.4	DS555.42	Laos—Civilization
956.9404	DS126.4	Palestine—History—Partition, 1947	959.4	DS555.5-86	Laos—History
			959.4004	DS555.44-.45	Ethnology—Laos
956.9405	DS126.5	Israel—History—Declaration of Independence, 1948	959.4042	DS555.84-.86	Laos—History—1975-
			959.5	DS594	Malaysia—Civilization
956.94052	DS126.5-126.99	Israel—History—1948-1949	959.5	DS595.8-597.21	Malaya—History
			959.5004	DS595-.2	Ethnology—Malaysia
956.94054	DS119.7	Entebbe Airport Raid, 1976	959.503	DS596.6	Malaya—History—Japanese occupation, 1942-1945
956.9442	DS109-.94	Jerusalem			
956.9442	DS109.85-.94	Jerusalem—History	959.504	DS597	Malaya—History—Malayan Emergency, 1948-1960
956.944203	D175-195	Jerusalem—History—Latin Kingdom, 1099-1244			
			959.55	DS650.4	Brunei—Civilization
956.95	DS153-154.9	Jordan	959.55	DS650.44-.83	Brunei—History
956.95	DS153.4	Jordan—Civilization	959.55004	DS650.42-.43	Ethnology—Brunei
956.95	DS153.7-154.55	Jordan—History	959.6	DS554.42	Cambodia—Civilization
956.950(3-44)	DS154.5-.55	Jordan—History—20th century	959.6	DS554.5-.842	Cambodia—History
			959.60(3-41)	DS554.7-.73	Cambodia—History—1863-1953
956.95004	DS153.5-.55	Ethnology—Jordan			
956.95043	DS154.55	Jordan—History—Intervention, 1958	959.6004	DS554.44-.46	Ethnology—Cambodia
			959.601	DS554.6-.64	Cambodia—History—To 800
956.953	DS110.S3	Samaria Region			
957	DK751-781	Siberia (Russia)	959.602	DS554.6-.64	Cambodia—History—800-1444
958	DK845-860	Asia, Central			
958	DS327-329.4	Asia, Central	959.603	DS554.6-.64	Cambodia—History—1444-1863
958.1	DS354	Afghanistan—Civilization			
958.1	DS355-371.2	Afghanistan—History	959.604(1-2)	DS554.8-.83	Cambodia—History—1953-1975
958.1004	DS354.5-.6	Ethnology—Afghanistan			
958.104(5-6)	DS371.3	Afghanistan—History—1989-	959.6042	DS554.84-.842	Cambodia—History—1975-
			959.6042	DS554.84	Cambodia—History—Civil War, 1970-1975
958.1045	DS371.2	Afghanistan—History—Soviet occupation, 1979-1989			
			959.7	DS556-559.916	Vietnam
958.1047	DS371.414	Afghan War, 2001—Prisoners and prisons American	959.7	DS556.42	Vietnam—Civilization
			959.70(3-4)	DS556.8-.83	Vietnam—History—19th century
			959.7004	DS556.44-.45	Ethnology—Vietnam
958.43	DK911-919.5	Kyrgyzstan	959.703	DS556.6-.63	Vietnam—History—To 939
958.45	DK901-909.5	Kazakhstan	959.703	DS556.7-.73	Vietnam—History—Later Le dynasty, 1428-1787
958.5	DK931-939.5	Turkmenistan			
958.6	DK921-929.5	Tajikistan	959.703	DS556.815	Vietnam—History—August Revolution, 1945
958.7	DK941-949.5	Uzbekistan			
959	DS524-526.7	Asia, Southeastern—History	959.704(2-44)	DS556.9-.93	Vietnamese reunification question (1954-1976)
959.1	DS527.9	Burma—Civilization			
959.10(2-4)	DS529.7-530.32	Burma—History—1824-1948	959.704(2-44)	DS556.9-.93	Vietnamese reunification question (1954-1976)
			959.7042	DS553.3.D5	Dien Bien Phu (Vietnam), Battle of, 1954
959.1004	DS528-.2	Ethnology—Burma			
959.1004	DS538-539	Ethnology—Burma	959.7043	DS557-559.8	Vietnamese Conflict, 1961-1975
959.102	DS527.2-.3	Burma—History—To 1824			
959.104	DS530	Burma—History—Japanese occupation, 1942-1945			

Dewey	LC	Subject Heading	Dewey	LC	Subject Heading
959.7043	DS558.4	Vietnamese Conflict, 1961-1975— Regimental histories— United States	959.9035	DS686.4	Philippines—History—Japanese occupation, 1942-1945
959.704342	DS557.8.I	Ia Drang Valley (Vietnam), Battle of, 1965	959.904(1-6)	DS686.5-.6	Philippines—History—1946-1986
959.704342	DS557.8.K5	Khe Sanh, Battle of, 1968	959.904(7-8)	DS686.614	Philippines—History—1986-
959.704342	DS557.8.E23	Easter Offensive, 1972	959.9047	DS686.6	Philippines—History—Attempted coup, 1987
959.704342	DS557.8.S6	Sontay Raid, 1970			
959.70437	DS559.4	Vietnamese Conflict, 1961-1975— Prisoners and prisons	959.9047	DS686.62	Philippines—History—Revolution, 1986
959.8	DS625	Indonesia—Civilization	959.9047	DS686.6	Philippines—History—Coup d'etat, 1989
959.8	DS633-644.4	Indonesia—History	960	DT	Africa
959.80(15-21)	DS641.5-642.22	Indonesia—History—1478-1798	960	DT14	Africa—Civilization
			960	DT17-39	Africa—History
959.8004	DS631-632	Ethnology—Indonesia	960.(1-21)	DT25	Africa—History—To 1498
959.80049922	DS632.B25	Balinese (Indonesia people)	960.(1-23)	DT24-28	Africa—History—To 1884
959.8012	DS641	Indonesia—History—To 1478	960.(23-326)	DT29-30.2	Africa—History—1884-1960
959.8022	DS643-.22	Indonesia—History—1798-1942	960.(23-314)	DT29	Africa—History—1884-1918
959.8022	DS643	Indonesia—History—British occupation, 1811-1816	960.04	DT15-16	Ethnology—Africa
			960.3(26-3)	DT30.5	Africa—History—1960-
959.8022	DS643	Indonesia—History—Java War, 1825-1830	961	DT160-177	Africa, North
			961	DT160-176	Africa, North—History
959.8022	DS643	Indonesia—History—Achinese War, 1873-1904	961.0(22-45)	DT172	Africa, North—History—647-1517
959.8022	DS643.5	Indonesia—History—Japanese occupation, 1942-1945	961.0(3-5)	DT176	Africa, North—History—1882-
			961.004933	DT193.5.B45	Berbers
959.803(5-6)	DS644-.1	Indonesia—History—1950-1966	961.1	DT241-269	Tunisia
			961.1	DT252	Tunisia—Civilization
959.8035	DS644	Indonesia—History—Revolution, 1945-1949	961.1	DT253.4-264.49	Tunisia—History
			961.1004	DT253-.2	Ethnology—Tunisia
959.8036	DS644.32	Indonesia—History—Coup d'etat, 1965	961.102	DT259	Tunisia—History—647-1516
959.8036	DS644.4	Indonesia—History—1966-	961.103	DT261-263.76	Tunisia—History—1516-1881
959.9	DS651-689	Philippines			
959.9	DS663-664	Philippines—Civilization	961.103	DT262	Tunisia—History—Expedition of Charles V, 1535
959.90(22-312)	DS674-.9	Philippines—History—1521-1898	961.103	DT262	Tunisia—History—Conquest, 1573
959.901	DS673.8	Philippines—History—To 1521	961.104	DT263.9-264.3	Tunisia—History—French occupation, 1881-1956
959.902	DS674	Philippines—History—1521-1812	961.105	DT264.35-.49	Tunisia—History—1956-
			961.2	DT211-239	Libya
959.902	DS675	Philippines—History—1812-1898	961.2	DT222	Libya—Civilization
			961.2	DT223.2-236	Libya—History
959.902	DS675.5	Philippines—History—Cavite Mutiny, 1872	961.2004	DT223-.2	Ethnology—Libya
			961.2022	DT229	Libya—History—642-1551
959.9027	DS676	Philippines—History—Insurrection, 1896-1898	961.2024	DT231	Libya—History—1551-1912
959.9031	DS679	Philippines—History—Insurrection, 1899-1901	961.203	DT235	Libya—History—1912-1951
959.9032	DS685	Dajo, Mount, Battle of, 1906			

Dewey	LC	Subject Heading	Dewey	LC	Subject Heading
961.204	DT235.5	Libya—History—1951-1969	962.4043	DT156.7	Sudan—History—Coup d'etat, 1985
961.2042	DT236	Libya—History—1969-	963	DT371-398	Ethiopia
961.2042	DT236	Libya—History—Coup d'etat, 1969	963	DT379.5	Ethiopia—Civilization
			963	DT380.5-387.95	Ethiopia—History
961.2042	DT236	Libya—History—Bombardment, 1986	963.0(1-2)	DT383	Ethiopia—History—To 1490
			963.0(2-4)	DT384-386.73	Ethiopia—History—1490-1889
962	DT43-154	Egypt—History			
962	DT70	Egypt—Civilization	963.0(43-6)	DT387-.92	Ethiopia—History—1889-1974
962.0(2-3)	DT95-107.4	Egypt—History—640-1882			
962.0(3-4)	DT107-.4	Egypt—History—Tewfik, 1879-1892	963.004	DT380-.4	Ethnology—Ethiopia
			963.041	DT386.3	Abyssinian Expedition, 1867-1868
962.0(3-55)	DT100-107.87	Egypt—History—1798-			
962.0(4-51)	DT107.3-.8	Egypt—History—British occupation, 1882-1936	963.054	DT387.7-.8	Ethiopia—History—Rebellion, 1928-1930
962.0(4-51)	DT107.8	Egypt—History—Fuad, 1917-1936	963.06	DT387.9	Ethiopia—History—Coup d'etat, 1960
962.0(4-55)	DT107.8-.87	Egypt—History—1919-	963.5071	DT397	Eritrea—History—1962-1993
962.004	DT71-72	Ethnology—Egypt			
962.02	DT95-.88	Egypt—History—640-1250	963.5072	DT397.3	Eritrea—History—1993-
962.02	DT95.8-.88	Egypt—History—Saladin, 1171-1193	964	DT179.2-.9	Africa, Northwest
			964	DT301-330	Morocco
962.02	DT95.8	Egypt—History—Invasion of Saint Louis, 1249	964	DT312	Morocco—Civilization
			964	DT313.7-325.92	Morocco—History
962.02	DT96-.7	Egypt—History—1250-1517	964.0(4-5)	DT324-325.92	Morocco—History—20th century
962.03	DT97-107.4	Egypt—History—1517-1882	964.004	DT313-.6	Ethnology—Morocco
			964.02(1-3)	DT319	Morocco—History—647-1516
962.03	DT103	Egypt—History—French occupation, 1798-1801	964.025	DT321-323.5	Morocco—History—1516-1830
962.03	DT104	Egypt—History—Mohammed Ali, 1805-1849	964.025	DT322	Kassr-el-Kebir, Battle of, 1578
962.03	DT106	Egypt—History—Ismail, 1863-1879	964.03	DT324	Morocco—History—19th century
962.04	DT107.8	Egypt—History—Insurrection, 1919	965	DT271-299	Algeria
			965	DT282	Algeria—Civilization
962.05(3-5)	DT107.821-.87	Egypt—History—1952-	965	DT283-299	Algeria—History
962.052	DT107.82	Egypt—History—Revolution, 1952	965.004	DT283-.6	Ethnology—Algeria
			965.022	DT289	Algeria—History—647-1516
962.053	DT107.83	Egypt—History—Intervention, 1956	965.024	DT291-292	Algeria—History—1516-1830
962.4	DT154.1-159.9	Sudan			
962.4	DT154.9	Sudan—Civilization	965.024	DT291	Algeria—History—English Expedition, 1620-1621
962.4	DT155.3-157.67	Sudan—History	965.024	DT292	Algeria—History—Expedition of Charles V, 1541
962.40(1-2)	DT156-.3	Sudan—History—To 1820			
962.40(3-4)	DT156.4-157.67	Sudan—History—1820-			
962.4004	DT155-.2	Ethnology—Sudan	965.024	DT291	Algeria—History—Spanish Expedition, 1775
962.4004965	DT155.2.D56	Dinka (African people)			
962.403	DT156.6	Sudan—History—1862-1899	965.024	DT291	Algeria—History—English Expedition, 1816
962.403	DT156.6	Fashoda Crisis, 1898	965.024	DT291	Algiers, Battle of, 1816
962.403	DT156.7-157.67	Sudan—History—1899-1956	965.03	DT294-295.3	Algeria—History—1830-1962
962.4041	DT157.67	Sudan—History—Civil War, 1955-1972			

Dewey	LC	Subject Heading	Dewey	LC	Subject Heading
965.03	DT294	Algeria—History—French Expedition, 1830	966.4004	DT516.42-.45	Ethnology—Sierra Leone
965.04	DT295-.3	Algeria—History—1945-1962	966.51	DT509.4	Gambia—Civilization
			966.51	DT509.5-.83	Gambia—History
965.046	DT295	Algeria—History—Revolution, 1954-1962	966.51	DT532.128	Fuladu (Kingdom)
			966.51	DT532.23	Niumi (Kingdom)
965.05	DT295.5-.55	Algeria—History—1962-	966.51004	DT509.42-.45	Ethnology—Gambia
966	DT331-346	Sahara	966.51031	DT509.8	Gambia—History—Coup d'etat, 1981
966	DT470-671	Africa, West	966.52	DT543.4	Guinea—Civilization
966.004963	DT530.5.D64	Dogon (African people)	966.52	DT543.5-.827	Guinea—History
966.02	DT476	Africa, West—History—To 1884	966.52004	DT543.42-.45	Ethnology—Guinea
966.03(12-26)	DT476.2-.23	Africa, West—History—1884-1960	966.52051	DT543.8	Guinea—History—Portuguese Invasion, 1970
966.03(26-3)	DT476.5-.523	Africa, West—History—1960-	966.52052	DT543.822	Guinea—History—Coup d'etat, 1984
966.1	DT554.4	Mauritania—Civilization	966.57	DT613.4	Guinea-Bissau—Civilization
966.1	DT554.52-.83	Mauritania—History	966.57	DT613.5-.83	Guinea-Bissau—History
966.1004	DT554.42-.45	Ethnology—Mauritania	966.57004	DT613.42-.45	Ethnology—Guinea-Bissau
966.105	DT554.8-.83	Mauritania—History—1960-	966.5702	DT613.78	Guinea-Bissau—History—Revolution, 1963-1974
966.23	DT507	Ashanti War, 1822-1831	966.5703	DT613.8	Guinea-Bissau—History—Coup d'etat, 1980
966.23	DT507	Ashanti War, 1873-1874			
966.23	DT551.4	Mali—Civilization	966.58	DT671.C23	Cape Verde—Civilization
966.23	DT551.45.S	Songhai Empire	966.58	DT671.C25-.C28	Cape Verde—History
966.23	DT551.5-.82	Mali—History	966.580(1-2)	DT671.C265	Cape Verde—History—To 1975
966.23004	DT551.42-.45	Ethnology—Mali	966.58004	DT671.C242-.C2	Ethnology—Cape Verde
966.23004963	DT551.45.D64	Dogon (African people)	966.5803	DT671.C28	Cape Verde—History—1975-
966.23051	DT551.8	Mali—History—Coup d'etat, 1968	966.62	DT629	Liberia—Civilization
966.25	DT555.4	Burkina Faso—Civilization	966.62	DT630.8-636.53	Liberia—History
966.25	DT555.52-.83	Burkina Faso—History	966.62004	DT630-.5	Ethnology—Liberia
966.25004	DT555.42-.45	Ethnology—Burkina Faso	966.6201	DT633-.3	Liberia—History—To 1847
966.25053	DT555.8	Burkina Faso—History—Coup d'etat, 1987	966.6202	DT634-.3	Liberia—History—1847-1944
			966.6203(2-3)	DT636.5-.53	Liberia—History—1980-
966.26	DT547.4	Niger—Civilization	966.62031	DT635-636	Liberia—History—1944-1971
966.26	DT547.5-.83	Niger—History			
966.260(1-3)	DT547.65-.75	Niger—History—To 1960	966.62031	DT636.2-.4	Liberia—History—1971-1980
966.26004	DT547.42-.45	Ethnology—Niger			
966.3	DT532.128	Fuladu (Kingdom)	966.62032	DT636.5	Liberia—History—Coup d'etat, 1980
966.3	DT532.23	Niumi (Kingdom)			
966.3	DT549.4	Senegal—Civilization	966.62032	DT636.5	Liberia—History—Civil War, 1989-
966.3	DT549.47-.83	Senegal—History			
966.30(1-3)	DT549.7-.73	Senegal—History—To 1960	966.68	DT532.12	Denkyira (Kingdom)
966.3004	DT549.42-.45	Ethnology—Senegal	966.68	DT545.4	Cote d'Ivoire—Civilization
966.30049632	DT549.45.D56	Diola (African people)	966.68	DT545.52-.83	Cote d'Ivoire—History
966.305	DT549.8-.83	Senegal—History—1960-	966.68004	DT545.42-.45	Ethnology—Cote d'Ivoire
966.3051	DT549.8	Senegal—History—Coup d'etat, 1962	966.6800496345	DT545.45.D85	Dyula (African people)
			966.7	DT510.4	Ghana—Civilization
966.31	DT507	Ashanti War, 1895-1896	966.7	DT510.5-512.34	Ghana—History
966.4	DT516.4	Sierra Leone—Civilization	966.70(1-3)	DT511-.3	Ghana—History—To 1957
966.4	DT516.5-.82	Sierra Leone—History	966.7004	DT510.42-.43	Ethnology—Ghana
966.40(1-2)	DT516.65-.72	Sierra Leone—History—To 1896	966.7004963374	DT510.43.E94	Ewe (African people)
			966.701(6-8)	DT511	Ghana—History—Danish Settlements, 1659-1850

Dewey	LC	Subject Heading	Dewey	LC	Subject Heading
966.7016	DT511	Ghana—History—Portuguese rule, 1469-1637	967.11004 + 96361	DT571.D68	Doyayo (African people)
966.705	DT512-.34	Ghana—History—1957-	967.11004 + 963962	DT571.D83	Duala (African people)
966.7051	DT512	Ghana—History—Coup d'etat, 1966	967.1102	DT578	Cameroon—History—Coup d'etat, 1984
966.7051	DT512	Ghana—History—Coup d'etat, 1972	967.15	DT615.5-.8	Sao Tome and Principe—History
966.7052	DT512.32	Ghana—History—Coup d'etat, 1979	967.15004	DT615.42-.45	Ethnology—Sao Tome and Principe
966.7052	DT512.32	Ghana—History—Coup d'etat, 1981	967.18	DT620.4	Equatorial Guinea—Civilization
966.81	DT582.4	Togo—Civilization	967.18	DT620.46-.83	Equatorial Guinea—History
966.81	DT582.5-.82	Togo—History	967.18004	DT620.42-.45	Ethnology—Equatorial Guinea
966.81004	DT582.42-.45	Ethnology—Togo	967.1804	DT620.27	Equatorial Guinea—Description and travel
966.81004 + 963374	DT582.45.E93	Ewe (African people)			
966.8103	DT582.75	Togo—History—1922-1960	967.21	DT546.14	Gabon—Civilization
966.83	DT541.4	Benin—Civilization	967.21	DT546.15-.183	Gabon—History
966.83	DT541.5-.845	Benin—History	967.21004	DT546.142-.145	Ethnology—Gabon
966.83004	DT541.42-.45	Ethnology—Benin	967.2101	DT546.165	Gabon—History—To 1839
966.8301	DT541.65-.67	Benin—History—To 1894	967.2102	DT546.165-.175	Gabon—History—1839-1960
966.83051	DT541.845	Benin—History—Coup d'etat, 1977	967.2104	DT546.18-.183	Gabon—History—1960-
966.9	DT515.4	Nigeria—Civilization	967.24	DT546.24	Congo (Brazzaville)—Civilization
966.9	DT515.53-.84	Nigeria—History	967.24	DT546.25-.283	Congo (Brazzaville)—History
966.90(1-3)	DT515.7-.72	Nigeria—History—1851-1899	967.240(1-3)	DT546.265-.275	Congo (Brazzaville)—History—To 1960
966.9004	DT515.42-.45	Ethnology—Nigeria			
966.900496333	DT515.45.E35	Egba (African people)	967.24004	DT546.242-.245	Ethnology—Congo (Brazzaville)
966.9004 + 963642	DT515.45.E34	Efik (African people)	967.3	DT1302	Angola—Civilization
966.901	DT515.65-.67	Nigeria—History—To 1851	967.3	DT1314-1436	Angola—History
966.903	DT515.7-.77	Nigeria—History—1900-1960	967.30(2-3)	DT1385-1396	Angola—History—1885-1961
966.905	DT515.8-.84	Nigeria—History—1960-	967.3004	DT1304-1308	Ethnology—Angola
966.9051	DT515.832	Nigeria—History—Coup d'etat, 1966 (January 15)	967.301	DT1357-1369	Angola—History—1482-1648
966.9051	DT515.832	Nigeria—History—Coup d'etat, 1966 (July 29)	967.301	DT1357	Angola—History—To 1482
966.9052	DT515.836	Nigeria—History—Civil War, 1967-1970	967.302	DT1373-1382	Angola—History—1648-1885
966.9053	DT515.84	Nigeria—History—Coup d'etat, 1983	967.303	DT1398-1417	Angola—History—Revolution, 1961-1975
967.0(1-2)	DT352.65	Africa, Central—History—To 1884	967.304	DT1428	Angola—History—Civil War, 1975-
967.03(1-26)	DT352.7	Africa, Central—History—1884-1960	967.41	DT546.34	Central African Republic—Civilization
967.0312	DT363	Emin Pasha Relief Expedition, 1887-1889	967.41	DT546.348-.384	Central African Republic—History
967.11	DT569.5	Cameroon—Civilization	967.410(1-3)	DT546.365-.37	Central African Republic—History—To 1960
967.11	DT572-578.4	Cameroon—History			
967.11004	DT570-571	Ethnology—Cameroon	967.41004	DT546.342-.345	Ethnology—Central African Republic
			967.4103	DT546.37	Kongo Wars, 1928-1931

263

Dewey	LC	Subject Heading	Dewey	LC	Subject Heading
968.052	DT1933	South Africa—History—Rebellion, 1914-1915	968.9402	DT3091-3101	Zambia—History—1890-1924
968.06	DT1945-1970	South Africa—History—1961-	968.9402	DT3103-3106	Zambia—History—1924-1953
968.0627	DT1959	South Africa—History—Soweto Uprising, 1976	968.9403	DT3108-3111	Zambia—History—1953-1964
968.29	DT1760	Homelands (South Africa)	968.9404	DT3113-3119	Zambia—History—1964-
968.81	DT1552	Namibia—Civilization	968.97	DT3187	Malawi—Civilization
968.81	DT1564-1648	Namibia—History	968.97	DT3194-3237	Malawi—History
968.81004	DT1554-1558	Ethnology—Namibia	968.97004	DT3189-3192	Ethnology—Malawi
968.8101	DT1587-1601	Namibia—History—To 1884	968.9701	DT3211-3214	Malawi—History—To 1891
968.8102	DT1603-1622	Namibia—History—1884-1915	968.9702	DT3216-3225	Malawi—History—1891-1953
968.8103	DT1618	Namibia—History—Herero Revolt, 1904-1907	968.9702	DT3225	Malawi—History—Chilembwe Rebellion, 1915
968.8103	DT1625-1636	Namibia—History—1915-1946	968.9703	DT3227-3230	Malawi—History—1953-1964
968.8103	DT1638-1648	Namibia—History—1946-1990	968.9704	DT3232-3240	Malawi—History—1964-
968.8104	DT1648	Namibia—History—1990-	969.1	DT469.M274	Madagascar—Civilization
968.83	DT2452	Botswana—Civilization	969.1	DT469.M282-.M39	Madagascar—History
968.83	DT2464-2502	Botswana—History	969.10(1-3)	DT469.M34-.M342	Madagascar—History—1885-1960
968.830(1-2)	DT2483-2493	Botswana—History—To 1966	969.1004	DT469.M276-.M277	Ethnology—Madagascar
968.83004	DT2454-2458	Ethnology—Botswana	969.101	DT469.M31-.M313	Madagascar—History—To 1810
968.8303	DT2496-2502	Botswana—History—1966-			
968.8304	DT2448	Botswana—Description and travel	969.101	DT469.M32-.M335	Madagascar—History—Hova rule, 1810-1885
968.85	DT2582	Lesotho—Civilization	969.103	DT469.M34	Madagascar—History—Menalamba Rebellion, 1895-1899
968.85	DT2604-2660	Lesotho—History			
968.850(1-2)	DT2630-2648	Lesotho—History—To 1966			
968.85004	DT2592-2596	Ethnology—Lesotho	969.103	DT469.M34	Madagascar—History—French Invasion, 1895
968.8503	DT2652-2660	Lesotho—History—1966-			
968.87	DT2742	Swaziland—Civilization	969.103	DT469.M34	Madagascar—History—Revolution, 1947
968.87	DT2754-2806	Swaziland—History			
968.87004	DT2744-2746	Ethnology—Swaziland	969.6	DT469.S44	Seychelles—Civilization
968.91	DT2908	Zimbabwe—Civilization	969.6	DT469.S452-.249	Seychelles—History
968.91	DT2914-3000	Zimbabwe—History			
968.910(2-4)	DT2959-2979	Zimbabwe—History—1890-1965	969.6	DT469.S48	Seychelles—History—Coup d'etat, 1977
968.91004	DT2910-2913	Ethnology—Zimbabwe	969.6	DT469.S48	Seychelles—History—Coup d'etat, 1981
968.9102	DT2968	Zimbabwe—History—Ndebele Insurrection, 1896	969.6004	DT469.S442-.S443	Ethnology—Seychelles
968.9102	DT2970	Zimbabwe—History—Shona Insurrection, 1896-1897	969.8	DT469.M39	Mascarene Islands
			969.81	DT469.R37	Reunion—Civilization
968.9104	DT2981-2994	Zimbabwe—History—1965-1980	969.81	DT469.R5	Reunion—History
			969.81004	DT469.R38-.R39	Ethnology—Reunion
968.9104	DT2988	Zimbabwe—History—Chimurenga War, 1966-1980	969.8102	DT469.R44-.R443	Reunion—History—To 1764
			969.8102	DT469.R45-.R453	Reunion—History—1764-1946
968.9105	DT2996-3000	Zimbabwe—History—1980-			
968.94	DT3052	Zambia—Civilization	969.8102	DT469.R45	Reunion—History—British occupation, 1810-1815
968.94	DT3064-3119	Zambia—History			
968.94004	DT3054-3058	Ethnology—Zambia	969.8104	DT469.R455-.R458	Reunion—History—1946-
968.9401	DT3079-3089	Zambia—History—To 1890			

Dewey	LC	Subject Heading	Dewey	LC	Subject Heading
969.82	DT469.M44	Mauritius—Civilization	971.27	F1061-1065	Manitoba—History
969.82	DT469.M45-.M497	Mauritius—History	971.27005	F1061	Manitoba—Periodicals
969.82004	DT469.M442-.M445	Ethnology—Mauritius	971.3	F1056-1059.7	Ontario—History
			971.3005	F1056	Ontario—Periodicals
969.8201	DT469.M465-.M463	Mauritius—History—To 1810	971.4	F1051-1055	Quebec (Province)—History
			971.4005	F1051	Quebec (Province)—Periodicals
970	E	America			
970	E16-18.85	America—History	971.5	F1035.8	Maritime Provinces—History
970	E31-45	North America	971.51005	F1041	New Brunswick—Periodicals
970	E40	North America—Civilization	971.6	F1036-1040	Nova Scotia—History
970	E45-46	North America—History	971.6005	F1036	Nova Scotia—Periodicals
970.00497	E51-73	Indians	971.7	F1046-1049.7	Prince Edward Island—History
970.00497	E58	Indians—History			
970.00497	E99.A35	Algonquian Indians	971.7005	F1046	Prince Edward Island—Periodicals
970.005	E11	America—Periodicals			
970.005	E31	North America—Periodicals	971.8	F1121-1124	Newfoundland—History
970.01	E101-135	America—Discovery and exploration	971.8005	F1121	Newfoundland—Periodicals
			971.82	F1135-1139	Labrador (Nfld.)—History
970-989	F	America—History	971.82005	F1135	Labrador (Nfld.)—Periodicals
971	F1001-1040	Canada			
971	F1021-.2	Canada—Civilization	971.91	F1091-1095.5	Yukon Territory—History
971.0(632-7)	F1034.2-.3	Canada—History—1945-	971.91005	F1091.A1	Yukon Territory—Periodicals
971.004114	F1027	French-Canadians	971.92	F1060-.97	Northwest, Canadian
971.005	F1001	Canada—Periodicals	971.94	F1106-1110.5	Keewatin—History
971.01	F1030-.9	Canada—History—To 1763 (New France)	971.94005	F1106.A1	Keewatin—Periodicals
			972	F1201-1392	Mexico
971.018	F1030	Lake of the Woods Massacre, 1736	972	F1210	Mexico—Civilization
			972.0(1-2)	F1229-1231	Mexico—History—To 1810
971.0188	F1030.9	Canada—History—1755-1763	972.0(3-6)	F1232-.5	Mexico—History—1821-1861
971.02	F1031	Canada—History—1763-1791	972.0(3-84)	F1231.5-1236.6	Mexico—History—1810-
			972.00497	F1219-1221	Indians of Mexico
971.02(2-49)	F1032	Canada—History—1763-1867	972.00497452	F1219.73-.75	Aztecs
			972.00497452	F1219.73-.75	Nahuas
971.024	F1032	Canada—History—1775-1783	972.005	F1201	Mexico—Periodicals
			972.018	F1228.98	Mexico—History—To 1519
971.03	F1032	Canada—History—1791-1841	972.02	F1230	Mexico—History—Conquest, 1519-1540
971.038	F1032	Canada—History—Rebellion, 1837-1838	972.02	F1231	Mexico—History—Spanish colony, 1540-1810
971.04(2-8)	F1032	Canada—History—1841-1867	972.03	F1232	Mexico—History—Wars of Independence, 1810-1821
971.049	F1033	Canada—History—Fenian Invasions, 1866-1870	972.07	F1233	Mexico—History—European intervention, 1861-1867
971.05	F1033	Canada—History—Confederation, 1867	972.08(16-21)	F1234	Mexico—History—Revolution, 1910-1920
971.06(12-32)	F1034	Canada—History—1914-1945	972.08(16-26)	F1234	Mexico—History—1910-1946
971.1	F1086-1089.7	British Columbia—History	972.08(27-31)	F1235-.5	Mexico—History—1946-1970
971.1005	F1086	British Columbia—Periodicals	972.08(35-41)	F1236	Mexico—History—1988-
971.23	F1075-1080	Alberta—History	972.081	F1233.5	Mexico—History—1867-1910
971.23005	F1075	Alberta—Periodicals	972.0816	F1234	Mexico—History—Decena Tragica, 1913
971.24	F1070-1074.7	Saskatchewan—History			
971.24005	F1070	Saskatchewan—Periodicals	972.0816	F1234	El Ebano, Battle of, 1915

Dewey	LC	Subject Heading	Dewey	LC	Subject Heading
972.0822	F1234	Mexico—History—Revolution, 1923-1924	972.84052	F1488	El Salvador—History—1944-1979
972.083(2-4)	F1236	Mexico—History—1970-1988	972.84052	F1488	El Salvador—History—Revolution of 1948
972.8	F1421-1577	Central America	972.84052	F1488	El Salvador-Honduras Conflict, 1969
972.8	F1430	Central America—Civilization	972.84053	F1488.3	El Salvador—History—1979-1992
972.8	F1435.4-1439.5	Central America—History	972.85	F1521-1537	Nicaragua
972.800497	F1434-1435.3	Indians of Central America	972.85	F1523.8	Nicaragua—Civilization
972.8005	F1421	Central America—Periodicals	972.85	F1525.5-1528.22	Nicaragua—History
972.81	F1461-1477	Guatemala	972.850(1-42)	F1526.25	Nicaragua—History—To 1838
972.81	F1463.5	Guatemala—Civilization	972.850(44-51)	F1526.27	Nicaragua—History—1838-1909
972.81	F1465-1466.7	Guatemala—History			
972.810(1-3)	F1466.4	Guatemala—History—To 1821	972.85005	F1521	Nicaragua—Periodicals
972.810(4-52)	F1466.45	Guatemala—History—1821-1945	972.8503	F1526.25	Nicaragua—History—English Invasion, 1780-1781
972.81005	F1461	Guatemala—Periodicals	972.85044	F1526.27	Nicaragua—History—Filibuster War, 1855-1860
972.8105(2-3)	F1466.7	Guatemala—History—1985-	972.8505(1-2)	F1526.3	Nicaragua—History—1909-1937
972.81052	F1466.5	Guatemala—History—1945-1985	972.85051	F1526.3	Nicaragua—History—Revolution, 1909-1910
972.82	F1441-1457	Belize	972.85051	F1526.3	Nicaragua—History—Revolution of 1912
972.82	F1443.8	Belize—Civilization			
972.82	F1445.5-1448	Belize—History	972.85051	F1526.3	Nicaragua—History—Revolution, 1926-1929
972.82005	F1441	Belize—Periodicals	972.85052	F1527	Nicaragua—History—1937-1979
972.83	F1501-1517	Honduras			
972.83	F1503.8	Honduras—Civilization	972.85052	F1527	Nicaragua—San Carlos Barracks Attack, 1977
972.83	F1505.5-1508.33	Honduras—History	972.85052	F1527	Nicaragua—History—Uprising, 1978
972.830(1-4)	F1507	Honduras—History—To 1838			
972.83005	F1501	Honduras—Periodicals	972.85052	F1528	Nicaragua—History—Revolution, 1979
972.8305(1-2)	F1507.5	Honduras—History—1838-1933	972.85053	F1528	Nicaragua—History—1979-1990
972.8305(2-3)	F1508-.22	Honduras—History—1933-1982	972.85054	F1528	Nicaragua—History—1990-
972.83051	F1507.5	Honduras—History—Coup d'etat, 1904	972.86	F1541-1557	Costa Rica
			972.86	F1543.8	Costa Rica—Civilization
972.83051	F1507.5	Honduras—History—Revolution, 1919	972.860(1-3)	F1547	Costa Rica—History—To 1821
972.83053	F1508.3-.33	Honduras—History—1982-	972.86005	F1541	Costa Rica—Periodicals
972.84	F1481-1497	El Salvador	972.8604	F1547.5	Costa Rica—History—1821-1948
972.84	F1483.8	El Salvador—Civilization	972.86044	F1547.5	Costa Rica—History—Uprising, 1932
972.84	F1485.5-1488.53	El Salvador—History			
972.840(1-42)	F1487	El Salvador—History—To 1838	972.86051	F1548	Costa Rica—History—1948-1986
972.840(4-52)	F1487.5	El Salvador—History—1838-1944	972.86052	F1548.2-.23	Costa Rica—History—1986-
972.84005	F1481	El Salvador—Periodicals	972.87	F1561-1577	Panama
972.8405(3-4)	F1488.3-.53	El Salvador—History—1979-	972.87	F1563.8	Panama—Civilization
972.8405(3-4)	F1488.5-.53	El Salvador—History—1992-	972.87	F1565.5-1567	Panama—History
972.84052	F1487.5	El Salvador—History—Revolution, 1944			

267

Dewey	LC	Subject Heading	Dewey	LC	Subject Heading
972.870(1-3)	F1566.45	Panama—History—To 1903	972.9105	F1786	Cuba—History—Revolution, 1895-1898
972.87005	F1561	Panama—Periodicals	972.9106(1-2)	F1787	Cuba—History—1899-1906
972.8705(1-3)	F1566.5-1567	Panama—History—1946-1981	972.91062	F1787	Cuba—History—American occupation, 1906-1909
972.87051	F1566.5	Panama—History—1903-1946	972.91062	F1787	Cuba—History—1909-1933
972.87051	F1566.5	Panama—History—Revolution, 1903	972.91063	F1787.5	Cuba—History—Revolution, 1933
972.87051	F1566.5	Panama—History—Coup d'etat, 1968	972.91063	F1787.5	Cuba—History—Moncada Barracks Attack, 1953
972.87053	F1567	Panama—History—1981-	972.91063	F1787.5	El Jigue (Cuba), Battle of, 1958
972.87053	F1567	Panama—History—American Invasion, 1989	972.91064	F1788	Cuba—History—Revolution, 1959
972.9	F1601-1629	West Indies	972.91064	F1788	Cuba—History—Invasion, 1961
972.9	F1609.5	West Indies—Civilization	972.92	F1861-1896	Jamaica
972.9	F1620-1623	West Indies—History	972.92	F1874	Jamaica—Civilization
972.9	F2155-2191	Caribbean Area	972.92	F1878-1887	Jamaica—History
972.9	F2173-2191	Caribbean Area—History	972.920(1-5)	F1884-1886	Jamaica—History—To 1962
972.9(1-5)	F1741-1991	Antilles, Greater	972.92005	F1861-1896	Jamaica—Periodicals
972.9(7-8)	F2001-2151	Antilles, Lesser	972.92034	F1884	Jamaica—History—Maroon War, 1795-1796
972.900497	F1619	Indians of the West Indies	972.92034	F1886	Jamaica—History—Slave Insurrection, 1831
972.9005	F1601	West Indies—Periodicals	972.9204	F1886	Jamaica—History—Insurrection, 1865
972.903	F1621	English West Indian Expedition, 1654-1655	972.9206	F1887	Jamaica—History—1962-
972.903	F1621	English West Indian Expedition, 1695	972.921	F2048.5	Cayman Islands
972.903	F2151	English West Indian Expedition, 1759	972.93	F1931-1941	Dominican Republic
972.903	F1621	English West Indian Expedition, 1793-1794	972.93	F1935	Dominican Republic—Civilization
972.903	F1621	English West Indian Expedition, 1795-1796	972.93	F1937-1938.58	Dominican Republic—History
972.91	F1751-1854.9	Cuba	972.930(1-4)	F1938.3	Dominican Republic—History—To 1844
972.91	F1751-1849	Cuba—History	972.930(4-52)	F1938.4	Dominican Republic—History—1844-1930
972.91	F1760	Cuba—Civilization			
972.910(1-4)	F1779	Cuba—History—To 1810	972.93005	F1931	Dominican Republic—Periodicals
972.910(5-6)	F1786-1788.22	Cuba—History—1895-	972.9305(3-5)	F1938.5-.58	Dominican Republic—History—1930-
972.91005	F1751	Cuba—Periodicals	972.9305(4-5)	F1938.55-.58	Dominican Republic—History—1961-
972.9103	F1781	Cuba—History—British occupation, 1762-1763	972.93052	F1938.45	Dominican Republic—History—American occupation, 1916-1924
972.9105	F1783	Cuba—History—1810-1899			
972.9105	F1783	Cuba—History—Black Eagle Conspiracy, 1830	972.93053	F1938.5	Dominican Republic—History—1930-1961
972.9105	F1783	Cuba—History—Negro Conspiracy, 1844	972.93053	F1938.5	Dominican-Haitian Conflict, 1937
972.9105	F1783	Cuba—History—Insurrection, 1849-1851	972.93053	F1938.5	Dominican Republic—History—Invasion, 1959
972.9105	F1785	Cuba—History—Insurrection, 1868-1878			
972.9105	F1785	Cuba—History—1878-1895			
972.9105	F1785	Cuba—History—Revolution, 1879-1880			

Dewey	LC	Subject Heading	Dewey	LC	Subject Heading
972.93054	F1938.55	Dominican Republic—History—Coup d'etat, 1963	972.9722	F2136	Virgin Islands of the United States
972.93054	F1938.55	Dominican Republic—History—Revolution, 1965	972.9725	F2129	British Virgin Islands
			972.973	F2033	Anguilla
972.93054	F1938.55	Dominican Republic—History—Revolution, 1973	972.973	F2091	Saint Kitts and Nevis
			972.974	F2035	Antigua
972.93054	F1938.55	Dominican Republic—History—Uprising, 1984	972.975	F2082	Montserrat
			972.976	F2050	Desirade (Guadeloupe)
972.94	F1900-1930	Haiti	972.976	F2066	Guadeloupe
972.94	F1916	Haiti—Civilization	972.976	F2070	Saintes Islands (Guadeloupe)
972.94	F1918-1939	Haiti—History			
972.940(1-3)	F1923	Haiti—History—To 1791	972.976	F2076	Marie Galante
972.940(6-72)	F1927-1928	Haiti—History—1934-1986	972.976	F2103	Saint Martin
972.94005	F1900	Haiti—Periodicals	972.977	F2088	Saba (Netherlands Antilles)
972.9403	F1923	Haiti—History—Revolution, 1791-1804	972.977	F2097	Saint Eustatius (Netherlands Antilles)
972.9404	F1924	Haiti—History—1804-1844	972.98	F2011	Windward Islands
972.9404	F1924	Haiti—History—Revolution, 1843	972.981	F2041	Barbados
			972.982	F2081	Martinique
972.9404	F1926	Haiti—History—1844-1915	972.983	F2116-2123	Trinidad and Tobago
972.9405	F1927	Haiti—History—American occupation, 1915-1934	972.9841	F2051	Dominica
			972.9843	F2100	Saint Lucia
972.94073	F1928.2-.23	Haiti—History—1986-	972.9844	F2061	The Grenadines
972.94073	F1928.2	Haiti—History—Coup d'etat, 1991	972.9845	F2056	Grenada
			972.986	F2048	Bonaire
972.95	F1951-1983	Puerto Rico	972.986	F2049	Curacao
972.95	F1960	Puerto Rico—Civilization	972.99	F1630-1640	Bermuda Islands
972.95	F1970-1976.3	Puerto Rico—History	972.99	F1633	Bermuda Islands—Civilization
972.950(1-4)	F1973	Puerto Rico—History—To 1898			
972.950(4-52)	F1975	Puerto Rico—History—1898-1952	972.99	F1635-1637	Bermuda Islands—History
			972.99005	F1630	Bermuda Islands—Periodicals
972.95005	F1951	Puerto Rico—Periodicals			
972.9504	F1973	Puerto Rico—History—Insurrection, 1868	973	E151-887	United States
			973	E162-168	United States—Civilization
972.95052	F1975	Puerto Rico—History—Nationalist Insurrection, 1950	973	E169.1-.12	United States—Civilization
			973	E171-183.9	United States—History
972.95053	F1976-.3	Puerto Rico—History—1952-	973	E179.5	United States—Territorial expansion
972.96	F1650-1660	Bahamas	973	HN51-90	United States—Social conditions
972.96	F1654	Bahamas—Civilization			
972.96	F1655.3-1657.2	Bahamas—History	973.(1-2)	E186-199	United States—History—Colonial period, ca. 1600-1775
972.96005	F1650	Bahamas—Periodicals			
972.97	F2006	Leeward Islands (West Indies)	973.(1-26)	E82	Indians of North America—Wars—1600-1750
972.9722	E263.W5	Virgin Islands of the United States—History—1775-1793	973.(1-7) + 0496073	E185.18	Afro-Americans—History—To 1863
			973.(1-8)	E81-83.895	Indians of North America—Wars
972.972	E263.W5	Virgin Islands of the United States—History—1775-1783	973.(26-53)	E83.(759-813)	Indians of North America—Wars—1750-1815
972.9722	F2096	Saint Croix (V.I.)			
972.9722	F2098	Saint John (V.I.)	973.(51-68)	E338	United States—History—1815-1861
972.9722	F2105	Saint Thomas (V.I.)			

Dewey	LC	Subject Heading	Dewey	LC	Subject Heading
973.(53-82)	E83.8(17-75)	Indians of North America—Wars—1815-1875	973.26	E199	United States—History—French and Indian War, 1755-1763
973.(63-82)	E415.6-680	United States—History—1849-1877	973.26	E199	Necessity, Fort, Battle of, 1754
973.(63-82)	E671-680	United States—History—1849-1877	973.26	E199	Braddock's Campaign, 1755
973.(7-82) + 0496073	E185.2	Afro-Americans—History—1863-1877	973.26	E199	Fort Oswego (Oswego, N.Y.)—Capture, 1756
973.(83-923) + 0496073	E185.6	Afro-Americans—History—1877-1964	973.26	E199	Fort William Henry (N.Y.)—Capture, 1757
973.(8-9)	E660-887	United States—History—1865-	973.26	E199	Forbes Expedition against Fort Duquesne, 1758
973.(8-913)	E660-783	United States—History—1865-1921	973.26	E199	Ticonderoga, Battle of, 1758
973.025	E154.5-.7	United States—Directories	973.3	E201-298	United States—History—Revolution, 1775-1783
973.04	E184-185.98	Ethnology—United States	973.3	E301-655	United States—History—1783-1865
973.04	E185.86	Afro-Americans—Social life and customs	973.3112	E215.3	Non-importation agreements, 1768-1769
973.04(2-8)073	E184.E95	European Americans	973.3113	E215.4	Boston Massacre, 1770
973.043931073	E184.D9	Dutch Americans	973.3115	E215.7	Tea tax (American colonies)
973.043981073	E184.S19	Danish Americans	973.3115	E215.7	Boston Tea Party, 1773
973.0468073	E184.S75	Hispanic Americans	973.314	E277	American loyalists
973.046872073	E184.M5	Mexican Americans	973.318	E303-309	United States—History—Confederation, 1783-1789
973.04687293 + 073	E184.D6	Dominican Americans	973.33	E230-241	United States—History—Revolution—1775-1783—Campaigns
973.04914073	E184.E2	East Indian Americans			
973.04917073	E184.E17	East European Americans	973.33(1-2)	E231	Canadian Invasion, 1775-1776
973.0494541073	E184.F5	Finnish Americans			
973.0496073	E185	Afro-Americans	973.3311	E241.C7	Concord, Battle of, 1775
973.0496073	E185.18-.98	Afro-Americans—History	973.3311	E241.L6	Lexington, Battle of, 1775
973.0496073	E185.86	Afro-Americans—Social conditions	973.3312	E241.B9	Bunker Hill, Battle of, 1775
973.0497	E75-99	Indians of North America	973.333	E241.B4	Bennington, Battle of, 1777
973.0497	E98.S7	Indians of North America—Social life and customs	973.333	E241.B8	Brandywine, Battle of, 1777
			973.333	E241.P2	Paoli Massacre, 1777
973.049921073	E184.F4	Filipino Americans	973.334	E234	Clark's Expedition to the Illinois, 1778-1779
973.05	E151	United States—Periodicals			
973.072	E175-.7	United States—Historiography	973.334	E241.M7	Monmouth, Battle of, 1778
			973.335	E235	Sullivan's Indian Campaign, 1779
973.1	E75-99	United States—Antiquities			
973.1	E159.5	United States—Antiquities	973.335	E241.K48	Kettle Creek (Ga.), Battle of, 1779
973.25	E196	United States—History—King William's War, 1689-1697	973.337	E241.C56	Clapps Mill, Battle of, N.C., 1781
973.25	E197	United States—History—Queen Anne's War, 1702-1713	973.337	E241.E	Eutaw Springs, Battle of, 1781
			973.337	E241.G9	Guilford Court House, Battle of 1781
973.26	E198	United States—History—King George's War, 1744-1748	973.338	F454	Blue Licks, Battle of the, Ky., 1782
			973.339	E239	Evacuation Day, Nov. 25, 1783

Dewey	LC	Subject Heading	Dewey	LC	Subject Heading
973.34(4-5)	E259	United States. Continental Army—History	973.6242	E406.M7	Monterrey (Mexico), Battle of, 1846
973.35	E271	Dominica, Battle of, 1782	973.64	E423	Compromise of 1850
973.4	E310-337	United States—History—Constitutional period, 1789-1809	973.7	E457	Lincoln, Abraham, 1809-1865
973.4(6-8)	E331-337	United States—History—1801-1809	973.7	E461-656	United States—History—Civil War, 1861-1865
973.41	E83.79	Indians of North America—Wars—1790-1794	973.7	E83.863	Indians of North America—Wars—1862-1865
973.43	E315	Whiskey Rebellion, Pa., 1794	973.70223	E468.9	United States—History—Civil War, 1861-1865—Cartography
973.44	E326	Fries Rebellion, 1798-1799	973.711	E415.7	Squatter sovereignty
973.44	E328	Kentucky and Virginia resolutions of 1798	973.711	E441-453	Slavery
973.46	E333	Louisiana Purchase	973.7113	E373	Missouri compromise
973.47	E335	United States—History—Tripolitan War, 1801-1805	973.7113	E423	Compromise of 1850
			973.7115	E450	Underground railroad
973.48	E334	Burr Conspiracy, 1805-1807	973.713	E458-459	Secession—Southern States
973.48	E336.5	Embargo, 1807-1809	973.713	E482-489	Confederate States of America
973.5(1-4)	E341-370	United States—History—1809-1817	973.713	E487-488	Confederate States of America—History
973.52	E83.812	Indians of North America—Wars—1812-1815	973.713	E487	Confederate States of America—Social conditions
973.52	E351-364.9	United States—History—War of 1812	973.73(1-3)	E473.6-.68	Peninsular Campaign, 1862
973.523	E356.D4	Detroit (Mich.)—Surrender to the British, 1812	973.73(4-5)	E475.81	Chickamauga (Ga.), Battle of, 1863
973.523	E356.C4	Chateauguay, Battle of, 1813	973.73(6-7)	E476.66	Shenandoah Valley Campaign, 1864 (May-August)
973.523	E356.C8	Crane Island, Battle of, 1813	973.731	E472.14	Big Bethel, Battle of, 1861
973.523	E356.D8	Dudley's Defeat, 1813	973.731	E472.18	Bull Run, 1st Battle of, Va., 1861
973.523	E356.C	Champlain, Lake, Battle of, 1814	973.731	E472.28	Belmont (Mo.), Battle of, 1861
973.523	E356.B2	Baltimore, Battle of, 1814			
973.523	E356.B5	Bladensburg, Battle of, 1814	973.731	E472.63	Ball's Bluff, Battle of, 1861
973.5239	E356.N5	New Orleans (La.), Battle of, 1815	973.731	E472.96	Fort Henry (Tenn.), Battle of, 1862
973.525	E357.2-.3	Impressment	973.731	E473.54	Shiloh, Battle of, 1862
973.5254	E356.E6	Erie, Lake, Battle of, 1813	973.731	E473.55	Chattanooga Railroad Expedition, 1862
973.53	E365	United States—History—War with Algeria, 1815	973.732	E473.68	Seven Days' Battles, 1862
973.54	E371-375	United States—History—1817-1825	973.732	E473.7	Shenandoah Valley Campaign, 1862
973.54	F2324	Carabobo, Battle of, 1821	973.732	E473.77	Bull Run, 2nd Battle of, Va., 1862
973.55	E376-380	United States—History—1825-1829	973.732	E473.77	Chantilly (Va.), Battle of, 1862
973.561	E384.3	Nullification	973.733	E474.65	Antietam, Battle of, Md., 1862
973.57	E398	Aroostock War, 1839			
973.62	E401-415.2	Mexican War, 1846-1848	973.733	E474.85	Fredericksburg (Va.), Battle of, 1862
973.6242	E405.2	Doniphan's Expedition, 1846-1847	973.733	E475.35	Chancellorsville (Va.), Battle of, 1863
973.6242	E405.2	Kearny's Expedition, 1846			

Dewey	LC	Subject Heading	Dewey	LC	Subject Heading
973.7336	E474.61	Maryland Campaign, 1862	973.913	E766-783	United States—History—1913-1921
973.734	E474.9	Chalk Bluff (Ark. and Mo), Battle of, 1863	973.917	E806-812	United States—History—1933-1945
973.734	E475.3	Kelly's Ford (Va.), Battle of, 1863	973.918	E813-816	United States—History—1945-1953
973.7349	E475.53	Gettysburg (Pa.), Battle of, 1863	973.92(2-3)	E838-851	United States—History—1961-1969
973.735	E475.76	Droop Mountain (W. Va.), Battle of, 1863	973.92(3-9) + 0496073	E185.615	Afro-Americans—History—1964-
973.7359	E475.97	Chattanooga (Tenn.), Battle of, 1863	973.921	E835-837.7	United States—History—1953-1961
973.736	E476.52	Spotsylvania Court House, Battle of, Va., 1864	973.922	E841.W49	Cuban Missile Crisis, 1962
973.736	E476.65	Lynchburg (Va.), Battle of, 1864	973.924	E860	Watergate Affair, 1972-1974
973.737	E476.66	Maryland Campaign, 1864	973.925	E865	Mayaguez Incident, 1975
973.737	E477.16	Big Blue, Battle of the, Mo., 1864	973.931	HV6432.7	September 11 Terrorist Attacks, 2001
973.737	E477.21	Fort Harrison (Va.), Battle of, 1864	974	F1-15	New England—History
			974	F106	Middle Atlantic States
973.737	E477.33	Shenandoah Valley Campaign, 1864 (August-November)	974.0(1-2)	F7-.75	New England—History—Colonial period, ca. 1600-1775
973.737	E477.33	Cedar Creek (Va.), Battle of, 1864	974.0(2-3)	F8	New England—History—1775-1865
973.7371	E476.7	Atlanta Campaign, 1864	974.0(2-3)	F8	New England—History—Revolution, 1775-1783
973.7378	E476.69	Sherman's March to the Sea	974.004971	E99.A12	Abitibi Indians
			974.004973	E99.A349	Algonquin Indians
973.738	E477.65	Shenandoah Valley Campaign, 1865	974.0049734	E99.A13	Abenaki Indians
			974.00497345	E99.D2	Delaware Indians
973.738	E477.67	Dinwiddie Court House, Battle of, Dinwiddie, Va., 1865	974.005	F1	New England—Periodicals
			974.02	E83.72	Eastern Indians, Wars with, 1722-1726
973.738	E477.67	Appomattox Campaign, 1865	974.02	E199	New England—History—French & Indian War, 1755-1763
973.75	E476.85	Mobile Bay (Ala.), Battle of, 1864			
973.752	E473.2	Hampton Roads (Va.), Battle of, 1862	974.02008825	F7	Puritans
973.771	E611-612	Confederate States of America. Army—Prisons	974.03	E357-359	New England—History—War of 1812
973.8(1-7)	E83.866	Indians of North America—Wars—1866-1895	974.1	F16-30	Maine—History
			974.10(1-2)	F23	Maine—History—Colonial period, ca. 1600-1775
973.8(1-8)	E660-735	United States—History—1865-1898	974.10(1-3)	F24	Maine—History—1775-1865
973.81	E83.869	Indians of North America—Wars—1868-1869	974.1005	F16	Maine—Periodicals
973.893	E717.1	El Caney, Battle of, 1898	974.102	F23	Maine—History—King William's War, 1689-1697
973.895	E717.7	Manila Bay, Battle of, 1898	974.102	F23	Maine—History—King George's War, 1744-1748
973.91	E740-887	United States—History—20th century			
973.91(3-6)	E784-805	United States—History—1919-1933	974.103	F24	Maine—History—War of 1812
973.911	E740-760	United States—History—1901-1909	974.2	F31-45	New Hampshire—History
			974.20(1-2)	F37	New Hampshire—History—Colonial period, ca. 1600-1775
973.912	E761-765	United States—History—1909-1913			

Dewey	LC	Subject Heading	Dewey	LC	Subject Heading
974.20(2-3)	E263.N4	New Hampshire—History—Revolution, 1775-1783	974.50(1-2)	F82	Rhode Island—History—Colonial period, ca. 1600-1775
974.2005	F31	New Hampshire—Periodicals	974.50(2-3)	E263.R4	Rhode Island—History—Revolution, 1775-1783
974.202	E198	New Hampshire—History—King George's War, 1744-1748	974.5005	F76	Rhode Island—Periodicals
			974.502	E198	Rhode Island—History—King George's War, 1744-1748
974.203	E520	New Hampshire—History—Civil War, 1861-1865	974.503	F83.4	Dorr Rebellion, 1842
974.203	F38	New Hampshire—History—1775-1865	974.503	E528	Rhode Island—History—Civil War, 1861-1865
974.2043	F40	New Hampshire—History—1951-	974.6	F91-105	Connecticut—History
974.3	F46-60	Vermont—History	974.60(1-2)	F97	Connecticut—History—Colonial period, ca. 1600-1775
974.30(2-3)	E263.V5	Vermont—History—Revolution, 1775-1783	974.60(2-3)	F99	Connecticut—History—1775-1865
974.3005	F46	Vermont—Periodicals	974.600497344	E99.M83	Mohegan Indians
974.303	E359.5.V3	Vermont—History—War of 1812	974.6005	F91	Connecticut—Periodicals
			974.604(1-3)	F100	Connecticut—History—1865-1950
974.303	E533	Vermont—History—Civil War, 1861-1865	974.604(3-4)	F101	Connecticut—History—1951-
974.303	F52	Vermont—History—To 1791	974.7	F116-130	New York (State)—History
974.4	F61-75	Massachusetts—History	974.70(1-2)	F122-.1	New York (State)—History—Colonial period, ca. 1600-1775
974.40(1-2)	F67	Massachusetts—History—Colonial period, ca. 1600-1775	974.70(2-3)	F123	New York (State)—History—1775-1865
974.40(2-3)	E263.M4	Massachusetts—History—Revolution, 1775-1783	974.70(2-3)	E263.N6	New York (State)—History—Revolution, 1775-1783
974.40(2-3)	F69	Massachusetts—History—1775-1865	974.70049734	E99.M12	Mahican Indians
974.4005	F61	Massachusetts—Periodicals	974.7004975542	E99.M8	Mohawk Indians
974.402	F68	Massachusetts—History—New Plymouth, 1620-1691	974.7005	F116	New York (State)—Periodicals
974.402	E83.67	Falls Fight, 1676	974.702	E83.655	Esopus Indians—Wars, 1655-1660
974.402	E198	Massachusetts—History—King George's War, 1744-1748	974.702	E83.663	Esopus Indians—Wars, 1663-1664
974.402	E199	Massachusetts—History—French and Indian War, 1755-1763	974.702	E196	New York(State)—History—King William's War, 1689-1697
974.402008825	F68	Pilgrims (New Plymouth Colony)	974.702	E197	New York (State)—History—Queen Anne's War, 1702-1713
974.403	E197	Massachusetts—History—Queen Anne's War, 1702-1713	974.702	F123	New York (State)—History—French and Indian War, 1755-1763
974.403	E359.5.M3	Massachusetts—History—War of 1812	974.703	E359.5.N6	New York (State)—History—War of 1812
974.403	E513	Massachusetts—History—Civil War, 1861-1865	974.703	F128.44	Draft Riot, New York, N.Y., 1863
974.404	F70-71	Massachusetts—History—1865-	974.71	F128-.9	New York (N.Y.)
974.461	F73-.9	Boston (Mass.)	974.74	F124-125	New York (State)—History—1865-
974.5	F76-90	Rhode Island—History			

Dewey	LC	Subject Heading	Dewey	LC	Subject Heading
974.8	F146-160	Pennsylvania—History	975.210(2-3)	E263.D3	Delmarva Peninsula—History—Revolution, 1775-1783
974.80(1-2)	F152-.2	Pennsylvania—History—Colonial period, ca. 1600-1775	975.256	F189.A6	Annapolis (Md.)
974.8004310748	F160.G3	Pennsylvania Dutch	975.26	F189.B1	Baltimore (Md.)
			975.3	F191-205	Washington (D.C.)
974.80049755	E99.I7	Iroquois Indians	975.3005	F191	Washington (D.C.)—Periodicals
974.8005	F146	Pennsylvania—Periodicals			
974.803	F153	Buckshot War, Harrisburg, Pa., 1838	975.302	E356.W3	Washington (D.C.)—History—Capture by the British, 1814
974.804	F154-155.3	Pennsylvania—History—1865-	975.4	F236-250	West Virginia
974.811	F158.1-.9	Philadelphia (Pa.)	975.4005	F236	West Virginia—Periodicals
974.9	F131-145	New Jersey—History	975.402	E83.775	Indians of North America—Wars—1775-1783
974.90(1-2)	F137	New Jersey—History—Colonial period, ca. 1600-1775	975.403	E536	West Virginia—History—Civil War, 1861-1865
974.90(2-3)	E263.N5	New Jersey—History—Revolution, 1775-1783			
974.90(2-3)	F138	New Jersey—History—1775-1865	975.403	E582	West Virginia—History—Civil War, 1861-1865
974.9005	F131	New Jersey—Periodicals	975.404(3-4)	F245-.42	West Virginia—History—1951-
974.903	E521	New Jersey—History—Civil War, 1861-1865	975.5	F221-235	Virginia—History
974.903	F138	New Jersey—History—War of 1812	975.50(1-2)	F229	Virginia—History—Colonial period, ca. 1600-1775
974.904	F139-140.22	New Jersey—History—1865-	975.50(2-3)	E263.V8	Virginia—History—Revolution, 1775-1783
975	E482-489	Confederate States of America	975.50(2-3)	F230	Virginia—History—1775-1865
975	E487-488	Confederate States of America—History	975.5005	F221	Virginia—Periodicals
975	E487	Confederate States of America—Social conditions	975.502	F229	Bacon's Rebellion, 1676
			975.502	E83.77	Dunmore's Expedition, 1774
975	F206-220	Southern States—History	975.503	E359.5.V8	Virginia—History—War of 1812
975.0049738	E99.M95	Muskogean Indians			
975.00497557	E99.C5	Cherokee Indians	975.503	E534	Virginia—History—Civil War, 1861-1865
975.1	F161-175	Delaware—History	975.503	E581	Virginia—History—Civil War, 1861-1865
975.10(2-3)	E263.D3	Delaware—History—Revolution, 1775-1783	975.503	F234.E	Emporia (Va.)—History—Civil War, 1861-1865
975.1005	F161	Delaware—Periodicals			
975.103	E359.5.D3	Delaware—History—War of 1812	975.6	F251-265	North Carolina
			975.60(1-2)	F257	North Carolina—History—Colonial period, ca. 1600-1775
975.103	E500	Delaware—History—Civil War, 1861-1865			
975.104(3-4)	F170	Delaware—History—1951-	975.60(2-3)	F258	North Carolina—History—1775-1865
975.14(1-3)	F169	Delaware—History—1865-1950	975.6005	F251	North Carolina—Periodicals
975.2	F176-190	Maryland—History	975.60(2-3)	E263.N8	North Carolina—History—Revolution, 1775-1783
975.20(1-2)	F184	Maryland—History—Colonial period, ca. 1600-1775	975.602	F257	North Carolina—History—Regulator Insurrection, 1766-1771
975.20(2-3)	E263.M3	Maryland—History—Revolution, 1775-1783	975.603	E524	North Carolina—History—Civil War, 1861-1865
975.2005	F176	Maryland—Periodicals			
975.203	E359.5.M2	Maryland—History—War of 1812	975.603	E573	North Carolina—History—Civil War, 1861-1865

Dewey	LC	Subject Heading	Dewey	LC	Subject Heading
975.604	F259-260.42	North Carolina—History—1865-	975.904	E83.835	Seminole War, 2nd, 1835-1842
975.7	F266-280	South Carolina—History	975.905	E558.1-.9	Florida—History—Civil War, 1861-1865
975.7005	F266	South Carolina—Periodicals			
975.70(1-2)	F272	South Carolina—History—Colonial period, ca. 1600-1775	975.906	F316-.23	Florida—History—1865-
			975.906(3-4)	F316.2-.23	Florida—History—1951-
			976	F296	Gulf States—History
975.70(2-3)	F273	South Carolina—History—1775-1865	976	F396	Southwest, Old
			976.00497387	E99.C8	Choctaw Indians
975.702	E197	South Carolina—History—Queen Anne's War, 1702-1713	976.1	F321-355	Alabama
			976.10(5-63)	F326	Alabama—History—1819-1950
975.703	E471.1	South Carolina—History—Civil War, 1861-1865	976.1005	F321	Alabama—Periodicals
			976.105	F326	Alabama—History—To 1819
975.703	E529	South Carolina—History—Civil War, 1861-1865	976.106(3-4)	F330-.3	Alabama—History—1951-
			976.2	F336-350	Mississippi
975.703	E577	South Carolina—History—Civil War, 1861-1865	976.20(1-4)	F341	Mississippi—History—To 1803
975.704	F274-275.42	South Carolina—History—1865-	976.2005	F336	Mississippi—Periodicals
975.8	F281-295	Georgia	976.202	F347.A25	Ackia, Battle of, 1736
975.8005	F281	Georgia—Periodicals	976.204	F351-353	Louisiana Purchase
975.80(2-3)	F290	Georgia—History—1775-1865	976.205	E516	Mississippi—History—Civil War, 1861-1865
975.80(2-3)	E263.G3	Georgia—History—Revolution, 1775-1783	976.205	E568	Mississippi—History—Civil War, 1861-1865
975.803	E359.5.G4	Georgia—History—War of 1812	976.3	F366-380	Louisiana
			976.30(1-3)	F372-373	Louisiana—History—To 1803
975.803	E83.813	Creek War, 1813-1814			
975.803	E83.836	Creek War, 1836	976.30(2-3)	E263.L	Louisiana—History—Revolution, 1775-1783
975.803	E503	Georgia—History—Civil War, 1861-1865	976.30(4-5)	F374	Louisiana—History—1803-1865
975.803	E559	Georgia—History—Civil War, 1861-1865	976.3005	F366	Louisiana—Periodicals
975.804	F291-.3	Georgia—History—1865-	976.304	E359.5.L8	Louisiana—History—War of 1812
975.8231	F294.A8	Atlanta (Ga.)			
975.9	F306-320	Florida—History	976.305	E510	Louisiana—History—Civil War, 1861-1865
975.90(1-3)	F314	Florida—History—To 1821			
975.90(2-3)	F314	Florida—History—English colony, 1763-1784	976.305	E565	Louisiana—History—Civil War, 1861-1865
975.90(4-5)	F315	Florida—History—1821-1865	976.306(1-3)	F375	Louisiana—History—1865-1950
975.9004	E99.S28	Seminole Indians	976.306(3-4)	F376-.3	Louisiana—History—1951-
+ 973859			976.335	F379.N5	New Orleans (La.)
975.9005	F306	Florida—Periodicals	976.357068	GV879.5	Baseball fields
975.901	F314	Florida—History—To 1565	976.4	F381-395	Texas
975.901	F314	Florida—History—Spanish colony, 1565-1763	976.40(1-4)	F389-390	Texas—History—To 1846
			976.40(5-63)	F391	Texas—History—1846-1950
975.901	F314	Florida—History—Huguenot colony, 1562-1565	976.4004974572	E99.C85	Comanche Indians
975.903	F314	Florida—History—Spanish colony, 1784-1821	976.4005	F381	Texas—Periodicals
975.903	E83.817	Seminole War, 1st, 1817-1818	976.402	F389	Texas—History—1810-1821
975.903	F314	Florida—History—Cession to the United States, 1819	976.403	F390	Texas—History—Revolution, 1835-1836

Dewey	LC	Subject Heading	Dewey	LC	Subject Heading
976.404	F390	Texas—History—Republic, 1836-1846	977.2	F521-535	Indiana
			977.20 (1-2)	F526	Indiana—History—To 1787
976.405	E532	Texas—History—Civil War, 1861-1865	977.2005	F521	Indiana—Periodicals
			977.204(3-4)	F530-.22	Indiana—History—1951-
976.405	E580	Texas—History—Civil War, 1861-1865	977.252	F534.I3	Indianapolis (Ind.)
			977.3	F536-550	Illinois
976.406(3-4)	F391.2-.4	Texas—History—1951-	977.30(1-2)	F544	Illinois—History—To 1778
976.41411	F394.H8	Houston (Tex.)	977.30(2-3)	F545	Illinois—History—1778-1865
976.42812	F394.D21	Dallas (Tex.)			
976.481	E99.P244	Panhandle culture	977.3005	F536	Illinois—Periodicals
976.6	F691-705	Oklahoma	977.303	E83.83	Black Hawk War, 1832
976.6005	F691	Oklahoma—Periodicals	977.304	F546-.4	Illinois—History—1865-
976.603004973	E78.I5	Five Civilized Tribes	977.304(3-4)	F546.2-.4	Illinois—History—1951-
976.603004975	E78.I5	Five Civilized Tribes	977.311	F548-.9	Chicago (Ill.)
976.604	F699	Oklahoma—History—Land Rush, 1889	977.4	F561-575	Michigan
			977.40(1-3)	F566	Michigan—History—To 1837
976.604	F699	Oklahoma—History—Land Rush, 1893	977.40(3-4)	F566	Michigan—History—1837-1950
976.604004973	E78.045	Five Civilized Tribes	977.4005	F561	Michigan—Periodicals
976.604004975	E78.045	Five Civilized Tribes	977.404(3-4)	F570-.2	Michigan—History—1951-
976.7	F406-420	Arkansas	977.434	F574.D4	Detroit (Mich.)
976.7005	F406	Arkansas—Periodicals	977.5	F576-590	Wisconsin
976.8	F431-445	Tennessee	977.50(1-3)	F584	Wisconsin—History—To 1848
976.800497317	E99.S35	Shawnee Indians			
976.8005	F431	Tennessee—Periodicals	977.50(3-4)	F586-.42	Wisconsin—History—1848-
976.804	E531	Tennessee—History—Civil War, 1861-1865	977.500497313	E99.M44	Menominee Indians
			977.5005	F576	Wisconsin—Periodicals
976.804	E579	Tennessee—History—Civil War, 1861-1865	977.503	E537	Wisconsin—History—Civil War, 1861-1865
976.9	F446-460	Kentucky—History	977.595	F589.M6	Milwaukee (Wi.)
976.90(1-2)	F454	Kentucky—History—To 1792	977.6	F601-615	Minnesota
			977.60(1-4)	F606	Minnesota—History—To 1858
976.9005	F446	Kentucky—Periodicals			
976.902	F454	Estill's Defeat, 1782	977.60(4-5)	F606	Minnesota—History—1858-
976.903	F455	Kentucky—History—1792-1865	977.6005	F601	Minnesota—Periodicals
			977.6579	F614.M5	Minneapolis (Minn.)
976.904	F456-.26	Kentucky—History—1865-	977.7	F616-630	Iowa
976.9041	F456	Black Patch War, 1906-1909	977.7005	F616	Iowa—Periodicals
			977.702	E507	Iowa—History—Civil War, 1861-1865
977	F350.5-358.2	Mississippi River Valley			
977	F476-485	Northwest, Old	977.703(3-4)	F625-.42	Iowa—History—1951-
977	F516-520	Ohio River Valley	977.8	F461-475	Missouri
977	F551	Northern boundary of the United States	977.8004	E99.08	Osage Indians
977.00497333	E99.C6	Ojibwa Indians	+ 975254		
977.1	F486-500	Ohio			
977.10(1-2)	F495	Ohio—History—To 1787	977.8005	F461	Missouri—Periodicals
977.1005	F486	Ohio—Periodicals	977.803	E517	Missouri—History—Civil War, 1861-1865
977.102	E263.0	Ohio—History—Revolution, 1775-1783			
			977.803	E569	Missouri—History—Civil War, 1861-1865
977.103	F495	Ohio—History—1787-1865			
977.103	E359.5.02	Ohio—History—War of 1812	977.866	F474.S2	Saint Louis (Mo.)
			978	E470.9	West (U.S.)—History—Civil War, 1861-1865
977.103	E525	Ohio—History—Civil War, 1861-1865			
977.104	F496-.2	Ohio—History—1865-	978	F590.3-596.3	West (U.S.)—History

Dewey	LC	Subject Heading	Dewey	LC	Subject Heading
978	F598	Missouri River	978.701	F761	Fetterman Fight, Wyo., 1866
978	F721-722	Rocky Mountains	978.752	F722	Yellowstone National Park
978.0(1-2)	F592-.7	West (U.S.)—History—To 1848	978.8	F771-785	Colorado
978.0(2-32)	F595	West (U.S.)—History—1890-1945	978.8004	E99.U8	Ute Indians
978.00497353	E99.C53	Cheyenne Indians	+ 974576		
978.00497354	E99.A7	Arapaho Indians	978.8005	F771	Colorado—Periodicals
978.0049752	E99.O3	Oglala Indians	978.80(1-2)	F780	Colorado—History—To 1876
978.0049752	E99.T34	Teton Indians	978.802	E83.863	Sand Creek Massacre, Colo., 1864
978.004975243	E99.D1	Dakota Indians			
978.004975272	E99.C92	Crow Indians	978.802	E83.868	Beecher Island, Battle of, 1868
978.02	F593	West (U.S.)—History—1848-1860	978.803(1-3)	F781	Colorado—History—1876-1950
978.02	F594	West (U.S.)—History—1860-1890	978.803(3-4)	F781.2-.3	Colorado—History—1951-
978.033	F595-.3	West (U.S.)—History—1945-	978.883	F784.D4	Denver (Colo.)
978.1	F676-690	Kansas—History	978.9	F791-805	New Mexico
978.1005	F676	Kansas—Periodicals	978.9004974	E78	Pueblo Indians—Antiquities
978.102	F685	Kansas—History—1854-1861	978.9004974	E99.P9	Pueblo Indians
			978.9004974	E99.P9	Cliff-dwellers
978.1031	E508	Kansas—History—Civil War, 1861-1865	978.900497496	E99.T2	Taos Indians
			978.9005	F791	New Mexico—Periodicals
978.2	F661-675	Nebraska—History	978.90(1-3)	F799-800	New Mexico—History—To 1848
978.200497933	E99.P3	Pawnee Indians			
978.2005	F661	Nebraska—Periodicals	978.90(4-5)	F801-.2	New Mexico—History—1848-
978.3	F646-660	South Dakota			
978.3005	F646	South Dakota—Periodicals	978.904	E522	New Mexico—History—Civil War, 1861-1865
978.302	E83.86	Dakota Indians—Wars, 1862-1865	978.904	E571	New Mexico—History—Civil War, 1861-1865
978.302	E83.876	Dakota Indians—Wars, 1876	979	F786-790	Southwest, New
978.303	E99.D1	Wounded Knee Massacre, S.D., 1890	979.0049725	E99.A6	Apache Indians
			979.0049745	E99.S39	Shoshonean Indians
978.303031	E83.89	Dakota Indians—Wars, 1890-1891	979.004975722	E99.M77	Mohave Indians
978.3031	E83.89	Wounded Knee Massacre, S.D., 1890	979.02	E83.84	Pacific Coast Indians, Wars with, 1847-1865
978.4	F631-645	North Dakota	979.1	F806-820	Arizona
978.4005	F631	North Dakota—Periodicals	979.10(1-4)	F811	Arizona—History—To 1912
978.402	E83.86	Dakota Indians—Wars, 1862-1865	979.10049726	E99.N3	Navajo Indians
978.402	E83.876	Dakota Indians—Wars, 1876	979.1004974 + 5529	E99.P6	Pima Indians
978.403031	E83.876	Dakota Indians—Wars, 1876	979.100497458	E99.H7	Hopi Indians
			979.100497994	E99.Z9	Zuni Indians
978.6	F726-740	Montana	979.1005	F806	Arizona—Periodicals
978.6005	F726	Montana—Periodicals	979.105(2-3)	F811	Arizona—History—1912-1950
978.602	E83.876	Little Bighorn, Battle of the, Mont., 1876	979.105(3-4)	F815-.3	Arizona—History—1951-
978.603(3-4)	F735-.2	Montana—History—1951-	979.173	F819.P57	Phoenix (Ariz.)
978.7	F756-770	Wyoming	979.2	F821-835	Utah
978.7005	F756	Wyoming—Periodicals	979.2005	F821	Utah—Periodicals
978.701	E83.863	Shoshoni Indians—Wars, 1863-1865	979.202	E83.863	Shoshoni Indians—Wars, 1863-1865
			979.202	E532.95	Utah—History—Civil War, 1861-1865

| --- | --- | --- | --- | --- | --- |
979.202	F826	Morrisite War, 1862	980	E	America
979.3	F836-850	Nevada	980	E16-18.85	America—History
979.3005	F836	Nevada—Periodicals	980	F1408.3-.4	Latin America—Civilization
979.4	F856-870	California	980	F2201-3799	South America
979.40049757	E99.D5	Diegueno Indians	980	F2201-2239	South America—History
979.4005	F856	California—Periodicals	980.00498	F2229-2290	Indians of South America
979.40(1-3)	F864	California—History—To 1846	980.005	E11	America—Periodicals
			980.005	F1401	Latin America—Periodicals
979.40(3-4)	F865	California—History—1846-1850	980.0099	F2217	Gauchos
			980.01	E101-135	America—Discovery and exploration
979.40(4-53)	F866	California—History—1850-1950	981	F2501-2656	Brazil
979.405(3-4)	F866.2-.4	California—History—1950-	981	F2510	Brazil—Civilization
979.461	F869.S3	San Francisco (Calif.)	981	F2520.3-2538.5	Brazil—History
979.49	F867	California, Southern	981.005	F2501	Brazil—Periodicals
979.494	F869.L8	Los Angeles (Calif.)	981.0(1-33)	F2526-2534	Brazil—History—To 1822
979.5	F851.7	Cascade Range	981.0(4-6)	F2535-2538.5	Brazil—History—1822-
979.5	F871-885	Oregon	981.03(1-2)	F2526	Brazil—History—1500-1548
979.5005	F871	Oregon—Periodicals			
979.50(1-3)	F879-880	Oregon—History—To 1859	981.032	F2528	Brazil—History—1548-1580
979.503	F880	Oregon Trail			
979.504	F881-.35	Oregon—History—1859-	981.032	F2528	Brazil—History—1549-1762
979.504(3-4)	F881.2-.35	Oregon—History—1951-			
979.6	F741-755	Idaho	981.032	F2528	Brazil—History—War of the Emboabas, 1707-1709
979.6004 + 974574	E99.S4	Shoshoni Indians			
			981.032	F2529	Brazil—History—French colony, 1555-1567
979.6005	F741	Idaho—Periodicals			
979.60(1-2)	E83.863	Bear River Massacre, Idaho, 1863	981.032	F2530	Brazil—History—1580-1640
979.602	E83.863	Shoshoni Indians—Wars, 1863-1865	981.032	F2532	Brazil—History—Dutch Conquest, 1624-1654
979.603(3-4)	F750-.22	Idaho—History—1951-	981.033	F2534	Brazil—History—1763-1822
979.7	F853	Columbia River Valley			
979.7	F886-900	Washington (State)	981.033	F2534	Brazil—History—United Kingdom, 1815-1822
979.7004 + 974124	E99.N5	Nez Perce Indians			
			981.033	F2536	Brazil—History—Declaration of Independence, 1822
979.7005	F886	Washington (State)—Periodicals			
979.70(1-3)	F891	Washington (State)—History—To 1889	981.04	F2536	Brazil—History—Empire, 1822-1889
979.704	F891	Washington (State)—History—1889-	981.04	F2536	Brazil—History—Revolution, 1842
979.7772	F899.S4	Seattle (Wash.)	981.04	F2536	Brazil—History—Quebra Quilos' Revolt, 1874
979.8	F901-951	Alaska	981.05	F2537	Brazil—History—1889-1930
979.8004971	E99.E7	Eskimos			
979.8004971	E99.E7	Nunamiut Eskimos	981.05	F2537	Brazil—History—Naval Revolt, 1893-1894
979.8004971	E99.E7	Yupik Eskimos			
979.80(3-4)	F908-909	Alaska—History—1867-1959	981.05	F2537	Brazil—History—Canudos Campaign, 1893-1897
979.8004971	E99.E7	Koniagmiut Eskimos	981.05	F2537	Brazil—History—Naval Revolt, 1910
979.80049719	E99.A34	Aleuts	981.05	F2537	Brazil—History—Contestado Insurrection, 1912-1916
979.8005	F901	Alaska—Periodicals			
979.80(1-2)	F907	Alaska—History—To 1867	981.05	F2537	Brazil—History—Revolution, 1922
979.805	F910-.7	Alaska—History—1959-			
979.84	F951	Aleutian Islands (Alaska)			

Dewey	LC	Subject Heading	Dewey	LC	Subject Heading
981.05	F2537	Brazil—History—Revolution, 1924-1925	982.061	F2848	Argentina—History—Revolution, 1930
981.05	F2538	Brazil—History—Revolution, 1930	982.063	F2849.2	Argentina—History—Revolution, 1955
981.061	F2538	Brazil—History—1930-1945	982.063	F2849.2	Argentina—History—Peronist Revolt, 1956
981.061	F2538	Brazil—History—Uprising, 1935	982.063	F2849.2	Argentina—History—Coup d'etat, 1966
981.061	F2538	Brazil—History—Revolution, 1938	983	F3051-3285	Chile
981.061	F2538	Brazil—History—1945-1954	983	F3060	Chile—Civilization
			983	F3081-3098	Chile—History
981.062	F2538.2-.22	Brazil—History—1954-1964	983.005	F3051	Chile—Periodicals
			983.0(1-3)	F3091	Chile—History—To 1565
981.063	F2538.2	Brazil—History—Revolution, 1964	983.0(1-3)	F3091	Chile—History—To 1810
			983.0(4-6)	F3093	Chile—History—1810-
981.063	F2538.25-.27	Brazil—History—1964-1985	983.0(4-63)	F3095	Chile—History—1824-1920
981.064	F2538.3-.5	Brazil—History—1985-	983.03	F3091	Chile—History—1565-1810
982	F2801-3021	Argentina			
982	F2810	Argentina—Civilization	983.04	F3094	Chile—History—War of Independence, 1810-1824
982	F2827-2849.22	Argentina—History			
982.0(1-22)	F2841	Argentina—History—1515-1535	983.05	F3095	Chile—History—Insurrection, 1851
982.0(1-24)	F2841	Argentina—History—To 1810	983.05	F3095	Chile—History—Insurrection, 1859
982.0(3-4)	F2846	Argentina—History—1817-1860	983.06(3-45)	F3099	Chile—History—1920-1970
982.0(3-7)	F2843	Argentina—History—1810-	983.061	F3095	Chile—History—War with Spain, 1865-1866
982.0(4-5)	F2847	Argentina—History—1860-1910	983.062	F3098	Chile—History—Revolution, 1891
982.0(61-7)	F2849-.22	Argentina—History—1943-	983.064	F3099	Chile—History—20th century
982.0(64-7)	F2849.2	Argentina—History—1983-			
982.005	F2801	Argentina—Periodicals	983.0641	F3099	Chile—History—Naval Revolt, 1931
982.02(2-3)	F2841	Argentina—History—1535-1617	983.0642	F3099	Chile—History—Uprising, 1938
982.023	F2841	Argentina—History—1617-1776	983.0646	F3100	Chile—History—1970-1973
982.023	F2841	Argentina—History—1776-1810	983.065	F3100	Chile—History—Coup d'etat, 1973
982.024	F2845	Argentina—History—English Invasions, 1806-1807	983.065	F3100	Chile—History—1973-1988
982.03	F2845	Argentina—History—War of Independence, 1810-1817	984	F3301-3359	Bolivia
982.04	F2843	Argentina—History—19th century	984	F3310	Bolivia—Civilization
			984	F3320.3-3327	Bolivia—History
982.04	F2846	Argentina—History—Revolution, 1833	984.005	F3301	Bolivia—Periodicals
			984.0(1-3)	F3322	Bolivia—History—To 1809
982.05	F2847	Argentina—History—Revolution, 1890	984.041	F3323	Bolivia—History—Wars of Independence, 1809-1825
982.06(1-2)	F2849	Argentina—History—1943-1955	984.04(2-5)	F3324	Bolivia—History—1825-1879
982.06(3-4)	F2849.2	Argentina—History—1955-1983	984.0(45-51)	F3324-3325	Bolivia—History—1879-1938
982.061	F2848	Argentina—History—1910-1943	984.05(1-2)	F3326-3327	Bolivia—History—1938-
			984.05(1-2)	F3326	Bolivia—History—1938-1982

Dewey	LC	Subject Heading	Dewey	LC	Subject Heading
984.051	F3326	Bolivia—History—Coup d'etat, 1943	986.105	F2273	Colombia—History—19th century
984.051	F3326	Bolivia—History—Revolution, 1946	986.105(2-61)	F2276	Colombia—History—1832-1886
984.052	F3326	Bolivia—History—Revolution, 1952	986.1053	F2276	Colombia—History—Civil War, 1860-1862
984.052	F3326	Bolivia—History—Revolution, 1964	986.106(2-31)	F2277	Colombia—History—1903-1946
984.052	F3326	Bolivia—History—Coup d'etat, 1979	986.1062	F2276.5	Colombia—History—1886-1903
984.052	F3326	Bolivia—History—Coup d'etat, 1980	986.1062	F2276.5	Colombia—History—Revolution, 1899-1903
984.052	F3327	Bolivia—History—1982-	986.1063(2-3)	F2278	Colombia—History—1946-1974
984.06(5-6)	F3100	Chile—History—1988-			
985	F3401-3619	Peru	986.10632	F2278	Colombia—History—Coup d'etat, 1953
985	F3410	Peru—Civilization			
985	F3430.3-3448.4	Peru—History	986.1063(4-5)	F2279-.22	Colombia—History—1974-
985.005	F3401	Peru—Periodicals	986.6	F3701-3799	Ecuador
985.0(1-2)	F3442	Peru—History—To 1548	986.6	F3710	Ecuador—Civilization
985.0(1-4)	F3442-3444	Peru—History—To 1820	986.6	F3723.3-3738.4	Ecuador—History
985.0(2-4)	F3444	Peru—History—1548-1820	986.6005	F3701	Ecuador—Periodicals
985.02	F3442	Peru—History—Conquest, 1522-1548	986.60(1-2)	F3733	Ecuador—History—To 1809
985.033	F3444	Peru—History—Insurrection of Tupac Amaru, 1780-1781	986.60(2-4)	F3734	Ecuador—History—Wars of Independence, 1809-1830
985.0(4-5)	F3446	Peru—History—War of Independence, 1820-1829	986.60(5-6)	F3736	Ecuador—History—1830-1895
985.0(5-631)	F3447	Peru—History—1829-1919	986.60(6-72)	F3737	Ecuador—History—1895-1944
985.05	F3447	Peru—History—Spanish question, 1864	986.606	F3736	Ecuador—History—Revolution, 1895
985.06(4-5)	F3448.2	Peru—History—1980-	986.6071	F3737	Ecuador—History—20th century
985.061	F3447	Peru—History—Revolution of 1872	986.607(2-5)	F3738	Ecuador—History—1944-
985.063(1-2)	F3448	Peru—History—1919-1968	986.6072	F3737	Ecuador—History—Coup d'etat, 1925
985.0632	F3448	Peru—History—Revolution, 1930	986.6072	F3737	Ecuador-Peru Conflict, 1941
985.0633	F3448.2	Peru—History—1968-1980	986.6072	F3738	Ecuador—History—Coup d'etat, 1944
985.0633	F3448.2	Peru—History—Coup d'etat, 1968	986.6074	F3738	Ecuador-Peru Conflict, 1981
986.1	F2251-2299	Colombia	987	F2301-2349	Venezuela
986.1	F2260	Colombia—Civilization	987	F2310	Venezuela—Civilization
986.1	F2270.3-2279.22	Colombia—History	987	F2319.5-2328.52	Venezuela—History
986.1005	F2251	Colombia—Periodicals			
986.10(1-2)	F2272	Colombia—History—To 1810	987.005	F2301	Venezuela—Periodicals
986.10(3-6)	F2273	Colombia—History—1810-	987.0(1-3)	F2322	Venezuela—History—To 1556
986.10(3-4)	F2274	Colombia—History—War of Independence, 1810-1822	987.0(1-3)	F2322	Venezuela—History—To 1810
986.102	F2272.5	English West Indian Expedition, 1739-1742	987.03	F2322	Venezuela—History—1556-1810
986.102	F2272	Colombia—History—Insurrection of the Comuneros, 1781	987.03	F2322	Venezuela—History—Insurrection of the Comuneros, 1781
986.104	F2275	Colombia—History—1822-1832			

Dewey	LC	Subject Heading	Dewey	LC	Subject Heading
987.03	F2322	Venezuela—History—Miranda's Expedition, 1806	988.3032	F2425	Surinam—History—Coup d'etat, 1980
987.0(4-5)	F2324	Venezuela—History—1810-1830	988.3032	F2425	Surinam—History—Coup d'etat, 1982
987.0(4-6)	F2322.8	Venezuela—History—1810-	989.2	F2661-2699	Paraguay
987.0(4-5)	F2324	Venezuela—History—War of Independence, 1810-1823	989.2	F2670	Paraguay—Civilization
			989.2	F2679.35-2689.23	Paraguay—History
987.061	F2325	Venezuela—History—1830-1935	989.2005	F2661	Paraguay—Periodicals
987.062	F2325	Venezuela—History—Federal Wars, 1858-1863	989.20(1-3)	F2683-2684	Paraguay—History—To 1811
987.063(1-3)	F2326-2327	Venezuela—History—1935-1974	989.203	F2683	Paraguay—History—Revolution of the Comuneros, 1721-1735
987.0631	F2325	Venezuela—History—Revolution, 1902-1903	989.203	F2683	Paraguay—History—War of Independence, 1810-1811
987.0631	F2325	Venezuela—History—Anglo German Blockade, 1902	989.20(4-5)	F2686-2687	Paraguay—History—1811-1870
987.06313	F2325	Venezuela—History—1908-1935	989.20(6-71)	F2688-.5	Paraguay—History—1870-1938
987.063(14-2)	F2326	Venezuela—History—1935-1958	989.207	F2688	Paraguay—History—20th century
987.0632	F2326	Venezuela—History—Revolution, 1945	989.207(1-3)	F2689	Paraguay—History—1938-1989
987.0632	F2326	Venezuela—History—Coup d'etat, 1948	989.2071	F2688	Paraguay—History—Revolution, 1904
987.063(3-4)	F2328-.52	Venezuela—History—1974-	989.2071	F2688	Paraguay—History—Revolution, 1922-1923
987.0633	F2326	Venezuela—History—Revolution, 1958	989.2071	F2688	Paraguay—History—Revolution, 1936
987.064	F2328	Venezuela—History—Attempted coup, 1992 (February 4)	989.2072	F2689	Paraguay—History—Revolution, 1947
			989.2073	F2689.2-.23	Paraguay—History—1989-
987.064	F2328	Venezuela—History—Attempted coup, 1992 (November 27)	989.2073	F2689.2	Paraguay—History—Coup d'etat, 1989
988.1	F2361-2391	Guyana	989.5	F2701-2799	Uruguay
988.1	F2369.8	Guyana—Civilization	989.5	F2710	Uruguay—Civilization
988.1	F2380.3-2391	Guyana—History	989.5	F2720-2729.52	Uruguay—History
988.1005	F2361	Guyana—Periodicals	989.5005	F2701	Uruguay—Periodicals
988.10(1-31)	F2384	Guyana—History—1803-1966	989.50(1-3)	F2723	Uruguay—History—To 1810
988.101	F2383	Guyana—History—To 1803	989.504	F2725	Uruguay—History—1810-1830
988.1032	F2385	Guyana—History—1966-			
988.2	F2441-2471	French Guiana	989.50(5-61)	F2726	Uruguay—History—1875-1904
988.2	F2449.8	French Guiana—Civilization			
988.2	F2460.3-2464	French Guiana—History	989.505	F2726	Uruguay—History—1830-1875
988.2005	F2441	French Guiana—Periodicals	989.505	F2726	Uruguay—History—Great War, 1843-1852
988.3	F2401-2431	Surinam			
988.3	F2409.8	Surinam—Civilization	989.506(1-5)	F2728	Uruguay—History—1904-1973
988.3	F2420.3-2425.23	Surinam—History			
988.3005	F2401	Surinam—Periodicals	989.5061	F2726	Uruguay—History—Revolution, 1886
988.30(1-31)	F2424	Surinam—History—1814-1950	989.5061	F2726	Uruguay—History—Revolution, 1897
988.301	F2423	Surinam—History—To 1814			
988.303(1-2)	F2425-.23	Surinam—History—1950-	989.5063	F2728	Uruguay—History—Revolution, 1935

Dewey	LC	Subject Heading	Dewey	LC	Subject Heading
989.5066	F2729	Uruguay—History—Coup d'etat, 1973	995	DU490	Melanesia
989.5066	F2729	Uruguay—History—1973-1985	995	DU739-747	New Guinea
			995.3	DU740	Papua New Guinea
989.5067	F2729	Uruguay—History—1985-	995.93	DU850	Solomon Islands
990	DU	Oceania	995.95	DU760	Vanuatu
993	DU418	New Zealand—Civilization	995.97	DU720	New Caledonia
993	DU419-422	New Zealand—History	995-996	DU28.11-66	Oceania—History
993.004	DU422.5-424.5	Ethnology—New Zealand	996	DU510	Polynesia
993.01	DU420.12-.14	New Zealand—History—To 1840	996.9004	DU624.6-.7	Ethnology—Hawaii
			996.11	DU600	Fiji
993.02(1-2)	DU420.16-.18	New Zealand—History—1840-1876	996.12	DU880	Tonga
			996.1(3-4)	DU810-819	Samoan Islands
993.021	DU420.16	New Zealand—History—Maori War, 1845-1847	996.1(3-4)	DU817	Samoan question
			996.13	DU819.A1	American Samoa
993.022	DU420.22-.34	New Zealand—History—Taranaki War, 1860-1861	996.14	DU819.A2	Western Samoa
			996.15	DU910	Tokelau
993.0(23-31)	DU420.22-.24	New Zealand—History—1876-1918	996.16	DU920	Wallis and Futuna Islands
			996.18	DU800	Pitcairn Island
993.032	DU420.26-.28	New Zealand—History—1918-1945	996.18	F3169	Easter Island
			996.21	DU870	Society Islands
993.0(35-4)	DU420.32-.34	New Zealand—History—1945-	996.211	DU870	Tahiti
			996.31	DU700-701	Marquesas Islands
994	DU108-117.2	Australia—History	996.4	DU650	Line Islands
994.004	DU120-125	Ethnology—Australia	996.5	DU500	Micronesia
994.0049915	DU125.D59	Diyari (Australian people)	996.6	DU560-568	Caroline Islands
994.01	DU98.1	Australia—History—To 1788	996.6	DU565-567	Caroline Islands—History
			996.7	DU640-648	Mariana Islands
994.01	GN871-875	Australian aborigines—Antiquities	996.81	DU615	Kiribati
			996.81	DU790	Phoenix Islands (Kiribati)
994.0(2-3)	DU114-115.2	Australia—History—1788-1900	996.83	DU710	Marshall Islands
			996.9	DU624.5	Hawaii—Civilization
994.02	DU115	Australia—History—1788-1851	996.9	DU625-629	Hawaii—History
994.04	DU116-117.2	Australia—History—20th century	999	QB54	Life on other planets

About the Author

After working in the fields of teaching and counseling, Ms. Scott earned her Masters in Library and Information Sciences summa cum laude from Catholic University, specializing in library automation.

In Federal Libraries, Ms. Scott has been the Head of Cataloging at the U.S. Bureau of the Census Library, Systems Librarian at the Judges' Library for the U.S. Court of Appeals in Washington, and Head of Technical Services and Systems at the NASA Goddard Space Flight Center Library. She also directed cataloging projects for the National Library of Medicine, National Oceanic and Atmospheric Administration, and NASA Langley.

Ms. Scott automated the library at the Harvard Center for Hellenic Studies, and a special military library at Ft. Belvoir, Virginia, and organized a digitization project for the architectural drawings used in the Pentagon Renovation Program.

Ms. Scott's interests are in providing information to users remotely through digitization and automation, and the arrangement of materials in manners most useful to the end user. Reflecting these interests, she provided access to needed materials for a special military library's branch sites scattered around the country utilizing a website, a customized web-based OPAC with pre-configured searches, and linking fields in cataloging records. She also developed a classification system reflecting the Agency's information needs and the type of materials in a special collection within the military library.

CPSIA information can be obtained at www.ICGtesting.com
Printed in the USA
BVOW051029270812

298702BV00005B/1/P